THE HISTORY OF THE HOLOCAUST IN ROMANIA

THE COMPREHENSIVE HISTORY OF THE HOLOCAUST

THE HISTORY OF THE HOLOCAUST IN ROMANIA

JEAN ANCEL

Translated by Yaffah Murciano
Edited by Leon Volovici
With the assistance of Miriam Caloianu

Published by the
UNIVERSITY OF NEBRASKA PRESS, *Lincoln*
and YAD VASHEM, *Jerusalem*

Map adapted from the original at the U.S.
Holocaust Memorial Museum.

Library of Congress
Cataloging-in-Publication Data
Ancel, Jean.
[Toldot ha-Sho'ah. English]
The history of the Holocaust in Romania /
Jean Ancel; translated by Yaffah Murciano;
edited by Leon Volovici with the assistance of
Miriam Caloianu.
p. cm. — (The comprehensive
history of the Holocaust)
Includes bibliographical references and index.
ISBN 978-0-8032-2064-5 (cloth: alk. paper)
1. Jews — Persecutions — Romania — History.
2. Holocaust, Jewish (1939–1945) — Romania.
3. Antisemitism — Romania. 4. Jews —
Romania — History — 20th century.
5. Romania — Ethnic relations. I. Title.
DS135.R7A719813 2011
940.53'1809498 — dc23
2011030180

Set in Ehrhardt by Kim Essman.
Designed by Richard Hendel.

The publication of this series was made possible by the generous gift of the Ike and Roz Friedman Family Foundation, in loving memory of Ike Friedman and Janis Friedman Yale and all those who perished in the Holocaust.

Publication of this series has also been supported by a grant from the Conference on Jewish Material Claims Against Germany.

Claims Conference   ועידת התביעות
The Conference on Jewish Material Claims Against Germany

Contents

Illustrations

Foreword to the Hebrew Edition

The purpose of the Holocaust History Project, launched by Yad Vashem in the late 1970s, was to summarize the achievements of the first generation of academic Holocaust research. It soon transpired that this aim was too ambitious and that several countries, including Romania, lacked even the most basic research infrastructure. Clearly, there was a need for primary research in these countries.

Although in the interwar period Romania boasted the second largest Jewish community in Europe after Poland, it has been awarded a relatively marginal position in Holocaust research in Israel and abroad. The history of Romanian Jewry, from Romania's establishment after the Berlin Congress in 1878 until the Holocaust, has not been adequately researched either.

As in other countries, the monstrous dimensions of the Holocaust in Romania sprang from the encounter of popular and traditional antisemitism rooted in ancient and deep-seated religious sentiments, on the one hand, with socioeconomic considerations, the power of the modern state, and the tools at its disposal, on the other. The Germans' preoccupation with precision and fastidiousness engendered a need for a "workforce" that would carry out their dirty work for them. This workforce was made up of their allies and the occupied nations of Eastern Europe. The riots and pogroms that had been, and in some places still were, an integral part of Jewish life could never have reached the monstrous proportions of the Holocaust without the meticulous planning, systematic implementation, and dedication that were the hallmark of Nazi ideology and German resolve.

In most Eastern European countries during the Holocaust, therefore, historical Eastern European antisemitism operated alongside Nazi ideology and power. The Nazis exploited popular anti-Jewish sentiments and channeled them to serve the modern liquidation factory that was erected during the war. Romania was unusual in that it was the Romanian, not the German, regime that operated the death machine that butchered Romanian Jewry, at its own initiative and under its own free will. Germany's involvement was secondary only.

The Holocaust in Romania, therefore, took place within a dual context: (1) the context of the religious, national, and socioeconomic antisemitism that had typified Romania since its establishment as a sovereign state, and (2) the context of the Second World War, which served as a convenient backdrop to the annihilation of European Jewry by the Nazis, their satellites, and their collaborators.

Although part of the Holocaust of European Jewry, the Holocaust in Romania was primarily Romanian. As Dr. Ancel has shown so clearly in his research, the Holocaust in Romania was the result of ideological stereotypes that Romanian intellectuals and politicians, with the backing or tacit consent of large sections of Romanian society, created in Romania after its independence, especially in the interwar period. The entire apparatus of the Romanian regime—government ministries, the various security services (the army, gendarmerie, and police), the civil administration in the occupied territories, the national bank, and district and local authorities—participated in this crime.

The fact that the Holocaust in Romania was initiated and implemented by Romanians explains both its savagery and its incompleteness. Their modus operandi, as indicated by the horrific descriptions Ancel brings into his research, was often unusually cruel, primitive, contemptible, and depraved. On the other hand, they were far less efficient than the Germans. This, no doubt, explains why there were people left to tell the tale.

Unlike the Germans, the Romanians, and other nations in and outside the Balkans, drew a distinction between "their" Jews and other Jews and related to the two groups differently. "Other Jews" includes Jews in the districts that were annexed to Romania after the First World War and in areas that were occupied and annexed to the Romanian military administration after the Soviet invasion in June 1941. The Jews of the Regat, the core Romanian principality, may have suffered pogroms, decrees, and degradation, but on the whole they survived the Holocaust. Nevertheless, as Ancel shows, there were several moments during the war when it seemed as if they too were about to suffer the same fate as their brethren. There is ample evidence that the Romanian government was preparing itself for such an eventuality. Although the survival rate of Romanian Jewry as a whole was the highest in Europe, the survival rate in areas where Jews were liquidated was one of the lowest.

Jean Ancel's research offers one of the most detailed, or possibly the most detailed, accounts written so far of the history of the Holocaust. Although details as a rule can be tiring, they have a power of their own, and it is this that makes this work so special. Ancel does not gloss over any place, person, organization, or unit connected with the massacre of Jews in Romania and Transnistria, from head of state to the most lowly sergeant and gendarme. Despite his concern for detail and accuracy, Ancel still manages to present us with a full picture of events. He also provides us with a comprehensive and accurate analysis of Romanian society, its motives and behavior, on the one hand, and of Jewish society and its modes of operation and responses, on the other.

In this work, Ancel makes use of an immense and varied corpus of sources, such as archival documents, all shades of the Romanian press, numerous survivor testimonies, and statements by defendants in the war criminals' trials held in Romania after its defeat. The archival material includes an impressive amount of official, semiofficial, and even private Romanian documents; Soviet documents that have become available in recent years; and German political, military, and administrative documents, as well as Jewish documents of the community and its institutions and of parties and organizations. The memorial literature as well as the many testimonies assembled immediately after the war and published in the communities' Black Books, or later by Yad Vashem, add a moving and more immediate personal dimension that the archival material lacks.

Many of the above sources were hidden until the downfall of Ceaușescu's regime in the late 1980s. The strong affiliation and partial overlap between the fascist regime of wartime Romania and the subsequent Communist regime, which absorbed many high-ranking officials from the fascist regime after they were ideologically reprogrammed, led to the suppression of many files that contradicted the official version of Romanian historiography—a version that downplayed the role played by the Romanians in the annihilation of Romanian Jewry and placed most of the blame on the Germans.

The author, therefore, faced two challenges: (1) to reconstruct, describe, and analyze the Holocaust in Romania, and (2) to refute the standard theses that guided Romanian historiography under Communist rule and influenced all academic research on the subject outside Romania. His critical approach led him to uncover many cases of documents that were forged in order to hide events or conceal responsibility for them or that were "fabricated" in order to deliberately deceive officials, opponents, or critics at the time, as well as future researchers.

As one who has followed the vicissitudes of this work for many years, I can testify that the author has put his whole heart into the enterprise. He has presented us with a monumental research project, the fruit of many years of work that demanded an immense psychological investment. This highly admirable work will also serve as a springboard for monographs on specific issues relating to the Holocaust of Romanian Jewry that deserve further study. Although it sometimes seemed as if Jean Ancel's intense involvement might interfere with the objectivity required of an academic researcher, he always managed to pull himself together in time and exercise caution and restraint. The result is a book that combines scholarship and feeling, description and analysis, empathy and detachment. This is a monumental and, as far as one can tell, also definitive work.

Yoav Gelber

Editors' Note

This English edition of Jean Ancel's *The History of the Holocaust: Romania* is a revised version of the original Hebrew book, published in two volumes in 2002 by Yad Vashem. Dr. Ancel undertook various revisions to the English edition, based on suggestions from the University of Nebraska Press's peer reviewers. Unfortunately, Dr. Ancel died on 30 April 2008 after a long illness, before he could revise the manuscript. These revisions, including bibliographical corrections and updates, were done by the editors based on the detailed correspondence on this subject between the author and the University of Nebraska Press in 2007. The final touches were by the editors, but the work and the spirit are those of Jean Ancel.

THE
HISTORY
OF THE
HOLOCAUST IN
ROMANIA

Introduction

It has taken me over sixteen years (1984–2000) to prepare this study on the Holocaust of Romanian Jewry, and I owe the reader an explanation as to why this is so. The first version of this book was completed in 1990. It was based on copious documentation that I had collected over a decade and that, with the generous assistance of the Beate Klarsfeld Foundation, was published in twelve volumes in 1986. After the collapse of the Communist regimes, the East European archives suddenly became available. Between 1992 and 1997, at Yad Vashem's behest and also independently, I visited the Ukraine, Russia, and Moldova (former Romanian Bessarabia), with stays in Moscow, Kiev, Odessa, Nikolayev, Kherson, and Kishinev. From 1994 on, I also visited the U.S. Holocaust Memorial Museum in Washington DC, which began amassing important collections of documents that came from Romanian archives. After my first visit to Moscow, and especially after four repeat visits to Odessa and Nikolayev that lasted over half a year, I realized that my book was deficient. The inaccessibility of the archives in Romania and the former Soviet Union had led to substantial errors in my understanding of Antonescu's regime, its objectives, it modus operandi, the role antisemitism played in its considerations, the extent of its participation in the liquidation of the Jews, and especially the kind of relationship it had with the Third Reich. I had to choose between publishing the book as it was, with updates and additions, or rewriting it almost from scratch. I chose the latter course.

Despite the size of this book (the result of an attempt to write an integral history of Romanian Jewry during the Holocaust based on primary sources), I have omitted several themes I originally intended to include. Nevertheless, I think I can state with some satisfaction that all issues relating to the Holocaust of Romanian Jewry have been covered. One major chapter of this book, dealing with the pogrom in Iași and the survivors (chap. 33), has become a book in its own right. This is *Hakdamah leretsah: Peraot Yasi, 29 beyuni 1941* (Prelude to murder: The pogrom in Jassy, 29 June 1941) (Jerusalem: Yad Vashem, 2003). The current work includes an abridged account of the pogrom in Iași. The Romanian translation of *Hakdamah leretsah* was published in Romania in 2005: *Preludiu la asasinat: Pogromul de la Iaşi, 29 iunie 1941*.

This work is the culmination of years of collecting Jewish sources, especially the testimonies of survivors of the mass liquidation operations. I believe that a history of the Jewish people in the Holocaust cannot rely only on the documentation left behind by the murderers and their accomplices; it must also invoke Jewish sources where they exist, provided they are reliable. After many years of considerable effort, I managed to track down several survivors of the genocide operations perpetrated by the Romanians in Transnistria. Their accounts breathe life into the dry documents I came across in the Ukrainian archives.

Romania joined the war Nazi Germany declared on the Jews and launched a campaign of mass destruction and deportation in the "liberated territories"—Bessarabia and northern Bukovina. Under the new situation that was emerging in Europe, Antonescu's regime sought to implement what I have called the Romanian antisemitic dream, namely, the desire to rid the country of Jews. Already in the autumn of 1941 Antonescu's regime wished to purge the Regat of Jews, and it was only the intervention of the German Foreign Ministry and the Reich Central Security Office (RSHA, the security department of the Nazi Third Reich), which were reluctant to overburden the murderers of Einsatzgruppe D, that averted this plan at such an early stage of the Holocaust. The antisemitic ideology of Antonescu's regime, which drove it to participate in the plan to liquidate the Jews, was based on local antisemitism as it had evolved over a century, especially A. C. Cuza's classic version and Corneliu Zelea Codreanu's fascist version, and not on the Nazi racist version. It was not by chance that the looting of Jewish property was termed *Romanization* rather than *Aryanization*. The death camps and the ghettos of Transnistria were intended as transit camps pending the transfer of the deportees to German occupied territory for liquidation.

The participation by Romanians in the liquidation of the Jewish people was, therefore, predicated on an antisemitic ideology that preceded Nazi racism and was the result of free choice, not German pressure or coercion. Indeed, when Marshal Ion Antonescu reached the conclusion that the liquidation of the Jews who remained in his territory no longer served Romania's national interests as he defined them, he stopped the liquidation, despite German pressure. The plan to deport the Romanian Jews to the Bełżec death camp in occupied Poland was put on hold by the Antonescu regime in early October 1942, that is, before Stalingrad and with no direct connection to it.[1]

The Romanian soldiers, gendarmes, and policemen who were ordered to "cleanse the ground" (the Romanian equivalent of the Final Solution) worked for, and were equipped and rewarded by, the Romanian state, and they carried out orders they received in Romanian from Bucharest, not Berlin. Nor were they content with merely obeying orders. There were soldiers in uniform and civilians who carried out acts of murder and looting at their own initiative to satisfy their own base instincts, in the atmosphere created by the regime in which the Jews were no longer considered human beings and in which it was permitted to cast off the shackles of humanity. It is important, however, to bear in mind that although the "evil" was of Romanian origin, without Germany's domination of Europe and help in freeing its Romanian allies from their complexes it would not have amounted to much. Romania's democratic legacy was nothing to boast of, and no opposition worthy of the name emerged that might have prevented or at least openly condemned the murder and looting of the Jews perpetrated by Antonescu's regime and the majority of the Romanian people. The royal family was no exception, while the Romanian Orthodox Church, which supported the regime throughout, provided it with a Christian justification for its dastardly acts.

The new German and Romanian documentation that I obtained revealed the surprising fact that the Antonescu regime had its own plan to deport most of Romanian Jewry to Transnistria in the second half of 1942. Again, as in 1941, it was only the intervention of the German Foreign Ministry, which wished to dispatch all Jews to the death camps and receive sole credit for their liquidation, that prevented the implementation of this plan. One final fact deserves emphasis: at no point in the decision-making processes affecting the Jews did the Romanian administration ever entertain humanitarian considerations or consider the genocide of Jews a crime against humanity.

The cross-fertilization of old and new documentation, particularly the files of the Securitate (Romanian Information Service during the Communist regime), the heir to the Siguranța (Romanian Security Police), enabled me to clarify the role of the Jewish leadership in organizing Jewish life during the period under review, its abortive attempt to prevent the deportation of the survivors of the first wave of destruction to the camps of Transnistria, and especially its successful struggle to prevent the deportation of the Jews of the Old Kingdom and southern Transylvania to the death camps in occupied Poland. The documentation confirms the major role played by the Jewish leader Wilhelm Filderman (1882–1963) in the struggle to save Romanian Jewry from destruction, his understanding of the dangers awaiting the Jews already in the autumn of 1941, and his ties with the leader of the opposition and with Antonescu and his ministers. It also shows that neither the Zionist movement nor Rabbi Alexandru Safran (1910–2006), the chief rabbi in Romania from 1939 to 1948, had any real part in thwarting the plan to liquidate the Jews.

I would like to thank Beate and Serge Klarsfeld, who sponsored the publication of the collection of documents on the fate of Romanian Jewry in the Holocaust and chose me for the task; the U.S. Holocaust Memorial Museum in Washington DC, which, on a number of occasions, allowed me to study and copy numerous documents; the Rosenzweig Family Fellowship for the Study of the Fate of Jews in Transnistria; Dr. Michael Berenbaum, former director of the Holocaust Museum Research Institute, Dr. Paul Shapiro, its current director, Henry Mayer, director of the Museum Archives, and Dr. Vassily Fisher, head of the museum's PR department; my colleague Dr. Radu Ioanid, who did his utmost to obtain copies of numerous documents from Romanian archives; Yad Vashem, for the fellowship from the International Institute for Holocaust Research; Esther Aran, Dr. Tikva Fatal, and the late Esther Hako, former coordinators of the Holocaust History Project; special thanks to Dr. Bella Guterman, Yad Vashem's director of publications, who swiftly and skillfully oversaw publication of the book; Dr. Yosef Govrin, Israel's ambassador to Romania from 1985 to 1989, for supporting, encouraging, and believing in me, and his wife, Hanna; Abraham Ben Amitai, the editor of the Hebrew version of the book, who worked alongside me for over ten years, improving the book's style and catching many errors; and Mr. Felix Dan, the printer, who also printed my first contribution to the study of Romanian Jewry, thirty-three years ago.

I would also like to thank Professor Yehuda Bauer, who read my work and made valuable comments; Professor Israel Guttman, who promoted its publication in the later stages; and Mr. Avner Shalev, chairman of the Yad Vashem Directorate. It is thanks to them that this book has been published in its present form.

This work has benefited from the guidance and active support of Professor Yoav Gelber of Haifa University, who not only stood by me as I wrote the book but also encouraged me to broaden and deepen the scope of the research. I cannot thank him enough. Last but not least, I would like to thank my wife, Susanna. The research and effort that went into the writing of this book, which sapped most of my energy and time for many years, would never have been possible without her support and help.

I would like to dedicate this book to the memory of my father, Shmuel Ben Chanoch Halevi, may he rest in peace.

"The L—d has chastened me sore; but he hath not given me over unto death" (Psalms 118:18).

Jean Ancel
Jerusalem, May 2002

In 1912 about 239,967 Jews (about 3.3 percent of the total Romanian population) lived in the Regat, the Old Kingdom that included Moldavia, Walachia, and Dobroudja before 1918. Upon the establishment of Greater Romania after the First World War, the Jewish population numbered 760,000, or 4.2 percent of the total population.[2] The Jewish population in the expanded country was divided into four historical units—the Regat, Bessarabia, Bukovina, and Transylvania—each of which integrated differently with Romanian society and culture.[3] There were also marked linguistic, cultural, and social differences between the Jews of the Old Kingdom and those of the other three provinces.

Historical circumstances bestowed special importance upon the Jewish community of the Old Kingdom. Nevertheless, the Jews of the Old Kingdom lagged far behind their brethren in Britain, France, or Germany. Romanian gentiles and Jews kept their distance from each other. From the mid-nineteenth century until the emancipation of Jews after the First World War, the stereotyping of Jews prevented their integration. By the end of the First World War, only a few Jews had been granted citizenship. "Europe's last serfs," as the Jewish Italian politician Luigi Luzzatti called them, were granted Romanian citizenship after a struggle lasting some seventy years and only at the behest of the Western powers and against the wish of the Romanian political establishment.

The Romanians granted Jews civil rights, therefore, not out of a desire to integrate them into Romanian society but rather at the urging of the victorious powers, international Jewish organizations, and the local Jewish leadership. The powers made their recognition of Romania's territorial gains (Greater Romania) contingent on the emancipation of the Jews.

After the new Constitution of March 1923 granted the Jews and other minorities full citizenship, the Jews of the Old Kingdom underwent a rapid process of transformation. The most prominent representative of the "new Romanians" who were affiliated with the Union of Romanian Jews was Dr. Wilhelm Filderman, the union's president. He also served as president of the Union of the Jewish Communities in the Regat (Old Romania) and of the Federation of Jewish Communities of Romania and headed the local branches of the American Jewish Joint Distribution Committee and ORT (the society for trades and agricultural labor) and most Jewish organizations in Romania, apart from the Zionist movement. Filderman, like most of those termed "assimilationist" by the Zionists, did not advocate total assimilation or the denial of the Jewish faith. The stream Filderman represented and led sought swift solutions to the problems of the Jews, whose situation was deteriorating. Although the Zionists, through their organization and its leadership and through influential youth movements, offered their own solutions to the plight of Romanian Jewry, they tended to overlook the petty problems of day-to-day life in the Diaspora. Consequently, there were serious confrontations among the Jewish leaders, particularly when the Zionist leadership in Romania was headed by one as forceful and as intransigent as Abraham Leib Zissu (1888–1956).

Due to the hatred and scorn the Romanian nationalists felt toward them, most Jews secluded themselves in their own Jewish world. Unlike their brothers in Germany, France, or Italy, most of them did not even wish to become Romanians. They took part in Romania's political life as Jews or as members of Jewish organizations. On the other hand, the Romanian government and elites, unlike their Hungarian and German counterparts, did not pressure the Jews to assimilate or change their national identity. Despite nationalist outbursts and antisemitic tendencies, no spiritual pressure of any significance was brought to bear on the Jews. Unlike Jews in Germany, France, or even neighboring Hungary, very few Romanian Jews converted or intermarried.

Following the unification of Bessarabia, Bukovina, and Transylvania under Romanian rule, the number of Romanian Jews tripled. To the 240,000 or so Jews of the Old Kingdom were added about 500,000 "foreign" Jews who spoke Hungarian, German, and Russian. Their integration into the Romanian Jewish community was slow and fraught with many administrative and cultural obstacles.

Most Jews of Greater Romania were considered foreigners not only because they were Jewish but also because of linguistic and cultural differences—a natural outcome of historical and geopolitical factors. Their situation contrasted sharply with the relatively comfortable situation of the Jews of the Old Kingdom. The Jews of Greater Romania were a far cry from the image of the foreigner dressed in a capote, speaking a foreign language, and cut off from the world around him, an image that was touted by nationalist antisemites in the mid-nineteenth century.

The interwar period may be considered the heyday of Jewish integration into Romanian society and culture. It was a period in which Jewish authors, playwrights, and artists made important contributions to Romanian culture. And yet Jews were still considered foreigners—and not only by overt antisemites. This proved to be an insurmountable hurdle, which, together with objective cultural, economic, social, and political obstacles, prevented the Romanian Jews from fully integrating into the ambient culture.

Although some Romanian politicians and intellectuals, guided by a broad humanistic perspective, their admiration for the Jewish people, and their wish to enrich Romanian life and create a better Romania, sincerely advocated the integration of Jews into Romanian society, they were a minority in the 1930s—a decade in which antisemitism, and with it Nazi and fascist influences, was on the rise. The Romanian Jews themselves entertained no illusions concerning their integration into the Romanian environment. The oscillation between a desire for integration on the one hand and rejection by the ambient society on the other—which was peculiar to Romanian Jewry—prepared the Jews of the Old Kingdom, psychologically at least, for the difficult years of the Iron Guard and Antonescu's regime.

Demographic Data

General population censuses were conducted in Romania in 1889, 1912, and 1930. After the 1912 census the Romanian Institute of Statistics began publishing statistical and demographic yearbooks with up-to-date information on the number of citizens, including births and deaths. Even so, the question of the size of the Jewish population in Romania served as one of the main pretexts for antisemitic incitement throughout the history of modern Romania. The antisemitic leader Alexandru Constantin Cuza estimated the number of Jews in the Regat after the First World War at 500,000—twice the official number. This number was inflated to 742,321 by an antisemitic demographer.[4] The antisemitic organizations placed the number of Romanian Jews at 2 to 3 million. Upon assuming power, Ion Antonescu himself was convinced that there were 3 to 4 million Jews in his country.[5] Jewish organization and institutions were also partly responsible for this state of affairs. They had inflated the number of Jews in Greater Romania to about 1 million in a bid to stress their importance and the importance of the community in whose name they spoke.

Two serious accusations underpinned this statistical distortion—"the Jewish danger" and the "Jewish invasion" that threatened Romania. Antisemitic propaganda on this issue paid off, creating a feeling, even among decent Romanians and politicians who were not antisemitic, that the official data were not accurate.

Table 1, based on official Romanian data, shows the Jewish population in the Regat in various periods.

Between 1930 and 1939 no change took place in the size of the Jewish population. A census conducted by the Ministry of the Interior in 1939 within the borders of Greater Romania placed the number of Jews at an estimated 765,000. The Romanian population, on the other hand, grew swiftly in this period,

TABLE I. JEWISH POPULATION IN THE REGAT

	1859	1899	1910	1912	1916	1930
Number of Jews	135,000	266,652	243,729	239,967	230,000	264,038
Percentage of population of of Romania	3.0	4.5	3.5	3.3	2.9	3.1

SOURCE: Ministrul Domeniilor, *Buletinul statistic*, 605–710; Colesco, *La population de réligion mosaïque*, 4, 14, 15–19; Ancel, *Documents*, 1:257–73. For official annual data on the number of Jews in the Regat between 1899 and 1915 and on the percentage of Jews in the population, see the demographic study published by the Jewish Center in 1943: Centrala Evreilor din România, *Breviarul statistic*; for selected pages of the study, see Ancel, *Documents*, 1:297–329. For annual statistics on natality and morbidity of Romanian Jews in general in the years 1870–1940 and in Bucharest in particular in the years 1907–40, see Ancel, *Documents*, 1:38, 277–78.

numbering 20,050,520 in 1939.[6] The number of Jews who converted to Christianity was negligible, as we shall have occasion to see. On the eve of the Second World War, therefore, there were fewer than 800,000 Jews in Greater Romania.

NATIONALISM AND ANTISEMITISM — ANTECEDENTS

Christian Roots

Until the twentieth century Romanian Jews had not experienced religiously motivated persecution of the kind that had left many victims in other European countries. However, they lived in the shadow of the religious preconceptions woven around them by Romania's Christian citizens. A study of epistles written by the metropolitans (heads of church in the Romanian principalities), folksongs, sayings, jokes, and even superstitions that prevailed among the Romanian people even before the establishment of modern Romania in 1859 shows that Jews were considered divinely accursed creatures ruled by the devil.[7]

When the first antisemitic movements emerged in modern Romania, they were not working in a vacuum. They simply took the negative Jewish stereotype, a legacy of the Romanian Orthodox Church and local folklore, and refined it. It was not fortuitous that on the eve of the establishment of Antonescu's government (September 1940) the antisemitic press began publishing early church canons and rules that were later adopted by the various synods (assemblies of bishops), such as canon 11, which prohibited any contact with Jews under penalty of excommunication.[8]

The Historical Background of Modern Antisemitism

Right from the dawn of the modern Romanian state, hatred of Jews was an overt and constant feature of Romanian society. Antisemitism left its imprint on Romanian nationalism and was the fuel that catalyzed national consolidation. It accompanied the nation from the dawn of its collective consciousness and did not abandon it even after the realization of its dream of liberation and the unification of all Romanian territories. Already by the mid-nineteenth century the idea that Jews constituted both an internal and external threat, and that they were part of a world conspiracy aimed at destroying the Romanian state, had penetrated the consciousness of many Romanians.

This does not mean that Romania was the most antisemitic country in the world or that Jews there suffered a worse fate than in other European countries. In Romania there was a huge disparity between principles and reality, laws and enforcement, intentions and deeds. This was largely due to the ineptitude of the corrupt government apparatus and the corruption that prevailed in all walks of Romanian life.

The development and consolidation of Romanian Jewry as an entity distinct from other Jewish collectivities in Eastern Europe took place at the height of the Romanians' struggle for liberation and national renewal. At that time the Jews played an important role in socioeconomic processes that were evolving in Romania. Together with several hundred thousand foreign Christians (Greeks, Hungarians, Germans, and Armenians) they stepped into the vacuum left by the absence of a middle class in traditional Romanian society, effecting a partial change in the quasi-feudal structure of Romanian society. This early process of change, or "progress," did not bring about a better or fairer way of life. The partial industrialization that took place in Romania did not bring about the same progress as widespread industrialization had in other countries. Under these conditions any initiative or creativity, especially on the part of Jews, was considered a disruptive force. Members of the new, romantic, Romanian intelligentsia viewed the changes that accompanied the industrialization and urbanization processes as endangering the good old Romanian customs and heritage. From the mid-nineteenth century until the emancipation of Jews in 1923, the integration of Jews in the Old Kingdom was obstructed by a series of prejudices that underlay the policy of the Boyars who ruled Romania until the early twentieth century and their successors, the representatives of the petty bourgeoisie.[9] The new ruling class accepted indiscriminately the antisemitic theories and ideas imported from the West that had evolved under the previous regime.

The National Poet Mihai Eminescu and the Jews

The greatest Romanian poet, Mihai Eminescu (1850–89), played a key role in educating generations of Romanians in the spirit of intolerance, extreme nationalism, and xenophobia. Eminescu's attitude toward the Jews was influenced, inter alia, by German antisemitic publications that he read during his studies in Vienna as well as by German and French newspapers. He was vehemently opposed to the idea of the emancipation of Jews. With his special talent and "sensitivity," he created negative stereotypes of Jews based on their characteristics, appearance, and customs. Eminescu was opposed to any formula granting civil rights to Jews. Like intellectuals both before and after him, he considered peasants, despite their many failings, as the quintessence of Romanianism and the basis of Romania's existence and renewal.

Eminescu was not the only Romanian poet or author who was hostile to Jews. Bogdan P. Hașdeu (1838–1907), one of Romania's most antisemitic intellectuals, listed three negative traits—a tendency to earn money without working, the lack of a sense of dignity, and hatred of all peoples—that were, in his opinion, common to all Jews, and he accused them of plotting against the rest of humanity.[10] The national poet, Vasile Alecsandri (1821–90), described Jews as "leeches" in his antisemitic play *The Village Leeches* (*Lipitorile satului*) and interspersed his poems with antisemitic allusions. Although many intellectuals supported the integration of Jews into Romanian society, the major poets and authors did not. Many antisemitic members of the Romanian intelligentsia also held political positions, and their antisemitic speeches, such as Vasile Conta's (1845–82) parliamentary address, later became compulsory propaganda material for the young members of the Iron Guard.[11] The proposals proffered by these intellectuals for a "solution" to the "Jewish problem" in Romania were quoted in the antisemitic laws of Antonescu's regime.

The first party based on a clear antisemitic platform—the Nationalist Democratic Party (Partidul Naționalist Democrat)—was set up in 1910 by Nicolae Iorga (1871–1940), a brilliant intellectual then at the start of his career, and Alexandru C. Cuza (1857–1947), who already was a virulent hater of Jews. Cuza became the standard-bearer of antisemitism in general and of Christian-based antisemitism in particular. In 1919 Cuza split off from the party and called his faction the Christian Nationalist Democratic Party (Partidul Naționalist Democrat Creștin). The addition of the word *Christian* was not fortuitous, and from this point on it differentiated between regular antisemitic groups or organizations and movements that predicated their hatred of Jews on Christian racist grounds. The platform of the new antisemitic party, as drawn up by Cuza and published in a pamphlet, stated that the purpose of the party was "to fight with all legal means in order to support economic, political, and social interests against the Jews." The party attacked the Minorities Treaty that awarded civil rights to Jews, and it emphasized that the granting of the vote to all citizens served the Jews only and that the only solution to the Jewish problem was to "remove them from the country, after a transitional stage during which all their influence on the Romanian people would be eliminated."[12] The party's work plan explicitly stated that the party's ultimate objective was to oust the Jews from Romania and that the means for attaining this goal were: the abolition of emancipation, the dismissal of Jews from the army, a ban on the employment of Jews in academia and in the civil service, the removal of Jewish children from state schools and the establishment of Jewish schools, and the gradual evacuation of Jews from the villages and their concentration in cities in preparation for their removal from Romania. Upon its establishment in February 1922, the party adopted the swastika as its symbol.

On 4 March 1923 Cuza set up in Iaşi an antisemitic organization called the League of National Christian Defense (Liga Apărării Naţional Creştine, LANC), the largest antisemitic organization in Romania at the time. It should be noted that all the events that led up to the League's establishment, including the ceremonies and speeches, as well as its platform bore no relationship whatsoever to the emergence or ideology of the National Socialist Party in Germany. The League created, fostered, and channeled hatred on a Christian Orthodox basis. The attempt to accuse the Jews of collective subversion against the Christian peoples and against the Romanians in particular—a subversion based on an imperative, a kind of genetic code, that arose from the very essence of Judaism, the Jewish nature, faith, and God—placed Cuza and his generation's hatred of Jews on a religious Christian basis. Cuza saw Christianity not only as a faith but also as a doctrine of the struggle against Romanian Jewry.[13] Already in 1899 Cuza claimed that Judaism was instinctively working to take control of Romania like a robot programmed by its Jewish God (unlike the *Protocols of the Elders of Zion*, which held that it was the Jewish leadership that set goals). Cuza's doctrine was sufficient for the Romanian antisemites, who had no need for the *Protocols of the Elders of Zion*, which had been translated into Romanian in 1923. Cuza's new explanation of the Jewish faith and his "disclosure" of its hidden agenda served as proof that the Jews were the only minorities in Romania who were unable to assimilate.

The extreme nationalist antisemitic movement in Romania, the cradle of the Romanian fascist movement, was not a product of existing political parties, marginal elements, the petty bourgeoisie, or those impoverished by the war—as was the case in Germany—but was first and foremost a student movement. In Romanian schools the sons of peasants and urban Romanians studied alongside the sons of the rural intelligentsia—teachers, clerks, clerics, and army officers. These youth from different social backgrounds created the most extreme and violent antisemitic right-wing movement in that period in Europe. The students of the gymnasia served as a natural pool for the fascist organization that made a bid for power in the late thirties.

Another feature that distinguished the antisemitic-fascist movement in Romania from similar movements in Europe at the time was that their main ideologues were themselves intellectuals (professors of medicine, law, history, and economics) as well as philosophers and poets. These intellectuals were able to speak in the name of Romanian values, which they, and to a certain extent, public opinion, believed expressed continuity with the past and with the Romanian reality, as against the parting with tradition that the new thinking represented.

CODREANU'S IRON GUARD

The Legion of the Archangel Michael (Legiunea Archanghelului Mihail) was set up in June 1927 by Corneliu Zelea Codreanu (1899–1938) and two of his followers. On 12 April 1930 its name was changed to the Iron Guard (Garda de Fier), but it continued to be referred to as the Legion (Legiunea), too.

Although the leaders of the Iron Guard adopted the Christian hatred of Jews typical of the Cuzist school, they did not enter into theological disputes in order to prove the superiority of Christianity and the irrelevance of Judaism. The legionnaires denied not only the Jewish God but also all the values of contemporary society, seeing them as a Jewish invention or as a social order (democracy) that served Jews. They broadened the scope of Christian hatred, adding to it their own exclusive invention—Christian legionary mysticism—that condoned any crime and promised universal absolution.

Youth from both antisemitic movements—the League and the Iron Guard—took part in attacks against Jewish institutions and objects, such as synagogues, Torah scrolls, religious objects, and cemeteries. The Youth (*tineretul*), as Codreanu liked to call his organization, were not all Legionnaires. In practice, many of those willing to attack Jews belonged both to the League (and to its successor organization, the National Christian Party) and to the Iron Guard. Although the link between Christianity and antisemitism was evident in both movements, the Legionnaires in particular attempted to portray their leader as a Christian martyr who dedicated his brief life to fighting Judaism and the Jews and even to identify him with Jesus (according to Cuza's dogma, which they accepted uncritically). In the election campaign of September 1931, Legionary propaganda depicted Codreanu as the messenger "sent by divine providence," who was ready to sacrifice himself fearlessly in order to "save the Romanians from the Jews."[14]

Although the Iron Guard was set up in 1927, its roots stretched back to the late nineteenth century. The debate concerning the authenticity of Romanian fascism is still controversial. The sources are scanty, and studies that have been published inside and outside Romania are few and far between. Most attention has been directed toward Mussolini's and Hitler's fascism. And yet, the definition of Mussolini's fascism as "a new principle"—the antithesis of democracy, plutocracy, the Freemasons, and the "immoral principles" of 1789—fits Codreanu's movement like a glove. Moreover, like Mussolini, Codreanu did not believe in dogmatic political programs and argued that his attitudes—which reflected the Romanian extreme right—were revolutionary and represented a new stage in furthering the Romanian nation.

The Iron Guard belonged, as stated, to the extreme right, and like its Italian counterpart, it was noted for its aggressive nationalism. Under the circumstances, it was directed mainly inward, as militant anti-Marxism or as adulation for a new Romanian state purged of foreigners and harmful foreign influences. Like Italian fascism, the Legion rejected the basic ideas of the French Revolution. To a lesser extent, it rejected the ideals of the bourgeoisie and the middle class (which it believed was overrun by Jews) and promised a new kind of relationship between the new Romanian state and its citizens (after both were purged of Jews).

Thus far we have considered the features common to both Romanian and Italian fascism. But there were differences, too, particularly in their raisons d'être and in their attitudes toward Jews. Romanian fascism, unlike its Italian counterpart, was not the product of military defeat or the injustice of peace treaties (the Minorities Treaty apart). Nor was it the product of a sense of deep moral or social crisis or the sense of the end of an era. Unlike Italian fascism, Romanian antisemitism was not the result of anti-Marxist or nationalist ideas but the driving force behind the movement's very existence.

The antisemitic creed advocated by Codreanu—the Legion's founder and first commander until his assassination in November 1938 by King Carol II's gendarmes—embraced extremes such as good and evil, pure and impure, white and black. To these was added another element—the satanic Jew—who was portrayed, as in Christian works, as a force as strong as, if not stronger than, God himself. Although the Iron Guard resembled Italian fascism in its general ideology, in its hatred of Jews it was closer to the German national socialist brand of fascism.

Codreanu, like Hitler, harbored a pathological hatred of Jews. Like Hitler, his hatred was based on feelings, not facts. As far as he was concerned, modern Romanian history was a constant war between Jews and Romanians. Jews were members of an accursed nation that, directly and through its lackeys, controlled the Romanian economy and sought to gain control of the state, too. The Jews sowed the seeds of hatred and dissension among the Romanians, and their revolutionary Marxist and Communist ideas were a destructive element. There was no compromise in the war between the Romanian people and the Jews. Antisemitism was an existential war for the Romanians, a war that justified all means, however barbaric. The Jewish conscience and morals, which the satanic Jews had disseminated throughout the world via Christianity, were not the morals of the Romanians or true Christians, and the conscience of the Romanian people had to be delivered from their harmful influence. Codreanu, like Hitler, ranted against the power of the Jewish press, which, he claimed, was conducting an unremitting war, trampling the proud ideals of healthy nationalism, and daily poisoning pure Romanian souls. Romanian Jews and their French brothers were guilty of destroying the old Romanian values, such as patriotism, self-sacrifice, and Christianity.

FROM PROPAGANDA AND INCITEMENT
TO ORGANIZED FASCISM AND TERROR

Antisemitic Incitement and Its Repercussions for Political Life, 1919–27

Until, and even a little after, the establishment of the Iron Guard in 1927, antisemitic organizations had only a marginal influence on the masses of the Romanian people and on the political system. Although the large parties were nationalist, they were not extreme, and nearly all of them stressed their commitment to democracy and their support of the democratic powers and of the political mechanisms that had been set in motion in order to prevent the strengthening of Germany and Hungary.

Two phenomena, however, pointed to the danger of fascism in Romania. First, all parties of any significance cultivated antisemitic activists and spokesmen, and their organs included publications of a distinctly antisemitic nature. So-called public opinion of the times focused obsessively on the Jewish "problem" and "danger." These issues were kept in the headlines by antisemitic propaganda and activity, although the government, political parties, and to a lesser extent parliament did not regard them as issues of national importance.

The second phenomenon that should have given grave cause for concern was that the standard-bearers of the new nationalist antisemitism were youth, particularly students. It is hard to find a rationale for the antisemitic ferment that took hold of these youth or their political and social iconoclasm. The First World War had not destroyed Romania's belief in progress or totally shaken the foundations of the Romanian bourgeoisie, with its desire for law and order. Although the war exacted a heavy toll—approximately eight hundred thousand Romanians dead and injured—it nevertheless culminated in the realization of a national dream close to the Romanians' hearts: the unification of all Romanian territories into a single country. When the Romanian soldiers, most of whom were peasants, returned after the war, they were rewarded with the promised prize—a plot of land—under the agrarian reform. Their children, too, along with the children of the urban intelligentsia, were accepted into the ranks of the civil service that had been expanded in order to absorb the newly annexed territories.

Unlike their German counterparts, the demobilized Romanian soldiers were not prepared to take to the streets or engage in illegal activity. On the contrary, there was an atmosphere of jubilation, euphoria, elation, and exaltation and a feeling of self-satisfaction on the part of the leadership and the regime, which, despite the human toll, had succeeded, with the help of the democratic Western powers, in defeating the enemy and establishing Greater Romania. The national ferment that took hold of some Romanian youth after the war may have been partially due to the economic crisis that engulfed Greater Romania from 1919 to 1923 or to the rejection of the Minorities Treaty in November 1919, which, like its predecessors (the 1856 Paris Treaty and the 1878 Berlin Treaty), was perceived as outside interference in Romania's domestic affairs.

The nationalist ferment also had a broader, intellectual base. Greater Romania, although victorious, had not fulfilled the hopes of the youth who had been influenced by the nationalist views of the "forerunners" (*precursori*), as the Legionnaires called them. Brilliant Romanian intellectuals, like their nineteenth-century predecessors, took up the torch of totalitarian nationalism. They incited the youth by providing them with new enemies, both real and fictitious, and laid the ideological foundations of a transformation that turned social and intellectual unrest into a wholly Romanian brand of fascism—although they were not always aware of the implications of their actions.

The antisemitic propaganda—hate literature that was disseminated in public places—raucous rallies, and tacit support of the establishment could not remain an academic debate on the role, or rather relevance, of the Jews in Romanian society. Indeed, since 1919 successive Romanian governments had adopted a national policy that had been widely supported by the political establishment—a policy that preferred Romanians to members of minority groups, who, according to official censuses, accounted for 27 percent of the population. In the three new territories—Bessarabia, Bukovina, and Transylvania—Jews were branded as foreign implants who did not speak the language of the majority. They were accused of helping disseminate the culture of the internal, ethnic enemy and of supporting the struggle of former rulers to change borders and peace treaties. In Bessarabia Jews were also accused of supporting Communism. The Romanian establishment, for its part, made no real attempt to integrate the Jews of the three new territories, who numbered over half a million, into Romanian society and culture. These Jews, more than other minority groups (Hungarians, Germans, Russians, and Ukrainians), became the main focus of hatred—a hatred concocted of traditional xenophobia (largely induced by the behavior of the aforementioned people toward the Romanians), traditional antisemitism, modern nationalism, and fear of an international revisionist conspiracy.

This hostility was further exacerbated by a flurry of accusations in the wake of the emancipation of the Jews of the Regat. These accusations led to demands to curb the intake of Jewish students to universities, through the introduction of a "Numerus Clausus" (limit on the number of Jewish students) and later a "Numerus Nullus" (total interdiction of Jewish students).

The brutal struggle against the Jews between 1919 and 1927, when the Iron Guard was established, was spearheaded by Romanian youth and students who belonged to the League and others. This struggle sent shock waves through Romanian society and political life by demanding a response, making a stand, and adopting unpopular measures. Anyone who remained faithful to the principles of democracy—and there were still many who did—was deemed a traitor and a "Yid-lover." Many politicians, party leaders, heads of movements, members of the establishment, government ministers, and intellectuals were opposed to this violent antisemitic incitement. In most cases, however, this opposition was not consistent, forceful, or explicit. A kind of tacit consent to the illegal actions the antisemitic youth perpetrated against the Jewish minority could be discerned among some of the aforementioned actors. Yet others hoped or believed that it was possible to differentiate between antisemitic activities and actions aimed at undermining the country's internal stability and for two different systems of morality and justice to coexist, while still preserving a democratic system of government. The playwright Eugène Ionesco (1909–94) referred to this "rhinocerization" of values in his play *The Rhinoceros*, in which the gradual transformation of the main characters into rhinoceroses served as a metaphor for their attraction to fascist ideas. In the mystical lexicon of the Legionnaires this transfiguration (*schimbarea la față*) took place after the Nazis' rise to power in Germany. Although the Romanian government helped foster a climate of antisemitism, it was held in check by international agreements, its wish to maintain the support of its traditional democratic allies in the West, and its need for loans and foreign capital.

The question of the roots of Romanian fascism, a question that has preoccupied many researchers, has been totally distorted by Romanian Communist historians.[15] The Communist Party, and many Romanian intellectuals in exile, favored the theory that Romanian fascism, although predicated on Romanian roots, was largely shaped by influences outside Romania. Ironically, in the thirties Codreanu and Cuza considered any suggestion, in parliament or in the press, that their movements were imitating Nazi ideology or work methods or Italian fascism to be a personal affront. Indeed, until the midthirties Codreanu had no ties with Hitler's movement.

Fascism and Antisemitic Terror, 1927–37

The period between the rise of the Romanian fascist Legion of the Archangel Michael, the second movement of its kind in Romania, in 1927, and the establishment of the Goga-Cuza government in December 1937 was marked by the rise of antisemitic and new, right-wing forces, most of which grew out of the existing political system. The brutal solutions to the Jewish problem proposed by the various antisemitic organizations from the early twentieth century were no longer mere antisemitic propaganda but an integral part of party platforms. Threats against Jews became the centerpiece of national and public debates. The democratic or self-styled democratic forces were in constant ebb, while the antisemitic leaders gained legitimization from respected political parties and public opinion and even the king. The economic crisis that engulfed the world from 1929 to 1933, coupled with the Nazis' rise to power, strengthened those elements that were proposing a new way of solving Romania's ills by jettisoning democratic values. They thereby hoped to cure the ailments of Romanian politics and lead Romania into a new era, in which the "nation," "resolve," "action," and the "elites" would turn Romania into a bastion of "Romanianism" and a natural ally of Italy and Germany.

The above notwithstanding, many powerful elements, guided mainly by a sincere concern for Romania's territorial integrity, opposed this trend. These elements were capable of neutralizing the nationalist monster they had themselves helped create. Under the prevailing political conditions (the relentless power struggle between the two large democratic parties, the constant reelection of the governing party, the appointment of cabinet ministers by the king, and the perpetuation of illegal acts under the cover of nationalism), however, it was impossible to unite all the democratic forces necessary to deliver a solid and fatal blow to Romanian fascism and its adherents. Moreover, the vacillating foreign policy of the Western powers in the Balkans as against the resolve, consistency, and assertiveness of the Nazis and the Nazi support, in 1934, of local antisemitic forces helped undermine Romania's internal stability and transformed the formal value system of the thinking Romanian public.

The nationalist, antisemitic, and vocal right grew from year to year, and with it the verbal and physical hatred of Jews. It was in this period that the students' intransigent nationalism turned into authentic Romanian fascism. This fascism spread beyond the university campuses to the political system and all strata of public life. The young hooligans of the early twenties were now politicians and leaders who were courted by the rich bourgeois intelligentsia and even by the aristocracy.

Although verbal and physical attacks against Jews continued unabated throughout the period, the greatest danger to Romanian Jewry in this period was the attempt to delegitimize Jews by demonizing and depersonalizing them. Depicting them as non-persons and the abstract embodiment of evil made it possible, and even necessary, to eradicate them. The Romanian fascist movement ventured to advocate a total social revolution, a national renewal in all fields, and the destruction of the entire political system headed by the "parasitic parties . . . addicted to foreigners."[16] The campaign, which began with the debasement of the Jewish faith and a demand for the introduction of the Numerus Clausus and the provision of Jewish cadavers to medical schools, became an all-out existentialist war against Romanian Jews as well as a ruthless war against the government and its values. The idea that inspired the Legionnaires' "ideology of the act" (*ideologia faptei*) was a local product, not a Nazi or fascist import. The Legion was predicated on the rejection of Jews as a social ill that was contaminating the healthy body of the Romanian nation; hence its rejection of democracy (which favored the Jews) and its resolve to take action. The Legionnaires branded all personalities, parties, and ideas that, in their opinion, served the Jews or protected the system that served them as a national danger. Under Nazi and fascist influence, the Legionnaires attempted in this period to define and clarify their doctrine in an attempt to publicly emphasize the authentic Romanian character of the movement and its roots in the Romanian reality and tradition.

THE ESTABLISHMENT OF NEW ANTISEMITIC FRAMEWORKS

The Romanian Front

One characteristic of the political arena after 1935 was the consolidation of antisemitic and fascist tendencies within the parties and splinter parties, which openly declared their support for the various solutions to the Jewish problem and the desire to reform the democratic parliamentary system (leading ultimately to the curtailment of civil liberties and to dictatorship). Although the political lexicon does not always stretch to defining these parties and lists, one thing is clear: they were all fascist. They produced personalities whom Antonescu later incorporated into his government, some of whom had served in the quasi-fascist regimes that preceded him. They formed a kind of school of extreme nationalism and active antisemitism, whose outstanding alumni were awarded positions in the Goga-Cuza government, in the king's last governments, in the Legionary government, and in Antonescu's government.

The split within the National Peasants' Party in 1932 engendered national political and antisemitic activity that turned hatred of minority groups in general and of Jews in particular into an electoral prize. The leader of the Romanian Front (Frontul Românesc) was Alexandru Vaida-Voevod (1872–1950), head of the party's right-wing arm and Romanian prime minister from 1932 to 1933. Born in 1872 in Hungarian-controlled Transylvania (like Goga), Vaida-Voevod served as one of the leaders of the Romanian National Party that had fought against Hungary's oppressive rule and as a member of parliament in Budapest had informed the world of the Romanians' suffering. The group that, together with Vaida-Voevod, split off from the original party, the National Peasants' Party (considered the pillar of Romanian democracy), demanded in effect the renunciation of the democratic regime that had, at least on paper, granted rights and equal opportunities to minority groups, particularly the Jews. Slogans such as "Romania for the Romanians" and especially "Numerus Valachicus" (to promote the ethnic Romanian majority in every institution or enterprise) became the hallmark of the Romanian Front. In a special pamphlet he published in April 1935, Vaida-Voevod claimed that Romania and the Romanians had been brought to the brink of extinction by the foreigners who were ruling them.[17]

Prior to his secession from the main party, Vaida-Voevod asked its executive committee to introduce the Numerus Clausus. The Front's platform, published on 12 May 1935, stated that Romania's policy must have a single objective: to safeguard the existence and development of the Romanian nation. The "principle of proportional representation" (*principiul proporționalității*) was the corollary of such a policy, since it allowed ethnic Romanians to control all branches of the economy.[18] Vaida-Voevod swallowed wholesale the contention of the nineteenth-century antisemitic nationalists that Romania had no "ethnic" Romanian middle class engaging in commerce and industry and that therefore it had to create such a class, with the help of the Romanian state, through a national credit system and close supervision of the various branches of industry for the good of the ethnic Romanians. (This was exactly the same policy Antonescu espoused after stripping the Jews of their assets). Vaida-Voevod sought to apply the principle of proportional representation to intellectual life, the press, education, and the universities by preparing and training Romanian children to serve the Romanian nation and state.

Although the Front's doctrine was effectively turned against all minority groups, in practice the new right-wing organizations bolstered the antisemitic political establishment. A nationalist party headed by the prime minister and deputy leader of the National Peasants' Party conferred greater respectability on the national idea, its followers, and activists in Romania's political life. This party's slogans served to legitimize the call for purging Romanian society of Jews.

In the course of the Front's three years of activity, its antisemitic attitudes became increasingly pronounced. Although the public considered the Front a right-wing party, it did not really consider it antisemitic, like the Iron Guard or the National Christian Party. In the nationalist context the Front's attitudes toward the Jewish question were, evidently, minimalist. Even this minimum, however, included the revocation of the emancipation of Jews, as Dr. Mihai Isacescu, the party's parliamentary representative, specified on 24 November 1936 when he called for a review of citizenship, since "there are over half a million cases of fraud."[19]

The history of this right-wing party of fascist hue (*de coloratură fascistă*) — as a Romanian historian put it when describing the radicalization of people and organizations that had formerly not been considered extreme — was yet another manifestation of the unprincipled nature of Romanian politics, the king's gross intervention in the political debate in an attempt to safeguard his interests, a disdain for democratic values, and a total lack of concern about the fate of Jewish citizens.[20] As Filderman stated at the time, antisemitism gradually evolved into a true "collective psychosis."[21]

The National Christian Party

The third antisemitic fascist party that was largely responsible for the demonization and marginalization of Jews (or rather, for the erosion of the partial acceptance of Jews before and after the emancipation) was the National Christian Party (Partidul Național-Creștin). The party was founded on 14 July 1935, following the fusion of Goga's National Agrarian Party (Partidul Național-Agrar, founded in 1932, after Octavian Goga broke away from the National Peasants' Party) and Cuza's League.

Goga's political message resembled his literary one: Romanian nationalism. The close "love affair" between Goga and Cuza (which to a large extent was reminiscent of that between Cuza and Iorga at the start of the century) was a foregone conclusion, both because of political developments in Romania and because of their political aspirations. Both were disillusioned with what they had set in motion, with students turned terrorists and murderers, and wished to destroy the doctrine and regime on which Greater Romania was predicated. Goga was keen to gain power, while Cuza, born in 1857, was old and tired enough to comply, although he was the new party's formal leader and most of its cadres were members of the League. What united them were hatred of Jews and foreigners and a common perception of the Romanian cultural heritage. In a collection of essays published in 1930, Goga ascribed to Eminescu copyright over more than just his contribution to Romanian literature:

> He is the father of the contemporary national ideology. . . . [M]ore than us all, he believed in the people, felt the people, and understood its historical mission. . . . Read his "Doina," the poem of our eternal aspiration: It is the definitive political evangel of Romanianism, a national, political orientation based on purity of blood. . . . Likewise, on the issue of the removal of the exploitative foreigner, there is no more brilliant doctrinarian than the poet. . . . Read his works and see for yourselves that you are standing before truths that are valid to this day.[22]

The new party was supported by the "urban bourgeoisie and several established rural elements" as well as by petty entrepreneurs in Moldova, Bessarabia, and Transylvania "who were unhappy with the tyrannical competition of big capital." The party's leadership included "intellectuals, teachers, lawyers, engineers, journalists, and students" as well as some dissatisfied politicians who had abandoned other parties.[23] This description of the social composition of the National Christian Party by two Communist historians shows to what extent this antisemitic-fascist party won the support of all sectors of established Romanian society. Goga and Cuza complemented each other: while the former attracted peasants and the rural intelligentsia, especially in Transylvania, the latter enjoyed traditional support in Bukovina and in parts of Moldova and Bessarabia.

King Carol and his entourage skillfully played off Goga, who supported the monarchy, against Cuza, the party's leader, hoping thereby to prepare Goga and his party for the role they had assigned for him in the Romanian political chess game—that of alternative to the Iron Guard, which like the National Christian Party was fascist, antisemitic, and pro-Nazi, but unlike the party retained its allegiance to the king.

The merger between the two parties was celebrated on 14 July 1935 in the Moldavian capital of Iaşi in the presence of several thousand supporters and delegations of the two parties who had congregated in the train station and the station concourse. Cuza and his son, Gheorghe Cuza, welcomed the national poet Octavian Goga (1881–1938), who was accompanied by a delegation of youth from the League. They continued their way on foot, dressed in the League's uniform—blue shirts, leather belts, and swastikas on their sleeves. A military band and three hundred Romanian flags bearing the sign of the swastika completed the scene. Cuza stood outside his house and read out the party platform, which stated, inter alia: "We want the spiritual principle of Christianity to serve as the foundation of the Christian State and therefore we consider the national church the supreme representative of the force creating the moral foundation." Goga-Cuza's country, therefore, was by definition a Christian country, in which Christian law prevailed and the clergy had special rights and privileges. The party platform called for:

1. an amendment to the Constitution that would apply the national principle to the country's life in order to bring about a moral transformation in Romanian society and restore the principle of state authority;
2. the establishment of a corporative senate and the introduction of a constitutional clause ensuring political power for ethnic Romanians;
3. nationalization of the press, so that minority groups would be banned from writing in Romanian, except in their own journals; and
4. Romania for Romanians of "Romanian blood": that is, application of the "national principle" to the government and government institutions and application of the principle of proportional representation in its "ethnic" sense to all private enterprises.[24]

According to the party platform, all civil service and government jobs, all state commissions, and all trading in state monopolies would be open to ethnic Romanians only. The platform also called for some Romanization of the private sector, through the dismissal of workers who were not of ethnic Romanian stock in order to ensure that 73 percent of all factory jobs (even in factories owned by members of minority groups) remained in Romanian hands. The platform differentiated between three types of minority groups:

1. Minority groups that were loyal to the Romanian state (the Germans). Members of this group could be awarded public positions on a proportional basis.
2. Minority groups belonging to the revisionist states (states aspiring to change the borders stipulated in the peace treaties, namely the Hungarians and Bulgarians). Members of these minority groups could also be awarded "certain" public positions and were allowed to engage in commerce, industry, and the liberal professions on a proportional basis.

3. Jewish nationals, as "newcomers" who were still subject to the influence of foreign Jews and of their countries of origin, "constituted a divisive element that thwarted the country's progress. Consequently, the country was obliged to protect the Romanian administration and workforce." What this effectively meant was a "Numerus Nullus in public service and probably also the denial of the right to work."[25]

The platform included three other points that had a significant bearing on the fate of Romanian Jewry, dealing with the refugee problem, the review of citizenship, and urban Romanization and nationalization of property—all traditional elements of antisemitic thinking.

The National Christian Party sought to deny Romanian citizenship to all those who had entered the country after the signing of the peace treaties, namely, to large sections of Jews in the annexed territories. It also established the need to nationalize the property of urban and rural minorities (i.e., the Jews) for reasons of "national expediency," to encourage Romanians to settle in key localities, and to Romanize the cities. The platform did not overlook culture, either, but demanded "administration and supervision by the Ministry of Propaganda to ensure a constructive national orientation to all facets of Romanian culture—publications, the press, theater, cinema and radio."[26]

We may sum up the general principles of the National Christian Party's platform by quoting Cuza's words, delivered in a faltering tongue, on the occasion of the merger with Goga: "Cuza's new Romania will be a Romania without Jews, since this is Hitler's policy. Or, rather, Hitler's policy is Cuza's policy, since it preceded Hitler."[27]

Even though the Nazis took part in the establishment of the new fascist party (see chap. 5), its founders were right in stating that Romanian fascism had Romanian roots. The National Christian Party's platform was largely based on the Romanian antisemitic dream of classical antisemitism—namely the minimalist program of the anti-Jew stream that began coalescing before the establishment of the Romanian state in 1859.

The Romanian antisemitic dream was formulated in 1935, when Britain and France (the powers behind the establishment of Greater Romania and the unification of all Romanians) as well as the League of Nations, which was still operating in Geneva, were forces to be reckoned with. The platform, therefore, stopped short of calling for the total revocation of the emancipation of Jews. It left certain positions open to members of minorities other than Jews and did not deprive all Jews of their livelihoods. The platform also contained a semblance of human rights in order to avoid the condemnation of the League of Nations.

The program, which became even more antisemitic after the collapse of the Western powers and the dissolution of the League of Nations, was adopted wholesale by Antonescu's administration and became the official antisemitic policy in the Regat and southern Transylvania. After the alliance with Nazi Germany, Romanian nationalist statesmen no longer had to couch their language in acceptable terms or resort to linguistic ambiguities (unlike the Legionnaires, who spoke openly of their plans to solve the Jewish problem). This policy was preceded by an intense and consistent delegitimization and demonization campaign that stripped Jews of their humanity and turned them into social evils and dangerous parasites that hindered Romania's regeneration and, ultimately, had to be eradicated.

I

The Goga Government
Europe's Second Antisemitic Government, 28 December 1937–10 February 1938

In the elections held in Romania on 20 December 1937, Gheorghe Tătărescu's ruling National Liberal Party received only 36 percent of the vote; Iuliu Maniu's National Peasants' Party, 20 percent; the Iron Guard, 16 percent; and Octavian Goga's party, 9 percent. King Carol II now faced the task of appointing the new prime minister, a task granted to him under the Romanian Constitution. According to this constitution, a ruling party had to gain at least 40 percent of the vote in order to form a new government. Therefore, Tătărescu (1886–1957) was not eligible for the premiership, even though his party received most of the votes. Maniu (1873–1953) and Codreanu were also out of the running, Maniu due to his unbridled criticism of King Carol II and Codreanu because the king wished to curb him. Therefore, the king charged Octavian Goga with the task.

Goga's "forty-four-day" government comprised the representatives of political antisemitism in Romania: members of the National Christian Party, leaders who had defected from the National Peasants' Party (notably Minister of the Interior Armand Călinescu [1893–1939]), and newcomers to the political scene, such as Gen. Ion Antonescu. This heterogeneous government was formed at the king's behest and was designed to serve his interests. Through his loyal followers in the government, the king hoped to retain control of the country. He therefore turned a blind eye to the National Christian Party's antisemitic platform (formulated in Iaşi in 1935 when the party was established), and even predicated the government's basic guidelines on the National Christian Party's political and social platform.

King Carol II encouraged the formation of an extreme right-wing government run by someone who supported the king and the monarchy in general. As a seasoned western diplomat in Bucharest stated, King Carol sought "to give Nationalism a chance to express itself within the present Government rather than be forced to call on the Iron Guard at some future date."[1] Even though this political maneuver was directed against the Iron Guard, it was welcomed by Berlin—which at the time still considered Goga, not Codreanu, its closest ally. This approval notwithstanding, the king managed to persuade Goga to include in his government loyalists such as Călinescu, the Iron Guard's sworn enemy, and Antonescu, at the time a staunch sympathizer of England and France.

King Carol's manipulations were largely driven by his deep contempt for political life, politicians, and the entire "democratic" system in Romania. "This is my government, and it must have my approval. The day I am not satisfied with its conduct of affairs, I shall require a change," the king declared in public after the establishment of the Goga government.[2] As the Italian historian Mariano Ambri explained, the king sought to exploit Romanian fascists of the Goga and Cuza ilk in order to block fascists of the Codreanu ilk.[3]

Christianity was the cement that bound Cuza to Goga and the nationalist circles in general and that largely neutralized opposition from the two large parties and the Iron Guard. "We believe first and foremost in the spiritual awakening of Romania through the doctrines of the Christian Church and its luminaries," declared Goga at a public gathering convened to outline his government's plans in early January 1938.[4] Cuza and Goga, the leaders of Romanian Christian fascism, invoked God, Christianity, and the church in stressing their will to solve Romania's problems and "restore Romania to the Romanians." Immediately after the establishment of his government Cuza announced, "Under no circumstances shall we relinquish [even] the slightest paragraph of our platform. Goga and myself have sworn [in the Cathedral of Iaşi] before God to restore Romania to the Romanians. We shall surmount the obstacles I have been contending with for fifty years, unflinchingly."[5] The tenets on which Goga's government was based—"Jesus, the monarchy, and the nation"—were the tenets on which Romanian nationalism had been predicated since 1864.[6] No wonder, then, that Goga was angered by allegations that these tenets were fascist or Nazi in origin. "We have no ties with National Socialism," he declared. "These ideas are of local provenance; they are pure ideas that, in my opinion, shall bring about a radical change in the history of mankind."[7]

The world Goga wished to set to rights was, according to him, basically a good world that had been spoiled and exploited by foreigners. It was a world that had suffered much, that had been oppressed and suppressed, but that had finally embraced the nationalist idea that accompanied the National Christian Party's rise to power "after a period of ostensible weakness of the State organism. The suffering, pain, and exploitation that had been the Romanians' lot," explained Goga in his government's guidelines, "triggered the revival of a proud and imperious [*poruncitor*] country aware of its own destiny." "We propose to compensate the [Romanian] nation," he declared in a radio broadcast, "as it expects."[8] Thus, seventy years after Mihai Eminescu launched the theme of national protest, Goga, also a poet, took up the same theme—that of a pure and glorious Romania, spoiled only by the foreigners and their ideas.

King Carol's political gambit exacerbated the situation of the Jews. Even before assuming office, the new minister of religious affairs, the historian Ion Lupaş (1880–1967), announced, "[The emergence of] the National Christian Party is justified because of the huge danger of the Jewish invasion."[9] The new prime minister's nationalist rhetoric was reminiscent of the basic tenets of Romanian nationalism. This nationalism, which ultimately developed into Romanian fascism, left no doubt as to who were the country's real enemies and how to deal with them.

Fascist and antisemitic nationalism, plans "to right wrongs," concern for the fate of the peasants, and the necessity of "purging" Romania of half a million vagabonds (*vagabonzi*) who had found in it a "new California" helped raise antisemitism to its greatest pinnacle yet: state antisemitism.[10] King Carol himself encouraged state antisemitism, spreading the antisemitic fiction that "250,000 Jewish invaders" had entered Romania. It was King Carol, too, who explained at length to a *Daily Herald* correspondent that he had appointed Goga prime minister because "the public spirit in Romania tends towards nationalism." There were "strong antisemitic feelings," and the Jewish problem was the country's main domestic problem.[11]

This anti-Jewish policy was founded on the myths and aspirations of the classical Romanian antisemitic dream. Goga the intellectual—like his predecessors in the Romanian intelligentsia—introduced irrational elements into his rhetoric. He used his literary talent and imagination to provide a graphic description of the genetic flaws of the Jewish people. He differentiated between the "olive-skinned" oriental Jews of "the pure Semitic type," who were "fairly refined," and western Jews, who were "crude, red-skinned, had almond-shaped eyes and flat Slavic features, and who had come over later from Poland and Russia."[12] Romania, stated Goga, might have come to terms with its oriental Jews, as had the French, English, and Dutch. Over the past twenty year, however, Romania had "suffered four consecutive invasions, each more dangerous than the last."[13]

Goga depicted Jews as pests and rodents that destroyed anything in their path. He described the "long-toothed" Galician Jews who had fled to Romania in 1916 as "formidable rivals."[14] He argued that Romania had no obligation to honor its undertakings under the peace treaties toward the half a million Jews (a fictitious number) that had infiltrated its borders, "and no-one can oblige us to keep them." In short, concluded Goga, the Jews were a "calamity."[15]

The anti-Jewish measures adopted by the Goga government were of three kinds: (1) Romanization; (2) exclusion of Jews from intellectual life, in particular from the press; and (3) denial of civil rights. The government investigated the possibility of expelling all Jews from Romania. In his address to the Romanian people Goga stressed that, as long as it was in power, his government planned to "create a new framework for our people."[16] In the same vein Cuza promised, "As long as I am in power, I shall implement my plan" — and rejected any possibility of flexibility in its application.[17]

All municipal councils were dissolved in order to rid them of members of minority groups and to steer them "toward the national idea." This measure, presented as "a prelude to further reforms," affected in the main Hungarians, Germans, and other minority groups, which accounted for as much as 60–70 percent of the population in certain Transylvanian cities.[18]

As part of the Romanization process, Jewish physicians and lawyers employed in public institutions were dismissed from their jobs. The National Insurance Fund, in its haste to get rid of its Jewish employees, dismissed them on New Year's Day 1938, a public holiday. The public found out what had happened the following day, when the press provided a list of Jews who had been made redundant and their Romanian replacements.[19]

S. Cunescu, general director in the Ministry of Labor, Health, and Social Security, announced that "Jews employed Romanian women in their homes in order to turn them into prostitutes."[20] The law forbade them to employ Christian servants or cooks under the age of forty.[21] Despite protestations, neither Goga's government nor the ensuing government (under the patriarch Miron Cristea) did anything to refute this collective accusation.[22]

Immediately upon assuming power, Goga announced his intention to appoint commissars to supervise the implementation of the Law for the Protection of the National Labor in factories belonging to minority groups.[23] Although the government was too short-lived to ever implement this law, the commissars effectively took control of the factories and their employment policies. In a similar vein, a committee was set up to discuss the "Romanization of factories and corporations that rely on local capital and receive profits from the State [but] which favor foreign workers over Romanian ones."[24]

The committee was set up to discuss the problem of Jewish-owned factories that employed Jewish workers, officials, or experts. The prime minister himself explained that this stage of the Romanization process called for confiscation of the factories for the benefit of those who supported the government. In an attempt to ruin them, a directive was issued forbidding the factories to carry out any transaction with the state, and special committees were established in order to purge commerce, industry, and labor of undesirable elements.

Goga made no secret of his intention to nationalize Jewish factories and dismiss Jews. In an interview with the British *Evening Standard*, he explained that this move was triggered by the Jews' monopolization of most of Romanian industry: "Foreigners have taken over taken our major industries, such as iron, mining and oil. Of Romania's 18 million inhabitants, a million-and-a-half are Jews. I intend dismissing Jews, in accordance with the principle of 'Romania for the Romanians.' I shall see to it that all jobs currently held by Jews are handed over to Romanians."[25] These attempts to marginalize Jews, which began even before Goga's appointment, received greater impetus during his tenure thanks to the Law for the Revision of Citizenship, which was promulgated on 22 January 1938.[26] This law was loosely interpreted as granting the authorities the right to retract the work permits of Jews whose citizenship was called into question and led to the dismissal of tens of thousands of Jews from their jobs, especially in the liberal professions.

Another antisemitic measure, largely prompted by stereotypes of Jews promulgated by the Romanian intelligentsia in the nineteenth century, was the passage of a bill confiscating all licenses from Jewish rural innkeepers and vendors of alcohol, tobacco, cigarettes, matches, and other goods over which the state had a monopoly. The licenses, which were usually assigned to war invalids or widows, "would be reassigned to Romanian war invalids" announced Goga on the radio.[27] In Nicolae Iorga's newspaper *Neamul Românesc*, Goga added that "150,000 Jewish-owned country taverns had been closed, because they endangered public health."[28] This figure was grossly inflated. According to official data submitted to the representative of British Jewry during his visit to Romania, there were 52,796 tavern owners in Romania, of which only 11,700 were Jews.[29]

Jewish lawyers were also a thorn in the government's side. The Romanian Bar Association in Bucharest, Foreign Minister Micescu's fiefdom, immediately passed an internal resolution to provisionally revoke the right of about 1,540 Jewish lawyers to practice their professions.[30]

The revocation of work permits in order to exclude Jews from the bar association was not significant in itself. What was significant was that this was the first time an attempt was made to anchor such a measure in law. The call for a law stipulating the collective dismissal of 1,540 lawyers for no other reason than that they were Jewish was in its simplest form a racist scheme cooked up by Romanian lawyers.

Although the bill was not passed, many Jewish lawyers were prevented, sometimes forcibly, from exercising their professions. In four districts Jewish lawyers were dismissed from bar associations despite being Romanian citizens.[31] Minister for Minorities Silviu Dragomir (1888–1962) expressed his "regret" at this "local activity," but the practice was never revoked, even after the Goga government's collapse.

The exclusion of Jews from the country's intellectual life began with the banning of three reputable Romanian newspapers—*Lupta*, *Dimineața*, and *Adevărul*—which, the prime minister claimed, were run mainly by foreigners whose interests conflicted with Romanian ideals.[32] These newspapers were targeted in particular for their open criticism of extremist nationalism and Romanian fascism in its various guises, their staunch support of the Western democratic powers, and their condemnation of Goga's pro-Nazi orientation.

Goga had been perturbed by these papers already in 1922, and Cuza even earlier than that. A stereotype commonly entertained by Romanian nationalists was that of the Jewish journalist who "bought" or blackmailed Romanian politicians in the cause of international Judaism. Goga, explaining the rationale behind the closure of the newspapers, described them as "foreign bodies in the country's cultural heritage, the creative struggle of which must not be obstructed by devious or subversive interventions." This was censorship of a new kind, designed to "eliminate at [the] source all obstacles to the National Christian idea . . . while recognizing that the directives to be addressed to the Romanian nation are a domestic problem of the people constituting the State."[33]

Jewish newspapers in Bukovina and Bessarabia were also banned, such as the German-language *Czernowitzer Blaeter*, the Hebrew *Darkenu*, and the Yiddish-language *Dos Yiddische Vort* and *Aufbau* (Oifboy). Members of the ruling party snatched Jewish newspapers from kiosks and burnt them in public squares. Likewise, over 120 Jewish journalists were deprived of permits to travel on Romanian railways.[34]

The government ordered Ion Alexandru Hodoș, a deputy minister in the prime minister's office, to draft a bill restricting journalism to ethnic Romanians. Non-ethnic Romanians were permitted to write for their own newspapers in their own languages only.[35] The purpose of the law was to prevent Jewish journalists access to Romanian newspapers. The new minister of education, Ion Petrovici (1882–1972), advised members of other minority groups "not to segregate themselves from Romanian culture, or isolate their youth from the spirit of the ruling people."[36] Iorga's newspaper *Neamul Românesc* accused Jewish publishers of polluting the Romanian soul, although, as Filderman pointed out, the publishing industry in Romania had been set up by Jews, and many books written by Iorga himself had been put out by Jewish publishers.[37]

The new government sought to exclude Jews not only from journalism and publishing but also from the cinema and theater. The minister of culture drew up a bill for the nationalization of all theaters and cinemas in Romania, adding that he would not wait for the bill to be approved but would adopt resolutions "accordingly."[38] Although this law was not implemented, neither was it revoked.

The Goga-Cuza government attempted to make capital out of this array of antisemitic laws in preparation for the approaching elections. Its election manifesto of 7 February 1938 emphasized its achievements in eliminating the Jewish influence from the country's intellectual life and its intention to continue doing so. In an impassioned appeal it exhorted the electorate to give the National Christian Party a chance to implement the rest of its platform: "See what we have achieved in only one month of rule, through simple administrative directives, pending the approval of new laws that we shall, in the future, bring before a new parliament that shall be elected. We have banned the publication of Jewish newspapers . . . the poisonous product of foreigners who have taken up residence among us, and who, under assumed names, warp our language, interfere in our domestic affairs, and desecrate the holy altar of Romanian sentiment."[39] The Law for the Revision of Romanian Citizenship, the embodiment of a fundamental tenet of the Romanian antisemitic platform, dealt the Jews a heavy blow, the effect of which was felt for many years to come.

Upon assuming power Goga informed the nation that preparations were underway for reviewing the citizenship of Jews who had been naturalized after the war.[40] This measure was based on the antisemitic fiction that "hundreds of thousands of citizens of Jewish extraction or religion were refugees or immigrants who were not entitled to Romanian citizenship or who had obtained it through fraudulent means."[41]

In 1936 the Central Bureau of Statistics determined that, according to the 1930 census, 758,000 Jews were living in Romania, constituting 4.2 percent of the population. The number of refugees from Russia—both Jewish and non-Jewish—totaled 11,000.[42] Even so, Romanian newspapers and politicians from all shades of the political spectrum claimed that hundreds of thousands of Jews had stealthily entered the country after the First World War.[43]

After ten days in power Goga, in an interview with a French newspaper, claimed that over half a million Jews had entered Romania illegally. Four days later he "downscaled" this figure to "half a million at the most."[44] The spokesman for the Romanian embassy in Paris set the number of Jewish refugees in Romania at a million. In an interview with an English paper the king stated, "Some say as many as 800,000 . . . [but] the maximum was [actually] about 250,000."[45]

Alongside the tendency to inflate the number of Jewish refugees in Romania was a tendency to inflate the number of Jews in Romania as a whole. Antisemitic demographers published fictitious assessments of the Jewish population in Romania. "The Jews number almost three million," stated the statistician I. D. Bârsan in the early twenties. A few months later he modified this to "over two million." His colleague, E. Vasiliu, spoke of "1,590,000 Yids."[46] Goga himself claimed that there were 1.5 million Jews in Romania, a figure a reputable Romanian paper denied, stating that Romania "had only 1,200,000 Jews."[47]

This practice of inflating estimates of the number of Jews—both established residents and newcomers—was not new. What was new, however, was the way in which the National Christians turned propaganda into seemingly incontrovertible facts. The promulgation of the Law for the Revision of Citizenship immediately gave antisemitic incitement a strong impetus. This and other antisemitic measures introduced by the government intensified hatred of the Jews and fueled the feeling that the Romanians were no longer the masters of their own country.

Jewish spokesmen and organizations made an abortive attempt to show that these figures were inflated by invoking official data showing that there were no more than 760,000 Jews in Romania (a figure corroborated by subsequent censuses, particularly the 1942 one).[48] Filderman himself estimated that 10,000 Jews had entered Romania illegally, and he was not even opposed to their expulsion.[49]

The Law for the Revision of Citizenship brought into question the citizenship of all Jews, not just those considered refugees, vagabonds, or illegal immigrants. It was a total and patent breach of the peace treaties and all international agreements for the protection of minorities—as well as of the Romanian Constitution and all the naturalization laws that had been passed after the Berlin Congress of 1878. The law had repercussions not only for the legal status of Jews but also for all aspects of their lives, such as accommodation, business permits, work permits, permits to exercise certain professions, membership in trade unions, and the like. These rights were automatically revoked with the abolition of citizenship and sometimes—depending on the whim of the various authorities—as soon as a Jew's citizenship was brought into question.

This law went further than other, similar laws by placing the burden of proof on the Jews, not the courts.[50] The law divided Jews into three main categories: (1) residents of the annexed territories (Bessarabia, Transylvania, and Bukovina); (2) residents of the Regat who had been granted citizenship on the basis of an affidavit (as specified in the peace accords); and (3) residents of the Regat who had been granted citizenship by court decision. Jews in all three categories immediately lost their right to participate in the approaching elections (which, ultimately, never took place).

Mayors were given thirty days to draw up lists of citizens whose citizenship was considered questionable. A copy of each list was delivered to the local magistrates court and another copy was posted in the municipality. All Jews had to check whether their names appeared on the list. Those in the first category were given thirty days to submit documents and permits proving their eligibility for Romanian citizenship. If their papers were in order, their citizenship was confirmed. If their papers failed to meet the new requirements, they were deprived of their citizenship and automatically became foreigners. The procedure for Jews in the second category was similar, except that they were given only twenty days from publication of the law in the official gazette to submit the requisite documents. The citizenship of Jews in the third category was reviewed only in cases of suspected fraud.

In order to prove their entitlement to Romanian citizenship, Jews had to overcome major administrative and technical hurdles. Many had to travel vast distances to former places of residence in order to obtain the relevant permits, often to find that the public archives had disappeared, been destroyed, or were now part of another country (due to boundary changes); they were not always informed of the criteria (birthplace, previous place of residence, etc.) whereby the lists of Jews were drawn up; they had to deal with a corrupt and ignorant bureaucracy; and most importantly, they had very little time in which to obtain the requisite documents. These factors turned the process into an obstacle course that many failed to complete.

The antisemitic atmosphere generated by the antisemitic organizations was not confined to the peasants. Silviu Dragomir, the commissar of minority affairs, who served both in the Goga government and in the ensuing government, later told Neville Laski, one of two presidents of the Joint Foreign Committee, a British Jewish organization, that "the only part of Goga's legislation that remained was due solely to the fact that public opinion seemed to demand its retention."[51] Note that Dragomir's assertion that this was the only law to remain intact was wrong. All antisemitic laws were either implemented or became law after the collapse of the Goga government. For example, plans "to ban Jews from villages, to nationalize their estates . . . to dismiss all Jewish artistic, technical or administrative staff from national theaters, opera houses, etc., . . . and [to forbid Jews] to work for the Romanian press under Romanian pseudonyms" were commonplace.[52]

After its collapse, the Goga government was perceived as a nationalist-antisemitic experiment that had failed due to the intrigues of the enemies of the nationalist idea and as a model of antisemitic activity that had to be followed through to the end. The cataclysm that this government brought upon Romanian Jewry permeated all aspects of their daily life and intensified with the publication on 8 August 1940 of the Jewish Statute. It was further exacerbated by the Legionnaires' rise to power in September 1941. The Legionnaires took it upon themselves to continue implementing the Romanian antisemitic dream where Goga had left off.

THE JEWISH RESPONSE AND INTERNATIONAL
INTERVENTION ON BEHALF OF THE JEWS

The rise of antisemitism, the establishment of the National Christian Party, and the indifference to, and sometimes even encouragement of, antisemitic propaganda by the Tătărescu government impelled the Union of Romanian Jews (the veteran political organization of Romanian Jewry, headed by Filderman) and the Jewish Party (set up in order to ensure Jewish national representation in the Romanian parliament) to set up a joint front, headed by Filderman. The two constituent organizations of the Central Council of Romanian Jewry (Consiliul Central al Evreilor din România), which was set up on 29 January 1936 by Filderman and Rabbi Jacob Isaac Niemirower (1872–1939), chief rabbi of Romania between 1936 and 1939, continued to function as two separate entities. The purpose of the Central Council was to defend the rights of Jews as stipulated by the Minorities Treaty and the Romanian Constitution of 1923.[53]

It did not take the leaders of Romanian Jewry long to conclude that the damage inflicted by the Goga government on the Jewish minority was irreparable, as they informed Laski during his visit to Bucharest: "The storm might pass, but will nevertheless affect about one-fifth of the Jewish population."[54] The strategy they adopted was discrediting the government in all possible ways. At first, before the enactment of the Law for the Revision of Citizenship, the leaders were still hopeful that the government might refrain from adopting extremist measures. The contemporary Jewish press, for example, expressed the hope that the government would clarify the demographic issue, acknowledge the Jews' loyalty to the state, and rein in any attempts to cause them harm.[55]

The World Jewish Congress, the Jewish organization most active on behalf of Romanian Jewry, based its campaign on two elements: (1) the 1919 Minorities Treaty and Romania's concomitant undertakings, and (2) the principles of the League of Nations "on matters relating to the defense of minorities." The congress asked the League of Nations to "declare all proclamations, speeches, announcements, administrative orders, and the like, that contravened the principles of the Minorities Treaty, null and void," to reinstate the rights of Romanian

Jewry, and to compensate them for the Romanian government's discriminatory policy toward them.[56]

In 1938, however, the prestige of the League of Nations plunged. In Romania itself a violent debate raged on the "dictates" the Minorities Treaty and the League of Nations had placed on Romania. Foreign Minister Istrate Micescu (1881–1951), a renowned jurist, stated after his government's collapse that "the Romanians gave up their national demands so that the Jews could preserve their international privileges" — an allusion to the rights specified in the Minorities Treaty.[57] Micescu became the chief spokesman of a heterogeneous movement of antisemites whose members belonged to all shades of the political spectrum. They challenged the legitimacy of the principles obliging the government to grant citizenship to "foreigners," especially Jews, who had no country or government of their own. Micescu even once informed the Tătărescu government "that he would not be surprised if the nation responded with violence to the indiscriminate granting of Romanian citizenship."[58]

The World Jewish Congress began alerting the European public to the situation of Romanian Jewry on 21 December 1937, issuing material to the press on Romania's undertakings toward its minorities.[59] It also dispatched protests to the British Foreign Office and the French Foreign Ministry as well as to Joseph Avenol, secretary general of the League of Nations, quoting extensively from the sections of the Minorities Treaty that guaranteed the rights of Jews. The response was swift: the foreign ministries of Britain, France, and the United States issued an invitation to members of the congress's executive.

What really influenced Bucharest, however, was not the protests of Jewish organizations but diplomatic pressure by the representatives of Britain and France. Of all the protestations issued by the Jewish world at the time, one sentence in particular stands out. This sentence, part of a memorandum issued by the Workers Circle Friendly Society in conjunction with Jewish trade unions in England, stated, "If the Minorities Treaty became 'scraps of paper,' how long will the other treaties, seeking to establish co-operation between nations, remain?" British Jewry appealed to the champions of peace and freedom, drawing attention to the link between antisemitic elements in Romania and "countries of Europe which are driving forward to a new war. . . . The forces persecuting the Jewish people are the same as the forces undermining peace and raining death and destruction upon millions of peaceful people." This prophetic statement shed new light on the significance of the antisemitic rampage in Romania and the nature of the forces participating in it.[60]

The establishment of the Goga government had been greeted with concern by the democratic powers and with delight by the fascist-Nazi camp. The journal put out by Cuza's League had for years carried articles, some penned by Cuza himself, supporting the Nazi Party, even before its rise to power in Germany. The Nazi government in Germany, for its part, admired Cuza's antisemitism. In 1933 Hitler awarded Gheorghe Cuza, and through him, his father, the Order of the Swastika, which in Romania was considered one of the highest decorations of the Nazi Party. Goga, for his part, had contacts with the leaders of the Nazi regime, and the merger of Goga's movement with Cuza's League was to some extent orchestrated by them. Germany and Italy, therefore, welcomed the National Christian government, and the press of both countries expressed the hope that Romania would change its foreign policy and cooperate with Germany and Italy.[61]

The German press could not praise Goga and Cuza enough for their nationalist past and their uncompromising struggle against the Jews. In their articles on Romania, Nazi newspapers highlighted the ideological ties between the two regimes, as reflected in their common symbol, the swastika, "the symbol of the peoples' regeneration, that has, overnight, become Romania's hallmark."[62]

Of Romania's allies, only Poland expressed support for the Goga government. One of its newspapers even called for the Polish border to be closed before Poland became swamped by a wave of Jewish refugees from Romania—as if Romanian Jews had no greater ambition.

Encouragement from the fascist camp on the one hand and awareness of the king's true aspirations on the other caused Goga to steer a middle-of-the-road course that ultimately satisfied neither side. It got him into trouble with Britain, France, and the Soviet Union and led to the disillusionment of the fascist camp. Already in his political platform speech, Goga promised to honor existing alliances while attempting "to further expand the circle of support across the border."[63]

Although Goga did not hide his sympathy for fascism, and later for the Nazis, he was not as outspoken as Codreanu, who declared, "48 hours after the Legion's victory, Romania will have an alliance with Rome and Berlin."[64] Goga trod a middle path, seeking to pacify the king and maintain the Western alliance on the one hand while strengthening ties with the fascist states and persecuting Jews on the other.

Throughout his forty-four days in office, Goga continued to sound the alarm of a "Jewish invasion" of Romania. Among his fictitious claims was that, for the past eighteen years, thirty-three thousand Polish Jews in possession of a border pass had been living in Maramureş. "Let these foreigners continue their journey," he declared in an interview with a Dutch paper in early January 1938.[65] Meanwhile, the Romanian delegate at the League of Nations made sure to stress

Romania's support for the League's principles, drawing "surprise and some amusement . . . among members of the delegations and the public."[66]

The firm and united stance of the democratic powers and pressure by the Soviet Union prove that in early 1938 it was still possible to curb the rise of fascism and prevent yet another country from jumping on to the fascist bandwagon. The efforts of the non-fascist powers were partly facilitated by the organized response of Romanian Jewry itself, although its importance should not be overstated. The Jewish public obeyed its leaders' call for passive resistance, or "Ghandism," as they called it. The basic tenets of this resistance, which were transmitted orally, were to refrain as far as possible from economic activity. The Jews should "abstain from buying anything at all for a few weeks, in order to bring commerce to a standstill, paralyze local industry, and have the peasants return to their villages with their products unsold." This economic boycott was designed to stir up discontent and to prove that antisemitic measures affected the entire population, not only Jews. Were it not for their leaders' intervention, the reaction of the Jewish population would have been close to panic.[67]

The rural exodus of thousands of Jews—most of them craftsmen, petty merchants, and service providers—the expected division of Jewish property, and the Jewish boycott of economic activity led to the paralysis of various industries. Fear of nationalization also prompted many Jews to withdraw their deposits from banks. According to Minister of the Interior Călinescu, by 4 January 1938 panic-stricken Jews had withdrawn 400 million lei from Romania's banks. This atmosphere of panic was contagious, and soon the Romanians, too, began withdrawing their deposits, emptying the banks of 2 billion lei. Călinescu stated that although the Jews were initially panic-stricken, "they [turned the tables] by declaring a boycott and themselves created economic hardships."[68]

Until his death in May 1938 Goga took further measures to harm the Jews and destroy any future they had in Romania. He blamed the Jews for the collapse of his government—thereby affecting the policy of his successors toward the Jews. He also blamed the international Jewish press for ranting against his government and its just measures against the Jews: "The oh so delicate nerves of the Jews have burst! I received a wave of protests, ranging from the plaintive to the impudently threatening." Goga further claimed that the Jewish organizations that had complained to the League of Nations over Romania's attitude toward the Jewish minority had no right to do so, since the Jews were "not a local ethnic minority" like the Hungarians or Germans and had no state to represent them.[69]

According to Goga, that mysterious, powerful, and influential body known as international Jewry had incited France to act on behalf of Romanian Jewry. In actual fact, France had long been singled out for criticism, slander, and ultimately hatred by the Romanian nationalists. The fascists and sympathizers of the "national idea" from across the political spectrum could not forgive France for condemning antisemitism and for the fact that its prime minister Léon Blum was a Jew.

Goga was largely responsible for implanting the myth of international Jewish power—a power strong enough to recruit personalities and organizations to its cause—in his successors' conscious and subconscious minds. This myth affected the policy of Goga's antisemitic heirs toward the Jews and worked both for and against them.

Immediately after his resignation, Goga's parting shot to the Jews was a message of revenge for their so-called war against the Romanian national idea: "Do not rejoice," he warned them, "since your laughter awakens too deep a protest, and your impudence makes our faces pale with outrage."[70] Although Goga initiated a program to realize the Romanian antisemitic dream, he was unable to complete it. This task was left to his successors, who took over where he left off.

The Goga government was never meant to be a lasting government but was set up more as a stopgap in the wake of the 1937 elections and the ensuing political crisis, as a means of blocking the Iron Guard's rise to power. However, the king's gambit provided the extreme fascist right with a golden opportunity for applying its ideology and goals. This in turn provoked a powerful international response on the part of the democratic Western powers. The diplomatic pressure exerted by these powers in January 1938, their remarkable resolve (unlike their conciliatory policy in Munich in September of that year), and Bucharest's fear of a possible Soviet response in Bessarabia forced the king to abandon his first nationalist experiment. The Jewish leadership under Filderman, together with international Jewish organizations, managed to alert the democratic world, the League of Nations, and the foreign ministries in the West to the fascist aspects of the new Romanian administration and the danger of another country falling into Nazi Germany's net. The influence of the Jewish leadership and of international Jewish organizations should not, however, be exaggerated. In the final analysis, the struggle was not between Judaism and Goga but between the democratic camp and the fascist camp, and in early 1938 the democratic camp proved that it could keep fascism in check.

2

King Carol II's Dictatorship and Its Policy toward the Jews, February 1938–August 1940

King Carol's policy toward the Jews can be divided into two main periods: (1) from February 1938 until the death of Patriarch Miron Cristea (1868–1939) and the Nazi conquest of Czechoslovakia in March 1939; and (2) from March 1939 until the Soviet ultimatum, the annexation of Bessarabia and Bukovina, and the first pogroms against the Jews in late June 1940.

During the first period (the Miron Cristea period), antisemitic sentiment even more than political measures determined the fate of Romanian Jewry. The king's ambivalent policy toward the Jews was fueled by fear of the Nazis and the Iron Guard on the one hand and the wish to strengthen ties with Britain and France in order to offset mounting German pressure on the other. As long as the situation was fluid and the king and politicians who supported him could still hope that the West would be able to ward off the Nazi threat an effort was made to temper the antisemitic sentiments that had been cultivated for generations among the Romanian people and that now threatened to erupt into violence.

Although on the face of it the new constitution endorsed the rights of citizens and minorities, in actual fact it deprived the Jews of most of their rights. Legislators adopted the antisemitic legacy of the Goga government, such as the fiction that the country was being inundated by Jews or that "the greatest part of industry and commerce was in the hands of Jewish proprietors."[1] The king ratified the Law for the Revision of Citizenship and measures to oust Jews from their jobs and positions in industry, commerce, and finance. Minister for Minorities Silviu Dragomir, while terming Goga's law "a just law," tried to placate the Jews with the promise that "if we are patient, we shall see that things will quieten down and that the situation will gradually return to normal."[2]

The difference between this promise and similar ones in the past was that, already at this stage, leaders linked the fate of Romanian Jewry to the Nazi invasion of Europe. After March 1938 the situation of Romanian Jewry was linked with the struggle for hegemony in Europe. As a leader of British Jewry noted after a meeting with Dragomir: "He [Dragomir] thought fit to point out that events in Czechoslovakia and their outcome would have a profound influence on the Jewish question, but that nobody, of course, could make predictions with any certainty."[3]

Many of the moderately antisemitic personalities on whom the fate of the Jews depended turned overnight into active antisemites. Even personalities known for their liberal outlook surprised the Jewish leaders with their antisemitic outbursts. In a radio address to the nation after his appointment on 1 February 1939, Foreign Minister Grigore Gafencu (1892–1957) promised justice and respect for minorities but qualified this by stating, "There is one minority in the country which is numerically too strong, and which, on its own behalf and in the interests of the national economy, must be made to emigrate in large numbers."[4]

During the first two years of the dictatorship, "voluntary" emigration along Nazi lines, proposed in collaboration with the antisemitic Polish government in the League of Nations and international forums, was considered the best solution to Romania's Jewish problem. This proposed solution further intensified hatred of Jews, although Romanian leaders still tried to cloak their plans in a European veneer. A report from the World Jewish Congress in January 1939 stated that Romania's policy in all spheres was based on antisemitism: "They want to disgrace the Jews politically, and ruin them economically, so that they are forced to emigrate."[5] Members of the government still hoped that it was possible to restrain the Nazis and emphasized that all anti-Jewish measures would be implemented in a legal and civilized manner. On this assurance, the World Jewish Congress report had the following to say: "In the minds of those gentlemen, the word 'civilized' means that they will not start any pogroms; 'legal' means that all measures against the Jews will be carried out by administrative means."[6]

Nazi pressure on Romania, the impotence of the Western powers, and the fear of German support for the territorial demands of its neighboring countries drove the Romanian establishment to make economic concessions to Germany. Through their authoritarian form of government and the anti-Jewish measures they adopted, Romanian leaders hoped to propitiate Germany and prevent it from taking action against Romania. It is worth nothing, however, that prior to January 1939, the Nazis asked no concessions from Romania on the Jewish question.[7] If anything, it was Romanian antifascist and pro-Western politicians who cynically linked the persecution of Jews to the situation in the region. In the eyes of these politicians — and their successors — the Jewish "coin" was the cheapest Romania was willing to pay in order to conserve its vital interests. Foreign Minister Gafencu informed the Jewish delegation he met with that he was as much a democrat as ever but unfortunately, due to changing circumstances, the Romanian government had to take account of Germany and its demands for an antisemitic policy. "If a change occurs in this state of affairs, the situation of the Jews in Romania may improve; if not, it will get worse."[8]

Prime Minister Armand Călinescu (who also held the interior and defense portfolios)—the sworn enemy of the Legionnaires and the Nazis—upon hearing of the Molotov-Ribbentrop Pact, informed the king on 23 August 1939 that "Germany is the real danger. An alliance with it is tantamount to a protectorate. Only Germany's defeat by France and Britain can ward off the danger."[9] In the government guidelines he drew up he portrayed antisemitism as a function of external events.[10] Romania's antisemitic policy, he implied, was directly contingent on Nazi successes. These statements were all made before the Jewish problem was even raised in political talks between Germany and Romania. Călinescu—who had many Jewish friends and abhorred antisemitism—informed a Jewish delegation that revocation of the citizenship of hundreds of thousands of Jews was irreversible.[11] "These Jews," he stated, "will not be able to earn a living and Romanian Jews must take into consideration [the need] to feed these poor and impoverished Jews . . . lest they perish." The most the king's regime was prepared to do was to discuss the matter "from a human and legal aspect."[12]

Frequent meetings of the heads of world Jewish organizations with Romanian politicians in Bucharest, Geneva, Paris, and London convinced them that the monarchy had resolved to undermine Romanian Jewry, impoverish it, and pressurize it to emigrate.[13] This policy, however, was not consistent but characterized by alternating periods of leniency and stringency.[14] In March 1939 the World Jewish Congress pointed to a single ray of light that pierced the hardships that were the lot of Romanian Jewry at the time: "In the opinion of people fully conversant with the situation in Romania, the Romanian Government, in view of the international situation and for other reasons, cannot permit itself to apply the same measures against the Jews as other nations have, so far, done."[15] This restraint would disappear with the collapse of France and the Soviet ultimatum in June 1940. The moral constraints were gradually eroded by domestic struggles, the calamities that overtook the Romanian nation and state (the surrender of a third of Romania's territory in June–August 1940), and the growing rhinocerization of public opinion fomented by many intellectuals, journalists, authors, and teachers, who dehumanized and demonized Jews.

In the second stage of the dictatorship, particularly after the conquest of Czechoslovakia in March 1939, the Jewish problem ceased to be of interest to the democratic powers and the League of Nations. The world Jewish organizations still tried to help, but the outbreak of the Second World War and the terrible situation of Polish Jewry lessened interest in the fate of Romanian Jewry.[16] In this period (1939–40) the fate of Romanian Jewry was affected not only by external events (the advance of the Nazis) but also—and perhaps even more—by internal events.

The first of these events, the assassination of Codreanu and other leaders of the Iron Guard, totally undermined the rule of law. On the night of 29–30 November 1938, the king ordered the assassination of fourteen leaders of the Iron Guard: Codreanu (who had been arrested in April 1938 at the king's order, together with all leaders of the Iron Guard the police were able to trace), the three assassins of Prime Minister I. Gh. Duca (on 29 December 1933), and the ten assassins of Mihail Stelescu (a Legionnaire who defected and set up his own rival organization). The Legionnaires, who were strangulated by gendarmes and then shot, were buried in a communal grave in the courtyard of Jilava prison near Bucharest.[17] Most of Romania's leaders—including Maniu; Constantin Brătianu, the head of the Liberal Party; Iorga; Călinescu; and Grigore Gafencu—had condemned Codreanu and his fascist movement. Nevertheless, the elimination of the Legionnaires had been conducted in an arbitrary and willful manner and on a feeble pretext (attempted escape from prison). The security police, the gendarmerie, and even to the Romanian army were not strangers to such liquidations and had in the past been deployed to eliminate Jews in a similar manner.

According to the testimony of one of the king's confidants, King Carol ordered Codreanu's assassination after he rejected Hitler's demand, in a meeting between the two, to set up a government under the Legion, to change Romania's foreign policy, and to revoke all agreements and pacts with the Western powers.[18] Needless to say, Codreanu's assassination angered Hitler greatly. The German press was given the go-ahead to attack the king and rake up his sordid past, especially his liaison with Elena Lupescu, a Jew. In the Nazi press Codreanu's assassination was portrayed as "a victory for the Jews."[19]

The second event that undermined the rule of law in Romania—the assassination of Prime Minister Călinescu and the chain of events it set in motion—was also connected with the Legionnaires. Călinescu assumed the premiership on 7 March 1939, after the death of Patriarch Cristea. He led the struggle against the Iron Guard "not because of its anti-Jewish program, but because of its opposition to the King Carol," although he was aware that it wanted "to throw the Jews into the sea."[20] Călinescu's assassination on 21 September 1939 by a gang of Legionnaires was masterminded by Horia Sima, Codreanu's successor, who had fled to Berlin when his movement was under attack. The king's response to the assassination was swift and bloody. The nine assassins, who in this case made no attempt to escape, were summarily executed the following day, and their corpses were left at the scene of the crime.[21] In the same week (22–28 September), 242

Legionnaires were executed (3–15 per district) and their corpses displayed in public.

The slaying of the Legionnaires took place during the last week of the fighting in Poland, and other such slayings took place after the signing of the Molotov-Ribbentrop Pact. Călinescu's assassination and reprisals against the Legionnaires, the German-Soviet alliance, and the collapse of Poland further intensified the atmosphere of chaos and anarchy and instilled fear in the hearts of Romania's leaders. Romania faced the German and Russian giants alone.

Contrary to expectations, the Jews were far from happy with the king's swift response to Călinescu's assassination. Still the object of persecution, they understood that the ease with which the Legionnaires had been dispatched and their bodies publicly exhibited signified the end of the rule of law in Romania, and they realized that they could be the next in line.[22] Those who had ordered the execution of "ethnic" Romanians could just as easily order the liquidation of the "Jewish Satan." The elimination of the Legionary leaders did not help ease the plight of the Jews or change attitudes toward them, as reflected in the censored press. The Romanian fascists believed that any step against them was part of a Jewish-Masonic-Communist plot, and the assassination of their leaders who had not fled to Germany merely intensified pressure on the Romanian establishment and caused it to panic.

The internal pressure was compounded by external pressure. As the Nazis advanced in Europe, they subjected Romania to increasing pressure, likened by Foreign Minister Gafencu to a "brain tumor."[23] This pressure led the Romanian establishment to make rash decisions, such as mobilization of the army and formal promises to protect the integrity and independence of Romania at any cost. Concomitantly, it intensified the hate campaign toward those it considered responsible for Romania's weakness, for its former pro-Western policy, and effectively for all its political, cultural, and ideological development since the unification of Romania in 1859, a development that ran counter to the "national idea."

The blow fell several months later, on 26 June 1940, with the Soviet ultimatum to Romania to evacuate Bessarabia and northern Bukovina (and even some of the Regat) within four days. Romania immediately gave in to the ultimatum and evacuated over sixty thousand square kilometers populated by some 3.5 million citizens. Hungary, Germany's ally, also made territorial demands on Romania. The Jews became the scapegoat of the national disaster: laws, decrees, and orders of all kinds were published daily, and the press became violent.

In the midst of this political-administrative chaos, a typically Romanian "miracle" occurred: the Legionary movement was resurrected after King Carol granted Horia Sima amnesty and appointed him undersecretary of education—the first time a Legionnaire sat in a Romanian government. All Legionnaires in prisons and camps were set free. On 25 June 1940 Sima urged his friends to join the king's new party, the Party of the Nation (Partidul Naţiunii).

On 3 July King Carol asked Germany, via its ambassador in Romania, to expedite a military delegation to Romania in the hope of obtaining Nazi support against Hungary's territorial demands. This heralded the start of Romania's political, economic, and military subjugation to Germany—and the realization of one of Germany's major objectives in Eastern Europe.

ANTISEMITIC LEGISLATION AND
ADMINISTRATIVE MEASURES AGAINST JEWS

Goga's fall and Codreanu's arrest gave the Jews breathing space. Although the Law for the Revision of Citizenship was still in force, Jewish merchants and businessmen who had not lost their citizenship began reopening their businesses, and Jewish lawyers resumed their practices in places where it was safe to do so. The only Jewish professionals who were barred from exercising their profession were journalists.[24]

Nevertheless, the political measures adopted by the king and his various governments affected the Jews more than other citizens. They were deprived of the little participation they had enjoyed in political life and of any political influence they had wielded.[25] Their legal status was even worse than it had been before emancipation.

Despite the anarchy that prevailed toward the end of the royal dictatorship, the Jewish public was convinced that the measures launched against them were part of a systematic and premeditated strategy. From early 1938 until the first pogroms against the Jews following the withdrawal from Bessarabia and northern Bukovina and the publication of the Jewish Statute, Goga's law (as implemented by the Cristea government) and its economic implications affected them more than surrounding events. There was no shortage of pretexts for revoking citizenship, and lawyers, doctors, clerks, merchants, and salaried workers were hardest hit.[26] State-controlled institutions, associations, and marketing networks summarily dismissed Jewish workers "because their citizenship papers had not yet been reviewed" and instructed all their branches to employ Christian workers only. The courts used the same pretexts to prevent Jewish lawyers from exercising their professions.[27] In many places Jewish lawyers were physically prevented from entering courts, such as the High Court of Justice (Palatul Justiţiei) in Bucharest.[28]

The above measures were not the product of the Nazis' influence in Romania or an attempt to imitate their policies. Rather, they were the continuation of an autochthonous Romanian policy that had roots in the past and a product of the refusal by broad sectors of Romanian society to countenance equal rights for Jews. On 29 July 1938 Filderman submitted a special memorandum on the tactics employed by Romanian lawyers to exclude their Jewish colleagues from the Romanian Bar Association.[29] The chambers of commerce, too, did their bit toward realizing the dream of Romanization by striking all Jews who had lost their citizenship from the register of businessmen. Bukovinian Jewry, which controlled a large portion of the retail trade, suffered most from Goga's law. According to July 1938 estimates, 75–80 percent of applications by Bukovinian Jewry for revision of citizenship were rejected.[30] Although a similar percentage pertained for Transylvania, the Jews there fared better economically than the Jews of Bukovina.[31] "As a result, thousands upon thousands of Jews were ruined," Filderman wrote in his memoirs.[32]

A Ministry of the Interior ordinance of 15 September 1938 stipulated that all Jews who had lost their citizenship would henceforth be considered aliens. The same ordinance also stated that Jews who had been living in Romania prior to 1916 would be granted certain concessions, although the nature of these was not specified.[33] This ordinance therefore created a paradoxical situation whereby many Jews who had completed their military service and had served as reservists or been sent to the border as backup troops were now classified as aliens who required special work permits. In June 1938 the Czernowitz municipality issued a circular "inviting" all Jews who had lost their citizenship to liquidate their businesses within fourteen days.[34]

The insecurity created by the Law for the Revision of Citizenship heightened tension among the Jewish masses and paralyzed economic activity. The directives concerning eligibility for citizenship were so muddled and contradictory "that even those who made them and those who had to implement them had no idea how to apply them."[35] No wonder, therefore, that the application of this law varied so much from region to region.

Many Jews who were deprived of their citizenship had nowhere to turn. They knew no language other than Romanian, held no citizenship other than Romanian citizenship, had no passports (theirs had been confiscated), and were not wanted by any other country. Most of them were too poor to pay the necessary bribes to officials and judges in order to obtain the requisite papers. In a special memorandum to the government, Filderman asked that Jews whose application had been turned down "be awarded the same rights as the Jews before the war, since they had served in the Romanian army, and had no other country." The list of those whose application was turned down included war widows, war orphans, and war invalids, Jews with military decorations, and Jews who had been considered Romanian subjects for many generations.[36]

Article 42 of the Law for the Granting or Annulment of Romanian Citizenship, passed on 20 January 1939 to buttress the Goga law, stated that "citizenship could be revoked if it had been obtained by deceitful or fraudulent means, or if certain activities that were relevant to the granting or annulment of citizenship had been concealed." Article 43 also approved the annulment of the citizenship of people "coming from a country with which Romania was in a state of war," while article 41 invalidated the citizenship of certain categories of Romanian citizens residing abroad (the citizenship of many Jews holding Romanian passports and residing abroad were confiscated as a result of this law). The Ministry of Justice was authorized to confiscate the property of all citizens whose citizenship had been revoked by articles 41, 42, or 43 of the law. This law was bolstered by two additional laws, passed on 20 July and 20 December 1939. With this legislation, "the last vestiges of human rights that were achieved by a century of struggle were blown away like dust," wrote Filderman.[37]

The other legislative bedrock (the Constitution being the first) on which the dictatorship's policy toward the Jews rested was the General Commissariat for Minorities, established on 3 May 1938. After 4 August 1938 the commissariat acted in accordance with a special Statute of Minorities, which listed all the freedoms and obligations of Romanian citizens, including members of minority groups.[38] King Carol's Constitution of 1938 recognized the right of all minority groups (including Jews) to use their own language in their religious and cultural life (including the press), in their personal and commercial dealings, and in "statutorily approved" meetings and gatherings. Minorities were allowed to set up their own welfare, religious, and social organizations and have access to public education in their mother tongue. The statute upheld the rights of members of minority groups to hold public office and exercise any profession under the same conditions as other citizens. Jews, however, unlike their Hungarian, German, Bulgarian, and Ukrainian counterparts, did not organize themselves into a separate ethnic entity and were not therefore recognized as a minority.[39] This was due less to the internal conflict between the assimilationists (under Filderman) and the nationalists (under the Jewish Party and the Zionist movement) than to the authorities' refusal to recognize Jews as a minority with national and cultural rights.

Jewish leaders were far from happy with this turn of events. Although there was little cooperation between the two camps, it is clear in retrospect that the adoption of either one of these approaches (assimilation or Jewish nationalism) would not have changed the Romanian establishment's attitude toward the Jews. In the summer of 1938 Dragomir, the minister for minorities, informed Laski that although many Romanian Jewish leaders had met with him to discuss their problems, "Dr. Filderman had not . . . because he wished to regard himself not a member of a minority but as a Romanian of Jewish persuasion."[40] Filderman was unable to maintain this position for long, and soon he, too, agreed to meet with Dragomir.

By mid-1938 it was clear that the government intended to target all Jews, regardless of whether their citizenship had been confirmed or not. As such, the royal dictatorship may be viewed as a prelude to the era of Romanization ushered in by the Legionary regime. During this period legislative and administrative measures were completed to bar Jews from the import-export trade, from representing foreign industries and plants in Romania, and from trading in the stock market or representing shareholders.[41] The antisemitic policy espoused by the National Bank of Romania and its manager, Mihail Manoilescu (1891–1950), ruined Jewish businessmen and merchants and caused Jewish-owned factories to shut down.[42] As a report by the World Jewish Congress stated, by refusing to redeem the promissory notes of Jewish firms, the bank hastened their collapse. The authorities revoked almost all licenses for the sale of tobacco, matches, and salt (licenses to sell alcohol had already been revoked by the Goga-Cuza government) as well as other items for which the state held a sales monopoly.[43]

Although the dictatorship's antisemitic policy was based on strong precedents, it was innovative inasmuch as its laws were aimed specially against Jews. An example of such legislation was the August 1938 law barring Jewish technicians and engineers from exercising their professions, even though Romania needed such experts.[44] The new law stated that only members of the new Engineers' Union were permitted to exercise their profession. What this meant was that Jewish engineers depended on the goodwill of the union branches for the renewal of their licenses, an issue on which Filderman remained skeptical. On 27 November 1938 the Architects' Union followed suit, publishing a list of Romanian architects from which Jews were excluded.[45] A government initiative of 9 June 1938 discriminated against graduates of foreign universities, including thousands of Jews who had been forced to study abroad in the twenties and thirties due to the violent antisemitic campaigns that were prevalent in Romanian universities at the time. The new directive stipulated that all university degrees and diplomas had to be certified and that all applicants for certification also had to provide proof of their ethnic origins.[46] This administrative measure mainly affected Jewish doctors who had qualified in France and Italy and had to have their qualifications "endorsed" if they wished to continue in their profession.[47] A directive of 17 March 1938 prohibited (Romanian) owners of pharmacies from renting out their pharmacies to Jews or even renewing existing rentals.

The unions, in an unusual degree of initiative, gave as broad an interpretation as possible to the antisemitic laws, especially Goga's law. The Union of Accountants (in Ilfov District), for example, had long been waiting for a convenient legal loophole to expel Jews, whose competition they feared, from their ranks. The Law for the Revision of Citizenship, together with the general antisemitic atmosphere that spawned it, gave the union the chance to succeed where formerly it had failed. In a public session the union unanimously decided to strike all foreigners and Jews off its list, to submit a new list to the authorities for approval, and to invalidate all forms signed by Jewish or foreign accountants. In this way they no longer had to contend with the threat of competition from Jewish accountants.[48]

These antisemitic measures were applied with particular stringency in Bukovina, the rulers of which were granted extraordinary powers under the new administrative constitution. Gheorghe Alexianu, the governor of Bukovina and a staunch antisemite, not content with the existing laws, introduced his own anti-Jewish measures. Bukovina served as an electoral base for Cuza's League and subsequently for the Goga-Cuza government's National Christian Party. Manifestations of physical violence against Jews, including attempts to organize pogroms, existed already during the period of the Goga government. The "minor excesses" referred to by the Romanian ambassador in London in describing the reign of terror instigated by the National Christian Party's storm troops in Bukovina in March 1938 (with a reassurance that they would not be repeated) metamorphosed, in February 1939, into a call for the wholesale abolition of the citizenship of Jews, their dismissal from their jobs, the revocation of their work permits, harassment, and threats. These same "minor excesses" led to the introduction of administrative measures that led to the collapse of industrial and commercial enterprises. As stated above, a July 1938 report stated that 75–80 percent of applications for the revision of citizenship were rejected in Bukovina (and Transylvania). Many Jews were required to submit documents that had been issued by the Austro-Hungarian Empire in order for their applications even to be considered.[49]

The administrative measures devised against the Jews of Bukovina, particularly those aimed at confiscating their work permits, were more brutal than anywhere else in Romania. Many Bukovinian Jews—as well as world Jewish leaders—became increasingly convinced of the hopelessness of the struggle to safeguard the rights, citizenship, and livelihoods of Bukovinian Jewry. As their certainty grew that the very existence of the Jews was at stake, they realized that the solution could not be found either at the local or the national level. They drew the conclusion that only emigration could save the Jews of Bukovina.[50]

PLANS FOR THE "CIVILIZED" EXPULSION
OF JEWS FROM ROMANIA: EMIGRATION

The feeling among Romanian Jewish leaders that behind the campaign to revoke the citizenship of Jews and deprive them of a livelihood was a plan to expel the Jews from Romania received official and public confirmation over the course of 1938. This plan was referred to in private talks between leaders of the Romanian establishment and representatives of Romanian and world Jewry. The official spokesmen made no attempt to conceal their intentions but used code words taken from the Romanian antisemitic lexicon. Thus, Jews who were forced to emigrate were referred to as "foreigners," "invaders" (*invadatori*), or "illegal immigrants," all terms divesting them of the right to live in the Romanian homeland. In a press interview King Carol denied the existence of a Romanian plan to expel the Jewish masses or transfer them to other countries but added, "We would be relieved to see some of our Jews leaving of their own free will."[51] In this way King Carol determined the rudiments of emigration policy for the following two years—a policy that was shaped by the international situation and by pressure from Romanian nationalists and fascists. The Jews' fears were justified.

On 12 March 1939 the Romanian government sent a memorandum to all countries that had a Romanian ambassador, excluding Germany, reaffirming the need to find an "effective" solution to the Jewish problem in central and Eastern Europe. The Romanians, who claimed that there were over 1.2 million Jews in Romania, sought to set up a Jewish state or dominion to accommodate the Jewish populations of Romania, Poland, and other European countries.[52] This plan, which was submitted at the height of the Czechoslovakian crisis, met with a generally poor response, apart from Brazil and Argentina, which welcomed it.

Europe was immersed in its own problem. In September Călinescu, the main proponent of the plan and the strongman in the Cristea government, was assassinated. Jewish refugees from Germany, Czechoslovakia, and, later, from Poland sought temporary shelter in Romania on their way to Palestine or other countries. Following appeals by Jewish organizations in Romania, the Romanian government and Jewish institutions there helped these refugees and eased their passage from Romania.[53]

It is clear from the above that, on the eve of the Holocaust, a unique opportunity existed in Romania for the emigration of thousands of Jews to Palestine or overseas. The dictatorship and antisemitic incitement in Romania, and especially Nazi Germany's victories, created conditions that favored emigration. The Romanian administration, for its part, had its own emigration plans and was prepared to do its bit to hasten the departure of the Jews. There was only one problem: no country was willing to have them.

3

The Rhinocerization of the Romanian Intelligentsia

THE DEMONIZATION OF JEWS

In the summer of 1934 a dispute took place between Mircea Eliade (1907–86), a young philosopher sympathetic to the Legionary movement, and George Racoveanu (1900–67), a priest and Christian Orthodox theologian and journalist, as to whether all Jews were damned or not. Racoveanu invoked Christian sources such as John 8:24 in support of his argument that all Jews were eternally damned.[1] Eliade disagreed with Racoveanu's interpretation of the verse and cited two other verses (John 8:29 and 8:44) that indicated that all Jews were damned as "Satan's sons" and not because of their refusal to adopt the true faith and recognize the Messiah. It was therefore necessary, stated Eliade, to determine whether all Jews were Satan's sons. Basing his argument on Christian Orthodox and Catholic sources, he came to the conclusion that this was not the case.[2]

The architects of this new brand of antisemitism were not only the antisemitic movements and their leaders but first and foremost the intellectuals. It was they who propagated the myth of the Jew as a monster eager to seize control of the country and its citizens. It was they who formed a bridge between the uncouth authors of the antisemitic and nationalist manifestos at the dawn of the century and the modern Romanian intelligentsia, with its eloquence and broad Western education. These intellectuals reformulated or expanded old antisemitic concepts and molded them to a reality in which the fascist idea had triumphed in Europe. They redefined the terms *Jew* and *Judaism* and invoked intellectual-spiritual arguments to delegitimize them.

This antisemitic ideology was based on a denial of the Jews' contribution to world and Romanian culture; presentation of the struggle between democracy and totalitarianism as a struggle between Judaism and nationalism; justification of the antisemitism of the founders of modern Romanian culture (*precursorii*) and an attempt to rid them of their persistent sense of inferiority vis-à-vis Western culture; comparison of Jews to animals, rodents, insects, and the like; and yearning for a strong leader who would solve Romania's basic problems, especially the Jewish problem, even if democracy had to be jettisoned along the way.

Contemporary Jewish intellectuals were aware of the role played by Romanian intellectuals in fueling antisemitism and fascism in the thirties.[3] This chapter attempts to outline the contribution of Romanian intellectuals to the delegitimization of Jews in Romanian society. This represented a new phase in the evolution of Romanian antisemitism, one that made it easier for successive Romanian fascist governments to deal with the Jewish problem.

Romanian intellectuals used a variety of means in their attempts to delegitimize the Jews: manifestos, articles in prestigious journals, speeches, and literary essays, as well as "scientific" papers on the subject. Not all of the new Jew-haters supported the Iron Guard or had met with Cuza. They included known writers who had become antisemitic in their old age, such as Ioan Alexandru Brătescu-Voinești (1868–1946); promising young intellectuals who supported the Iron Guard, such as Mircea Eliade and Emil Cioran (1911–95); literary and ideological critics such as Nicolae Roșu (1903–?) and Nicolae Davidescu (1888–1954); eminent philosophers such as Nae Ionescu (1890–1940) and the historian Nicolae Iorga; and prominent media personalities such as Pamfil Șeicaru (1894–1980).

Although it would be difficult to find a common denominator among them, each undoubtedly played a part in creating what Filderman described as "an antisemitic psychosis." This psychosis engulfed Romanian society, the press, and the intelligentsia until the newspaper *Porunca Vremii* was able to state, "Antisemitism is currently part of the catechism of national defense."[4]

In their smear campaigns, antisemitic publications resorted to the stereotype of the parasitic Jew, the destroyer of Christian nations, who used international organizations (such as the Alliance Israélite Universelle) and secret societies (such as the Freemasons) in his or her desire to conquer the world and world finance. Their theories contained new elements, too, as they attempted to adapt the antisemitic dogma of the intellectual elites who laid the foundations of contemporary Romanian culture to the twentieth-century reality of industrialization and economic and social transformation. They emphasized the negative traits of Jews that had been shaped by their faith and by the Talmud and that, they claimed, had now passed into the genetic pool. They openly blamed the Jews for some of the negative aspects of capitalism and the industrialization process that Romania was undergoing at the time. The antisemitic intellectuals of the thirties did their best to disparage their Jewish counterparts and denied the contribution of the Jews in general, and of Romanian Jews in particular, to world and Romanian culture.

In proposing solutions to the Jewish problem, these ideologues tended to resort to terms such as "eradication" and "expulsion." Although the rise of fascism in Europe left its mark on all intellectuals, their ideas evolved almost totally independently of Nazi ideology. More than ever, Jews were depicted as close to achieving their covert aim of world hegemony. According to these Romanian antisemites, Communism and capitalism had helped promote the Jews' global strategy, while democracy had almost delivered Romania into their hands. Brătescu-Voineşti accused the Jews of monopolizing "world capital," the press, and commerce and of attempting to achieve their goals by force, despite the fact that they had no army. Jews, he claimed, were trying to undermine the church and the family and values such as modesty, patriotism, and nationalism — in short, "anything that constituted an obstacle to achieving their goals."[5] Roşu, a young ideologue on the Romanian right who was the first to write a manual of right-wing doctrine, accused the Jews of "dissolving" traditional values, through liberalism (i.e., democracy) and socialism (i.e., Communism).[6] The triumph of these two doctrines, he added, was a victory for the Jews, who would always support rationalism and individual rights.[7]

This antisemitic diatribe against the Talmud and the Jewish faith for having created the Jewish monster gained momentum on the eve of the establishment of the Legionary regime. In 1936 Roşu accused the Jewish religion of having evolved into "a pragmatic political ethic that constituted a fertile breeding ground for economic and capitalist [expansionism]." He likewise charged that the Talmud fostered negative character traits in Jews that later became absorbed into their genetic blueprint. The Talmud and other Jewish works, he claimed, were governed by "material principles" that ran counter to the principle of spiritual harmony fostered by the Christian or Greco-Roman tradition. The Jew not only was alien to European culture but was its enemy, too.[8]

Ionescu, the foremost philosopher of the Romanian right at the time, summed up these characteristics as follows: "Their faith orders them to subvert the Christian order of things and values." In all spheres, he added, there was a "structural incompatibility between Christian and Jew, and therefore there is no solution to the Jewish problem. Judah suffers because it is Judah. . . . The *Jewish drama is not a problem but a phenomenon, and cannot therefore be solved*."[9] Jews were also guilty on another score, according to Roşu: "All Jews have a prophetic propensity, a cruel and fanatical individualism that turns them into trouble-makers wherever they go. . . . Anarchy and revolutionism are typical features of the Semitic psyche."[10] Russia's fate was, according to Brătescu-Voineşti, a product of Jewish destructiveness inspired by the Jewish religion: "To what depths have they brought an Empire of 160 million people!"[11]

"The Jews," stated Ionescu, "do not bring about progress . . . they bring about change, not progress."[12] Brătescu-Voineşti, basing his argument on "facts," maintained that while Romanian Jewry's material situation had improved, "it had not contributed to progress" or "made any useful contribution to intellectual life. . . . Which Jewish invention has ever led to a significant advance in human progress?" He even denied that the Jews were the founders of monotheism."[13]

The antisemitic ideologues all agreed that the Jews had brought antisemitism upon themselves and that there was no solution to the Jewish problem. Brătescu-Voineşti was pessimistic about the possibility of the Jews leaving Romania of their own free will. After all, he argued, why should they wish to leave a land over which they had gained control or relinquish their positions of power? It followed, therefore, that the struggle against the Jews was a struggle for survival. The instinct of survival in individuals and nations "is so strong it defies logic," stated Brătescu-Voineşti, hinting at a possible solution to the Jewish problem.[14]

These right-wing intellectuals were responsible not only for shaping the ideology of Romania's authoritarian regime but also for the metamorphosis of the Jew in the public consciousness into a less than human creature whose behavior differed from that of others. Hitler's likening of Jews to bacteria was not foreign to the antisemitic mindset of nationalist Romanian intellectuals. They themselves had reached similar conclusions early in their careers. Brătescu-Voineşti, for example, related how his observation of insect life in his garden had helped him decode the behavior patterns of Jews. A keen gardener, Brătescu-Voineşti would "spend many hours intently observing the movements of various insects," a hobby that fostered his "liking for truth and aversion for lies and deceit."[15]

Equating Jews to rodents (mice, rats), reptiles (snakes), amphibians (frogs), and insects (spiders, locusts, and other pests) was just another facet of the traditional branding of Jews.[16] The antisemitism Cuza cultivated over half a century merged with Christian antisemitism fostered by leaders of the Orthodox Church and Legionary antisemitism to create an image of the Jew as an unnatural, inhuman, demonic, and base creature—the antithesis of the purity, beauty, and intelligence of Romanian Christians. These ideas, which had percolated into the subconscious of Romanian intellectuals, matured in the years preceding the Holocaust.

The Romanian intellectuals perceived Jews as the embodiment of a destructive and relentless force that was attempting to seize control of Romania, enslave its people, spoil its character, and pollute its soul. The Jewish Satan could bring poverty and disease on the Romanians "and bring about their death through a process of gradual starvation."[17]

Nae Ionescu, in his preface to Mihail Sebastian's novel *De două mii de ani*, predicted a bitter fate for himself and his people. "Do you not feel that cold and darkness are enfolding you?" he exclaimed, in a sentence that well described the subsequent fate of the deportees in Transnistria.[18] Roşu took this idea even further when he stated that Iosif Hechter (Sebastian's protagonist) was facing an "irrevocable sentence," not realizing that he was echoing the fate of Joseph K, Kafka's protagonist in *The Trial*: "Unless, one day, you are far away in Eretz Israel [*sic*, not Palestine], darkness and cold will enfold you."[19] The sensitive and assimilationist Hechter sensed the approaching calamity but found no solution: "Individually, each Jew panics: What should he do? Escape, die, commit suicide, or apostatize himself? As a collectivity, there is only one thing we can do: passively await our fate."[20]

4

The Romanian Orthodox Church and Its Attitude toward the "Jewish Problem"

The Romanian Church was an integral part of the Romanian establishment, and its leaders played an important role in the country's affairs. However, they had to contend with issues of principle that were more complex than those the rest of the Romanian establishment faced. Officially, Romania emulated the progressive Western nations and had signed agreements to protect its minorities. On the other hand, it felt an aversion toward Jews. These factors, together with local and imported brands of antisemitism, were combined into a single dogma. On the one hand, the ecclesiastical establishment, as part of the larger establishment, had to respect the so-called protected religions of the greater Romanian state. On the other hand, the antisemitic movements, especially Cuza's League, obliged the church to continuously deal with questions of principle on which it was necessary to take a stand—something the religious establishment found hard to do.

All antisemitic-fascist movements in Romania considered themselves Christian movements and professed to defend Christianity and the Christian tradition from invaders who were polluting the Romanian country and soul. The church and its leaders were uncertain how far to identify with these movements without violating the fundamental doctrines of the Christian faith and without crossing the fine line between upholding antisemitic tradition and inflaming passions. The combination of militant Christian nationalism and active antisemitism was to a large extent new, and the Romanian Church was unsure how to handle it. In the past it had not initiated wars of religion or inquisitions against heretics and Jews but had almost always identified with Romanian nationalist goals and suffered together with the people during periods of conquest and foreign rule. The church was hardly likely to oppose Cuza's platform, which adopted the slogan "Jesus, the King and the Nation" and obliged prospective members to swear allegiance to the church, the king, and the national flag, which now sported a black swastika in a white circle.[1]

Codreanu and members of his Iron Guard were the heirs of Cuza's Christian antisemitic legacy. Codreanu was wont to declare that his movement "was free of atheists" and that the Legion would only admit Romanians who were capable of believing in God: "Let anyone who believes without reservation, join our ranks."[2] The church served as a role model, and Codreanu's movement strove to emulate it and to reach that place that is "situated thousands of meters above us."[3] Codreanu's close associates were aware of or involved in matters of faith. Ionel Moța's father, for example, was an orthodox priest in the small town of Orăstie, Transylvania, while Vasile Marin's works emphasize the role of Romanian Orthodox Christianity in "defending Romanian nationalism."[4] The Christian principles adopted by the leaders of the Iron Guard served as a basis for the growing rapprochement among Romanian nationalism, the Orthodox Church, and antisemitism, even after the murder or death of Codreanu and his close friends.

Many priests joined the two antisemitic movements, delivered incendiary sermons against Jews, or participated in antisemitic activities. Some priests took their zeal even further. On 15 December 1928, for example, a priest named Stănescu led a gang of students on a rampage through the city of Buzău looking for Jewish boys to attack. The students' teachers also led the gang, which ended up fatally wounding a Jewish boy.[5] This teacher-priest combination was able, in the thirties, to create an antisemitic generation of a new kind — one that was active, aggressive, and aware of its power.

The Education Ministry made no attempt to prevent teachers from joining Cuza's movement or any other antisemitic movement. The Romanian intelligentsia played a large part in shaping public opinion. Journalists, teachers, priests, and civil servants increasingly absorbed, and even began disseminating, the fascist dogma of the antisemitic movements, as the following excerpt from Filderman's memoirs testifies: "It attracted church clerics because the ignorant masses were uninterested in the precepts of Christian morality but readily accepted the primitive harangues of anti-Semitism — which enabled the clerics to exploit them for their own profit."[6]

Theology students in the thirties were agents of antisemitic ferment. Many of them joined the antisemitic movements and initiated attacks against Jews. In January 1930 gangs of students of the theology faculty in Kishinev organized riots against Jewish firms and later marched through the center of town shouting slogans such as "death to the Jews." All the students who were arrested and tried after the demonstration were subsequently acquitted.[7]

In September 1932 Christian antisemitic incitement gained a new patron—the newspaper *Porunca Vremii* (The need of the hour). *Porunca Vremii* began publishing the antisemitic pronouncements of church leaders as well as the anti-Jewish decrees issued by Moldovan and Walachian church leaders over the generations. It even published a separate edition of these decrees and decisions for its readers' enlightenment. Antisemitic priests used the newspaper as a forum for expounding the significance of the Christian festivals and the life and passion of Christ, as well as current events, from an antisemitic angle. The paper began publication as the organ of the League and of the National Christian Party, continued as the mouthpiece of the Iron Guard, and ended up as the Christian antisemitic voice of the Antonescu regime.

Almost all the leaders of the Romanian Orthodox Church depicted Jews as the enemies of Christianity, as a disruptive and divisive force that polluted the Christian soul and values and was responsible for Romania's misfortunes. They branded Jews as traitors, Communists, and Bolshevik sympathizers. First and foremost, however, they accused Jews of deicide. In 1937 Nicolae Bălan (1882–1955), the metropolitan of Transylvania, accused the Jews of being the founders of the Freemasons, "a secret kabalistic sect" and a relentless adversary of Christianity.[8] In 1936 Marin Popescu, a "researcher" into Judaism, wrote that if the Germans found stifling the presence of the Jews, who constituted only 1 percent of Germany's population, "how will we be able [to continue] to bear the burden of 17–20 times as many Yids?" Popescu considered the Jews "a separate people" whose parasitical characteristics and avarice were the product of "a sick mentality fostered by the Talmud." He predicted that Jews could constitute a fifth column in times of war: "Over 90% of all Communist agents and terrorists are Yids," which was why Hitler had decided "to get rid of them once for all. . . . In actual fact, the 'chosen people' is nothing but a formidable organization of international crooks . . . a unique mafia that aims to destroy Christianity and plunder the entire world."[9]

Ion Moța was yet another priest who was known to express fundamentalist antisemitic views. His son's death in the Spanish Civil War heightened his popularity among the Legionnaires, the Transylvanian peasants, and Romanian youth in general. He proposed that the Romanians model themselves on Hitler in their dealings with the Jews: "Since we cannot burn the Jews or drown them in the Danube or the Black Sea to wash up in their Dead Sea, let us do what the experts, namely the pragmatic and rational Hitler, did. . . . And just as the world no longer brands Hitler a thug but take off their hats to him, so will they do to us."[10]

In the summer of 1937, without any apparent reason, Patriarch Cristea began expressing antisemitic sentiments that soon took the form of a Christian campaign against Jewish existence in Romania. The adoption of a public position such as this at a time of antisemitic nationalist ferment, growing Nazi influence in Romania, and a Legionary attempt to seize power led to the institutionalization of the antisemitic campaign and its adoption by several church leaders. The patriarch not only denied the right of Jews to exist in Romania but also rejected the Western democratic values on which the Romanian state was based. In his eyes France symbolized the harmful influence that had destroyed Christian tradition and national values.[11] The rationale for the antisemitic campaign launched by the patriarch was no different from that advanced by Cuza and Codreanu. The patriarch absorbed all the antisemitic jargon, gave it a kind of Christian stamp of approval, applied it to world Jewry, and blessed the nationalist struggle against the Jews. All in all, he revived the main antisemitic myths.[12] According to Cristea, a solution was possible only if the Jews were expelled from Romania. On this issue, however, he departed from traditional antisemitic thought. It was no longer "Yids to Palestine" — the pet slogan of the traditional antisemites. In an eruption of Christian hatred, the patriarch denied the Jews the right to their ancient land, since the land of Israel belonged to the Arabs and also since the Jews, by nature, exploited and controlled the resources of each nation with which they came into contact "through ethnic and Talmudic sophistry." The patriarch rejected the traditional interpretation of the Christian precept of "brotherly love." The rationale he provided demonstrated that for him, as for the Legionnaires and many politicians, the Jew had ceased being a human being and did not even qualify as a "brother" deserving of Christian love and absolution.[13]

The patriarch's "declaration of war" was enthusiastically received by the antisemitic movements. Under the patriarch's influence, Cuza changed one of his principles and declared, "Palestine should be left for the Arabs," while the Jews should be sent elsewhere, "to Africa, Australia, or Asia."[14] According to the leader of the Romanian Orthodox Church, with a few exceptions, Jews were perceived as the Antichrist, a subversive and disparate element, dangerous to the soul of the Christian, responsible for its moral decline and for the calamities that had befallen Romania, traitors, disseminators of left-wing views, the allies of the Bolsheviks, and primarily, the killers of Jesus. Under the patriarch's influence, prelates of the church who addressed the Jewish question also sought a pragmatic and immediate solution to the Jewish problem, namely the expulsion of the Jews.

The Romanian Orthodox Church (and to a lesser extent the Romanian Catholic Church) became an antisemitic institution in the years preceding the Holocaust, thanks to Patriarch Cristea, who also played an extremely important part in Romanian politics. Christian antisemitism was propagated by "theologians" such as Cuza, Codreanu, and others, and the church, without officially adopting their dogma, succumbed and even contributed to the atmosphere of antisemitism. With the temporary weakening of the veteran fascist elements toward the end of the pre-Holocaust period, the church became the standard-bearer of Christian-inspired antisemitism.

The church as an institution joined other influential organizations and entire sectors of the Romanian public that were, or had become, antisemitic and was a main determinant of how the Romanians perceived the Jews during the Holocaust. Its influence extended to the army and police, the judicial system, the civil service, the press, the education system, trade unions, members of the liberal professions (particularly lawyers, doctors, pharmacists, engineers, and architects), thousands of businessmen, and most of the youth, who for years had been soaking up fascist and antisemitic propaganda. Given its moral and national influence on the Romanian masses, the church caused inestimable damage to Romanian-Jewish relations.

5

The Nazi Influence on Romanian Political Life and Its Effect on the Situation of the Jews

In the period leading up to the Second World War, Nazi Germany had nothing to offer Romania to induce it to abandon its traditional pro-Western policy and alliances with France and neighboring countries and join the Axis forces. The Nazis were able to offer Hungary and Bulgaria slabs of Romania and Yugoslavia. The 1919 unification had satisfied the national aspirations of Romania, however, and in any case it had never sought to expand beyond its ethnic borders.

On the other hand, the Nazis could not afford to ignore Romania because of its convenient location and natural resources, especially oil. In February 1938 Walther Funk, Reich minister of economics, informed Nicolae Petrescu-Comnen, the Romanian ambassador in Berlin (1 May 1932–17 February 1938), "Romania is the richest country in Europe" and proposed that economic ties between the two countries be strengthened.[1] One of the directors of Funk's ministry emphasized that Germany needed raw material from Romania and informed Petrescu-Comnen's deputy, "In a few years' time, we shall be on your doorstep."[2]

Several options were open to Germany in seeking to realize its goals in Romania: it could try to persuade the press and the Romanian public of the truth of its ideology and the effectiveness of its regime; it could support sympathetic right-wing parties and movements in Romania; it could exploit the large concentrations of *Volksdeutschen* (ethnic Germans) in Transylvania and other areas (about 750,000 individuals in 1930); it could activate its secret services; it could conduct an intensive campaign of economic penetration; it could use ordinary diplomacy and turn the full force of its leaders' charisma on the Romanian government; or finally—if all that failed—it could achieve its aims through threats, intimidation, extortion, and coercion. Nazi Germany used all the above in order to obtain oil, grain, food, and other natural resources as well as a military foothold in Romania. Addressing the Jewish problem was only part of the Nazis' broader strategy.

As Germany began rearming itself, the importance of Romanian oil grew, and its interest in Romania grew concomitantly. In late January 1935 Hitler suggested that Alfred Rosenberg (director of the Foreign Affairs Department [APA] of the National Socialist German Workers' Party) should himself travel to Romania in order to influence King Carol to change his policy.[3] In order to prepare the ground for this visit, Radu Lecca, a Romanian Gestapo agent, was sent to Romania "to deliver a long letter and to expedite Rosenberg's visit to Bucharest."[4] Lecca, the scion of a famous and respectable boyar family from Oltenia (Walachia) and Cuza's cousin, worked for several years as correspondent for the Nazi periodical *Voelkischer Beobachter* and the German News Agency (Deutsche Nachrichten Büro) in Bucharest.[5] The king, however, saw the letter as "an act of extreme political pressure."[6] He and his establishment remained faithful to their pro-Western orientation, which served their national interests, and Rosenberg's visit never materialized.

In March Berlin sent Lecca to Romania to carry out another assignment: the establishment of a large, popular pro-Nazi movement in Romania. In the final analysis this plan, too, failed. Lecca brought large sums of money to finance pro-Nazi propaganda and set up the movement, and Cuza boasted in private talks that he "would set up the largest party in Romania," with the help of Lecca's millions.[7] Lecca approached Nichifor Crainic, a former sympathizer of Italian fascism and currently a Nazi sympathizer, asking him to help lead the campaign to reorganize the propaganda activities of the National Christian Party. Lecca promised Crainic "as much money as he would need to organize propaganda activities."[8] Goga, who had already been allotted seven hundred thousand deutsche marks to wage a campaign against the pro-Western foreign minister Nicolae Titulescu, received another 4 million lei for the reorganization of the National Christian Party and propaganda activities. (Ion Antonescu was forced to reimburse Germany from state funds after he came to power.) Nae Ionescu, the Iron Guard's ideologue, received 20 million lei.[9] The money was sent to Lecca directly from Berlin, not via the German legation in Romania. Members of the German legation were known to have remarked, "He uses it [the money] as he sees fit."[10]

The Nazis were interested in influencing right-wing parties but also journalists and intellectuals, antisemites, extremist nationalists, and those who were generally dissatisfied with the democratic system and Western values. The main objective of Nazi foreign policy was to dissolve Romania's alliances with the Western powers, its regional pact with Yugoslavia and Czechoslovakia (the Little Entente), and other treaties that had been made in the aftermath of the First World War. The Nazis' propaganda efforts were directed against France in an attempt to undermine the sympathy many Romanian intellectuals felt toward French culture and toward democracy in general. Romanian Jews, who only fifteen years previously had enjoyed full civil rights, were now depicted by the propaganda machine as part of a world conspiracy hatched by Jews in general and French and English Jews in particular—the friends of Léon Blum, Lev Trotsky, and the Bolsheviks who backed them.

The Nazis, therefore, were responsible for the internationalization of Romanian antisemitism. The Jews of Romania were portrayed as participating in a secret plot to undermine the Romanian nation, which had, for the first time, managed to unite into a single country. The Jewish problem came to occupy an important place in the public debate regarding Romania's political future.

Romanian newspapers that received Nazi funds, such as *Universul* and *Curentul*, continued to portray Jews as Communist agents bent on destroying Romania.[11] They accused France of weakness, of pruning its assistance to the Romanian armament effort, of ignoring Romania's commercial and industrial interests, of failing to keep up with the German arms race, of being inconsistent, and of endangering Romania's borders in the Laval-Stalin Pact. Germany, on the other hand, was portrayed as capable of safeguarding Romania's territorial integrity. The Nazi top brass dispensed such promises liberally, and all Romanian politicians and diplomats who met with the Reich's leaders received promises of this kind.

Antisemitism proliferated not only in the antisemitic press but also in the mainstream press, which began receiving Nazi backing, too. Only Germany, argued the advocates of an alliance with the Nazis, would guarantee Romania's territorial integrity and revitalize the country's economy.[12] Pro-Nazi antisemitic propaganda spread, even though many leading intellectuals and several Romanian politicians considered the Iron Guard and Cuza abhorrent, even before the latter began incorporating Nazi terminology into his rhetoric.[13]

As the right became increasingly forceful and aggressive, its opponents became progressively weaker. France's supporters were silenced: "They were paralyzed by the fear of compromising themselves, by fear of terror, by discouragement, by indolence, by ideological repression."[14] Even before the Nazis came to power most liberal Romanians were afraid of identifying with the Jews and therefore chose to deny that the excesses of the radical right constituted a real existential threat to the Jews. Some of these prominent persons manifested a sort of tacit acquiescence in the illegal activities of the antisemitic youth. Others hoped or believed that one could make a distinction between antisemitic acts and those aimed at undermining the regime—that there could be two different systems of ethics and justice without undermining democracy as a system of government. This great change in values took place after the Nazis rose to power. Even the most relatively courageous voices in the opposition pushed their temerity just enough to murmur that it was incomprehensible why the country's leaders encouraged these antisemitic diversions.

There were indeed many politicians and intellectuals who supported democracy as a system, maintained good relations with Jews and especially with Filderman, and were repelled by fascism and antisemitism. But what almost all these people had in common was that they did not protest when the Jews were denied their civil rights; when the first steps were taken to expel Jews from the civil service, discharge them from their jobs, and exclude them from various sectors of economic and cultural life; when their property was expropriated; or when the campaigns of mass annihilation began in Bessarabia and Bukovina. No one resigned in protest; no one left Romania to avoid living under a fascist regime. They all adapted themselves to the dictatorship and were happy enough if they were not personally implicated in repressive acts.

The Nazis controlled a number of newspapers, including the nationalist *Curentul*, a daily with a circulation of forty thousand, and the antisemitic *Porunca Vremii*. Klaus Schickert, a correspondent for the German News Agency, also took over *Timpul*, a popular daily put out by the politician Grigore Gafencu, after dismissing Gafencu's Jewish partners.[15] German firms, Romanian firms with German capital (which proliferated in Romania after 1934), subsidiaries of the giant German concern Farbenindustrie (with their Romanian-sounding names, such as Ferrowolff Romanil, Coloranil, and Ferrostall), the Great Romanian Bank (Societatea Bancară Românească—effectively a front for the Dresdner Bank), and other companies based on German capital and technology all kept Nazi Germany informed of Romania's economic and military policies and supported the antisemitic Romanian press in its various guises.

In the first half of the thirties a change occurred in Romanian antisemitism, not so much in its methods, contents, or objectives but rather in its scope and intensity. The themes were still the same as those invented by Codreanu, Cuza, and their nineteenth-century predecessors. Despite the caricatures of Jews with Semitic features, the question of racial purity and the superiority of the Aryan or Nordic race was a sensitive issue for the Romanians, who had not been included by the Nazis in the super-race. Recurrent themes in antisemitic propaganda and caricatures were the superiority of Christianity versus the shortcomings of Judaism, the cruelty of Jews, their diabolical traits, the issue of Jewish "blood," the superiority of the Romanian "soul," and the satanic nature of the Jewish religion.[16]

With German assistance, Romanian antisemites learned how to organize, print, and disseminate propaganda. The Nazis also reinforced the rejection of Western values and the values of the French Revolution—a trend that already existed in

Romanian culture. For the first time, Romanian antisemites challenged the need for Romania's alliance with democracy. In particular, they fostered the yearning for a strong leader who would solve Romania's problems, put an end to the farce of its politics and to "anarchy," and implement the "national idea." The pre-Goga governments, while not initiating such a process, supported it indirectly.[17]

The Molotov-Ribbentrop Pact (23 August 1939) sent out shock waves in Romania. The Romanians feared that Britain and France would abandon them, as they had Czechoslovakia, or would be unable to save them in their time of need. When Goga passed away in the summer of 1938, the APA feverishly sought a replacement to lead the Romanian pro-Nazi nationalist camp. There was, as yet, no mention of Codreanu as Goga's successor. The department believed that it was important "not to alienate [the king], but to enlist his support." The German legation in Bucharest decided to reorganize Romania's propaganda apparatus "as long as the psychological impact of the Soviet-German alliance outweighed the British influence."[18]

After demanding "adequate means," the German ambassador, Wilhelm Fabricius, determined that Schickert, the German News Agency's correspondent, should take over the propaganda apparatus and work together with the ambassador himself, "without [such cooperation] becoming public." Fabricius determined that Schickert's first step must be "to influence the Romanian press in Bucharest and in the provinces. A staff of collaborators is essential," he added, "to write articles," since articles sent over from Germany arrived too late. The APA and the German legation agreed to "organize German propaganda services in Romania." Karol Otto Suprian, secretary-general of the German Institute of Sciences in Bucharest, was appointed executive director of the new propaganda service, while Himmler himself appointed Edith Von Kohler as its supervisor.[19] Posing as a correspondent for the *Deutsche Allgemeine Zeitung* in Bucharest, Von Kohler managed to penetrate the Romanian establishment, publish articles in the Romanian press, "and recruit sympathizers among Romanian journalists."[20]

Fabricius and his associates began assailing the Romanian government directly with their antisemitic propaganda, emphasizing the Jews' hunger for power, their greed, and the harm they were causing relations between the two countries. Prestigious Nazi weeklies and monthlies, including some that "specialized" in the Jewish problem, were circulated free of charge in German bookstores in Romania.[21] Textbooks, academic works, and courses were offered free of charge to Romanian students.

Although few Romanians mastered German, antisemitic articles from German journals were translated and disseminated in the local press. Antisemitic propaganda was also disseminated via the four newspapers belonging to the German minority in Romania—two in Bucharest, one in Sibiu, and one in Czernowitz. These ethnic Germans happily participated in the overall attempt to delegitimize the Jewish people. German firms in Braşov, which had a large German minority and was considered the center of the Volksdeutschen in Romania, contributed hundreds of thousands of lei to Rosenberg's propaganda fund in Romania.[22]

The local fascist antisemitic movements and organizations were the vehicles whereby Nazi propaganda was imported into Romania, exploiting the silent consent of successive Romanian governments, particularly after the Anschluss, which, in the absence of an adequate response by Britain and France, turned Germany into the dominant power in the region. Nazi propaganda in its local manifestation intensified antisemitism, undermined and eventually weakened the intelligentsia and the free press, and eroded the foundations of Jewish existence in Romania. The tenuous ideological link between Nazi antisemitism and Romanian antisemitism, especially on racial and religious issues, did not prevent them from closing ranks against the Jews.

Nazi support for the Iron Guard, which began with Codreanu's declaration in November 1937 that "48 hours after the Legionary movement's victory, Romania will have an alliance with Rome and Berlin," intensified after Germany's disillusionment with Goga and the abortive attempt to draw the king into the fascist camp.[23] On 21 December 1937, after assuming the premiership, Goga hastened to assure the German ambassador that he would sign a friendship treaty and expand trade relations with Germany and abandon Romania's alliances. He did not, however, keep his promises.[24] For the Nazis, "the second antisemitic government in Europe," as Alfred Rosenberg had proudly described it, was a disappointment, having failed, inter alia, to apply antisemitic principles, as the German ambassador stated in a report dated 19 January 1939: "All these antisemitic measures, however unpleasant for the Jews, are simply . . . superficial barbs. . . . It remains to be seen if the Goga-Cuza government will dare to adopt truly decisive measures."[25]

The APA, which had been cultivating Goga since 1934, tried to effect a reconciliation between him and Codreanu and found partial success after Goga asked the Germans, via the Nazi ambassador Fabricius, not to favor "one right-wing party in Romania [i.e., the Iron Guard] over another."[26] Foreign Minister Istrate Micescu, a favorite of the king's, informed Fabricius that the Goga government's task was to fight the Iron Guard and asked the Reich to cease supporting the Legionnaires.[27] In Prague Micescu emphatically informed the foreign minister of Czechoslovakia, Eduard Beneš, that "Goga was not Codreanu," after agreeing to continue with the Little Entente. Rosenberg was disappointed with Goga's failure to apply the APA's advice to set up party branches throughout the country "and saturate police ranks with his supporters."[28] When he was forced to resign, Goga apologized to the German ambassador for his failure and for dashing the hopes his Nazi supporters had pinned on him, now that "Israel had won!"[29]

Between February 1938 and the Soviet ultimatum of 26 June 1940, Germany's foreign policy toward Romania was divided between the official policy of the Foreign Department in Berlin and the foreign policy of the various Nazi organizations. The latter used tactics such as destabilization of the current regime in Romania, supporting fascist rather than "classical" antisemitism, subversion, espionage, and encouraging local Germans to form a fifth column. Berlin at the time was vacillating between two opposite trends: strengthening ideological ties with its fascist allies or realizing economic, political, and strategic goals with the existing regime. This dilemma persisted during Antonescu's regime. Correspondence between the German ambassador in Bucharest and his superiors in Berlin testifies to the extreme caution Germany officially exercised in its dealings with the king (it refrained from publicly identifying with the Iron Guard even after Codreanu's death). The German secretary of state, Ernst Von Weizsäcker, clearly illustrated this aspect of Nazi policy when he ordered Fabricius, in June 1938, to assure the Romanian government "that we had no ties with Codreanu."[30] On the other hand, King Carol's insistence that Hitler recall Heinz Konradi, the economic attaché and agent of the Nazi Foreign Department through whom the Nazis funded the Iron Guard, illustrates the other side of Nazi policy toward Romania.[31]

Nazi disillusionment with the classical strain of Romanian antisemitism had repercussions for the fate of Romanian Jewry. The Nazis transferred their support to the Iron Guard, while the king and most of the political establishment tried to prevent Romania's immolation on the altar of German interests. They understood that the system of alliances of which Romania was a part would not hold out against German might and hoped that the West would be able to curb German expansionism. Meanwhile, they sacrificed grain, meat, food, raw material, and especially oil in order to appease Germany's voracious appetite.

The above helps shed light on Romania's antisemitic policy—a policy based on a traditional schism between foreign and domestic affairs, between its desire to impress its Western allies as to its democratic nature while at the same time espousing an antidemocratic domestic policy (not only in relation to the Jews, either). Nazi support for the Legionnaires—more even than support for Cuza and his associates—succeeded in undermining Romania's political stability and discrediting democracy by resuscitating the idea that democracy served Jewish interests only and was diametrically opposed to the true interests of the Romanian people. The result was an intensification of the yearning for a strong leader

(Codreanu) who would solve Romania's problems, particularly the Jewish problem. Nazi support for the Iron Guard legitimized the Legionnaires' antisemitic ideology in the eyes of Romanian politicians who were afraid of Germany because of the threat it posed to Romania's territorial integrity and autonomy. External German pressure coupled with the internal Legionary threat impelled the royal dictatorship, in its latter days, to adopt an overtly antisemitic policy in order to appease the Nazis on issues that did not appear to impinge on Romania's vital interests. Filderman's prediction in December 1934 that "the adoption of a racist policy would inevitably lead to an alliance with Nazi Germany" was substantiated in September 1940.[32]

ECONOMIC INFILTRATION

The situation of Romanian Jewry was influenced during this period by the Nazis' recurrent attempts to control Romania's economy, change its export policy, and take the place of the Western powers as exporters of machines, weapons, and other goods to Romania. Although economic penetration of Romania had been a German goal since the late nineteenth century, it now constituted part of the Nazis' war preparations and part of the Reich's ideological struggle against the democratic powers and "world Judaism." Moreover, this policy was clearly directed against the Jews and used the Jewish problem for its own ends. The APA wished to turn the Balkans into Germany's main supplier of raw materials and foodstuffs, instead of overseas countries, and to strengthen the rail link with Romania and other countries in the region. This policy was successful even before the economic and political enslavement of these countries.[33]

Germany's antisemitic allies in Romania also helped the Reich strengthen its economic ties with Romania at the expense of the democratic countries. Already in 1934 Cuza called for an economic and political "pact" with Germany.[34] Upon assuming office Prime Minister Alexandru Vaida-Voevod of the National Peasants' Party also hastened to send a senior envoy to Berlin in order to strengthen economic ties with Germany.[35]

Although German capital investments in Romania were inferior to those of France, Britain, and Czechoslovakia even after the Anschluss, Germany's relative share of Romania's commercial balance continued to grow. By 1938 Romania was importing machines, motors, and cars mainly from Germany, even though it continued to export most of its products to the West. It was these exports that brought foreign currency into the country.[36]

The Nazis were mainly interested in Romanian oil, which they wished to pay for with commodities rather than with currency. During 1938–40 Germany pressured Romania to export most of its raw materials to the enlarged Reich in exchange for machines, weapons, and other goods (mostly plundered from Romanian's former allies). Such a measure would have deprived Romania of its foreign currency sources at a time when the price of raw materials and foodstuffs was rising monthly due to the outbreak of war. The failure of the German Four Year Plan to achieve a breakthrough in the production of synthetic oil and the danger of a British-French embargo on oil shipments from Mexico and the United States—countries that supplied 60–65 percent of the Reich's total oil consumption—enhanced the value of Romanian and Soviet oil as an exclusive source of liquid fuel in the case of a general war.[37]

In the struggle against German economic penetration, Romania was not helped by Britain and France, its traditional allies. Britain and France had economic interests in Romania and had a large say in the Romanian economy. They were able to influence Romania's commercial balance and, through their hold on Romania's capital market, its economy, too. Even so, right from the start, neither Britain nor France made any attempt to curb Germany's economic expansion. France remained indifferent to the signals of distress emanating from Bucharest, while London recognized, in late November 1938, the supremacy of German economic interests in Romania and in the Balkans in general. Neville Chamberlain told King Carol during his visit to Britain in November 1938 that, due to a series of natural circumstances, Germany "should enjoy a preponderant position in Romania's economy."[38] Britain's renunciation was brought to the attention of the economic adviser at the German Embassy in London, who immediately understood its significance: "a definite recognition of German priority in the Balkans."[39]

This news reached Berlin on the eve of King Carol's arrival for an official visit. Hitler asked King Carol to deliver the goods Goga had failed to deliver: dissolution of Romania's ties with the West and its regional allies, cancellation of its membership in the League of Nations, and according to one Romanian report, the establishment of a government led by Codreanu. The murder of Codreanu and his associates did nothing to temper Nazi ambitions, and for several months the king was forced to make more economic concession in favor of Nazi Germany.[40] Romanian politicians from all ends of the political spectrum began to doubt the wisdom of a pro-Western policy. The Munich agreements and the West's indifference to the disintegration of Czechoslovakia sent out shock waves in Bucharest and led it to reconsider the entire basis of Romanian policy. The vulnerability of the democratic powers was exposed. Czechoslovakia, an important ally, was now supplanted by Nazi Germany as Romania's main supplier of weapons—weapons that were still manufactured in Czech factories, under old orders, but sanctioned by the new bosses.[41]

The Nazis also appropriated firms and factories belonging to citizens and countries that fell into the hands of the German army. The Oil Treaty, which was debated for months, was signed on 29 May 1940, the day of the German victory over France. In return, the Romanians received weapons looted from Poland and refrained from demanding foreign currency in payment for their oil.[42]

After Hitler's speech of 30 January 1939 the German legation in Bucharest and the Reich leaders began to show an interest in the part played by Romanian Jews in the Romanian economy. They tried to supplant the Jews from entire industrial sectors and from the Romanian economy in general and to replace them with ethnic Germans.

6

Pogroms and Persecutions
in the Summer of 1940

The transition from antisemitic policy and incitement to pogroms took place suddenly in the summer of 1940. It was the result of a national calamity — the cession of Bessarabia and Bukovina to the Russians — and had no connection with the Nazis (it occurred before the first German soldier even set foot on Romanian soil).

The Romanian army's hasty retreat from Bessarabia and northern Bukovina in the summer of 1940 following the Soviet ultimatum of 26 June was used by the Antonescu regime to justify the liquidation of the Jews of Bessarabia and Bukovina in the summer of 1941. Even later, this regime continued to justify its participation in the extermination of European Jewry on national grounds rather than on grounds of Nazi antisemitic ideology. On 19 October 1941 Antonescu rejected Filderman's request to halt the liquidation of Bessarabian and Bukovinian Jewry on the grounds that their behavior during the retreat of the Romanian army in the summer of 1940 warranted it. "Even before the arrival of the Soviet forces, the Jews . . . of Bessarabia and Bukovina spat on our officers, ripped their tunics, tore their uniforms, and wherever possible, clubbed soldiers to death. We have proof of this."[1]

The proof Antonescu referred to came in the form of reports and telegrams by army units to the General Staff, reports from the police inspectorates, and accounts by Romanian refugees on the behavior of the Jews and other minority groups during the Romanian retreat. These reports accused Jews of attacking soldiers, displaying hostility toward the Romanian government, being overly sympathetic toward the new Soviet regime, offending Romanian national sentiments, desecrating churches, killing priests and government officials, and inciting the non-Romanian, and even the Romanian, population against the Romanian administration. They depicted all Jews as enemies and as Communists. Romanian Communist historiography also helped foster this myth.[2]

The Romanian public was shocked at the rumors Romanian refugees disseminated about Jews willfully attacking churches and murdering priests. Although such accusations were fabrications, they had serious implications. The first to spread the rumor of the desecration of churches by Jews were refugees from Czernowitz who claimed that "the Jews destroyed churches" even prior to the entry of the Soviet army.[3] The Communists, the report stated, "have removed the crucifixes from the Czernowitz Cathedral, and replaced them with the red flag and Stalin's portrait, and have destroyed the interior [of the church] with grenades."[4] Already on 27 June a Bessarabian newspaper reported that Jews had attempted to disrupt a service in the Kishinev cathedral.[5] On 3 July a general report stated that Jewish Communists, not satisfied with acts of terror and offenses to the national sentiments of the Romanian people, "had looted churches and ridiculed and mocked [priests]."[6] A report titled "A Jewish Operation," dated 4 July, described how gangs of Jews (bande de evrei) in Bălți "broke crucifixes in churches and waved the red flag" over them. A similar report stated that the Jewish Communists destroyed churches in Chilia-Nouă.[7] Communist Jews were also blamed for the murder of a Pravoslav priest in Bălți, a Catholic priest in Czernowitz, and two Romanian priests in Cetatea-Albă.[8]

The Romanians were less critical of the behavior of the Russian, Ukrainian, and Bulgarian minorities, even though Ukrainians were among the instigators of the riots. Sometimes Jews and members of other minority groups were described as joining forces to attack the Romanian population and stray soldiers.[9] In southern Bessarabia, where Jews were scarce, Jews were accused of setting up joint committees with members of other minority groups and taking over the local government.[10] A report of 5 July stated, "The Jews, led by government officials of foreign extraction, were most active in the mistreatment of the [Romanian] population and in preventing the evacuation of the army and civil authorities."[11] Unlike the enormous publicity the press afforded to the "crimes of the Jews," the active hostility of the Ukrainians, Bulgarians, and to a lesser extent, the Russians toward the Romanians was hushed up. Even decades later, reports on the hostile acts of members of minority groups other than Jews were withheld from the author of this research.[12] Testimonies by refugees about the Ukrainians' hostility toward the Romanian authorities, their delight at changes of government, or the warm reception they gave to the Red Army were concealed or inconspicuously slipped into reports.[13] Numerous testimonies collected from Jewish survivors from Bessarabia and Bukovina confirm this.

In the face of the national tragedy, the Romanian military establishment scapegoated the Jews for the humiliating retreat of the Romanian army and its failure to fulfill the promises military spokesmen and army commanders made to the nation at the outbreak of the Second World War. Army and police reports are full of false and tendentious information about Jews who had remained within the borders of Romania and could not be blamed for participating in anti-Romanian acts. Most of Iaşi's Jews, stated one report, "openly showed their delight at the Bolsheviks' proximity to the River Prut, and adopted a defiant posture."[14] In Iaşi, another report by the local military authorities stated that "liaison officers stayed with [the Jews] who left" for the Soviet Union. The report went on to say that Jews from Iaşi who had decided to move to Soviet Bessarabia did so, on their own admission, "in order to incite public opinion against Romania and persuade the Soviets to conquer Iaşi, too."[15]

On 1 July 1940 the Cluj police reported that the Hungarians were rejoicing at the calamity that had befallen Romania and that the Jews, although not expressing it openly, "felt satisfaction at Russia's expansion."[16] The Jews, in an attempt to parry Romanians' furious responses to rumors of Jewish atrocities in Czernowitz and as proof of their loyalty, prayed in the synagogues for the king's well-being. Reports of Communist activities in Transylvania did not blame the Jews but implied rather that the Hungarians were at fault. The military authorities accused Jews of expressing their antagonism toward Romania by "spreading false rumors and ridiculing anything Romanian." All sorts of Jews "expressed their pleasure" at Bessarabia and Bukovina's cession to the Soviets.[17]

In a spate of false allegations, the Jews of the Regat were accused of launching terrorist attacks, instigating attacks against military personnel, and assaulting soldiers. "A group of Jews, encountering several Romanian soldiers who were retreating toward Huşi, stripped them of their clothes and weapons, left them in their underwear and spat on them in public."[18] Another report accused Communist Jews of "shooting and killing four Romanian officers in Herţa," although in actual fact the Russians had shot a Romanian officer and a Jewish soldier had tried to defend his commander.[19] Similar items stated that "a policeman in Roman was shot to death by four Jews," and "an arms cache in Rădăuţi was attacked by four Jews who, encountering resistance, shot four people dead." In Cucuteni, near Iaşi, "a uniformed Jew who aimed his gun at a general was severely disciplined" (two Jewish reservists were killed by the masses). In Târgul Frumos a Jew "carrying a gun and grenade" was killed by the masses, and so on and so forth.[20]

Attempts by Jewish leaders to show solidarity with the Romanian people were interpreted as "stratagems to exonerate Jews from blame for terrorist activities carried out by members of the Jewish people in the occupied territories."[21] The authorities were aware of the anxiety felt by the Jews of the Regat. According to one report, despite efforts to keep the peace, "nationalist youngsters, particularly former Legionnaires, will carry out reprisals against the Jews."[22] The Jews' anxiety was intensified by "the tone of the national press," which the authorities did not even attempt to curb, despite censorship. A report by the Romanian General Staff stated that the Jews were sure that "in light of recent events in Bessarabia and Bukovina, Romania would not hesitate to implement forthwith a definitive solution to the Jewish problem in our country."[23] Anxiety levels rose even further following a rumor that Nicolae Iorga, King Carol's adviser, was intending to submit a memorandum demanding "the immediate expulsion of all Jews."[24] Based on information they had collected on Iaşi's Jews, the Iaşi police decided "to closely monitor the new manifestation of the Jewish problem." Nevertheless, the police did admit that some Jewish inhabitants of Iaşi and of the Regat condemned the actions of Bessarabian Jews and their attitudes toward the Romanian government.[25]

These reports were delivered to the heads of the military establishment and the administration, who accepted in part the accusations of the antisemitic press regarding "Soviet plans to step up propaganda efforts," in an attempt to persuade the Jews that "under current circumstances Communism was their only hope."[26] A heavy shadow fell over the Jews of the Regat, who were accused, en masse, of sympathizing with the sworn enemy of the Romanian nation.

Did Jews in Bessarabia and northern Bukovina really participate in anti-Romanian activities, as army and police reports claim? The answer is yes, although this answer must be qualified by stressing that most Jews barricaded themselves in their homes, fearing this sudden development that had cut them off from their relatives and changed their way of life. Although the Romanians perceived the Russian occupation as a national disaster, many Bessarabian Jews openly expressed their pleasure at this turn of events, "and some participated in attacks against Romanian soldiers and policemen."[27]

Testimonies of Jews from central Bessarabia and survivors' Yizkor (memorial) books corroborate that Jews—mainly youth—did harm, insult, and jeer at fleeing Romanian soldiers; they also ripped insignia from their shirts and tore the Romanian flag. They did not, however, participate in acts of murder. In northern Bessarabia, moreover, Jews played no part in attacks against retreating soldiers or the evacuating authorities. In Secureni, where retreating Romanian soldiers beat up many Jews, the Jews barricaded themselves in their homes upon the entry of the Soviet army, "since we did not know what to expect of the new rulers." It was the Ukrainians who actually welcomed the Russians: "Dressed in festive garb and carrying garlands of flowers, bread and salt, they afterwards began dancing in honor of the invaders." The author of this testimony added, "We Jews breathed with relief thinking that it was all over and that we were saved. But we soon realized we were wrong."[28] In Hotin most Jews were "confused, panic-stricken, and worried by the uncertainty of the situation" and refrained from participating in demonstrations or in hostile acts against the Romanians.[29]

The Jews' attitude toward the retreating Romanian authority was not, therefore, uniform or consistently hostile. However, one cannot summarily dismiss reports by military units concerning Jews' attacks against soldiers, although these were inflated. Jews did not attack churches or assassinate priests and military personnel. Although many Jews were appointed to managerial positions or jobs in the propaganda service by the new administration, this was only until suitable candidates were recruited from among the Romanians in Bessarabia and the Ukrainians in northern Bukovina and Bessarabia.

THE POGROMS OF SUMMER 1940

The ignominious retreat from Romanian territory, antisemitic incitement before and during the retreat, the humiliation suffered by the Romanian soldiers, the fact that many units comprised reservists and armed followers of Cuza and Codreanu, and particularly the need to find a scapegoat were the main elements that facilitated the transition from threats to the butchery of Jews in the summer of 1940. Most of the pogroms took place in Bukovina, a region noted for its support of Cuza and the Legionnaires. The orders to kill did not emanate from the high command or from the Romanian General Staff but from the brigadier rank and below. The pogroms were a spontaneous expression of anger following the ignominious retreat, in which the Jews served, as usual, as scapegoats. This time, however, domestic and international factors were such that the Romanians were no longer satisfied with smashing windows and breaking bones. The army units withdrawing from Bessarabia and Bukovina left in their wake a trail of brutal acts of murder, whose victims were not only Jews on either side of the new Bukovinian border but also Jews from the northern Regat and Jewish soldiers who still served in the Romanian army.

The Dorohoi pogrom was planned and carried out by the officers and soldiers of two brigades of the Romanian army—Brigade Three (the border guards) and Brigade Eight (the gunners)—and possibly other brigades, too.[30] The officers' motivation in planning the pogroms was clearly delineated in a military report stating that the brigade "has retaliated for the enormous problems it encountered with the Jews north of the Prut" in Bessarabia. Soldiers had "killed 40 and wounded 15. . . . Our brigade sustained no losses."[31] Although the number of victims was actually higher, the report speaks for itself. On 28–29 June long army convoys passed through Dorohoi, retreating from Hotin and northern Bessarabia. At the same time convoys of panic-stricken Romanian refugees flowed through Dorohoi, spreading rumors that the Jews had attacked the retreating Romanian soldiers. Dorohoi, a town of sixteen thousand inhabitants, a third of whom were Jews, was already notorious for its antisemitic climate and for attacks against Jews.[32]

Army units also looted Jewish stores and firms and murdered Jews in the new border town of Siret. Two young Jewish conscripts were killed by soldiers, thrown off a train, and sprayed with shots as an extra precaution. "We have saved them from reserve duty," the soldiers joked to the other passengers. The gendarmes arrested and cruelly tortured a number of Jews in Siret "for having signaled to Russian planes."[33]

In addition to these acts of murder, the Jews of the new border region suffered for several months from the Communist witch hunt that followed the retreat. Soldiers, policemen, and local authorities "tracked down Communists, dug up Communists, and cooked up Communists." Anything that was reminiscent of the Red Army was considered sufficient "grounds" for arrests, beatings, torture, and extortion of ransoms from Jews. The military court worked overtime to keep up with the caseload, in most cases imposing heavy sentences.[34]

The garrisons stationed in the Jewish towns of northern Moldova and southern Bukovina (which had now become border towns) helped foster a climate of terror. Their commanders initiated and carried out collective punishments of Jews, particularly Jews living in towns near Dorohoi — the place where the taboo on the systematic murder of Jews had been broken.

In August 1940 Captain Mihailescu, commander of the gendarmerie unit in Mihăileni, together with one of the commanders of the army regiment stationed in Mihăileni, launched a joint offensive against local Jews. Soldiers and gendarmes surrounded the town and began a house-to-house search for "weapons and Bolshevik material." They did not even spare the funeral parlors or tombs of pious sages in the Jewish cemetery.[35] Some families were forbidden to leave their homes, and armed soldiers were stationed at the entrances to their homes to enforce the ban. Among the "incriminating" objects turned up during the search was a red synagogue curtain, purportedly meant to serve as a red flag to welcome the Red Army when the time came. Red fabrics and a book by a Russian author were confiscated, and an entire family was arrested because of a red thread that was tied to the wrist of a three-day-old baby to ward off the Evil Eye.[36] An affluent Jew was also arrested for ostensibly plotting to deliver the town into the hands of the Soviet army.

Several Jews were arrested and cruelly interrogated in local police stations. After a rigorous selection process, during which several Jews were released after paying the high ransoms that were demanded even by the pretor (the military officer in charge of administrative matters), eleven Jews remained in custody.

They were escorted under heavy guard to the military court, where they were tried for making preparations to welcome the Soviet army. Women who tried to find out what had happened to their husbands were detained and sent back to Mihăileni. The eleven Jews, including the local rabbi, were court-martialed by the Fourth Army in Roman. After the court clerk was bribed to put forward the trial, they were acquitted on grounds of insufficient evidence and released.[37]

Meir Teich, the president of the Suceava community, summed up the situation of Bukovinian Jewry under Romanian rule as "wretched," with frequent riots, looting, beatings, "and even murder."[38] The same was true of the Jews of northern Moldova, thousands of whom were evacuated from dozens of villages, while many others fled for fear of the army. Neither the Jews nor their property were safe any longer. The Legionnaires and Cuzists launched local initiatives with impunity. The army imposed a rule of terror that paralyzed almost all economic activity and brought the Jews to the brink of starvation. Thousands of Jews were impoverished.

Estimates of the number of casualties in the summer of 1940 range from several hundred to several thousand. The absence of data on the number of Jews who were killed during the retreat from Bessarabia and Bukovina or the number of Jewish recruits who were killed by their peers or pushed off trains makes it hard to assess the exact number of casualties. The severance of northern Bukovina and Bessarabia from the Regat added to the confusion surrounding the number of casualties. The work of collecting testimonies on the pogroms began only in mid-1944, after the entry of the Soviet army.

The Dorohoi pogroms in northern Bukovina were a landmark in the destruction of Romanian Jewry. The patterns that were set in the summer of 1940 were repeated in the summer of 1941 when the Romanian army, now Nazi Germany's ally, served as a tool for solving the Jewish problem and "wreaked its great revenge." In the summer of 1940, before one German soldier had even set foot on Romanian soil and before most soldiers had even heard of Nazi ideology, certain brigades of the Romanian army proved that they were capable of planning and carrying out pogroms against Jews even without explicit orders from above as well as enlisting the cooperation of some civilian populations. They did this by:

1. Accusing Jews of shooting soldiers as a pretext for starting a pogrom.
2. Giving Romanian citizens advance notice of imminent attacks to enable them to mark their houses.
3. Eliciting the support and cooperation of other security units and of the Romanian public.
4. Allowing the rioters to kill, rape, and loot as a reward for their deeds.

The pogroms, as stated, were local initiatives, and the government had no say in their planning or implementation. The Dorohoi pogrom laid the groundwork for the Iași pogrom in the summer of 1941 that resulted in over fourteen thousand casualties. It is worth noting that the perpetrators of the pogroms were never disciplined, not even during the Communist regime.

THE ION GIGURTU GOVERNMENT AND ITS POLICY TOWARD THE JEWS

The king's last government, which lasted for two months (4 July–4 September 1940), was a government of a new kind. It included fascist elements, was run by a pro-German statesman, and had a markedly German orientation in its foreign policy. France's collapse and Britain's isolation from the European continent completely altered Romania's geopolitical situation and the balance of political power in the country. The king hoped that a government headed by a pro-Nazi politician that contained three Legionnaires and thirteen Cuzists and was willing to meet all German demands would save the country from having to make territorial concessions to Hungary and protect it against additional Soviet advances.[39] To this end, he officially asked Hitler to send a German expeditionary force to Romania. The Jewish problem thus became a bargaining chip in Romania's foreign policy, an indication of its wish to strengthen ties with the Reich, and a symbol of its wish to belong to the club of fascist and totalitarian countries. It was the price the Romanians were willing to pay in return for protection by Nazi Germany.

During his visit to Berlin on 26 July 1940, Prime Minister Ion Gigurtu (1886–1959) promised the German foreign minister Joachim von Ribbentrop that Romania would meet all Germany's economic demands. "Romania could also solve the Jewish question definitively if only the Führer were to carry through a total solution for all of Europe."[40] On the same occasion Gigurtu assured Ribbentrop that his country was prepared "to adapt itself fully to the Führer's plan for a new order in Europe," and in the same breath he promised "to solve the Jewish problem definitively" with the führer's help.[41] In return, he received a promise from Ribbentrop that Germany would solve the Jewish problem in Germany and perhaps throughout Europe. In his meeting with Hitler, Gigurtu did his best to convince him that, with German cooperation, "Romania planned to reorganize everything on the German model, and above all to carry out reforms in the economic and social sphere." As to the Jews, continued Gigurtu on his own initiative (Hitler did not even raise the issue), "they had started on a solution, to be sure, but no final settlement could be undertaken without the assistance of the Führer, who must carry out a total solution for all of Europe."[42] To Hitler, this represented the acme of antisemitism.

The Gigurtu government achieved the antisemitic movement's basic demand: the abolition of civil rights for Jews, which, according to the movement, Romania had been "forced" to grant in 1921. Despite its preoccupation with Transylvania, the government turned its attention to the legal aspects of compulsory Romanization, such as the exclusion of Jews from all economic activity, the confiscation of their property, and the introduction of forced labor to replace military service, which had been abolished at the end of August by the Jewish Statute. All these measures, it will be noted, were adopted prior to the establishment of the Iron Guard's fascist regime. Already on 27 June 1940 Filderman remarked to Minister of the Interior Mihail Ghelmegeanu (1896–1984), "An idea is forming in the brains of some people for the expropriation of Jewish property in villages and towns, to be followed by the expropriation of commerce, industry and the liberal professions."[43] It was during Gigurtu's rule that this trend was born.

Over the course of just two months, the government ministries dismissed hundreds and possibly even thousands of Jews—physicians, pharmacists, teachers, engineers, architects, nurses, medical orderlies, technicians, and the like—even those who were not required to forfeit their citizenship under Goga's Law for the Revision of Citizenship. A law requiring civil servants to be registered in the Party of the Nation—membership in which was barred to Jews—served as a pretext for the dismissal of Jews. Although Minister of the Interior Ghelmegeanu tried to convince Filderman and Chief Rabbi Alexandru Safran on 27 June that "the order barring Jews admission to the Party of the Nation . . . is not racist in nature, but is the product of current circumstances," the letters of dismissal sent to many Jews openly stated: "Dismissed on grounds of Jewish ethnic origins and on suspicion of endangering State security."[44] On 16 July Filderman declared before the leaders of the Union of the Jewish Communities in the Regat that the exclusion of Jews from the Party of the Nation "was tantamount to revoking their civil rights."[45]

The first to be dismissed were thirty-five Jewish physicians and pharmacists employed by the Ministry of Health's Medical Insurance Funds.[46] On 6 August the press published a long list of Jewish doctors who had been dismissed from the Ministry of Health and Social Insurance as of 1 July 1940.[47] In a communiqué issued several days earlier, the Ministry of Health seized the opportunity to totally Romanize its ranks by limiting eligibility for vacant positions to doctors of Romanian, German, Russian, or Hungarian extraction. After the enactment of the Jewish Statute the ministry continued dismissing Jews, this time by virtue of the new law. On 16 August it dismissed forty doctors and solicited applications for the vacant positions. On 22 August another twenty-nine Jewish doctors and pharmacists were dismissed, and the activity continued until there were no Jewish doctors left in the state's employ.[48]

It cannot be stressed enough that all these decisions, measures, and events took place before the establishment of a fascist government in Romania. During the darkest period of Romania's history, the nation saw antisemitic legislation as a significant, and perhaps only, point of light. It was perceived as the beginning of the realization of the Romanian antisemitic dream—a dream the Goga-Cuza government had failed to implement—and as an example of national courage that was so sorely lacking at the time. During this period hundreds of thousands of Romanians abandoned their homes at a few hours' notice and tens of thousands of families were separated for many years. Cultural institutions were unable to transfer all the rare documents, books, and important archeological finds testifying to the antiquity of the Romanians to those parts of the homeland that were still under Romanian rule. Entire arsenals of weapons, ammunition, and provisions fell into Russian and Hungarian hands. No wonder, then, that the population was overjoyed when the Law for the Revision of Citizenship and the Jewish Statute stripped 73,253 Jewish families of their civil rights, sorted them into categories, and barred their access to nearly all economic, industrial, and cultural institutions.[49] Each new law or order that was passed to further restrict the Jews' freedom of action and movement—and there were plenty—was considered a historic achievement, the realization of the Precursorii's dreams and predictions. Romanians from all social strata, including members of the clergy, the military, teachers, and industrialists, shared in the general euphoria. The trade unions in particular, which had always considered the Jews a threat, were overjoyed.

The Jews' status at the time was governed by two decrees that had the force of law: the decree of 22 June 1940 establishing the Party of the Nation and barring Jews from membership in it, and the Jewish Statute of 9 August 1940 that banned intermarriage, inter alia (see chap. 7).

The first decree, as Filderman pointed out to the minister of the interior, effectively abolished civil rights for Jews and brought about their dismissal en masse from the civil service and public institutions. The Party of the Nation served, as stated in a prestigious Romanian paper, as "a most important tool for eliminating Jews from Romanian's public and economic life."[50] The party also collected data for drawing up antisemitic legislation. From mid-July 1940 many communities reported to the Union of the Jewish Communities in the Regat that party branches were taking steps "to classify Jews into categories."[51]

The Jewish Statute was not confined to the juridical status of the Jews but had far-reaching repercussions on every aspect of their lives. It led to the destruction of village factories owned by Jews, the expulsion of Jews from their villages, and the confiscation of their property. It banned various categories of Jews, especially lawyers, pharmacists, doctors, engineers, architects, and accountants, from exercising their professions. It expelled Jewish pupils from state schools. It set impossible deadlines for handing in documents and certificates, even when their owners preserved some of their rights (specifically, the right to work, to retain a work permit, or to belong to a trade union). Each day the press published a list of Jews who had lost their right to practice their profession.

The heads of the Bucharest Bar Association and many lawyers were delighted when hundreds of Jewish lawyers "who had failed to submit the requisite documents" were expelled from the bar.[52] The bar association spearheaded the struggle to rid the courts of Jewish lawyers. It drew up a list of 289 lawyers who were expelled from the bar, followed by another list of 789.[53] The picture was completed by lists of doctors, civil servants, engineers, and other professionals who were forbidden to exercise their professions. "Despite being censored," protested Filderman to the minister of the interior, "newspapers continue to incite public feeling against the Jews and to criticize the Statute for being 'too mild.'"[54]

For three weeks following the passage of the statute (until new problems intervened), the press celebrated this "victory" over the Jews. It made a point of emphasizing the lengthy battles waged by successive Romanian governments since the 1878 Berlin Congress to deprive Jews of their civil rights and the right to purchase land. The statute emphasized the moral, economic, and spiritual "renewal" that would take place once all Jews had been expelled—a renewal also known as "the New Order."[55] What all these statements shared was the sense that the statute was not a final but rather an initial stage in the solution to the Jewish problem. *Neamul Românesc*, Iorga's paper, which represented the views of the "moderate" right, saw the statute as the beginning of "a new judicial order" based on the Romanian reality and as the start of a struggle that was to be continued by legal means.[56] This contrasted with the torrent of antisemitic ideas that flooded the regular antisemitic press, which had no reservations about demanding the total and violent exclusion of Jews from all spheres of activity. The proposals raised between 11 August and 3 September 1940 formed the backbone of the laws, decrees, decisions, and directives passed by the National-Legionary government and by the Antonescu government. A proposal to nationalize real estate belonging to urban Jews spoke of Jewish ownership of real estate in Iaşi as "Iaşi's tragedy."[57] The same source equated Romanian cities where Jewish landowners preponderated with Tel Aviv. The press and most government ministers concurred that the next stage in the antisemitic campaign was to speed up the process of Romanization. During a public debate on the significance of the statue, the minister of national economy set forth the government's plans for the Romanization of the economy. These plans, according to Minister Gheorghe Leon (1888–1949), an economics professor, included the transfer of entire sections of the economy into Romanian hands, the nationalization of industry, a monopoly over large-scale commerce, the promotion of national elements, and fund-raising activities to finance the operation.[58] These declarations of intent, which were never enacted by the Gigurtu government, became law during the fascist regime. A journalist, speaking for many, described the statute as: "The first stage in the solution of the Jewish problem . . . a new perspective on the Jewish issue. . . . Complementary measures and special directives are necessary, in the spirit of true national government. There is only one solution: recapturing lost ground in all areas. The Statute is just a pointer to future activities."[59]

The law forbidding intermarriage was welcomed, although to a lesser extent than the statute itself. Intermarriage at the time was a marginal phenomenon. Following the Vienna Dictate (30 August 1940) only 4,145 cases of intermarriage were registered in Romania, of which 2,077 were Jewish men married to Aryan women (not all of whom were Romanian). In 1941 there were 2,942 children of mixed marriages.[60] Immediately after passage of the law, a number of Romanian women married to Jewish men submitted a memorandum to the minister of justice requesting that their children be considered Romanian.[61] Iorga's paper used a Nazi racist vocabulary to praise the law as being of "historic importance . . . designed to preserve the pure Romanian race."[62] There is no need to dwell on the reaction of the "pure" antisemitic camp.

The statute delivered a fatal blow to the Jewish intelligentsia, which was, in effect, part of the Romanian intelligentsia. Until the Soviet occupation in August 1944 Jews lost the right to exercise their professions and were excluded from all cultural endeavors within Romanian society. Their existence depended on the wretched jobs offered them by the various communities, which generally involved a painful socioeconomic restratification, or on the generosity of some Romanian intellectuals who continued to employ their Jewish friends in secret.[63]

THE JEWISH LEADERSHIP

The Jewish leadership under Filderman faced an unprecedented challenge in the history of Romanian Jewry: how to respond to the murder of Jews? The monarchy's last months gave the lie to the views of Filderman and other Jewish leaders concerning the gravity of the threat antisemitism posed to Jewish existence and ways of combating it. Filderman failed to understand, until it was almost too late, that antisemitism could not be fought with facts, logic, or reason.

An article Filderman wrote on the Jewish problem, published in the nationalist newspaper *Curentul* on 12 August 1937, illustrates his views. In it he attempted to prove to the Romanian intelligentsia that Romania had no Jewish problem since its population density was much lower than that of other European countries. In a comparative study of the population densities of several European countries, he "proved" that Romania had room for everyone, including Jews. A greatly incensed Nicolae Iorga retorted by publishing *Judaica*, an antisemitic treatise. He interpreted Filderman's argument regarding population density as an attempt by Filderman and others to seize control of Romanian land.

Even discounting the tendency of Diaspora Jews to indulge in hyperbole, the prevailing consensus was that Filderman was the most important and representative personality of Romanian Jewry. The leaders of the Zionist movement, as well as local antisemites and Nazi hardliners, shared this view. They incited the Romanians against Filderman and called for his neutralization.[64] On 27 June the *New York Times* wrote that the campaign against Filderman caused Romanian Jews much apprehension since, for the time being, he was the only person who had the courage and standing to defend Jewish interests and intervene with the authorities.[65]

On 27 June 1940, when the retreat from Bessarabia and Bukovina began, Mihail Ghelmegeanu, the minister of the interior, asked Filderman to ensure that "all leaders of the Union [of the Jewish Communities in the Regat] place themselves at the government's disposal and silently await developments" (i.e., that the Jews of the Regat remain passive).[66] He failed, however, to inform him of the retreat of the Romanian soldiers from Bessarabia and Bukovina. When news of this development trickled through, some of the union's leaders, abandoning the role of passive bystander, called for a strong response. On the other hand, during the initial two days of the army's withdrawal some leaders of the union, including Filderman, were overwhelmed by a sense of impotence, as the situation was out of control. According to Rabbi Safran, immediately after he and Filderman heard of the violence against Jews, "we returned to the Ministry of the Interior in order to ask Ghelmegeanu to order the cessation of the pogroms against the Jews but the ministry was in panic and disorder and it was impossible for us to get another appointment that day."[67]

According to Rabbi Safran, news of attacks on Jews began to reach the union's offices already on the evening of 27 June, after the meeting with the minister of the interior. A heavy atmosphere prevailed at union board meetings, with some members clamoring for action without really knowing what kind of action was feasible. There were proposals for a total restructuring of the union, for "injecting new blood," expanding its welfare institution, and opening up its debates to as many people as possible so as to broaden its consultative base.[68] Some of these proposals were later implemented.

These debates took place at a time when hundreds of Jews were being butchered in northern Romania, although news of these atrocities was sporadic. During the retreat from Bessarabia and Bukovina, ties with the communities in the annexed territories, as with many communities within Romania proper, were severed.[69] Moreover, the authorities intercepted correspondence between the union and the communities, even inside the Regat.[70] As a rule the local authorities did not allow community councils to meet, and a special permit had to be obtained from the military commander of the region for each meeting.[71]

By early July the union's leaders as well as the Jewish leadership began to change their tune, as they realized that they were dealing with a catastrophe—even though they still believed it to be a local catastrophe that was unrelated to the calamity that had beset European Jewry or neighboring Poland. This change was occasioned not only by the news that began filtering through to the union's offices but also, and especially, by the campaign of verbal incitement against Jews in the censored press. Based on past experience, the Jews felt that they were about to be scapegoated for the failure of Romanian politicians, the king, and the army to preserve the homeland's territorial integrity. "An atmosphere of contempt for, and revulsion towards, the Jews prevails throughout the country," wrote *Curentul* on 1 July 1940.[72] The following day the paper's director, Pamfil Şeicaru, published an "appeal to Romanians" in which he accused not only the Jews of Bessarabia and Bukovina but also the Jews of Bucharest of treachery: "In Bessarabia and Bukovina, too, the Jews have removed their mask. Is this surprising? We should have anticipated this manifestation of Jewish degradation. But what concerns me more, and lies behind this appeal, is the deliberately provocative attitude of the Jews . . . in the country's capital. . . . The Jews now have the misfortune of atoning for their sins."[73]

Jewish leaders' concern was rooted in the distant and not so distant past. In the First World War and its aftermath, the Jews of Walachia were accused of collaborating with the German conqueror and of sympathizing with Germany and Austro-Hungary and spying for them. Many paid for this accusation with their lives. In the 4 July board meeting of the Federation of Jewish Communities of Romania, Filderman spoke of potential "disastrous consequences" after the retreat, especially in the wake of "rumors concerning the Jews' behavior during the unfortunate times we are going through."[74] In a meeting with Minister of the Interior Ghelmegeanu two or three days before the collapse of the Tătărescu government (24 November 1939–4 July 1940), Filderman, in an attempt to defend the Jews, said, "We never know how riots based on misinformation will end," intimating that the riots could well have the effect of undermining the regime. Filderman also asked the prefecture of police "to protect the Jewish population and the synagogues."[75]

Under Romania's authoritarian regime, the Jewish leadership did not have many options for responding to the news of Judeocide. They were unable to alert public opinion either at home or abroad. There was no freely elected parliament and no access to the radio, and the censored press was not only antisemitic but spearheaded the antisemitic campaign that supported Judeocide. The pro-democratic opposition was totally paralyzed, and most (although not all) of the political forces the king rallied round him did all they could to curry favor with the Nazis and their lackeys. The Jewish leadership's inability to protect the property and lives of the Jews was immediately apparent to Filderman and his associates and largely shaped their reactions to events during the Antonescu regime. Romanian Jewry was left defenseless—although some degree of goodwill still existed among some members of the old guard that led Romania during the interwar period and did not identify excessively with the antisemitic branch of Romanian politics. Foreign support, never very strong, consistent, or sincere, disappeared altogether, as *Porunca Vremii* testified on 27 July 1940 in an article on the inability of the democratic powers to save Romanian Jewry.

The help the democratic Western powers gave Romanian Jewry existed largely in the minds of the Romanian antisemites, who believed that democracy served Jewish interests, while nationalism served Romanian interests. The governments of France, Great Britain, and the United States did not subject Romania to heavy pressure to force it to preserve Jewish rights, with one exception (during the Goga-Cuza government, when it suited them). Filderman, therefore, was left with only one option: to try and influence the establishment from within.

One issue that preoccupied the Jewish leadership even more than the Jewish Statute itself was the implications of banning the conscription of Jews into the Romanian army. Filderman submitted five memoranda to the minister of national defense, who was, however, too preoccupied with preparations for the withdrawal from Transylvania to relate to them.[76] It was clear to Filderman that the Romanian government's ruling on this matter was based on similar legislation in Hungary.[77] The press began to speak openly of forced labor for Jews. Already before the end of July (and before publication of the statute), the leaders of the Jewish community announced that the police were drawing up lists of Jewish men who were to be assigned to various tasks.[78] Fear that Jews were to become vassals of the military establishment prompted Filderman to ask the prime minister for a written assurance that he would "amend" the statute, reinstate Jews into the army, and assign more rights to Jews who had been conscripted in 1939–40.[79] A copy of the memorandum was also delivered to the king.

Meanwhile, the situation of the Jews took a sudden turn for the worse. Wealthy Jews from the northern or annexed territories became bankrupt, while members of the liberal professions were impoverished. The well-to-do were forced to sleep in synagogues and community buildings. Events followed upon one another so rapidly that community leaders, despite their concern, were unable to keep up with them and take suitable steps to meet the new contingencies. By way of example, on 22 August, after the annexation of Bessarabia and northern Bukovina, the Jewish Federation was still discussing solutions for the 110,000 Jews who were being expelled from their villages, out of a total of 456,000 Jews who were left in Romania according to official data.[80] Filderman described the problem as follows: "The problem of the Jews in the villages is the most difficult yet. If suitable statistics were available, we could, with their aid, prepare restratification options, and help those who are victims of the law [and likewise] submit concrete proposals to the government to at least delay their expulsion from the villages."[81]

After northern Transylvania's annexation to Hungary on 2 September 1940, only 330,000 Jews remained in Romania according to official statistics (in actual fact, there were about 10 percent fewer, as later transpired). The problems, however, got only worse. "A third have lost their livelihood," and even worse, tens of thousands of Jews began drifting from place to place: "We shall be required to help a population that has no means of sustenance—lawyers, civil servants, teachers, and the like. *Although the problem has diminished in scope, it has not diminished in severity*. We must do all we can, while there is yet time, to prevent a situation of total chaos in six months' time."[82]

Above all, as Filderman remarked in one of his petitions to the minister of the interior, "our physical safety [as well as our property] is being jeopardized." Daily life also grew harder as measures were introduced to undermine the Jewish way of life, such as the prohibition on ritual slaughtering and the order to open shops and businesses on the Sabbath. The ban on ritual slaughtering affected communities "whose income derived from the meat tax [*gabela*] and burial tax."[83]

The issue of ritual slaughtering was so important that Rabbi Safran decided to call a meeting of the Council of Rabbis to discuss the issue. The council ruled that "it is permissible to kill animals, even by shooting, immediately after the ritual slaughtering. As to the slaughtering of fowl, [we must request] that it be allowed in private courtyards."[84] The chief rabbi's effort bore fruit, at least in respect to the slaughtering of fowl. In mid-August Petre Nemoianu, the undersecretary of state in the Ministry of Agriculture, sanctioned the slaughtering of fowl in courtyards. "As far as the slaughtering of cattle is concerned, it is a lost case."[85] This ban remained in force until the end of the Antonescu regime, and many Jews in Moldova refrained from eating beef, even when it was available.

One of the Jewish Federation's most difficult tasks was to organize classes for the tens of thousands of children who were expelled from state and private schools. This task became even harder after the German army entered Romania and took control of many schools and Jewish institutions. One of Filderman's close associates in the union, M. Zelțer-Sărățeanu, stated, "No Jewish pupil will be left without a school, and no Jewish teacher will be left without a job."[86] The Bucharest Jewish community alone ran twenty-three Jewish schools, before Jewish pupils were expelled from state and private schools.[87] Many of these expelled pupils now found themselves in Jewish schools, much to their chagrin and that of their assimilated parents.

In this period frustrated Jewish authors and artists also began besieging Filderman with urgent requests for assistance. The requests were contentious and contemptuous of the obtuse and uneducated rich and of Filderman himself for being insufficiently attuned to their special needs. The writer I. Peltz, for example, lambasted the wealthy for their inability "to understand the drama of the most epic author the Jews have bequeathed to Romanian literature" (referring to himself) before professing his admiration for Filderman and asking him for 30,000 lei "to be delivered on the spot."[88] Even the intellectual Henric Sanielevici, an assimilationist literary critic and anthropologist who belonged to a family "that symbolized, perhaps, the cultural progress of Romanian Jewry over the preceding fifty years as well as the terrible decline of Moldovan Judaism," was reduced, in the final analysis, to asking the Jewish community for help.[89] Filderman's memoirs provide us with a true picture of the chaotic atmosphere that prevailed during the last weeks of the dictatorship, before the fascist regime took over:

> I wrote memoranda, I intervened personally, I laid siege to ministers and top functionaries. . . . Occasionally, when a decree went far beyond all sense, I was able to get it changed and in some small way brought a bit of relief to our sad fate. . . .
>
> Of the great number of times I sought to meet with the authorities, they usually agreed to receive me. They listened to me and made promises, some of which they kept. I wrote and dictated hundreds of pages of memoranda, many of which required long and difficult preparation. My collaborators kept me constantly up to date on what was happening.
>
> I intervened when refugees from Bukovina were threatened with deportation at such short notice that they had no time to pack their belongings. I

pleaded for the ritual slaughter of cattle, which had been forbidden on some pretext. When a tax of twenty million lei was imposed on the Jewish communities and all the subsidies to the Mosaic cult were dropped, I intervened to delay payment of the tax. . . .

There were some students about to be deported to Yugoslavia who had to be extricated from their predicament; there were many people incarcerated in prison camps who had to be helped . . . there were masses of refugees that the army was transferring from one place to another for military reasons.

Day after day, at all hours, I tried to move heaven and earth. . . . Where was one to find the money, the food, the medicines, the roofs?[90]

7

The National-Legionary State

The fascist regime in Romania was established suddenly after a short and acute political crisis that led King Carol II to appoint Ion Antonescu president of the council with extensive powers. Antonescu subsequently forced Carol to abdicate in favor of his son Mihai (who was granted limited powers only) and leave the country. The collapse of Romania's political system and of the interwar regime was primarily the outcome of Soviet and German policy. The regional interests of these two allies led to territorial losses for Romania in three regions: Bessarabia (and northern Bukovina) to Soviet Russia (in the Molotov-Ribbentrop Pact), northern Transylvania to Hungary (in the Vienna Award, mediated by Germany and Italy in late August 1940) and southern Dobruja to Bulgaria, on 7 September 1940, at Germany's instigation.

In early September 1940 it might still have been possible to prevent the fascist forces from taking total control of the country but for the hatred that Iuliu Maniu, the most senior of Romanian politicians and head of the National Peasants' Party, felt toward the king. He and other representatives of the veteran Romanian parties refused to go along with the king's request to set up a national unity or provisional government. Maniu and Brătianu rejected any coalition that would keep King Carol II in power. Their refusal paved the way for Antonescu, an ambitious general "whose hands were clean," to set up a government together with the one Romanian movement that was identified with Germany and fascism and that would receive Nazi Germany's blessing and support. At the time this sequence of events was not viewed as a political turning point but rather as a political exercise of the kind that had taken place in 1918, when Alexandru Marghiloman established a pro-German government that was supposed to guarantee the best possible capitulation terms from Germany after the Romanian army's defeat on the front and the disintegration of the Russian army.

Despite the Legionary movement's attempts to portray its inclusion in the government as "a Legionary revolution," it did not seize power by force.[1] The antipathies of the leaders of the two major parties and direct and indirect

German intervention were what brought the Romanian fascists to power. At the time Maniu stressed that, under the circumstances, the democratic forces in Romania were powerless to oppose Germany. A government headed by Antonescu could play an important role "in preventing new concessions . . . and in tempering the conditions the Germans would impose." The leaders of the National Peasants' Party felt obliged to support Antonescu even though his regime was totalitarian and opposed to the principles of parliamentary democracy: "The party does not intend . . . to place obstacles in the way of the new government, but shall allow it to reconstruct the country, reinstate its moral order . . . and reorganize the army."[2]

Antonescu's appointment as president of the council on 4 September 1940 took the leaders of the Iron Guard by surprise. At the time the movement was no longer outlawed, and three of its members had served as cabinet ministers in the king's previous government, under Gigurtu. In late June 1940, after the Soviet ultimatum, in a desperate attempt to curry favor with Nazi Germany, the king offered cabinet positions to Horia Sima, the commander of the Iron Guard, and several Legionary leaders.[3]

The king's volte-face was so sudden that the police force had no time to inform its men to call of the search for the "assassin Horia Sima," whose picture they carried on their persons.[4] The Legionnaires were catapulted into power on 28 June 1940 as cabinet undersecretaries and members of the king's party. They were no longer persecuted: prisoners were released, and fugitives who had sought sanctuary in Germany returned to Romania to resume their activities. Nonetheless, this was no longer the same movement as the one led by Codreanu. Most of its senior leaders had been killed at the king's behest, while the mass support the Legion had enjoyed in the previous elections in late 1937 was greatly diluted. After the execution of Codreanu and other key activists, most of the remaining leaders surrendered without putting up a fight and hastened to assert their allegiance to the king. The observation by Romanian historian Aurică Simion that "the Legionaries were 'fearless fighters' only when supported or tolerated by the authorities" is accurate.[5]

Thus, a combination of international and internal events conspired to bring to power a movement whose slogan was to find a "solution to the Jewish problem," a movement that was dissatisfied with its secondary role in political life, in which it served the interests of the ruling parties. The king's suppression of political life during the dictatorship—the disbanding of parties, the banning of political demonstrations (except those by the king's National Renascence Front), and the introduction of strict censorship—all worked in favor of the Iron Guard. The Iron Guard had only to carry on from where it had left off and place itself at the forefront of the political system. In the vitriolic antisemitic propaganda the Iron Guard disseminated after 1930, the Legionnaires undertook to solve the Jewish problem as part of their plans to do away with democracy and all that it implied. However, apart from the desire to deprive Jews of their property and remove them from any position of power or influence, the Iron Guard lacked any clear political strategy on the Jewish question. Their platform focused on two objectives: getting rid of the Jews and confiscating their property.

Certain strata of Romanian society—peasants, workers, and particularly the petty bourgeoisie—supported the Legion. As a Romanian historian pointed out, "Tens of thousands, and perhaps even hundreds of thousands, of men and women, young and old, dressed in green shirts and national costume, marched in procession in Bucharest and Iaşi under the Legionary flag."[6] In January 1941 Sima claimed that the movement had half a million official members.[7] The Legion's supporters were not only simple folk but also members of the intelligentsia, the clergy, and the affluent middle classes—artists, writers, journalists, and senior civil servants, who had their own special frameworks, such as the Răsleţi Corps (Corpul Răsleţi), which, according to Sima, had over four thousand members.[8]

It is worth noting that party affiliations in Romania were a matter of expediency—the expectation of perks and exploitation of a general climate of corruption—rather than ideology. The Iron Guard's new followers were mostly former members of the king's party, Cuza's antisemitic movement, and even Maniu's party.

According to Antonescu's supporters, the Legionary leadership had three goals: vengeance, terror, and confiscation of Jewish property (becoming rich).[9] The attainment of these goals depended on control of the state's apparatus of oppression. Of the ministers and junior ministers who were members of the National-Legionary government that was set up on 14 September, fifteen were member of the Iron Guard and only five (in addition to several members of the military who served as undersecretaries in the Ministry for National Defense) were nonaffiliated. The nonaffiliated ministers, who owed their appointment to Antonescu, were: the minister of justice (Mihai A. Antonescu), the minister of the national economy (Gheorghe N. Leon), the minister of finance (George Cretzianu), and the minister of agriculture (Nicolae Mareş), as well as the undersecretary of the Ministry of Fuel and Mines (Victor Dimitriuc). Sima served as vice president of the council without portfolio, while Gen. Constantin Petrovicescu, a fanatical Legionnaire (and a relative newcomer to the Legion) served as minister of the interior (14 September 1940–21 January 1941).

Sima blamed the Jews in general and Romanian Jewry in particular for the calamities that had befallen the Romanian people and for the royal dictatorship's excesses. His main grievance, however, was the part they had played in Codreanu's assassination and in the executions of 21 September 1939: "Although the Jews did not participate directly in these executions, but simply acted behind the scenes . . . the entire country knew who was behind [these acts], who advocated the murder of the Legionary commander: The secret government of Jews in Romania, obeying orders from the Bolshevik Jewish Command in Moscow. . . . Unable to deny their involvement, they [the Jews] began to fear the consequences [of their actions], and dread the terrifying (as they saw it) vengeance of the Legionnaires."[10]

The Legionnaires did not lay the entire blame for the persecution of their movement on the Jews but also accused the entire establishment of suppressing it. This establishment had to pay the price. The Legionary press ran daily articles and features calling for revenge against the leaders of the previous regime, who had unleashed the campaign of suppression against the Iron Guard and ordered the executions of its leaders in 1938–39. Nicolae Iorga, who was blamed for Codreanu's arrest and the trial that led to his execution, was the press's prime target. The movement's mouthpiece, *Buna Vestire*, published a list of offenders that included presidents of the council, ministers, police commissioners, and heads of the security service, many of whom were subsequently targeted by the Iron Guard during its revenge campaign.[11]

Antonescu acceded to the Legionnaires' demands, and on 23 September 1940 he ordered "the establishment of commissions of inquiry and the trial of the perpetrators of crimes who had a share in suppressing political activity."[12] It soon transpired, however, that Antonescu and the leaders of the Iron Guard did not see eye to eye concerning the punishment to be meted out to members of the former establishment. While Antonescu favored due process (investigations and trial), the Legionnaires were thirsty for revenge. In late September and early October 1940 a number of personalities on the list of wanted people were placed under house arrest, in a clear attempt to protect them. It became increasingly difficult to uphold law and order as the various branches of government — particularly the Ministry of the Interior — became swamped with Legionnaires and as the Legionnaires set up their own alternative institutions, such as the Legionary Police. The tension between Antonescu and Sima soon came to a head. On 21 September 1940 Antonescu asked members of the Legionary movement to refrain from interfering in the government's activities and from barging into government offices: "The Legionnaires may no longer enter [the prime minister's] Office at will, as they did to start off with. That was a romantic period, and [their behavior] was understandable. Now, however, law and order must be restored."[13]

The schism was deeper than it appeared in September. For Sima, the establishment of the National-Legionary regime did not mark the end of the struggle for power. In his opinion, the movement's true victory was contingent on "the entire nation becoming Legionary."[14] For Antonescu, on the other hand, the army was the nation's main bastion.[15] When the head of the Legionary movement, "exploiting the purity of national ideas," attempted to win over officers, "in particular, young officers and cadets," by any means (such as exerting pressure on relatives), the conflict escalated from one of misunderstanding and differences of approach to a direct confrontation between Antonescu, the army, and members of the former establishment on the one hand and the Legionary movement on the other.[16] Antonescu used his full authority to protect the army—on which his rule depended—from the influence of Legionary ideology. As Sima himself put it, "He passionately protected his officers from adopting the Legionary spirit."[17]

It did not take long for the Iron Guard to restructure as a ruling party, but this process highlighted the internal problems from which the movement had suffered since Codreanu's assassination and the liquidation of an entire core of activists in 1938–39. Sima wanted his supremacy recognized by movement leaders who had remained in Romania or fled to Germany. Among the latter were two whom Codreanu had named as his heirs and who, but for their arrest and flight to Germany, would have assumed leadership of the movement (before his death Codreanu drew up a list of successors, on which Sima was placed fourth). Sima also had to contend with the hatred of Ion Zelea Codreanu, Corneliu Codreanu's father, who considered himself his son's "heir" and "replacement on earth."[18] It was also necessary to reinstate the movement's organizational frameworks "post haste" and establish and arm the paramilitary organizations that terrorized Jews and Romanians alike until the end of Legionary rule.[19]

THE JEWISH STATUTE: THE
PREVIOUS GOVERNMENT'S LEGACY

Any discussion of antisemitic legislation during the Legionary period cannot fail to take into account prior trends toward the restriction of civil rights for Jews and limitations on their economic activity, particularly under the Goga-Cuza government. Such a discussion must also consider the extent to which the new regime was influenced by Nazi racist legislation.

First, it is worth noting that the Ministry of Justice, which launched most of the antisemitic laws, was run not by a member of the Iron Guard but by one of Antonescu's men, a professor of international law at Bucharest University by the name of Mihai Antonescu (the two were not related). Second, the National-Legionary government inherited a body of laws—mainly dating back to the

Goga-Cuza government but also to King Carol II's dictatorship—greatly restricting the activity of Jews in various economic spheres.[20] Col. Traian Borcescu, author of *A Study on the Jewish Problem in Romania* and a member of the General Staff of the Romanian army, who studied the problem of antisemitic legislation in 1943, was right in saying, "The Jewish problem was a constant [factor] in Romania and antisemitism [in Romania] long preceded the current racist principles of the National-Socialist ideology [and was organized] into political frameworks long before it."[21]

The main problem that members of the Romanian fascist movements encountered in the interwar period was their inability to come to terms with the emancipation of Romanian Jews and the civil rights awarded them under the peace treaties and Minorities Treaty, which, they claimed, had "paved the way for extensive Jewish penetration in all fields in the Romanian State." The authors of the study claimed that the antisemitic organizations were hampered by "the country's legislative situation, the democratic spirit in Europe, and a certain apathy among the parties." Change and temerity, stressed the study, came about with the establishment of the Nazi regime in Germany, whose "pure antisemitic [principles] and the creation of a new spirit, and a new European dogma based on the principle of race and nations, have exerted a decisive influence in Romania, too."[22]

The Goga-Cuza government was the first to introduce overtly antisemitic legislation through the Law for the Revision of Citizenship of 22 January 1938, which restricted the number and rights of Jews who were eligible for emancipation.[23] This law, which was received in the "new spirit" Nazism had fostered in Europe, was the culmination of a protracted struggle on the part of Romanian antisemitic movements, particularly the League of National Christian Defense and its successor, Goga and Cuza's National Christian Party, as well as the Iron Guard (even before Germany's influence became a major factor in Romanian life). All these organizations, which were based, inter alia, on the antisemitic ideas of the fathers of modern Romanian culture in the second half of the nineteenth and the early twentieth centuries, vehemently opposed citizenship for Jews. Although the law abolished the citizenship of over 360,000 Jews, it did not fulfill the expectations of the Romanian government until the establishment of the Legionary government, which "excluded [Jews] from economic life" by classifying them as foreigners and passed "new laws in order to protect and foster the Romanian element."[24]

The second stage of the antisemitic movements' attempt to deprive Jews of civil rights was the promulgation of the Jewish Statute on 9 August 1940, toward the end of King Carol II's reign.[25] The statute, which divided the Jews into three categories, effectively abolished the civil rights of most Jews. Category B (the preferred category) applied to Jews of the Regat who had been Romanian citizens before the First World War or who had been granted citizenship for their participation in the war.

The Jewish Statute introduced an innovation into Romanian legislation by defining Jews on the basis of race and also by drawing a legal distinction between "blood Romanians" and ordinary Romanians—without, however, defining what constituted a "blood Romanian." The Romanian legislature's definition of a Jew was based on two interwoven principles—religion and blood—so as to "avoid the difficulties attendant upon the application of similar legislation in other European countries."[26] Thus, the legislature defined Jews as:

1. Those believing in the Jewish faith (religion).
2. Those born of parents of the Jewish faith.
3. Christians whose parents were of the Jewish faith.
4. Christians whose mothers were Christian and fathers were members of the Jewish faith who had not converted to Christianity.
5. An illegitimate child whose mother was of the Jewish faith.
6. Women who met any of the above criteria and were married to Christians or had converted to Christianity after June 1939 (a year before the establishment of the Party of the Nation).

Finally, the law defined "atheists of Jewish blood" as Jews, too. It stipulated that a Jew who converted to Christianity after the passage of the law would still be considered a Jew for all intents and purposes. Thus, although the definition of a Jew "by blood" was an innovation, the attempt to confine full civil rights to "ethnic" Romanians dates back to the early thirties, when the government tabled parliamentary bills granting priority to Romanians in the merchant fleet (March 1934) and enhancing the proportion of Romanians in factories and industry to 80 percent (July 1934). Filderman unsuccessfully attempted to prove that there was no serious unemployment problem in Romania and that "the preference of the Romanian element" and the protection of the Romanian workforce were modeled on "Hitler's methods." He tried in vain to influence Romanian public opinion by invoking statistics, tables, studies, and various publications indicating that "the country was already in Romanian hands."[27] The legal definition of *Romanian ethnic origin* was the standard definition before the new term *Romanian blood* was introduced.

The Jewish Statute, the "natural" continuation of Goga's 1938 legislation, was considered insufficiently "revolutionary" because (a) it relied on the Constitution of February 1938, (b) it did not totally abolish Jewish entitlement to Romanian citizenship (it retained some rights for Category B Jews), and (c) in particular, because the definition of a Jew "was confused, and still required . . . clarification and reformulation."[28]

During Antonescu's reign the Jewish Statute was considered "the starting point for a solution to the Jewish problem."[29] The statute was inspired by the Nuremberg Laws, as Minister of Justice Ion V. Gruia (4 July–4 September 1940) took care to explain. He also pointed out that he had based the law not only on the concepts of "a common soul" (a term taken from the Iron Guard's antisemitic lexicon) and a common "race, language, land, royal dynasty, and past and shared ideals" but first and foremost on blood and on the Christian faith—the two forces that together defined the nation: "I have arrived at an original Romanian formula that considers Romanian blood an ethnic and moral element, the definition of which relies on legal distinctions of religion and extraction. The definition of the Jew [on this basis] receives, in addition to its hitherto legal structure, a political connotation."[30] Gruia coined the slogan adopted by all the Romanian antisemitic movements and by Nicolae Iorga himself: "Romania is the land of the Romanians only."[31]

When the National-Legionary government and its successor, Antonescu's fascist regime, came to power, they found a ready-made legal framework for depriving Romanian Jews of their rights and banishing them from Romanian society. These two governments merely continued and extended an already existing trend.[32]

ANTISEMITIC LEGISLATION PASSED BY THE NATIONAL-LEGIONARY GOVERNMENT

Antisemitic legislation passed by the National-Legionary government was primarily triggered by the wish to realize the Romanian antisemitic dream, as interpreted by both Antonescu and the Legionnaires. As far as we know, the regime was not pressured directly by Berlin or by the German legation in Bucharest to introduce antisemitic legislation, and the antisemitic laws that were adopted were not based on a Nazi initiative. Rather, the anti-Jewish laws were a reflection of Antonescu's basic outlook: "The Jews are to a large extent responsible for the calamities that have befallen this country."[33]

The Legionnaires, for their part, did not enjoy the same freedom of action or inaction as Antonescu. They were bound by "undertakings" they had given the Romanian public. It was up to them to prove that the degradation of the Jews, the confiscation or theft of their property, and their dismissal from their jobs and sources of livelihood would solve Romania's socioeconomic problems, as they had claimed for almost a decade and a half.

The laws and the administrative orders that were issued by the various government ministries had several objectives: (1) the Romanization of Jewish property; namely, the expropriation of Jewish-owned property on behalf of the state or citizens "of Romanian blood"; (2) the dismissal of Jews from their jobs and their replacement by Romanians, particularly the three hundred thousand or so refugees who had fled from the territories ceded to the Soviet Union, Hungary, and Bulgaria; and (3) the creation of a Jewish "artistic ghetto," as secretary of the Jewish Federation and historian Matatias Carp defined it, namely, the exclusion of Jews from Romanian intellectual and cultural life.[34] The gaps left by this legislation were filled in by administrative measures adopted by government ministries, local government institutions, and even voluntary associations.

The Legionary movement viewed the expropriation of land as a question of principle. The land, as the commander of the Iron Guard stated in 1982, "had become a social problem that threatened the peasants' physical health and moral integrity. The law was designed to protect the peasant class."[35] The laws expropriating land owned by Jews were important from the Legionnaires' perspective but failed to bring them any personal advantage. The main beneficiary of the land expropriations was the state. Despite Sima's call "to live in poverty," most members of the movement were keen to get rich fast. While the Romanization laws enabled them to become rich legally, terror enabled them to become rich "illegally." The Romanization of the economy led to a further decline in the country's already depleted economy following shipments of food and raw material to Germany, as promised by Antonescu at his first meeting with Hitler in September 1940, and the loss of about a third of Romania's territory.

Three laws for the expropriation of Jewish property were passed:

1. The Law for the Expropriation of Assets in Rural Districts was enacted on 5 October 1940.[36] Agricultural land, fodder, pasture, ponds, manor houses, vineyards, nurseries, dairy barns, sheepfolds, chicken coops, beehives, and flower gardens were expropriated from Jews of all categories, as well as land that was not suitable for agriculture or other uses. This land was transferred to the state along with all the animals, machinery, and stores of grain and fodder.
2. On 12 November 1940, forest land, including all structures and facilities built on them, as well as wood-processing plants, with all their structures, land, and equipment, were expropriated from Jews and corporations with Jewish majority stockholders.[37]
3. On 4 December 1940 ocean liners and riverboats were expropriated from Jews. A total of 152 vessels, including 80 tugboats, were affected.[38]

Note that these three laws expanded the definition of who was a Jew. The first of them defined a Jew as anyone with at least one Jewish parent, whatever his or her religious faith or citizenship. Jews owned about forty-five thousand hectares of land. After expropriation, the land was leased by public tender to "ethnic Romanians who could demonstrate that they had the financial and technical ability to make the best use of the leased property." Many refugees received clerical positions in the flour mills and wood-processing factories confiscated from Jews.[39] The chief beneficiary of the expropriations was the state, along with individual Legionnaires who seized land and other property that had been owned by Jews.

The main Romanization laws relating to employment were as follows:

1. The Decree-Law of 5 October 1940 authorizing the Ministry of the National Economy to appoint a commissioner for each factory "at its sole discretion . . . to ensure that the factory's activities conform with overall State policy."[40] The commissioner's powers and functions were not anchored in law but determined by directives issued by the relevant government ministry. The Legionnaires, unhappy with this law, demanded a law that would enhance the commissioner's powers. This resulted in:

2. The new Decree-Law of 5 October 1940, awarding the commissioners of Romanization unlimited powers and supervision of transactions, accounts, and other business activities of the factories to which they were appointed.[41]

3. The law of 17 October 1940, limiting the jurisdiction of Jewish lawyers who still belonged to the bar (Category B Jews) to matters concerning "their coreligionists" only.[42] The law and, particularly, the reasons that prompted it were based on racist principles.

4. On 9 November 1940, the permits allowing Category B Jews to sell commodities that were a government monopoly were revoked under the Jewish Statute. Those affected were mainly widows, the handicapped, and war orphans.[43]

5. On 15 November 1940 Jewish doctors were forbidden to treat Romanians. Jewish doctors, even converts who had married Romanians, were dismissed from the Doctors' Union.[44] They were allowed to form "their own organization," headed by a Jewish physician appointed by the president of the Doctors' Union. The law emphasized that this situation would continue "until a radical solution were found to the Jewish problem." Jewish doctors were required to wear a distinguishing mark as determined by the union and to specify "Jewish doctor" on their signs

and prescriptions. They were forbidden to publish articles in scientific or scholarly journals or magazines and to belong to scientific or scholarly associations or participate in their conventions.

6. On 16 November 1940 a law "for the Romanization of factory employees" effectively dismissed Jewish employees from factories and businesses.[45] Only Jewish employees in institutions of a religious or cultural nature were allowed to remain. Jewish businessmen were allowed to carry on their businesses (for the time being only) but were required to dismiss all Jewish workers and employees (including nonsalaried workers and the business owners' wives and children). The law broadened the definition of Jew to include anyone who had a Jewish father, even if he had converted to Christianity. The only exception was the offspring of Jews who had fallen in the 1877 Independence War "if they are currently Christians." Most of those dismissed received only nominal severance pay, if anything.

7. On 19 November 1940 the permits of Jewish cinema managers and directors of travel and tourist agencies were revoked. Commissioners were appointed to supervise these establishments pending their transfer to Romanian ownership.[46]

On 24 December 1940 the Ministry of Labor refused to grant or renew permits attesting to the professional skills of Jewish craftsmen and workers (they had to be renewed annually).[47] This meant that Jewish craftsmen were unable to find work in their field of expertise and would be considered unskilled workers.

In this period laws were also passed dismissing Jews from the Romanian army. Initiated by Antonescu in his capacity as minister of national defense, these laws provided the legal basis for the establishment of labor units. Under the Jewish Statute, Jews in Category B (basically Jews from the Regat) were allowed to do army service but not to serve in the regular army. Jews in categories A and C were banned from the army altogether. In practice almost all Jews were expelled from the army, except for servicemen in the regular army whose professional contribution was considered vital.

The last such law to be promulgated by the National-Legionary regime abolished the position of commissioner of Romanization.[48] This law, which amounted in fact to a public admission of the Legionnaires' inability to run the country and its economic affairs, was designed to put an end to abuse on the part of the commissioners of Romanization, who confiscated Jewish property for their own ends rather than for the state. Initiated by Antonescu, the law was also signed by two non-Legionary ministers, Mircea Cancicov, minister of the national economy

(10 November 1940–27 January 1941) and Mihai Antonescu, minister of justice. The law, which was passed on 19 January 1941, two days before the outbreak of the Legionnaires' rebellion, was one of the direct causes of the military coup.

Another kind of antisemitic legislation focused on the Romanization of intellectual, cultural, and artistic life. Traian Brăileanu, the Legionary minister of national education and culture (14 September 1940–21 January 1941), was the main architect of this kind of legislation. The Jewish author Felix Aderca described Brăileanu as "a hooligan-philosopher," a "total Romanian . . . of Armenian extraction" whose intellectual ability was questionable.[49] The Legionnaires, however, respected him as a thinker. Like other antisemitic intellectuals and supporters of the movement, he found a receptive audience among the students of Bucharest University. Brăileanu published a collection of the translated works of German thinkers, juxtaposing the works of Immanuel Kant with excerpts from Alfred Rosenberg's "ideology." This minister single-mindedly adopted every means at his disposal to oust Jews from all spheres of intellectual life.

On 22 September 1940 he forbade Jewish actors to perform in Romanian theaters and ordered all Jewish theaters to append the term *Jewish Theater* to their name. Jewish theaters were not allowed to put on original plays and could perform only Romanian plays that were not "anti-national or anti-Romanian in character."[50]

On 14 October 1940 Brăileanu ordered the expulsion of Jewish pupils from Romanian state schools, while authorizing the establishment of private Jewish schools.[51] Before passing this law Brăileanu summonsed Chief Rabbi Alexandru Safran and informed him personally of his decision. When Rabbi Safran protested, "Sir, what are we to do with these children? They too have to be educated," Brăileanu replied with unconcealed hatred, "It's not our business what you do with them. Do as you please."[52]

The law stipulated that the new schools were meant exclusively for Jewish pupils and were to be staffed by Jews. Romanian teachers were forbidden to teach in Jewish schools, and vice versa. Jews who held any teaching or managerial post within the Romanian education system were dismissed, and Jewish pupils and students were expelled from all state, private, and church schools. The Ministry of Education was authorized "exceptionally" to permit the enrolment of children "who had been baptized before the age of two" in private or church schools, provided the mother was Christian (even if not of Romanian extraction) and the father a convert to Christianity. There was one exception to this law: the children of decorated Jewish servicemen or of Jewish servicemen who had fallen in Romania's Independence War or in the First World War, provided "they had been Christians on 9 August 1940," were allowed to continue their education in state schools.[53] Jewish schools lost the right to award accredited certificates.

On 16 October 1940 an order was passed forbidding Romanians to submit their research or essays on educational or scientific topics to publishing houses owned by Jews.[54] Another order, of 18 November 1940, forbade Jewish artistes to join unions or artists' syndicates but made receipt of a work permit contingent on "payment of taxes and membership dues."[55] Romanian actors and musicians (even amateurs) were forbidden to perform in Jewish companies or orchestras or in halls owned by Jews. Romanian impresarios were forbidden to have dealings with Jews.

On 24 October 1940 the deputy minister of the press placed the finishing touches on the "Jewish cultural ghetto" by sending a special circular to public libraries stating that, pending the law on "the nationalization of the 'Romanian printed word,'" the "use or study" of Jewish works was banned.[56] The circular stated that every public library would soon be sent a list of Jewish authors. This list was subsequently sent not only to public libraries but also to any important library in Romania.[57]

The last law the Legionary movement managed to squeeze through before it disappeared from the political scene, passed on 15 January 1941, ordered a special census of the Jews under Legionary supervision, as part of the general population census that was scheduled for 1941. This was in response to the deep-rooted Romanian antisemitic myth that Romania was overrun by Jews (the "Jewish invasion"). Both the Legionnaires and Antonescu were convinced that the number of Jews living in Romania far exceeded the official figures and that Jews had paid bribes to officials to distort the figures. Even after Romania had lost over 450,000 Jews (those living in the territory it had ceded), they still believed that there were well over 339,000 Jews (the official figure, which in itself was about 40,000 more than the actual figure) in the country.

In view of the above, it is safe to conclude that antisemitic legislation in Romania during the period under discussion was not the result of Nazi pressure or recommendations but was purely of a home-grown variety, the purpose of which was to realize the Romanian antisemitic dream as reflected in the antisemitic literature of the late nineteenth century, especially after the emancipation of Romanian Jewry. The laws were proposed, drawn up, and implemented by the Romanian right together with the fascist movement and were firmly anchored in local antisemitic ideology. Even the Jewish Statute, which was modeled on the Nuremberg Laws and was passed before the Legionnaires' rise to power, attempted to provide a local definition of a Jew that would tie in with the Christian antisemitic tradition. Nevertheless, some allowances must be made for the general antisemitic climate fostered by Nazi anti-Jewish legislation and its indirect role in dispelling doubts and anxieties.

The inconsistency of the racist definition of the Jew in Romanian legislation bred confusion, a confusion that not only intensified as time went by but that was compounded by the laws Antonescu's government continued to pass after the ouster of the Legionnaires. Adding to the confusion was the distinction some of the laws drew between "Romanian citizens" and "Romanians by blood" without specifying the difference between the two.[58] The concessions granted various kinds of Jews, all of whom belonged to Category B (war veterans, war widows and war orphans, decorated servicemen, and converts), varied from law to law and generated even more chaos. As a general rule, in referring to their duties, the definition of Jew was expanded to include as many Jews as possible, while in speaking of their rights, the definition of Jew was narrowed so as to exclude as many Jews as possible.

It is also worthy of note that the laws passed by the National-Legionary government were not the consequence of parliamentary debates or professional deliberations. The National-Legionary regime operated basically as an extra-parliamentary institution. Its laws were generally decree-laws (*decret-lege*) that had the force of law. The initiators of these laws were usually the ministers of the relevant ministries. The orders were signed by Antonescu, the respective ministers, and occasionally King Mihai before being ratified and published in *Monitorul Oficial* (Official gazette).

SOCIAL SEGREGATION AND CONTINUED RHINOCERIZATION

The exclusion of Jews from society, a process that had begun in the early thirties, continued with a vengeance during this period. The National-Legionary regime succeeded in undermining the legitimacy of Jewish existence in Romania. Thus far Legionary propaganda had failed to penetrate all strata of Romanian society, and a significant section of the Romanian intelligentsia considered the Iron Guard brand of antisemitism to be uncivilized and opposed to Western values, on which Romanian culture was based. While in power, however, the movement succeeded in breaking down the barriers that had formerly prevented many from accepting the Iron Guard's antisemitic ideology. The moral restraint and sense of shame that had formerly characterized many of the undecided evaporated, while the climate of virulent antisemitism and fear of Legionary revenge silenced the rest.

The expulsion of Jews from professional associations and unions, particularly from voluntary ones, was accompanied by many incidents of collective antisemitic behavior. In July 1940 the Jewish author Alexandru Dominic noted with some satisfaction that the Association of Romanian Authors' attitude toward its Jewish members was "irreproachable": "Only a short while ago, the current president [of the association], the renowned Professor Herescu, informed several young members who raised the issue of the presence [of Jewish authors] in the Association, that all politics ceased at the gates of the Association, and rejected antisemitic proposals. The Association has also behaved exceptionally well toward Jewish authors who are not affiliated with it."[59]

During the first two months of Legionary rule a spate of antisemitic activity was unleashed by the bar association, the most antisemitic of all professional associations, which, during the thirties, had surpassed itself in its activities against Jewish lawyers and its demands for the Numerus Clausus to be introduced into the law profession and the universities. The Bucharest district branch of the association hastened to expel Jewish lawyers who were unable to present documents attesting to their Category B status and published in the press the names of 289 Jewish lawyers who had been expelled from the bar.[60] The bar association decided to celebrate the establishment of the new regime by expelling 55 more lawyers on the pretext that they, too, had failed to submit documents attesting to their right to work under the Jewish Statute.[61] In the six successive sessions that were held daily from 6 September to 13 September, almost all Jewish lawyers were expelled from the bar association, until only 177 of 1,479 former Jewish lawyers, including Filderman, remained.[62] The "vetting process" was performed superficially, the declared intention being to prevent Jews from practicing the law and to eliminate Jewish competition.

On 13 September, a day before the establishment of the Legionary government, the General Union of Romanian Engineers expelled some of its Jewish members and announced that it would not take into account any law that allowed Jews to preserve their rights. The union promised to continue its effort to "get rid" of Jews, and in a meeting held on 10 October it carried out its promise.[63]

Subsequently, all restraint was abandoned, as other professional associations and unions followed suit. The Federation of Sports Unions revoked all permits granting Jewish journalists access to sports stadiums and halls. The Romanian Opera dismissed all Jews on its staff (21 September 1940). The Syndicate of Journalists expelled all Jews (25 September 1940) and the Association of Professional Journalists followed suit (27 September 1940).[64] On 29 September the Association of Merchants announced its decision to "homogenize" its leadership and reinforce it with "Romanian elements [to facilitate] it integration in the Legionary State."[65]

The Institute of Chartered Accountants asked its Jewish members to prove their Category B status, although the law did not require such proof.[66] Even the Association of Romanian Authors was affected. On 4 October the executive of the association convened and decided to expel all Jewish authors from the association. The Union of Journalists in Bukovina and the Association of Electricians in Bucharest followed suit (6 October and 7 October 1940, respectively). The Faculty of Medicine in Bucharest barred Jewish students "of all categories" from enrolling (21 September 1940).[67]

The College of Physicians asked the government to forbid Jewish doctors to treat Christians and to force Jews to fill prescriptions at Jewish pharmacies only. The college reserved the right to treat Jewish patients, however, probably for reasons of personal gain.[68] The College of Pharmacists likewise requested that the government draw up a law forbidding Romanians to rent out pharmacies to Jews.[69] Both requests were granted. Many Romanian physicians accused board members of the College of Physicians of dragging their feet in implementing the law.[70]

After the collapse of the Antonescu regime, when the College of Physicians hastened to reopen its doors to Jewish doctors in the spirit of the new times, Dr. Max Poper, the president of the Jewish Doctors' Union, took the opportunity to remind members of the college of their shameful past. What had upset Jewish doctors most, he stressed, was the medical community's almost total indifference to the humiliation of the Jewish doctors and the savagery with which both civilian and military doctors' committees behaved toward the Jews who were at their mercy.[71]

The trend toward the exclusion of Jews from trade unions and professional organizations knew no bounds. The Tuberculosis Hospital in Bucharest discharged its last nine Jewish patients in late November 1940.[72] As a crowning insult, the Bucharest municipality informed the Jewish community of its intention to disinter the bodies of converted Jews from Christian cemeteries and reinter them in Jewish cemeteries.[73]

These measures caused the Jews not only tremendous material hardship but also untold psychological harm. Generations of Romanian Jews who had advocated assimilation felt cheated. Even before the establishment of the National-Legionary regime (after the promulgation of the Jewish Statute) Arthur Zelţer Sărăţeanu, a secretary of the Union of Romanian Jews, stated that the Jews objected to "the humiliation and degradation" of a population that "had always been loyal and devoted to Crown and State."[74] The humiliation and degradation were daily occurrences in the Legionary state, while the exclusion of Jews from Romanian society continued unabated. For example, the Law Governing the

Organization and Management of the College of Physicians, published in *Monitorul Oficial* on 15 November 1940, stated, "The right to exercise the profession [medicine] is granted to physicians of Romanian, Aryan, Hungarian or Turkish ethnic extraction. Physicians of Jewish ethnic [extraction] may not be admitted to the College, even if they have converted."[75]

The use of Christian symbols and slogans to justify its racist policy was a sign of the hypocrisy of the Legionary movement and of its total abandonment of Western democratic values. In light of the above, the antisemitic legislation of the National-Legionary government, far from having a revolutionary component, merely reflected a tendency and mood that had already existed in the thirties. It was not the result of direct German influence or pressure. The Christian and national principles that constituted an integral part of Legionary ideology applied to gentiles only. The humanitarian concepts espoused by the Legionnaires did not extend to Jews, and Jews were excluded from the population the Legionnaires were meant to lead and whose interests they wished to promote. Legionary personalities and newspapers reflected this attitude clearly, especially when debating the concept of justice. "A state without justice cannot be victorious. . . . Do as you would be dealt with," declared Alexandrina Cantacuzino, president of the National (Christian) Orthodox Society of Romanian Women.[76] On the very day these words were printed (10 December 1940), a Legionary journalist described the reality he envisaged after the collapse of "the democratic world": "The 'better' that will ensue after the collapse of the democratic world will bear no resemblance to the 'good' that existed before 1938. This 'better' will be the 'best' for the Christians of Europe only, not for the Jews and their associates. In the Europe of tomorrow, they will feel the 'better' as the 'worse.'"[77] Legionary racist legislation cannot be separated from this mood, which bore no relationship whatsoever to Nazism or its ideological base.

8

Romanization

Romanization as a national objective was not born with the Legionary movement nor did it die with it. The motif of Romanization appeared on the national agenda already in the late nineteenth century. The National Legionary regime, however, in its single-minded use of terror and victimization of Jews, gave new meaning to the term. The terror tactics adopted by the Legionary movement had no parallel in Romanian history.

After the Legionnaires were ousted from the government, it transpired that the appropriation of Jewish factories and property, supposedly on behalf of the state, had served as a front for a massive looting and robbery operation perpetrated by Legionary members and sympathizers and even by ordinary citizens who seized the opportunity to get rich at the Jews' expense. The state was none the stronger for the Legionary attempt to put the Romanization dream into practice. On the contrary, the movement, in the course of its experiment, clashed with traditional Romanian forces that vehemently opposed the Legionnaires' principles and modus operandi. These forces were at least as strong, if not stronger, than the Legionary movement. General Antonescu's open support for his Legionary partners soon turned to cautious compromise and finally extreme opposition to their economic principles and their modus operandi.

Antonescu's attitude toward the Legionnaires changed after their terror tactics led to the paralysis of the Romanian economy. The Jews, for their part, were pawns in the hands of the two camps, neither of which cared for their fate, let alone their property. This situation left them little room for maneuver, especially since any attempt to influence the Legionnaires was doomed to failure at the outset. If some Jews still had a livelihood, this was due more to bureaucratic errors and time constraints on the part of the Legionary leaders than to any premeditated plan.

Overestimating their own strength, the Legionnaires attempted to wrest both political and economic power from the old establishment and impose their principles by force. As Sima notified Antonescu in late October 1940, "A Legionary

State signifies monopoly of politics and the press by the movement, . . . and a [government-]controlled economy that is totally opposed to the former liberal economy." The members of the old establishment, who controlled most economic positions, naturally resented the Legionnaires' attempts to divest them of their power. "The old world is putting up a tremendous opposition. The new world wishes to establish a new order, but [the old world] prevents it from so doing," grumbled Sima to Antonescu.[1]

The Legionary heads' second mistake was to denounce all opponents of their political and economic creed as members of "the plutocracy, the Jews, and the Free Masons."[2] At that time, the establishment was still strong enough to thwart the Legionnaires' plans to turn Romania into a totalitarian state like Germany. The Jews and their property constituted the weak link in the liberal economy, while the Legionary terrorist regime rendered them powerless to oppose the Legionary spirit.

One might have expected values such as humanity and justice to stand in the way of the Legionnaires. These values, however, which had never been very strong in Romania in the first place, crumbled during the five months of National-Legionary rule. Antisemitic and racist legislation distorted the country's judicial system. Moreover, the Legionnaires' impatience with the slow pace of Romanization and fear that the Jews might exploit the old establishment's opposition for their own purposes pushed them to adopt terror tactics against Jewish individuals and groups and the Jewish community as a whole.

The implementation of Romanization began in Walachia and Oltenia, two regions in southern Romania with a small Jewish population. The first towns to be targeted were Găiești, Turnu-Măgurele, Târgoviște, Caracal, and Corabia. The campaign moved on to southern Transylvania, where all important localities, excluding Timișoara, were affected and then to Bucharest, from where it spread to all the large Jewish communities of Moldova. By the time of the rebellion of 21 January 1941, "most Jewish businesses and real estate had been looted . . . through criminal means."[3]

Although many strata of Romanians took part in the Romanization campaign, it was the Legionnaires who instigated and directed it. It is their name, too, that is associated with the intimidation and corruption that accompanied the operation that was supposed to usher in a golden era in Romanian history. Antonescu himself attributed the Legionnaires' criminal activities to their "greed."[4]

Once in power, the Legionnaires' methods for funding the Romanization operation became synonymous with corruption and greed. They spared no locality and no Jew, however poor. Many Legionnaires and ordinary citizens exploited the situation to confiscate Jewish property in the movement's name, without authorization. In most cases, however, the movement was careful to register confiscated property in its name. At least some of the looted cash was handed over to the movement, which used it for its own purposes.

Against Romania's difficulties and the Legionnaires' ineptitude, the confiscation of Jewish property represented a concrete act with immediate and visible results. When Constantin Muşat, a Romanian lawyer whom the Jewish Federation hired to report on what was happening in the various Jewish communities, visited Braşov, he made a copy of a standard "sales deed" drawn up between a Jew and the Legionary movement. The deed stipulated that the "purchaser" (a Legionary loyalist) would hand over 40 percent of his profits for the "purchase" and give the remaining 60 percent "to the Legionary movement." The purchaser would run the business "under Legionary supervision [and employ] Legionary officials and salesmen."[5]

In remote localities such as Făgăraş the movement did not even bother to draw up such deeds but forced "all Jewish merchants to . . . sign blank sales deeds . . . handing over their property to the Legionary movement."[6] These blank deeds contained only the heading "Sales Deed," the name of the Jewish owner, the name of his business, and his signature. Later on the Legionary movement filled in the remaining details, such as the amount paid and the name of the purchaser who had been rewarded by the movement for his loyalty. Sometimes the movement retained the property itself, in which case it was careful to register it with the Land Registry and receive legal endorsement by the courts or a public notary, as was the custom.

The chaos caused by the swift transfers of ownership raised concern among the old establishment. In order to placate Antonescu, Sima issued a special circular on 16 November 1940 forbidding anyone to use the movement's name without his authorization: "The name of the Legionary movement may not be used . . . without prior permission. No-one may attach the name of the Legionary movement to a factory or industry without my express permission. Membership in the movement does not confer the right to call a factory belonging to an individual a Legionary [factory]. . . . Organizations that have already begun [to purchase] such factories must report the exact circumstances [of the purchase] and request permission."[7]

In its efforts to mobilize funds, the Legionary movement did not differentiate between rich and poor Jews. All Jews were required to give generously to the cause. In a book published in the autumn of 1941, after the suppression of the Legionnaires' rebellion, the Antonescu regime stated, "There was no accountability. Receipts did not specify the name of the recipients. The movement's leaders appropriated hundreds of thousands [of lei] without issuing receipts."[8]

During this period Legionary institutions, many of which paralleled national institutions, expanded. The largest of these was Legionary Aid (Ajutorul Legionar), a charity organization that granted generous humanitarian aid to other Legionnaires and ordinary Romanian citizens. Legionary Aid helped poor families during the winter and at festival times and supported the families of Legionnaires who had been executed or killed in clashes with the police or who were in jail. It opened canteens and soup kitchens in neighborhoods and towns. Such activities, together with the Legionary movement's attempts to improve worker's living standards (e.g., by ceding to their demands for higher wages), endeared the movement to the masses. Sima, convinced that his movement would win in an election, tried to persuade Antonescu to call new elections: "We are tremendously popular and must exploit this historic moment to the full."[9]

The Jews "contributed" to the movement's success by providing most of the funds, buildings, and equipment necessary to set up the canteens and other welfare projects. They provided the raw materials and buildings for the movement's cooperatives, as well as telephones and cars. They even provided new and used clothing for Legionary orphans and poor children. The printing presses that the Legionnaires used for their publications were confiscated from Jews. Finally, Jewish factory owners (tolerated by the Legionnaires, who lacked the know-how to run the factories) and other businessmen were required to raise workers' salaries and Romanize their factories (dismiss Jews and hire Romanians in their place). These factory owners funded the most coveted position the movement could award its rank-and-file members—that of commissioner of Romanization. As Sima explained, "The Commissioners of Romanization earned . . . 50,000 lei per month from the factories. This sum was large even in comparison with the salaries of top government officials. A minister's salary at the time was 35,000 lei at the most. . . . In order to prevent preferential treatment within the movement, I issued a circular stating that the salary of all government officials [and officials] in the private [sector] who have been appointed by the new regime shall not exceed 20,000 lei. Any surplus must be handed over to the movement's treasury."[10]

As a measure of how bad things were, "in Piatra Neamț Jews were not allowed to bury their dead unless they contributed to the local [chapter of the] Legion."[11] In Brașov cars owned by Jews were impounded "without authorization or payment." Also in Brașov, a Legionary commander, after placing his watch on the table, gave a Jew two minutes in which to sign over his business to the Legionary movement.[12]

Toward the end of the National-Legionary regime the Legionnaires began using coercion and torture, even in Bucharest, in order to raise funds for Legionary Aid. A Jew in Bucharest was tortured into handing over 10,000 lei to

Legionary Aid.[13] Jews were forced to hand over cash as well as their businesses in order to fund the organization. Those who refused were tortured.[14]

Legionary Aid served as a legal front for extortion. In Hârlău, in northern Moldova, for example, a shop owner whose stolen wares returned after he enlisted the help of the local authorities was forced to sign a written declaration to the effect that he had handed over his goods to Legionary Aid. The Legionnaires thus gave the impression of abiding by the law, while Jews lost out on all fronts.[15]

Other Legionary institutions and organizations, in particular chambers of commerce, workers' organizations, and various paranational institutions (those set up as an alternative to state institutions over which the Legionnaires had no control), participated in the looting of Jewish property. One of these institutions was the infamous Motorized Legionary Guards (Gărzile Legionare Motorizate), a police squad set up by Radu Mironovici, commander of the Bucharest police force.

The Legionary motorcycle squad, set up to escort Legionary vehicles, was modeled on its German equivalent. Unlike Antonescu, who as chief of state had control of the army and its fleet of vehicles, the Legionnaires had to build up their own fleet of vehicles, especially as the showdown with Antonescu approached. The movement gave its members driving lessons and spared no effort to obtain vehicles of all sorts.[16]

As part of this effort the Legionnaires began confiscating vehicles owned by Jews or their political rivals, in complete defiance of legal niceties. After the suppression of the Legionary rebellion the authorities were required to return all confiscated cars to their lawful owners. The new prefect of the Făgăraş district asked Antonescu for instructions regarding the "special case of a truck owned by a Jew that had been handed over to the Legionary movement." To the prefect's query as to whether "the confiscation and transfer of Jewish property to members of the Legionary movement" was anchored in law, Antonescu replied with an unequivocal "no!"[17]

In January 1941 the Legionary Economic Council, an umbrella organization coordinating the movement's various economic units under the direction of Ilie Gârneaţă, set up a new unit, the Legionary Workers' Corps (Corpul Muncitoresc Legionar), which later distinguished itself in the riots in Bucharest. This unit, which was headed by Dumitru Grozea, was responsible for the appropriation of Jewish property in Bucharest. Grozea had distinguished himself by supervising the assassination of high-ranking officials (ministers, police commanders) of the former regime who were being held in Jilava jail, near Bucharest. The corps' headquarters in Bucharest served as a torture chamber for Jews during the January 1941 rebellion (see chap. 11). Hundreds of Jews were summoned to the center or taken there by force and tortured into signing over their businesses to the Legion.[18]

A popular activity among the Legionnaires was the theft of radios, because it yielded immediate results with minimal effort. At the time radios were very expensive, and not many Romanians could afford them. The radios were an easy target for the Legionnaires, who sold them off immediately for cash at a cut-rate price. Once the police joined in this operation, it became semiofficial.[19] The confiscation of radios began even before the establishment of the National-Legionary state in mid-September 1940. In August 1940 the police had begun registering and in some cases (usually in remote localities) confiscating radios owned by Jews. On 30 October 1940 the Jewish Federation demanded that the radios be returned to their owners.[20] A day after the request was submitted, radios were still being confiscated in Vaslui.[21]

When the radios were confiscated by regular policemen, their owners were generally issued a certificate of expropriation. Once the distinction between Legionary and regular police was blurred, however, the Legionnaires impounded not only the radios but also the certificates of expropriation, so that the Jews had no way of retrieving their radios.[22] It was not uncommon for Legionnaires — at the movement's behest or on their own initiative — to break into Jewish homes and seize radios.[23]

In November the operation became so widespread that it became difficult to keep track of it, especially since not all radios that were confiscated reached the Legionary or police inspectorates.[24] The operation was extremely profitable. In Vaslui alone the value of the confiscated sets was estimated at 2 million lei.[25] The looting of radios continued until the collapse of the Legionary state. On 11 January 1941 radios were still being confiscated from the Jews of Craiova.[26] In Petroșani the Legionnaires forced the owners of confiscated radios to "donate" them to the Iron Guard.[27] By April 1941 Filderman estimated the value of confiscated radios at around 100 million lei.[28]

The Legionary Ministry of the Interior gave retroactive cover to this operation by issuing a directive for the confiscation of radios owned by Jewish "suspects." The exact contents of the directive are unknown, but in Piatra Neamț, for example, the head of the security police was at a loss as to how to implement the directive because the list of suspects did not specify who owned radios. But he soon found a solution. Enlisting the help of the local postmaster, he obtained a list of Romanian Broadcasting Corporation subscribers, all of whom were Jewish, and simply marked off all odd numbers on the list as "suspicious."[29]

The Antonescu regime completed what the Legionnaires had begun. In late June 1941 Antonescu ordered the confiscation of all radios still owned by Jews, "without exception," and the prosecution of all Jews who owned radios.[30] The confiscated radios were distributed to various government ministries, public institutions, and the army. Gen. Grigore Georgescu, the minister of public works and communications (27 January–10 July 1941), had no scruples about asking the minister of the interior for three confiscated radio sets, while the minister of the interior had no scruples about granting the request.[31]

STATE–ORDAINED ROBBERY

The looting of other Jewish property was also instigated by the authorities, who did not even bother to try and find a legal pretext, even in the antisemitic legislation of the new regime. The historian Matatias Carp, for example, describes Jewish factories and goods being stolen from the Jews of Craiova and the vicinity in the presence of the prefect of the Dolj district, the local police commander, and the deputy president of the chamber of commerce. On this occasion, a commissioner of the State Police advised the Jews not to protest if they wished to be spared "terrible torture." Carp dubbed the incident "impotence in the face of authorities turned thugs."[32]

Similar gangs operated throughout Romania, as three long memoranda written by the Jewish Federation and hundreds of petitions sent to government ministries testify. These gangs usually comprised police commanders (from the State Police), public notaries, representatives of the Ministry of the Interior, and sometimes even the minister of the interior himself, mayors, commissioners of Romanization, and the heads of various other public institutions. The chambers of commerce also played an active role in the confiscation of Jewish businesses. They served as a front both for the Legionnaires and for other antisemitic groups who had dreamt of purging Romania of the "taint" of Jewish commerce. The Bucharest Chamber of Commerce, for example, banished Jewish peddlers and suppliers from the textile industry.[33] Three non-Legionary heads of the same institution summoned Jewish merchants and factory owners and informed them that "the Legion had decided to transfer their factories to Legionnaires whose names would later be disclosed."[34] In the days preceding the rebellion, the Chamber of Commerce no longer summoned Jews but had the Legionnaires bring them in by force.

The police commander in Turnu Severin, a member of a local gang of notables, ordered the chamber of commerce to inform the city's forty Jewish merchants that their businesses had been seized by Legionnaires. "Upon returning home, you will each be required to sign over your commercial assets to people chosen by the Legion." The merchants were also forced to sign pledges "to stay on as long as necessary in order to teach the new owners the tools of your trade."[35]

When the Jewish merchants of Slatina were summoned to the local chamber of commerce they found armed Legionnaires waiting for them, who forced them, at gunpoint, to hand over their business permits and sign over their property for a token payment. In Ploieşti gangs organized by Marin Stănescu, prefect of the Prahova district, and the police commander attacked and destroyed the community's religious and cultural institutions.[36]

In Râmnicu Vâlcea the local gang of notables produced a scenario of several acts. On 23–25 November six Jewish merchants were taken to Legion headquarters, where they were severely beaten (one had all his teeth pulled out). They were released only after agreeing "to leave the city quietly, without breathing a word of what had happened." On 29 November the city's physician-general declared all Jewish businesses "contaminated" but conveniently forgot to submit an official report to that effect, in order to prevent appeals against his decision. The local commander of the Legionary Police ordered Jewish storekeepers to close their shops and gave them three days in which to draw up an inventory of their stock, sign over their shop to the Legionnaires, and leave the city. Following this, Victor Bărbulescu, the prefect of the Vâlcea district (formerly a public prosecutor), summoned the Jewish merchants and reprimanded them for closing their stores and thereby causing hardship to the local citizens. When the merchants protested that they had closed their stores on the physician-general's order, "Bărbulescu ordered them to evacuate their stores by the evening." While Bărbulescu was speaking to them, Legionnaires broke into the stores and took their stock, paying them in return a mere 10–14 percent of its true value.[37]

Gangs of regular and Legionary police operated in Bucharest even after Antonescu disbanded the Legionary police. These gangs searched the apartments of wealthy Jews for weapons and documents, on the pretext that they were suspected to be members of the Freemasons or B'nai B'rith. The gang would usher all tenants into one corner of the room, assign one member to keep watch over them at gunpoint, and then set about ransacking the apartment for cash, foreign currency, jewelry, and any other valuables they could lay their hands on.[38] Policemen who searched the home of Ilie Stângă, a commander of the Legionary Police in Bucharest, after the suppression of the Legionary rebellion found the following items in his possession: 901,064 lei, FF 92,300, FF 6,000 in gold coins, 340 Turkish lira, $1,415, £1,515, 500 Bulgarian leva, 3,400 Yugoslav dinars, and other notes of foreign denomination.[39]

The theft of cash and jewelry did not require much ingenuity. The mere sight of armed, uniformed policemen and green-shirted (in winter, leather-coated)

Legionnaires was sufficient to strike fear into Jews' hearts. The theft of shares was a more complex matter that required legal counsel and recourse to public notaries and the courts. A law of 5 October 1940 ordering all shares to be registered in their owners' names within a period of thirty days, subject to the commissioner of Romanization's approval, paved the way for this kind of institutionalized theft.[40]

The fact that the gangs operated illegally and left no official traces of their activities makes it almost impossible to reconstruct their modus operandi. The only information we have comes from isolated incidents that reached the courts after the dissolution of the Legionary movement.

In sum, the Romanization campaign was carried out by the Iron Guard in accordance with the program devised by its Economic Council under Gârneață, with Sima's support and the help of the Legion's administrative and police systems. The seizure of Jewish assets, which was prompted by political and ideological considerations, turned the Iron Guard, within a few months, into Romania's richest institution. In April 1941 the President's Office published data on Jewish property that had been seized by the Legionnaires during their term in office. In that period there were 1,162 compulsory sales transactions ratified by the courts, at least 1,081 property confiscations, and 260 appropriations of buildings and apartments. In Romania as a whole (excluding Bucharest) the Legionnaires seized Jewish assets worth 1,018,624,911 lei, for which they paid a mere 52,176,783 lei, or 5.12 percent of the true value.[41] These official statistics relate only to cases that reached the courts. It "goes without saying that the list falls far short of the tragic reality," since "victims lodged complaints in only a few instances and [even] then, were reluctant to do so in writing."[42]

In some cases the Legionnaires forcibly confiscated and looted the property of their political rivals or members of the old guard. Even so, Jewish property was the movement's main and acknowledged target. The despoliation of the Jewish community was governed by ideological considerations. The assertion by some Romanian historians, therefore, that the Legionnaires "used the same methods indiscriminately against Romanian, Jewish and Hungarian citizens" is untenable. Theft of Romanian property was insignificant in both relative and absolute terms, as the figures published by the Antonescu regime after the Legion's ouster from power show. "Legionary headquarters and many apartments belonging to members of the Iron Guard became caches for stolen property looted in the tradition of classical crime."[43]

Later attempts to gloss over the Legionnaires' almost total and obsessive preoccupation with the Jewish problem for the four and a half months it was in power cannot conceal that the appropriation of Jewish property was virtually the only means whereby the movement attempted to keep some of its promises to those

Romanians who believed in its ideology. These were basically the peasants, who were promised a plot of land each, and the workers, who were promised an end to their exploitation. The theft of Jewish property served as camouflage for the social demagoguery the Iron Guard propagated for over a decade. The Jewish question played a leading role in its election propaganda during the 1937 election campaign.

After assuming power the movement's leaders soon realized that they could not fulfill all their promises. For a start, the amount of land owned by Jews was insignificant, while the nationalization of food-processing industries enriched only a small stratum of capitalists and high-ranking Legionnaires. The most the movement could do for the peasants, according to Sima, was "to prevent them being intimidated and abused by the gendarmes." In the long term the movement's leaders hoped "to make cheap credit available to the peasants . . . to save them from Jewish usury." By late 1940, however, Romanian banks and financial institutions were no longer owned by Jews.[44]

Once the National-Legionary state was established, the movement focused on improving the workers' lot. "The workers' problem [their economic situation and exploitation] was easier to solve, since all we had to do was to force the factory [owners] to treat them more humanely and revise salary scales."[45] The Jews could not significantly "contribute" to the fulfillment of these promises, however, since most of the large mines and industrial plants that employed hundreds of thousands of Romanian workers were owned by the state or by foreign concerns. Legionary ministers tried, via the commissioners of Romanization, to introduce higher salaries for workers and a minimum wage, in accordance with National-Legionary principles. The movement attempted to persuade workers that it faithfully represented their interests: "You are now the masters of the country . . . exploitation has ceased. There is no longer any need for strikes."[46] It soon transpired, however, that the movement's social principles were not consistent with the actions of most of its leaders and activists, many of whom had grown rich on the proceeds of factories, shares, businesses, restaurants, stores, or workshops looted from Jews, and some of whom even sat on the boards of firms or banks.[47]

The movement and its spokesmen were constantly contradicting themselves. On the one hand, Sima urged movement members and activists "to live modestly and to conquer the desire to get rich easily."[48] On the other hand, the movement's leaders attempted to incite the workers against "their exploiters," to destroy the existing social order, and to build a Legionary society and Legionary centralist economy on its ruins. In publications and official speeches and at the frequent reinterment ceremonies of the movement's slain, the Legionary leaders promised workers that the "Legionary revolution" was the way to overthrow their exploiters.[49]

During the short period of the National-Legionary state's existence, the Romanian economy suffered many setbacks. Some of them had external causes, such as the presence of German troops in Romania; economic pacts with Germany that were detrimental to Romania; the rise of the Deutschmark vis-à-vis the lei; exports of food, clothes, oil, and meat to Germany in exchange for weapons, machinery, and training; the collapse of Western markets, which struck a serious blow to foreign currency reserves; and the funneling of almost all natural resources and oil to Germany and its allies. On the domestic front, the Legionnaires also contributed to the collapse of the economy. Delays in production and the serious blow to commerce induced by the confiscations of Jewish properties paralyzed industry, while the atmosphere of instability led to a general decline in the value of property and a lull in investment. Soon inflation set in, causing the cost of staples to jump and leading to a shortage of basic commodities and to economic, political, and even physical insecurity. The situation was one of total chaos. Speeches on the movement's plans "to get rid of the bourgeoisie" were imprudent, not to say politically unwise, since many Legionnaires themselves had joined the ranks of the "bourgeoisie" on the backs of the Jews.[50]

"The Legion cannot tolerate the bourgeoisie . . . a Legion made up of the bourgeois is inconceivable."[51] Such declarations, at a time when Legionnaires throughout the country were confiscating property, factories, and houses, antagonized the Romanian old guard as well as Antonescu, before he became Hitler's ally. "I cannot sponsor such actions," declared Antonescu to Minister of the Interior Petrovicescu after a cabinet session in which the latter described acts of pillage and looting. "I cannot take property belonging to others, even if they are Jews."[52]

While in power, the movement had to choose between accepting the bourgeois ethic and enjoying the fruits of power, as other parties had done before them, or adopting a revolutionary strategy that involved confiscation of property and resources in order to fulfill their promises and win over as many Romanians as possible to its cause. Its heterogeneous composition and lack of competent leadership and the circumstances that catapulted it to power caused the Legion to behave with a lack of restraint toward the old guard that antagonized broad sectors of the Romanian establishment.

The Legionary movement's heterogeneous composition developed before the Iron Guard came to power, when it was a popular movement that recruited its members from all strata of society. According to one of its staunch opponents, the democratic journalist Tudor Teodorescu-Braniște, the Legion attracted "all the malcontents who undermined the order of the country: Unemployed or underpaid teachers, out-of-work graduates, doctors without a practice, lawyers without a clientele, and the like. In the villages, the movement attracted the scum of the earth."[53]

Toward the end of King Carol II's reign the movement began homing in on more specific populations in an attempt expand its base. All these populations had something in common: disillusionment with the political situation and dissatisfaction with their own lives. They were poor peasants, youth, the lumpenproletariat, and members of the urban petty bourgeoisie, as well as rural workers who had recently migrated to towns.[54] Finally, when it seemed as if democracy in Romania was dead and as if Romania was searching for its roots in a blend of extremist nationalism and mysticism, "new converts" began joining the ranks of the movement en masse. The new converts comprised "titled women, influential industrialists seeking their own advantage, privileged youngsters, young women seeking thrills, failed politicians who were excluded from all parties, . . . a substantial proportion of our intellectuals, gnawed by ambition and animated by flattery."[55]

Upon assuming power the Iron Guard had many bills to foot. It began by liberally dispensing ministerial positions to its members in Bucharest and in the provincial towns and awarding its members senior positions in the country's major industrial concerns. It sent its frustrated intellectuals to university. It took over Romanian radio and tried, albeit unsuccessfully, to take complete control of the country's intellectual life. A commission "for the revision of the university professors" was established in November 1940 with an aim "to adapt higher education to the structure of the National-Legionary State." Three hundred forty professors, doctors, senior lecturers, assistants, and others were interrogated, and dozens were dismissed from their positions. Among other things, the commission asked the intellectuals invited to appear before it to prove that they were not Freemasons, philo-Semites, communists, and so on. The commission warned many professors that if they would not adapt themselves "to the Legionary conduct," the "current regime," or the "legionary labor" they would be fired.[56] Despite the generous rewards it bestowed on its members, the movement itself lacked talented and skilled statesmen to run the country.

The Legion had almost nothing to offer its rank-and-file supporters, who came from a variety of social strata and were united in their sense of frustration and hatred of Jews. Thus the attacks on Jews, their property, their livelihood, and their occupations was not merely the result of ideology or a desire to emulate the Nazis. They were governed by pragmatic considerations, too. The exclusion of Jewish lawyers from the bar and the restriction of their jurisdiction to "matters affecting their coreligionists only" was simply a means of rewarding members of the Romanian bar who were loyal to the movement. Similarly, ethnic Romanian physicians were rewarded for their loyalty by the dismissal of thousands of Jewish doctors from public institutions, government ministries, government health funds, and hospitals and by prohibiting them from having Romanian patients. University graduates were inundated with jobs that became available after the dismissal of "the lackeys of the kings' dictatorship," as the Legionary press dubbed them. Other members of the movement were granted Jewish stores, businesses, apartments, houses, household utensils, and cash as a reward for their support.

At the bottom of the ladder were the poor and destitute. Although in the nature of things they had no share in the above pie, the Legionary welfare organizations catered to their needs, again at the Jews' expense. In this way the movement was able to look after its own interests while upholding the Christian ethics by which it supposedly operated.

9

Legionary Terror

The Iron Guard was set up by Codreanu in part because he was dissatisfied with the modus operandi of Cuza's League of National Christian Defense. For, while the League never questioned the parliamentary system, Codreanu sanctioned the use of terror in his attempts to "purify" the Romanian nation and "defend" the Christian Orthodox faith. The Iron Guard invoked Christian dogma to rationalize its use of terror and demanded blind obedience to its leader. The youth who broke away from the League to set up the Iron Guard gradually shed Cuza's ideological influence as they geared up for "antiparliamentarian and revolutionary" activity.[1] According to Codreanu, to realize their objectives the Romanian nationalists had to resort to "violence, if necessary, and sacrifice human life, if the circumstances so demanded."[2] The inauguration of the National-Legionary government removed any residual restraints that still curbed the hard-core Legionnaires and gave them license to vent "their predatory instincts" on the Jews.[3]

The Legionary regime was set up in early September 1940, shortly before the start of the academic year. Students, "encouraged by their Legionary teachers, abandoned their studies and devoted themselves instead to singing Legionary songs, marching in Legionary parades, and [seeking ways of obtaining] weapons."[4] Statistics published by the Antonescu regime after the suppression of the Legionary rebellion stated that 1,109 teachers neglected their responsibilities and over 18,500 students abandoned their studies in order to participate in meetings of the movement: "Most of these students carried weapons in their schoolbags which they placed on benches during classes. . . . Many schools served as arms and munitions caches, with the help of teachers and students."[5]

The movement heads were convinced that they represented the pure national sentiments of Romanian youth. No wonder, therefore, that Hora Sima entertained such rage, contempt, and antagonism toward the Guardian of the Country (Straja

Țării), the rival youth movement set up by King Carol II during his dictatorship, which "while claiming [it was set up] under the influence of Italian fascism, really aimed at usurping the place of the Legionary youth in the new Europe."[6]

According to Sima, the Legionary youth represented the new Romania, "kindling the entire nation with its enthusiasm," both literally and metaphorically. The movement's leaders ordered these youth to perpetrate crimes while absolving them of all material and moral responsibility and arguing that the day of reckoning had arrived and that it was time to take revenge against all former opponents of the Iron Guard. At the same time, the Legionary clergy promised them absolution "in the world to come." The leaders of the National-Legionary regime accused members of the old guard of being in thrall to Jews, belonging to the Freemasons, and "lacking ideals and . . . bringing about the collapse of the country's borders." In a speech delivered on 10 December 1940, three days after the assassination of the movement's opponents in Jilava jail, Sima deliberately invoked Christian themes (absolution, crucifixion) in order to justify the assassinations: "Those [who themselves are guilty of] thousands of transgressions and crimes are now demanding pure and saintly behavior of the Legionnaires after having assassinated our leader who alone could have forgiven them, and after having humiliated and crucified our youth for twenty years."[7]

From the above we see that Legionary terror was not inspired by Italian or even German fascism but had its roots in Romanian antisemitism.

THE LEGIONARY POLICE

The Legionary police, the most dangerous of all terrorist institutions, was set up, organized, designed by, and modeled on Nazi units. It was set up on 6 September 1940, the day after the king's abdication, in order to protect the new regime and suppress opposition to the Legionary movement. As such, it was initially welcomed by Antonescu. The movement's leaders saw the establishment of an alternative police force as "natural, akin to a fascist militia or the German SA." At the same time, the proportion of Legionnaires in the state police grew apace, largely due to the party's hold on the ministry of the interior and key positions in the national police. The movement also embarked on an intensive campaign to recruit members of the state police. "In Bucharest, the State police has effectively become a tool in the Legionnaires' hands."[8]

The Legionary police, which were based in Bucharest, ran an independent network of operatives who were directly subordinate to Sima. Its internal organization and activities were a closely guarded secret, kept even from Legionary members of the state police. In late October 1940 Reinhard Heydrich, head of the German Security Police, sent one of his subordinates to Romania on Himmler's instruction, ostensibly to organize a "Legionary liaison unit" but actually to remodel the Iron Guard along German lines. According to a German intelligence chief, the Legion, although initially none too pleased at this intervention, nevertheless welcomed the delegation, which achieved its objective of setting up a Legionary militia largely modeled on the SS.[9]

In a matter of weeks the Legionary police became so powerful that its creators were no longer able to control it. It also encouraged other terrorist organizations inside and outside the movement to undertake anti-Jewish activities. The Legionary police were motivated by violence for its own sake and by the desire to make a quick buck. In September 1941, after the movement's ouster from power, an official publication of the Antonescu regime described the Legionary police as comprising: "totally unqualified people, people *sans* culture or morals, the dispossessed, the scum of the earth."[10]

The Legionary police's main raison d'être was to defend the government and arrest those who had actively opposed the movement during King Carol II's reign—an operation that, according to the Legionary heads, "could not be handled by traditional police cadres."[11] In other words, the Legionary police was set up to avenge the persecution of members of the Iron Guard in the thirties by members of the old regime.

Upon the establishment of the Legionary government, the Jewish problem did not figure high on the Legionary agenda. The existence, however, of an extraparliamentary (and therefore illegal) police force encouraged the formation of other illegal militias, whose main aim was to terrorize Jews into handing over their money and property. These "policemen," operating in gangs or on their own, often kept all or part of the loot for themselves instead of transferring it to Legionary institutions.

This situation of economic and general anarchy exacerbated the tension between Sima and Antonescu. In early November Sima appointed Ion Boian as the new commander of the Legionary police in Bucharest, since the previous commander "had shown himself to be . . . incapable of locating [people and groups] that were violating the law in the capital in the name of the Legionary police, as their victims testified."[12]

On 27 November 1940 several of the movement's terrorist organizations—especially the Union of Legionary Workers, some heads of the Legionary police, and Legionnaires who had infiltrated the state police—"avenged" Codreanu's assassination by murdering sixty-five leaders of the old establishment who had been arrested at the start of the National-Legionary government and held in prison in the village of Jilava. This massacre and the assassination of

Nicolae Iorga two days later were the straws that broke the camel's back, incensing Antonescu against the Iron Guard in general and against Sima in particular. On 30 November Antonescu ordered the dissolution of the Legionary police.

Members of the Legionary police who were not assigned to the regular police were detailed to the Order Service (Serviciul de Ordine), an internal organization Sima set up "in order to ensure order within the movement."[13] Boian, the commander of the Legionary police, was also appointed head of the Order Service. The incorporation of fanatical students into this service resulted in the establishment of a new terrorist organization that usurped the Legionary police, whose members were subsumed into the regular police. Moreover, the Union of Legionary Workers, notorious for its cruelty toward Jews, set up its own militia with the sole aim, as the commander of the Iron Guard himself put it, "of breaking into Jewish homes and stealing their valuables."[14] All these terrorist groups operated alongside, and sometimes instead of, state police institutions (the regular police, the security police, and the gendarmerie).

TORTURE CENTERS

The Iron Guard's terror institutions and affiliated state institutions set up torture centers in which Jews were incarcerated and tortured in order to coerce them into handing over their money and property. These centers were set up in police inspectorates and stations, municipalities and municipal institutions, schools, movement "nests" and "green houses," Legionary institutions, income tax offices, and during the rebellion, even synagogues and Jewish community institutions (which were subsequently burnt down and destroyed). As the Legionnaires' hold on the government grew, the division between movement and state became increasingly blurred. Apart from the Romanian army (with a few exceptions), all other institutions cooperated willingly or unwillingly in applying the Iron Guard's policy of terror. The police and security police were inundated by Legionnaires, "who tried, often successfully, to take them over."[15] District prefects, who were responsible for the police in provincial towns, were also affiliated with the movement. The Ministry of the Interior and all its branches (apart from one) were overrun by Legionnaires or Legionary sympathizers. The movement had virtually free access to the police inspectorate in Bucharest.

The terror tactics applied in the various Romanian towns and localities differed only in their intensity and cruelty. As the confrontation with Antonescu approached, riots and violence against individual Jews and entire communities escalated. The army was not always a neutral bystander—in some remote localities, it actively participated in the rioting.

THE EXPULSION OF JEWS FROM
THEIR HOMES AND LOCALITIES

In many regions the Legionnaires began realizing an ancient antisemitic dream—to purge the villages of Jews. The purge had two objectives: (1) to loot Jewish property, and (2) "to protect the peasants from the harmful effects of Judaism" and fulfill "an ancient aspiration of our nation's greatest ideologues."[16] The operation, which was premeditated, was carried out in a totally random manner and did not even pretend to conform to the antisemitic legislation introduced by the National-Legionary regime. The order to expel Jews from the villages (sate) and other small localities (comune) was given verbally by the minister of the interior. The Union of the Jewish Communities tried unsuccessfully to find out if there was a written order to expel Jews from villages so that it could bring the issue to the courts. The existence of a "verbal order" to expel the Jews from the villages of Suceava district was mentioned by the mayor of Iţcani-Gara, Strobl, to the president of the community, Dr. Hellman.[17]

Although the call to purge the villages, and indeed the entire country, of Jews was a leitmotif of the times, in the summer of 1940 such incitement constituted an immediate threat to the very existence of Romanian Jewry, as the following passage from the antisemitic organ *Porunca Vremii* indicates: "The preferred solution—albeit audacious and frequently entailing cruel acts of reprisal—is expulsion. The Jews must be expelled, in order to expunge all memory of them. True, this solution has all the ingredients of a surgical operation, but what's wrong with that?"[18]

Meanwhile, the antisemitic press in Romania was closely following the persecution of Jews in Nazi Germany and advocated adopting similar methods. There were also some purely Romanian proposals to limit the number of Jews in Romania, such as "a 2000-lei tax for each Jewish child born," as a petition by the Jewish Federation to the minister of the interior testifies.[19]

In the course of October 1940 Jews were expelled from dozens of villages that had been inhabited by Jews for over a century. The federation was unable to keep abreast of developments due to restrictions on freedom of movement and on telephone and postal services and the danger of railroad travel (Jews were thrown out of moving trains). Most of the expulsion orders never even reached the courts. An exception was the case of a ritual slaughterer from the village of Murgeni who moved to Bârlad because "there were no more Jews left in Murgeni. The municipal authorities [of Bârlad], however, refused to let him stay, but ordered him to return to Murgeni, even though all its Jewish families had been evicted."[20]

The expulsions were not always collective but were sometimes selective, targeting specific Jews whose property the Legionnaires had set their eyes on. Expulsion as a way of getting rich quickly without legal complications was a popular expedient among the Legionnaires, especially during the initial stages of National-Legionary rule. Thus, for example, in Vaslui three wealthy Jews were given eight to ten hours to leave their homes, and on 29 September sixty-four Jewish families were ordered to evacuate their homes in the city center.[21]

In the villages the local authorities and Legionnaires issued expulsion orders at will, without feeling any need to justify their actions. In the cities, however, they could not get away with this so easily but had to account for their deeds, even if only verbally. The expulsion from Sibiu, for example, was justified on the grounds that buildings were needed to house Cluj University and the Cluj Court of Appeals, which had been partially transferred to Sibiu after Cluj was ceded to Hungary.[22] In Bucharest an attempt to evacuate tens of thousands of Jews from their apartments by declaring the area in which they lived a military zone was vetoed by Antonescu after the Jewish Federation intervened.[23] On 21 October 1940 the minister of the interior was forced to issue a written declaration categorically stating that "there was no order to revoke residence permits in the military zone [of Bucharest]."[24]

In many localities that were "cleansed" of Jews, committees "to administer Jewish property" were set up to make provisions for the distribution of immovable property (usually real estate) through the magistrate's court. Such a committee was set up in the village of Comănești in the Suceava district, from which Jews had been expelled during the cession of northern Bukovina to the Soviet Union.[25] The committee, which comprised an official from the Ministry of the National Economy, the local mayor, a representative of the Iron Guard, and the commander of the local Legionary unit, drew up a report on 10 December stating that Jews had "fled" and even "left the country. . . . Some have died, while there is no information on others . . . their abandoned and unattended homes have been looted and destroyed. . . . Nearly all their houses are open to the elements." In order to stop this vandalism the committee proposed "that all Jewish homes be handed over to the custody of local residents," who would be entitled to live in them "and cultivate the surrounding land as a reward for looking after them, and to cover the costs of any repairs."[26]

By mid-December the Legionnaires were using similar methods in Bucharest, too. They seized apartments and buildings and evicted their Jewish occupants, after "beating them cruelly and forcing them to sign declarations that they were renouncing their rental contracts of their own free will."[27] In Bucharest the

Legionnaires were careful to give their terror campaign a "legal" guise and to evict Jews only from their homes, not from the city.

A special evacuation project initiated by the Legionnaires with Antonescu's blessing was the evacuation of the Jews of Panciu, a town north of Bucharest. On the night of 9–10 November 1940 a large earthquake destroyed almost the entire town, leaving its inhabitants homeless. The residents, including some six hundred Jews, were evacuated to the nearby town of Focşani, a hotbed of Legionary activity. The Focşani authorities restricted residency to "natives of the district," while Panciu was declared "a Legionary city" and out of bounds to Jews.[28] The refugees were not even allowed to collect their personal belonging that were scattered among the ruins. All their property was looted. On 21 March 1941, two months after the suppression of the Legionary uprising, the Jewish Federation was still petitioning the minister of the interior to allow the Jews to return to Panciu: "Of the 48 heroes of Panciu who fell in the War of Unity [the First World War] 22 were Jewish, and their names are inscribed on the communal grave in honor of our fallen heroes."[29] This appeal, however, fell on deaf ears. Antonescu himself, influenced by the Legionary idea, subsequently issued a special order declaring Panciu a "Christian town." The Jews of Panciu was not allowed to return to the town until the collapse of the Antonescu regime.

Legionary pressure on small Jewish communities and sometimes on isolated Jews scattered among hundreds of villages throughout Romania soon left its mark. By early December the Jewish Federation was able to present Antonescu with accurate data on thirty-nine localities from which "the entire Jewish population had been expelled after their property had been confiscated."[30]

In Moldova the use of terror escalated toward the end of the National-Legionary regime. The Legionnaires refused to allow Jewish refugees from villages in the Suceava, Câmpulung and Rădăuţi districts to remain in Rădăuţi, where they had fled and were being supported by the local Jewish community. On 8 December seventy refugee families were given twenty-four hours to leave Rădăuţi.[31] Similarly, thousands of Jews who had settled in villages in the Dorohoi district were given until 20 January 1941 to leave.[32] Bolfan, the mayor of Hârlău in the Botoşani district, ordered local Jews to evacuate their homes, which were to be converted into "Legionary workshops."[33] Young Jews who wished to return to Dorohoi after having been dismissed from their jobs in Bucharest and other cities were not allowed back.[34]

A particularly sorry fate awaited "foreign Jews" (Jews who did not have Romanian citizenship). It was Antonescu who gave the order for "all Jews who had been in the country for only a few years to leave within two months" after the issue was debated in the cabinet session of 4 October 1940.[35] "Anyone who fails to leave shall be incarcerated in one of the camps that are being set up for this purpose."[36] Antonescu blamed Petrovicescu, the minister of the interior, who was in charge of the operation, for failing to set up camps and collect data "on Jews who had entered Romania illegally."[37]

The following incident testifies to the fate that awaited foreign Jews who were tracked down by the authorities. In October twelve families of supposedly Hungarian origin were taken to the no-man's land between Hungary and Romania, where they were left to fend for themselves. The Hungarian border guards refused to let them in, while the Romanian border guards refused to take them back.[38] They were never heard of again.

After his public scolding, the minister of the interior attempted to restore himself to Antonescu's good graces by providing an extensive list of candidates for expulsion. In the absence of illegal immigrants, he padded the list with legal ones, including immigrants who had been naturalized or whose parents had been naturalized. Even army veterans (and their children and parents) or Jews who had been awarded residence permits for 1941 were not spared but were given a few hours or days in which to leave the country.[39]

The expulsion of Jews from the villages marked a turning point in the relationship between Jews and Romanians. These rural Jews had adopted the language and some of the customs of their Romanian counterparts, while retaining their Jewish identity. They were the prototypical Romanian Jews — dressing almost like their Romanian neighbors, somewhat lax in their religious observance, but fiercely loyal to their faith. During the nineteenth century Jews had been expelled from their villages on several occasions, and the presence of Jews in villages always provided fodder for Romanian antisemitic literature. The 1940 expulsions, however, were not based on any law or "legal" provision but on a "verbal order" that was transmitted from the upper echelons down to the lowest ranks. Antonescu did nothing to stop these expulsions, although Filderman and the Jewish Federation were careful to inform him of each specific expulsion operation and violation of the law. It should be pointed out that the expulsion of Jews was consistent with Antonescu's antisemitic outlook and his wish to purge the villages of Jews.

The purging of the villages continued until the last day of Legionary rule (21 January 1941), and it was only due to lack of time that certain villages were spared. Those who were expelled were never allowed back. The expulsion policy clearly reflected Antonescu's weltanschauung, and he was simply waiting for the right opportunity to bring it to fruition. The 1930 census shows that the operation turned about 10,000 (of a total of 110,000) Jewish villagers into impoverished refugees.

Subjecting Jews to forced labor was also the brainchild of the Iron Guard. Like the expulsions, this operation was not anchored in any law, order, or provision—at least until 5 December 1940, when the Law on the Military Status of Jews was introduced, obliging Jews to pay taxes and work for the state in lieu of military service. Officials from all governmental authorities, such as district prefects, police officers, and army commanders, subjected Jews to forced labor at their own initiative.

On 21 November 1940 all the Jews of Ploieşti, regardless of age or gender, were ordered by Marin Stănescu, the prefect of the Prahova district, to clear the ruins of three synagogues and a Jewish school that had been demolished by the Iron Guard (ostensibly for being "unsafe" following the earthquake of 9–10 November).[40] One detachment of Jews was sent to clear the ruins in the nearby town of Vălenii de Munte. The Jews of Câmpina, near Ploieşti, were also forced to carry out various public works. Maziliu, the police superintendent of Brăila, ordered "all Yids—intellectuals, lawyers, physicians, rabbis, young and old" to clear the snow over Christmas and the New Year.[41]

Sometimes forced labor was used to punish a community or communities that dared to report acts of looting or violence to Antonescu or the courts. For example, on 12 December 1940, a day after the director-general of the security police ordered an investigation into looting by Legionnaires in Târgovişte, "the Jews there, including veterans and decorated soldiers, adults aged 50–60, and even the community rabbi were forced to clear the mud and sweep the streets." At this stage the Jewish establishment still tended to view such actions as illegal initiatives and in their petitions and memoranda emphasized that forced labor was not anchored in "any order of the administrative [as opposed to Legionary] authorities."[42]

At this stage even Antonescu considered the imposition of forced labor irrespective of social class and profession as inhuman, and in the last joint government session on 10 January 1941 he criticized the practice harshly.[43] Although the forced labor was relatively mild at the time (things got much worse after the Legionnaires were ousted from power and the work detachments were introduced), it demoralized the Jewish public, making them feel they had lost control not only of their property but also of their bodies. Although the Law on the Military Status of Jews was originally legislated in order to offer forced labor as an alternative to military service, it was used by the authorities to get the Jews to carry out various jobs on their behalf.

One of the Iron Guard's objectives was to wage a war without quarter against the Jewish religion. For a start, the establishment of the National-Legionary regime was considered a victory against Judaism and its symbol—the synagogue. The Iron Guard always claimed that Judaism had brought about the moral, economic, and political decline of Romania and the Romanians. Although the Legionnaires were not the founders or sole disseminators of Christian Orthodox antisemitism, it was they who brought antisemitism to new heights. Already toward the end of King Carol II's reign the restraints were removed and the press—even those newspapers that had formerly shown a certain degree of moderation—ranted against the Jews and their faith and blamed them for the disaster that had befallen the Romanian state. The famous author Cezar Petrescu welcomed the Jewish Statute as the basis for a future nationalist Romania and claimed that as far as antisemitism was concerned Romania could hold its own and had no need to be taught by others (i.e., the Nazis): "We have no need to borrow from others or emulate them. The pioneers were here and belong to us: Alecsandri, Eminescu, Conta, Kogălniceanu, Haşdeu, A. C. Popovici, Goga."[44]

Indeed, all these authors but one were precursors of Romanian-type antisemitism. On 7 August 1940 *Neamul Românesc*, the historian Iorga's newspaper, demanded that government subsidies to the Jewish cult be abolished and that the money thus saved be used to offset tax evasion and illegal export of capital abroad by Jews and to set up a fund for the "Romanization of commerce and the training of Romanian merchants."[45] Nicodim, the patriarch of the Romanian Orthodox Church, in an attempt to console Romania for the loss of Bessarabia and northern Bukovina to the Soviet Union, declared in a press interview about a month before the establishment of the National-Legionary government: "Even now, the Jews have remained true [to type]. Everything goes to show that we have admitted a serpent into our midst. . . . They have bitten us without considering that it is thanks to us that they live and eat in this country."[46]

The invective against Jews, synagogues, rabbis, and the Jewish religion was simply a prelude to the physical assault against Jews and peaked before the establishment of the National-Legionary regime. This smear campaign took place at a time when Romania, disillusioned with Great Britain and France, who were unable to guarantee its territorial integrity, publicly dissociated itself from democratic Western values. The call for Romanian society to take stock to determine the reasons for Romania's weakness and for the calamities that had befallen it went hand in hand with a call to purge Romania of Judaism.[47]

The theme of Judaism's responsibility for all of Romania's ills was a daily refrain. International Judaism was accused of almost dragging Romania into war.[48] Judaism was guilty of inventing "materialistic messianism . . . which was seizing control of international finances," wrote the priest Gheorghe Butnariu, a spokesman for Christian antisemitism under the fascist regime. Judaism was also accused of inventing democracy, which "was hostile to the Church, inimical to the Romanian soul, and anathema to the idea of Romanianism . . . as well as being immoral."[49] Judaism had, moreover, brought about the collapse of the Romanian theater, "as well as of the press, literature, music and politics."[50] Jewish physicians were responsible for the high rate of infant mortality and abortions.[51] "Judaism's spirit of segregation" had prevented a rapprochement with German culture. Nichifor Crainic, an important fascist and antisemitic ideologue who served as minister of the press and propaganda between July 1940 and May 1941, argued in a speech at the Institute of German Culture in Bucharest: "The Jews are to blame for the fact that the Romanians have not sufficiently recognized the superiority of German culture. We have to destroy once [and] for all this Jewish mask, that has hidden the true face of Germany from us."[52]

Although the word *fascism* was not part of the Legionnaires' vocabulary, they presented their ideal of the totalitarian state as the polar opposite of democracy, which had, according to them, destroyed the qualities of the Romanian people and created a culture that was foreign to its traditional Christian values: "Our culture has been influenced by the bogus elements of yesterday's Jewish, Masonic and anti-Christian, or anti-Romanian, State."[53]

The Legionnaires' campaign against Judaism was fueled not only by Christian antisemitism but also by more immediate goals relating to the movement's activities and ideology. When it first came to power, the movement's primary goal was to take over government institutions and avenge Codreanu's murder. Indeed, it was Codreanu himself who had placed revenge firmly on the movement's agenda when, in 1936, he had reminded the Legionnaires "not to confuse the right and duty to forgive those who have wronged them with the nation's right and duty to punish those who have betrayed them."[54]

Legionary revenge was directed at all those responsible for the tragedy of the Romanian people, as defined by the Iron Guard.[55] It was the Legionnaires' belief that the Jews were partly responsible for this tragedy, as well as for Codreanu's murder: "The situation of the Jewish community in Romania appears to be worse than desperate in the eyes of the synagogue leaders, because they had a part in the government's activities during King Carol's dictatorship. They have the murder of Corneliu Codreanu and the massacre of 21 September 1939 [the execution of Legionary leaders at King Carol's instigation] on their consciences. Although the Jews did not participate directly in these executions . . . the entire country knows who was behind them."[56]

The dilemma facing the Legionnaires when they came to power was whether to apply the "Talmudic principle" [*sic*] of the *lex talionis* ("an eye for an eye and a tooth for a tooth") immediately or to defer revenge to some future date. This dilemma was resolved when the Legionnaires began executing Romanian "traitors" whose "day of reckoning" Codreanu had presaged prior to his death.[57]

During this period the church played an important role in the movement, and many priests held important positions within it. Antonescu's men found that 55 priests were members of the Legion's administrative and leadership cadres, including some district prefects and commanders.[58] Many of these priests not only preached violence but also practiced it. After the suppression of the uprising, 218 priests who had fought against the army were arrested.[59] The participation of priests in numerous Legionary ceremonies and events (in the presence of Reich and Nazi Party representatives) highlighted the difference between the Nazis and the Romanian fascists.

For the four and a half months they were in power, the Legionnaires' ideological war against Judaism and the Jewish religion continued unabated, peaking shortly before and during the rebellion. Legionary propaganda at the time reflected the entire gamut of antisemitism in Romanian society. The Legionnaires invoked Christian symbols to demonize Jews and called for the expulsion and—even at this early stage of the Holocaust—destruction of the Jews:

> Let them go wherever their God takes them. Let them leave behind, in our hospitable homeland, the wealth they have accumulated at our expense. Let them pack their cases at once. Let them consult the object they put on their foreheads when they pray, and go.[60]

> Since Romanians are true Christians, they cannot associate in any way with Jesus's murderers.[61]

> We do not wish to utter dire prophecies, but merely to establish the fact that the Jewish serpent is breathing its last. The day is nigh on which the Legionary boot shall crush the last head of this beast of prey.[62]

> Let us rid ourselves of the element [whose name is] Israel.[63]

To the accusation of deicide was added that of Communism. The Legionnaires equated Jews with Communists and hence with the Russians—the Romanian nation's archenemy.

It should be borne in mind that the war against Judaism did not reflect the mood of most of the Romanian intelligentsia or even the public at large. The fear of Legionary retaliation, however, silenced most of the opposition. Those who determined the attitude toward the Jewish minority were the Legionnaires and their sympathizers—both real and bogus.

The all-out war against Judaism was one of the main differences between Legionary and traditional antisemitism in Romania. Only the Legionnaires' determination to fight this war to the bitter end can explain their obsessive preoccupation with the Jewish religion, as reflected in the desecration of synagogues; the expropriation of cemeteries; the imprisonment, humiliation, torture, and murder of rabbis; the expropriation and destruction of community institutions; and during the rebellion itself, the torching and destruction of synagogues. This aspect of Legionary terror belied a myth dear to the Romanians' hearts — that they were a kind and tolerant nation, especially when it came to freedom of religion and worship. This myth was so firmly entrenched that even the Jewish establishment was taken by surprise. In his petition to Antonescu, Filderman stressed that the orders issued by Minister of Cults and Arts Radu Budișteanu against the Jewish faith violated Romanian law and ran counter to "the Romanian people's ancient tradition of religious tolerance."[64]

Filderman's arguments, his direct ties with Antonescu, and more importantly, the fact that Antonescu's antisemitism was still of the traditional type (not the fascist totalitarian kind that he was later to embrace) led Antonescu to revoke the order and even dismiss Budișteanu following his first meeting with Filderman on 14 September 1940 (see chap. 12). On 15 September 1940 Antonescu even ordered Budișteanu to publish a statement forbidding "attacks against other religions, people, or property."[65] The following day the new minister of national education, cults, and arts, Traian Brăileanu, deferred the implementation of two orders "until the final status of the country's religions has been determined by law" and also abolished "any decision, provision or other administrative measure that runs counter to this [deferment] order."[66]

In this climate clearly it was Judaism, not only the Jews, that was the target of attacks. Gangs of Legionnaires organized by the district prefect and the police destroyed Jewish religious and cultural institutions in Ploiești.[67] The great synagogue, the Sephardi synagogue, and the community school were destroyed on the pretext that the buildings had been rendered unsafe by the earthquake. The destruction and looting extended to other community institutions, too. The community building was stripped of furniture, the community archives and safe were impounded, as were furniture and holy objects from the destroyed synagogues and school, and the firewood and clothes that had been collected for distribution to the poor were confiscated.

The violence against local Jews was so brutal that it drew sympathetic responses from the Romanian public. An envoy sent by the Union of Jewish Communities to report on the situation in Ploiești testified that "an atmosphere of panic, fear and terror prevails in the city."[68] When Nicolae Iorga was assassinated, eleven Jews were also killed in the city, including Rabbi David Friedman, who was "shot in the head from above," the Jewish Federation reported to Antonescu.[69] The corpses were piled on either side of the streets, where they were later collected by gendarmes: "That day, on the floor of the building belonging to the Prahova Legionary Headquarters [Legiunii de Jandarmi], the blood of Professor Iorga mingled with that of Rabbi David Friedman."[70]

The above is but one example of how the Legionnaires conducted their war against the Jewish religion. A similar pattern was followed in other communities. On the day the Legionnaires destroyed the synagogues of Ploieşti, members of the Iron Guard broke the windows of Bucharest's Choral Temple — the symbol of Romanian Judaism — and threw stones and bricks at four nearby synagogues.[71]

Legionary attacks on synagogues reached a peak during the rebellion. Attacks on synagogues, however, was simply one facet of the Legionary war against the Jewish presence in Romania. By early December it was already clear to the Jewish leadership that the National-Legionary government was intending to "paralyze the activities of the Jewish communities."[72] Community institutions, schools, cemeteries, rabbis, and ultraorthodox Jews were targeted.

The rabbis were the prime target. The first to be arrested were rabbis from Transylvania and Walachia. Rabbi Moses Reich and the ritual slaughterer Drach, of Mediaş, were tortured and had their beards shaved off because Jewish store-owners had sold their businesses to the Germans (at the synagogue's behest, according to Sima).[73] On 30 November the rabbi and leaders of the Caracal community were arrested and tortured for three consecutive days for helping Jewish prisoners interned in the camp that had been set up in the city.[74] Legionnaires arrested Rabbi Abraham Schönfeld from Adjud, dragged him to the nearby forest, and tortured him all night long on a whim.[75] On 27 September Rabbi Leizer Hager of the Vizhnitz Hasidic dynasty was arrested in Arad. Filderman attempted — unsuccessfully — to obtain his release on the grounds that he "was one of the country's foremost rabbinical scholars . . . whose life was wholly devoted to the worship of God."[76]

THE EXPROPRIATION OF JEWISH CEMETERIES

Another facet of the war against Judaism was the desecration and destruction of Jewish cemeteries, which struck a blow at the heart of Jewish tradition. At first these acts appeared to be initiated by local fanatical Legionnaires who were determined to extort money in any possible way. A precedent was set by the Legionary authorities of Piatra Neamţ, who made the burial of Jews conditional on a donation to Legionary Aid. This was followed by a "legal" initiative to close down the cemetery and expropriate its grounds. The community of Piatra Neamţ, it should be mentioned, was one of Romania's most ancient Jewish communities, with a synagogue dating back to the early sixteenth century.[77]

By mid-October it was already clear that the new regime, especially the Legionary movement, wished to destroy Jewish cemeteries and wipe out any trace of Romania's Jewish past. In most cases they rested their case on the Law for the Nationalization of Jewish-Owned Land, which expropriated Jewish rural land and therefore did not apply to cemeteries that were situated in cities, even if they had formerly been situated outside cities. On 12 October the Ministry of the National Economy closed three cemeteries in Bucharest, and impounded the Hevra Kadisha (Sacra) building and its property.[78] The vacant section of the Bacău cemetery was also expropriated and turned over to agriculture, although no administrative order had been given to that effect.[79] The Ploieşti municipality informed the local Jewish community that it could no longer bury its dead in the new part of the cemetery and revoked its sales contract to the community.[80] Leşu, a priest of the Postal Church (Biserica Poştei) in Buzău, orchestrated the destruction and expropriation of the Jewish cemetery that dated back to 1834. Almost all its tombstones were overturned and stolen. Special Legionary squads were sent to destroy the cemeteries with hammers and chisels. The cemetery's fence was also destroyed, and the site was converted into a parking lot for horse- and ox-drawn carts. Leşu even used building material he had collected from the cemetery to renovate his church. In late November the Piatra Neamţ and Vaslui municipalities also announced the expropriation of Jewish cemeteries.[81]

In Bucharest, the Sephardi community, which had only one cemetery that had served it for centuries — since its arrival in Romania after the expulsion from Spain — was hit particularly hard when the authorities ordered the community to exhume their dead. Note that all orders to evacuate the cemeteries (both new and old) were verbal. The authorities knew that it would be hard to rationalize such orders and that any written order would be contested in the courts. The Union of Sephardi Communities in Romania was unsure whether it was required to exhume its dead or simply to shut down its cemeteries. "The closure of the cemeteries signifies the destruction of our communities," announced the union.[82] Sometimes expropriation orders came from two different authorities simultaneously. For example, the Bucharest municipality and the Ministry of the National Economy both ordered the expropriation of the cemetery on Giurgiului Road in Bucharest, leaving the community uncertain as to whom to obey. The situation throughout Romania grew steadily worse: "We are forbidden to operate cemeteries in urban areas for reasons that are unclear, while our cemeteries in rural areas have been appropriated."[83]

In December the Bucharest municipality took matters a step further by deciding that the time had come to "cleanse" Christian cemeteries of the graves of converted Jews. It therefore gave a written order to the Bucharest Jewish community to exhume a number of corpses, included that of Constantin Dobrogeanu-Gherea, the founder of Romanian Socialism.[84] The expropriation and desecration of cemeteries continued even though Corneliu Georgescu, the undersecretary for colonization and refugee affairs, had promised Filderman in late October 1940 that he would put a stop to such practices.[85] His promises were in vain. Hârlău's old Jewish cemetery was impounded and partly destroyed, while Huşi's only Jewish cemetery was expropriated.[86] In late October General Antonescu intervened and forbade the expropriation of Jewish cemeteries.[87] In Bucharest, for example, the cemetery on Sevastopol Street was closed down, but the Filantropia cemetery and the cemetery on Giurgiu Street were left open. Antonescu's order, however, was ignored by the Legionary authorities in provincial towns and by Legionnaires in central government, who continued to order expropriations and held on to territory that had already been impounded. On the day the Jewish Federation discovered that Antonescu had issued a directive forbidding the expropriation of cemeteries, an antisemitic newspaper announced the Bucharest municipality's decision to expropriate the Sevastopol cemetery.[88] The destruction of this important cemetery was completed after the Legionnaires were ousted from power.

"COMMUNISTS"

The struggle against the Communist party — or, in Legionary terms, against "those guilty of Communism" — served as a pretext for carrying out some of the cruelest terrorist operations against Romania's Jewish population. Jews were considered Communists, members of the Communist party, or Communist sympathizers. The antisemitic and Legionary press daily identified Jews with Communism. In actual fact the Communist party in Romania was negligible, and its activity had almost come to a standstill after the cession of Bessarabia and Bukovina to the Soviet Union. Florea Becescu, head of the anticommunist division in King Carol II's secret service and a security expert in the National-Legionary government, met with Sima and assured him that the Communist Party generally, and in Bucharest in particular, constituted no threat to the new regime. It comprised several dozen men only, about half of whom were undercover agents. A demonstration by the Communist Party on 3 November 1940 resulted in the death of only one person — an undercover agent, who was killed by friendly fire.[89]

Nevertheless, in early October a witch hunt was unleashed against Communists throughout Romania, which peaked on the eve of 7 November, the anniversary of the Bolshevik Revolution. During this witch hunt Communists in many cities, the vast majority of them Jews, according to Sima, were arrested.[90] In actual fact, the arrest of Communists (i.e., Jews) by the Romanian security police and regular police was not an innovation. What was new in 1940 was the random arrest of Jews by gangs of Legionnaires and policemen.[91] Hundreds of Bucharest Jews, with their hands raised above their heads, were marched through the city's streets to police or Legionary cells. The movement's torture centers were notorious, especially the one situated in the police inspectorate in Bucharest and the Legionary cells in Traian, Cercului, and Roma Streets. In these and other centers Jews were subjected to torture, hung by their hands or feet, robbed, and then released to make way for other Communists.

The Jews of Iaşi, "the Legionary movement's stronghold," were victims of the most violent anticommunist campaign in the whole of Romania. Iaşi was chosen as a center of terror by the Legionary movement not only because of its antisemitic history but also because its university and high schools supplied a steady reservoir of passionate youth influenced by Codreanu and the climate of violence fostered by the Legionary regime. Communities in other localities were also victimized for being Communist. In Giurgiu "almost the entire Jewish population was arrested irrespective of age or social status . . . [for being] Communists."[92]

The anticommunist campaign was directed first and foremost against Jewish youth, who had no shops, businesses, or property that could be confiscated. In their case the Communist witch hunt was a pretext for the arrest, torture, sexual abuse, and murder of Jews. Given the paucity of true Communists, membership in a Zionist youth movement was considered sufficient grounds for arrest and torture, although most of the Legionary investigators themselves were unaware of the difference between Zionism and Communism.

The Legionary movement was the only political movement in Romania to adopt terror as its methodology in the political arena and to justify it on Christian grounds. Revenge against the Jews, against those considered to be in the Jews' pay or enemies and traitors (all those who, according to Codreanu, had betrayed the interests of the Romanian people) were the leitmotifs of Legionary ideology. The Jews were an important element in the negative symbolism created by the founders of the movement. The Legionary movement encouraged the removal of Christian and moral restraints against the use of terror against Jews long before the Nazis came to power, as the 1924 pogroms in Oradea and Cluj testify. And yet the assassination of prime ministers and statesmen who opposed the movement and the settling of accounts inside the movement indicate that before September 1940 the Legion did not unleash its full terror potential against the Jews.

In September 1940, when an opportunity arose to inflict vengeance on the Jewish minority, the movement merely exploited preexisting terrorist frameworks, such as youth and student organizations and military, paramilitary, and police institutions. These organizations, as well as the Nazi-trained Legionary police that was set up during the National-Legionary regime, and government ministries and institutions controlled by the movement were the perpetrators of Legionary revenge against Jews. As such they also influenced the attitudes of ordinary antisemites toward the Jews. Once in power, the Legionary movement effectively exonerated anyone who attacked, robbed, or murdered Jews. Terror was a tool wielded by the Legionnaires to gain control of Jewish money, property, stores, and houses. The use of terror in its various forms cannot be divorced from the true goal of Romanian fascist ideology — to expunge the Jewish presence from Romania.

Terror also served the antisemitic goals of classical antisemitism and the credo of all antisemitic movements in Romania: Purging villages of Jews, subjecting Jews to forced labor, and attacking their community institutions. The Legionary state declared war against the Jewish community and its leaders (as representatives of a despised people) and against the Jewish religion, its institutions, and its symbols. Christian dogma was invoked to justify the eruptions of murderous hate, which took the form of a campaign of all-out terror against the Jewish minority, during which Jews were attacked and murdered, usually but not solely for their property.

The Confrontation
between Antonescu and the
Legionnaires and Its Impact
on the Situation of the Jews

The fate of Romanian Jewry during the short-lived National-Legionary regime was directly dependent on the relationship between Antonescu and the Legionnaires and on the power struggle between them. The Nazi presence in Romania (the German legation in Bucharest, the envoys of the various services, and the German minority in Transylvania), by largely determining the outcome of this power struggle, also influenced, albeit indirectly, the plight of the Jews.

The Jewish community was flung into this power struggle without being able to influence either side, barring some small influence on Antonescu for a short while. His antisemitism had been absorbed from traditional Romanian sources—education, the army, and the church. During the 1930s Antonescu was drawn to Cuza and had close ties with Codreanu (on one occasion he even tried to mediate between Codreanu and the king).[1] It is not, therefore, surprising that Goga and Cuza chose him to serve as defense minister in their government. Until 1940 he was considered pro-French and pro-British and anti-German, like most Romanian officers. This earned him the support of the leaders of the historical Romanian parties and was a contributory factor in his appointment as prime minister. Antonescu was, therefore, part of the establishment that led Romania during the interwar period, as indicated by the fact that until 1940 he advocated reform of the system, unlike the Legionnaires, who were bent on its destruction even before they came to power.

Antonescu was born in 1882 in the town of Piteşti, into a family of peasants and military men without any social standing.[2] In 1907, while a lieutenant in the Romanian army, he participated in the suppression of the peasant's revolt, showing remarkable determination and initiative as well as a notable disregard for human life.[3] This detail drew the attention of his superiors.

In 1911 Antonescu graduated from the military academy. In 1913 he took part in the Balkan War and received the highest military decoration. During the course of the First World War Antonescu gained a reputation as a talented staff officer, and he was quickly promoted. In 1916 he was appointed operational chief of staff to army commander Gen. Constantin Prezan. Toward the end of the war Antonescu's record earned him the post of chief of operations on the General Staff. His tenacity, disregard for both soldiers and fellow officers, and malice, along with his red hair, earned him the nickname "red dog" (*câinele roşu*). Nevertheless, he was an excellent officer who, unlike most of his colleagues, had not succumbed to corruption.

In the mid-1920s Antonescu was appointed military attaché to Britain and subsequently to France. He quarreled with King Carol II, whom he accused of failing to prepare the army and state for war, and proposed reforming the military forces.[4] He had few social contacts and, as a military man who had no friends in political circles, was not supported by any party or movement. Over the years he began to feel contempt for the democratic system and accused the king and the two historical parties—the National Peasants' Party and the National Liberal Party—of being responsible for Romania's tragedy: its isolation, its unpreparedness for war, and the ignominious surrender that led to the cession of parts of its territory to its neighbors.

Before he came to power Antonescu, unlike most Romanian politicians, had had hardly any contact with Jews. The first Jew with whom he had contact was Filderman, with whom he had attended high school in Bucharest. During Filderman's first meeting with Antonescu as *Conducător* (leader) on 14 September 1940, the two spoke about their school days. "He [Antonescu] recalled my activities at school and how he had always taken a liking to me," Filderman noted.[5] Antonescu's second significant contact with Jews was in the Second Balkan War (16 June–16 July 1913) and then in the First World War, when tens of thousands of Jews fought in the Romanian army. Most of these Jews were subjected to spontaneous or organized outbursts of antisemitism. Many were deliberately accused of defecting to the enemy and spying for the Germans. They were beaten, tortured, humiliated, and shot to death in their units and at the front, after trumped-up charges were brought against them. General Prezan, Antonescu's superior, ordered the execution of hundreds of Jews.[6]

Antonescu's recognition that Jewish soldiers had fought and fallen in the service of their country partly explains the rare concessions he made in the antisemitic legislation introduced by his regime. Another factor that may have influenced him was his short-lived marriage to a French woman of Jewish extraction, whom he apparently divorced in France before he returned to Romania in 1936. This woman bore him his only son, who died in his infancy. Very little is known of his first marriage, about which he was extremely secretive. His marriage to his second wife, Maria, who had also formerly been married to a Jew, sparked a political and legal storm after people in circles close to King Carol II spread rumors that she was guilty of bigamy. Mihai Antonescu, a young lawyer, successfully defended Antonescu and later became his right-hand man.[7]

Antonescu's initial encounter with antisemitism was through Romanian culture and literature and in the streets. Antisemitism fit with his nationalist and right-wing propensities. His love for his fatherland contained an element of xenophobia, especially in relation to Jews. These tendencies existed alongside an admiration for the democratic West, as represented by Britain and particularly France, which had brought about the unification of the Romanians and the creation of a Greater Romania. Moreover, Antonescu had received a French military education, and French was the only foreign language he spoke. Like most members of the Romanian military establishment, he had no liking for the Germans and was not even familiar with their culture and language. It is fair to assume that until the blitzkrieg in Poland, with its political repercussions for Eastern Europe, followed by Germany's victory over France and the Soviet ultimatum to Bucharest, Antonescu did not believe in Germany's military superiority.[8] When he assumed power, however, a different reality prevailed, and Antonescu believed Germany to be the only power capable of safeguarding what remained of Romania after it had ceded large chunks of its territory to neighboring states. (At the time, Antonescu was not aware of the secret addendum to the Molotov-Ribbentrop Pact, whereby Germany agreed to Bessarabia's annexation by the Soviet Union.)

ANTONESCU THE ANTISEMITE

In his book on the plight of the Jews under Legionary rule the historian Matatias Carp wrote that anyone who believed that Antonescu's policy toward the Jews was guided by "sensitivity, benevolence or concern" was wrong: "General Antonescu began by knowingly permitting the torture and looting of Jews, and attacks and crimes against them . . . and ended by initiating, approving and ordering measures that inevitably led to the looting and mass murder of the Jewish population."[9]

Carp describes Antonescu's attitude toward the Jews during National-Legionary rule. Legionary criticism of Antonescu and his policy, however, would seem to indicate that Antonescu was on occasion understanding toward the Jews and even intervened on their behalf. This hypothesis is corroborated by Antonescu's statements regarding the values on which his government was predicated. "Public opinion," he wrote on 14 January 1941 in his final letter to Sima, "does not belong exclusively to Free Masons, Jews, criminals and plutocrats." On the contrary, public opinion condemned violence "and inhumanity. It is for humanity that I have been fighting these last forty years."[10] Antonescu often took up the theme of humanity in talks, cabinet sessions, and correspondence with Sima. Evidently the Conducător had his own principles regarding the government's attitude toward its citizens and the values of justice and humanity in general. Filderman emphasized this point in his first memorandum to Antonescu, on 11 September 1940, even before the National-Legionary government was established: "Your address, which was read out in synagogues throughout the country, has reassured the Jewish population that the regime through which his Excellency hopes to bring about a national revival shall rest, inter alia, on faith, justice, law, order and humanity."[11]

These reassurances blinded the Jewish leadership at the beginning of the new regime. Filderman himself assured his colleagues in the Union of Jewish Communities and the Jewish Federation that "General Antonescu respects human life."[12] The many petitions and memoranda the Jewish leadership submitted to government ministries to protest antisemitic policy frequently referred to the "lofty" principles advocated by the prime minister in an attempt to persuade ministers and other influential personalities to stop the persecutions: "The Head of State has declared that the new regime is predicated on law and order, and these [values] are the legacy of everyone and anyone who seeks them."[13] Antonescu himself invoked these principles when speaking to the Legionnaires or when seeking the intervention of his new allies, Germany and Italy, on behalf of the Romanians in northern Transylvania who were at Hungary's mercy. In mid-November 1940, for example, when Antonescu visited Italy to ask the Italians to intervene on behalf of the Romanians living in areas annexed to Hungary, he declared himself to be guided "both by humanitarian considerations and by considerations of pure justice. I demand that the Hungarians cease their persecution and harassment of the Romanians."[14] In government sessions and direct appeals to the Legionary heads Antonescu condemned attacks against Jews. For example, on 11 January 1941 he reprimanded the Legionary leaders for having subjected the Jews of Brăila to forced labor: "Intellectuals, lawyers, physicians, and rabbis, regardless of age, were forced to clear snow from the city streets. In Buzău, an elderly rabbi was ordered to clear the snow."[15]

In his condemnation of Legionary activity Antonescu used the term *Yid* (*jidan*) to refer to Jews. The Romanians (like the Russians and unlike the Poles and Czechs) had two words for Jews—*evreu* (Jew) and *jidan* (Yid). The second term, used by Romanian antisemites throughout history, had negative associations. Antonescu used the two terms selectively. In orders, cabinet sessions, and correspondence with Sima he used the term *jidan*, but in talks with Jewish leaders and leaders of the opposition and in publications of that period he used the more neutral term *evreu*.

The use of the term *jidan* as such does not prove that Antonescu was antisemitic. His true feelings and opinions on the subject of Jews can be gauged from a study of his public and private statements about Jews. Like Cuza, Antonescu believed that Jews had invaded Romania after the First World War, and he believed in a Jewish world conspiracy against Romania. He was also convinced that Jews were the cause of his country's troubles and that they had seized control of Romania's wealth through methods known only to them. Even before he truly came under Hitler's influence Antonescu believed that Jews who had "sinned" against the Romanian state and people, particularly those who had been ordered to leave the country but had failed to do so in time, should be held in detention camps (*lagăre*). Although his enemies included Hungarians, Russians, Ukrainians, Freemasons, and Communists, he regarded the Jews as the most dangerous internal enemy. Though not as passionate and obsessive about the subject as the Legionnaires, Antonescu also saw the Jews as evil incarnate.

Like Romanian antisemites before him, Antonescu sought to expel Jews from Romania. In October 1940 he ordered all Jews who "had arrived in Romania after 1913 . . . even if naturalized" to leave the country within two months.[16] Constantin Petrovicescu, the minister of the interior, proved unequal to the task. He was unable to trace the masses of Jews who had supposedly entered Romania illegally after 1913. In a cabinet session of 10 January 1941 Antonescu asked Petrovicescu for a report. Petrovicescu, who also subscribed to the myth of a Jewish invasion, sought a way out of his predicament by declaring many legal Jews illegal.

Antonescu viewed the expulsion of Jews from Romania as a debt of honor to the nation, similar to the return of Transylvania or Bessarabia:

> I have undertaken a commitment toward the country that I have failed to honor—namely the incarceration in camps of all Yids who entered the country illegally. Why have we failed to carry out this commitment? . . . I hereby insist that all Yids who entered the country illegally be incarcerated. This step is necessary, because they have begun to practice commerce, support Communism, and undertake all sorts of propaganda acts. Let them stay in these camps until they decide to leave the country. I must honor my word. I made a clear commitment that I have failed to honor. Meanwhile, the Yids are making a laughing stock of me.[17]

Around the time he was calling for the incarceration of Jews (even before his first meeting with Hitler), Antonescu shook hands with Filderman, the Jewish Federation's president, and gave him his word of honor that he would restrain the Legionnaires.

Antonescu equated the Jewish problem with two other serious problems that threatened the existence of the Romanian state: the Hungarian problem, and the Communist threat. On 29 October 1940 he asked the minister of the interior to deal with the Hungarian problem, the Jewish problem, and the Communist problem, in one breath.[18] Antonescu retaliated for the Hungarian authorities' arrest and expulsion of the Romanians in northern Transylvania by subjecting the Hungarians in Romanian towns to a similar fate. In their case, however, he emphasized that the evacuation from Bucharest and other towns "in present-day Romania" would "naturally, be carried out without brutality." In applying the law, therefore, he drew a clear distinction between Romanians and "foreigners." When the Legionary minister of education, Traian Brăileanu, demanded that the celebrated Professor Iorgu Iordan be expelled from Iaşi University for being a "known Communist," Antonescu was determined that his expulsion be implemented "within the framework of, and in accordance with, the law": "The army, the judiciary and the education system are all institutions with a strong tradition and foundations. If we undermine them, the entire country will collapse. We have to deal with these institutions cautiously. . . . I cannot do things today that may, tomorrow, be condemned as arbitrary."[19] At this stage of his career Antonescu was far removed from the leader who would issue instructions for the liquidation of the Jews. It was Hitler and the Nazis who were instrumental in converting Antonescu from a classical antisemite into a Nazi racist antisemite.

The dispute between Antonescu and the Legionnaires regarding the confiscation of Jewish property is reflected in contemporary documentation. This documentation shows that the dispute was not one of humanitarianism versus antisemitism but rather one of brutal antisemitism versus a milder form of antisemitism that was contingent on the needs of the country and the times. "Do you imagine that all Jews can be replaced immediately?" Antonescu asked the Legionary ministers. "Political problems must be solved one by one, like in chess."[20]

Antonescu was split between his European self, the result of years spent in Britain and France and his admiration of their culture, and his Romanian self. He adopted one or the other personality depending on the circumstances. His Romanian self was predominant in his dealings with the Legionnaires, while his European self came out in his dealings with members of the old establishment and the Jewish leaders, to whom he spoke of justice, humanity, and law.[21] He was particularly angered by the Legionnaires' blatant disregard of his commitments and by their impatience with his policy toward the Jews.

Like other antisemites Antonescu believed that the Jews used special "methods" to exploit Romania and demanded an "immediate halt to the use of such methods."[22] Unlike the Legionnaires, his approach to the looting of Jewish property was rooted in his strong statist outlook: looting in the name of the state, on behalf of the state, and through the state for the good of the Romanian people was justified. He believed in "giving back to the Romanian what was theirs by right," unlike the Legionnaires, who resorted to looting for its own sake: "I, too, am in favor of confiscating Jewish property. I believe, however, that the operation must be carried out in a legal framework and in stages, i.e., in a systematic fashion, and for the good of the public only."[23]

Jewish leaders, who were more familiar with Antonescu's European persona, were ignorant of the other persona that emerged during cabinet meetings. In many ways Antonescu's antisemitism was a more sophisticated brand than that of the Legionnaires. Through his "rational" statist arguments Antonescu hid behind a guise of integrity and even humanity that deceived his victims almost until the end.

Another factor shaping Antonescu's attitude toward the Jews was the Legionnaires' allegations that he was associated with and perhaps even a member of the Freemasons. As the power struggle between him and the Legionnaires escalated, these allegations intensified. In actual point of fact, Antonescu never joined the Freemasons, rarely alluded to the order in his speeches, and even ridiculed the Legionnaires for their obsessive harping on the theme. His opposition to some of the measures the Legionnaires adopted against people and institutions they associated with the Freemasons (such as the YMCA in Romania) was partly anchored in the distinction he drew between Romanians and Jews. According to him Jews were, in the best case, "foreigners," while Romanians, even if Freemasons, were "brothers" (*frați*), and therefore any punishment meted out to them had to be within the framework of the law: "I, too, endorse the destruction of the Free Masons and their exclusion from public life. This, however, has to be done in a legal and humanitarian framework, and not by violence, since violence between brothers is intolerable."[24]

As the rebellion approached, Antonescu's invective intensified, and he became increasingly antagonistic toward both the Legionnaires and the Jews (any defense of the Jews would have been taken as further proof of his affiliation with the Masonic lodge). Nazi antisemitic propaganda in Romania was rife with condemnation of the Freemasons. Antonescu, whose family history was not entirely unsullied from a nationalist standpoint, was extremely sensitive to this accusation and the damage it could cause to his reputation with the leaders of the Nazi regime. After his meeting with Hitler on 14 January 1941, in which he agreed to send Romanian troops to fight alongside German soldiers against the Soviet Union in return for the führer's support against the Legionnaires, he took Sima to task for accusing him of belonging to the Freemasons: "This ingratitude [of yours] has reached a point whereby Legionary circles are spreading the rumor that I, too, am a member of the Free Masons, and that I have therefore adopted a position in their favor."[25] The Nazis were aware of this problem, and Manfred von Killinger, the Nazi ambassador in Bucharest, referred to it at length in his first report to Berlin after the suppression of the rebellion, on 11 February 1941.

The allegation that he was a Freemason haunted Antonescu even after the suppression of the uprising and influenced his policy toward the Jews, including his adoption of the extermination plan. He passed a special law to quash all rumors concerning his alleged ties with the Freemasons and tried to behave in a way that belied any connection with the order. On 6 February 1941, two weeks after he annihilated the Iron Guard, he issued a special law "forbidding acts that endangered the State's existence and interests." Article 12 laid down the death penalty for anyone "who accused cabinet ministers or heads of State of sympathizing with the Jews or Free Masons, without being able to substantiate such allegations."[26]

Antonescu's need to exonerate himself of blame was evident in his talks with German ambassador Killinger immediately after the suppression of the rebellion. In these talks, in an evident attempt to cover his back from his erstwhile partners in government, Antonescu accused them of harboring Communist sympathies. "The Legion," asserted Antonescu, "has accepted many Communists into its ranks. We have proof that many of those calling themselves Legionnaires received a payoff from the Bolsheviks." Similarly, he tried to convince the German ambassador that two ringleaders of Legionary terror had "apparently received sanctuary in the Soviet embassy." He even adduced proof of his former partners' betrayal of the fascist idea: "We have proof that British Intelligence still exerts a strong influence on the Legionnaires."[27] Finally, he took upon himself a long-term commitment to clear his name, in Killinger's presence. As Killinger reported, "When I mentioned the Legionnaires' claim that he [Antonescu] is close to the Free Masons, the general declared that he would convince the youth [i.e., the Legionnaires] that he has nothing to do with the Free Masons, and added that he hopes that by autumn he will settle the issue satisfactorily, without having to fire a single shot."[28]

The Jewish problem did not affect Nazi Germany's attitude toward the Romanian heads of state. At first Berlin viewed the Legionnaires' rampage against Jewish property as part of the fascist revolution that was taking place in Romania, as it had in Germany. In Antonescu's first two meetings with Hitler, on 22–23 November 1940 and 14 January 1941, the Jewish problem was not even raised. Romania's complex political situation and vital German interests (preparing for war against the Soviet Union and the invasion of the Balkans) meant that German leaders (Hitler, the Foreign Ministry, the Military Mission in Bucharest, and the German legation) were more interested in Romanian resources (food and fuel) and troops than the implementation of an antisemitic policy in a country that espoused an antisemitic stance anyway. Furthermore, the Germans had not yet formulated the Final Solution and therefore had no interest at the time in pressurizing the Romanians into adopting their policy. Despite the absence of German pressure, many Romanians approved of Romanian antisemitic policies (exclusion of Jews from economic and cultural life, confiscation of property, dismissal from jobs), even before the establishment of the National-Legionary government. Some of the propaganda fueling this antisemitism was financed by the German embassy in Bucharest, which paid off men, journalists, and newspapers and supported both antisemitic parties.

It thus transpired that the establishment of the Legionary government served merely as a catalyst for preexisting antisemitic trends. For example, the Jewish Statute was promulgated on 9 August, before the Legionnaires even came to power. As an antisemitic newspaper wrote on 15 August 1940, "Any attempt to strengthen Romania is bound to fail unless we first find a solution to the Jewish problem based on the brilliant German model."[29] This is but one example of hundreds of statements, declarations, and threats that were uttered from early 1940 (especially after the Soviet ultimatum of 26 June) until the establishment of the National-Legionary government. This incitement peaked in early July 1940, during the Dorohoi pogroms. When the Legionary regime came to power, therefore, it inherited a climate of violent antisemitism, a few pogroms against Jewish communities, and a desire to emulate Nazi policy.

The three foci of power within the National-Legionary regime — the Iron Guard, Antonescu and the army, and the Nazis — all entertained basic assumptions that turned out to be totally fallacious but that had an indirect bearing on the fate of the Jews in that period. The Legionnaires believed — with some justification — that the Nazis preferred their movement to all others and that the existence of a fascist government was a prerequisite for German guarantees of

Romania's new, post–August 1940 borders. On 23 January 1941, the final day of the uprising, when the Romanian army massacred the Legionnaires, the Legionary newspaper warned Antonescu that the suppression of the movement would endanger the existence of the Romanian state: "It is only because Germany has a similar national movement that it agrees to safeguard our future."[30] Antonescu himself initially believed that the Germans trusted and supported the Legionnaires. As Sima put it, "He believes, erroneously, that the movement is popular in Berlin."[31] As for the Nazis, they, including Hitler, thought "it was impossible to govern in Romania against the Iron Guard."[32]

They were all wrong! The first to realize his mistake and try to turn the situation to his advantage was Antonescu. Germany's victories and the situation in eastern and central Europe convinced Antonescu that only Nazi Germany could guarantee Romania's sovereignty. Upon assuming power Antonescu hastened to declare that he and Romania "were 100% behind the Axis powers. We shall fight with it to the bitter end, until we either prevail or are defeated. I would, however, like to abolish the Vienna arbitration." To those of his ministers who still remembered his pro-English leanings and antipathy toward the Germans, he hastened to add, "I am no sentimentalist. When the interests of my nation are at stake . . . I would side even with my archenemy in order to save the State. *In this case, however, I bear no ill will, nor ever did, against the Germans.*"[33]

At the time the Iron Guard was engaged in bloody acts of revenge and its "battle for Jewish homes and stores." In the course of this operation members of the Iron Guard clashed with local Germans as well as with Germans from the Reich, who began flowing into Romania "in order to get rich in a Romania that was as good as conquered," as the German embassy in Bucharest reported while seeking "to put an end to this undesirable invasion."[34]

Thus, for both Antonescu and Hitler the Jewish problem took second place. Hitler found Antonescu's brand of classical antisemitism sufficient to qualify him as a partner for his plans. The Jewish problem, therefore, was not an important feature of contacts between Antonescu and the official Nazi representatives. Nazi intervention in the Jewish problem was minimal at the time, although the very presence of Germans in Romania influenced the fate of the Jews and, in particular, their property.

Once the National-Legionary government was established, the Germans attempted to teach the Romanians the basics of Aryanization. On 19 October 1940 Hermann Neubacher, German minister plenipotentiary charged with economic matters in the Balkans, promised to send Antonescu an Aryanization expert, among others.[35] The German adviser evidently was unaware that the Romanians had their own brand of Aryanization — Romanization — that was rooted in a long tradition of Romanian antisemitism and the Romanians' ancient desire to rid themselves of foreign exploitation. In the late thirties this term became synonymous with the fulfillment of the antisemitic dream of ousting Jews from the economy and seizing their property.

Haupfsturmfuehrer ss Gustav Richter, who was appointed adviser on Jewish affairs to the German embassy in Bucharest in the spring of 1940, appeared in Bucharest for the first time in November 1940.[36] At the time his services were not required by the Legionnaires or by Antonescu. As far as racist legislation was concerned, the Legionnaires' objectives far predated the appearance of the Nazi advisers and were advancing swiftly toward realization. Moreover, as far as the so-called legal confiscation of Jewish property was concerned, the Legionnaires' greed, cruelty, and determination surpassed even the Nazis'. Antonescu's desire to realize the Romanian antisemitic dream, as entertained by most veteran antisemites, was part of his program for reforming Romanian society. Neither the Legionnaires nor Antonescu proposed the nationalization of Jewish-owned firms and factories (in the Legionnaires' case, this was because they wished to keep Jewish loot for themselves). In the area of expropriation of Jewish property the Romanians still had much to learn from their German counterparts.

The Germans were also eager to have a share in the loot. Most German, and especially Austrian, businessmen were interested in French-, Dutch-, or Belgian-owned firms or in Romanian firms of mixed or Romanian-Jewish ownership.[37] In some cases they sought to "purchase" 50 percent of all the company's stocks or its equity.[38] The Gestapo agent Artur Tester (who, in late 1942, played an important role in the abortive attempt to organize the emigration of seventy thousand Jews from the Transnistrian ghettos and camps to Palestine) got rich during Legionary rule by stripping Jews of their property with the help of Legionary associates.[39]

The Jewish problem was one of the reasons for the informal schism between the Iron Guard and Nazi Germany. Negative reports concerning the Legionnaires' economic ineptitude proliferated in Germany. The way the Legionnaires handled the Jewish problem did nothing to mitigate the negative impression these reports created.

Even before the Hitler-Antonescu meeting on 14 January 1940, when Hitler gave Antonescu a free hand to crush the Legionnaires, it became clear that everyone with an operational role in Berlin supported Antonescu: Hitler, Ribbentrop, the Wehrmacht generals who met with Antonescu, the head of the military delegation in Bucharest, various economic officers, and the soon-to-be-replaced chief of the German legation in Bucharest, Wilhelm Fabricius. Security chief Himmler and all his organizations, as well as propaganda minister Goebbels, supported the Iron Guard.[40] Himmler's emissaries in Romania (i.e., the Nazis) saved the Legionnaires' commander, Sima, and other leaders of the movement from execution and helped them escape to Germany, dressed in German military uniforms. After the defeat of the Legionnaires Antonescu ordered the Gestapo envoys to leave Romania because they had supported and armed the Iron Guard rebels.

Ultimately the Nazi envoys did not have any choice but to support the Iron Guard against Antonescu, contrary to Hitler's orders. The Nazis had preached active antisemitism and the exclusion of Jews from economic life for years. The Legionnaires were simply practicing in their own way what the Germans had preached all along. Even so, German economic, strategic, and territorial interests led the official representatives of the Third Reich to patronize the Romanian conservatives rather than the revolutionaries.

At this stage the Reich approved of Antonescu's plans for the gradual exclusion of Jews from the economy and for the nationalization of Jewish property, as Antonescu himself outlined early in his political career in the Italian newspaper *La Stampa*.[41] Neubacher, Germany's special economic attaché, enlightened Col. John P. Ratay, the U.S. military attaché in Bucharest, on Germany's attitude toward the Jewish problem in Romania: "The Jews must go, but they will be liquidated gradually and according to laws and regulations which will be promulgated. These laws will be closely patterned after the laws which I have had promulgated for that purpose in Vienna. A plenipotentiary commission will be set up for that purpose, and I shall have an expert come from Vienna who, as 'adviser,' will take charge of the work."[42] This policy survived until the formulation of the Final Solution and the eruption of hostilities along Romania's new border with the Soviet Union.

II

The Legionnaires' Rebellion and the Bucharest Pogrom, 21–23 January 1941

The Legionnaires' rebellion and the Bucharest pogrom that took place during the rebellion were closely intertwined. The fact that the Iron Guard continued to act as an underground terror organization when in practice it held most of the power plunged it into a fateful confrontation with the Romanian army. This confrontation alienated the guard from the masses and thereby saved most of Romanian Jewry from extermination.

By early January 1941 Antonescu realized that the Legion's activities no longer served the interests of Romanian nationalism and that the Iron Guard had turned into an organization for the provision of perks (jobs, stores, apartments, and money) to its members: "If we continue in this way, and fail to put a stop to all the illegal activities, the State will collapse, we ourselves shall be engulfed in a wave of anarchy, and Romania shall be carved up among its neighbors."[1]

The National-Legionary government had failed. Sima and his movement no longer represented the Romanians in Nazi Europe, and they had lost their justification for holding power. As soon as Antonescu found Hitler and the Wehrmacht leaders amenable and even sympathetic to him, following the painful concessions he had made, the link between an independent Romania and the National-Legionary regime was severed. The movement's leaders failed to understand this, relying instead on the ideological link and the identity of interests that existed, so they believed, between National Socialism and their movement. Sure of themselves and of their power and confident of the support of sections of the population—at least those that had grown fat on the spoils of stolen property and lucrative positions—they responded to Antonescu's criticism with attacks of their own. Antonescu, however, maneuvered them into staging a premature rebellion, with the aim not only of ousting them from power but also of basing his rule on a show of force, as Hitler had done on 30 June 1934. Hitler himself alluded to this in their meeting in January.

During preparations for the rebellion the Legionnaires openly attempted to identify the Jews and Judaism with Antonescu and his followers and during the rebellion itself, with the army and its commanders. The Legion repeated one of its worst mistakes—accusing Antonescu of having connections with the Jews and the Freemasons—in order to persuade the Nazis and the Romanian public that the Old Regime and Antonescu's supporters were part of a world Jewish conspiracy. The once-veiled attacks against Antonescu turned into vicious character assassination: "We see a return to the old motif of Free Mason sympathizers even in the government, and it is rumored that the Conducător himself is a Free Mason."[2]

The Legion's use of antisemitic themes was not arbitrary but designed to woo the Nazis by impressing upon them that they shared a common ideology. Although this propaganda made an impact on several leaders of the Nazi regime—notably Goebbels and Himmler—what Antonescu failed to tell his partners in government was that Hitler had already vouched his support for Antonescu. Hitler himself omitted to inform his ministers (except for Ribbentrop, who was present at the meetings with Antonescu) that he had decided to support Antonescu in his struggle against the Iron Guard.

During the three weeks leading up to the confrontation antisemitic propaganda grew to proportions unknown even under National-Legionary rule. Every article and every newspaper warned that the day of reckoning was nigh. At the same time the Legionary movement intensified its attacks against public figures they identified as Freemasons or British agents, in an attempt to delegitimize Antonescu and his men in the Nazis' eyes. In the days preceding the confrontation the Legionary and antisemitic press was characterized by:

1. a direct incitement to murder;
2. attacks against the Freemasons, underscoring their affiliation with England and the Jews;
3. an intensification of Legionary indoctrination, with an emphasis on the imminent confrontation between the movement and Judaism; and
4. an emphasis on the relationship between Legionarism and National Socialism.

Yet again the Legionnaires resorted to the pretext of a Jewish invasion to launch a campaign of intimidation against the Jews. The Legionnaires argued that at least 1 million Jews remained in what was left of Romania, whereas in reality—as corroborated by the official statistics—there were a little under 300,000.[3] The day before the start of the pogrom against the Jews, the Legionary organ *Cuvântul* alarmed its readers by reporting that Romania had the third largest

Jewish community in the world and that "Romanian is now the third language of the Jews, who number a million."[4] On 14 January, after reporting that there were 1.3 million Jews left in Romania after the territorial concessions, the paper stated, "The final solution is expulsion. [Even] one Yid is contagious."[5] The message was clear: the Iron Guard would settle accounts with the Jews and their lackeys. "The destruction of Judaism is now a commandment of the national survival instinct."[6]

The German legation in Romania also fed the Romanian press with antisemitic propaganda. This propaganda, however, was notorious for its lack of imagination, its use of inappropriate clichés, and its misplaced emphases, many of which rang false to Romanian ears. For example, an article titled "Jewish Control of Romania," which appeared in early January in the Frankfurt paper *Welt-Dienst*, claimed that the Minorities Treaty of 9 December 1919 had turned Romania into "a State controlled by Jews." This assertion did not ring true even to Ilie Rădulescu, the antisemitic journalist who translated and analyzed the article, since the Romanians viewed the Versailles Treaty first and foremost as a recognition of the Romanians' historic national rights and as the fulfillment of the dream of unification. In his article Rădulescu added, "The political rights of the Jews are meaningless, since they were obtained from us under duress."[7] The following day the newspaper again referred to the German article. After quoting passages that claimed that the Jews were responsible for the fall of the Goga government and Codreanu's assassination, the paper added, "The Yids are the true assassins, and will be the assassins of tomorrow, unless we exterminate them completely before it is too late."[8]

During the twenty days leading up to the Bucharest pogrom the press took up the refrain of the urgent need to solve the Jewish problem. Clear indications of what was about to take place were evident almost daily. The writing was on the wall. In hindsight, it is clear that the Bucharest pogrom was not spontaneous but was planned by the Iron Guard, which also planned to take control of the entire state.

The leaders of the Iron Guard realized that a confrontation with Antonescu would present them with an opportunity for wreaking their revenge on the Jews. In the days preceding the crisis the Iron Guard stepped up its declarations of support for the Reich's antisemitic policy in an attempt to underscore the shared ideology between the two countries. At a public rally on 19 January Vasile Iaşinschi (perhaps the most antisemitic of the Legionary ministers) explained that the German nation had no choice but to launch a war against Judaism, which "had tried to supplant it" and create a Jewish state and had been the cause of Germany's downfall. The League of Nations was "a tool used by the Free Masons and the Jews to destroy national states." Professor Eugen Chirnoagă, dean of the Bucharest Technological Institute, declared that the Jews were fighting the führer because they wished to gain control of the whole world. "The Legion saw through them and showed up their true colors, and that is why the Sanhedrin sentences it to death." At a rally Brăileanu, the minister of culture, education, and religion, gave a logical, step-by-step breakdown of the Jewish danger:

> Throughout Europe, the signal has been given for a revolution against Judaism. The propaganda [*prigoana*] against the Legion is the fruit of British agents in our midst, *namely the Yids*, who have planned to place the State in the service of British-Jewish imperialism. The aim of the proletarian [Bolshevik] revolution, which was organized by the Jews, was to destroy the national borders set up by the bourgeoisie, to destroy the nation-state, and to organize Europe into a united economic system that relies on the core Jewish leadership that has settled in London. This Yid-inspired strategy was foiled here, as it was in Germany and Italy.

Professor P. P. Panaitescu, a specialist on the Freemasons and Bucharest University's new dean as well as the editor of *Cuvântul*, also made a contribution to the antisemitic propaganda. After describing how the Jews had taken over the parties in Romania, he concluded, "The blow that National-Socialism has dealt Judaism is an act of kindness to the entire world." Constantin Papanace, who would have succeeded Codreanu as the movement's leader had he not been arrested on 25 July 1938, condemned Romanian and world Jewry and accused members of the Old Regime of glossing over the Jewish danger "and of diverting the Romanian people's attention from the arch enemy, namely the Yid." He went on to describe Jewish attempts to destroy "the noble Aryan soul," which was "suffocating in a climate of Jewish ordure." The conclusion reached by this close friend of Codreanu, who had spent many years in Nazi Germany, was concise and to the point: "We shall finally solve the Jewish problem together with the Axis powers."[9]

Antonescu's tactics ensured that the Romanian army, which remained loyal to him, "was in a state of active defense almost until the evening of 22 January" (until two o'clock in the afternoon, according to one source).[10] For two days the army confined itself to acts of retaliation and to surrounding the main areas under Legionary control. Meanwhile, Antonescu gave the Legionnaires a free hand in certain neighborhoods, allowing them to torch rows of houses and stores for kilometers on end (along Dudeşti and Văcăreşti Streets, for example) and murder hundreds of people. He allowed them to flex their muscles for at least two days without any interference from the military.[11]

Thus the destruction of Jewish neighborhoods was simply part of the general's tactical and strategic game. Antonescu needed chaos in the capital, with the paralysis of public transport and dozens of corpses strewn in the streets, in order to prove to Germans and Romanians alike that only he could impose order, discipline, and security and reinstate regular economic activity. As early as 1946 the Jewish historian Matatias Carp wrote that although the Jewish neighborhoods were most vulnerable, "as the instigators of the rebellion knew full well," no one did anything to preserve "human life, at the very least, if not property. By apathy or perhaps even design, a population of almost a hundred thousand people was left to the mercy of murderous hordes."[12]

Antonescu was fully aware of the situation in the neighborhoods. An eyewitness in the same building as Antonescu confirmed that even on the first day of the rebellion Antonescu knew what was going on in the streets of the country and the capital and was aware the lootings, murders, and torching perpetrated by the Legionnaires. "Inconceivable atrocities are being perpetrated. Dozens of Jews have been taken from their homes to Băneasa Forest, where they have been shot dead, and their corpses stripped naked and left to rot."[13]

The Legionnaires, blinded by their hatred of Jews, repeated the mistake of associating the army with the Jews. Labels such as collaborator, stooge, Freemason, and the like were attached indiscriminately to people, institutions, the Conducător, and finally the army itself. The Romanian generals were incensed by the Legionnaires' accusations that they had surrendered Bessarabia, Bukovina, and Transylvania without a fight. The tanks that were shooting at Legionnaires, a Legionary newspaper informed the city of Constanța on 22 January, "are the same tanks that retreated while the country was being dismembered." The following day the newspaper dubbed army members "cowards" and "hired assassins."[14]

Toward the evening of 23 January, a few hours after the suppression of the rebellion, Antonescu addressed the nation for the first time since the unrest began, declaring that he would tell them the "whole truth and nothing but the truth." He described Legionary actions against soldiers, particularly one incident in which the "rebels poured gasoline on [a captured soldier] and set fire to him in the presence of his horrified comrades."[15] He completely omitted, however, any reference to Legionary crimes against Jews.

Antonescu's victory and new hold on domestic affairs had a decisive bearing on the fate of the Jews. By suppressing the Legionnaires Antonescu also freed Romania of supervision by the Nazi murder and intimidation agencies. In 1956 the former military attaché to Berlin Ion Gheorghe declared, "Had the Legion remained in power, the fate of Romanian Jewry would no doubt have been similar to that of [European] Jewry." On the other hand, he added, were it not for the escalation of Germany's anti-Jewish policy, antisemitism in Romania would have continued as in the past and would never have become such a destructive force.[16]

LEGIONARY INCITEMENT AGAINST
JEWS DURING THE REBELLION

"The Jews have rebelled!" stated one of the flyers the Legionnaires distributed in the villages on the first night of the rebellion, when they discovered to their dismay that the army had remained loyal to Antonescu. Their aim "to incite the peasants and lure them to the cities" was partly successful. From the start the Legionnaires sought to implicate the Jews in the rebellion, turning them into a scapegoat and target upon which the frustrated masses could vent their anger. They disguised their power struggle as a crusade against the Jewish minority and their butchery as a campaign against Judaism, which was hiding behind Antonescu and his lackeys. All newspapers, flyers, and radio broadcasts (which the authorities had a hard time silencing during the three days of the rebellion) directly incited antisemitic activities and as the situation deteriorated escalated into a call for murder. All the rebel organs published prominently placed manifestos and articles praising "chaos and anarchy." Each hour the rebels' radio station, named Romania, reminded the public that "at this very moment, the Free Masons and Jews are fighting to destroy the National-Legionary State." After specifying who the enemies were, it warned that "for each legionnaire killed, we shall shoot ten [of the enemy]." They portrayed the army's retaliatory strikes as actions "to protect the Jews."[17]

During the rebellion the Legionnaires fully exploited the theme of a god who suffered on behalf of his children (the Legionnaires), who were the victims of the satanic acts of the enemies of Christ and of the movement (the Jews and their stooges). One of their publications even stated, "The killings [i.e., the government's actions against the Legion] must be stopped immediately! The enemies are delighted, the Jews rejoice." The Iron Guard commander who signed this manifesto made a point of reminding Antonescu that "he, too, had worn the Green Shirt" and topped this with flattery by comparing Antonescu to a father (God) who was "shooting at his children." The manifestos to officers and soldiers contained direct incitements to murder Jews: "If we are forced to shoot, we must make sure that we don't shoot each other. You know whom to shoot. The Jews and Free Masons are the sole beneficiaries of the current lack of understanding."[18]

Throughout the three days of the rebellion, the Legionnaires did their best to portray the conflict as a confrontation between the Romanian state (of which only they were the true representatives) and "Jewish capital," Judaism, and its stooges. They warned the Romanians that the destruction of the Legion would plunge Romania back into the days of the "Jewish-Masonic hydra—that had tried to topple the National-Legionary government."[19]

The Legionary dailies—the only newspapers that appeared during the rebellion—continued the incitement until the army seized their offices and printing houses. The newspapers continued to discuss Jewish affairs as if nothing untoward were happening. "Who do you think are the chief violators of the law to prevent sabotage of the economy?" asked the veteran organ of the antisemitic movement on the second day of the rebellion. It answered, "The Jews! . . . And they must be punished accordingly, and ruthlessly!"[20]

On 22 January *Porunca Vremii* called for a new census of the Jews in order to prove that "Romania had more Yids than indicated by the official statistics." According to the author of the article the census was supposed to determine: "How many Yids are Romanian citizens, how many have changed their names, how many have converted to Christianity, how many carry another citizenship, how many have a [foreign] passport, how many entered the country in the last decade, how many emigrated in the last decade, and how many have intermarried."[21]

Cuvântul, the Legion's official organ, served as a mouthpiece for the movement's ideology and political aspirations during the three-day crisis. Its pages were full of terms such as "death," "love of death," "revival," the "crucifixion of Codreanu," "enemies," "vengeance," and especially, the satanic monster that was responsible for all the calamities that had befallen and would befall the Christian Romanian nation—namely, the Jew.

On 22 January, before anyone knew that Antonescu was about to give the order to open fire on the Legionnaires, *Cuvântul* wrote that "the Free Masons' gold" had undermined the nation's independence, freedom, and sense of social justice. "Three Jewish billionaires alone are able to assume the entire cost of the current war."[22] On 23 January the newspaper blamed the Jews and their stooges for the tragedy of the civil war. On 24 January the organ's last issue bequeathed its antisemitic will to the following generations by attempting to explain to the public why the movement had come to such an end and why it had plunged the nation into chaos and anarchy. Prominent headlines informed the soldiers of "how the Jewish-Masonic plot was devised," and the paper's center page again carried the infamous call to kill Jews: "You know whom to shoot at." "The dark forces" (namely, "Jewish capital and the Free Masons") had collaborated in an attempt to "destroy the Romanian people" and the Romanian state, which was founded on the "Captain's spirit." The Jews were not the only guilty party in this conspiracy; equally guilty were the democratic foundations of the previous regimes and the Liberal Party. The editorial used Christian symbols and disinformation in order to persuade the army to lay down its arms and unite with the Legionnaires against their common enemy — the bloodthirsty "Jewish beast" (*fiara iudaică*) that had incited the two camps to kill each other. "Its thirst will be quenched only when this people's seed has been extirpated."[23] The paper's editor, Panaitescu, wrote a long editorial in which he made substantial use of his expertise on Freemasonry. The article was primarily directed at the Romanian intelligentsia and reflected the Legionary movement's mistaken belief that the Nazis would not permit its eradication.

As it turned out, all of Panaitescu's assumptions were mistaken: Antonescu did not want a Legionary Romania, and the Nazis were able to manage very well without the Legionnaires. Many Legionnaires were arrested or fled, and the movement was supplanted by Antonescu and his regime. *Cuvântul*, meanwhile, published a new oath of allegiance to Antonescu, including a commitment to die for him in the war launched by the movement "against all the country's Jews and criminals."[24]

The ideological will offered in *Cuvântul* on 24 January was the Iron Guard's swan song. Only a comparison with Antonescu's political will, presented on the last day of his trial in June 1946, or Hitler's last will, which he drew up in his bunker in Berlin in April 1945, can show what part antisemitism played in the lives of these public personalities and fascist movements.

The fate of the Jews on the second day of the rebellion was discussed on the inner pages of *Cuvântul*, in a long article describing the battles with the army that also alluded to anti-Jewish riots. The article described how the police were unable to maintain order, since most of the policemen had been paralyzed by the "siege" imposed upon them by the "criminal Alexandru Rioşanu, Undersecretary for Public Order in the Interior Ministry and Antonescu's confidant [in retaliation for firing at the building of the Council of Ministers]."[25]

The movement's other organs also continued with their anti-Jewish incitement throughout the rebellion.[26] The propaganda was so intense and the smear campaign against Antonescu and his associates so virulent (he was portrayed as a stooge of the Freemasons) that Antonescu himself decided to clear his name to the Romanian people on the evening of 22 January: "Do not believe this childish nonsense. Surely you cannot believe that General Antonescu, the country's shield, a true friend of our German and Italian allies, would have tolerated any involvement, however small, by [the connivers] of the Jewish and Masonic conspiracies, in the country's and government's affairs."[27]

The pogrom against the Jews of Bucharest was planned and organized by the Legionary leadership. It was not a spontaneous rampage or an attempt to exploit the situation of anarchy that prevailed. The pogrom was no isolated incident but rather the natural consequence of the persecutions and antisemitic atmosphere that prevailed under the National-Legionary government. Although the Bucharest pogrom is usually considered a by-product of the rebellion, the two were parallel events that were planned and executed by the same authority and leadership.

The army, the gendarmerie, and the police who accepted Antonescu's authority did not participate in the pogrom. The police under Legionary control did. They included regular and Legionary policemen in the Ministry of the Interior, the Siguranța (Romanian Security Police), and the police prefecture in Bucharest. They also included members of Legionary terror organizations set up under Legionary rule, such as the workers' union, the students' union, the Legionary cells, the economic council, and the Legionary movement as a whole. Their numbers were boosted by high school and even primary school students as well as Gypsies, criminals, and other marginal elements from the city outskirts who were only too happy to participate in any antisemitic event from which they stood to gain, irrespective of who organized it.[28] Several dozen Christian Orthodox priests, and perhaps hundreds, also played a significant role in the rebellion and pogrom.

It was Iașinschi, the Legionary minister of health and social protection, who gave the order to burn down the Jewish quarters on 22 January.[29] The Legionnaires' thirst for revenge was directed at Jews, their property, and their religion. They stormed Jewish homes, community institutions, and synagogues, desecrated holy books and Torah scrolls, and torched and destroyed everything in their path. The movement's headquarters and branches in Bucharest were turned into centers in which Jews were tortured and killed. Constantin Matei, the commander of Nicador's Legionary nest (Cuibul Nicador), wrote to Antonescu immediately after the suppression of the rebellion informing him that the leaders of the Iron Guard "have ordered us to destroy Jewish stores."[30]

The storming of the two Jewish quarters and adjacent areas (which also had a sizable Jewish population) began on the afternoon of Tuesday, 21 January, several hours before the start of the rebellion, and ended in the early morning of Friday, 24 January, after the suppression of the rebellion. Already on 20 January Legionnaires had begun arresting Jews and detaining them in the police prefecture of Bucharest.[31] The litany of crimes they perpetrated in the Jewish quarters comprised: looting, arrests, beatings, rape, detention in torture centers, and spontaneous murders and organized executions as well as the seizure and torching of synagogues and community offices and the burning of immovable property, shops, businesses, and houses. From the second day of the pogrom the Legionnaires were joined by ordinary Romanians, even from the affluent classes, as well as Gypsies, criminals, and other undesirables. Many of them, not content with looting, broke into houses and added their crimes to those of the organized Legionnaires.

At noon on 21 January (in some cases even earlier) gangs of armed Legionnaires stormed the Jewish neighborhoods and began beating and arresting Jews indiscriminately in the streets, synagogues, and Jewish institutions. About two thousand Jews, "irrespective of gender or age—aged between 15 and 70, and some even 85," were forced into trucks or marched to torture centers.[32] Legionary gangs broke into private homes and arrested affluent Jews and Jewish officials representing community institutions, the Union of Jewish Communities, the Jewish Federation, and other Jewish public institutions, according to pre-prepared lists. The detainees were taken to prepared or improvised torture centers (see chap. 12).

In the torture centers the Jews were deprived of all valuables and then tortured for hours and days. In most cases torture and murder served as an outlet for the sadistic impulses of the Legionnaires, women as well as men. Affluent Jews—or Jews who were considered affluent—were also tortured in order to force them into handing over hidden property, while Jewish officials were tortured in order to coerce them into handing over community funds. On 21 January the Legionnaires rounded up Jews in the synagogues. Several dozen victims succumbed while being tortured, others were thrown from the upper stories of the police prefecture or slaughtered in abattoirs, but most were shot to death by special, organized Legionary squads.[33]

On the first day of the rebellion the Legionnaires arrested many policemen who were loyal to Antonescu. During the three days of the rebellion, 76 police officers, 4 supernumerary police officers, 10 police agents, and 453 regular policemen were disarmed, and some were forced to hand over their uniforms.[34]

THE TORTURE CENTERS

The Legionnaires planned or improvised about twelve torture centers in institutions and police buildings under their control: the police prefecture in Bucharest, police stations in precincts fifteen and twelve, the branch offices of the Union of Legionary Workers, the main branch of the union in Roma Street where the leaders of the rebellion were stationed, the branch office of the union in Cercului Street, the Captain's Farm near Bucharest, and the council offices in the village of Jilava.[35] They also used Jewish institutions that had been seized for this purpose, such as the Malbim Synagogue and the offices of the Union of Jewish Communities. The municipal abattoir served as a special torture center. Several dozen to several hundred Jews were taken to the torture centers.[36]

The scale of torture, abuse, and murder depended not only on the Legionnaires' whims but also on the amount of time at their disposal and the means of transport available to them (to take their victims to execution sites outside the city and to transport the loot). These factors account for the disparity between the large number of detainees and the relatively small number of mortalities.

Jews were arrested either according to a pre-prepared list of names and addresses or randomly. Most Jews were arrested when the Legionnaires broke into synagogues, houses, and Jewish institutions or during roundups in the streets, although some were arrested after their neighbors informed on them. Houses and stores "that were designated as Christian" were left intact.[37] Signs such as "Christian business," "Christians live here," "German enterprise," "Aryan owner," or "Christian tenants" stood out against the destruction and torching of Jewish-owned buildings and provided additional proof that the pogrom was premeditated.

The Legionnaires used a variety of techniques in their attempt to satisfy their hunger for revenge. The fact that many of those who took pleasure in torturing Jews were young (some of them adolescents) and female added a new, hitherto unknown, and sometimes perverted dimension to Legionary crime. In almost all cases the young Legionnaires attacked their victims immediately after their arrest. The first stage of torture took place at the police prefecture, with the Legionnaires giving vent to their anger by beating detainees with "anything that came to hand, slapping cheeks, punching, and beating with rifle butts, steel helmets, and whips."[38] The torture usually lasted for hours and even days without interruption, with the Legionnaires working in shifts. In police precinct fifteen the Jews were beaten "almost continuously from 6 pm on 20 January until 1 pm on 23 January." In the Union of Legionary Workers' headquarters "[the men] were beaten and tortured unremittingly from 7 pm to dawn." In the Captain's Farm Jews were subjected to two days of torture.[39]

In all torture centers the Jews were robbed of any valuables they had on their person and sometimes even their clothes. Often the victims (especially those on the prepared lists) were subjected to further torture to force them into revealing where they (or their relatives) had hidden money and valuables. They were then taken or driven back to their homes, ordered to hand over their belongings, and in most cases, shot to death. The Bucharest community's treasurer, Sigmund Colin, was forced to open the community safe before he was murdered.

Execution was the last stage in the process of torture, the details of which, once revealed, shocked not only the Romanian public but even the Nazis. Jewish leaders were arrested and tortured as Jews and as the representatives of Judaism: "They tortured me into revealing where I had taken the hundred million that were given to Rioşanu," Matatias Carp reported to Filderman five days after the suppression of the rebellion. "They beat me to try and force me into handing over a written affidavit. I resisted, however, and in the end they agreed to accept a suicide note." Horia Carp's father was accused of "amassing hundreds of millions of lei from JNF charity boxes."[40] The Legionnaires forced Jews to sign fictitious transactions and suicide notes as well as requests to the state prosecution to refrain from conducting postmortems of the more high-ranking victims. Suicide notes were particularly popular, since they gave the Legionnaires license to murder with impunity.

Another scene of murder was the municipal abattoir. On the last day of the rebellion, fifteen Jews, picked at random from among the hundreds who were being detained in the police inspectorate in the capital, were taken in vans to the abattoir. Their corpses, or parts of them, were found after the rebellion was suppressed. They had been shot, mainly in the head and neck.[41] The bodies were molested, usually while the Jews were still alive. The military prosecutor in charge of investigating the Legionnaires' crimes at the time stated that "the corpses of those murdered in the abattoir were hung by the back of their necks on butchers' hooks."[42] Mihai Antonescu's personal secretary testified that the victims were hung on hooks while still alive: "Live men were hung on hooks where they were carved with large butchers' knives. The plant [the abattoir] remained closed for a week. The halls had to be disinfected."[43]

By late January rumor had it that 2,000 Jews had been killed, although the actual figure was 125. The Jews latched on to this inflated figure, perhaps because of their collective memory of the atrocities that had accompanied the pogrom. The Legionnaires' torture and murder techniques and the way they mutilated their victims' corpses may be considered a Romanian "contribution" to the inventory of human atrocities. Had this pogrom been committed in some period other than the Holocaust, it would probably have gone down in history as the largest pogrom against Jews since Kishinev (1903).

The Bucharest pogrom also broke an unwritten taboo vis-à-vis Jewish women. Legionnaires, soldiers, gendarmes, and ordinary people treated Jewish women as sexual objects with which they could do as they wished. Raping Jewish women was not considered wrong from an ideological perspective, although marrying Jewish women was. In general, the Legionnaires were not overly concerned with the issue of race, especially since the Romanians did not figure high in the hierarchy of racial superiority devised by the Nazis. It is not fortuitous that such an important element of Romanian antisemitic legislation glossed over Nazi ideology, and Jewish women were arrested, beaten, tortured, and raped. A natural reticence and the fact that the Jewish family had not disintegrated meant that the issue of rape was kept under wraps in the testimonies that were given immediately after the pogrom. The military prosecutor, however, pointed out that "while the synagogues were burning, these brutes broke into houses and raped women in front of their husbands' and children's eyes."[44]

The Romanian Jewish poet Arthur Axelrad, whose poem on the suffering of Romanian Jewry was inspired by the Bucharest pogrom, had to keep adding verses to his poem as the Bucharest pogrom was followed by pogroms in Iaşi, Bukovina, and Bessarabia. His resultant lengthy dirge on the fate of Romanian Jewry alludes to the defilement of Jewish women and girls in the Bucharest pogrom and refers explicitly to the cruelty of the Legionary women, who tortured, murdered, and looted their Jewish victims.[45]

SYNAGOGUES

From the establishment of the Iron Guard in 1927 until its demise, there was not a single large-scale Legionary event that did not involve an attack against synagogues—which for the Legionnaires was *the* symbol of Judaism. Even dozens of years later, the Legionary leaders in exile continued to use the term *synagogue* to denote Judaism, Satan, and intrigues against the movement and against the Romanian people.

The synagogue offensive began on the afternoon of 21 January (when the arrests, tortures, and murders also began) and peaked toward evening. During the offensive the Legionnaires attacked almost all of Bucharest's synagogues (the official estimate handed to Antonescu listed twenty-five synagogues that were attacked, but an enclosed note stated that the list was not complete). All synagogues that were attacked were desecrated. Torah scrolls were thrown to the ground, torn, and in many cases burnt. Holy artifacts and valuables were looted. Whatever was not looted was destroyed. Finally, the Legionnaires set fire to almost all the synagogues, although only two of them were completely destroyed. In cases where deliveries of fuel or gasoline failed to arrive, the synagogues were spared.

The Legionnaires, like the Nazis, did not destroy all the holy artifacts they confiscated. After the suppression of the rebellion the authorities found "ten Torah scrolls and eighty prayer shawls" as well as several hundred "Jewish ritual objects" that had been stolen but not destroyed.[46]

A third target of Legionary violence was Jewish houses, businesses, workshops, clinics, and pharmacies. This time no holds were barred. The Legionnaires acted as the vanguard of an operation in which the masses also participated. The masses comprised the poorer populations on the city outskirts, Gypsies, and criminals from Bucharest and its environs as well as respectable citizens who found it hard to resist the temptation. The description Filderman sent Antonescu after the pogrom did not leave much to the imagination: "There are no words to describe this ruthless pogrom in which entire streets were destroyed and looted in the commercial and poor neighborhoods." The Legionnaires broke into businesses and stores along entire highways, boulevards, and streets, looted and destroyed their stock, and sometimes also set fire to them. The Legionary tornado did not spare a single Jewish concern.[47]

The rabble also broke into Jewish homes, leaving havoc in their wake. They raped and murdered the inhabitants; looted, wrecked, and torched property they could not remove; and set fire to entire apartment buildings.[48] Sometimes fires spread from businesses and stores to entire buildings. The Legionnaires would not allow the firefighters near the scenes. This operation, like others specified above, was also the result of careful organization and planning, as proven by the fact that the rioters came equipped with fuel containers, cans of benzene, and even fire grenades. The Legionnaires' trucks were stationed nearby to take all the looted property to the movement's centers, headquarters, and branches as well as to private homes.

The movement was unable to control the masses who had jumped onto the Legionary bandwagon. These people were motivated by greed and defied Sima's instructions to lay down their arms. Unlike the organized Legionary gangs who drew up lists of their victims, the rabble plundered "indiscriminately and arbitrarily, store by store, house by house, apartment by apartment, from the mansions of the rich to the slums of the poor, from thriving businesses to bagel stalls, from the rich [Jew's] penthouse to the beggar's hovel—their axes and trucks spared nothing."[49]

As a rule, the indirect damage outweighed the direct damage. The rabble destroyed craftsmen's livelihood and means of production, doctors' and pharmacists' laboratories, factory equipment and machines, electricity and water systems, windows and doors. Even after the organized Legionnaires left, mobs of Romanians and Gypsies broke into the Jewish quarter and into neighborhoods adjoining the affluent commercial area that were inhabited by tens of thousands of impoverished Jews, whose possessions they coveted. The residents of Lipscani

Street, the most important and affluent commercial area, were not harmed. The Legionnaires had managed to "purchase" only several stores in this prestigious street. They were in no hurry to confiscate other, destroyed businesses that they thought would soon be theirs.[50]

The pogrom, during which 1,274 business, stores, workshops, and apartments were damaged or wrecked, affected an entire class of independent Jewish merchants and craftsmen. The Jewish Federation estimated the damage (including the damage to synagogues) at some 383 million lei.[51] After the suppression of the rebellion the army tracked down "almost 200 trucks of booty, as well as cash and jewelry."[52] The authorities commissioned by Antonescu to investigate the riots described them "as acts of terror that are reminiscent of those used in the [Russian] Communist Revolution."[53]

Legionary rage was a prominent feature of this operation as well, as the participants behaved "like the cruelest barbarians." Even German soldiers who were passing through Bucharest after the suppression of the rebellion were taken aback by the Legionnaires' savagery.[54] The military attaché at the German embassy collected data on the number of dead and visited the local morgue. "In Bucharest you can see hundreds of corpses, most of them Jewish," he reported.[55] What was so shocking about the Bucharest pogrom was not so much the kinds of acts the Legionnaires resorted to—after all, the desecration of synagogues, torching, looting, and sabotage were nothing new to the Legionnaires—but their scale. "Whoever visited Dudeşti and Văcăreşti streets immediately after the mobs had passed through, were shocked not so much at what they saw, as by the unusual techniques of destruction—[techniques] used by another kind of carnivore—namely, the green ants."[56]

SHORT-LIVED MORAL STOCK-TAKING BY ROMANIAN SOCIETY

"We parents, teachers, clergy, and politicians must all examine our consciences and ask ourselves whether we did all we could to mold our souls in the Romanian and humanitarian spirit."[57] This heartfelt cry of despair by a Romanian journalist—one of the few voiced immediately after the rebellion—inaugurated an extremely short-lived period of soul searching in which an attempt was made to rehabilitate the self-esteem of Romanian society. The Bucharest pogrom shocked the Romanian public and the non-Legionary section of society that was not pro-Nazi. What was different this time was that the pogrom had taken place in the capital itself, not in some remote town like Dorohoi where the army had taught Jewish "Communists" a lesson. Those who had welcomed the Legionnaires so enthusiastically now condemned them with the same vigor and determination. This change of heart, although radical, was not unusual in Romanian society. The press and many intellectuals launched a debate on how to rehabilitate the regime after the Legion's collapse.

The Legion's disintegration not only brought down the National-Legionary government but also caused a partial collapse of its ideology. Questions arose concerning the true nature of Legionarism, a belief system that had disturbed and poisoned political life in Romania for a decade and a half, at a time when Europe was controlled by the Nazi Party, a sister to the Iron Guard. A true soul searching naturally should have included an open public debate on antisemitism and an analysis of the reasons behind the deterioration of moral norms in whose existence some members of Romanian society and the intelligentsia believed. Such a debate never took place. Indeed, the period of taking stock was extremely short lived and hardly alluded to the Jewish question at all. Nor did the voluminous collection of telegrams and letters of support sent to Antonescu from all strata of the public after the suppression of the rebellion mention terror against Jews.

12

The Jewish Leadership under the National-Legionary Regime

The establishment of the Legionary regime took the Romanian Jewish leadership by surprise. One reason why the Jewish leadership — both assimilationist and Zionist — was so unprepared for this turn of events was because of its lack of involvement in the fate of Jews in other European countries and in the political situation in general. It was only after the establishment of the Legionary regime that Filderman began taking an interest in the fate of Jews in occupied Poland, Germany, Italy, and Hungary, in order to warn Antonescu that his Legionary partners wished to emulate Nazi fascism. This does not imply that the Jews felt no sympathy for the suffering of their siblings, including the Jews of Bessarabia and northern Bukovina, upon whom the Iron Curtain had already descended. They were, however, often ignorant of their fate due to the lack of reliable information. As a rule, Romanian Jewry was preoccupied with the problems brought about by the new regime: rural migration, dismissals from jobs, evictions, confiscations, looting, terror, and the like. The Jewish leadership operated under the belief that it had to contend, alone, with an idiosyncratic but essentially Romanian regime, whose decisions were adopted in Bucharest, not Berlin.

The veteran Jewish community organization, which operated under two names (Union of Jewish Communities of Romania and Federation of Jewish Communities of Romania), stood at the forefront of the struggle against the Legionary regime. The two main Jewish political organizations — the Union of Romanian Jews (presided over by Filderman) and the Jewish Party — had been disbanded on 1 February 1938, when King Carol II set up his dictatorial regime banning all political parties. The Zionist movement, however, existed throughout the period of Legionary rule until August 1942. By nature, however, it was not equipped to lead the struggle against the Legionary regime. At the most, all it could do was help as many Jews as possible escape from Romania. "It was, therefore, natural that it maintained a passive attitude" about what was going on.[1] Moreover, at that time and shortly after there was a change of guard within the movement, following the aliyah (emigration) of the veteran, experienced leadership.[2] The leaders of the Zionist organization were divided in their attitude toward aliyah. Leon Mizrachi, the chairman of the Zionist executive, who left Romania in late March 1941, claimed that if a leader felt he was no longer useful and "someone else could step into his shoes," he should emigrate and "build up Eretz Israel."[3] There were, however, many elements in Eretz Israel who did not view this advice favorably: "We wish to express our great concern at the fact that all our most important members [of our movement] are leaving together for Eretz Israel. Since only a few select members of Romanian Jewry and of the Zionist movement will be entitled to emigrate to Eretz Israel, it is inconceivable that the erstwhile leaders of Zionism could abandon it [Romanian Jewry] to its own devices."[4]

These differences of approach vis-à-vis contemporary developments led to decisions, or a state of indecision, that ultimately paralyzed the few Zionist leaders who were capable of steering Romanian Jewry through the crisis. Failure to understand the true nature of the Soviet regime as well as the turmoil within the Zionist organization in Bukovina and Bessarabia caused most of the Zionist leaders in Czernowitz and Kishinev to stay put.[5] A year later most disappeared in the Russian steppes or were killed by the Germans and Romanians.

In Romania the Zionist organization and its branches and institutions confined their activities to promoting aliyah. This restriction in the scope of organizational activities was not merely a response to Legionary terror but also part of a deliberate policy not to provide the Legionnaires with any pretext for harming the Zionist organization.[6] Abraham Leib Zissu, a leader of the Zionist organization and later one of the main opponents of the Antonescu regime, "fled to Germany for six months . . . at the start of the Legionary regime, when the situation first became worrying."[7] Zissu, who had many assets in Germany and Switzerland, spent the better part of ten years (1928–38) with his family in Germany. He then evidently moved to Switzerland, returning to Romania only after the collapse of the Legionary regime.

In view of the above, Romanian Jewry could turn only to the Union of Jewish Communities of Romania and the Federation of Jewish Communities of Romania for help. Formally, the union represented the communities of the Old Kingdom (Regat) that had existed prior to 1919, while the federation represented all Romanian Jews, including the unions of Bessarabia, Bukovina, and Transylvania.[8] After the geopolitical changes in the summer of 1940, only the Jews of southern Bukovina (about 26,000 out of 93,000 Jews in Bukovina) and southern Transylvania (about 40,000 out of 155,000) remained within the federation. In his petitions to the authorities Filderman often spoke in the name of the union or the federation, or both, regardless of the community's location or the subject being discussed. When discussing issues affecting the entire Jewish population, he spoke under the aegis of the federation (consequently, almost all his petitions to Antonescu were in the Jewish Federation's name). Issues relating to the Jews of the Regat or petitions to ministers were submitted on behalf of both organizations. By speaking in the name of both organizations, Filderman hoped to get as many officials as possible recognized by the authorities, so as to facilitate the acquisition of telephone permits and car licenses and enhance their freedom of movement—which was, generally speaking, very restricted.[9] Filderman, who was the president of both organizations, had three secretaries—Emil Costiner, Matatias Carp, and Dadu Rosenkrantz—who were signatories to petitions to the authorities.

In May 1940 Filderman masterminded an attempt to set up a strong central framework capable of operating on the political and, especially, the economic planes. By early September 1940 the Jewish Federation's financial situation was critical, so much so that Filderman resigned in protest at the communities' failure to pay their share of ongoing expenses at the rate determined for them. Of the sixty-three communities that remained in Romania after its dismemberment, "only 11 paid the full amount; thirty communities paid only 37% of their dues, while 22 paid nothing at all." The organization, "which, for over a year, served as the Jews' only shield against the barrage of hatred pouring in from all sides," as Carp put it, was a modest institution "with a small directorate and a meager budget, which encountered dangerous apathy among the Jews."[10]

Fear of the situation of being abandoned by Filderman, the representative of Romanian Jewry par excellence, drove the community leaders, albeit grudgingly, to cover the deficit.[11] Filderman stressed that he was working "up to 16 hours a day on the community's behalf" and added that his resignation would be final "if the communities failed to acknowledge the critical nature of the situation."[12]

Legionary resolve versus Jewish apathy: this was the backdrop to the battle between Romanian Jewry and the authorities—a battle that aimed at dispossessing Romanian Jews, expelling them from the villages, depriving them of their livelihood, and "solving" the Jewish problem in ways that were not yet clear even to the Legionnaires. Antonescu, unlike the Legionnaires, was still open to logic and could be persuaded that antisemitic measures harmed the Romanian state, people, and economy and jeopardized his own plans. In order to lend substance to his arguments, Filderman conducted his own research into the political, social, and economic beliefs of state leaders (particularly Antonescu) as well as their habits, their friends, and whom they admired. He even attempted to predict their responses to events and challenges.

Filderman's claim that it was in the Romanians' interest to safeguard the rights of Jews was not new. It was an argument he had used right from the start of his career. As he wrote to Antonescu, "I have always defended my coreligionists' rights, provided their demands do not run counter to the economic interests of the country and of the Romanian people."[13] His training as a lawyer equipped him to foresee the impact of antisemitic legislation on the life of the Jews, and he began to prepare early on for such an eventuality. "We must collect data . . . through a well-organized Bureau of Statistics." At his recommendation, such a bureau was set up under M. D. Camil, an outstanding Jewish statistician.[14]

In the same vein, Filderman and the Jewish Federation arranged for Jewish journalists and lawyers to review the press, particularly the antisemitic press, on a daily basis. The idea was to comb the antisemitic press for antisemitic statements or references to antisemitic laws and levies designed to ruin the Jews, so as to enable the Jewish Federation to contest them. Press statements that ran counter to official policy were later used by the Jewish Federation as "incriminating" material in its petitions and memoranda to the authorities.[15]

After the establishment of the Legionary regime, it soon transpired that much courage was required to serve as a federation head or as board member or head of a community, especially in a remote locality. All community leaders were primary targets for intimidation, surveillance, torture, and expulsion. The Legionnaires saw the community leaders, rabbis, and synagogue officials as their main ideological rivals, whom they had to subdue before they could crush the entire community.

TACTICS ADOPTED BY THE JEWISH LEADERS

In Romania there was no real opposition to the Antonescu regime. At his trial in 1946 Antonescu declared with some justification that he had defended the opposition and that, even though he was portrayed as a dictator, he had not eliminated his rivals. "During my rule, there had never even been a strike," he added.[16] The opposition — individual leaders of the large parties that had been banned in 1938, who had turned down Antonescu's offer of government positions — took no action to topple Antonescu's regime until nearly 23 August 1944, the day King Mihai ordered the Conducător's arrest in his palace. Until then the opposition's dissidents had confined themselves to letters of protest or advice delivered to Antonescu via mediators or common friends and letters to Britain and the United States, frequently sent with Antonescu's knowledge and consent.

In view of the above, the almost daily reports and protests by the Jewish leadership to Antonescu concerning Legionary crimes were nothing short of acts of heroism. Filderman assumed personal responsibility for corroborating the accuracy of the reports. Antonescu, who at first relied only on the reports "of the Legionnaire from the Ministry of the Interior, had absolutely no idea of what was going on in the country." On 11 October 1944 the newspapers quoted General Aldea, who was appointed to investigate the Legionary ministers after the suppression of the rebellion, commenting on Antonescu's "total ignorance" of what was going on in the streets of his country. It was the ignorance of a military leader whose main concerns were foreign policy and rebuilding the army, who left everything else to his aides.[17] Filderman's memoranda and meetings, therefore, apprised Antonescu of facts he was not too happy to hear about. As a military man, Antonescu abhorred anything that disturbed the public order. Consequently, the gap between him and the Legionnaires widened. Filderman and the Jewish leadership were convinced, even at this early stage of the Holocaust, that any leader other than Antonescu spelled total extermination for the Jewish population, although the word *extermination* had not yet entered the European lexicon.[18] Matatias Carp summarized the Jewish strategy as follows: "The hundreds of memoranda on the suffering of the Jews throughout the country, that exposed the true extent of the terror and atrocities that the murderous and destructive Legionnaires perpetrated, were not meant to refine the Conducător's feral inclinations, but rather, to broaden his field of vision . . . so that he could see how the foundations of the country were being undermined, and with them, his personal status."[19]

The Legionnaires' actions, as we saw above, took the Jewish leadership by surprise. Outraged, they tried to soften the Legionary onslaught, which was but the first stage in the realization of the Romanian antisemitic dream. Federation leaders repeatedly stated how they suffered together with Romania and the Romanian people in these hard times. A memorandum on the expulsion of Jewish pupils and staff from state schools, submitted in early September, emphasized the sense of outrage at this terrible injustice perpetrated "against children who were loyal to the State" and against the professional competence of Jewish teachers "who had been educated in Romanian schools and who were imbued with Romanian sentiments."[20] Such reactions, however, made no impression on the authorities. If anything, they were proof of the failure of the integrationist policy espoused by generations of assimilationist Jewish intellectuals.

Federation leaders, apart from Filderman, believed that this was a passing phenomenon. A study of the protocols of federation meetings shows that many of them did not yet understand that the very existence of the Jewish minority in Romania was at stake; they still believed that they were simply dealing with discriminatory laws. Filderman, on the other hand, realized that the main problems were not to do with education, synagogues, communities, and the like but with the danger of forced labor and the expulsion of tens of thousands of Jews from the villages, following the implementation of the Jewish Statute.[21] The regime's daily assault on Jewish property and livelihoods caused all strata of the Jewish public to storm the Jewish Federation's offices seeking advice and aid. Many (ironically, mostly simple folk) understood that this was not a passing phenomenon but a true war and that the authorities wanted to deprive them of their livelihood, starve them, dispossess them of their houses, and expel them from their localities. Many Jews risked their lives to travel to Bucharest by train in order to report on the situation, while others sent lengthy descriptions of their suffering to Filderman, asking him to find a swift solution. Neither Filderman nor the Jewish Federation, however, was able to offer them salvation, and they had no choice but to turn them away empty-handed, to the petitioners' great resentment.

Filderman tried to arrange a meeting with Antonescu in order to present the anti-Jewish campaign as part of a Romanian problem that would, in the final analysis, be detrimental to Romania's economy and well-being. Thanks to his ties with Romanian politicians, he was granted an audience with the Conducător on 14 September 1940—the day the National-Legionary Regime was established. Antonescu, who believed that world Jewry was responsible for the downfall of the Goga-Cuza government, asked Filderman "to order your coreligionists not to sabotage the government." Filderman was surprised by the general's lack of political savvy. "He did not understand that the [international] political situation had changed since 1938, and that Europe was currently under Nazi control, and there was no longer anyone to whom one could address complaints about the rampage of Romanian antisemitism."[22] Antonescu ended the talk with the following promise, which later served as a basis for demands by the Jewish leadership: "If your coreligionists will not sabotage the government, whether directly or behind the scenes, politically or economically, the Jewish population shall not suffer at all. General Antonescu's word is law."[23] His letter, which arrived four days after the meeting, caused euphoria among the Jews, but the promises he made did not stand up.

The Romanian establishment, especially its antisemitic element, had always favored the idea of Jewish emigration. When Antonescu raised the idea in his first meeting with Filderman, the latter retorted that in 1937, when emigration from Romania had been feasible, the General Staff had foiled his emigration plan because "it was reluctant to lose a hundred thousand soldiers on the eve of war," and now there was no country willing to accept the Jews. However, continued Filderman, "the number of Jews has dwindled enormously since then, and I will order the relevant committee to adapt the former plan to current circumstances so that as soon as large-scale emigration becomes possible, the first transports of Jews can leave."[24]

In October 1940 the Jewish leadership realized that it was powerless to prevent the confiscation of property or dismissals from jobs, even where such acts were illegal and even in cases where Antonescu himself intervened. For example, even though Antonescu ordered the removal of notices in the town of Călăraşi calling for a boycott of Jewish stores, the boycott was not revoked but spread throughout Romania. Antonescu intervened mostly in cases involving disturbances of the public order, harm to the country's institutions, or excesses by the Legionary police. On 4 October, in the wake of Filderman's protests, he instructed Rioşanu, the deputy minister of the interior, to inform police commanders throughout the country that "the Legionary policy or any other green-shirt [Legionary] organization was forbidden to carry out arrests or conduct house-to-house searches or any other activities that were subject to the jurisdiction of the Ministry of the Interior or the Security police."[25] This order was never obeyed, partly because the Legionary police disregarded it and partly because much of the ordinary police force was already under Legionary control.

In guiding the community's desperate struggle for survival, the Jewish leadership, especially Filderman, was partly successful. Although Filderman symbolized decades of attempts at Jewish integration into Romanian society and was considered assimilationist by his Zionist rivals, he read the Romanian political map accurately and managed to use the Jewish problem to drive a wedge between warring camps within the government. He achieved this without betraying Jewish values and without degrading himself or the few who helped him in this desperate attempt to save the lives, if not the property, of the Jews.

During this struggle for survival Romanian Jewry exposed its weaknesses, its trivial concerns, and its Diaspora mentality of fearfulness, subservience, and insularity. The success and heroism of the Jewish leadership in Romania can only be evaluated against the Jewish leadership's response to the fascist threat in other countries. Such a comparative study has yet to be undertaken.

The Jewish Federation was unable to prevent the expulsion of Jews from villages or the theft of their livelihoods and property. It was unable to prevent the passage of antisemitic laws, the dismissal of Jews from their jobs, or the wave of antisemitic fervor that engulfed not only Cuza and Codreanu's disciples but also entire sectors of Romanian society. And yet, in a country wherein the Holocaust was symbolized by severed limbs and violated corpses strung on meat hooks in abattoirs, the Jewish leadership deserves some credit for the fact that the vast majority of Jews remained alive — albeit stripped of their possessions, beaten, and tortured. Moshe Ussoskin, who emigrated to Eretz Israel at the time at Filderman's instigation, summarized Filderman's role as follows: "The Jew in the street saw Dr. Filderman as the symbol of his own security."[26]

13

The Political and Ideological Foundations of the Antonescu Regime

This chapter and the next shall cover the period between the suppression of the Legionary rebellion on 24 January 1941 and the beginning of Romania's active participation in Germany's war against the Soviet Union on 22 June 1941. During this period Antonescu ruled Romania single-handedly. His dictatorship was based on control of the army, Hitler's trust in him, and his popularity with the masses, as one who had saved Romania in September 1940 from the fate of neighboring Poland and Yugoslavia (occupation and division). In many ways this period marked the transition from a right-wing dictatorial regime based on nationalist and antisemitic principles to an out-and-out fascist regime (albeit without a fascist party) that perpetrated war crimes and crimes against humanity.

Antonescu himself described his regime as "the totalitarian national regime, a regime of order and national and social revival."[1] An outcome of the political and social circumstances that evolved in Romania in the thirties, this regime sought to realize the national aspirations that preceded the crisis of June 1940 and precipitated Antonescu to power. This regime owed its genesis and existence to Nazi domination of Eastern Europe.

The Antonescu regime cannot be easily understood or classified due to its inherent ideological contradictions and idiosyncrasies that distinguished it from other fascist regimes in Europe. On the face of it, a regime that abolished parliament, aligned itself with the Axis countries, joined the war against the Soviet Union, adopted the Final Solution in part of its territory, and passed antisemitic and racist laws was a fascist regime. A series of facts complicate the issue, however: the Antonescu regime followed in the wake of a similar, albeit weaker, dictatorial regime (King Carol II's). All Antonescu did, in fact, was abolish a parliament that had not been elected democratically and was not representative of the people's will. Moreover, he based his antisemitic legislation on antisemitic laws that had been promulgated by the previous regime, such as the Jewish Statute of 9 August 1940.

Antonescu and his ministers never considered themselves or their regime fascist. On the contrary, they brutally neutralized the Romanian fascist movement; destroyed its apparatus; dispersed, suppressed, and outlawed its members; condemned its terror methods; and alluded to it as a Nazi stooge. The political and ideological foundations of Antonescu's regime were laid before his time by intellectuals and established right-wing movements, politicians who despised democracy or at least Romanian-type democracy, the nationalist organizations and parties that were set up in the thirties, and finally by the king himself, with his loathing of Romanian democracy and its politicians and his dictatorial leanings.

No wonder, then, that in February 1941 most Romanians did not feel that an illegitimate power had taken over, a foreign power that was alien to the tradition of Romanian democracy and served German interests. On the contrary, there was a general sense of relief and gratitude to Antonescu for having suppressed the Legionnaires without turning the country into a German satellite to be carved up among its neighbors. In the years leading up to the establishment of the Antonescu regime, there had been a gradual erosion of the principles that underpinned democracy and the parliamentary system. Many Romanians throughout the social strata were put off by politicians, whom they perceived as lacking moral fiber, and many even questioned the desirability of a free press. The corruption that existed at all levels of government became synonymous with democracy in general. At the same time, there was greater public tolerance of verbal and physical expressions of extremism by people and organizations working for the "national idea."

Throughout the thirties, politicians, intellectuals, journalists, organizations, and the press took up the refrain of a leadership crisis. They demanded the dissolution of parliament, the reinstatement of censorship, and the strengthening of the police, gendarmerie, and army. They provided fodder for the king's dictatorial tendencies and his contempt of politicians. These circles were marked by a sense of disillusionment and frustration stemming from the regime's failure to realize Romanians' national aspirations and from the erosion of Romanian national interests under a regime that did not uphold the political and spiritual traditions of the Romanian people.

These fissures in the democratic system were amplified by Codreanu and his associates, who, in their blind hatred of Jews, lured an entire generation or two into the mesh of totalitarianism. They justified their hatred of democracy by claiming that it led to Jewish control of the Romanian state, enriched a group of immoral politicians and businessmen who had sold out to the Jews, enslaved the economy and the state, and subjected the souls of Romanians to foreign control. The struggle that these circles waged against democracy, the political parties, politicians, the press, journalists, and intellectuals and against all forms of government that were based on compromise assumed a murderous and terrorist guise that was alien to the Romanians and Romanian political life, despite all its shortcomings.

The Jewish Statute, which was passed before Antonescu became head of state, introduced racism into Romanian legislation. It was the basis for the Romanian definition of a Jew, "based on the hypothesis that a nation is not composed of one race only, but of a mixture of races."[2] Hence the need to define the nation on the basis of "blood" and religion.

Nicolae Davidescu, a right-wing journalist and ideologue who became active in the midthirties, wrote that race "is not an absolute concept" and that every European nation was composed of a mixture of peoples and races. The Germans, too, he added, had Slavic blood that came "from east of the River Elba." Against this he posited the idea of nation and nationalism as elements that "were shared by the majority of the people, and that created a community of interests, sorrows and joys," a shared past and a common future.[3] Ovidiu Vlădescu, secretary general in the prime minister's office and a lecturer at Bucharest University, also attempted to provide a definition of *nation* in the Antonescu regime. In a broadcast on Radio Bucharest, he defined the characteristics of a nation as a shared ethnic and religious origin, the memory of a shared past, and the expectation of a shared future, adding that there were many differences even within a single race.[4]

This uncertainty and even official restraint regarding race and Nazi racist theories was a feature of the Antonescu regime throughout its existence. This does not imply that the Jews were able to change their wretched status or that Antonescu was not a racist. On the contrary, Antonescu's desire to purge the country of Gypsies, tens of thousands of whom were expelled with the Jews to Transnistria, was inspired mainly by racist considerations.[5]

This regime considered itself to be continuing the objectives of Romanian fascism as preached by Cuza and incipiently implemented by Goga. The regime set up by Antonescu rejected democracy, parliament and parties, the free press, and the right of individuals to determine their fate—as well as the Legionary movement. This seeming paradox can be explained as follows. Although Antonescu rejected the Legionnaires' modus operandi and method of governance and their leaders' behavior, he did not reject the Iron Guard's nationalist doctrine or Codreanu's heritage.

Antonescu's regime was based on this antisemitic heritage rather than on the principles of National Socialism. Indeed, he was always very careful to refrain from any reference to racial theories. He was convinced that it was his destiny to restore Romania to its roots and traditions, to rehabilitate a system of government that had been undermined by irresponsible Romanian politicians, and to solve social and national problems that had been created by a policy that ran counter to Romanian interests. These beliefs were predicated on his conviction that he was the redeemer of Romania and of the Romanian people.

Antonescu's foreign policy, which was governed by his wish to realize the national aspirations of the Romanians, including those who were under foreign rule, was also an expression of his political outlook and his aversion to democracy. At the start of the war he was convinced that only his alliance with Germany in its war against the Soviet Union would ensure the return of Bessarabia and Bukovina, and later also northern Transylvania, through negotiations or, if necessary, by brute force. On the eve of the war against the Soviet Union Antonescu believed that, having set up a stable government and quietly prepared a revamped army for war, he was about to realize his third objective, which he defined unambiguously as follows: "First eastwards, by brute force; then westwards, at the green table or by the sword."[6]

During the initial stages of the war Antonescu represented the broadest Romanian national consensus, which embraced the entire political spectrum apart from the Communists. This created an equation between the regime's existence and the realization of the Romanians' national aspirations. Unlike the opposition, which supported joining the war only for the sake of liberating Romanian territories, Antonescu was convinced that his foreign policy was correct. He accused the "politicians" of having failed to adapt to the tremendous changes that were sweeping through Europe and of having failed to discard, while there was still time, a policy "based on [an alliance with] the governments of the western democratic powers and inspired by the pacifist delusions propagated by that institution in Geneva [the League of Nations]."[7]

At the pinnacle of his power Antonescu attributed the insularity of Romanian foreign policy to the politicians' inability "to devise a foreign policy that supported the totalitarian powers, since such a policy contradicted the foundations of democracy." The parties' fear of dissolution, he claimed, caused them to prefer their narrow interests to the national weal. What was needed was an internal structural change, a new regime that would alter Romania's system of alliances and earn the recognition and cooperation of the fascist powers: "The new totalitarian regime I established on 6 September [1940] demands, inter alia, this right. . . . Any policy other than a pro-Axis policy would inevitably have led us to a fate similar to that of Poland."[8]

During the initial stages of the war, influenced by easy victories and ideological ties with the Nazi regime, Antonescu, and even more so his deputy, Mihai Antonescu, aligned themselves with the ideological war the Nazis were waging against the Slavic nations, Communism, and the Jews, thereby weakening Romania's justification for participating in the war—the liberation of its land. The opposition, especially Iuliu Maniu, condemned statements that turned Romania's participation in the war, even at the initial stage (for the liberation of Bessarabia and Bukovina), into a "holy war [against] the Soviet Union's sociopolitical system." They added, "Let us reserve the holy war for a Greater Romania with all its territories."[9] Note that at the start of the Antonescu regime, Antonescu enjoyed the silent, and sometimes even semipublic, consent of the leaders of the opposition. "The Head of State is honest and patriotic . . . and he deserves our full support," declared Constantin Brătianu to his associates on 14 February 1941. "He [Antonescu] is the only person capable of running the country under current conditions at home and abroad."[10]

Until late August 1941, when the Romanian army crossed the Dniester River (Romania's former border), Maniu and Brătianu supported Antonescu in the belief that his military government was the best solution under the prevailing circumstances. At the time, none of his internal critics, including Maniu, believed that any other policy was viable. The Conducător occasionally taunted the two "politicians" in a sarcastic vein, suggesting they take over and implement a different policy if they could.[11] He clung to power until the last moment, however, because he did not trust the Soviets' assurances regarding the independence and sovereignty of Romania.

Despite the painful economic concessions he was forced to make to the Germans, Antonescu was supported by the Romanian bourgeoisie—industrialists, bankers, capitalists, shareholders, and large factory owners—many of whom had thrived under his government. His Romanization policy benefited them, enriched them, removed competition by talented individuals, and turned many government officials and their supporters into owners and shareholders of Jewish factories, companies, and businesses. Unlike other fascist regimes, however, the Antonescu regime did not intervene in the country's economic life. Antonescu did not try to reform the economy or adapt it to the regime's needs other than those needs resulting from the war. His regime put an end to the Legionary attempt to build a totalitarian economy and, as far as possible, resisted Germany's attempts to seize control of the country's economy and subordinate it to the Reich's needs.

After forbidding Jews to exercise their professions, the regime handed over their practices and clientele to Romanian doctors, lawyers, pharmacists, dentists, engineers, architects, chemists, laboratory technicians, teachers, and unemployed members of the clergy, as well as graduates of the various vocational and high schools. After the Legionnaires' ouster, Antonescu won over the productive elements of the Romanian intelligentsia without harming members of King Carol II's Old Guard, who had been demoted by the Legionnaires. Antonescu never outlawed outstanding intellectuals, even if they were identified with previous regimes.

Losses at the front (including army officers) and the recruitment of intellectuals left a power vacuum that was filled by young (and not so young) candidates, who enjoyed various perks. The ideology of the Antonescu regime—which became more nationalist and less fascist as the war progressed and the Germans became weaker—was acceptable to most of the Romanian intelligentsia, which chose to see it as part of the national cultural heritage. At the same time, Romania's democratic opposition was not strong enough to overthrow the dictatorial regime. Moreover, not every intellectual appointed to the government was necessarily a fascist or antisemite, and all cabinet members were able to tender their resignation without any fear of the consequences. Indeed, some officials resigned for reasons of conscience.[12] It is clear, therefore, that Romania was inherently different from Nazi Germany in terms of personal responsibility for crimes against the Jewish people.

After the Legionnaires' ejection, the Antonescu regime did nothing to mitigate the attacks against Jews and Judaism. These attacks were designed to delegitimize "Jewish values" (especially humanity), which distorted "true" Christianity and enabled the Jews to rule Christian nations. This smear campaign, in which Mihai Antonescu also participated, frequently resorted to terms such as *Satan, humanity, Christianity, Freemasons, converts, enemies of Jesus, Talmud,* and the like. The image of the Jew–Satan continued to appear in articles in the Christian antisemitic press. "The Jewish Satan is the cruelest enemy of Christianity," stated one such article.[13] The antisemitic press also condemned attempts by Jews to convert to Christianity, on the pretext of safeguarding "the ethnic purity of the people and the sanctity of the Church."[14]

14

The Government's Attitude toward the Jews

IDEOLOGY AND POLICY

The ouster of the Legionnaires did nothing to change the Antonescu regime's attitude toward the Jews. As an antisemitic newspaper hastened to clarify, the sense of relief felt by some Jews was based on a false premise, since Antonescu's confrontation with the Legionnaires and his campaign to restore order was not "intended to appease the Jewish communities."[1]

Antonescu's friend Alexandru C. Cuza was in the habit of reminding Romanians that it was he who had initiated the struggle against Romanian Jewry and that Antonescu was merely continuing what he had started. On the eve of the opening of the International Antisemitic Congress in Frankfurt in March 1941 Cuza declared the goal of antisemitic policy to be the expulsion of Jews—a goal Antonescu's government had not yet officially declared. "A solution to the Jewish problem is emerging. This solution is the expulsion of Jews from the midst of other nations and their forcible resettlement—since their religion prevents them leaving of their own free will—on their free land. All nationalists in the world must unite in order to expel the Jews forthwith."[2] The congress was attended by delegates from all occupied countries and German allies.

In calling on the nation to show remorse for the crimes committed by the Legionnaires during the Legionary revolt, Nicodim, the patriarch of the Romanian Orthodox Church, never once alluded to the main victims of these crimes.[3] Meanwhile, the government decided to conduct a population census that would enable it "to inspect the family from both a racial and spiritual perspective," in order to "purify the nation once [and] for all from Semitic infiltrations."[4] After the suppression of the Legionnaires, Nichifor Crainic, the minister of propaganda (1 April–27 May 1941) summed up government policy as follows: "We want to be masters of our country . . . the local spirit must struggle to purge the country of Jews."[5]

In view of the above, how did the Antonescu regime differ from the National-Legionary regime (also headed by Antonescu) in its attitude toward the Jews? Although both wished to purge the country of Jews, the Antonescu regime proposed a systematic and final solution to the Jewish question — one that the state would initiate and implement to the end. "What will the hundreds of thousands of Jews who have been removed from their sources of livelihood do, especially since the nationalization of apartments is just the first of similar measures? At present, timorous gangs of Yids are hanging around the streets, in the hope of finding a loaf of bread. Once their savings are finished, what will they do? Romania's antisemitic policy shall be accomplished only after the foreigners leave our national land once [and] for all."[6]

For the Romanian nationalists the Antonescu regime symbolized the triumph of the national idea, a concept that embraced more than the mere expulsion of Jews. The new regime undertook to base all its policies on a more radical interpretation of the principle of Romanian ethnicity, Romanian values, Romanian virtues, the ideas of the great pioneers, "holy egotism" (as defined by Octavian Goga in 1920), and the promotion of Romanian interests in all spheres. This policy, while unfavorable to the Jews, did not advocate their extermination but at the most their deportation.

Ideologically speaking, the Romanians perceived the Antonescu regime as the incarnation of Cuza's brand of antisemitic nationalism. From a political standpoint Antonescu was perceived as the heir of the transitory Goga-Cuza government. No wonder, then, that the contemporary Romanian press highlighted the antisemitic nationalist accomplishments of the Goga-Cuza government while accusing Romanian Jewry, world Jewry, and the democratic powers of being responsible for its collapse.[7] The antisemitic press saw the new regime "as a national authoritarian regime — a regime [based] on Cuza's inspired doctrine" — one that raised aloft "Cuza's ideological flag" under "the Conducător's astute leadership."[8]

Every generation, declared *Porunca Vremii* (the mouthpiece of Romanian antisemitism), believes that history begins with it and that the present eclipses the past. This is not so, however. History merely repeats itself. "The nation's foremost intellectuals have risen up against the foreigners. No doubt had Mihai Eminescu not been antisemitic, he would not have suffered the fate he did. Nor is he the only one to have been crucified for his national beliefs. . . . Who toppled Goga's glorious, nationalist regime in late 1937?"[9] The press celebrated the victory of the "national idea" over the Jews and published speeches and declarations by the Precursorii — intellectuals and politicians who objected to a Jewish presence in Romania, opposed civil rights for Jews, and favored anything that would curb Jewish "expansionism."[10]

The nationalists perceived the Antonescu regime as the symbol of the realization of the antisemitic dream: namely, the expulsion of Jews from Romania (although how this was to be accomplished was not specified). The web of restrictions and prohibitions that antisemitic legislation wove around the Jews, on top of the delegitimization of the Jews during the thirties, turned them into nonentities. No wonder, then, that the Antonescu regime and public discourse bandied around terms such as *universal values*, *morality*, and *humanity* without feeling the need to justify the absence of these values in their dealings with Jews. For over a decade Jews had been banished from the national conscience, and double standards were the order of the day. Romanian society, wrote a journalist who was not antisemitic, was suffering a crisis fueled by hatred. Only a return to national traditions could solve this crisis. "We must resuscitate our Romanian faith, humanity and morality."[11]

Xenophobia, wrote Nicolae Davidescu, a famous nationalist ideologue, "is a sentiment unknown to us."[12] And yet all government echelons were aware that "the nationalist and authoritarian principles" that guided Romania, according to the minister of labor, health, and social services, were diametrically opposed to the "spirit of the democratic, anti-nationalist, foreign State," in the words of the journalist Pamfil Șeicaru. Such principles were also antisemitic.[13]

It was Antonescu who determined the scope and pace of implementation of the antisemitic policy he launched as part of the fulfillment of the "national idea," as the Precursorii put it. After the Legionnaires' expulsion from the government, it was Ion Antonescu, aided by Mihai Antonescu, who directed Jewish affairs, as well as all other matters of state. Ion Antonescu's antisemitic views were shared by many ministers, district prefects, police officers, and mayors, who themselves initiated antisemitic measures, either in support of the regime or from personal conviction.

Leaving aside the hypocrisy of the claim that the Romanization policy was an act of justice, Antonescu simply continued the policy he had launched at the start of his career as a dictator, before the Legionnaires turned it into a competition for Jewish property in which terror, torture, and murder were means that justified the end. The main features of this policy were:

1. A gradual and controlled continuation of the policy of excluding Jews from all walks of life. Such efforts began with the Romanization policy of the Goga-Cuza government and were later resumed by the National-Legionary government. The difference this time was that

the government resorted to means such as legislation and the judiciary rather than force and terror. Antisemitic legislation and Romanization continued throughout the Antonescu regime, without reprieve.

2. Regulation of the pace and scope of Romanization so as not to harm the economy, war preparations, or the interests of the population. This circumspection grew out of the government's erroneous belief in the enormous economic power wielded by Romanian Jewry, a belief that was far from the truth, especially in the post-Legionary period.

3. Presentation of the antisemitic program as part of a plan to rehabilitate the nation, create a middle class, and promote Romanian commerce. This plan was meant to remedy all the shortcomings of Romanian society, many of which the Precursorii blamed on the Jews. The Jewish policy was, therefore, an integral part of the government's internal policy. It was also perhaps the only area in which the government could carry out reforms and keep its promises.

4. Antonescu's hypocrisy in furthering his aims. At this time Antonescu still felt obliged to keep the promises he had given Filderman (see chap. 12), but he lied to Filderman and even blamed the Nazis for the anti-Jewish measures he had personally ordered. An illustration of his hypocrisy was the way he used the derogatory term *jidani* (Yid) in government sessions, private conversation, internal documents, correspondence, and written comments in the margins of reports while using the term *evrei* (the regular term for Jew) in his increasingly infrequent meetings with Filderman and other Jewish personalities. It is worth noting, however, that certain categories of Jews "who had made a real contribution to the country," particularly decorated veterans, were exempted from the antisemitic legislation.

5. A waging of war against the Jewish religion, as well as against Jews, pursued by the Antonescu regime as heir to the Cuza-Goga ideology. This war was based on the antisemitic perception of the Jewish faith and Jewish values as the work of the devil, repugnant, and diametrically opposed to Christian values. The campaign was spearheaded by newspapers and journalists, leaders of the Romanian Orthodox Church, and members of the fascist establishment. Most Romanian intellectuals dissociated themselves from the campaign against Judaism, if not from the campaign against Jews.

6. The victimization and scapegoating of Jews by government authorities, semi-official organizations, and the press. Until mid-1943 Jews were presented as the main cause of the country's internal problems,

especially the food shortage and poor living conditions. In reality, these problems were the by-product of Antonescu's growing commitments to Hitler and the Third Reich.[14]

The above notwithstanding, the Antonescu regime was not the most extreme expression of Romanian nationalism. There were more fanatical circles that, governed by sheer hatred and cruelty, were prepared to attack Jews without any logic or even expediency. Antonescu, on the other hand, was guided by a semblance of logic (at least until the summer of 1942 and at least in his policy toward the Jews of the Regat and southern Transylvania) and by a concern for the Romanian people. In this he differed from the politically emasculated former Legionaries and followers of Cuza, who, impatient with the slow pace of Romanization, were infused with a hatred that defied logic. No wonder, then, that throughout the war the Jews were pursued by fear of the worse alternative—the Legionary alternative—avoidance of which depended on Hitler and his policy toward the Antonescu regime.

EXPROPRIATIONS, DISMISSALS, AND ATTEMPTED DEPORTATIONS

Despite Antonescu's anti-Legionary policy, he did not order the return of confiscated property but allowed the Romanians to keep it, through a variety of bureaucratic and legislative expedients that eschewed violence. From 6 September 1940 until the end of the National-Legionary regime, most Romanian Jews were plunged into a state of extreme poverty. In addition to direct damages totaling over 21 billion lei (over $100 million, according to official exchange rates), they also suffered indirect damage due to loss of income and livelihood.[15] Their poverty notwithstanding, Antonescu continued to believe that the Jews controlled the country's economy.

The exclusion of Jews from various spheres of activity (one of the underpinnings of the national idea) took different forms. It began with the ban on Jews participating in two referenda, the first in March, after the Legionnaires were ousted from the government, and the second on 9 November 1941, after the end of the first campaign on the eastern front.[16] All Romanians "except for Jews and women" participated in these referenda, which Antonescu held to obtain *post facto* approval of his policies. In another anti-Jewish development, the security police ordered all Jewish passports to bear the stamp *evreu* (Jew), thereby becoming the second official document to bear the red stamp (reserve ID cards being the first).[17]

The Antonescu regime reaped the fruit of the Romanization policy initiated by the Goga-Cuza government and pursued by King Carol II and the National-Legionary government in connection with the dismissal of Jews from their professions and their workplaces. Those hardest hit were Jewish workers and professionals, especially lawyers, doctors, engineers, factory workers, and commercial employees, who were barred from exercising their professions or jobs.

Approximately 1,000 of Bucharest's 1,200 Jewish lawyers lost their livelihoods. Only about 150 (decorated veterans, Jews naturalized before a certain date, etc.) were allowed to continue working, and even then, only for other Jews. After the Bucharest pogrom a Jewish Telegraph Agency correspondent, writing about the plight of the lawyers and their families, described them as "destitute and desperate. They do not have the economic resources available to German Jews under similar circumstances."[18]

Doctors, too, were permitted to serve Jewish patients only. Since the Jewish doctor–patient ratio was high, some doctors were automatically deprived of a livelihood. According to the Jewish Telegraph Agency correspondent, only about one hundred of Bucharest's six hundred Jewish doctors were able to eke out a modest living for a while, "as long as their Jewish patients are not completely impoverished."[19] All the Jewish doctors at Bucharest's Elias Hospital (built in 1938 thanks to the donation of a Sephardic philanthropist who bequeathed all his wealth to the Romanian Academy) were dismissed as early as 1940, except for one who was dismissed in early 1941.

The Legionary Law for the Romanization of Labor, which was to be implemented by late 1941, added momentum to the purge of factories and businesses. "Many [Jewish workers] have already been discharged and this process continues from day to day. Members of this class have been unable to save anything, for in general their earnings have been below 5000 lei [$10–12] a month." Most Jewish breadwinners fell into this category. "They have no capital, and can live only as long as they can work and earn."[20]

Although the expulsion of Jews from Romania was never a serious option until the outbreak of war, once the option presented itself Antonescu did not hesitate to make use of it. Groups of Romanian Jews were brought nightly to the new border point in Dornești and forced to cross over at gunpoint. About one hundred Jews were killed in crossfire between the Romanian and Soviet border guards. Meanwhile, orders were given to expel 1,400 Jews with Polish or Nansen passports (passports issued by the League of Nations to stateless people). Upon the intervention of the Jewish Federation and Romanian institutions, Antonescu was finally forced to revoke the order. Unlike antisemitic legislation and the Romanization process, this operation lacked overall coordination and planning. This situation changed after 22 June 1941, due either to Nazi intervention or to the Romanians' desire for more coordinated action.

The Continuation of Romanization

The Antonescu regime sought to complete the Romanization process for the good of the Romanians, without resorting to violence, as the Legionnaires had done. In place of violent means, they introduced antisemitic legislation. The architects of this legislation described it as "a civilized approach," based on "the principle of respect for ownership" and conformance with the new spirit sweeping through Europe. This approach, which gave priority to the nation's interests at the Jews' expense, considered Jews as less than human, as non-persons, devoid of needs or rights. As a Romanian newspaper put it, "We may have bent the principles of law," and old legal textbooks may "point an accusatory finger at us," but "we have also expressed our highest esteem for true nationalism and the new European spirit of rebirth."[21]

Antisemitic legislation was meant to solve internal problems, boost the "plan for the rehabilitation of the nation," and turn more Romanians into property owners, as part of "a complete social pact" that the new regime wished to implement "without bloodshed, though a creative national spirit."[22] The philosophy behind the antisemitic legislation is best described by a Christian Orthodox priest, in this passage published in a former Legionary newspaper:

> Surely a nationalist State that controls the entire judiciary and legislature may dispense with the need to resort to violence in order to solve the Jewish problem! Surely we, who control the entire apparatus of government, including the legislature, and who have [the power] to apply the most draconian laws, need no longer break into a Yid's house, thrust a pistol into his chest, and yell [like a gangster] in the forest: Your money or you[r] life! Violence and looting have become redundant. Instead, the government shall systematically undermine the Yids' power through legal means, with justice and restraint. Jewish property shall legally and systematically be taken over by the State. This is the only effective way to destroy the life and property of the Jews.[23]

This philosophy underlay the antisemitic and racial legislation of the Antonescu regime. As early as April 1941 the Jewish leadership realized that the regime's laws were "far more extreme" than those of the National-Legionary government and that it was out to "destroy the Jews before it could even ensure their replacement" with Romanians—one of Antonescu's favorite slogans.[24] The cluster of antisemitic laws that governed all aspects of life had several common denominators:

1. the continued implementation of the antisemitic laws passed during Legionary rule, especially laws relating to the expropriation of property and Romanization of labor;
2. the continued expropriation of Jewish property by Romanians;
3. the passage of new, sometimes racist, antisemitic laws, as riders to previous laws;
4. the passage of laws designed to "legitimize" illegal actions; and
5. the passage of laws on forced labor and fines, at the military's instigation.

The antisemitic legislation was largely the handiwork of three ministers in Antonescu's government: Deputy Prime Minister Mihai Antonescu, Minister of Labor, Health, and Social Affairs Petre Tomescu (27 January 1941–23 August 1944; also dean of the Faculty of Medicine at Bucharest University), and Justice Minister Constantin C. Stoicescu (15 February 1941–8 August 1942; also professor of Roman law at Bucharest University). These three ministers together were responsible for drawing up new laws and riders to old laws in order to further the cause of Romanization.

One of the laws that specifically targeted Jews was a special provision of the Law for the Containment of Acts Endangering State Security, which specified a particularly harsh penalty for Jewish offenders.[25] In March 1941 Jews renting apartments from Christians were denied the extension on rental contracts that was granted to the population as a whole through a decree-law. Under this law, converts to Christianity or those with only one Jewish parent were also considered Jews.[26] (The previous law of 21 September 1940 had extended rental contracts for the entire population, regardless of ethnic origin.) On 24 February a special law determined that those wishing to register private and corporate businesses had to provide information on their ethnic origins to the Central Board of the Chambers of Commerce, already notorious for their hatred of Jews and for having cooperated with the Legionnaires in expropriating Jewish businesses and stores. The Chambers of Commerce reserved the right to reject applications "without having to account for their decision."[27]

In late April the Romanian Credit Institute (Institutul de Credit Românesc, ICR) was set up in order to grant credit to Romanian businessmen and industrialists who wished to buy up businesses from "foreigners."[28] By law, the institute (effectively a bank) was staffed exclusively by ethnic Romanians. An amendment to the Law for the Organization of the Grain Trade infused it with "a Romanian and Christian character," by banning all grain companies owned by Jews with foreign passports.[29] The grain trade was one of the industries in which Jews had been prominent since the nineteenth century, and the amendment affected thousands of Jews. Municipalities throughout Romania followed suit by introducing measures targeting wholesale meat merchants (which had no legal backing) and dismissing Jews from abattoirs and the meat trade.[30]

The impact of the dismissal of Jewish physicians was felt throughout Romania, which already suffered from a shortage of doctors, especially in provincial towns and villages.[31] The Association of Physicians occasionally advertised in the local press for doctors or dentists, while penalizing Jewish doctors for attending to non-Jewish patients.[32] Jewish physicians who gave in to the pleas of Romanians (mainly peasants) to see them or write out prescriptions for them were disciplined, as the minutes of the Disciplinary Committee of the Buzău Association of Physicians testify. This committee sat on 12 May 1941 to discuss the case of Boris Camerman, a Jewish physician who was indicted on three counts: (1) "examining and treating . . . a Christian patient"; (2) "examining and prescribing for a Christian patient"; and (3) "prescribing for a Christian patient." All three patients were from nearby villages. After a drawn-out debate the committee found the doctor guilty, and in accordance with the decree-law of 15 November 1940 he was suspended for two months.[33]

Intermarriage

On 9 April 1941 the Antonescu regime introduced a patently racist law forbidding civil servants to marry Jews or anyone who was not of ethnic Romanian extraction. Although the law contained a proviso authorizing the Ministry of Justice to issue marriage certificates in such cases "for exceptional reasons," the proviso did not extend to Romanians who wished to marry Jews. Anyone who violated the law was liable to be dismissed from his job. This law was partly based on the law of 9 August 1940 banning intermarriage.[34]

Antonescu, himself the architect of this law, ordered the minister of justice to instruct all ministers and government officials to draw up "lists of staff . . . who were married to Jews." The lists had to specify whether the Jewish spouse had converted to Christianity and the religion of the children.[35] In response to this request, lists began flowing in detailing hundreds of civil servants in the prefectures, municipalities, police, and so on who had intermarried (usually men marrying Jewish women).[36] The Ministry of Justice issued a circular explaining the law and its ramifications and clarifying that it applied to the military, too, "with one exception." Offenders in the military would be punished not under the new law but "under the Law on the Marriage of Army Personnel," the existence of which was hitherto unknown and which was formally enacted only after the outbreak of war.[37]

The minister of justice instructed the various ministries on the criteria for granting a marriage license to Romanians wishing to marry Germans or Italians "for exceptional reasons," adding the following qualification: "The law aspires to promote the foundations of Romanism in all spheres of the State's activities. On the other hand, the law demands allegiance from its functionaries. . . . Therefore, each functionary must give the matter due consideration before reaching a mature decision. In doing so, he may even have to choose between his job and his home."[38]

Following passage of this law some functionaries (policemen and other civil servants) did indeed divorce their Jewish wives. Many others, however, did not, in the hope that somehow or other the situation would resolve itself. On 22 May 1941 *Porunca Vremii* published a reminder for functionaries with Jewish wives who had not yet submitted marriage annulment forms.[39]

The offspring of mixed marriages was another problem that was even harder to resolve. The treatment of these children shed light on the way the Romanians in general, and the Romanian legislature in particular, viewed the issue of race. The baptized child of a Romanian (or Aryan) father and Jewish mother was considered Romanian (or Aryan) in all respects and was entitled to attend public schools and serve in the army.[40] The Bucharest Court of Justice set a legal precedent by ruling that F. Kell, a convert to Christianity who had a "pure" Aryan father and a Jewish mother, was not subject to the provisions of the Jewish Statute.[41] On the other hand, the child of a Jewish father was considered Jewish even if the child or the father, or both, had converted; the child was subject to all the provisions of antisemitic legislation.

The moderate press demanded clemency for all children of mixed marriages — "children who are not guilty for having been born and baptized here, educated in Romanian schools and for having served in our army. Sometimes, humanity and justice should also have a place in the legislator's considerations."[42] This plea fell on deaf ears, however. On 21 March 1941 a special rider was added to the Law of Religions of April 1928, stating that any person age eighteen or over was entitled to convert, except Jews. This was the result of the "the nation's" need, as an antisemitic paper put it, to preserve "purity of blood and religion."[43]

Laws Relating to Army Conscription and Expropriation of Jewish Homes

During this period the Romanian military passed a new law to solve the shortage of professional manpower caused by the expulsion of Jews from the army. While a law passed on 21 January subjected Jews to penalties and forced labor in lieu of army service, a new law of 13 February permitted the recruitment of physicians, pharmacists, engineers, architects, and other experts "in periods of prolonged mobilization and in wartime." Professionals thus recruited were granted certain rights depending on their rank and position and were allowed to wear army uniforms and insignia (yellow and white hexagonal metal stars, the number and size of which were determined by rank).[44] The Romanian army exploited this law to recruit Jewish professionals, especially doctors. The public became aware of this phenomenon only after Romanian soldiers, unable to believe that the army had recruited these Jewish officers, accused them of having insinuated themselves into the army under false pretenses and humiliated and attacked them. Such incidents took place during the pogroms in Iaşi and other places. Unlike Jews who were fired under the Law for the Romanization of Labor, who received no compensation, Jews dismissed from the standing army were awarded pensions under military law.[45]

The Law for the Expropriation of Urban Buildings Belonging to Jews, more popularly known as the Law for the Confiscation of Jewish Homes, completed the realization of the antisemitic dream that had begun under the Goga-Cuza government, limped along under the royal dictatorship, and picked up momentum under the National-Legionary government. This law, passed on 27 March 1941, declared that all houses, buildings, and built-up plots of land belonging to Jews were to be handed over to the state, except for those used for industrial purposes. Firms with one Jewish partner, or where at least 40 percent of the capital belonged to Jews, were defined as Jewish firms for the purposes of this law.

The law specified seven exceptional categories: (1) Jews who were naturalized before 15 August 1916 (when Romania joined the First World War); (2) decorated Jewish war veterans, or veterans who were noted for acts of bravery in Romania's wars; (3) war orphans; (4) Jews who had converted to Christianity twenty or more years prior to the law and who were married to Romanians; (5) Jews who had been converts for ten years or more, were married to Romanians, and had children; (6) single Jews who had been converts for at least thirty years; and (7) descendants of those in the preceding categories. Likewise, certain Jews who had "shown exceptional loyalty to the country" and their children were exempted from the law.[46] The exemptions were not automatic but were granted on an individual basis through special rulings.

Jewish First World War veterans were not exempted from the provisions of the law, possibly because they were too numerous or because the antisemitic lobby assumed that most had not fought on the front. The law forbade all Jews, irrespective of category (even those with preferred status), from purchasing houses, buildings, or plots of land. The homes of deceased Jews had to be sold within three months. Liens or mortgages on houses transferred to the state were waived. Jewish mortgage providers received no compensation; gentiles received three years' compensation from the rental of the property. Jews were allowed to remain in their homes until the expropriation took effect (since the state had to deal simultaneously with tens of thousands of apartments and buildings, this often took time). Jews whose homes were expropriated were granted compensation through government bonds that yielded a yearly interest of 3 percent but were frozen on the day they were issued. The property's value was assessed by the government on the basis of property taxes paid to the income tax authorities. This compensation was minimal and made a mockery of the poor.

The Law for the Expropriation of Jewish Apartments, which transferred to the state 75,387 apartments situated within the April 1941 borders, was the product of classical Romanian antisemitism.[47] The rationale behind the law, which accompanied its publication, as was customary, serves as a lesson in Romanian nationalism and hatred of Jews as it evolved in Romania for over a century. All articles, analyses, lectures, and radio broadcasts stressed that General Antonescu, the architect of this law, was implementing the nationalist platform in his own inimitable, "civilized" style and at his own pace.[48] In the final analysis, the only real difference between Antonescu and the Legionnaires was that while the former offered Jewish houses and jobs to the Romanians, the latter seized Jews' cash, jewelry, and personal items for themselves.

Privileged Jews and Category 2 Jews

The High Court of Appeals was asked to intervene several times during this period to extend the validity of the 1938 Law for the Revision of Citizenship passed by the Goga-Cuza government. It determined that the law "was consistent with the [1923] Constitution" and that all decisions to deprive the Jews of their citizenship adopted under this law were "legal and constitutional."[49] These rulings were handed down in cases where Jews, in a desperate attempt to save some of their property, appealed to the court for recognition of the naturalization that had been granted them in 1918 under the Marghiloman Law (Legea Marghiloman, the first attempt to prevent the granting of universal citizenship to Romanian Jews) or under the 1919 Citizenship Law (the second such attempt). The rulings stated that the 1923 Constitution revoked their citizenship retroactively, since such citizenship had not been granted under the terms of the peace agreements.

A legal precedent handed down by the appeals court would have broadened the categories of those eligible for citizenship and allowed them to hold on to some of their property. Many Jews turned to the administrative courts (Curtea Administrativă—parallel to the ordinary courts) in an attempt to obtain the desired "Category 2" status (decorated war veteran) that theoretically granted them certain rights, particularly home ownership. Very few, however, were successful. Most were rendered homeless. The only authorized Jewish newspaper—the Zionist *Renașterea Noastră* (Our revival)—kept its readers informed of court rulings on this issue. The courts rejected all claims for recognition of citizenship under the Marghiloman Law or under the 1919 Citizenship Law.[50]

In March 1941 the Bucharest court determined, in a legal precedent, that "Jewish physicians who had worked in hospitals during the [First World] War did not qualify for Category 2," although many Jewish doctors who had fought in the war had died of the typhus epidemic that had raged among the military at the time.[51] The Timișoara and Suceava courts ruled that Jewish youth who had joined the premilitary units as volunteers while under conscription age could be considered Category 2 citizens, but a similar application heard by the Bucharest court was rejected. The Administrative High Court, which dealt exclusively with such cases, accepted the application of a decorated volunteer.[52]

This travesty of justice with respect to Jews who appealed for recognition as Category 2 citizens was exacerbated by hypocrisy—a hypocrisy that hid behind a laconism that was perfected to an art. For example, the right of a decorated Jewish war veteran who had been recognized as a Category 2 Jew to own his apartment was revoked under the Law for the Expropriation of Jewish Apartments.[53] The claim of a Jewish woman whose father had already been naturalized in 1916 was turned down on the grounds that "a woman's status was determined by her husband's status," not by her father's status, although the law specifically stated that the offspring of Category 2 Jews also belonged to Category 2.[54] Similarly, the application of an orphaned man whose Jewish father had fallen on the front was rejected because, in the court's opinion, "the term minor applied only to those who were minors at the time of their father's death." As a consequence of this ruling, the petitioner lost his right to practice as a lawyer.[55] The Administrative High Court also determined a legal precedent whereby the children of a naturalized Jewish woman were not automatically considered Category 2 Jews, after several lower courts had ruled otherwise.[56]

Although this and several other laws awarded privileges to injured or disabled Jewish First World War veterans, in practice they were not always accorded these privileges. For over twenty years many military units refused to issue permits to injured or disabled Jews. "The regiments in Iași do not issue such permits" (although they had, as early as the twenties, granted certain benefits to holders of these permits).[57] For many years the War Ministry had omitted the Jewish dead or wounded from the lists they compiled, including them instead in the number of the missing. The issue of citizenship, which began as a struggle against antisemitism, turned into a question of life and death at the start of the Antonescu regime. With a rising tide of complaints by privileged Jews, Filderman appealed to the Ministry of National Defense, which promised to instruct the recruitment centers to issue permits to wounded Jewish veterans. The Union of Jewish Communities sent written notification of this promise to all the communities, but to no avail.

The head of the Iaşi recruitment center informed one of the Jewish community's leaders that he was not obliged to abide by the instructions he had received "since it was the responsibility of the commander of the unit in which the Jew had served at the time to adjudicate" each case on its own merits. "To date," continued the commander, "twenty years or more after [the end of] the last war, no Jew has managed to obtain a document confirming his war injury from the center [the capital] or from local headquarters."[58] The same was true regarding confirmation of military decorations, without which no privileges were granted.

The National Romanization Center

The laws for the expropriation, nationalization, and confiscation of Jewish property turned Romania into the owner of an extremely large and varied fortune. The huge number of properties, some of which housed factories, coupled with the ineptitude of the Romanization commissioners who had been appointed to take over and run these factories, convinced the architects of Romanization of the need to seek a different way of organizing nationalized property. There was a concomitant need for legislation to determine who would be the beneficiaries of these Jewish assets, in view of repeated promises by the government to help the Romanians at the Jews' expense.

Legislation was likewise introduced to grant credit to Romanians who wished to take over factories or firms and to pay "compensation" to their Jewish owners (usually in payments that stretched over dozens of years). On 2 May 1941 the Law for the Establishment of the National Romanization Center (Centrul Național de Românizare, NRC) was introduced to coordinate the smooth transfer of property. A few days later the Law for the Provisional Administration of the National Romanization Center was introduced.[59] The NRC was accountable to the Undersecretariat for Romanization and Colonization, which was responsible for monitoring the NRC, directing the Romanization police force, and dealing with administrative problems relating to minorities.[60] The Undersecretariat for Romanization was itself accountable to the prime minister's office, and its director was virtually of ministerial status. The NRC was put in charge of all assets seized by the state "under the expropriation laws" — that is, not only Jewish assets but also assets belonging to local Germans and Bulgarians after the repatriation of the Germans and the population exchange with Bulgaria.[61]

The Romanization of industry was more complex than the Romanization of homes because the country needed skilled Jewish manpower and know-how, especially in light of the shortage of industrial goods caused by the war. The NRC, which insinuated itself into almost all aspects of the life of the Jewish population, inspired terror and dread in the hearts of all Jews during the Antonescu regime.

Problems Caused by the Antisemitic Legislation

The antisemitic legislation promulgated by the Antonescu regime caused a great deal of confusion, particularly on the issue of Jewish identity, Romanian identity, and the definition of Jewish property, Jewish firms, privileged categories, and the like. For example, the Law for the Expropriation of Urban Buildings based its definition of a Jew on the Law for the Expropriation of Land, which differed slightly from the way Jews were defined by the Jewish Statute. In the decree-law annulling apprenticeship contracts the minister of justice defined anyone who had a Jewish grandparent as a Jew, unless the grandparents had converted to Christianity before the parents were born. The confusion among the various categories of exemption — soldiers who had fought on the front, Jews who had been naturalized before a certain date, or decorated war veterans — was even greater. A special memorandum on antisemitic legislation put out by the High Command in late 1941 referred to this confusion: "A study of the decree-laws defining the status of Jew in various contexts clearly indicates that the legislation is inconsistent, improvised, incomplete, unprofessional, imprecise, flawed, and altogether lacking in legal method." The examples quoted in the study were ones with which the Jewish Federation's jurists were already acquainted:

1. The legislator drew a juridical and political distinction between "those of Romanian blood" and regular Romanian citizens, without clarifying the criteria determining who was of "pure" Romanian blood.
2. The definition of Jew varied from one law to another.
3. The categories of privileged Jews who enjoyed various exemptions also varied from law to law.
4. Some decrees targeted Jewish companies without determining the criteria that defined a Jewish company.
5. In cases where a Jewish company was defined, the criteria varied from one decree to another.
6. The Decree for the Expropriation of Urban Land specified a number of exceptions that were germane to this law only.
7. The decree-law that banned marriage between Jews and people of "Romanian blood" failed to define who was an ethnic Romanian: "Is

someone who has a German or French grandfather considered to be of Romanian blood? Is he allowed to marry a Jewess? These issues of personal status have implications for the offspring of such unions."

8. Certain measures, such as the expulsion of Jews from theaters, were anchored in ministerial decrees only. The Romanization of healthcare professionals was the offshoot of a decree mandating the establishment of the Association of (Jewish) Physicians.

9. Various decrees, such as that relating to physicians, required certification of Romanian ethnic origin, without determining who counted as an ethnic Romanian or who was authorized to issue such certification. Moreover, while the law required certification of ethnic origin, an official announcement forbade anyone "to grant a document on ethnic [origin]."

10. The Jewish Statute of 9 August 1940 divided Jews into three "categories," with Jews in the second category still retaining some civil rights. "All decrees issued after 6 September 1940 disregard these categories."[62]

Some of the legal confusion was due to the haste with which the Antonescu regime issued the many laws (in an attempt to transfer Jewish property to Romanians as swiftly as possible), the initiatives adopted by the relevant ministers and institutions, and the lack of judicial coordination.

The antisemitic legislation of the Antonescu regime rested on the basic premise that there were two parallel systems of justice: one for the Romanians and one for the Jews. This double standard became possible once the Romanians ceased seeing Jews as human beings. Legislation that blatantly discriminated against Jews was presented by the legislature as the epitome of justice in Romanian law. For example, the nationalization of apartments was euphemistically described as a means of "consolidating the principle of the inviolability of ownership."[63] Time and again the Romanians were assured that the expropriation of Jewish homes in no way impinged on the right to private property, since "ownership is inviolable" and Romania "is a land of legality and humanism."[64] A law book published in early June 1941 and bearing the signature of Mihai Antonescu, the main architect of the antisemitic legislation, stated, inter alia: "Justice is the invisible testimony that God exists within us."[65]

15

Romanization (II)

On 26 February 1941 the Romanian press launched a campaign to publicize the achievements of the Antonescu regime. On the first day of the campaign the press focused on the expropriation of Jewish property, initiated under the National-Legionary government—the nationalization of land, flour mills, sawmills, and other rural industries.[1] The following day it vaunted "the nationalization of labor" and the dismissal of Jews from factories and businesses. The press, which was censored and received background material from the authorities, made much of "General Antonescu's accomplishments": namely, expropriation, nationalization, confiscation, dismissals, and segregation. Newspapers reported the hiring of tens of thousands of refugees in factories and businesses expropriated from rural Jews or on land confiscated from Jews. They saluted the government's effort to promote "Romanian commerce," as witnessed by the fact that the number of "pure" Romanian firms had risen by 21 percent between September 1940 and February 1941 compared to the same period the previous year.[2]

The Ministry of National Defense proudly announced the exclusion of Jews from the army and hinted at "forthcoming provisions," a veiled allusion to forced labor. It likewise bragged about the dismissal of all Jewish officers, NCOs, and skilled personnel from the regular army and the confiscation of 126 ships "owned by Jews or Jewish firms." The government, for its part, announced the Romanization of all propaganda and culture institutions that, prior to 6 September 1940, had been run by Jews and the "integral" Romanization of the Romanian printed word. Most Jewish-owned movie theaters (95 percent) and tour operators (75 percent) were taken over by Romanians. In the field of education, the government announced "a radical solution . . . to the Jewish problem," namely, the wholesale expulsion of Jewish teachers and pupils from Romanian schools and the establishment of Jewish schools with "exclusively Jewish staff, and which catered only to Jewish pupils." All private theaters were nationalized in an attempt to promote Romanian ethnic art (*curat românești*). In the field of healthcare, the Association of Physicians was reorganized to exclude Jewish doctors, who were allowed to treat Jews only. Jews were also forbidden to rent pharmacies.[3]

The implementation of Romanization was the regime's main goal in its domestic policy, just as the liberation of Transylvania was its main goal in its foreign policy. Antonescu clarified on a number of occasions that "the Romanization of economic life" was one of his regime's basic goals. The Conducător linked the principles of "integral nationalism" on which he had based his regime with the Romanian people's social problems, Romanization, and the solution of the Jewish problem. Unlike the Legionnaires, he undertook to carry out Romanization without violence, "systematically and consistently" (*metodic şi progresiv*), and he conditioned the removal of the Jews on their replacement by "local forces," namely, ethnic Romanians, in order not to undermine economic life.[4] Antonescu's method of robbery was presumed to be "civilized" (*civilizată*), in contrast to the "savage and criminal Legionary method."[5]

The government's tendency to harp on the progress of Romanization and the difference between Legionary tactics and its own was an indication of the failure of the antisemitic legislation to fully implement Romanization, as well as the enormity of the task that the government, as heir to the Cuzist legacy, had undertaken. The government wished not only to lay its hands on Jewish property—a feat easily accomplished through antisemitic legislation—but also to expropriate Jewish capital, purge all factories and industrial plants (some of which were still owned by Jews) of Jewish employees and professional staff, and drive Jewish physicians, engineers, pharmacists, architects, and other members of the liberal professions out of the labor market.

The Antonescu regime wished to deprive Jews in practice—after it had done so through legislative measures—of the right to free speech and the right to publish and disseminate their ideas. Likewise, following on the expropriation and Romanization of Jewish factories and firms, the regime attempted to set up new industries that were totally free of Jews. The regime offered easy credit terms and financial concessions to Romanians who wished to take over businesses, stores, and jobs that had formerly belonged to Jews. This colossal enterprise required a complete economic revolution, one that each successive government since Romanian independence had longed for but that none had been able or dared to implement. Despite the paucity of accurate data on the Jewish contribution to the Romanian economy in general, especially during the Antonescu regime, it is safe to assume that even after the expropriation and looting operations the Romanian economy still could not manage without Jewish experts, technicians, and skilled labor.

Another factor that the Legionary regime, and to some extent also the Antonescu regime, overlooked was the rivalry—both overt and covert—that existed between the Germans and the Romanians. The Germans (businessmen from the Reich or locals) were waiting for the right moment to take over Jewish factories and possibly entire industries from which Jews had been dismissed through the Romanization laws and illegal initiatives. In this contest the Romanians were the losers. This, and the fact that Romania was almost entirely under Germany's hegemony, made the architects of Romanization aware that in the balance of things Aryanization took precedence over Romanization. Along with the outbreak of war in June 1941, this led to an immediate deceleration in the pace and intensity of Romanization, which was already hampered by its failure to take into account true Romanian interests.

Between February and June 1941 the three economic objectives of Romanization were:

1. the expropriation of Jewish capital that remained in Jewish hands;
2. the Romanization of factory personnel; and
3. the limitation of Jewish involvement in economic life and all other possible spheres.

The decree-laws for the nationalization of Jewish property (land, forests, factories that processed agricultural produce, ships, and urban houses and buildings) were broadly interpreted as granting permission to expropriate Jewish capital, too. The decree-law of 4 March 1941 restricting the commercial freedom of Jewish factories and firms also sanctioned the confiscation of Jewish capital by ordering all company owners to deposit their stock in the National Bank of Romania for registration purposes.[6] By late March it was clear that "the National Bank and the Finance Ministry were refusing to return stocks and bonds deposited by Jews."[7] This law, therefore, served simply as a front for divesting Jews of the stock they had been unable to sell in time, or unable to sell illegally to Romanians or Germans at a loss after passage of the law. On 25 March a new decree-law stated that the stocks of shareholders who refused to disclose their identity and register shares in their name would be transferred to the state.[8] On 26 September 1941 all shares in travel and tour operations held by Jews were confiscated.[9]

The expropriation of Jewish firms and factories (except for factories processing agricultural produce, sawmills, lumber mills, flour mills, and alcohol refineries, which had already been nationalized) was further hampered by the lack of reliable data concerning Jewish involvement in the economy and by Mihai Antonescu's plans for "differential" Romanization, depending on the type of property being confiscated. In the ideological material he appended to the Law for the Establishment of the National Romanization Center, Mihai Antonescu specified, "The Romanization of certain types of property must be executed resolutely, systematically, speedily and authoritatively, while the Romanization of other [types of property] must be executed methodically, gradually and have sufficient financial backing." By the first type of property, Mihai Antonescu meant landed property (especially urban land), while by the second type of property he meant commercial and industrial property, which included also "productive assets." Mihai Antonescu's concern, one shared by Ion Antonescu, was that unless the nationalization of Jewish factories was accompanied by a concomitant investment in "capital, training, experience and funding," they would prove to be "dead assets."[10] The raison-d'être of the NRC was to prepare the infrastructure for such investment. It is thus easy to understand why, despite the rapid expropriation of most types of Jewish property, the expropriation of certain factories that relied on skill and expertise took place in a far more circumspect manner.

It is safe to say that the Romanian economy relied extensively on Jewish skilled labor and on factories established, maintained, run, and managed by Jews. Despite the absence of accurate data on the number of Jewish factories that were taken over by Romanians, Germans, or others, we know that in August 1944 some factories were still owned, even if partially, by Jews.

The composition of the Jewish professional workforce was a subject of considerable interest to the Army High Command, which conducted periodic surveys in order to determine how best to utilize the Jewish workforce for the purposes of forced labor. These surveys, the results of which were passed up through the political echelons, provide an accurate picture of Jews by profession and occupation. In May 1941, for example, the High Command reported that 74,240 out of a total of 300,000 Jews in Romania proper (excluding Bessarabia, northern Bukovina, and northern Transylvania) were professionals, students, and craftsmen. These statistics did not include those under the age of twenty-one or age fifty-two or over.

Less accurate data on the Romanian reliance on Jewish skilled labor is reflected in results from a survey of factories published the same year. For the purposes of the survey the factories were divided into two types — those employing over a hundred workers and those employing fewer than a hundred workers. The workers were divided not into Romanians and Jews but rather into Romanians, minorities (including Jews), and foreigners (holders of foreign passports, many of whom were Jews who had been deprived of their citizenship following the Goga-Cuza government's Law for the Revision of Citizenship). All factories in Bucharest employing Jews asked to be allowed to continue employing Jews. In Romania as a whole, 6,894 factories and plants that still employed Jews asked to be allowed to continue doing so. Press headlines on this issue elicited a furious response among the architects of Romanization, who, from February to June, were

TABLE 2. THE JEWISH WORKFORCE IN ROMANIA, 15 MAY 1941

Lawyers	761	Elementary school teachers	14
Architects	57	Postgraduates	34
Actors	29	Liberal professions	23,696
Chemists	22	Physicians	1,082
Accountants	194	High school teachers	81
Merchants	5,722	Artists	121
Dentists	519	Rabbis	122
Druggists	69	Students	2,220
Pharmacists	423	Yeshiva students	24
Bank clerks	1,043	Journalists	79
General clerks	8,872	Total	51,475
Commercial clerks	5,652		
Photographers	198	Jewish craftsmen	22,765
Engineers	441	Grand total	74,240

SOURCE: Table of the "situation of the Jews," drawn up on 15 May 1941 by the Army High Command, with a breakdown of the Jewish workforce by profession, in Ancel, *Documents*, vol. 10, doc. 20, p. 76. The craftsmen category includes Jews whose profession was unknown to the authorities. It follows that there were actually fewer craftsmen than indicated in the table.

responsible for the dismissal of about 4,100 Jewish factory workers in Bucharest alone.[11]

Later a more general picture emerged of the conflict between the dismissal of Jews on the one hand and the need for Jewish labor on the other. Table 3 provides official data on the various stages of the Romanization of factories and workshops (some of them owned by Jews) from the passage of the Law for the Romanization of Labor on 16 November 1940 to 1 March 1943.

Despite the dismissal of most Jews, a number of Jews still continued to work—sometimes in the same jobs—for a mere pittance. In the Army High Command's estimation, by late 1942 the Romanization of the national economy had been fully achieved in the case of agricultural and industrial property in the villages, only partly in the case of commercial property, and only 50 percent in the case of the Romanization of labor.[12]

On 1 March 1943 there were still 4,301 factories employing Jews. In publishing these data in March 1943, the undersecretary for labor attributed the number who remained employed to the difficulty of the task of Romanization and to the failure of the November 1940 law to lay down adequate penalties for infractions. Moreover, the war situation rendered the continued employment of Jews imperative "due to the conscription of [Romanian] youth who were meant to replace the

TABLE 3. NUMBER OF WORKERS AND CLERKS IN PRIVATELY OWNED
FACTORIES, NOVEMBER 1940–MARCH 1943

	In Romania		In Bucharest	
	Jews	Romanians	Jews	Romanians
16 November 1940	28,225	210,472	17,906	117,262
1 August 1941	21,137	—	—	—
31 December 1941	16,292	210,297	9,672	133,826
1 March 1943	5,608	214,016	3,019	142,708

SOURCE: *Timpul*, 4 June 1942; *Universul*, 13 June 1943; study of the Jewish problem in Romania
compiled by Division 1 of the Romanian army's High Command, undated, in Ancel, *Documents*,
vol. 10, doc. 107, p. 276. See also statistics on the Romanization of factory workers, 1940–42, drawn
up by Filderman, in his draft memoirs, YVA, Filderman Archive, P-6/58, p. 94. Of 6,508 Jews
who were still officially employed on 1 March 1943, 5,199 were clerical staff and 1,209 laborers.

Jews, and the shortage of Romanian experts."[13] At the same time, the undersecretary took credit for the establishment of vocational schools designed to train
Romanian youth to replace the few remaining Jewish employees.

The regime waged a stubborn war "to restrict the activity and number" of
Jewish craftsmen, according to a confidential report put out by the High Command.[14] This was achieved through legislation and through the recruitment of
Jews to forced labor. A law was passed forbidding extensions of the work permits
of Jewish craftsmen and laborers and another forbidding "Jews to learn a profession in industry, crafts, and commerce so as to prevent the rise of a new cadre of
Jewish craftsmen." Although the recruitment to forced labor may have met the
ideological requirements of Romanization, it did not solve the practical need for
skilled Jewish craftsmen. The need was so strong that some Jewish craftsmen
were reinstated in their jobs. These craftsmen were granted "exemptions from
forced labor" (that is, they were forced to pay a penalty for the right to work) or
employed in military industries, where, although not paid a salary, they could,
according to a tacit understanding, undertake private work.[15]

Nor did the engineers of Romanization completely accomplish their goal of
Romanizing commerce. Despite the offer of easy credit terms and tax concessions
to Romanians who wished to take over stores and businesses from Jews, there
was no significant response. Even so, a report published by the Ministry of the
National Economy in May 1942 on the "Romanization of Commerce" to the
effect that tens of thousands of Jewish businessmen were still working was grossly
inflated. A year earlier there had been a mere 5,722 Jewish merchants, and their

numbers were constantly on the decline. The Ministry of the National Economy, which studied ways of "reorganizing commerce" with a view to Romanizing it, was forced to admit that the full Romanization of commerce was a mammoth task that required, first and foremost, the establishment of basic vocational training courses. The ministry promised to set up business schools on the lines of the one in Galați. The National Bank of Romania, together with the Ministry of the National Economy and the undersecretary of state for Romanization, worked out a program for granting generous credit to ethnic Romanians who were willing to take over Jewish businesses.[16]

The results were disappointing. Ethnic Romanians failed to come forward in the hundreds to take over Jewish stores and businesses that had barely provided Jewish storekeepers and petty merchants with the means for survival. In certain parts of southern Transylvania and Walachia the government's plans were thwarted when Jewish stores and business were taken over by local Germans and Hungarians, not by ethnic Romanians. In discussing the reasons for the revocation of the plan to deport Jews to extermination camps in Poland, which was supposed to begin with the evacuation of Jews from Transylvania and Banat, we must bear in mind this aspect of the partial success of Romanization.

The Romanization of the economy was enthusiastically backed by Romanian capitalists and industrialists, irrespective of past party affiliation. The National Bank of Romania, which was still controlled by members of the Liberal Party, and an economics circle that was not aligned with the Antonescu regime but represented Romanian economic interests supported the government's Romanization policy. On 4 March 1941 an advisory council was set up under the Ministry of the National Economy, headed by the president of the High Court, a representative of the national bank, and a representative of the Ministry of the National Economy. The purpose of the council was to prevent foreigners (i.e., Germans) from taking over factories and firms and to ensure that the Romanian state had first choice in their acquisition.[17]

The Antonescu regime considered it its mission to openly turn its ethnic citizens into industrialists and businessmen at the expense of the Jews. It therefore made a point of stressing the link between Romanization and the national idea and adherence to the national goal, in its broadest sense.

INTELLECTUAL AND CULTURAL ROMANIZATION

The Antonescu regime continued the policy of excluding Jews from the country's intellectual life. The Romanization of the written word, the Romanization of the intellect, and the Romanization of the spirit that began under the Goga-Cuza government with the dismissal of Jewish journalists and the closure of Jewish newspapers continued under the royal dictatorship and gained momentum under Legionary rule. The Legionnaires barred Jewish intellectuals from all branches of Romanian cultural life—literature, education, the press, cinema, theater, and sport. Romanian intellectuals of Jewish extraction were forced to fall back on the Jewish community—a framework many had tried hard to escape. They were thrown back on the generosity of the Jewish community, Jewish philanthropists, and the few Romanian colleagues who had not totally abandoned them. The Antonescu regime attempted to Romanize its culture in the same way that it attempted to Romanize its industry and trade.

The antisemitic press continued its obsessive harping on the "damage" caused by Jewish authors and intellectuals who, after the First World War, had "infiltrated" Romanian cultural life and had "dallied" with new literary currents and ideas. The propaganda minister, Nichifor Crainic, was especially vindictive, claiming in an article published in Germany that "the Jewish spirit had, over the past twenty years, built a dividing wall" between Romanian and German culture and had created "a completely distorted image of Germany in order to drive a wedge between us and the Third Reich."[18]

Other "crimes" perpetrated by Jewish intellectuals, especially authors, were described bluntly by the antisemitic press and in a more refined but no less antisemitic manner by serious journals. Jewish authors, claimed *Porunca Vremii*, the organ of the antisemites, were attempting to destroy the values of the Romanian heritage and the local literary tradition and were contaminating the Romanian cultural environment with various intellectual frauds in an attempt to hasten the disintegration of society, a process they were promoting with "Satanic resolve."[19]

The Antonescu regime based its decisions on this kind of hyperbole rather than on the humanitarian outlook of many Romanian intellectuals. The latter, however, failed to speak out but instead tolerated and even collaborated with the regime, which rewarded them in turn with positions and honors. The issue of the attitude of Romania's intellectuals toward their Jewish colleagues and toward the regime's antisemitic policy is a complex one that is beyond the scope of this book.[20]

The policy of intellectual Romanization was consistently implemented throughout the Antonescu regime. On 13 November 1941 Mihai Antonescu, in his capacity as minister of propaganda, ordered that the matrices and records of "Jewish composers, authors or musicians" be destroyed.[21] He also ordered that a catalogue be drawn up of acceptable records and matrices. At the same time the Ministry of Propaganda began publishing lists of Jewish authors, which "for the next three years, shall be displayed on the bookshelves of Bucharest's large book stores."[22] In late December 1941 Liviu Rebreanu, director general of theaters and opera houses, sent a "last reminder" to all theater managers that "current laws and regulations banned Jews from undertaking any artistic activity other than in an exclusively Jewish environment."[23]

Cultural Romanization continued throughout the regime's rule and complemented the Romanization of property and labor. Cultural Romanization dealt a serious blow to Jewish intellectuals, who were convinced that their talent and love of Romanian culture had won them a place in Romanian culture and society. Although the attitude of Romanian intellectuals to this cultural Romanization was not unequivocal and was largely influenced by the progress of the war, in the final analysis the regime succeeded in winning over the intelligentsia. Many Romanian intellectuals were given positions and honors and felt reasonably at ease in the nationalist climate fostered by the regime, although many were not overtly antisemitic and some even came to the aid of their beleaguered Jewish colleagues.

16

The Antonescu Regime and the Final Solution, 1941–42

THE DEADLY TRIANGLE: ANTONESCU, THE LEGIONARY LEGACY, AND THE NAZIS

Between February and June 1941 Antonescu's policy and the fascist government reached a turning point that made it possible for them to adopt the Nazi Final Solution and actively participate in its implementation. Such a turning point in the government's antisemitic ideology could never have occurred without certain predisposing factors. Among these were Hitler's growing influence on the Romanian dictator, Antonescu's total identification with the Nazi regime as the antithesis of democratic liberalism, and the need to contend with the antisemitic Legionary legacy left behind by the fascist movement—the natural ally of the National Socialists—after its ouster from the political arena. Nor should one forget that at the time this turning point occurred and preparations were being made to implement the Final Solution in both Germany and Romania a large German expeditionary force—including many armored units—was stationed on Romanian soil.

In February the German military presence in Romania reached a peak, with the expeditionary force numbering 680,000 soldiers.[1] Indeed, the British ambassador closed the embassy after sending a letter to the government in Bucharest stating that his country no longer saw Romania as an independent state due to the large concentration of German troops in its territory.[2] Mussolini as well as the Budapest government considered Romania an occupied state (the latter notified all its embassies to this effect).[3] In a memorandum he sent to the Conducător, Constantin Brătianu stated, "We are under German occupation," adding that he knew full well that such a statement would anger the general.[4]

Antonescu, against Manfred von Killinger's advice and German pressure, had no intention whatsoever of rehabilitating the Legionary movement, assimilating it, or incorporating its members in his government. On the contrary, in his desire to rid the government of the Legionary presence, he hastened to set up a new government without them. In this context Antonescu again demonstrated his tactical skills, cunning, and hypocrisy by pulling the wool over the eyes of the leaders of the Nazi regime. He persuaded Killinger, for example, that "out of respect for the Army, it was impossible to integrate the Legionnaires into the government. The Army would not understand this." At the same time, he assured him that "the government would naturally be guided by the positive ideas that the healthy element of the Legionnaires wished to see prevail." He also promised to appoint a new leader for the Iron Guard—a promise he failed to keep.[5]

Antonescu did not forget the assistance that the Legionnaires received from the German secret services (the Gestapo, Sicherheitsdienst [SD], and SS) and various German diplomats. During the weeks following the Legion's suppression these envoys had hidden numerous leaders of the rebellion in the buildings they controlled and later smuggled them out of the country dressed in German uniforms.[6] In December 1942, at the height of the battle of Stalingrad, after Iron Guard leader Horia Sima had fled from Germany to Italy and there were fears in Bucharest of a Nazi-Legionnaire plot, Antonescu recalled the affair in a letter of 9 December 1942 to Marshal Erich von Manstein, the German commander sent to help the encircled German and Romanian troops on the outskirts of Stalingrad: "Your officers and NCOs, who were given an extremely warm welcome in this country, paid [us] back by arming the Legionnaires against me and covertly guiding them in their criminal actions with the aim of toppling the government and assassinating me. After the [suppression of the] rebellion, they disguised the leaders of the rebellion in German uniforms, and smuggled them out of the country, hidden in German trucks or among German soldiers."[7]

As he prepared to attack the Soviet Union, Hitler attached increasing importance to military considerations and therefore showed less interest in Antonescu's relationship with the Legionnaires. In practice, the Nazis were quite satisfied with Antonescu's achievements: he had restored calm, kept his economic agreements with Germany, and proved that he was able to fill the political void left by the Legionnaires, even without the existence of a fascist party. Romanian nationalism, together with incitement against Jews, Communists, and the many enemies of the Romanian state, filled this void.

The disappearance of the Iron Guard, therefore, did not leave an ideological void. As early as 19 April 1941 Killinger, speaking at a ceremony at the German legation in Bucharest to mark Hitler's birthday, stated that the führer considered Antonescu Romania's true representative and forbade any other Romanian party or movement to use the führer's name for its own purposes.[8] Antonescu, for his part, promised Killinger that he would govern the new Romanian state "on the basis of Legionary ideology."[9]

The radicalization of Antonescu's policy toward the Jews in 1941 was also prompted by personal consideration, in particular his acute sensitivity to his image in Nazi Germany—a sensitivity fueled by several real or rumored scandals in his past. One of the rumors spread by the Iron Guard was Antonescu's affiliation with the Freemasons, which, they claimed, rendered him unfit to serve as head of state. Other embarrassing episodes from his past were his service as military attaché to Britain and his pro-British and anti-German pronouncements at the time. Sima used these points against him in his confidential letter to Hitler on the eve of Antonescu's second meeting with the führer in January 1941.[10] Equally embarrassing was that Antonescu's military glory came from the battles he waged against the German army in the First World War.

There is evidence that Antonescu's alleged affiliation with the Freemasons was of considerable concern to the Nazi leaders in Berlin. On 17 February 1941, for example, Goebbels noted that Antonescu, who enjoyed Ribbentrop's support, had been unable to enlist the support of the Romanian people because he was not a fascist. Once again, Goebbels declared, "the Free Masons are forcing their way back into the old positions, and even the Jews are coming back. Poor Antonescu! Now that he has officially destroyed the Legionary character of the State. It is hard to say where things will lead if he continues in this unhappy direction." On 6 March, after Antonescu held a referendum to gain public support (Antonescu's policy was approved by a vast majority, as is customary in totalitarian regimes), Goebbels again derided the German Foreign Ministry and its diplomats, saying, "The Jews are becoming arrogant again. The generals and Free Masons rule."[11] In early February Killinger informed Antonescu that the Iron Guard leaders believed "he was surrounded by Free Masons."[12] The outgoing German ambassador, Wilhelm Fabricius, also referred to Legionary rumors of Antonescu's closeness with the Freemasons and Jews. These accusations, which we now know to be false, played a major part in shaping Antonescu's attitude toward the Jewish question in the months leading up to the German invasion of the Soviet Union.

The Conducător himself strongly denied any affiliation with the Freemasons. In early February 1941, even before the establishment of the new regime, the Presidency of the Council of Ministers announced, "Anyone who dares to imply that General Antonescu's government has, or had, members who were Free Masons, shall be brought to justice." Until the fall of 1941 the censored Romanian press harped continuously on the theme. So keen was Antonescu to disprove the accusations against him, he even asked the public prosecutor "to investigate the activities of the Free Mason lodges, and to determine whether any members of the former government had been Free Masons."[13]

In early May the press announced that a Committee of Inquiry into confiscated

Masonic material had completed its work and submitted its finding to the court. "A full list of Free Masons operating as [various] associations in Romania has been officially reconstructed."[14] On 20 June 1941 the public prosecutor of the Bucharest court, after examining the material, published an official statement: "Most members of the Free Masons' Lodge belong to the Judaic element. The Lodge's struggle is one of surreptitious destruction . . . it is a struggle that aims at undermining the nation. The Lodge's weapons are money and political power. The raids on private homes did not unearth incriminating documents of punishable offences committed by members of the Free Masons' Lodge. Among the documents examined by the Committee, none was found that indicated that a member of General Antonescu's former government . . . belonged to the Free Masons."[15]

Despite the lack of evidence the committee concluded that all Freemasons were pawns in the hands of international Judaism and were out to destroy and enslave "our bodies and souls." The Bucharest court, after refuting the claim that some members of the previous government were Freemasons, stressed that "the slanderers have been sentenced to a year's imprisonment and fined two thousand lei." Even so, the press continued publishing the names of Freemasons selected from the "comprehensive" list, which included several hundred names.[16]

The list of Freemasons contained several surprises, including as it did the names of certain well-known nationalists, such as Alexandru Vaida-Voevod, the leader of the Romanian Front, who had served as prime minister in 1933. Equally surprising was that the list contained none of the Iron Guard's sworn enemies—such as Prime Minister Armand Călinescu, who was ultimately assassinated by the Iron Guard, or Gabriel Marinescu, head of the Bucharest police and one of King Carol II's loyal minions, or then-Minister of the Interior Victor Iamandi.

Once the list of Freemasons was complete, the government leaders, especially Antonescu, were in the clear. Thus, when Killinger reminded him of the Legionary claim that he was affiliated with the Freemasons, Antonescu retorted that "he would convince the young people [i.e., the Legionnaires] that he entertained no Masonic ideas of any kind and hoped by autumn to clarify matters in this regard, too, without firing a shot."[17] Once Antonescu had cleared his name and ordered the extermination of Bessarabian and Bukovinian Jewry—a measure that earned him Hitler's esteem—he was in a position to inform Killinger that as far as the Legion and he were concerned "the Marshal is totally deaf" and that his new state would be based on combatants at the front, "but without the Legion."[18]

The Nazis in Berlin and their representatives in Bucharest were by no means a passive element of the deadly triangle that led to the radicalization of Romanian policy. They used a variety of means, including direct public threats to Jews and members of the Romanian opposition. They alluded to the Judaic threat that had grown since the suppression of the Legionary movement and asked for a free hand in handling Romania's Jewish problem—even though this would violate Romanian sovereignty—as part of an "international" solution to the Jewish problem. Within the deadly triangle, the Jewish problem became an important element in the Legionary campaign to blacken Antonescu's name—a campaign that was conducted from Germany after the suppression of the rebellion and that exploited the discomfiture and even regret that many Nazi diplomats felt following the Legionnaires' removal from government.

Berlin saw the Jewish question in Romania as the state's main problem or, as Goebbels put it, "the key to Romania's problems." According to Goebbels, there was still much ground to cover. Hitler himself maintained, even after the ethnic "cleansing" of Bessarabia and Bukovina, that Antonescu would be unable to rehabilitate his country without first "getting rid of the Jews."[19] Killinger intervened at least twice in public to warn of the Jewish danger in Romania and "promised" that Germany would deal with the Jews and their sympathizers—the opponents of the Antonescu regime (note the false implication that the Jews were responsible for the collapse of the Iron Guard). After taking opposition circles to task "for making the general's life difficult" and for attempting to undermine ties between Germany and Romania, Killinger continued, "The Jews are once again rearing their heads and opening their insolent mouths. They feel free to do so only in the wake of the Legion's suicide. I advise the band of Jews who wish to destroy Germany . . . not to be too self-assured, for the day of reckoning is nigh!"[20]

In early June *Deutsche Allgemeine Zeitung* published an editorial on "the start of the purge," emphasizing that General Antonescu "has decided to take action to solve the [Jewish] problem."[21] This was followed by a warning by Andreas Rüchrig, head of the Association of Ethnic Germans in Romania (Volksgemeinschaft der Deutsche in Rumänien), to the Hungarian Jewish minority in Transylvania not to oppose Antonescu's pro-German policy. In point of fact, this warning was directed specifically at Iuliu Maniu and his Transylvanian colleagues, who headed the opposition to Antonescu's regime and whose names were therefore linked by Rüchrig with the Jews. Those who opposed the current Romanian policy, added Rüchrig, were not only enemies of the state but also enemies of the Reich, "and will get their just deserts."[22]

The Nazis did not stop at warnings and threats in the press but played a far more active role in the metamorphosis of classical Cuzist antisemitism into active participation in the extermination of the Jews. This role is unfortunately not well documented, due to concealment on the part of both governments, lack of access to the Romanian archives, and selective transcriptions of talks between the leaders of the two regimes on anti-Jewish measures. Nevertheless, the Nazi envoys in Bucharest made no secret of the fact that they intended to solve the Jewish question themselves rather than leave it up to the incompetent Romanians.

March 1941 had seen the arrival in Bucharest of "special emissaries of the Reich and of Himmler"—Mihai Antonescu's expression—immediately following Antonescu's suppression of the Legionnaires' rebellion. "The political situation was still uncertain," as Mihai Antonescu euphemistically put it. The Nazi delegation, consisting of SS police officials such as Gustav Richter, Karl Hoffman, Karl Pflaumer, and a certain Eitzen, had come to discuss what to do with the Jews of Romania. Hoffman was an emissary of the RSHA; he later served as an attaché for police affairs in Bulgaria. SS-Brigadeführer Karl Pflaumer was interior minister of the state of Baden beginning in May 1937; later he served as police commander and head of administration in Alsace. From March 1941 to March 1942 he was advisor for administrative affairs in Romania, specifically responsible for organizing the administration in the occupied territories of Bessarabia and Bukovina. Richter, born in 1912, was a member of the Nazi Party from May 1933, serving with the SD from March 1934. In 1935 he was appointed official in charge (Referat) of Jewish and Freemason affairs for the entire southeastern region of Germany, and he filled other positions in the security police. He arrived in Romania from Dijon, France, where he had served as a representative of the German legation in Bucharest. This was not Richter's first visit to Romania. Hermann Neubacher's aide in Bucharest, the commercial attaché Heinrich Klugkist, recalled that Richter had first visited Romania in November 1940 as a liaison officer for the SD, which had a semiofficial legation in Romania (set up at the start of Legionary rule and dissolved after the suppression of the rebellion). Nothing is known about Eitzen.[23]

According to Mihai Antonescu the Germans "presented . . . an official request that responsibility for the handling of Romania's Jews be handed over to the Germans exclusively, since Germany [was] preparing the international solution to the problem." Writing in 1944, with the Red Army already in northern Romania, Mihai Antonescu claimed to have refused the German request. In that version the minister told the Nazi delegation in March 1941 that Romania opposed "any physical solution" or harsh forms of oppression, and that "it did not accept crime as an institution and as a political method." He was lying. The Romanian administration did work with the Nazi delegation, and did consent to the Germans' "international solution of the Jewish problem."[24]

The phrase "international solution of the Jewish problem" expresses Nazi demands at an early stage in the formulation of the Final Solution. This was the first attempt by Himmler and the RSHA to take over the handling of the Jews of Romania. It came at a moment when a German force of 680,000 troops was stationed on Romanian soil, one and a half months after the Romanian fascist movement had been tamed by the Antonescu government, and at a crucial juncture in relations between Germany and Romania. During this period the understandings reached with Mihai Antonescu regarding the deportation and extermination of the Jews of Bessarabia and Bukovina took shape. What did that "solution" actually mean in March 1941? The answer appears in Nazi ideologist Alfred Rosenberg's March declaration that "the Jewish problem in Europe will be solved only when the last Jew leaves the European continent."[25]

Richter's attitude toward the Jewish problem, as reflected in his first report, was far more extreme than that of the Romanian government, which aimed basically at "restoring national rights to our nation," as the Law for the Establishment of the National Romanization Center put it. Richter officially set the ball rolling on 1 May 1941 in a talk with Mihai Antonescu over anti-Jewish measures adopted by the Romanians. Both agreed that the main step toward solving the Jewish problem had already been taken — namely, the establishment of the Romanization Office. Mihai Antonescu boasted that he had thwarted any attempts by Jews to torpedo the anti-Jewish measures he had introduced. He was happy to be able to draw on Richter's experience in solving the Jewish problem and put him in contact with Gen. Eugen Zwiedinek, a Romanian general of German origin who served as undersecretary of state for Romanization, for further cooperation between the two countries.

Mihai Antonescu was not the only one who was delighted at Richter's arrival. On 7 May General Zwiedinek confessed that he had long awaited the chance to cooperate with a Nazi representative. He claimed that it was he who had advised the Conducător to ask the Germans to send over an expert on Jewish affairs to advise the Romanian government on Jewish matters. Zwiedinek immediately agreed to Richter's proposal to coordinate the handling of the Jews at the organizational level and subject them to state supervision in preparation for what Richer already termed the Final Solution.[26] Thus the groundwork was laid for the Final Solution in Romania, although most historians agree that at the time Hitler had not yet formulated his policy for the extermination of European Jewry.[27]

Other structural reforms proposed by Richter would have far-reaching consequences for the Jewish community. Foremost among these was his proposal for the establishment of a Central Office of Romanian Jews, supposedly based on the French model, the functions of which would be determined by special statute.

The office would be subordinate to the Head Office of Romanization (the term *head office* corresponded to the German *Hauptampt*, a name Richter apparently borrowed from the Reichssicherheitshauptamt—the ministry that had sent him to Romania) and would receive instruction from this office only.

Zwiedinek promised Richter that all decisions regarding the Jewish question would be kept confidential to prevent information leaking out from the office and potentially triggering resistance. They further agreed that only those who had been present at their talk should be allowed to participate in future talks on the Jewish question. In Richter's assessment, Zwiedinek showed a sincere desire to help solve the Jewish problem in Romania and was grateful for the opportunity to achieve this goal.[28]

Zwiedinek's enthusiasm for Richter's proposals was not shared by Ion Antonescu or his deputy, Mihai Antonescu. Indeed, the Nazi advisor on Jewish affairs was soon to discover that he could not rely on promises and that the Jews were an important element in the country's foreign policy and the higher interests of the Romanian state.

Further progress was made during Zwiedinek and Richter's second meeting, held on 12 May 1941. Richter drew up a working plan with the following provisions:

1. All draft laws from the Undersecretariat of State for Romanization shall be sent to Richter for confirmation before being presented to Antonescu.
2. A draft law shall be submitted for the dissolution of all Jewish political organizations except for the Jewish religious communities and for the blocking of their bank accounts and a total ban on their legal or underground activities. Their property shall be transferred to the Jewish Center.
3. A Jewish Center shall be set up as the sole organization authorized to represent the Jews before the authorities.
4. The property of Jews shall be confiscated. The Jews shall be obliged to report and declare all their property to the authorities.
5. An Evacuation Fund shall be set up. A certain percentage—20 to 25 percent—of the overall amount accruing from the liquidation of a Jewish business, as determined by the Undersecretariat of State for Romanization, shall constitute the financial resource for the evacuation of the Jews from Romania.

On 13 May Richter put the finishing touches on his work plan during a visit to the Central Bureau of Statistics by asking its deputy directors, Drs. Golopenția and Vlad, for demographic data on the Jews of Romania: "On the basis of the

Census of 6 April 1941, I proposed we begin with the [census] forms submitted by Jews, since the Head Office of Romanization requires them for its work."[29]

It did not, therefore, take long for Richter, Eichmann's man in Romania, to streamline the medley of antisemitic measures—in both the socioeconomic and intellectual fields—that had grown up randomly since 1938 in accordance with local antisemitic dogma. Despite rampant antisemitism, no systematic steps had been taken prior to Richter's arrival to segregate, evacuate, or isolate the Jews. Upon his arrival in Romania, the twenty-nine-year-old German expert began streamlining Romania's antisemitic policy and subjecting it to orders from Berlin, as the first condition of his work plan testifies. Ironically, despite wishing to "cleanse" Romania of the "inferior" Jewish race, the Germans never considered the Romanians to be full-blooded Aryans. Both Richter and his superiors considered the Romanians inferior to the Germans.

Romania's racist-religious formula for defining Jews, devised by King Carol II's legal advisors in August 1940, served Richter's purposes well. It should be noted that even before Richter's arrival anti-Jewish incitement was at its peak. A census of Jews conducted on 5 April, in which a Nazi expert and an Italian fascist expert acted as observers, showed that Jews had already been dismissed from their jobs and excluded from the country's cultural life and that most of their property had been expropriated, confiscated, nationalized or looted. Indeed, the Romanians had done such a thorough job that one might have thought there was little left for Richter to do. Not so, however. The enterprising Richter recommended a series of new measures, such as obliging Jews to wear a yellow badge and forcibly segregating them in ghettos in preparation for the Final Solution.

Richter's measures notwithstanding, and despite a huge German military presence on Romanian soil, Antonescu managed to retain considerable freedom of action on the domestic front. "The foreign army has not interfered in our home affairs," declared Antonescu on the eve of the invasion of the Soviet Union.[30] Richter soon discovered that the consent of the Bucharest government was a prerequisite for the implementation of his plans for the Jews of Romania proper (the Regat and southern Transylvania).

The Jews of Bessarabia and northern Bukovina were a different kettle of fish. First, these provinces were not under Romanian sovereignty. According to Alfred Rosenberg, who was actively participating in the affairs of the east as Hitler's commissioner for the central control of the question connected with the East European region, they belonged to the East European territories that had been divided into five regions on 29 April 1941, all of which required "a uniform approach to the Jewish problem."[31] It was in these regions that the Nazi extermination machine was subsequently deployed. On 7 May 1941 Rosenberg sent instructions to the future reichskommissar of the Ukraine to dismiss the Jews from their positions through the introduction of ghettos, labor battalions, and forced labor as a first stage of solving the Jewish problem.[32]

In March 1941 the so-called Führer's Decree (Führerbefehl) empowered the RSHA to set up mobile murder squads—the Einsatzgruppen—in the eastern occupied territories. On 3 March General Halder, chief of the Wehrmacht General Staff, was informed of Himmler's special mission. The first version of the protocol, setting forth the relationship between the German army and the Einsatzgruppen, was signed by General Von Brauchitz, the Wehrmacht's supreme commander, on 28 April 1941. The final agreement, permitting the Einsatzgruppen to operate near the front, alongside the assault units, was signed in late May.[33] Einsatzgruppe D, numbering four hundred to five hundred men, was assigned to the area south of the front (including Bessarabia and Bukovina) as part of General Von Schobert's Eleventh Army. The instructions Himmler sent to the commander of Einsatzgruppe D stipulated that its duties included killing Jewish men, women, and children.[34] The "Guidelines for the Behavior of the Army Units in Russia," issued on 19 May, exhorted the Wehrmacht's General Staff to take firm action against Bolsheviks, partisans, terrorists (members of the underground), and Jews. In late May Reinhard Heydrich, on behalf of the RSHA, and General Quartermaster Wagner, on behalf of the army, signed the final version of the understanding regulating the relationship and cooperation between the RSHA and the army.[35]

This was the background to Antonescu's third visit to Hitler on 12 June 1941—a visit that was to have such disastrous consequences for Bessarabian and Bukovinian Jewry. During this visit, the purpose of which was to finalize military and political coordination for the impending invasion of the Soviet Union, Hitler promised Antonescu unlimited territorial rewards in the east.[36] Antonescu requested that the Romanian army be allowed to participate in the fighting "right from the very first day" and asked Hitler to be allowed control over the Romanian forces and over the German forces that were stationed on Romanian soil. "Day and night," emphasized Antonescu, "the Romanian people had been thinking of the hour when they could settle account with Russia, and they wished that moment would come very soon for them to take revenge for everything Russia has done to them."[37]

A study of the practical measures Antonescu took to implement the Final Solution in the two former Romanian provinces shows that not only did he know of the existence of the Einsatzgruppen and of the coordination between them and the army but that he actually emulated their methods. That Hitler shared his big secret with Antonescu is a measure of the tremendous esteem in which he held the Romanian general who had been educated in a French military academy and spoke no German. The disclosure of the secret was ratified two months later by the German foreign minister, who in June had had no idea of the contents of their conversation.[38] This disclosure casts doubt on the reliability of the transcripts of talks between Hitler and his many non-German-speaking guests on the Jewish question, as well as on the reliability of the translator, Schmidt, who, in his memoirs, published after the war, claimed that he was but "a statistician on the stage of history."[39]

Less than a week after his return to Romania Antonescu, convinced of Germany's imminent victory, drew up his own plan for the solution of the Jewish problem in the two provinces Romania had been forced to cede to the Soviet Union in the summer of 1940. The original plan may have been drawn up even earlier, during the RSHA mission's visit to Romania in March–April 1941, in which case the June plan was simply the final version of it. In drawing up this plan Antonescu was doubtlessly impelled by his desire for revenge against the Jews, whom he held responsible for Romania's humiliating defeat and who identified with the Soviet regime. In any case, it was during the two weeks leading up to the invasion that the Romanian plan was finalized.

A conversation between Romanian foreign minister Mihai Antonescu and Ribbentrop in the latter's headquarters in Zhitomir, Ukraine, on 23 September 1942 sheds light on Romania's understandings with the SS concerning the fate of the Jews of Bessarabia, Bukovina, and Transnistria. At this talk, which was a prelude to Mihai Antonescu's talk with Hitler in Vinnitsa, Ukraine, Ribbentrop asked Mihai Antonescu to continue cooperating in the extermination of Romanian Jewry. They also discussed the fate of the Jews of the Regat and southern Transylvania: "In the regions from which all Jews have been evacuated, total calm prevails. Will Romania be able to order further measures of this kind? [Mihai] Antonescu responded that in Bessarabia and Bukovina, as well as in Transnistria, the implementation of such measures has been agreed upon with the SS."[40]

Mihai Antonescu's transcript of the conversation does not mention the understanding with the SS or with the RSHA and German envoys who visited Romania in March 1941, a year and a half earlier.[41] These understandings—and others like them—were evidently never committed to paper. Even Romania's participation in the war against the Soviet Union was never put into writing. Indeed, Antonescu boasted that, unlike previous Romanian statesmen who drew up numerous agreements, pacts, and conditions before agreeing to join the allies in the First World War, he relied simply on the führer's word.[42]

It is also worth noting that Antonescu adopted the Final Solution at a time when he was convinced that Germany was going to defeat the Soviet Union in the forthcoming war. His belief was based on Germany's easy victory over the French and British armies in 1940, the results of the Balkan campaign, the victory over the British Expeditionary Force in Greece, and Antonescu's personal conviction that the Wehrmacht had found a solution to the main problem in any war against Russia, namely, its sheer size. As Antonescu said in his meeting with Hitler on 12 June 1941, "Whereas Napoleon and even the Germans in 1917 had still had to contend with the huge problems raised by space, the motor in the air and on the ground have eliminated space as Russia's ally."[43]

Between 5 and 18 June the attitude of the Romanian authorities toward the Jews underwent a dramatic transformation with no forewarning apart from Antonescu's meeting with Hitler on 12 June. Antonescu's change of heart was noticeable in his attitude toward the Jews and in the disparaging way he referred to them. On 22 June 1941 he bragged that he "had courageously addressed" the problem of Romanization, dispossessed the Jews, and consolidated cooperation with Germany "in accordance with the permanent interests of our *vital space*."[44] In October 1942 he accused the Jews as well as the British and Americans of having "dictated the terms" of the 1919 Paris Peace Conference. He lamented that Ionel Brătianu, the founder of modern Romania, had been forced at the Berlin peace conference in 1878 to accept the "humiliating" condition that awarded Jews civil rights, resulting in the "Judaization of our country and the erosion of *the purity of our race*." He accused Constantin Brătianu, Ionel Brătianu's heir, of having caused Romania's moral decline by "capitulating" to the Jews and Freemasons and by introducing a democratic-liberal policy that granted rights to all ethnic groups.[45]

In its eagerness to take up the antisemitic refrain, the antisemitic press did not even wait for instructions from the Ministry of Propaganda. The German legation in Bucharest provided it with funds and background material. It was this same press that predicted a change in Antonescu's policy toward the Jews. On 1 June *Sfarmă Piatră* declared, "The Jewish problem must be totally eradicated." On 8 June it published an article on the "degeneracy" (*degenerare*) of the Jewish race. On 18 June the newspaper stated, "As usual, the Jews are the ringleaders of the traitors."[46] On 12 June (the date of the meeting between Hitler and Antonescu) another antisemitic newspaper, *Chemarea Vremii*, reported, "The Jewish problem not only has not been solved, it has not even begun to move in the direction of the Great Solution."[47]

On the eve of the war Antonescu gave full vent to his hatred of democracy, thereby remaining true to the Legionary heritage that rejected democracy because it favored Jews, awarded them rights, turned them into full-fledged citizens, allowed them freedom of expression, and undermined the national idea and the

Romanian ethnic state. Thus the long process of excluding Jews from the fabric of Romanian life that had been initiated by prominent intellectuals in the nineteenth century, obsessively promoted by Cuza and his movement, and raised to extreme nationalist heights for a decade and a half by the Legionary movement was completed on the eve of the outbreak of war by the Antonescu regime.[48] In a Europe overrun by fascism, what began as a just war for the liberation of land from foreign occupation turned, in the hands of a regime that closely identified with the fascist political outlook, into a unique opportunity for expunging the Jewish presence from parts of the Romanian country.

Internal and external pressures and personal problems impelled Ion Antonescu and his henchman, Mihai Antonescu, to adopt the Nazi Final Solution and apply it to Bessarabia and Bukovina and later to occupied Transnistria. These pressures may be symbolized by a triangle connecting Antonescu, the Legionary heritage, and the Nazi presence in Romania. Antonescu's need to prove himself to the Nazis after having crushed the Romanian fascist movement, to refute the allegation that he was a Freemason, and to atone for his past foibles, as well as his desire to impress Hitler and prove himself worthy of his trust, caused a mutation of the Romanian brand of antisemitism into one where the Nazi Final Solution became a possibility.[49]

The adoption of the Final Solution in Romania was, therefore, simply the last stage of a long process of antisemitic policy development. The Romanian order to cleanse the land (the Romanian version of the Nazi Final Solution) was the result not only of Hitler's sway over Antonescu but also of Romania's antisemitic past. The Final Solution was merely the end product of years of demonizing and delegitimizing Romanian Jewry, decades of antisemitic invective fomented by the Romanian Orthodox Church under the patriarch Miron Cristea, and the fanatical Romanization campaign waged by Romanian intellectuals against the Jewish "vermin." The gendarmes and soldiers who, in July 1941, began shooting at tens of thousands of Jews in Bessarabia and Bukovina—an act unprecedented in Romanian antisemitic history—had no moral scruples to overcome. They were merely finishing off the work of the army units that had unleashed the pogrom against the Jews of Dorohoi in the summer of 1940, even before German soldiers had set foot on Romanian soil, or of the Legionnaires who threw hundreds of Jews, alive, from moving trains and left their bodies to rot or who, in January 1941, strung up dozens of mutilated corpses in the Bucharest municipal abattoir.

17

The Romanian Solution to the Jewish Problem in Bessarabia and Bukovina, June–July 1941

In Romania the murder of Jews merely for being Jews began in June 1940, after the Romanian army's withdrawal from the areas ceded to the Soviet Union. These murders were isolated events and would have remained so but for explicit instructions for the implementation of an overt Romanian policy of genocide. This policy was devised under Nazi influence, probably in March–April 1941 after the arrival of special emissaries of the Reich and Himmler. These emissaries were sent over by Himmler to discuss the fate of Romanian Jewry and to officially transfer the handling of the Jews to Germany. After their arrival Mihai Antonescu concluded "understandings" with the SS, or rather with the Reich Central Security Office (RSHA), as discussed in the previous chapter. Although we know little of the true nature of these understandings, practical preparations for the liquidation of the Jews evidently began in late May or early June — shortly before Antonescu was informed of the exact date of Operation Barbarossa. Since the late thirties conditions in Romania had been ripe for the implementation of an extermination policy, although this was not obvious. Therefore, the orders for the liquidation of Jews neither shocked nor elicited any form of opposition among members of the army or the Romanian establishment. The Romanian army's General Staff drew up a plan to incite the Romanian population of Bessarabia to perpetrate riots against the Jews prior to the arrival of the Romanian forces (see below).

Ion Antonescu himself gave the order to liquidate a part of Bessarabian and Bukovinian Jewry. He entrusted the implementation of this order to the gendarmerie (which was attached to the Ministry of the Interior) and the army, particularly the pretors (types of military governors). Anticipating Germany's victory, Romania's leaders informed the government on 17–18 June 1941 of their plans for the Jewish population in the two provinces. The leadership left no doubt about the significance of the order to "cleanse the ground." Mihai Antonescu's speech of 3 July 1941 at the Ministry of Interior was distributed in limited-edition brochures titled "Guidelines and Instructions for the Liberation Administration." Guideline ten revealed the regime's intentions regarding the Jews: "This is the . . . most favorable opportunity in our history . . . for cleansing our people of all those elements foreign to its soul, which have grown like weeds to darken its future."[1] Mihai Antonescu elaborated on this theme during the cabinet session of 8 July 1941:

> At the risk of not being understood by traditionalists . . . I am all for the forced migration of the entire Jewish element of Bessarabia and Bukovina, which must be dumped across the border. . . . You must be merciless to them. . . . I don't know how many centuries must pass before the Romanian people shall again encounter such total liberty of action, such opportunity for ethnic cleansing and national revision. . . . This is a period in which we are masters of our land. Let's use [this opportunity]. If necessary, use your machine guns. I couldn't care less if history remembers us as barbarians. . . . I take formal responsibility in telling you there is no law. . . . So, no formalities, complete freedom.[2]

On 19 June Gen. Ilie Şteflea (the general who put down the Legionary rebellion in Bucharest at Antonescu's behest) sent a secret circular to the army informing it of Antonescu's instructions: "All Yids, Communist agents, and their sympathizers must be identified . . . to enable the Ministry of Interior to track them down, restrict their freedom of movement, and apply future directives."[3] This order resembled a similar instruction given by Field Marshal Wilhelm Keitel to the Wehrmacht.[4] Gen. Ion Topor, the grand pretor and commander of the gendarmerie units in the liberated territories, was given explicit orders regarding the Jews and Communist and Soviet functionaries in Romanian territories: "All pro-Communist Romanians and Ukrainians shall be sent across the Dniester, and all pro-Communist members of the minorities [a euphemism for Jews] shall be eliminated."[5]

The pretors implemented these orders with the army's full collaboration and with the tacit agreement of the High Command. Since the special orders issued to the army were not written down, very little is known about them today. These orders were usually given to officers, albeit not necessarily those of the highest rank, although almost all senior officers knew of them.[6] The special orders were invoked every time military or civil authorities were reluctant to kill Jews, whether out of fear of the consequences or because they did not believe such orders existed. In Cetatea Albă, for example, Major Frigan of the local garrison requested written instructions to execute the Jews. The pretor of the Third Army, Col. Marcel Petală, traveled to Cetatea Albă to inform the major of the directives concerning the Jews in the ghetto. The next day 3,500 Jews who had survived the main offensive were killed.[7]

The directives "on matters of security and policing" awarded the local military commanders total authority.[8] Usually the prefects and civil authorities took over only after the army units had completed their task. Although the military commanders were empowered to act directly in all matters relating to the liquidation of the Jews, they always preferred to leave this to the pretors and their men. The pretors thus became the chief executors of the special orders. In areas controlled by the army the orders to kill were given exclusively by the military commanders or pretors, even where officials of the Romanian civil authorities were present.[9] The orders were issued by the German or Romanian staff and were passed on by the pretors.

The military commanders appointed diehard Romanian nationalists as mayors of the cities they occupied. In Herța, for example (where the army, together with the new local authority, killed 132 Jews), the mayor was appointed by Maj. Gheorghe Vartic, pretor of the Seventh Infantry Division. The local government was subject to the army's authority and scrupulously obeyed all directives issued by the army, the gendarmerie, and especially the pretors, as long as the army was present. Frequently cooperation between them was obligatory, especially during the first phase of the liquidation (pinpointing the victims—Jews, Communists, or political suspects). In many cases the newly appointed mayors acted on their own initiative. The civil guard set up in Herța by the new mayor "informed the [army] patrols whom to arrest."[10]

The orders to kill Jews soon became an open secret, and all Christians in Bessarabia and Bukovina knew that the Jews were doomed.[11] Soldiers as well as local citizens knew of the directive, or rather special dispensation, issued by the army to do with the Jews' lives and property as they saw fit "within the first 24 hours of the occupation."[12] Although this written order was not discovered after the war, we know that it was circulated among both military and civilian officials. It was mentioned in the testimonies of Jews and non-Jews alike (the latter referred to a dispensation of three days rather than twenty-four hours) and was likewise referred to in the trials of Romanian war criminals.

THE RECAPTURE OF BESSARABIA AND NORTHERN BUKOVINA

The Romanian units that participated in recapturing Bessarabia and northern Bukovina belonged to a military division called "South," which comprised the Eleventh German Army, a Hungarian military force, and the Third and Fourth Romanian Armies.[13] Officially, Antonescu was supreme commander of both the German and Romanian forces on the Romanian front—a title officially bestowed upon him by the führer in Munich on 12 June 1941 in recognition of the general's talent.[14] Unlike other sectors on the German-Soviet front, the southern sector remained quiet during the first two weeks of the invasion. For the first ten days only a few sporadic exploratory forays took place, although these had serious implications for several border communities, such as Siret, Herța, and Noua Suliță.

On 17 July units of the Eleventh German Army reached Bălți, where they immediately unleashed a pogrom against the local Jews.[15] On 14 July a unit of the Eleventh German Army reached Orhei, and by mid-July German and Romanian forces of the Eleventh Army controlled all of northern Bessarabia. In central Bessarabia, however, the joint forces encountered fierce Soviet resistance.

On 16 July the soldiers of the Eleventh Army and a large gendarmerie unit entered Kishinev, where they were welcomed by the Romanians there. At the same time, units of the Third Romanian Army reached the area south of Kishinev, thereby completing the occupation of the part of Bessarabia most densely populated by Jews. In southern Bessarabia the Soviet front was breached in several places and collapsed several days later. On 26 July large forces of the Fourth Romanian Army reached the Dniester (only Romanian forces operated in southern Bessarabia).[16]

On the morning of 3 July the Romanian army launched a general offensive against northern Bukovina (where mainly Romanian units operated), and two days later they entered Czernowitz. The Third Romanian Army crossed the Prut near Noua Suliță and after two days of fighting, on the eve of 7 July, reached Hotin. The next day the Romanian forces resumed their offensive and reached the Romanian side of the Dniester.[17]

THE STAGES OF GENOCIDE

The destruction of the Jews of northern Romania took place in two stages: the spontaneous stage and the planned stage. Before we embark on a discussion of the various techniques the Romanians employed to liquidate the Jews, it is worth noting that the methods used in rural areas differed vastly from those used in urban centers. In rural and semirural areas (including some towns), the period between the withdrawal of the Soviet army and the entry of the Romanian and German forces was characterized by spontaneous waves of killing. Sometimes the local population exploited this interregnum to form gangs of terrorists, "whose main aim was to kill Jews."[18] Most of these spontaneous killings occurred in areas where no real tensions had existed between Jews and gentiles and where, on the contrary, a tradition of more or less peaceful coexistence had been characteristic for a century. This fact alone explains why, all in all, so few Jews tried to escape. In Bessarabia, however, many rural Jews did try to escape the first wave of killings, seeking refuge in towns, fields, or hiding places or with their Christian neighbors.

Almost overnight the feelings and attitudes of Romanian society underwent a sea change, as Romanians and Ukrainians turned against their former friends, comrades-in-arms, and fellow employees. The change was so swift that the Jews had no time to fully absorb what was happening. We now know that this change of heart was not entirely spontaneous but was preceded by a detailed plan drawn up by the chief of the General Staff's Second Bureau to incite the Romanian population against the Jews.

In Bessarabia and in parts of northern Bukovina the acts of pillage and murder evolved into a kind of popular uprising of sorts against Jews, both as Jews and as "allies" of the Soviets, the foreign occupier. This explains why the attacks on Jews occurred immediately after the withdrawal of the Soviet forces. Although there is no way of knowing the extent of the carnage against Jews during this period, we do know that their numbers ran into the tens of thousands.

THE ROMANIAN ARMY

On 8 July Iosif Iacobici, the chief of the General Staff, ordered the commander of the General Staff's Second Bureau, Lt. Col. Alexandru Ionescu, to implement a plan "for the removal of the Judaic element from Bessarabian territory . . . by organizing teams to act in advance of the Romanian troops." Implementation began on 9 July. "The mission of these teams is to create an unfavorable atmosphere towards the Judaic elements in the villages, thereby encouraging the population to remove them on its own, by whatever means it finds most appropriate and suited to the circumstances. Upon the arrival of the Romanian troops, the feeling must already be in place and even acted upon."[19]

Attached to the report was a detailed plan of the instructions given to the General Staff's Second Bureau and a map of the distribution of the teams. The special teams recruited Romanians from Bessarabia who "had proved their mettle," possessed valid Soviet documents, and had left their families behind in Romania—"an additional guarantee that they would carry out the assignment." These teams, duly reinforced, were dispatched to incite the peasants against the Jews and encourage them to loot, rape, and kill. They were sent along nine parallel itineraries from the central and southern sections of the Romanian–Bessarabian border toward the Dniester and spread from the Danube and Cetatea Albă in the south to Bucovici and Kishinev in the north. Each team comprised two to four men and was headed by an agent of the Second Bureau. After being provided with money, the members of the team were ordered "to exploit relatives, acquaintances, and anti-Communist elements, in order to disseminate the *idea of joint resistance to the Jewish danger*."[20]

The first killings took place at Siret, in southern Bukovina, five kilometers from the new Soviet border and home to many Vizhnitz and Sadagura Hasidim. Fifteen hundred local Jews were marched to Dorneşti, twelve kilometers away, where trains waited to deport them to southern Romania. A few women stayed behind to look after about twenty elderly and disabled Jews, including an ailing man who was looked after by his two daughters. These Jews were driven to a valley not far from town, where the two sisters were raped by several soldiers of the Seventh Division. Some elderly Jews, including the local ritual slaughterer and his wife, were brought to division headquarters and accused of "espionage and attacking the Romanian army."[21] That same day, all of the Jews who remained behind were shot near the bridge over the River Prut in the presence of the inhabitants of Siret, who had been invited along to witness the proceedings.

In Herţa the shooting of large groups of Jews posed certain technical problems, as no thought had been given to burial requirements. After the execution a heap of corpses lay in pools of blood, guarded by a soldier who "from time to time fired his rifle at one of the bodies that twitched."[22] The rabbi of the community was murdered in his home, along with his entire family. A five-year-old girl was thrown into a ditch and left to die.[23] Any survivors were later deported to Transnistria.

On 7 July 1941 the Sixteenth Regiment, followed closely by the Ninth and Tenth Regiments, occupied Noua Suliţă. Although members of the Tenth and Sixteenth Regiments killed "only" 50 Jews, the members of the Ninth Regiment more than made up for it. As soon as they entered the city they accused the Jews of shooting at the army and raided their homes. The next day 880 Jews and 5 Christians were found dead in the courtyards and streets.[24] An additional 45 Jews were shot at the behest of the regiment's commander, Colonel Cârlan, who took an active part in their murder.[25] On 8 July, when the Seventh Division entered the city, they found it in an appalling state.[26] Pretor Vartic, with the help of the gendarmes attached to the division, ordered 3,000 Jews to be detained in a distillery. Before entering the factory courtyard the detainees were ordered to place all their valuables in a bag. Fifty of the Jews were declared "suspects" and shot.[27] Lt. Emil Costea, commander of the military police, and Constantin Nicolau, an officer especially chosen for the task, refused to kill the Jews.[28] Their refusal, and the fact that four members of Vartic's murder squad were busy elsewhere at the time, forced the general to turn to the gendarmerie for help. The Hotin gendarmerie legion, which was idle at the time since Hotin had not yet been occupied, sent over several gendarmes, who murdered 87 Jews.[29]

Gen. Olimpiu Stavrat, commander of the Seventh Infantry Division, and Vartic were also responsible for the murder of Jews in Lipcani. Vartic's ruthlessness can be illustrated by the fact that he murdered with his bare hands a Jewish woman and her two daughters from Geamăna, a village near Lipcani, with whom he had lodged.[30]

On 3 July 450 local Jews were gunned down in the Bukovinian village of Ciudei.[31] Later that day 200 Jews in Storojineț were gunned down in their homes. On 4 July nearly all Jews in the villages of Ropcea, Iordănești, Pătrăuți, Panca, and Broscăuți, near Storojineț, were massacred with the active collaboration of local Romanians and Ukrainians.[32] On 5 July the wave of murder expanded to include thousands of Jews in the villages of Stănești, Jadova Nouă, Jadova Veche, Costești, Hlinița, Budineț, and Cireș as well as many of the surviving Jews of Herța, Vijnița, and Rostochi-Vijnița.[33]

On 4 July, after the combined German-Romanian armies entered Czernowitz, they began killing operations among the city's fifty thousand Jews — operations that continued for four days. Despite Russian resistance, the scope of the task, and challenging physical terrain, Bessarabian Jewry suffered the greatest losses in the Romanian campaign to "cleanse the ground." On 6 July, a day after the Romanian occupation of Edineți, about a thousand Jews were shot by Romanian troops, and sixty more were murdered at Noua Suliță. The next day it was the turn of those Jews who had buried their relatives in Edineți to be slaughtered.

On 7 July the Jews of Pârlița were liquidated, while the Jews of Bălți continued to be massacred. The next day thousands of Jews were shot in the towns of Briceni, Lipcani, Fălești, Mărculești, and Florești and in the villages of Gura-Camenca and Gura-Căinari.[34] By 9 July the wave of exterminations implemented by the combined German-Romanian forces reached the Jewish settlements of Plasa Nistrului (near Czernowitz), Zoniache, Răpujineț, and Coțmani in northern Bukovina, and dozens of small villages became *Judenrein* (cleansed of Jews).[35] On 11 July Lincăuți and the village of Cepelăuți were "purged" of their 160 or so Jewish inhabitants.[36] On the same day Einsatzgruppe D began its activities in Bălți.[37] On 12 July 300 Jews were shot in Climăuți.[38]

The seventeenth of July marked the beginning of the liquidation and deportation of Kishinev's fifty thousand Jews. On that day alone several thousand Jews — perhaps as many as ten thousand — were killed.[39] The destruction of this large Jewish center — the largest in Bessarabia — continued until the last of its Jews were killed or sent to camps in Transnistria in November 1941. The slaughter of the Jews of Cetatea Albă in southern Bessarabia followed a similar pattern.

Thus the first stage of the Romanian Holocaust was implemented with the help, but not under the coercion, of the German Eleventh Army and Einsatzgruppe D. This first stage spanned the period between the occupation of Bessarabia and northern Bukovina by the Romanian and German forces (Bălți, Czernowitz, and Kishinev, for example) and the partial or complete replacement of these forces by a civil Romanian administration (in large cities, by a garrison). From this point on the lives of urban Jews depended on not one but several, usually competing, civilian Romanian authorities. This meant further suffering for the Jews, as each authority attempted to outdo the other. These authorities were the regular police, the Siguranța, the prefect and mayor, and sometimes — as in the case of Bălți and Kishinev — even Einsatzkommando 10a, which stayed in these cities for short periods. In rural areas this stage ended with the arrival of the gendarmes.

THE GENDARMERIE

The Romanian concept of "cleansing the ground," as conveyed by Gen. Constantin Vasiliu, the commander-in-chief of the gendarmerie, to his subordinates, was partially influenced by the Nazi guidelines (*Richtlinien*). It comprised three parts: "The immediate liquidation of all Jews in rural areas, the ghettoization of all Jews in urban areas, and the arrest of all suspects, party activists, and Soviet civil servants."[40] Although all gendarmerie commanders received the same instructions, each of them interpreted them in his own way. This was due in part to their mentality and in part to the tremendous freedom of action to which they were accustomed. The vagueness of the instructions also allowed for a multiplicity of interpretations. For example, the instructions failed to specify which localities qualified as cities and which as villages. Consequently, many gendarmerie commanders defined certain localities as rural when strictly speaking they were not, spelling a death sentence for most of Bessarabian and north Bukovinian Jewry. The fact that urban and rural settlements in eastern Romania were often barely distinguishable from each other facilitated interpretations of this kind.

Although most of the Jewish population lived in towns, these were barely larger than the large Romanian and Ukrainian villages. Moreover, the outskirts of certain towns (for example Călărași, Edineți, Lipcani, Noua Suliță, and Rășcani) resembled villages and were considered as such.

Another aspect worth noting is that the commanders of the Romanian gen-

CHART 1. "CLEANSING THE GROUND" OPERATIONAL HIERARCHY

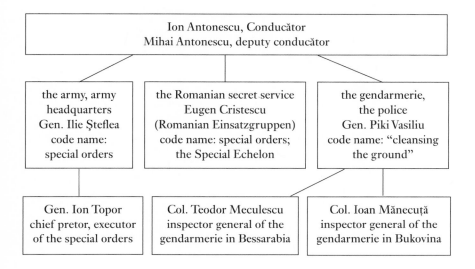

darmerie, unlike their Nazi counterparts, did not conceal the order to "cleanse the ground." In Roman, Maj. Filip Bechi, the commander of the Orhei Legion, openly informed his men that they were "going to Bessarabia to cleanse the terrain entirely of Jews." He later informed the heads of the sections (subdivisions of the gendarmerie legions) that "the Jews must be shot." Some days later, at Bechi's order and under the supervision of his deputy, Capt. Iulian Adamovici, the Orhei Legion was dispatched to the frontier village of Ungheni. Vasile Eftimie, secretary of the Legion and commander of the security police, mimeographed and distributed the orders for "cleansing the ground" to all sections and post heads.[41]

MURDER TECHNIQUES EMPLOYED BY THE GENDARMES

In rural areas the gendarmes were the principal executors of the orders for "cleansing the ground." Each gendarme knew in advance where he would be placed and the composition of the legions and sections he would command. The majority had served in the same villages before 1940, and their familiarity with the terrain and the Jewish inhabitants facilitated their task.[42] Col. Ion Mănecuță headed the gendarmerie in Bukovina, while Col. Teodor Meculescu headed the gendarmerie in Bessarabia. The territory was apportioned among the legions, each of which was headed by a colonel or lieutenant colonel. The legions were subdivided into sections (*secție*), which were in turn subdivided into posts. In certain (usually large) villages, such as the village of Ceneşăuţi-Orhei, there were both a section and post. In these villages not only local Jews but all Jews under the section's jurisdiction were shot.[43] Romanians age eighteen to twenty-one, known as the "premilitari," were also placed at the disposal of the gendarmerie after a short training period. These young people excelled at torturing and killing Jews. There were also volunteers who were motivated by patriotic sentiment to sign up for the gendarmerie; many of them were known to be antisemites. In 1950 the Bucharest Court noted, "Scattered at their posts, left to their own initiative, these noncommissioned officers and their aides did not limit themselves simply to the implementation of given orders. Most of them had a vested interest, to such an extent that no Jew escaped their attention. Some of them even devised new means of extermination in order to satisfy their sadistic impulses."[44]

The techniques the gendarmes used to exterminate the Jews, whether improvised or calculated, were efficient. The commander of the Orhei Legion, for example, destroyed "the entire Jewish population in the district" and instructed a section commander to make sure that all orders for the liquidation of the Jews had been properly executed. "The Major is vigilant," he warned, "and shall punish any show of weakness on the part of the noncommissioned officers."[45]

The gendarmes put to good use the firearms training they had received from the army. They developed an entire language of codes to realize their objectives. For example, they used the army code "enemy planes" to get the Jews to lie flat on the ground prior to being shot. The term "enemy planes" thus became synonymous with the shooting of small groups of Jews.[46] Such tactics were somewhat hampered by the fact that the women were not familiar with army commands. Another tactic was to call out "enemy attack" and, in the ensuing confusion, to open fire on the stunned Jews. In Sărăţeni, for example, eight Jews were shot by this method. Sometimes gendarmes would gun down Jews as they were marching.[47] Hundreds of Jews were killed in small groups in this way. The commander of the Bieşti Post "advised" a group of six women, three men, and a child whom he was escorting outside the village "to rest, since there is still a long way to go" and then ordered his men to shoot them.[48] In a similar episode, Dumitru Gavrilă, commander of the Ceneşeuţi Section, ordered a group of twenty-seven Jews he was escorting to the outskirts of the village to take a rest and then ordered his gendarmes to shoot them. He himself made sure that the victims were dead; if any were still breathing, he shot them.[49]

The speed with which the gendarmes killed Jews raised certain problems, such as the proximity of the front to a village as gendarmes arrived in the army's wake. The local commander of Horodiştea, for example, refused to execute Horodiştea's seven Jews for fear that the shots would draw the attention of enemy forces in the area and had them transferred to Minceni instead, where they were shot upon arrival.[50] For the same reason, fifteen Jews were transferred from Susleni, a village near the Dniester, to Vrapova.

Not all gendarmes were as disposed to relinquish an opportunity to kill Jews. Some of them went far beyond the call of duty. The commander of the Negureni Post, for example, took sixteen Jews to a cellar where he shot them with the help of two post commanders from a neighboring village, who came to assist him "just for fun." Likewise, the commander of the Alcedar Post, considering shooting too noisy, strangled a Jew with his own bare hands.[51]

It should be noted that not all gendarmes enjoyed killing Jews. Some post commanders sent Jews out of their jurisdiction, hoping that others would do their dirty work for them. Thus Constantin Bradie, the commander of the Tarsova Post, who had participated in the murder of the Jews of Negureni and of two Jews in Alcedar, sent two young Jews from his village to the commander in Alcedar to be disposed of. After that commander simply sent them back, Bradie dispatched the two youths to Sgt. Petre Diaconu with the message "do with them as you please." The two Jews, age seventeen or eighteen, begged Diaconu for mercy, whereupon he retorted, "May God have mercy on you," and shot them.[52]

Not all Jews were killed immediately—those who were useful to the gendarmes were kept alive for a few more months. Lt. Col. Nicolae Caracaş of Kishinev, for example, employed several Jewish furriers from the local ghetto to repair and alter fur coats that had been stolen from Jews in the ghetto. After completing the work, they, too, were shot or deported.[53] Some Jewish craftsmen were kept alive in Czernowitz and in certain Bessarabian towns after most of the Jews there had been liquidated or deported. When the Jews of Banila-pe-Siret and Seletin in Bukovina reached Hotin in October 1941, they found twenty-four local Jewish craftsmen who had been kept alive because they were useful to the Romanians and the authorities.

BURYING THE DEAD

The most serious problem for the gendarmes was how to bury the victims, not how to kill them. Burying them was considered "dirty" work, unlike killing them, which was considered "clean" work.[54] The gendarmes went to great pains not to sully their pristine army uniforms decorated with white braid or their polished boots. A report attached to the first five Einsatzgruppen reports sent by the chief of the security police and SD to Ribbentrop on 30 October 1941 stated, "The way in which the Romanians are dealing with the Jews lacks any method. No objections could be raised against the numerous executions of Jews, but the technical preparations and the executions themselves were totally inadequate.

The Romanians usually left the victims' bodies where they were shot, without trying to bury them. The Einsatzkommandos issued instructions to the Romanian police to proceed somewhat more systematically in this matter."[55]

It is important to note that the gendarmes, especially, used weapons looted from the Soviets. There is evidence that the use of Soviet weapons was not fortuitous.[56] Sometimes weapons and ammunition were specially brought from Legion headquarters, as was the case in Grigoriefca and Vaplova.[57]

Another popular murder technique was drowning. The Prut and Răut Rivers, and even more so the Dniester, soon became execution and burial sites favored by the gendarmes as well as the Romanian and German armies. The first three hundred Jewish victims from Storojineţ were thrown into the water by the gendarmes and shot. Another sixty managed to save their lives by swimming across the Dniester.[58] On 6 August the gendarmes of the Twenty-Third Police Company shot two hundred Jews and threw their bodies into the Dniester.[59] On 17 August members of Einsatzgruppe D shot eight hundred Jews on the bank of the Dniester because they were unable to swim back to Bessarabia as they had been ordered.[60] When the Jews of Noua Suliţă reached the banks of the Dniester on 6 August, they found the river covered with the corpses of the most recent victims.[61] The gendarmes operating in northern Bukovina in early July threw Jews into the Prut and shot them or, conversely, shot them and threw them into the river.[62] Cruelest by far was the way the gendarmes killed individual Jews or isolated Jewish families they came across in the villages, resorting to a variety of brutal practices designed to satisfy their sadistic inclinations and need to find new ways of killing.[63]

The gendarmes posted along the Dniester also used drowning as a murder technique—mainly during the second phase of the liquidation, when the number of Jews had declined and the gendarmes had plenty of spare time. The drowning of Jews had a symbolic value, signifying the "purification" of the ground from its foreign elements. Although no accurate statistics exist to document how many Jews were drowned in the Dniester, we know that at least twenty thousand suffered this sorry fate. Many Romanian citizens took an active part in these drowning operations and were later tried as war criminals in Romanian law courts. The following illustrates the techniques the gendarmes adopted: "Ion Foamete, Commander of the Zahaicani Post, together with his deputy, Dimitru Gigulie, used their rifle butts to force a Jewish woman and her two children—the only Jews in the village—to run to the bank of the Dniester, whereupon they forced the woman and her children to wade deeper and deeper into the water until the current swept them away and they sank."[64]

Shortly before 21 June 1941 Antonescu ordered the Romanian Special Intelligence Service (Serviciul Special de Informaţiuni, ssi) to establish a special unit of about 160 men to "obtain intelligence and protect the home front from acts of espionage, sabotage, and terror."[65] This unit, Operational Echelon no. 1 (Eşalonul I Operativ), known as the Operational Echelon (Eşalon Operativ) or the Special Echelon (Eşalon Special), belonged to the ssi and in some ways resembled the German Einsatzgruppe. Although the Operational Echelon was established on an ad hoc basis shortly before the invasion of the Soviet Union and its members had not undergone formal training, it was undeniably antisemitic. Like the Einsatzgruppe, the Operational Echelon was divided into smaller teams (echipe).[66] Although the issue of collaboration between the Einsatzgruppe and the Operational Echelon has yet to be adequately elucidated, some contact between the two groups almost certainly took place. We know, for example, that on 18 June Eugen Cristescu, the echelon's commander, left with his men for northern Moldova and was seen several days later (before 22 June) in Piatra Neamţ, at the Romanian army headquarters, where he is assumed to have met with Ohlendorf, the commander of Einsatzgruppe D. No written proof of that meeting exists, however.

The echelon's first operation was carried out in Iaşi along with the Romanian army and police and with the assistance of German military units. More than fourteen thousand Jews were murdered there on 29–30 June 1941 (see chap. 33). From Iaşi the echelon continued with the Fourth Romanian Army to Bessarabia. In Kishinev it collaborated with Einsatzkommando 11b in the pogrom described in its reports of 4 and 7 August.[67] It is a well-known fact that as soon as the echelon and the Romanian police units crossed the River Prut they collaborated with Einsatzgruppe units and in most cases were under their direct influence and acted under their guidance.

Such collaboration notwithstanding, the relationship between the various units of Einsatzgruppe D, on the one hand, and the Romanian army, gendarmerie, police, and Operational Echelon, on the other, left much to be desired. The Germans were content only when the Romanians acted according to their directives. In Kishinev, for example, the ghetto was erected after Sonderkommando 11A and Antonescu ordered the Romanian military commander of the town to do so.[68] In Bălţi cooperation between the Romanian police and Einsatzkommando 10a was successful, as reflected in a German report of 29 July that stated that the Romanian police acted "in accordance with the commando's directives" — that is, with a brutality toward the Jews that was already commonplace in Bălţi and in Bessarabia in general.[69]

If, however, the Romanians acted in an impulsive or unplanned manner, failed to remove the evidence of their mass murder operations (massacres, looting, and rape), or accepted bribes from Jews, they elicited the wrath of their Nazi counterparts. The exchange of letters among German and Romanian army commanders reflects the Germans' displeasure with the way things were proceeding. They were not displeased with the crimes themselves but rather with the inefficient way in which they were carried out. In a letter dated 14 July 1941 sent to Romanian army headquarters, General Von Schobert, commander of the Eleventh Army, criticized the way in which the Romanian soldiers killed Jews near the village of Taura in the Bălți district, allowing two Jews to escape and failing to bury their victims' corpses. Their behavior, he complained, "has lowered the prestige of the Romanian army, and at the same time, that of the German army in the eyes of world opinion." He demanded that steps be taken to prevent the repetition of such incidents.[70]

Reports by Einsatzgruppe D and the Feldgendarmerie on the lootings and killings carried out by the Romanians frequently referred to their "lack of organization." When such actions were taken not only against Jews but also against Ukrainians in Bukovina and Bessarabia, the Germans protested.[71] The Germans also protested against Romanian inefficiency or weakness in the way they handled the Jewish question. In a report of 11 July the commander of Einsatzkommando 10a complained of a rash of thefts in Fălești.[72] He also complained that "the measures adopted against Jews prior to the Einsatzkommando's arrival were totally lacking planning."[73] In another report, dated 14 August, the Reich Central Security Office pointed out that the solution to the Jewish problem in the area between the Dniester and Dnieper was in the "wrong hands" (the Romanians').[74] The Romanians, unlike the Germans, murdered and looted the Jews in a totally haphazard manner, as the following excerpt from a report dated 10 July 1941, from Einsatzgruppe D to Einsatzkommando 10b, indicates: "Proceed more vigilantly with respect to the Jewish question in Romanian territory; Jewish meetings should be surprised by us and plots uncovered in order to activate the Romanians against Jewish intelligence, and so that we ourselves may intervene."[75]

THE DEATH TOLL (STAGE 1 OF THE LIQUIDATION)

As of 29 December 1930, the Jews of Bessarabia (including Hotin) had numbered 206,958 and of Bukovina, 107,975.[76] Under the Soviets (June 1940–July 1941) their numbers increased, especially in the large cities of Kishinev and Czernowitz. Jewish survivors from Czernowitz, some of them officials of the Jewish community, also noted the increase in the number of the Jews, estimat-

TABLE 4. STATISTICAL DATA ON ROMANIAN JEWS, BY DISTRICT

District	29 December 1930	1 September 1941	May 1942
Bukovina			
Czernowitz	51,681	49,497	16,794
Câmpulung	7,748	6,572	76
Rădăuți	11,578	6,494	72
Storojineț	15,397	4,312	60
Suceava	6,697	5,074	31
Dorohoi	14,874	11,547	2,316
Total	107,975	83,496	19,349
Bessarabia			
Bălți	31,916	2,923	—
Cahul	4,444	47	—
Cetatea Albă	11,400	55	—
Hotin	36,132	21,468	126
Ismail (including Kilia)	6,433	1,389	1
Lăpușna (including Kishinev)	50,603	10,311	100
Orhei	19,566	360	—
Soroca	29,510	36,014	—
Tighina	16,954	58	—
Total	206,958	72,625	227
Grand total	314,933	156,121	19,576

SOURCE: General data on the official census of the Jewish population of the provinces of Bessarabia and Bukovina, 1930–42, YVA, 0-11/87; reprinted in Ancel, *Documents*, vol. 1, doc. 46, p. 324.

ing the number in the city at some 70,000–75,000 during the Soviet regime.[77] The majority of the Jews (and Romanians) who sought refuge in Bessarabia and Bukovina during Soviet rule were local people and their families who had left but decided to return to their localities. At the same time, there was also a stream of Jews moving from those two provinces to Romania, hindered in many cases by the authorities.

On 1 September 1941 the Romanian army conducted a special population census in the areas recaptured from the Russians.[78] Following this census, the Romanian authorities declared, "On that date, there were 126,434 citizens of Jewish nationality in the two provinces, some of them free, and some in camps."[79]

The total number of Jews deported by the Soviet authorities before the war or recruited to the Red Army or who fled from the Romanian-German invasion did not exceed 30,000–40,000. On 4 September 1941 the Romanian army reported that 64,176 Jews had been interned in camps before being sent to their death.[80] On 25 September another 44,397 Jews remained in these camps.[81] On 15 January 1942 the Inspectorate of the Transnistrian Gendarmerie reported that 118,847 Jews from Bessarabia, Bukovina, and the Dorohoi district had been deported to Transnistria.[82] Extrapolating from the above data, we see that in the space of two months (July–August 1941), at least 100,000 Jews perished or disappeared in these areas (including Herța and its surroundings).[83]

The chapter on demography (chap. 38) provides accurate statistics on the number of Jews interned in the camps and deported to Transnistria, based on information made available following the opening of the Romanian and Soviet archives after 1991. These data on the whole match the data contained in table 4.

The Romanian press did not tell the truth about the liquidation campaign. However, General Voiculescu, the governor general of Bessarabia, in an attempt to impress the Romanians with his contribution to the "reconstruction" of Bessarabia, declared in late August 1941, "The Jewish problem in Bessarabia has been solved. There are no more Jews in Bessarabia's villages, and ghettos have been set up for Jews who still live in the cities."[84]

18

The Camps and Ghettos in Bessarabia and Northern Bukovina, September–November 1941

It was Ion Antonescu who sealed the fate of the survivors of the first wave of killings in the two provinces. Antonescu himself relayed his decision to the Operational Echelon, while Mihai Antonescu relayed it to the Civil Administration Echelon. Like previous operations, this one was supposed to be conducted without written orders so as to leave no trace of the crimes and preclude Jews' demands for compensation or the return of property. The corrupt nature of the Romanian administration, however—both military and civil—occasionally prompted Antonescu and other high-ranking officers to set up committees of inquiry to investigate alleged irregularities. The reports of these committees of inquiry contained almost all the secret orders, even the ones transmitted orally, thereby exposing the Antonescu regime's responsibility for imprisoning the survivors of the first waves of murder in ghettos and camps, subjecting them to a reign of terror in the ghettos and camps, and subsequently deporting them.

Before leaving for Kishinev Gen. Gheorghe Voiculescu, governor general of Bessarabia, was summoned to meet with Antonescu for a briefing on the Conducător's policy in Bessarabia and Bukovina.[1] Among the unwritten prerogatives Antonescu gave Voiculescu was one empowering him "to mercilessly punish those who did not fit into the framework of his basic ideas." These basic ideas, as reflected in the verbal commands, determined that the first problem the governor general had to resolve was the Jewish problem. As the Conducător put it, "the Jews had to be disciplined for their attitudes and actions" during the withdrawal from Bessarabia in June 1940, during Soviet rule, and in the early stages of the war (June–July 1941). "Accordingly, and taking cognizance of the fact that Bessarabia and especially Kishinev is teeming with Jews," Voiculescu later reported, "I have issued, a mere five days after my arrival in Kishinev, Ordinance

No. 61 of 24 July 1941 . . . concerning the establishment of camps and ghettos. The same ordinance states that a ghetto must be set up in Kishinev forthwith."[2]

Voiculescu's reports to Antonescu in the months following the occupation of Bessarabia, as well as other sources, show beyond a shadow of a doubt that the initiative for the establishment of camps and ghettos—and the subsequent deportation of Jews to Transnistria—came from Bucharest, and the actions were not prompted by German pressure. Indeed, such pressure was unnecessary, given that Romania's policy toward the Jews of Bessarabia and Bukovina corresponded in every respect to Germany's.

THE HASTY DEPORTATIONS

Around this time Einsatzgruppe D units were engaged in killing operations in Soviet territory. The Einsatzkommando units advanced swiftly on the Wehrmacht's heels through huge expanses of Soviet territory inhabited by hundreds of thousands of Jews. The Romanian army began deporting tens of thousands of Jews across the Dniester—the Romanian-Soviet border until June 1940—to what later became known as Transnistria. This action, based on the talks between Hitler and Antonescu in Munich on 12 June 1941, was undertaken without any coordination with the German army. The operation began when the Romanian army reached the Dniester River and completed the occupation of the territories that had been annexed to the Soviet Union the previous year. On 18 July 1941 General Topor, the grand pretor, reported that 3,546 Jewish "men, women and children" from the Bălți district had been rounded up by the army and sent to an area adjacent to the front, because "their continued presence in Bessarabia is not desirable." These Jews, he added, had no food and no one to guard them and would be best sent back to Bessarabia and put to work, if transporting them across the river proved unfeasible.[3]

Toward late July the Romanian army rounded up about twenty-five thousand Jews near the village of Coslar on the Dniester. Some of these Jews had been marched over from towns in northern Bukovina; others had been arrested in north Bessarabian towns, particularly in and around Briceni. On 24 July, shortly after the combined German-Romanian forces entered the Ukraine, these Jews were deported across the Dniester to the village of Cozlov. The Romanian soldiers did not allow the deportees to buy food or water but took them that same day to an open field, which they enclosed with barbed wire. Anyone who attempted to escape was shot. After three days of solid rain the weak died, while the remainder were wracked by exhaustion, hunger, and thirst. Only on the last day they were held in this makeshift camp were a few Jews allowed to go to a nearby stream and fetch drinking water. They were then distributed among local villages and kolkhozes in contingents of five hundred to one thousand.[4]

German officers stationed in the vicinity ordered the deportees on to Mogilev. En route, several columns were interned in the village of Skazinets, in a former kolkhoz that was turned into a makeshift camp and surrounded with barbed wire. Although the Romanian soldiers were still responsible for guarding the deportees, many of them were shot by German soldiers.

At the same time, Romanian Fourth Army headquarters ordered its military and gendarmerie units "to catch those who had crossed [back into Bessarabia] and send them back to the Ukraine."[5] Meanwhile, the Romanian soldiers continued bringing convoys of Jews from northern Bessarabia to the Dniester. On 1 August their numbers were swelled with more than 2,500 Jewish survivors of the Hotin massacre.

The Romanian soldiers then proceeded to drown about four hundred Jews, shooting anyone who tried to get out of the river or swim to safety. Colonel Meculescu, inspector general of the gendarmerie in Bessarabia, reported the drowning of only two hundred Jews on 6 August by the gendarmes of the Twenty-Third Police Company.[6] The remainder were taken to the Secureni camp, where they were held pending German authorization for their deportation to the Ukraine.

On the other side of the river the roundup of Jews who had been deported by the Romanians in late July continued. By late July or early August 1941 30,000–32,000 Jews had been forced to cross the Dniester. This figure is derived from various SSI and police reports, from orders given to the gendarmerie to prevent the return of these Jews to Bessarabia, and from Einsatzgruppe D reports.[7] On 4 August most were taken to Mogilev and ordered by the Germans to stand in a vacant plot in the city center in the burning sun, without food or water, and await instructions. For the next three days the Germans subjected the deportees to a selection process, during which the old and sick were separated from the others on the pretext that they required hospitalization and then shot. The youth were then ordered to dig graves for them. During this operation a total of about 4,500 Jews either died of exhaustion or were shot by the Germans and Romanians.[8] The Romanian soldiers threw their victims' corpses into the Dniester, but the German soldiers made a point of burying their victims. The German units now took over and on 4 August, without informing their Romanian allies, forced a contingent of 3,000 Jews back to Atachi, on the Romanian side of the Dniester, facing Mogilev.[9]

In view of Antonescu's request to the German ambassador that Bessarabian Jews not be sent back (since their return "contradicted the guidelines which the

Führer had specified to him [Antonescu] in Munich regarding the treatment of the eastern Jews") and the Foreign Ministry's decision to comply with this request, the killing units in the area had to make a quick decision.[10] Sonderkommando 10B could not deal alone with the huge concentration of Romanian Jews deported eastward over the Dniester by the Romanians and those located in a village "some 50 km. up the Dniester from Mogilev Podolsk and packed with deportees."[11] Units under the command of Higher SS and Police Chief Friedrich Jeckeln (responsible for the rear lines of communication in the Army South area and the Reich Kommissariat Ukraine) murdered 22,200 Jews in three days in Kamenets-Podolsk.[12] Romanian sources reported that of about 30,000 deportees, a mere 12,600 escaped. The escapees were subsequently returned to Bessarabia from the Ukraine via Yampol and interned in the Vertujeni camp.[13]

It is worth noting that right from the start of the war the Soviet authorities forbade all its citizens (Jews and non-Jews alike) to cross over from Bessarabia to the Ukraine. The measure was lifted after about ten days, but in the meantime most bridges and railway bridges had been destroyed by German aviators, making an escape almost impossible. The Hotin and Atachi bridges as well as the entire Bessarabian border were heavily guarded. Jews attempting to cross the bridges into the Ukraine were repulsed by Red Army soldiers. The chaos grew as Jews began flowing in from near and far (including from northern Bukovina), fleeing from the advancing German and Romanian troops. Not only did the Soviet authorities not help the Jews escape, but in many cases they forcibly prevented them from doing so. All the evidence indicates that the Soviet army prevented its citizens from escaping across the Dniester in the early days of the war. A few Jews, however, escaped by train or crossed over to Odessa via bridges in southern Bessarabia.

In late June the masses of Jews gathered in Atachi were finally allowed to cross over a makeshift bridge the Soviets had built in the days preceding their withdrawal. The area served as a target for aerial bombardment, resulting in many casualties on the bridge and on either side of the river. In any case, the fugitives did not manage to get far before the Germans caught up with them. Some were shot on the spot, while others fled back to the Dniester.[14]

Thousands of Jews were shot on the Ukrainian and Romanian banks of the Dniester and dumped into the river or forced into the water at gunpoint and shot. The perpetrators of these crimes were never brought to justice, even when the authorities got wind of them. Investigations were ordered only because the gendarmes lined their own pockets with money and other valuables taken from the Jews they murdered, instead of transferring them to the National Bank of

Romania. It is thanks to their greed that we have documents attesting to the drowning of thousands of Jews in the Dniester in late July and August.[15]

The fact that the convoys of Jews were constantly on the move created a problem the Romanian General Staff had not anticipated. It meant—much to the Germans' annoyance—that thousands of Jewish corpses were strewn by the roadside, marking their itinerary and attracting the attention of the Ukrainian and Romanian peasants, who stripped the corpses of their clothes and prized out their gold teeth.

Many Jews were already ill, exhausted, or half-crazed when they arrived at the camps. As the commander of the Vertujeni camp testified in 1945, the Jews' plight there was "worse than abject. Many of them had been forced to march for days from place to place in the August heat. The technique of keeping Jewish prisoners constantly on the go was the greatest tragedy of the times."[16] It is clear from the above that the Romanian death marches—during which tens of thousands of Jews are said to have lost their lives—preceded the Nazi death marches by several years.

Thus, the camps and ghettos were set up in response to the failure of the attempt to hastily deport the Jews who had survived the first wave of "cleansing the ground." They were an improvised solution to the problem of finding a stopping place for the convoys of tens of thousands of Jews who were being marched from place to place.

On 8 August a special order was issued relating to the internal regime of the camps, delegation of responsibility, and sources of funding. The order stipulated that the Jews would be maintained by "foreign sources of funding" and not at the state's expense. "The deportees themselves shall provide the money for their upkeep, and in the case of any shortfall, the gendarmerie legion shall try to help. The internees shall be closely guarded to prevent them escaping."[17]

The camps were set up in coordination with the district governors, or prefects, who assumed their duties on 25 July 1941.[18] The camp's inmates provided these prefects with a steady source of labor: they were put to work clearing out ruins, repairing municipal services, rebuilding roads and bridges, cleaning government offices, and helping out in military hospitals. Although the special order stipulated that the Jews were to be paid for their services, they were not paid, and moreover, they received no food. Evidently this order was amended orally, as testified by Colonel Mănecuţă, the inspector general of the gendarmerie in Bukovina, reporting on the situation of the Jews in the Edineţi and Vertujeni camps on the eve of their deportation: "I was informed by telephone that the State shall not be financing their upkeep."[19]

The forced labor to which the Jews were subjected was ostensibly meant to

TABLE 5. CAMPS AND GHETTOS IN BESSARABIA, SEPTEMBER 1941

Camp	No. of Jews as of 1 Sept. 1941	Responsible gendarmerie legion	Units guarding the camp	Start and end of deportation	Comments
Secureni	10,356[a]	Hotin	Sixtieth Police Company	2 Oct.–8 Nov.	Including Jews of the Bârnova (3,000) and Brebeni (2,000) camps[b]
Edineţi	11,762[c]	Hotin	At first soldiers and cadets, later Sixtieth Police Company	11–15 Oct.	—
Limbenii Noi	2,634	Bălţi	Bălţi Gendarmerie Legion	—	Transferred from Mărculeşti camp on 28 September
Răşcani	3,072	Bălţi	Bălţi Gendarmerie Legion		
Răuţel	3,253	Bălţi	Bălţi Gendarmerie Legion		
Vertujeni[d]	22,969	Soroca	A soldiers' platoon	16 Sept.–8 Oct.	Including 1,600 Jews who were transferred from the Alexandrucel Bun camp on 19 August and 5,550 Jews who were transferred from the Rubleniţa camp on 19 and 20 August
Mărculeşti[e]	11,000	Soroca	Soroca Gendarmerie Legion	20 Oct.–10 Nov.	—
Chişinău ghetto[f]	11,252	Chişinău	Tenth Police Company; Company of Fiftieth Regiment; Company of Sixty-Eighth Regiment; Twenty-Third Police Company	8–31 Oct.[g]	Deported via Rezina to the death camp of Bogdanovka

		Per region	Gendarmes from the regional legions	23 Oct. 1941	Deported via Tiraspol to the death camp of Bogdanovka on the Bug River[h]
Small ghettos and camps in southern Bessarabia, Ismail, Cahul, Chilia, and Bolgrad	5,000	—	—	23 Oct. 1941	
Total	—	—	—	—	72,625, according to the census taken by the representative of the Central Bureau of Statistics with the help of the Romanian army

SOURCE: Collated from reports and tables submitted by the Gendarmerie Inspectorates to Pretor Topor or by the pretor to the Ministry of the Interior. Carp, *Cartea neagră*, 3:41, 61, 85, 88, 113, 115; Ancel, *Documents*, 5:52, 99, 131–33; Ancel, *Documents*, 10:100–102, 138.

a According to a count carried out by the gendarmes, there were originally 10,201 Jews. The municipal authorities later found only 8,302 Jews. Carp, *Cartea neagră*, 3:115.

b According to a count on 10 August 1941. Carp, *Cartea neagră*, 3:101.

c The gendarmes found 12,248 Jews. The army's Sanitary Service found only 11,224 Jews. Carp, *Cartea neagră*, 3:114.

d Carp, *Cartea neagră*, 3:104–6.

e Carp, *Cartea neagră*, 3:61.

f Carp, *Cartea neagră*, 3:61.

g See the schedule for the first six convoys that left Kishinev ghetto for Rezina and Tighina on 12–17 October 1941, USHMM/SSARM, RG 54.001M, roll 1, fond 706, opis 1, vol. 22, p. 61.

h See the schedule for the convoys that were deported on 15 October 1941 from Cahul, Ismail, Bolgrad, Chilia, and Vâlcov via Tarutino and from there to Tighina and Transnistria, drawn up by the inspector general of the gendarmerie in Transnistria, USHMM/SSARM, Kishinev Archive, p. 62.

pay for their food. In some cases, the deportees were expected to buy their food, although most did not have the means, since most of their valuables and money had been confiscated by the National Bank of Romania or looted by the gendarmes and guards.

Between 10 July and late August four large camps and two large ghettos as well as several smaller camps and ghettos were set up in localities that had been emptied of their Jewish inhabitants, in preparation for the start of the organized transports to Transnistria. By 31 August most Bessarabian and north Bukovinian Jews were interned in camps or in the Kishinev ghetto. (The Czernowitz ghetto was set up in October.) Romanian gendarmes (in the villages), policemen (in the towns), and soldiers (in Soroca and Kishinev) were responsible for guarding the camps and ghettos.

The commander of the gendarmerie in Bukovina, Mănecuță, reported to General Topor that despite all measures adopted by the urban and rural authorities and despite efforts by the gendarmerie, it was impossible to ensure food for these camps and in general "it was impossible to cater to their needs, taking into account the large number of people and the overcrowded conditions." Many Jews, he emphasized, were destitute and about to die of starvation.[20]

THE DEPORTATION TO TRANSNISTRIA

As Voiculescu reported to Antonescu, by late August 1941 the Jewish problem in Bessarabia had been solved, there were no more Jews in Bessarabia's villages, and ghettos had been set up for the Jews who remained in the cities.[21] This marked the successful completion of the first stage of Antonescu's campaign to "cleanse the ground," during which some one hundred thousand Jews were murdered and another thirty thousand to forty thousand fled (most were sent back to Bessarabia, where they suffered the same fate as the deportees). Those who survived this wave of murder were interned in several improvised ghettos in Lujeni and Văscăuți. From mid-July most were marched in columns to northern Bessarabia and then to the Dniester. The journal kept by Rabbi Horovitz of Banila on the Siret bears testimony of the tragedy suffered by the Jews in the villages and small towns of northern Bukovina.[22]

The Romanians' attempt to perfect the planning and implementation of the deportation operation was, in part, a response to criticism by various Einsatzgruppe units that the operations were unplanned (leaving corpses unburied and failing to cover their tracks) and corrupt (raping and looting). The Einsatzgruppe commanders' disapproval of this state of affairs is reflected in their

CHART 2. CHAIN OF COMMAND FOR THE INTERNMENT OF JEWS IN
CAMPS AND GHETTOS AND THEIR DEPORTATION TO TRANSNISTRIA

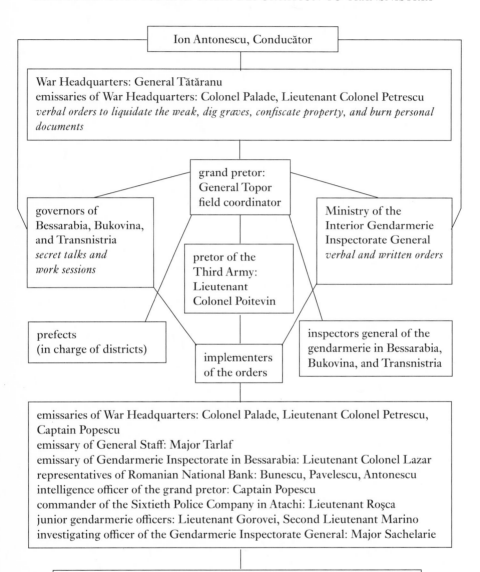

Ion Antonescu, Conducător

War Headquarters: General Tătăranu
emissaries of War Headquarters: Colonel Palade, Lieutenant Colonel Petrescu
verbal orders to liquidate the weak, dig graves, confiscate property, and burn personal documents

grand pretor:
General Topor
field coordinator

governors of
Bessarabia, Bukovina,
and Transnistria
secret talks and work sessions

Ministry of the
Interior Gendarmerie
Inspectorate General
verbal and written orders

pretor of the
Third Army:
Lieutenant
Colonel Poitevin

prefects
(in charge of districts)

implementers
of the orders

inspectors general of the
gendarmerie in Bessarabia,
Bukovina, and Transnistria

emissaries of War Headquarters: Colonel Palade, Lieutenant Colonel Petrescu,
Captain Popescu
emissary of General Staff: Major Tarlaf
emissary of Gendarmerie Inspectorate in Bessarabia: Lieutenant Colonel Lazar
representatives of Romanian National Bank: Bunescu, Pavelescu, Antonescu
intelligence officer of the grand pretor: Captain Popescu
commander of the Sixtieth Police Company in Atachi: Lieutenant Roşca
junior gendarmerie officers: Lieutenant Gorovei, Second Lieutenant Marino
investigating officer of the Gendarmerie Inspectorate General: Major Sachelarie

commanders of the convoys of deportees via Atachi, Cosăuți, and
Rezina: gendarmerie officers Lieutenant Cristea, Lieutenant Popovici,
Lieutenant Roşca, Lieutenant Popoiu, Captain Ramadan

periodic reports. In a report dated 14 August the RSHA stated that the area bordered by the Dniester and Dnieper was in the wrong hands, indicating that they expected the Romanians to take responsibility for the solution to the Jewish problem on the other side of the Bug, too.[23]

The Romanian General Staff planned and supervised the deportation operation through its envoys and through the grand pretor. The General Staff had at its disposal the various branches of the army, the Ministry of the Interior, the pretorate, and the gendarmerie and also, as necessary, the governors of Bessarabia, Bukovina, and Transnistria. The chain of command went from Ion Antonescu to the General Staff to the grand pretor (General Topor) to the gendarmerie legions. These provided the effectives, backed up, where necessary, by soldiers of the Third Army provided by the pretorate. The instructions issued by the inspectors general of the gendarmeries in Bessarabia and Bukovina regarding the deportation matched the instructions from the top echelons. Voiculescu's "Instructions for the Evacuation of the Jews from the Vertujeni Camp," for example, specified the timing of the deportation, the number of Jews in each convoy, the distance to be covered daily, the commanders of the convoys, and coordination with the prefectures "in accordance with the Grand Pretor's instructions."[24] The cooperation of the Railway Authority and Transportation Ministry was also enlisted, since some of the deportees were transported to Atachi or Mărculeşti by train. For the duration of the war the Railway Authority was subordinate to the General Staff.

On 30 August Gen. Nicolae Tătăranu, the representative of the Romanian General Staff, and Gen. Arthur Hauffe, the representative of the Wehrmacht, signed the "Agreement for the Security, Administration, and Economic Exploitation of the Territory between the Dniester and the Bug and the Bug and the Dnieper" (known as the Tighina Agreement). Paragraph 7 referred to the Jews in the camps and ghettos of Bessarabia and Bukovina and the Jewish inhabitants of Transnistria: "The Jews cannot, at present, be transported across the Bug. They must therefore be concentrated in labor camps and put to work, until they can be evacuated to the East, once the war is over."[25] This agreement confirms that right from the start the Romanians were meant to be responsible for solving the Jewish problem on the Transnistrian side of the Bug as well and that their final objective was to cleanse Transnistria, too, of Jews.

The agreement effectively put an end to the controversy between the two armies over the Romanians' right to deport Jews from Bessarabia and Bukovina and acknowledged their right to use Transnistria as a large concentration camp. Prior to the signing of the agreement negotiations took place between Mihai

Antonescu and representatives of the German Foreign Ministry, about which nothing is known apart from a few hints that Mihai Antonescu subsequently dropped. The envoys of the RSHA had already stated that, in their opinion, the solution to the Jewish problem between the Dniester and the Dnieper was in the wrong hands. Hitler, on the other hand, was more than satisfied with the way Antonescu was handling the Jewish problem. In late August 1941, several days before the signing of the Tighina Agreement, he told Goebbels: "As far as the Jewish problem is concerned, it may be stated with certainty that a man like Antonescu is pursuing much more radical policies in this area than we have so far."[26]

At a meeting with the governors of the provinces, Antonescu scheduled the first deportation for 15 September. General Topor's attempt to move up the date for crossing the river south of Atachi to 6 September failed for logistic reasons and also because heavy rain had caused the Dniester to overflow. He ordered "the route of the convoys to be determined, and the gendarmes to be prepared to begin the transfer on 6 September. . . . The convoys shall comprise a thousand [Jews] each."[27] The operation was conducted like a military operation. Before it began, the chief of General Staff asked Topor to report to him on "the exact status of all the Jewish camps and ghettos in Bessarabia and Bukovina," specifying the number of Jews in each camp and ghetto and the names of the guard units.[28] Topor received the order on 4 September and on the very same day reported back to War Headquarters (housed in the carriage of a special train used by Antonescu himself) with information regarding the location of the camps, the number of Jews being held in them, and the units guarding them. The information revealed no involvement on the part of the German military; on the contrary, the entire operation was an internal Romanian affair.

The deportations began on 16 September. The Vertujeni camp was the first camp that was ready to receive deportees, as the inspector general of the gendarmerie in Bessarabia reported to General Topor.[29] Although there were a number of bridges over the Dniester, the bombed bridge at Hotin, on the northernmost tip of the border, led over into German-occupied territory in Poland and was therefore disqualified. The five main crossing points from Bessarabia to Transnistria were, from north to south: Atachi–Mogilev Podolski (better known as Mogilev); Cosăuți–Yampol; Rezina–Râbnița; Tighina–Tiraspol; and Olănești–Iasca.

Both before and during the deportation hundreds of Jews were starved, beaten, or tortured to death each day. Women and girls were raped, and those who resisted were shot. More Jews were murdered during searches for their valuables. Even before the convoys headed for the Dniester the whole place was littered with corpses. More corpses were left by the wayside during the deportation.

On 4 October, the chief of General Staff, at Antonescu's behest, gave an impossible deadline of ten days for "the deportation of all Bukovinian Jewry across the Dniester."[30] On 9 October the deportation of 21,000 Jews from southern Bukovina began, using sealed freight wagons. The operation lasted for about four days. A month later, on 13 November, only 179 Jews remained in the entire area by special dispensation, at the request of the local authorities and local citizens, to operate the sawmills or serve as doctors. The deportation of Jews from the Czernowitz ghetto began on 12 October, several days after the establishment of the ghetto, and lasted until 15 November, in which short period about 30,000 of Czernowitz's 50,000 or so Jews were deported, on the verbal command of the General Staff's representatives.[31]

The deportation of the Jews in the Storojinetz ghetto began on 13 October, followed on 6 November by the deportation of the twelve thousand Jews who lived in the Dorohoi district. In mid-December 1941 the last convoys of Jews left southern Bukovina and the Dorohoi district, bringing the second phase of the Holocaust of Romanian Jewry to a close. A second wave of deportations took place in the summer of 1942.

On October 6 Ion Antonescu reported to his cabinet on the status of ethnic cleansing in Bessarabia: "I have decided to remove the Jews permanently from these regions, and the operation is currently under way. The 10,000 or so Jews who are left in Bessarabia shall, in a few days' time, be taken across the Dniester and, circumstances permitting, sent across the Urals."[32] The convoys of Jew that were led toward the Dniester had very few escorts (gendarmes, police, and soldiers), and it would have been easy to stage a riot or plan an escape. Even so, there are no known cases of Jews having tried to escape from the deportation convoys in Bessarabia and Bukovina.[33] On the contrary, the deportations gave the Jews a relative sense of security and were preferable to the alternative — torture and death. The Christians inhabitants of Bessarabia and northern Bukovina did not move a finger to help their beleaguered compatriots.

Official statistics that compare the number of Jews in Bessarabia on 1 September 1941 with those who arrived at the crossing points on the Dniester show that about twenty-five thousand Jews from the region "died of natural causes, disappeared or were shot" in the space of about two months.[34] Voiculescu wrote in his summary report, after mentioning the orders he received from Antonescu, that the deportations were well organized and conducted "in a civilized manner."[35]

Unlike the first stage of the holocaust of Romanian Jewry, in which Antonescu was still under some Nazi influence, in the second stage he, his partners in government, and the Romanian army acted entirely on their own initiative. The deportations were Antonescu's brainchild, prompted by his wish to purge the liberated territories of Jews. On 16 October 1943 the minister of the interior wrote a memorandum on the repatriation of some of the survivors in Transnistria in which he claimed that the Jews had brought the deportations on themselves "because of their attitude toward the Romanian Army when it had retreated from the Soviet-annexed territories, and toward the Romanians during the Soviet occupation."[36] There was not one verbal or written reference to German pressure as a predisposing factor in the deportations.

Likewise, in a special memorandum issued by Antonescu, the Presidency of the Council of Ministers claimed that the deportation of the Jews from Bessarabia and Bukovina was intended "to restore the dignity of the Romanian people," which had been hurt by the Jews' attitude toward the army and the Romanian people.[37] At the height of the deportation campaign Ion Antonescu informed the nation of his resolve "to punish the Jews for the crimes they have committed against the nation, the army, and our recaptured fatherland." In his idiosyncratic style, he added, "As long as I live, no-one and nothing can stop me from completing the cleansing operation."[38]

At this stage Antonescu was planning the deportation of Jews not only from Bessarabia and Bukovina but also from the Regat. In his trial, Alexianu, the governor of Transnistria, testified that Marshal Antonescu had dispatched two colonels to Tiraspol (his temporary headquarters until the occupation of Odessa) in September 1941 "to prepare Transnistria for the deportation of Bessarabian and Bukovinian Jewry, to be followed by the deportation of the Jews of the Regat."[39]

THE VERTUJENI CAMP

The Vertujeni camp, which was evidently set up on 11 August 1941 on the outskirts of the village of Vertujeni, on a hill overlooking the Dniester, served as an internment camp for the survivors of the first wave of killings in the Soroca district. The camp was set up to put an end to the death marches of deportees from northern Bukovina who were barred by the Germans from crossing over into the Ukraine. On 17 August a convoy of about 13,000 Jews, who had been marching for weeks, reached the camp. Large numbers had been tortured to death or killed by gendarmes and cadets before even reaching the camp.[40] On 18 August some of Lipcani's 4,000 Jewish survivors were taken to the forest near the camp, and on 21 August four convoys of survivors from the smaller camps of Alexandru cel Bun and Rublenița were transferred to Vertujeni. One of the convoys, comprising the disabled and about 1,500 women with small children, was transported to the camp in horse-drawn wagons.[41]

Colonel Palade, acting for the General Staff, initially ordered all Jews who were in the Bălți gendarmerie's area of jurisdiction to be interned in Vertujeni. However, the unexpected arrival in Vertujeni of the large convoy from across the Dniester thwarted this plan, and the colonel had to ask the General Staff for instructions as to what to do with the Jews in the Bălți area.[42] On 23 August the Vertujeni camp held about twenty-three thousand inmates; two weeks later the number had risen to twenty-six thousand. Occasionally Jews who were arrested or found in hiding places in the neighboring villages and those whom the gendarmes had spared (the gendarmes were entitled to shoot all Jews on sight in all rural areas) were taken to Vertujeni.

The Vertujeni camp was not equipped to accommodate so many people, especially as there was not enough drinking water. The Romanian authorities, however, were unconcerned, "packing the Jews into attics, sheds, and storehouses, like sardines. No medical care was provided. Each day, about 50–60 people perished. There was hardly any water. [The Jews] had to wait in line for many hours just for a cup of water."[43] This was the situation when there were 1,200 inmates in the camp, and things got much worse after the arrival of the second contingent of Jews from across the Dniester, who were in a much worse state. The mortality rate doubled to around 120 deaths per day.

The camp's first commander, Col. Alexandru Constantinescu, was shocked when he first caught sight of the convoys entering the camp: "They were in a state of indescribable exhaustion . . . an impossible mix of human creatures . . . women, children, young girls and men, the sick, the expiring, women giving birth. It was impossible to feed them all or provide them with enough sleeping places. . . . Before my eyes, I saw several Jews die, others faint, women giving birth. All were covered in lice and sores."[44] Colonel Constantinescu was so troubled by this sight that he asked to be discharged—a request that was granted largely because he was not a member of the standing army.[45]

THE DEPORTATION FROM THE VERTUJENI CAMP

On 10 September General Topor gave the signal to begin deporting the Jews of the Vertujeni camp in convoys of 1,600 each. Following this signal Colonel Meculescu issued the camp commander "instructions concerning the evacuation of Jews from Vertujeni" and sent verbal instructions to Capt. Victor Ramadan and, via Ramadan, to Agapie. The instructions permitted the shooting of Jews "during the transfer" from the camp. General Topor added a vaguely worded paragraph to his orders, stating: "Those who disobey [instructions] shall be treated in accordance with the standard regulations anchored in laws, decrees and decree-laws."[46] The gendarmerie officers who were in charge of the deportees had no problem interpreting this paragraph.

On the eve of the deportation the number of Jews left in the camp had dwindled to 22,150. In other words, in the space of a month and a half about 4,000 Jews had perished. The mortality rate in the camp rose to 200–300 a day as more Jews succumbed to hunger, disease, and torture and an increasing number of babies and old people died.

Meculescu decided to march the deportees along two different routes: via Cosăuți in the north and Rezina in the south.[47] He sent his personal representative, Lt. Col. Radu Lazăr, to coordinate the logistics of the operation with Colonel Palade and, later, to coordinate operations on the ground. The gendarmes of the camp, under the command of an officer, accompanied the columns of Jews to Soroca in the north and Mateuți in the south, where the Soroca and Orhei gendarmeries legions took over and escorted the deportees over the Dniester.

On the other side of the Dniester Transnistrian gendarmes were waiting for the convoys. The commanders of the convoys were given maps with the two deportation routes marked in red and blue, one of which has survived.[48] Captain Ramadan was in charge of the deportees who were taken to Cosăuți, while Lieutenant Popoiu was in charge of those taken to Rezina. The instructions specified, "There are to be no records of the crossing."[49] Before leaving the camp, all the Jews' personal documents testifying to their existence were confiscated and burnt. The Jews were counted before crossing the river and again upon arrival, using "metal rods."[50]

A special unit of trigger-happy gendarmes was placed at the disposal of the two officers in charge of the operation. The commanders of the gendarmerie legions in the two camps were responsible for "burying the dead with the help of local citizens, and to make in advance [temporary] billeting arrangements on the outskirts of villages, in barns, storehouses, and the like, so as to prevent epidemics."[51]

The official orders forbade looting and even specified that anyone caught looting would be shot. This order, however, was never obeyed. In most cases the local peasants connived with the gendarmes, offering them a share of the spoils. The order also stipulated that each convoy had to be provided with fifty horse-driven wagons to transport luggage and those who were unable to walk. In practice, each convoy was supplied with only six to eight wagons, and even those had to be paid for with hefty bribes to the drivers, the gendarmes, and the camp commander. Agapie collected 400,000 lei from all the deportees in exchange for promises to provide them with wagons.[52] These wagons were the gendarmes' last chance to extort money from the Jews, and they exploited the opportunity to the full, promising transportation for pregnant women, children, the sick, and the elderly. What they failed to reveal, however, was that at a certain point other gendarmes would be taking over, and they would want new arrangements and their share of the pie. The gendarmes did not guard the convoys well and failed, whether deliberately or inadvertently, to prevent Romanian and Ukrainian peasants from attacking the Jews en route and stealing items on their person or among their belongings. In the trials of war criminals it transpired that Agapie had not even bothered to inform the gendarmes that it was their duty to prevent the peasants from looting, if necessary by force.

The composition of the convoys was random, and many families were forcibly separated, at the camp officers' whim. In most cases the separation was final, since the convoys heading in different directions never met up again. The regime of covering thirty kilometers a day was strictly adhered to, without a pause even to drink water. At night the Jews slept in open fields. As the indictment against the camp's commanders stated, "The convoys of wretched deportees, worn out by hunger, abuse, disease, and looting, continued flowing into the 'province of death' [Transnistria]. Gendarmes forced them to run with shouts and blows, until they earned their long awaited rest [i.e., death] either in the forests of Cosăuți or in the 'province of death' across the Dniester."[53]

At night the new gendarmes and their aides chose girls from among the masses and abused them until dawn. By day they still managed to "earn" a little money by "selling" Jews to the peasants. This wholly Romanian practice, which combined theft with murder, took place along the deportation routes in Bessarabia and soon became an accepted practice. Peasants lying in wait for the convoys would approach the accompanying gendarme, point to a Jew whose clothes or shoes they wanted, and offer a price ranging from 1,000 to 2,000 lei ($1.00–1.50). After some haggling, the gendarme would summon the unfortunate Jew and shoot him or her. The peasant would pay the agreed-upon price and swiftly strip the corpse.

After the camp had been emptied of its inmates, the mayor of Vertujeni (which was, to all intents and purposes, now a Romanian village) sent a confidential report to the regional pretor describing the terrible conditions in the village, the streets of which were littered with Jewish corpses, and complaining that the gendarmes were confiscating furniture that had belonged to Jews and should have been turned over to the state. The report did not condemn the incarceration, abuse, and murder of the Jews but castigated the camp commanders for leaving the camp in a filthy condition and for stealing Jewish property that the mayor felt rightfully belonged to the villagers, who had appropriated Jewish land and houses and therefore were entitled (in the mayor's opinion) to the furniture, too.[54]

The Mărculeşti camp was set up by the Romanian gendarmerie to accommodate the survivors of the first wave of killings in Bessarabia. It also served as a transit camp for the Jewish deportees who were being marched by the gendarmes from northern Bukovina to Transnistria. Mărculeşti was chosen as a camp for the same reason as Vertujeni. Both were Jewish towns that had been emptied of their Jewish populations. Jewish Mărculeşti, called Mărculeşti Colonie in official documents, was about one and a half kilometers away from Mărculeşti proper. The village was situated on the Dniester, about forty-five kilometers from the district capital of Soroca and some four kilometers from the Bălţi-Soldăneşti railroad. It was the last station before the Dniester.[55]

Mărculeşti was founded in 1837. Until 1941 it had an exclusively Jewish population (of 2,319, according to the 1930 census). After the outbreak of war in June 1941 Jewish refugees began pouring in from Bălţi, Făleşti, and other places, fleeing the bombings. They were welcomed with open arms. Until 5 July the Soviets prevented the Jews from escaping to the Ukraine, but after the border was opened many refugees, including a small share of the Jews in Mărculeşti, left for the Dniester. A few privileged families drove there in horse-drawn wagons. On 7 July, before the entry of the Romanian army, hundreds of Romanian peasants entered Mărculeşti and looted Jewish property, murdered dozens of Jews, and raped women. Many Jews fled to the village's outlying fields, but they were followed there and killed. Only a few Jews who survived the pogrom actually reached the Dniester.

Upon the Romanian army's entry into Mărculeşti, on 8 July, eighteen Jewish community leaders were taken hostage and later shot to death. All the Jews of Mărculeşti were ordered to gather at the edge of the town, where a Romanian officer stripped them of their possessions. The men were ordered to deepen the antitank trenches that had been prepared by the Soviets. Before they were shot to death they were ordered to undress and were placed in groups of ten in front of the trenches. The men were shot first, followed by the women and children. Although we do not know the exact number of victims, official reports set it somewhere between 460 and 1,040, including Jews from Gura-Căinari. The massacre was perpetrated by soldiers from the Sixth Infantry Regiment under the command of Col. Emil Matieş.[56]

The Mărculeşti camp served primarily as a transit camp for the convoys of Jews who were being marched to Rezina. In early September 1941 about 11,000 Jews were concentrated there. On 6 September about 9,000 Jews were transferred to Mărculeşti from three small camps in the Bălţi district, pending their deportation: 2,634 from Limbenii Noi, 3,072 from Răşcani, and 3,235 from Răuţel. Over time, more than 10,000 Jews who were deported from Bukovina by train or by foot passed through the camp. From early October the camp also absorbed convoys of Jews from Czernowitz and southern Bukovina who were also being taken to Rezina. The Czernowitz convoy was taken to Mărculeşti station by train and then marched the four kilometers to the camp. The inmates of the camp were then taken by foot to the Dniester. From the moment the camp began absorbing convoys of Jews from southern Bukovina it turned into a "torture and looting camp."[57]

THE DEPORTATION FROM THE MĂRCULEŞTI CAMP

The same thieving practices that Agapie introduced in Vertujeni were adopted in Mărculeşti. As they testified during their interrogations, Agapie and Mihăiescu managed to fleece the deportees of 2,060,000 lei — which was probably a conservative estimate. Of this sum, only 560,000 lei were transferred to the national bank.[58]

Before the convoys left the camp, the camp officers ordered all deportees, under penalty of death, to throw all their valuables and personal effects into a large bowl.[59] Such attempts at extortion, fueled by the myth of Jewish affluence, were commonplace. Even exhausted Jews who were about to be shot were ordered to hand over their valuables. The officers who met the convoys in Cosăuţi conducted their own "fund-raising" operations before pushing the Jews off the bridge.[60] When the Jews arrived in Transnistria fleeced of all their belongings, the Transnistrian gendarmes, realizing there was nothing left to steal, vented their frustration on the hapless Jews.

The Mărculeşti-Cosăuţi road was strewn with the corpses of Jews who had been unable to keep up with the others. Immediately after the convoys passed by, peasants descended on the corpses and stole their clothes. "Places where the convoys had stopped for a while were littered with corpses. Deportees from previous convoys were left there dead or dying."[61] It was around this time that the deportees from Bukovina began to refer to these marches as "death marches" (*Todesmarsch*). According to a deportee's testimony, "The road was littered with Jewish corpses from previous transports, their eyes gouged out by ravens."[62]

The convoys of Jews constituted a ready source of income for the Romanian peasants. Some "bought" Jews from the gendarmes, some formed gangs that worked independently or in collusion with the guards, some stole their clothes, some agreed to bury them for payment, and some "sold" them cups of water in exchange for their valuables. As a survivor wrote, "They lay in wait for the wretched convoys and exploited our catastrophe."[63] By far the worst part of the trek to the makeshift bridge erected by the Romanian army in Cosăuți or to the rafts in Atachi was crossing the Cosăuți forest or spending the night there. These stopovers sometimes lasted for days.

THE BATTLE FOR THE BOOTY

Although the Mărculeşti camp was closed down in early November, it still served a purpose as far as the authorities were concerned. On 24 November 1941 the prefect of the Soroca district accused the military authorities of appropriating "valuables left by the Jews who were being taken across the Dniester" and of having them stored in the army depots of the Fourth Army Corps. Since the camp was under his area of jurisdiction, the prefect claimed, the Jews' property rightfully belonged to the prefecture. In an attempt to resolve this dispute, the Ministry of National Defense set up a committee representing the army, the Quartermasters Corps, the Ministry of the Interior and the prefecture. Ion Mihăiescu informed the committee that "when he realized that the Jews had left much of their belongings behind in the camps he had, at his own initiative, transferred all the property to safe places, under lock and key." Despite the value of this property, the entire process of storing, registering, and guarding it was totally chaotic because "2,300 Jews passed through the camp daily." Mihăiescu therefore decided to entrust the property to the gendarmes guarding the camp. He then notified the Bukovinian government of its existence "since the Jews whose property it was were under its jurisdiction." He likewise notified War Headquarters.[64]

The General Staff's Second Section, which was responsible for supervising Jews and other minorities, informed the Ministry of National Defense that "many of the personal effects that the Jewish deportees were unable to take with them had been left behind in the camp." The army could put these goods to good use, especially to equip military hospitals. Since the goods were being kept in "mice-infested" storerooms, the Second Section advised the General Staff to arrange for their immediate transfer to army depots. The minister of defense himself added a handwritten note instructing that immediate action be taken to salvage the property for the army's use and that the army be kept informed of such action.[65]

On 28 October 1941 Capt. Gheorghe Pârvulescu arrived in the Mărculeşti camp and contacted the representatives of the national bank, as he had been instructed to do, but not the district authorities. The representatives of the national bank took him on a tour of the camp, showing him all the valuables left behind by the deportees. Captain Pârvulescu began the job of sorting through the deportees' personal effects, but "with the arrival of new convoys each day" the goods continued to pile up. Meanwhile, the General Staff sent ten rail cars to Mărculești to transport the goods. Mihăiescu advised Pârvulescu "to load the goods [on the cars] now, and leave the sorting out for later, once the goods are unloaded."[66] Pârvulescu followed this advice, but between 3 and 9 November the army managed to load only three cars, and then only with the help of peasants who were recruited by the gendarmes to transport the goods from the camp to the cars that were waiting in the railway station. The outbreak of a typhus epidemic in the camp put an end to the operation, and the three cars were sealed by the representative of the General Staff. On 7 November representatives of the Bukovinian government arrived and claimed the goods on the ground that they were government property.

The situation grew even more complicated when the prefect of Soroca, his pretor, and a gendarmerie officer (a major) from Bukovina arrived in Mărculești Station, staking their claim to the goods. They all saw themselves as the deportees' rightful heirs. The prefect ordered the three rail cars, which the General Staff's representative had sent on to Bucharest, to be stopped en route. He was forced to defer his plan to appoint his own committee to sort through the goods left behind in the camp due to the outbreak of the typhus epidemic. Meanwhile he ordered all the goods to remain under the supervision of the camp commander.

In a desperate attempt to salvage the goods, the prefect appealed to the Defense Ministry, the Interior Ministry, and the Bessarabian authorities and even sent his pretor and gendarmerie officer in pursuit of the cars, but to no avail. On 24 November the sealed cars reached Bucharest, where they were transferred to the army's central warehouse. The cars were opened on 28 November 1941 in the presence of representatives of the Defense and Interior Ministries (both of which were responsible for the liquidation and deportation of Jews), who confirmed that "the lead seals and the locks . . . were intact." After the objects were sorted (28 November 1941 to 11 February 1942) they were divided up between the army's central warehouse, its main sanitary depot, and Maria Antonescu's Welfare Council (Consiliul de Patronaj).[67]

The ministerial committee concluded that the Bukovina government was to blame for allowing the Jews to take too many possessions with them and for failing to issue instructions as to what was to be done with the goods they left behind. It praised Mihăiescu's initiative in salvaging the goods for the army's use. The committee did not consider itself empowered to make decisions regarding the division of the booty, which was state property and, as such, subject to the discretion of the state's higher institutions.[68]

Edineți was a town in the Hotin district, which had 4,341 Jews (representing 90.3 percent of the total population of Edineți) in 1930. At the outbreak of war the Soviet army withdrew from the town, taking with it several senior government officials. Some Jews decided to escape, although most stayed put. On 2 July 1941 Romanian and German paratroopers were dropped onto a hill adjoining the cemetery and began bombarding the town. Groups of Jews began fleeing to Secureni, where they were interned in the camp there and then deported in convoys to Atachi, a point for crossing over the Dniester. When the paratroopers entered the town, the Romanian soldiers began shooting in the air to frighten the Jews and then raided their homes, killing hundreds of them. The Jews began barricading themselves into their homes. The soldiers incited the local Christian population to launch an anti-Jewish rampage, claiming that Jewish lives and property were up for grabs. Romanian soldiers, the Christian inhabitants of Edineți, and peasants from the surrounding villages took part in the pogrom. Any Jewish property that was not looted was expropriated by the Romanian state.

A week later the Jews were divided into two groups and marched in the direction of Rezina and Secureni. The first group was deported to Transnistria, while the second was made to wander among Secureni, Briceni, and Edineți in an endless cycle. After the Jews of Edineți were deported a transit camp was set up there for Jews from other areas, principally Jews from northern Bukovina who had been evacuated in mid-July from their villages and towns (Banila, Ciudei, Văscăuți, Jadova, Vijnița, Lujeni, and Herța) and moved in convoys toward the Dniester. The transit camp also took in Jews from northern Bukovina who had previously been concentrated in the Storojinetz camp as well as Jews from Bessarabia whom the Germans had not allowed to cross over to Transnistria.

The Edineți camp began operating officially on 20 August 1941, when the first group of deportees arrived from Bukovina and Bessarabia. Even before then thousands of Jews had fled to Edineți in a bid to save their lives, little knowing that the town was empty of Jews. Poitevin, the pretor of the Third Army, who was touring the area at the time to check how many Jews were left and where they were located, reported to General Topor on 9 August that he had found ten thousand Jews in Edineți. He described how they were "living in filthy conditions in abandoned houses," without food. Many of them were sick, due to poor sanitary conditions. The pretor lamented that "they are neither isolated nor guarded, and therefore constitute a constant source of contagion and danger to the population and the army marching [to the front]."[69]

The Edineți camp consisted of five streets surrounded by barbed wire. Over twelve thousand Jews were packed into its ruined houses, basements, and warehouses. Most of them were penniless when they arrived, having been fleeced by their guards and by gangs of peasants in the weeks prior to their arrival. Anyone who tried to escape from the camp was shot on the spot. Local peasants were allowed to approach the barbed wire fence in order to barter with the inmates. As Moritz Schechter from northern Bukovina stated in his testimony, the inmates of the Edineți camp knew only "hunger and hardship."[70] The most difficult existential problem in the Edineți camp was the shortage of drinking water. Although several wells existed in the camp, all but one had been poisoned by the local citizens and gendarmes to spite the Jews.

Unlike the Vertujeni and Mărculești camps, the Edineți camp was disorganized, due to a lack of manpower to run the camp. Since the gendarmes who were supposed to guard the camp failed to arrive, the entire camp was initially guarded by six gendarmes and fifty cadets who were hired on a daily basis. Colonel Mănecuță, the inspector general of the gendarmerie in Bukovina, reported that the cadets "stole and committed various other crimes [torture and rape], and were more of a liability than an asset."[71] Even the soldiers from the Engineers Corps who were stationed in the area and sent in as reinforcement committed crimes, according to Colonel Mănecuță. Finally, in mid-September, the arrival of three gendarmerie platoons of the Sixtieth Police Company solved the problem. All correspondence concerning the camp emphasized that the Jews had no food (nor money to buy any), no medical care, and no medicines, despite a typhus epidemic that had erupted on 20 September and four other epidemics. Gendarmerie lieutenant Victor Popovici, who was in charge of policing of the camp, informed the camp's committee that unless the epidemic were contained, all the Jews would have to be shot.[72]

THE DEPORTATION FROM THE EDINEȚI CAMP

The deportation of Jews from the Edineți camp took place from 10 to 18 October. The operation was conducted by Lt. Augustin Roșca, from the Roman gendarmerie legion in the Regat, and his deputy, Lieutenant Popoiu.[73] Prior to the deportation Roșca was given the *consemn special*, the special command that empowered him to shoot Jews who could not keep up with the convoys. He was also ordered to prepare graves large enough to accommodate a hundred people at ten-kilometer intervals along the deportation route. The order was scrupulously obeyed, as an official report stated, and in one convoy alone about five hundred Jews were shot. As was customary, peasants who had been lying in wait for the convoys "pounced on the corpses and plundered them."[74] Even before the deportation got under way all sick Jews and Jews who were recovering from typhus were shot to death. Despite the absence of precise data, Dr. Zeev Shärf's testimony informs us that many Jews fit into this category.[75]

The convoys comprised 2,500 people each. The gendarmes' policy was to deliberately split up families. One convoy was taken to Atachi (eighty kilometers away), while the other was taken east, to the notorious Cosăuți forest and Cosăuți crossing point (fifty-six kilometers away). The last contingent dispatched to Atachi arrived on 16 October, and the last dispatched to Cosăuți arrived on 18 October.[76]

The way to Atachi led through the Briceni forest, almost as notorious as the Cosăuți forest, although the tortures and murders perpetrated there were on a smaller scale. This was because Briceni forest served as a transit camp only, for convoys arriving from Edineți and Briceni, while the Cosăuți forest served as a night camp. Even so, according to a survivor's testimony, "unspeakable" crimes took place in Briceni forest, too. "On the way to the forest, we encountered countless corpses, body parts, and murdered children who had been left behind from previous transports."[77]

At the Atachi and Cosăuți crossing points Captain Popescu gave the order for the Jews' personal documents to be destroyed. A search committee consisting of representatives of the National Bank of Romania and gendarmerie officers was set up to search the Jews and their belongings. Any documents or money they discovered were confiscated.[78]

THE SECURENI CAMP

Secureni, a town in northern Bessarabia, had a Jewish population of 4,200 (representing 73 percent of the town's population). Once the town was Judenrein it made a suitable location for a camp because it was situated only two kilometers away from the Dniester and near the Bălți-Czernowitz railroad. On 6 July 1941 combined Romanian and German forces entered the town after Romanian soldiers had slaughtered Jews scattered in the small villages in the area. Cepelăuți's 160 Jews were killed near the flour mill, and some of them were hacked to bits. Jews who tried to escape were murdered by the Romanian soldiers, both on the roads and in the Sărbiceni forest.[79] In Secureni itself, gangs of peasants and local Christians, especially Ukrainians, egged on by Romanian soldiers, carried out atrocities for two days, killing about 90 Jews, raping women and girls, and looting most of the Jewish homes. These were the same Ukrainians who had welcomed the Soviet army with flowers and dances when it entered Secureni in late June 1940.

Toward the end of July all the Jews of Secureni were evicted from their homes by soldiers and taken forcibly to the main square. The Jews of Secureni were marched north to Mogilev, where they merged with an immense convoy of twenty-five thousand Jews whom the Germans were trying to drive back into Bessarabia. The town remained empty of Jews, its ruined and ransacked houses deserted. On 6 August a convoy of Jews from northern Bukovina, survivors from Seletin, Văscăuți, Noua Suliță, and Nepolocăuți, were brought there, after some of them had been shot or drowned in the Dniester, following the Germans' refusal to allow them to cross over.[80]

The camp, comprising the ruined homes of local Jews and an open field through which it was accessed, held some 17,000 Jews. Another 5,000 Jews were crammed into the smaller camps of Bârnova and Brebeni in the area. Mănecuță reported to the grand pretor that "despite measures adopted by the civilian and municipal authorities and efforts by the gendarmerie, the Jews have nothing to eat and could die of starvation" due to the cramped conditions.[81] On 15 August the Grand Pretorate informed the General Staff's Second Section that a solution had been found. About half of the 20,000 or so Jews in Secureni were transferred to Edineți, and the inspector general of the gendarmerie in Bukovina was charged with feeding and guarding the remaining half.[82] Although on 1 September there were only 10,356 Jews left in Secureni, the camp was still very overcrowded.

It would appear that officers close to Antonescu informed the head of the Federation of the Jewish Communities of Romania of the plight of the Jews in the Secureni camp. On 19 August the federation for the first time sent a petition to the minister of the interior demanding the repatriation of the twenty-five thousand Jewish inmates of the Secureni camp, who lacked proper food, shelter, and medicines, and demanding that aid be allowed through. The petition was returned a few days later with the suggestion that the federation address its request to the Presidency of the Council of Ministers.[83] On 28 August the federation asked Mihai Antonescu to allow "emissaries to bring food, clothes, medicines and money to Jews in the Secureni and Edineți camps."[84] Mihai Antonescu turned down the request. He agreed, however, to allow money through, via the Second Section's Prisoner of War Department.[85] However, Filderman and his colleagues did not trust the army after the disappearance of 500,000 lei that had been sent to Vertujeni and decided to err on the side of caution.

On 2 October all the Jews of the Secureni camp were told to gather in an open field, where they were randomly divided into two groups. Here, too, as in Vertujeni, families were split up. The first convoy was sent south, to nearby Atachi, while the second was sent to Cosăuți. Before the first convoy left for Atachi its members were ordered to lie flat on the ground while policemen searched them and their belongings, stealing their last, essential items.[86] The secret order given to Lieutenant Roşca, the commander of the operation, resulted in "the death of about 500 Jews who were being evacuated along the Secureni-Cosăuți route," according to an official document drawn up in December 1941.[87] Note that in the Romanian Holocaust lexicon, the number five hundred is not to be taken literally; rather, it denotes a massacre. Thus, for example, an official government communiqué referred to five hundred Jewish Communists who were shot in Iaşi in late June 1941, and similar figures were quoted in other gendarmerie reports.

Roşca was in charge of the deportation from Secureni, while his deputy, Lieutenant Popovici, was in charge of the deportation from Edineți. According to the report cited above, the Jews of Secureni, as in other places, were believed to be wealthy, and the peasants would pounce on the corpses to strip them of their clothes, even though this provided negligible returns. On 5 October the second contingent left Secureni for Atachi but was kept waiting until 11 October before being allowed to cross the river.

While the Jews were kept waiting in the open and muddy field adjoining the crossing point, the envoys of the National Bank of Romania searched them and confiscated and destroyed any personal documents they found. Dozens of Jews were killed during these searches by frustrated envoys of the National Bank of Romania who were unwilling or unable to understand that these Jews had arrived destitute, after having been robbed of all their possessions.

On 12 October the deportation of the Jews of the Secureni camp to Transnistria was completed. With the exception of the Kishinev ghetto, the Romanians had realized their aim of a Bessarabia cleansed of Jews.

19

The Kishinev Ghetto

In 1930 Kishinev, the capital of Bessarabia, had 41,405 Jews out of a total population of 114,896. In 1942 after the liquidation of the ghetto, the census of residents of Jewish blood recorded a mere 99 Jews in Kishinev, some of whom were defined as Jews by virtue of the Romanian racist laws only. During the thirties Jews moved into Kishinev due to an increase in anti-Jewish incitement in the towns and villages. Rapid economic development in Kishinev toward the end of the decade also attracted Jewish youth. Under Soviet rule (July 1940–July 1941) there was a further surge in the number of Jews in the town as tens of thousands of Jewish refugees, some of them natives of the Regat, fled from Romania to Kishinev. This was matched by an influx of Jews from the Ukraine and from Russia, who came of their own free will or were brought over as functionaries of the Soviet regime. Soviet publications, such as the Yiddish-language newspaper *Einikeit*, quoted a figure of 60,000 Jews in Kishinev on the eve of the occupation. This figure was probably a conservative estimate.[1]

On the morning of 22 June German planes bombed the city, killing thousands of citizens, including many Jews. Officials of the Soviet administration fled as all hell was let loose. The Soviet authorities also played a part in the tragedy of the Jews of Kishinev. Shortly before the outbreak of war they published announcements designed to dispel the population's misgivings. When they were proved wrong, they did nothing to help the Jews. They did not inform the Jews of available means of transport out of the city and made no attempt to prioritize their evacuation.

Before the Red Army finally withdrew from Kishinev on 13 July, the Soviets mined all public buildings, department stores, warehouses, and factories. For three days the city had no government. Occasionally one could hear blasts as buildings blew up from air raids or from mines that were set off as people attempted to break into buildings to loot them.[2]

Soviet bureaucrats, who had entered Kishinev only a year earlier and who were mainly from other regions of the Soviet Union, gathered on train platforms and on roads leading east, where they were joined by the new—mainly Russian and Ukrainian—citizens, who had also arrived the previous year. The fact that everyone was trying to escape all at once made things much harder for the Jewish fugitives. Thousands of men, women, and children poured onto the roads during the air raids, in an area densely populated with Romanians who were waiting for the day when they would be liberated from the hated Russian and Communist yoke. Some of these Romanians told the Jews that the day of reckoning was nigh, while others looted the homes of Jews who were leaving Kishinev.

At the outbreak of war Jews and non-Jews alike were hastily conscripted into the Red Army. Soldiers were recruited from government factories and businesses, which had a high percentage of Jews, to defend the city. In the final analysis only a few of those conscripted were actually deployed by the Red Army. Thousands of the recruits were taken to the Ukraine, ostensibly to be issued with uniforms and weapons. On the other side of the Dniester, however, they were abandoned by their escorts, who fled in an attempt to escape captivity. Most of the Jews began retracing their steps to Bessarabia and their families. Most never got there. They were caught by German soldiers and killed on the spot or else sent back to Bessarabia in the large convoys of Jews that were being forced back there.

On 16 July 1941 Romanian soldiers entered Kishinev. Conversant with the local language, they used local citizens to help track down Jews. Testimonies indicate that Kishinev was divided between the German and Romanian armies. Einsatzkommando 11a, led by Paul Zapp, reached Kishinev on 17 July at 4 a.m. and took control of the upper part of the city where members of the liberal professions, including the Jewish intelligentsia, lived, while the Romanian army occupied the poorer neighborhoods in the lower city. In addition to killing Jews, the soldiers and low-ranking officers stole their property.

On 24 and 25 July all the Jews from the upper city were rounded up and taken to the small market in the lower city, which, together with four surrounding streets, was designated as the ghetto area. Most of the houses in the ghetto had been torched by the retreating Soviet army or bombed. As soon as the Romanian officers told the masses they could disperse, they stampeded toward the ruined houses of the ghetto. The area designated as the ghetto was far too small to contain them all. Dozens of people were crammed into a single room, and many families were split up in the chaos and dark. For the first few days the ghetto was open, but the Jews were warned not to leave it for any purpose. Once the ghetto command was set up, the ghetto was surrounded by barbed wire, with several entrances, guarded by Romanian soldiers and policemen.

The establishment of the ghetto was a combined German-Romanian initiative. Zapp, for his part, wished to halt the messy killings, which were creating a terrible stench in the streets. Governor Voiculescu, who arrived in the city on 19 July, complained of "swarms" of Jews and issued Ordinance no. 61 of 24 July 1941, ordering the establishment of the Kishinev ghetto based on the "Conducător's fundamental ideas on the handling of Jews." He ordered a notice to be put up in the streets announcing the establishment of the ghetto and the obligation of the Jews to report to the authorities.[3]

Around that time Alexandru Giurgiuveanu, head of the Romanization Administration in Bessarabia, arrived in Kishinev. Giurgiuveanu was yet another serious contender for the custodianship of looted Jewish property. Unlike the government and the military, which were awarded special powers by Antonescu to deal with Jewish property under military law, the Romanization Administration was responsible for legalizing the theft of Jewish property through broad interpretation of the laws and their implementation. Since the Jews of Kishinev were either dead or interned in camps and ghettos, the Romanization Administration focused on real estate such as land, plots, houses, buildings, factories, flour mills, businesses, and workshops. Although most of this real estate had been nationalized by the Soviet authority, the Romanian authorities, who did not approve of the Soviet expropriation of property, returned it to its former owners. Thus, theoretically at least, the way Jewish property was handled in Bessarabia and northern Bukovina was specific to these provinces and did not apply to Romania proper.

Although the Romanian authorities did not promulgate new laws stripping Jews of their Romanian citizenship, the murder and deportation of Jews continued unabated. The Romanization Administration partly remedied the legal chaos concerning the status of Jews in the liberated territories by a blanket application of all the Romanization laws to these territories, irrespective of the legal status, citizenship, and prerogatives of their victims. Literally overnight the Romanization Administration became a powerful behemoth owning tens of thousands of apartments, houses, plots of land, businesses, and factories that had become absentee or abandoned property. The Romanization Administration clearly felt no need to even make a pretense of seeking out the owners of this property. Rather, it allocated assets to local ethnic Romanians or to Romanians from the Regat who had begun arriving en masse. This it did by renting out the property or selling it through fictitious sales deeds, in accordance with the racist legislation that already existed in Romania. Moreover, the National Bank of Romania, among others, offered Romanians easy credit terms to rent or buy up properties in order to encourage the establishment and expansion of Romanian enterprises.

At first Giurgiuveanu sided with Voiculescu against the military in the fight over Jewish property and criticized Col. Eugen Dumitrescu, the military commander of Kishinev, for his "independent stand" in this matter.[4] However, it was not long before Giurgiuveanu began looting abandoned Jewish property himself. In return for generous bribes, he offered factories and large estates to his cronies at "ridiculously low rents."[5] Similarly, he gave away raw material for free, without inventorying it as was required, and turned a blind eye to theft in return for a share in the proceeds. A secret conspiracy grew up between him and members of the military in the Bessarabian administration, who granted the new factory owners permits attesting that they were manufacturing goods for the war effort.

The ghetto was a constant source of tension between the provincial government and the army, both during and after its existence. Governor Voiculescu was under the impression that Antonescu had awarded him exclusive powers not only to direct the ethnic cleansing operation but also to carry out a purge of the military apparatus, if necessary. Since the military was directly subordinate to the General Staff and the General Staff to Antonescu, General Voiculescu asked the General Staff to dispatch two military judges to Kishinev to assist the Bessarabian government in the cleansing operation. The General Staff immediately sent over four judges, instead of the two Voiculescu had asked for, but assigned them to the military tribunal in Kishinev. Nevertheless, Voiculescu "placed them to the ghetto," where they were briefed to arrest anyone acting "unlawfully," as Voiculescu put it. The operation to purge the military of corruption failed, however, and the judges failed to live up to the governor's expectations. In fact, the governor claimed that they had botched the job because "several of them were married to Jews." Voiculescu next turned to the only service untainted by corruption—the ssi: "In the operation to eradicate theft, I engaged the services of the Kishinev branch of the Special Intelligence Service—the only institution, to my mind, capable of helping us in this cleansing operation."[6]

Voiculescu was particularly eager to arrest the corrupt officers who accepted large bribes to smuggle Jews out of the ghetto to the Regat. When the ssi discovered a plan to smuggle a group of thirteen Jews out of the ghetto, they decided to set a trap, with the main aim of "catching the officers who were responsible for smuggling Jews out of the ghetto" and only then "discovering how the Jews escaped." On 28 October 1941 the group of thirteen Jews, led by Kissil Kremer, boarded an army truck that, unbeknownst to them, was operated by undercover ssi agents. After Kremer paid the undercover agent 120,000 lei in cash and 40 gold coins, the ssi agents arrested the entire group on the spot. The military prosecutor ordered them searched, after which they were taken to the ssi prison in Kishinev for further interrogation. No sooner had the military prosecutor departed, however, than three ssi agents broke into the prison, searched the

Jews, and stole 352 gold coins the Jews had managed to hide. The SSI agents hid the stolen coins in a hole in the floor of SSI headquarters in Kishinev, where they were discovered after the whole incident came to light.[7]

It is clear from this account that not a single Romanian institution withstood the temptation to grow rich at the Jews' expense. The situation in the Kishinev ghetto was by no means exceptional. Similar corruption existed in other ghettos and camps in Bessarabia. The only difference was that the situation in the Kishinev ghetto, situated as it was in the Bessarabian capital, was far better documented by the Romanian bureaucracy than were activities in other, more remote camps.

THE KILLING OF JEWS IN THE GHETTO

The first deliberate act of murder was the execution, by order of the ghetto commander, of about one hundred hostages who had been arrested immediately after the ghetto's establishment. The hostages included intellectuals, members of the liberal professions, affluent members of the community, and a sprinkling of rabbis. Since the operation took place immediately after the establishment of the ghetto, when chaos reigned and the ghetto committee had not yet been set up, there is no record of the victims of the massacre. The incident came to light only through references to it in Einsatzgruppe reports and through the testimony of survivors of the Kishinev ghetto.[8]

After the establishment of the ghetto, Otto Ohlendorf, the commander of Einsatzgruppe D, ordered Zapp to execute the leaders of the Jewish community in the ghetto. Zapp immediately ordered the ghetto commander to deliver 2,000 Jews under age forty, particularly members of the liberal professions (engineers, doctors, teachers, and lawyers) for forced labor. Romanian soldiers immediately swarmed through the ghetto and began arresting Jews, to the accompaniment of their womenfolk's screams, and marched them to a vacant lot in the center of the ghetto. The Romanian ghetto commander advised the Jews to obey orders without resistance, assuring them that they would be allowed back into the ghetto once they had carried out their assignments. Zapp then selected 551 of the 2,000 Jews, who were told they were being "relocated" (*Umsiedlung*) for work purposes.[9]

The 551 Jews were forced into trucks and taken to a remote location about fifty kilometers outside the city. They were ordered out of the trucks and made to stand beside deep antitank trenches that had been dug at the start of the war, where they were shot in the neck by four murder squads belonging to the SD security service, the Waffen-SS, and the Schutzpolizei (Secret Police). The area was guarded by members of the SD. The Jews who were waiting their turn about ten meters from the trenches could see everything that was going on. As the Jews were shot they fell into the trenches, where they were laid out in an orderly fashion by about another ten Jews, who were then shot themselves.[10] The operation, which Zapp himself supervised, was not mentioned in any Romanian document and only emerged during the trials of the heads of Einsatzkommando 11 in Munich in February 1970, when the fact that no doctor was present at the execution site also came to light.

Not all the murder operations were carried out by the Germans. Some were carried out by the Romanians, in addition to the murders they committed as they looted and raped. On 7 August the Romanian inspector of roads asked the ghetto commander to supply him with 500 Jewish men to work in the Ghidighici quarries, about twelve kilometers north of Kishinev, and 25 women to cook for them.[11] About a week later 200 of the 525 Jews returned to the ghetto, exhausted. The remaining 325 were killed. A report of 28 August by the Tenth Gendarmerie Company — the company that murdered the Jews — describes how a Romanian military unit on its way to the front stopped at Ghidighici train station. The unit's sergeant, "believing" he recognized a Jew who had slighted him during the retreat from Bessarabia, set his soldiers on the Jews. The gendarmes guarding the Jews "were too few in number to stop the assailants." Although the report stated that "the quarrel ended with several Yids sustaining slight injury," in actual fact, 325 were killed by the Romanian soldiers.[12] Today, after the opening of the Moldovan Republic archives, we know that the Ghidighici massacre was no random event but a planned and deliberate massacre of Jews who were accused of insurrection.

THE GHETTO COMMITTEE

The Community of Jews in the Kishinev Ghetto, alias the ghetto committee, was set up to save Jewish lives, prevent the delivery of Jews into Einsatzgruppe hands, pressure the ghetto commander into controlling his men, and ensure the food supply in the ghetto. The committee's funds were provided by Jews who still had money and valuables.[13] It would appear that the committee was set up in early August and was approved by the ghetto commander, who was pleased to have a channel for his requests. The committee's elected leaders were Shapiro, an attorney (we do not know his first name), and Dr. Gutman Landau. One of the committee's first actions was to pay the ghetto commander a weekly bribe, in return for which he was supposed to refrain from handing Jews over to the Germans, irrespective of the purpose for which they were required.[14]

The ghetto commander's acceptance of the bribe did not prevent him delivering 350 Jews — of which 330 never returned — to the Nazi executioners in late

August. Despite blatant evidence to the contrary, the Jews clung to the belief that the commander could save them. The fact that the ghetto commander gave his promise shortly before the departure of the Restkommando that Zapp had left behind in Kishinev convinced the committee that the ghetto commander had managed to save the Jews from the hands of the Nazi executioners. (The Restkommando was a small unit of Einsatzkommando 11a left in Kishinev to complete their assignment after the Einsatzkommando was assigned to kill Jews in the areas newly occupied by the German army.)

The Jews also interpreted the fact that the ghetto commander had set up labor camps for the ghetto inmates as a positive sign. Every morning at six o'clock all able-bodied Jews were marched out of the ghetto and put to work under the supervision of Romanian soldiers. Unlike the Germans, the Romanians viewed the Jews first and foremost as a source of income, and for about a month relative calm prevailed in the ghetto. Although the terrible living conditions in the ghetto persisted, the killings ceased and the Jews even began trying to improve their lot by organizing medical and economic aid, distribution of food and clothes, and help for those who were worst off.

The committee conducted an internal census (the results of which have not survived) and managed to establish ties with Jewish leader Wilhelm Filderman and Chief Rabbi Safran. This was done through the good offices of Romanian officials who visited Kishinev and through telephone calls and telegrams. As far as is known, no written report was submitted, and neither Filderman nor his colleagues had a clear picture of the true extent of the tragedy of the ghetto. After the first message got through to Bucharest the Jewish Federation and private individuals sent sums of money illegally into the ghetto. A market was even set up in the ghetto where Romanian peasants were permitted to sell their crops twice a week. Men from the work detachments sometimes managed to bring food or clothes into the ghetto. Doctors who had managed to survive the selections organized a makeshift hospital, but without medicines and proper equipment were unable to offer any real medical assistance. Two synagogues were also set up in the ghetto.

On 11 September 1941 the ghetto committee asked Colonel Dumitrescu, the military commander of Kishinev, to "exempt them from forced labor" on Rosh Hashanah and Yom Kippur, in order to observe the festivals.[15] The commander gave his permission for the two days of Rosh Hashanah only. Despite this permission, the work detachments were made to work on the first day of Rosh Hashanah. While the rest of the community was engaged in prayer in the ghetto's two synagogues, the committee members were told to report to the ghetto commander. When they returned from the meeting they refused to disclose its purpose. The ghetto residents were profoundly shocked when they heard that Dr. Landau and his wife had resolved to commit suicide. Several days later Shapiro managed to reach Bucharest "in a military plane, with the help of a [Romanian] general with whom he was acquainted. He was dressed as a Romanian officer (he had [once] been a Romanian officer) and gave his word of honor that he would return [to Kishinev]. He returned, later, in the same plane." In Bucharest Shapiro met with community leaders—Rabbi Safran, Filderman, Filderman's secretary Charles Gruber, and attorney Fred Şaraga—in Rabbi Safran's house, where he informed them of the massacres that had taken place, the plight of the Jews in the ghetto, the forced marches, and the deportations. He described "how [the sick] were loaded on to carts daily, while the healthy were forced to march in the direction of the Dniester." Gruber subsequently described the meeting as follows:

> The way he spoke, his detachment, his lack of emotion . . . made more of an impression on us than any emotional appeal on his part could have done. . . . My impression was of someone half alive, half dead. He described the situation and urged us to do what we could to help. . . . Until then, we hadn't the slightest idea of what was going on. Even when he told us, we found it hard to believe. We never [imagined what was going on]. When you are actually there, you are choked by emotion. We were shocked, overcome by compassion, rage, and a sense of helplessness.[16]

Rabbi Safran also described the meeting in his memoirs: "We listened to him for hours—long, terrifying hours. Difficult hours. We tried to conceal our emotions from Shapiro, but it was impossible."[17] The meeting, it would seem, took place on 10 October 1941, after the start of the deportations. The following day Filderman notified Antonescu of "the desperate appeal from the head of the Kishinev Ghetto" and asked him to put a stop to the deportation, which "is death, death, death of innocent people with no other guilt than that of being Jews."[18] Antonescu replied with a letter justifying his policy, which was published on 19 October in all newspapers. This letter triggered a new wave of nationalist antisemitic sentiment.

In the face of Antonescu's resolve to eliminate any Jewish presence in Romanian Bessarabia, the leaders of Romanian Jewry were powerless. Both Filderman and Rabbi Safran advised Shapiro to stay in Bucharest, where he would be safe, but he decided to return to the ghetto and his family. He was deported over the Dniester on 20 October and later shot.[19]

The authorities decided to carry out the deportation in four convoys of 2,500 Jews each. The first convoy was scheduled to leave the ghetto on Yom Kippur itself, and therefore Colonel Dumitrescu did not accede to the Jews' request to exempt them from work. On Yom Kippur morning hundreds of horse-drawn carts entered the ghetto. The ghetto commander and his men tried to assure the Jews that they would come to no harm and that the deportation was ultimately for their own good, since it was dangerous for Jews to live in large concentrations, given the Germans' plans to liquidate the Jews. The ghetto committee managed to get the deportation postponed for a few days and immediately appealed to the Jewish Federation heads for help. Hundreds of telegrams bearing cryptic messages such as "Father is very sick . . . please send over medicine forthwith" were sent to the federation or to relatives in Bucharest, but to no avail.[20] The Jews of Kishinev were doomed.

The original plan to deport the Jews in four convoys of 2,500 Jews each had to be abandoned due to logistic constraints relating to the crossing of the Dniester bridges. In the end, the planned deportation turned into a long series of convoys of Jews wading through the deep mud that lined the main roads leading to the Dniester. Hundreds of Jews were shot on the way for failing to keep up or simply because of a verbal command to kill Jews (the existence of such commands came to light during the Romanian war criminal trials).

Before the start of the deportations Antonescu instructed all prefects to confiscate jewelry and valuables owned by Jews who were "being evacuated," in coordination with the national bank, and to reimburse them with German occupation marks (RKKS, which were valueless) or rubles.[21] These valuables and money were confiscated on behalf of the Romanian state from Jews in the camps prior to their deportation. In Kishinev, however, the bank's representatives did not arrive in time, and therefore several convoys left prior to being searched. For reasons mentioned above, most of the spoil failed to reach the Kishinev bank vaults. Colonel Dumitrescu therefore ordered that a special place be set aside for the orderly confiscation of the goods and that an inventory be kept of all confiscated money and valuables. The place assigned for this purpose was a warehouse used to breed horses for the Romanian army, about five kilometers from the city, a place in which about seven hundred Jews from the ghetto had previously been shot. Here the Jews were stripped of all valuables—money, gold, metals, and diamonds. This operation came to light only because of thefts by the army and bank representatives who, uncharacteristically, failed to keep an inventory of confiscated money and goods. They not only failed to obey Antonescu's orders—as the report drawn up by Capt. Ion Paraschivescu, commander of the Twenty-Third Police Company, stated—but went even further, confiscating "silver objects such as spoons, forks and candlesticks," which they threw into "an open wooden crate."[22] These thefts were never recorded. A midwife was ordered to carry out a thorough gynecological examination of the women to uncover valuables. The two drivers who were recruited to assist her were caught trying to hide valuables they had found. According to the report, they claimed that all they had taken were a few worthless screws and nails.

The searches took place at all times of the day and night, depending on the progress of the deportations. The overseer of the operation drew up a report recommending a supply of special pressure-powered kerosene lamps to facilitate night searches. He also recommended that the drivers employed to search the women be replaced by "trustworthy officials." The overseer ended the report with the following affirmation: "I, the undersigned, believe that this is the only way that this precious fortune confiscated from the Jews shall reach the State Treasury."[23]

At the same time that Colonel Dumitrescu called for order in the work of the confiscation committee, Governor Voiculescu called for order in the work of the Romanization Administration's committee. The Romanization Administration's committee, which was subordinate to Colonel Dumitrescu, was responsible "for the registration and storage of movable property and chattels left by the Jews in the Kishinev ghetto." Voiculescu gave Dumitrescu unwritten permission to register and store the good but forbade him "to deliver them in any form to any party." Dumitrescu, however, disobeyed this injunction and distributed items from the confiscated property to friends or to those who paid him enough. Voiculescu, in a condemnatory letter to Dumitrescu, ordered him to "report according to which criteria and with what authority" he had acted.[24] The argument between the colonel and the governor over Jewish property became the subject of a summary report drawn up by Voiculescu. Section 4 of this report, titled "The Registration and Storage of Movable Property," lamented "the Kishinev military commander's defiance of the Bessarabian authorities, leading to the waste and dispersal of valuable State property left behind by the Jews who have departed from the city in the direction of the Dniester."[25]

The ghetto committee played for time, trying to postpone the deportation of Jews in the hope that the Jewish Federation in Bucharest would manage somehow to get the deportation order revoked. It was also able to reduce the number of deportees dispatched in each convoy. After Shapiro's visit to Bucharest on 9 and 10 October, Filderman obtained a verbal promise from Mihai Antonescu to stop the deportations in Kishinev and Czernowitz so as to spare the intellectuals, merchants, craftsmen, and the like.[26] Meanwhile, the federation sent Constantin Muşat, its hired Romanian lawyer, to Kishinev. As Rabbi Safran stated:

> This Christian lawyer had been hired and well paid by the Federation to carry out important missions in places where only a Christian could enter and thus bring help on the wretched Jews. Only someone like him could bribe Romanian civilian and military clerks to obtain at least some temporary "easing" of the situation. This was in the hope that meanwhile in Bucharest we could secure some postponement of the anti-Jewish decisions. . . . He had been sent not only to inspect the situation in Kishinev, but also, if possible, to see what was happening throughout the region.[27]

On 14 October the deportations stopped for several days, but they resumed on 20 October. On that day a convoy of several hundred Jews, including Shapiro and his family, left for Tighina and Tiraspol and thence eastward toward the extermination camps on the River Bug. On 1 January 1942, after ten weeks of ceaseless marching, a few hundred Jews, including Shapiro, were shot near the village of Samakhatka, about seven kilometers from Karlovka, the site of a subsequent ghetto. Shapiro's family later perished in Karlovka.[28] The roads from Kishinev to Orhei were "awash with bodies."[29] The last three convoys to leave the ghetto, on 29, 30, and 31 October 1941, comprised 1,004 Jews and 123 carts, 882 Jews and 138 carts, and 257 Jews and 80 carts, respectively. All were bound for Orhei and later Rezina.[30] On 30 October Muşat sent a telegram from Kishinev to the Jewish Federation secretary stating, "We lost the case. All our clients have been convicted. We must appeal."[31] The U.S. embassy kept a close watch on the ghetto's fate and kept Washington informed of events. In June 1942 the Association of Romanian Jews in America published a detailed description of the liquidation of Bessarabian Jewry in its journal, *The Record*, including the fate of the Jews in the Kishinev ghetto. Already then it described the "sale" of Jews along the deportation routes for 2,000 lei apiece (see chap. 18).[32]

By early November 1941 hardly any Jews remained in the Kishinev ghetto. The ghetto, however, was not completely liquidated. At first about 130 Jews remained—families with children, as well as some wealthy men who had managed to bribe the ghetto commander, Dumitrescu, and Voiculescu. The governor, who had never shown the slightest interest in the deportees' health, suddenly allowed these Jews to remain in the ghetto on the grounds that they were too "ill" to be moved and needed time to recuperate before being assessed for deportation by a medical committee. The "small ghetto" also included some sick and mentally disturbed people.[33] Although a few of the remaining Jews managed to escape, their place was soon taken by other Jews who had been found hiding in Kishinev, so that the overall number remained constant at around 130. Richter, the adviser on Jewish affairs at the German embassy, reported how Schor, Kishinev's wealthiest Jew, placed 25 million lei at Marshal Antonescu's disposal. The latter sent him back a thank-you note, stating, according to Richter, that he was a "good Romanian."[34] Over the course of time the number of Jews in the small ghetto rose to 200. From the fall of 1941 the ghetto became a dumping ground for Jews of Bessarabian origin who had been arrested throughout Romania. The ghetto's streets remained abandoned, and its plundered houses were open to the elements. The city's many synagogues were ruined, and the Torah scrolls that had been taken to the ghetto lay in tatters in the streets. The house of the famous rebbe of Koritz was surrounded by Torah scrolls that had been torn and trampled on by soldiers and passers-by.

In May 1942 Voiculescu claimed that by 21 May — the day of his patron saint Constantin — no Jews would be left in Kishinev. Landau, the ghetto leader, and his wife immediately committed suicide. Among the last deportees were orphans, the sick, and fifty-eight mentally ill Jews who had been left in the psychiatric hospital in Costujeni. On 20 May all two hundred were concentrated in the city's military headquarters and after being fleeced of their possessions were herded onto freight cars and sent to Transnistria. Kishinev was left with ninety-nine Jews, some of whom were only Jews as defined by the Romanian racist laws.[35]

In early March 1944, about four months before the Soviet army recaptured Kishinev, the mayor of Kishinev published a description in the local press of the Romanian regime's achievements since the liberation in July 1941. The first achievement cited was the exclusion of Jews from the city's life. In 1941 Kishinev had 33,407 Romanians, 3,306 Russians, 265 Ukrainians, and 11,388 Jews. In late 1943 it had 80,979 Romanians, 751 Russians, 778 Ukrainians, and only 177 Jews. The "true" Romanian spirit was beating strong, added the mayor, in a city in which, prior to 1941, "the Romanian soul had been strangulated by foreign elements."[36]

20

Czernowitz

On the eve of the Romanian–German invasion Czernowitz was the largest Jewish city in Romania after Bucharest. In 1930 it had 42,932 Jews (about 38 percent of the city's population). In September 1941, after the first wave of massacres, there were 45,759 Jews (over 58 percent) according to German sources and 41,118 Jews (52 percent) according to Romanian sources. Taking into account the fact that Jews from the Czernowitz district fled or were transferred to the city, by the time of the deportations in October 1941 the city had 51,681 Jews, according to Romanian sources.[1] On the eve of the occupation the Jews of Czernowitz estimated their numbers at 70,000 or more.[2] The Jewish community in the city and Filderman placed the number of Jews in Czernowitz at 60,000 and the number of Jews whom the Soviet authorities had exiled to Siberia and other parts of the Soviet Union at more than 3,000.[3]

Until late 1940 Czernowitz had many German citizens who, under Austrian rule, had comprised about half of the city's population. After the Soviet annexation 25,000 Germans were evacuated from the city according to the terms of the Molotov-Ribbentrop Pact between Nazi Germany and the Soviet Union. At the same time, 10,000 Romanians fled from the city and became refugees in their own country. Consequently the proportion of Jews in the Czernowitz population rose from 40 percent to an absolute majority. When the Romanians recaptured the city, Jews comprised 58.1 percent of the total population while Romanians comprised only 23.6 percent of the population (18,608 individuals). From the perspective of the Romanian ethnic state, this situation was intolerable.[4]

The Jews of Czernowitz formed a distinctive bloc among the Jews of Greater Romania. They turned the city into an industrial and trade center as well as into a center for Jewish culture in German and Yiddish (including the press and theater). It was also a hub of national and Zionist activity and of Jewish and German national culture and education. After Bucharest, Czernowitz was the most influential Jewish center in Greater Romania.

Soviet rule (1940–41) was not kind to the Jews of Czernowitz. The Soviets introduced a reign of terror, targeting many Jews as members of the bourgeoisie and as antisocial and Zionist elements. Their identity cards were branded with a special stamp that marked them for deportation. As noted, thousands of Jews were deported in sealed freight wagons to Siberia and more remote areas of the Soviet Union.[5] "Every night, the streets of Czernowitz were rent by the wails and cries of relatives of [Jews] arrested by the NKVD. Most of the leaders of the community . . . disappeared without a trace, and no one knows where their bodies are scattered."[6]

During the early days of the occupation the Soviet authorities set in motion an organized evacuation of the local citizens according to criteria determined by the Soviets. All citizens were forbidden to leave the city by any other means. Once the city was bombed, however, the ensuing chaos made it impossible to continue with the organized evacuation. Most Jews, who historically felt an affinity for Austria, not Russia, did not even try to escape. They spoke no Russian, and a year under Communist terror had left them disillusioned with the Soviet experiment. Moreover, the false propaganda of the Soviet authorities after the Molotov-Ribbentrop Pact had blinded them to the reality of the German danger. Although there are no accurate statistics on the number of native Jews who fled along with the Russians, we may assume that there were no more than several hundred. An unknown number of Jewish youth—probably also no more than several thousand—were recruited to the Red Army.[7] Not all Jewish youth were called up, and of those who were, not all were sent to the front, due to the rapid advance by the Germans from the Lvov area, which turned the whole of Bukovina into an encircled zone. Even if many Jews decided to escape after the bombings, they were prevented from doing so by the lack of transport.[8]

Many Jews left the city on foot or by cart, little realizing that the Germans were waiting for them on the other side of the Dniester. Thousands of Jews, mostly youth, flocked to the local train station in the hope of boarding a train for Russia. After two to three days, many Jews who had boarded trains found themselves in Galicia, in the heart of Nazi-occupied territory.[9] A few thousand Jews who were sent to Russia by train under the organized evacuation during the early days of the occupation managed to reach Soviet territory. Most of them were Soviet Jews. The various censuses conducted by the Romanian authorities after the occupation show that most of Czernowitz's Jews remained in Czernowitz.[10]

As the Soviets began withdrawing from the city on the second day of the invasion, Ukrainian and Romanian gangs from the outskirts of Czernowitz broke into and looted Jewish stores and even Jewish homes. The first units of the Romanian army entered the city on 5 July 1941, after having killed thousands of Jews in and around Storojinetz and in the villages in the southern part of the Czernowitz district. On the night of 5 July dozens of Jews who lived on the city's outskirts were killed by Romanian soldiers who broke into their homes, looting and raping.[11] On the morning of 6 July regular Romanian and German units entered the city. The Jews, who had heard from peasants that Jews had been massacred in all the villages and towns along the way, hid in their homes.

Although no written order has survived, all the Jewish survivors testify that during the first three days of the occupation the invading armies were given a free rein to kill, loot, and rape, "with impunity," as one of the witnesses stated.[12] Many Ukrainians and some Romanian citizens helped the occupiers by identifying the houses of Jews—some of them their erstwhile employers. Jews were shot in their homes, in cellars, attics, gardens, the street or anywhere where they tried to escape. After the soldiers searched their homes for valuables, their non-Jewish neighbors came to take the pickings.

Members of Einsatzkommando 10b reached the city on 6 July in the evening and with the help of their Romanian colleagues took over the Schwarzer Adler (Black Eagle) Hotel in the city center, not far from the Great Synagogue—one of Romania's grandest synagogues. Members of the Einsatzkommando arrived equipped with lists of Communists and Jews, which were updated after their arrival with the Romanians' help. The following day they began arresting Communists and Jews. On 8 July they carried out a large *aktion*, during which they arrested the Jewish leadership and executed about a hundred Jews. Members of Einsatzkommando 10b estimated the number of Jews executed by them and by the Romanian soldiers and policemen at five hundred.[13]

The Einsatzkommando arrested 1,500 Jews, imprisoning some in the local Jewish Cultural Center and taking several hundred others to the Bilu suburb, where all were shot and buried in a mass grave. Among those in the cultural center, an unknown number were selected and ordered to stand in a row. The Germans then shot every tenth man on the spot. After killing about a hundred Jews, the Germans ordered the others to run. Anyone who lagged behind was shot by members of the Einsatzkommando. Hundreds of Jews were killed on 8 July in and around the Jewish Cultural Center by members of Einsatzkommando 10b. Jews who were arrested loaded the corpses onto garbage wagons in the streets and transported them to the Jewish cemetery, where they were buried in four mass graves.

Dr. Abraham Mark, the chief rabbi, was among the Jews arrested by the Einsatzkommando. He "was told to order the Czernowitz Jewish community to supply a thousand trucks [to] the German Army" and then taken to the top floor of the Great Synagogue, where he was made to watch while the temple was set on fire.[14] The Nazis also burnt sixty Torah scrolls that were stored in the synagogue.

The rabbi was then taken to the Schwarzer Adler Hotel, where members of the Einsatzkommando were billeted, and, along with two cantors and the beadle, was pushed into a lift. On 9 July, after being tortured for two days, they were taken to a hill overlooking the River Prut and shot, along with another 160 Jews (those who remained after the selection of the Jews imprisoned in the Jewish Cultural Center). A group of twenty Jews was then ordered to bury them in a mass grave.

All the five hundred Jews who were still under arrest were shot by members of the Einsatzkommando. The graves of some are unknown. The following day, when members of the victims' families turned up at Romanian police headquarters to find out what had happened to their relatives, they were savagely beaten by the guards. From 5 July to the end of the month an estimated two thousand Jews were killed according to Mayor Popovici, or an estimated five thousand according to the Jewish community.[15]

Ohlendorf, the commander of Einsatzgruppe D, proposed speeding up the "handling" of Czernowitz's Jews even before the implementation of the overall solution to the Jewish question in the European continent "within the German-Ukrainian framework." He proposed sending the Jewish masses to work in the Pripet marshes or sending them to the Dnieper River and even to the remote, as yet unoccupied, Volga River, in order to liquidate them. The last report on Czernowitz states that another 1,106 Jews and 34 Communists were shot to death in and around the city by late August 1941.[16] Einsatzkommando 10b operated in Czernowitz for over a month—longer than it had operated in any other place, including Kishinev.

IMPLEMENTATION OF THE ANTISEMITIC POLICY

As soon as the Romanians recaptured the city the Jews of Czernowitz were put to work for the Romanian and German armies, the newly reorganized municipality, the new factory owners, and the Christian citizens. The Jews of Czernowitz "became the city's servants," a preliminary report, published in 1945, stated.[17] Initially the thousands of Jews subjected to forced labor were mostly from the three makeshift detention camps run by the Romanians or were Jews arrested by the Einsatzkommando or the German army. After the departure of the army units and the reorganization of the municipality and other Romanian institutions in Czernowitz, the exploitation of Jewish labor became routine. The police took to raiding Jewish homes early in the morning, conscripting men, women, and children for work, irrespective of occupation, age, and gender. The Jews were made to remove rubble from the city center, rebuild the heavily bombed railway station, demolish unsafe buildings, rebuild the iron railway bridges over the Prut, work as porters in the train station, load coal, sweep the streets in the summer and shovel them clear of snow in the winter, and clean the homes of government officials and senior civil servants. Jewish women were made to clean the Romanian and German military field hospitals, launder soldiers' uniforms, work in warehouses, and sort objects that had been looted from Jews.[18] They received no payment for their work, had irregular work hours, and were beaten and even raped. The Jewish workers were entirely under the control of the Romanian policemen who supervised them.[19]

The yellow star that Jews were required to wear whipped up the aggressive instincts of the local citizens and the masses that had settled in Czernowitz after the occupation. Jews were attacked in the streets, beaten up, and humiliated. Many Jews subjected to forced labor died when unsafe buildings collapsed on them or when train wagons hit them. Some were killed by German soldiers and work supervisors, while others were injured or crippled while repairing the bridges over the River Prut.

Later, when the forced labor of Jews was taken over by the army's Regional Recruitment Bureau, many officers, especially the heads of the Jewish Bureau (Biroul evrei), became rich by exploiting the Jewish workforce. They were authorized to send Jews to work for the Bukovinian government or to do dangerous jobs under German supervision for the Romanian army or in forced-labor units.

The fear of deportation that constantly hovered over the Jews of Czernowitz and their proximity to the border of occupied Poland paralyzed their will and turned them, until the end of Romanian rule, into the most submissive and fearful Jewish community in Romania. Not only were they subjected to the anti-Jewish measures that applied to all Romanian Jews, but these measures (such as the order to wear the yellow star) often were maintained in Czernowitz long after they had been revoked in Romania.

The government's military cabinet (Cabinetul Militar), headed by Stere Marinescu, was responsible for the implementation of all anti-Jewish orders and regulations. The cabinet operated in parallel with Bukovina's military headquarters. Even by the standards of the Siguranța, Marinescu was considered a corrupt, vulgar, and violent man. Together with Governor Alexandru Rioşanu he had looted Jewish property and secreted large quantities of valuables and food in his home.[20] He headed the military cabinet from its inception until the spring of 1943, enjoyed the trust of the first and second governors, even though they were aware of his corrupt behavior, and was a close confidante of Gen. Corneliu Calotescu, the second governor. In the summer of 1942 he was appointed head of the Jewish Bureau and effectively directed the deportation operation.

The name Marinescu became synonymous with Romanian antisemitism in

Czernowitz and antisemitic initiatives that were triggered by pure malice. Mari-nescu applied directives from Bucharest rigorously and supplemented them with his own directives and orders. Since he considered the mayor "a stooge of the Jews" (*jidovit*), he never consulted with him and, most of the time, did not even inform him of his plans. Marinescu was not the only one to persecute and plunder the Jews. Others who did so were the directors of the Secret Service; the director of the Department of Internal Affairs; Tudor Popescu, the director of the Jewish Bureau prior to Marinescu; and the police commander.

Bukovina's only local newspaper, *Bucovina* (a semiofficial newspaper that was controlled by the Ministry of National Propaganda, under Mihai Antonescu), also played an instrumental role in anti-Jewish incitement. Like other antisemitic newspapers in Romania, it did not stop at anticommunist and antisemitic, or even anti-Ukrainian, incitement but proposed concrete measures against Jews and demanded their strict implementation. It blamed the Jews for all the province's economic problems and for the government's failure to rehabilitate the Bukovin-ian economy. *Bucovina* continued to attack Judaism and the fourteen thousand Jews who remained in Czernowitz after the second deportation in the summer of 1942, until the Soviet army entered the city in March 1944.

As early as August 1941 *Bucovina* called for the deportation of all of Czer-nowitz's Jews. It printed a list of Jews who failed to obey antisemitic regulations (wearing the yellow star, buying food at specific times, etc.) and closely followed the progress of Romanization. Three local dignitaries — Czernowitz's first mayor, Octavian Lupu Strejac; Professor Dimitri Marmeliuc of Czernowitz University; and the journalist Constantin Loghin — published a manifesto in the newspaper calling for the Romanization of all of Bukovina and the strict implementation and even expansion of the Romanization laws, due to the province's special status and the large Ukrainian minority that lived there. They demanded the immediate deportation of all Jews, Ukrainians, and other minorities in the region.

The establishment of a ghetto aroused opposition among some of Czernow-itz's leaders. They therefore decided to send a delegation to Germany, headed by the new mayor, Traian Popovici, to study the issue. Popovici hoped that this step "would dull the vigilance of the Presidency of the Council of Ministers and temper the impulsiveness of the supporters of Romanization, for whom the city reeked [with the presence] of Jews." The delegation's ports of call were Lublin, Cracow, and Frankfurt am Main. Antonescu himself had sent a similar delega-tion from Bucharest to Warsaw, headed by his advisor Dan Stănescu from the ssi, "in order to study the German concentration [of Jews] in the neighborhoods and to learn from their experience," as the Conducător informed his deputy.[21] Rioşanu's death on 30 August 1941 following unsuccessful surgery was a blow for the mayor, who had far less influence over the new governor's decisions regarding the fate of the Jews. The new governor, General Calotescu, and his military cabinet excluded Popovici from their discussions and plans on how to handle the city's Jews, so much so that the mayor was surprised to learn that the Jews knew more than he did about the dangers that lay in wait for them. "I think the instinct for survival has foreshadowed the danger," he wrote in 1945. The ghetto, added Popovici, had become the government's obsession. And yet Popovici, at the time, believed that the authorities would go no further: "[The idea] of mass deportation had not even occurred to me."[22]

Preparations for the establishment of the ghetto continued throughout September. The German legation in Bucharest also evinced interest in the plan. Himmler's special envoy from Berlin, Karl Pflaumer, who had been sent to help the Romanians govern Bessarabia, came to Czernowitz to discuss with Popovici what type of ghetto should be set up in the city. Czernowitz—a former Austrian city, strategically located on the route to Vienna and Berlin, with a rail link to the General Government (Generalgouvernement, the German administration that was set up in the middle and main section of occupied Poland)—was also frequently visited by Nazi officials on their way to Romania and the Balkans or returning to Germany.

On 29 September 1941 the governor convened a meeting with the director of the local Siguranța branch, a special SSI envoy from Bucharest, Stănescu (who had just returned from Warsaw), and others to discuss the establishment of the ghetto. At the meeting the governor called on the mayor to submit a concrete proposal for the establishment of the ghetto. Popovici refused: "I gave a lengthy exposé of the special attributes of the Jews of Bukovina, their contribution to the city's prosperity under Austrian rule, their contribution to commerce, industry, trades, crafts, medicine, the arts and the legal system, and other professions. I placed special emphasis on their contribution under the Romanian regime and their desire to integrate. I analyzed their political proclivities, and stressed their cooperation with the ruling parties. In short, their attributes outweigh their shortcomings. I opposed the ghetto."[23]

Unlike the ghettoization of the Jews, which was a local initiative, the deportation of the Jews was the brainchild of the Conducător himself (who had meanwhile assumed the rank of marshal). In the government session of 6 October 1941 Antonescu asserted that it was he who had ordered the deportation of the Jews from Bessarabia and Bukovina.[24] As early as 5 October the head of Antonescu's military cabinet had instructed the governors of Bessarabia and Bukovina to coordinate with the national bank the confiscation of gold, jewelry, and other valuables from the Jews and the conversion of their currency into German Occupation

Marks—a valueless currency restricted to the eastern occupation zones.[25] On the morning of 9 October Governor Calotescu ordered Bukovina's military commander to prevent the Jews from leaving Czernowitz by establishing a "cordon sanitaire" with the help of "an authorized team," the members of which would be assigned to all the city's exit points that same evening.[26] That day, shortly before the Jews of Czernowitz were apprised of their fate, Filderman pleaded with Antonescu to abolish the deportation of Bukovinian Jewry to the Ukraine—a fate, he argued, that was equivalent to death.[27] On 9 or 10 October General Topor, the grand pretor, and Lt. Col. Gheorghe Petrescu arrived in Czernowitz and relayed verbal orders to Calotescu, following which the governor informed the army commander of Bukovina of the decision to evacuate the Jewish population.

On the eve of the evacuation two gendarmerie regiments were dispatched to Czernowitz to guard the city's exits and the ghetto, "together with local forces." The military commander and the inspector general of the gendarmerie in Bukovina were jointly responsible for rounding up the Jews, herding them onto the trains, and accompanying them to the border points. One of the two gendarmerie regiments was detailed to guard the ghetto and accompany the convoys of deportees to the Dniester. The National Railways Authority offered two trains with fifty freight cars each for the operation. On 11 October the authorities began herding the Jews into the ghetto prior to their deportation. From that date on any property owned by Jews became government property.[28]

As well as instructions to deport all Czernowitz's Jews across the Dniester, the envoys of the General Staff gave the governor verbal instructions concerning the modus operandi. The military commander of Bukovina, Gen. Vasile Ionescu, asked to see the special orders in writing, but the envoys of the General Staff refused. "They tell me that these actions are done only by verbal order, so as to leave no evidence." The envoys of the General Staff listened to the mayor harangue the governor about the historic repercussions of such an action on the Romanian state and people. Lieutenant Colonel Petrescu tried to calm him down and reassure him that he would not bear any responsibility by saying, "*Mr. Mayor, who will write history? The Yids?*"[29]

All official documents and public notices refrained from using the term *deportation* (*deportare*). Instead, the word *evacuation* (*evacuare*) was used. The innovative use of the reflexive form of this verb (*a se evacua*) created further linguistic ambiguity by implying that the Jews had decided to relocate of their own volition.[30] Already, then, Popovici drew attention to the cynical misuse of language. The term *evacuation*, he pointed out, means "to provide sanctuary to the population and protect it from the enemy's wrath, the calamities of nature . . . and from harm . . . regardless of blood, religion or ideology." Evacuation was, moreover, confined to the borders of the sovereign state and was prompted not by hatred but by love for one's fellow citizens. Therefore, the "evacuation of the Jews from Bukovina and other areas was a travesty." Since the deportation implied uprooting a certain section of the population "against its own wishes . . . it was a punishment rather than a privilege."[31]

This cynical misuse of language by the leaders of the Antonescu regime was deliberate and only partly due to unfamiliarity with the finer aspects of the Romanian language. It was the authorities' way of avoiding facing up to the implications of their actions. The regime had not been set up by the Romanian fascist movement, for which the semantic definition of its anti-Jewish actions was the least of its concerns, but by nationalist elements from the traditional right, including jurists and civil servants from the Regat and servicemen (both regulars and reserves) as well as the governor himself and members of his military cabinet.

The Jews of Czernowitz soon realized the true import of the measures the Romanian government adopted against them. However, they were as yet unaware that the ghetto was merely a prelude to deportation. The community reorganized itself only after the Romanians resumed control of the city. The first mayor, Lupu Strejac, appointed Dr. Sigismund Neuberger, a retired leader of the Zionist movement in Bukovina, as head of the Jewish community. Strejac also appointed several individuals who had been prominent in the Jewish community before the Soviet annexation to be members of the new Jewish committee. This leadership (or any leadership, for that matter) was incapable of dealing with the calamity. The committee heads were notified of the imminent ghettoization of the Jews by General Ionescu. At 9 a.m. on 11 October 1941 Ionescu summoned the committee heads to government headquarters, where he read out to them relevant sections of Ordinance 38, issued by the governor; showed them the map of the ghetto; and demanded the relocation of all Jews to the eastern section of the city, the place assigned as the ghetto.[32]

This announcement did not take the committee heads by surprise. Just the previous day they had waited for the mayor—whom they considered their friend and protector—to leave a work session with the governor. Popovici recalled how the faces of the committee heads were "twisted in anxiety," but he was unable to offer them any reassurance, and they immediately realized that he had been unable to avert the calamity. They thanked him for his help, promised to remember him on their wanderings, and left weeping "like a funeral procession."[33] Words cannot describe the impact of the news, spread by word of mouth through the ghetto, on the Jews. "The Jews were thrown into despair and an indescribable pandemonium [ensued]."[34] The area assigned to be the ghetto could barely contain five thousand people, let alone fifty thousand. Many Ukrainian and Romanian families that had not been evacuated were still living there. Most Jews found out only at noon that they had to leave their homes, leaving them a mere six hours to get organized and move into the ghetto. Thousands of Jews began running around with backpacks they had prepared for emergencies, clutching objects that were of no immediate use, such as blankets, pillows, mirrors, lamps, and books. Most Jews did not know exactly where the ghetto was located or exactly which streets it encompassed. They scurried back and forth, dropping objects on the way, changing course at mere hearsay, and returning to bring more objects that seemed vital to them at the time.

The Jews were allowed to take only as much property as they could carry into the ghetto. Specially recruited policemen and aides supervised the operation, prodded Jews into leaving their homes, prevented them from returning, and generally sowed panic and despair. Ion Holca, police commander of the Second (central) Quarter, supervised the evacuation of his quarter from the balcony of the police precinct, shouting instructions to his subordinates: "Don't let them take too many things with [them]. Don't let them use carts to transport their possessions. Don't let them return for more possessions. Once they've left, they must not be allowed back."[35]

THE DEPORTATION

On the morning of 13 October 1941 gendarmes broke into the ghetto and took up positions in several streets, while soldiers set up barriers that prevented contact among various parts of the ghetto. Most Jews already knew that they were going to be deported but did not know where. The Jews selected for deportation were taken from their homes amidst curses and blows. "We had no idea where we were going," recalled Sarah Grosskopf, an intellectual, who was deported with the last convoys in early November.[36] On 13, 14, and 15 October convoys of about two thousand Jews each left the ghetto for the nearby train station.

At the station the Jews were taken to a loading bay and herded into windowless freight cars or freight cars with boarded-up slats. Each train had about fifty cars, into each of which fifty to eighty people were crammed. Once the cars were full the doors were nailed shut with wooden planks, which were removed only when the train reached its destination—Atachi or Mărculeşti. The journey was slow, with frequent halts in the open countryside (not in populated areas) to free the track for other purposes. Many deportees reached Transnistria empty-handed, having been fleeced of their belongings, or with tattered clothes, and sometimes even naked and barefoot, following weeks of vigorous marching after they left the train at Atachi or Mărculeşti.[37] No sanitary arrangements were made for the deportees during the journey, and they were forced to relieve themselves on the spot. The passengers were given no food or water before or during the journey, and all, especially children and babies, suffered from thirst. Several dozen sick and elderly people died on the way. Although the deportees were given the same reception in Atachi and Mărculeşti, those sent to Atachi were spared the horrors of the Mărculeşti camp and the Cosăuţi forest.

On 15 November the deportations suddenly ceased. The reason Antonescu agreed to change his original order to deport all of Bukovina's Jews was partly due to the fact that the Jews were necessary for Czernowitz's rehabilitation and partly due to pressure by the Germans on the Romanian authorities in Bucharest and in Transnistria to put an end to the unruly and unplanned deportations. Consequently, even Jews who had no permits and who had managed to evade the deportations were saved. All received permits issued by Popovici (known as "Popovici permits") and were ultimately allowed to go home once their permits had been ratified by General Ionescu's review commission (*comisia de verificare*).[38] This was simply a sorting committee that operated from the municipality: "There were about six tables. Next to each table was an officer, two to three soldiers and several lists. We had to go through these lists searching for the [names] of Jews. Jews who gave money, jewelry, and gold watches 'passed' the review."[39]

After the review was completed, the ghetto was closed. The commission reported that 5,619 permits had been issued by Calotescu (known as "Calotescu permits") to heads of families (16,569 people); 3,120 Jews had been spared deportation thanks to Popovici permits or because they had been in the ghetto on 15 November, the day the deportations ceased, even though they had no permit. An estimated several hundred Jews hid without permits. According to the mayor's estimates, a little over 20,000 Jews remained in Czernowitz.[40] In a little over a month (12 October–15 November 1941) 33,891 Jews had been deported from Czernowitz.[41]

The Jews were under the impression that Calotescu and Popovici were engaged in a power struggle. Popovici claimed that the municipality was authorized to issue permits and indeed was better equipped than the military to do so, since it knew which Jews were essential to the economy and which were a threat to public order.[42] Documentation that has recently come to light shows that what was going on was not a power struggle as such but rather anger on the part of Marinescu and his men and other extortionists, who neither forgot nor forgave, at Popovici's disinterested interventions to save Jews. Although Antonescu's order to halt the deportations put the situation on hold, Marinescu continued harboring a grudge against Popovici. In June 1942 an opportunity for revenge presented itself. Popovici was dismissed on the eve of the second deportation and was replaced by Maj. Dimitri Galeş, notorious for his hatred of Jews.

Upon their return the Jews of Czernowitz who were not deported found their homes vandalized and looted, despite the governor's explicit instructions that the looting of state property was forbidden under penalty of death (no one really expected the Jews to return home).[43] Many homes had been taken over by neighbors and Romanians from the Regat, who "refused to assign the Jews even a single room." "Every one of us had to sign a declaration that he had got back his lodging in best order. Naturally, it must be prevented that Romanian gentlemen could be suspected of having plundered Jewish houses."[44] Jews' requests to friends and neighbors to return the valuables they had placed in their safekeeping prior to the deportations were rudely turned down.[45] Some bolder Jews actually filed complaints with the Siguranţa. Life in Czernowitz returned to a semblance of normality:

> And now began what the Romanians called "normal life." All Jewish specialists and many others were ordered to work for ridiculous wages and to rebuild the economic life of the town. We managed our scanty lives by selling our last household goods. Need was crushing. Restricted in our movements, humiliated and insulted, with a yellow star that was recognizable to the Christian population, we sneaked like thieves through the streets. They were deserted in many parts of the city; the houses stared at us with tarnished windows. Most of them were broken, telling us what had happened. Poverty, cold and hunger, anxiety and fear were our bedfellows. The days were dismal and the nights without compassion. The reports from Transnistria set our nerves on edge. Rumors, which prophesied new deportations for the last days of May [1942], embittered our lives. The reports from Transnistria pointed out what deportation meant. Everything could be suffered: humiliation, poverty, contributions, toil, but the thought of the doom of deportation was intolerable, was terrifying. . . . Despair spread again over the Jewish homes.[46]

Such was the mood among the Jews of Czernowitz between 15 November 1941 and 31 May 1942—the day on which the deportations resumed.

THE ROMANIZATION PROCESS IN CZERNOWITZ

Decree-Law no. 2507 of 3 September 1941 legalized the transfer of Jewish property to the Romanian state.[47] This law applied the expropriation and Romanization laws that already existed in the Regat to Bessarabia and Bukovina. Most of the legally expropriated property no longer belonged to Jews, having been nationalized by the Soviet authorities. The purpose of the law was to prevent such property from reverting to its former owners, as had happened to non-Jewish property after the Romanians recaptured these provinces. The law stipulated that flour mills, alcohol distilleries, timber plants, pharmaceutical factories, oil factories, rural land in villages, and industries set up on this land, as well as urban buildings and apartments, would henceforth be considered state property. The difference between the application of this law in the provinces and its application in the Regat was that in the Regat the law had not mandated the direct expropriation of stores, businesses, or factories (apart from the aforementioned categories), the land on which they were built, or even the money used to run them. Formally, at least, this property remained in Jewish hands. Under Legionary rule the Legionnaires had deliberately excluded this property from the provisions of the Romanization laws, so as to be able to lay hands on it more easily.

A special law was passed in September 1941 granting the governor of Bukovina almost unlimited powers and making him directly subordinate to Ion Antonescu.[48] In order to fill the gaps left by the Romanization laws the governor issued Decree no. 2956 on 29 August 1941, stating that "all movable and immovable property, and all production means in plants and factories, the timber industry, businesses and other property owned by the Soviet State, Jews or Germans who have been evacuated to Germany under Soviet rule, shall be transferred to the Romanization Administration." The decree defined Jewish property as any of the aforementioned property that had belonged to Jews or to Jewish companies on 1 January 1939 or any company with at least one Jewish owner or shareholder on that date.[49]

Branches of the Romanization Administration were set up in Kishinev and Czernowitz and from their inception acted as if there were no Jews or Jewish property. After the Jewish property was inventoried, it was rented out or sold to ethnic Romanians. This generated "an illegal situation" whereby businesses and factories "not only were not transferred to State ownership, but were still owned by Jews," declared Emanoil Manu on behalf of the undersecretary for Romanization on 25 September 1941, upon visiting Czernowitz as part of a large delegation of representatives of government ministries dealing with the liberated territories.[50] These words were spoken during a special session on the subject of the Civilian-Military Cabinet for the Administration of Bessarabia and Bukovina.

Manu, who had no idea that the Jews were about to be deported from Czernowitz and Bukovina, was concerned that the illegal activities of the Romanization Administration might result in "the State having to pay large amounts in compensation." In order to prevent this happening and to facilitate the implementation of the "authentic" Romanization operation, he proposed "a supplementary decree-law" that applied to all Jewish businesses and industrial property "that had not been included in the Romanization laws." He likewise proposed that all functions of the Romanization Administration in Bessarabia and Bukovina be regulated by decree-laws rather than decrees issued by the governor.[51] This proposal, as far as we know, was never implemented. The deportation of the Jews from Bukovina put an end to this legal wrangling. Note that none of the resolutions, laws, orders, and debates concerning Jewish property related to the Jews themselves, who were in any case outside the law.

The second stage of the Romanization process involved drawing up an inventory of all Jewish property. Even half a year after the liberation the inventory was not complete, partly, but not entirely, due to the incompetence of the Romanization Administration, which had meanwhile changed its name to the Administration for Romanization and State Property (Direcția Românizării si Adminsitrării Bunurilor Statului) in order to emphasize its status as owner of large amounts of property. The inventory of property was designed to prevent theft. The Romanization Administration was headed by Professor Eugen Pavlescu of Suceava, a former director of a firm, who had been dismissed for financial misconduct. After Czernowitz's liberation he was, "to everyone's consternation," sent to Czernowitz to direct the Romanization operation there, even though he was under police interrogation at the time.[52] The Romanization Administration published tenders — far too late, to the chagrin of many — to lease industrial plants that had not been expropriated under the Romanization laws, thereby launching the third stage of Romanization.

The Romanization Administration, which until December 1941 was responsible for the transfer of Jewish factories into ethnic Romanian hands, worked slowly and raised all sorts of objections on the way. The head of the Romanization Administration's industrial section, an engineer named Bocancea, accepted bribes from Romanians who wished to lease Jewish factories. In so-called technical advice sessions held in his home he negotiated the amount of the bribes. Ultimately he was dismissed, after complaints were lodged against him by Romanians who refused to pay the bribes. Reports by Antonescu's representatives spoke of quarrels between members of the Romanization Administration and the district prefects of Bukovina over industrial property left behind by local Germans.

Another factor hindering the transfer of Jewish factories, businesses, stores, and houses was the reluctance on the part of the administrators of this property, who hailed from Bucharest and other cities, to relinquish their high salaries.[53] Meanwhile, machinery, raw material, finished goods, and the like kept disappearing from factories and storehouses, obstructing the operation of the factories. To make matters worse, conflicting directives were issued by the various government ministries involved in the transfer of Jewish property. The Ministry of the

Interior, for example, ordered the governor of the Rădăuți district to lease out all Jewish businesses by 30 November 1941, while the undersecretary of Romanization forbade him to lease out any stores.

Another reason why it was so hard to reactivate the factories was the lack of skilled labor. The dismissal of Jews and the emigration of Germans resulted in a severe shortage of craftsmen (even under Romanian rule Romanian craftsmen had been scarce, both in Czernowitz and throughout Bukovina). During the first month of the reactivation of the factories only 265 skilled laborers were available out of a requisite 3,959, and this at a time when not all factories had resumed operation.[54] Despite a variety of incentives and attempts to train craftsmen in vocational schools (reflected in a reduction of the apprenticeship period, the granting of generous stipends, and the transfer of Jewish and German workshops to ethnic Romanian hands), Czernowitz never recaptured its status as an industrial center. Attempts to encourage migration to Bukovina in general and Czernowitz in particular and the opportunities offered to war orphans to train in vocational schools or as apprentices did not appreciably alter the situation. In late 1941, of the city's 4,373 factories only 520 were running. Only 344 apprentices of a requisite 1,950 were available. Finally, 180 apprentices were enrolled in all the city's vocational schools, as compared to 1,800 in June 1940.

Another sphere of Romanization peculiar to Bukovina was the Romanization of land. Since Austrian rule, many Jews had become landowners or owners of farms and agricultural equipment. Looting of land, machinery, and livestock was widespread, and the deviousness of those in charge of allocating the loot caused considerable unrest among the Romanian peasants in Bukovina, as the Siguranța reports indicate.[55]

The first problem the authorities encountered in leasing out Jewish land was that the land registration records had been burnt. The Romanization Administration appointed committees to assess small and midsize estates (up to 125 acres) owned by Jews. The overall area of these estates was an estimated 75,000 acres, although we do not know for certain that this was exclusively Jewish land.[56] The large Jewish estates, on the other hand, are known to have totaled 58,750 acres. These estates were immediately identified and leased out. Things came to a head when Pavlescu's deputy, Stefan Romașcanu, one of the two officials responsible for the Romanization of land, donated the estates to relatives and friends who were not ethnic Romanians.[57] The Siguranța's list of land donated by Romașcanu to relatives and acquaintances comprised twenty-three Jewish estates totaling 24,900 acres, as well as two ponds.[58]

Soldiers and gendarmes posted to northern Bukovina, who by virtue of their capacity could not receive land, seized cattle, agricultural equipment, and other property belonging to Jews. Lieutenant Bologa, a meat supplier for the army, returned to southern Bukovina "with 4–6 cartloads of household items, linen, and furniture, which he sold in a public auction." The commander of the gendarmerie post in Şişcauţi village set a record by acquiring "an Arabian stallion, three cows and two calves," for which he had a receipt stating that he had bought the animals from a Jew the day after he arrived in the village. "On the third day [after his arrival], the Jew was shot dead by the same commander of the gendarmerie post," stated a confidential Siguranţa report.[59] We shall never know the full extent of the theft of Jewish property and related crimes perpetrated by Romanian gendarmes and soldiers and by (mostly Ukrainian) peasants.

The final stage of the Romanization process, affecting all Romanian returnees and Jews who survived the first wave of deportation, was the Romanization of Jewish homes and their contents. An estimated seven thousand to ten thousand apartments were handed over to Romanians. The Romanization of apartments began with looting by neighbors, continued with the removal of furniture and appliances by municipal clerks and officials from the Romanization Administration, and ended with the seizure of apartments by Romanians even before they applied for permits from the Romanization Administration. The beneficiaries (mostly civil servants from the Regat and southern Transylvania or Romanians who had returned to Czernowitz to work) begrudged the fact that the Romanization Administration had taken over the choicest apartments in the city center and residential neighborhoods — apartments they crammed full of furniture, carpets, and items looted from other apartments — especially since most of the government officials already owned houses, "while they [the civil servants] were not allowed to renovate their homes or acquire new houses [i.e., Jewish houses]."[60]

In early October the Siguranţa drew up a list of government officials, headed by the Czernowitz district prefect, who, despite already owning houses in the city, had expropriated Jewish homes and furniture.[61] The deportation of thirty thousand Jews had left thousands of houses vacant — more houses than there were Romanians seeking accommodation, even if one included those who had moved to the city. Affixed to these houses in prominent positions were placards stating "state property" (*averea statului*). Frequently whole houses, including furniture, were handed over to ethnic Romanians, who later had the option of purchasing them for next to nothing, in installments.[62] Many ethnic Romanians simply seized Jewish apartments, even if their owners were still living there (prior to being deported), without paying rent to the state. Since many of these apartments were five- to seven-room luxury apartments with valuable furniture and objets d'art, their theft by ethnic Romanians signified a loss of revenue to the Romanian state.

When the municipality took over the Romanization of Jewish apartments it simply exacerbated the injustice with which the system was already riddled. The municipality's clerks had no scruples about handing out furniture or omitting items from the inventory in exchange for bribes. Even after the deportations, Jews who returned to their apartments could be evicted by Romanians who wished to appropriate their homes.

We see from the above that all those who were involved in the handling of Jewish property, whether on behalf of the Bukovinian administration or independently, were corrupt officials who grew fat at the state's expense. This corruption had ideological implications, especially in view of the fact that Antonescu and his deputy had always professed pure intentions as far as Romanization was concerned.

Like the California gold miners who returned home once the fields played out, the scavengers who descended on Czernowitz left once the raw materials they had received for free ran out or once they had nothing left to sell: "They were not interested in an honest day's work, in developing an industry or trade. They came to steal, grab and consume. Why should they work and seek new raw materials? They simply turned tail and fled, leaving everything behind, including workers and clerks. They disappeared overnight, knowing that one day they would have to account for their deeds."[63]

One of these gold diggers was former minister Vasile Noveanu, chair of the Bukovina Association of Industrialists, who took over the Trianco sock factory. Among those who benefited from the free-for-all were engineers, lawyers, government officials, failed industrialists, and bankrupt merchants. They were made a present of the Hercules knitwear factory, the Caurom tire factory, several sawmills, and leading firms in the city center—a total of 245 plants and 2,282 businesses and stores.[64]

DORI POPOVICI'S MEMORANDUM

Dori Popovici, the mayor's uncle and former vice president of the Romanian National Council in Bukovina that had decided to unite with Romania in 1919, had, under Austrian rule, headed a Romanian youth organization that advocated unification and opposed Austrian rule. After the unification Popovici became a leader of the Bukovina People's Party and twice served as minister on its behalf. On 28 October 1941 he sought an interview with Antonescu on the corruption that permeated local government in Bukovina, or in his words, "the terrible decadence that has overtaken public life in this province."[65] Although Antonescu refused to grant him an interview, he instructed Ovidiu Vlădescu, secretary general of the Presidency of the Council of Ministers, to meet with Popovici after he had presented his complaints in writing. Popovici did so in a seventy-four-page memorandum detailing all the crimes perpetrated by the Romanian regime and its officials in liberated Bukovina, including crimes against Jews.[66]

Antonescu, angered by Popovici's criticism of his regime and without even reading the report, wrote in the margin of the letter requesting an interview that he blamed the corruption on "the suspect and rogue politicians who encouraged the Jews and use them to gain political control over the provinces . . . , and for growing rich." The situation, he added, would have been far worse "had I delivered the country to these politicians, who would have sided with the Yids and the Ukrainians."[67]

Popovici's memorandum was divided into four sections: (1) the situation in northern Bukovina after the liberation; (2) those responsible for the situation; (3) proposals for remedying the situation; and (4) "the solution to the Jewish problem." Romanization, wrote Popovici, had failed because the factories were not working. Commercial life had come to a standstill, and only about 150 stores—most of them bars, cafes, and hairdressing salons—of the 3,000 stores and businesses that operated in the city in June 1940 had reopened. Land expropriated from the Jews remained uncultivated due to the indifference of the Romanization Administration. Merchandise, machinery, and equipment had been stolen. Jewish owners had been forcibly evicted and their houses expropriated in a totally arbitrary manner. "The government's highest ranking officials" were implicated in the theft of furniture and goods from houses and warehouses. The deportation of the Jews had been implemented with extreme cruelty, and the Germans had made a point of photographing these tragic scenes. Looters, many of them government officials, had raided the homes of Jews who were interned in the ghetto. Permits to return home were granted to some Jews by a committee of corrupt officials. Jewish middlemen had aided and abetted the looting of Jewish property by local dignitaries and Romanian government officials. Among the latter were "men in the governor's immediate entourage," government officials, and civil servants, all of them "corrupt and immoral elements." As to the solution of the Jewish problem, while Popovici believed that their expulsion from Bukovina was inevitable, he argued the importance of doing this gradually, so as not to harm Romanian national interests "by traumatizing our economic structure and the State."[68] All in all, Popovici's memorandum, which became available only in 1994, sheds considerable light on the nature of the Romanian regime in Bukovina and its crimes against Jews and reflects a divergent view that refused to condone these crimes.

Romanization in Czernowitz was thus only partially successful. Although Jewish property was transferred to ethnic Romanians, the latter, unlike the Jews, failed to use it productively. The Romanization process demonstrated that the mere expropriation of property was not sufficient in itself to radically alter the socioeconomic structure of Romanian society and render it more productive.[69] The important objective underlying the establishment of a separate, autonomous government in Bukovina failed due to the corruption of its leaders, even if Bukovina was economically better off than Bessarabia. Popovici's memorandum caused government officials in Bucharest to admit that "inexcusable acts had been committed in connection with the deportation of the Jews and the seizure of property left behind by the Bolsheviks."[70]

Most Romanians in Bessarabia and Bukovina were overjoyed at their liberation from the yoke of Russian and Communist rule. Although many of them profited from the expropriation of Jewish property, many more were disillusioned with the corrupt behavior of the Romanian government. Such disillusionment was evident both after the unification in 1918–19 and after the liberation in 1941. A Siguranța report on the atmosphere in the liberated territories described the mood of the Romanians in Bessarabia and Bukovina in late November 1941, after the deportations had ceased: "Our Romanian brothers [from the Regat] brought with [them] their old habits — theft, nepotism, bribery — as well as the terror tactics of the gendarmes, who gave free rein to their baser instincts."[71] At the end of the day, the Romanization operation in Czernowitz, as elsewhere, simply intensified and highlighted the intrinsic flaws of the Antonescu regime.

21

Southern Bukovina

In August 1938 King Carol II decided to implement administrative reform in Romania. He divided the country into ten provinces (*ţinuturi*) and appointed a governor (called a "royal resident") for each province. He established a new administrative area in northeastern Romania called Bukovina, to which he attached Dorohoi—a district that had always been part of the Regat—and appointed Gheorghe Alexianu, a law professor, as its governor. In June 1940 when the Soviet Union annexed Bessarabia and northern Bukovina, the territory of Bukovina that remained within the borders of Romania became known as southern Bukovina. Populated primarily by Romanians and a small Ukrainian minority, this area included the districts of Câmpulung and Suceava and southern Rădăuţi. The two northern districts, Storojineţ and Czernowitz, as well as northern Rădăuţi, became part of the Soviet Union. The Dorohoi district remained in Romanian hands and reverted to the Regat. Following the reconquest of northern Bukovina in July 1941 the Dorohoi district again became part of Bukovina and was subject to the new administration in Czernowitz.[1]

This administrative exercise bore disastrous consequences for the Jews of the Dorohoi district by linking their fate with that of the Jews of Bukovina and Bessarabia. The new province of Bukovina was further enlarged by the addition of the Bessarabian district of Hotin, although this did not affect the fate of its Jews since the Jews of Bessarabia were already doomed to destruction.

In July 1941 thousands of Jews were expelled from the small towns and villages of the Suceava district to the district cities of Cacica, Solca, Ilişeşti, Arbore, Balaceanca, Comăneşti, and others. The deportees were put up in houses and synagogues and supported by the local Jewish communities. In the Câmpulung district the Jews were transferred to the district capital of Câmpulung as well as other large towns. Several hundred Jews were transferred from the villages of Iacobeni and Dorna Cândreni and evidently from other small villages, too, to the town of Vatra Dornei. About eight hundred Jews were expelled from villages in

TABLE 6. JEWISH POPULATION OF SOUTHERN BUKOVINA

District	1930 census	1939 estimate	1941 census	1941 deportees	1942 residents of Jewish blood
Câmpulung	7,748	7,673	6,572	6,118	76
Suceava	6,697	6,483	5,874	5,942	31
Rădăuți	8,609[a]	11,142[b]	6,447[c]	9,169	72
Total	23,054	25,298	18,893	21,229[d]	179

SOURCE: Jewish Center, Results of the census of citizens of Jewish blood in Bukovina, stenciled booklet, 20 July 1942, in Ancel, *Documents*, vol. 1, doc. 43, pp. 291–92; Institutul Central de Statistică, memoriu asupra populației evreești înainte și după detașările de teritorii din 1940 [Central Institute of Statistics, memorandum on the Jewish population before and after the annexation of the territories in 1940], in Ancel, *Documents*, vol. 10, doc. 16, p. 54; Foreign Ministry, data on the Jewish population of Romania in 1941, presented by the Central Institute of Statistics, 10 February 1942, in Ancel, *Documents*, vol. 10, doc. 92, p. 218.

[a] 9,512, according to Carp, *Cartea neagră*, 3:134.
[b] In the entire Rădăuți district, before it was partitioned.
[c] This figure is based on the census undertaken by the military authorities in the district and in the whole of Bukovina on 1 September 1941, after the expulsion of about 2,100 Jews from Siret to camps in southern Romania. The total figure should be about 8,500. The overall number of Jews from southern Bukovina should accordingly total at least 21,000.
[d] The author discovered this figure after the Hebrew version of the book was about to go to print. It appeared in a table drawn up by army headquarters on the eve of the second wave of deportations in June 1942, on the number of Jews who were deported from Bukovina or left behind, 9 April 1942. USHMM/RMFA, RG-25.006M, roll 10, "The Jewish Problem," vol. 21, p. 131.

the Gura Humorului region and transferred to its capital.[2] Hundreds of rural Jews were expelled or fled to the district capital of Câmpulung.

The decision to deport the Jews of southern Bukovina must be seen in the context of Ion and Mihai Antonescu's plan to carry out ethnic cleansing, as expressed by Mihai Antonescu in a cabinet meeting on 8 July 1941 and at a work session with the heads of the administration on the eve of their return to the liberated territories. Ion Antonescu's edict of 4 October 1941 to deport all the Jews of Bukovina included the Jews of southern Bukovina and was implemented through regular channels: War Headquarters, the Bukovinian administration, Bukovinian military headquarters, the gendarmerie and police force, the district heads (prefects), and the municipalities and local authorities. The command was delivered to the prefects of the three districts as well as to the military and civilian authorities via the administration in Czernowitz, not directly from Bucharest.

At the time of their deportation the Jews of southern Bukovina were already subject to a special regime that had been imposed on all Jews in Romania on the eve of the outbreak of war. This regime included forced labor for males, incarceration of hostages, restrictions on freedom of movement, the designation of some Jewish neighborhoods as ghettos, and the obligation to wear the yellow star (an obligation that was revoked in the Regat but remained in force throughout Bukovina).

The Jews were herded into cattle cars supplied by the Romanian Railway Authority (Căile Ferate Române, CFR) in coordination with army headquarters. The cattle cars, which departed from the district capital and from two or three other large towns, transported the Jews in a northerly and then easterly direction along the Czernowitz-Lipcani-Atachi line. The trains stopped in Volcineț (a station before Atachi), near muddy trenches, to force the Jews to abandon their belongings.

In general the authorities of southern Bukovina kept to their original plan. In a mere four to five days (9–13 October 1941) they succeeded in deporting all the Jews. The deportation was so sudden and swift that even the leaders of the Jewish community never guessed what the authorities were planning. The disruption in communication with Bucharest hampered the transmission of information to Jewish leaders in the capital. The deportation was so swift and total that certain towns in southern Bukovina were left without doctors, pharmacists, specialists, or artisans, and several dozen Jewish professionals had to be sent back from Atachi before crossing the Dniester.

The first transport, which included the Jews of Burdujeni and Ițcani, left Suceava on 9 October, according to plan. This was followed the next day by a second transport that deported Jews from Suceava and Gura Humorului. The third transport, which left on the same day, deported the Jews of Vatra Dornei and the surrounding area. Within five hours of the deportation order 2,650 Jews had been deported.[3] On Saturday, 11 October, an additional transport left Suceava with approximately 1,200 Jews, because there had not been enough room on the previous transport. On 13 October the last transports left simultaneously from Rădăuți and Câmpulung. After that only 179 Jews were left in the whole of southern Bukovina, including those who had been sent back from Atachi several days after their arrival. These Jews were spared deportation thanks to pressure by the owners of erstwhile Jewish factories, primarily sawmills, who could not run the factories without Jewish experts. Likewise, several doctors and one (female) pharmacist were spared deportation. In Rădăuți, for example, the town's only gynecologist (who was sent back from Atachi before being sent to Transnistria) and only dentist were left.[4] By October 14 southern Bukovina was already Judenrein.

The Jews of Câmpulung and the surrounding area were deported on 13 October, the first day of the Succot festival. News of the impending deportation had reached them unofficially the previous day.[5] A Jewish family even managed to telegram their relatives in Bucharest a coded message in German to the effect that they were about to be deported and would try and send their young daughter over, in the hope that "God is with us."[6] On the day of the deportation the town crier appeared in the streets early in the morning and, to the accompaniment of drums, ordered all Jews to report to the town hall, hand over their jewelry, gold, silver, and cash, and then proceed to the railway station of the neighboring village, some three kilometers away, with their personal belongings, for deportation. They were not told where they would be taken.[7] The prefect, Colonel Stăncescu, ordered them to report to the railway station within three hours, rejected a request that the elderly and physically and mentally sick be left behind, and refused to receive a delegation that came to beg for clemency.[8] The city's police chief, Inspector Stipor, and his aide, Inspector Bogdan, manhandled the Jews, threatened to execute laggards, and ordered the soldiers to be firm with them. "Ignorant of the true situation, we locked up our homes securely when we left," Hannah Scharansky testified. "However, they began looting our homes even before the transport had left."[9] The authorities did nothing to prevent the looting.

At the station a long train with dozens of cattle cars awaited the deportees. Approximately two thousand Jews from Câmpulung and the surrounding area were forced to board the train—sixty to seventy to a car—and were locked in. After a journey of about forty-eight hours the train came to a halt at night in an open field near Atachi. The deportees, afraid of the Ukrainian farmers who were waiting to attack them and steal their belongings, collected money from the occupants of each car and bribed the stationmaster into postponing their disembarkation until daylight. These Jews, too, were deliberately made to disembark in muddy trenches and were forced to choose between abandoning their belongings and helping their parents: "The situation was unbearable, and quite impossible for the elderly and sick. Indeed, it was here that the first victims—those who did not survive this harsh test—succumbed. Despite being hustled by the soldiers, many of the deportees stayed behind and were beaten to death. It was [only] with great difficulty that I managed to save my parents."[10]

The members of the depleted convoy were marched to Atachi, where they were assigned to demolished houses and the synagogue. At night the soldiers took the law into their own hands and attacked them, leaving a trail of injury and death in their wake. The following day (15 October) representatives of the National Bank of Romania, acting for the state and for themselves, sorted through the Jews' belongings, removing any valuables and throwing the rest in the mud. After they had finished their job the soldiers who were sent to accompany the Jews across the Dniester took the pickings—each according to his rank. On the morning of 16 October all the Jews of Câmpulung were taken to the riverbank, where they were kept waiting all day in the cold and rain. This transport was later taken across the Dniester on improvised rafts used by the Romanian army to ferry over horses and cows: "The crossing was via a pontoon bridge used to transport cattle, hay, and military personnel. The Jews were made to sit at the edges of the raft, to make it easier for their escorts to push them into the water. Many drowned. . . . We reached the other side of the river at dead of night, with the desperate cries of the drowning ringing in our ears."[11]

VATRA DORNEI

Vatra Dornei was a picturesque spa resort in the mountains of Bukovina, where many Jews lived off tourism. On 11 October the Jews of Vatra Dornei were ordered by the town crier, to the accompaniment of drums, to leave all their belongings behind and report within three hours to the local railway station. That summer the Jewish population of Vatra Dornei had grown due to an influx of Jews from Dorna Cândreni, Iacobeni, and other nearby villages. With the German invasion of the Soviet Union, dozens of Jews were taken hostage and held in a designated part of the town, while the rest were employed in various kinds of forced labor. Several streets on the outskirts of the town were turned into a ghetto, and some of the Jewish population was transferred there. Despite all these anti-Jewish measures the deportation order was so unexpected that the Jews took hardly any possessions with them: "It was a tremendous shock to us all, and we had no time. Many rich people suddenly found themselves penniless. We left with a knapsack on our back."[12]

The Jews were deported in two cattle trains that left on the same day, a few hours apart, each "congested and filthy" car carrying fifty to sixty Jews. After a three-day journey they all arrived in Atachi in the pouring rain and were made to disembark in a marshy location where they had to choose between discarding their belongings and losing their lives. As they emerged from the cars, Ukrainian farmers, according to prior agreements with the soldiers, fell upon the Jews and looted them. "They prized packages from our hands by force."[13]

In Atachi the deportees saw the messages that had been left behind by earlier deportees, most of them inscribed in blood. Alongside the names of victims were requests to recite kaddish. One Jew later recalled that even when they were in Mogilev, on the other side of the Dniester, "we didn't know where we were being taken."[14] The second search of personal belongings was supervised by a captain of the gendarmerie and inspectors of the national bank.

When the Jews of Vatra Dornei arrived in Atachi they found a ravaged town inundated with Jews from the numerous transports. The wagons "stretched in a column all the way to the railway station," some two kilometers away.[15] At the time, approximately twenty thousand Jews in Atachi were waiting to cross the river. Of these, two thousand at the most were transferred daily, in groups of a hundred each. Captain Popescu, representing army headquarters, gave the order to step up the pace of the deportation and evacuate the Jews within two days to make room for further transports. It was impossible to carry out this order, however, due to the searches for valuables, also ordained by army headquarters. In order to remedy this situation Captain Popescu ordered the searches to be conducted "by place of origin in the order in which the Jews arrived in Atachi."[16]

This created a new problem: how to prevent Jews who had already been searched but were still waiting to cross the river from coming into contact with Jews who had just arrived or who were waiting to be searched? The Jews of Vatra Dornei arrived just when the new search procedure was introduced. "Some of them were left for days on end under the pretext that they were being quarantined, or that they had not changed all their money," according to an official report by a police inspector sent to investigate the disappearance of money and valuables confiscated from Jews.[17] Finally, after being kept waiting for four days, Dan Popescu, inspector of the National Bank of Romania, together with army personnel, conducted the search. On 17 and 18 October the Jews of Vatra Dornei were transferred to Mogilev. Thus was one of Romania's most glorious communities, renowned at home and abroad, destroyed.

All in all, only twenty-one Jews remained in Vatra Dornei, some of whom had been brought back from Atachi at the request of the local authorities. The Klipper brothers (Fritz and Nathan), former owners of a timber factory, were allowed to stay in Vatra Dornei with their families, as their expertise was needed by the German army. On 31 October, twenty days after the deportation ended, gendarmerie detectives reported that "there were still many Jews" in Vatra Dornei and that "a radio transmitter had been seized in the basement [of the four Abramovici brothers] just as they were about to broadcast to Moscow." These Jews had been arrested and subsequently released and "were now doing business."[18] For the gendarmerie, however, even twenty-one Jews were too many.

The Jews of Rădăuţi learned of their impending deportation the day before it took place, on the festival of Succot, 13 October 1941. They too had had no inkling that the entire community was about to be deported. On 14 October all Jews were ordered to change their money into rubles and hand over their valuables at the National Bank of Romania. "There was a long line at the National Bank. . . . [E]ach Jew had to first pay all state and municipal taxes for a full year and then move on to another counter to change his money into rubles."[19] On 15 October the deportations proper took place.

The Jewish population of Rădăuţi had grown significantly following the expulsion of Jews from the surrounding villages prior to the outbreak of war and the transfer of the Jews of Siret to Rădăuţi about a month before the deportation. It took no less than four freight trains to transport Rădăuţi's 9,169 Jews.[20] Two of the trains were directed to Atachi and two to the Mărculeşti camp and from there via Rezina to Transnistria. Seventy-eighty Jews were packed randomly into each car. Unlike other transports from southern Bukovina, families were split up. The deportees were unaware that two of the trains were being directed to another crossing point.

The gendarmes accompanying one of the trains stopped it in an open field about fifty kilometers from Rădăuţi and demanded that the Jews "hand over all their gold and valuables, and the keys to their houses," arguing that they would be stripped of their valuables at the Mărculeşti camp anyway. The gendarmes collected an entire suitcase of gold and jewelry.[21] Nevertheless, in both Mărculeşti and Atachi the Jews were again subjected to a series of body and baggage searches. With each search the Romanians' pickings dwindled and with them the Jews' chances of survival in Transnistria.

The deportees sent to Atachi were taken off the trains and marched in the winter snow to the town, where they were crammed into gutted and ruined houses. It was here that the first deaths occurred. An eyewitness described the situation of the Jews in Atachi as follows: "The Bessarabian farmers exploited every opportunity to rob us of all our possessions, in exchange for basic foodstuffs. A man's suit went for two loaves of bread and a pot of unsugared tea. The Romanian gendarmes kept us on the run, to prevent us obtaining food even by this means."[22]

After being kept waiting for several days, two of the convoys from Rădăuţi crossed the Dniester. Most of the Jews were not allowed to stay in Mogilev but were marched farther to camps and ghettos in the heart of Transnistria. On 22 October 1941 the president of the Atachi community, Isidor Pressner, sent a desperate plea to Filderman "to save us from the jaws of death" and to intervene immediately with the authorities to prevent the transfer of the remainder of his community to a certain death in Transnistria. The deportation to the Ukraine, wrote Pressner in a letter that was smuggled to Bucharest, is "without destination, without purpose, and in an unknown direction." Many members of the community, added Pressner, had already been deported. Others had perished, gone crazy, or committed suicide. "We are unable to describe the enormity of the disaster that has befallen us. One thing, however, is clear. Unless we are saved *immediately*, no one . . . will remain alive." Filderman received the letter, but there was nothing he could do.[23]

Less is known of the fate of the two transports that reached Mărculeşti. The 1,500 Jews in one of the transports were marched from Mărculeşti to the Cosăuţi forest and then over the Dniester, after which they were marched for forty more days to the Tzibulevka ghetto near Berşad. Of the 1,500 Jews who crossed the Dniester, 1,270 reached Tzibulevka, and of these, only 210 were still alive three months later (February 1942). "Three unmarked mass graves in Tzibulevka, in which Jews were interred still clothed, bear testimony to the wretched fate of the deportees from Rădăuţi and other localities in Bukovina."[24]

On the day of deportation (15 October) the community leaders decided to entrust 157 Torah scrolls from the synagogues of Rădăuţi and other communities that had been evacuated to Rădăuţi to a trustworthy Pole by the name of Kuczinski for safekeeping. Army units passing through the town seized the Torah scrolls, however, and turned their parchment into drums, shoes, and sandals. In 1945, when the last one thousand survivors of the community returned from Transnistria, they collected the torn scraps of parchment "and buried the drums and shoes they discovered, in accordance with Jewish tradition." The soldiers also desecrated and destroyed the Jewish cemetery, dismantled its fence, smashed the gravestones, disinterred and scattered bones, and demolished the monument commemorating the soldiers of the Austrian army who had fallen in the First World War and the monument commemorating the Jews who had been massacred in the 1940 pogroms.[25]

The deportation operation did not end with the ethnic cleansing of Bukovina. The Antonescu regime wished to track down and deport all Jews born in Bukovina and Bessarabia who had, over the years, settled in other parts of Romania. An edict issued by the Interior Ministry, which was not officially publicized but was distributed to police stations, ordered all Jews originating from these two regions to return immediately to their places of origin, together with their wives and children, "even if the latter were born in the Regat." Filderman wrote to Antonescu at the time as follows: "They are being sent to their death, for no crime other than having been born in the wrong place." Their status, he wrote, was worse than that of foreign nationals who had entered Romania with or without a permit.[26]

On 17 October the police, using previously prepared lists, began arresting Bessarabian- or Bukovinian-born Jews and their families. The "culprits" included Jews who had moved to the Regat decades earlier, entire families where the father had been assigned to forced labor detachments at the time, or those who, in the summer of 1940, unwilling to live under a Communist regime, had fled with the Romanian army from the territories annexed to the Soviet Union. In Iași, which had a sizable concentration of Jews from Bessarabia, the Siguranța ordered all Bessarabian- and Bukovinian-born Jews to report to it by 26 October.[27]

The Jewish Federation's intervention was ineffective.[28] When Filderman asked the interior minister, Gen. Dumitru Popescu, to delay the deportation, the latter replied that had it been left up to him, these Jews would never have been deported in the first place but that "his authority was limited to the 1940 borders."[29] It was Antonescu who had decided to deport these Jews.

The above supports the hypothesis that, even had the Jewish leadership in Bucharest known in advance of the deportation, which was kept secret until its implementation, they could not have saved the Jews of Bessarabia and Bukovina. In this case, for example, even though the Jewish leadership knew about the deportation in advance, they were unable to prevent it because the order emanated from Antonescu himself.

Finally, it should be pointed out that the Jews who were arrested in the Regat and Southern Transylvania at that time or in the following months suffered an even worse fate than the rest of Bukovinian Jewry. The majority were taken in special trains directly to the extermination camps on the River Bug and murdered upon arrival. The vast majority never returned. We do not know exactly how many perished, but they almost certainly ran into the thousands.

22

The Dorohoi District

Dorohoi and the surrounding Jewish towns represented the quintessence of Romanian Jewry. Over two to three centuries these towns produced the type of Romanian Jew who spoke Yiddish and Romanian, was educated in Romanian-Jewish schools and later in public schools, spoke no "foreign" language, was not under foreign rule, and saw Bucharest as a spiritual center. Two months before the invasion of the Soviet Union the Dorohoi district (excluding Herța, which had been annexed to the Soviet Union the previous year) had 11,546 Jews, of which 5,389 lived in the district capital.

On the eve of the invasion of the Soviet Union (22 June 1941) the authorities arrested the head of the Jewish community, attorney Isidor Avramovici-Băluș, together with twenty-two other persons who had been categorized as suspects and transferred them in sealed cattle cars to the Târgu-Jiu camp. The journey took two weeks and was punctuated with "threats to kill us." Since the Târgu-Jiu camp was full to bursting, the prisoners were transferred to a special camp in Craiova, where they were held for two months.[1] When they returned to Dorohoi it was no longer the same. At the outbreak of war some five thousand Jews from the district's towns and villages (Mihăileni, Darabani, Săveni, Târgu, Rădăuți) had been evacuated to Dorohoi, and these were later followed by another one thousand. A special regime had been introduced in the city that differed from that of other towns in the Regat, since administratively the district was annexed to Bukovina. "Under such conditions, it was virtually impossible to represent or defend Jewish rights," testified one of the community leaders.[2]

The Jews of the Dorohoi district were subject to all the laws, decrees, and ordinances that applied to other part of Romania, such as Antonescu's decree of 21 June 1941, which gave the authorities forty-eight hours to transport all able-bodied Jews age eighteen to sixty from the villages between the Siret and Prut rivers to the Târgu-Jiu camp and their families to towns in the district where they lived.[3] In actual fact, the evacuation had already begun on 19 June.

The deportation of the Jews of the Dorohoi district is a well-known and well-documented chapter of Romanian history. Already at that time it was seen as a test case for the Antonescu regime's plans for the Jews of the Regat. In his last meeting with Filderman, on 8 September 1941, Antonescu promised that he "drew a distinction between the Jews of the Regat and other Jews, and planned to grant them preferred status."[4] The Jewish leadership in Bucharest believed him and was therefore totally taken unaware when the deportations from the Regat began. The Jewish Federation's emissary, the Romanian attorney Constantin Muşat, left for Dorohoi on 6 November, as soon as the first news of the deportation reached Bucharest.[5]

Documents from the 1945 trial of Bukovinian government leaders, Muşat's report of November 1941, information smuggled to Filderman by community leaders who were not deported, and information about attempts by the Jewish leadership in Bucharest to avert the decree constitute the documentation of this deportation operation. Here, even more than in southern Bukovina, the authorities tried to conceal any written documents or evidence of personal responsibility in the implementation of the deportation. These attempts at concealment continued under the Communist regime.

As far as the orders and administrative preparations were concerned, the deportation of the Jews from the Dorohoi district resembled that of the Jews from southern Bukovina. Although we know that the deportation order was issued by Romanian army headquarters, it has not thus far been traced. On 25 November 1941 Muşat stated that the garrison stationed in Dorohoi had received an order from Marshal Antonescu on 25 October forbidding Jews to leave the city "under any pretext" and abolishing all concessions in this respect (travel permits for students, court witnesses, etc.). The district governor, Col. Ioan Barcan; Mayor Jean Pascu; and the secretary of the Bukovinian administration, Nicu Lupu, drew up a document stating that "those who had been transferred to the city of Dorohoi from the outlying towns of Dărăbani, Săveni, Rădăuţi [Prut] and Mihăileni, must be expelled; this surplus population interferes with the sound conduct of life in the city of Dorohoi."[6]

On 5 November rumors spread that the Jews were about to be evicted from the city. That evening the heads of the Jewish community of Dorohoi and of the surrounding communities that had been evacuated to Dorohoi were summoned by the prefect. Surprisingly, he did not mention deportation but informed the apprehensive community leaders that within two days the evicted Jews would receive clothing and shoes collected from their abandoned homes in the district.

"To this day, we are waiting for these goods," added Muşat. The following day (6 November) the police commander made good this omission. He summoned the Jewish community leaders and informed them that the deportation from Dorohoi would begin the following day, with the deportation of the Jews of Dărăbani and Rădăuţi-Prut.[7] On 7 November the first transport left for Atachi with 1,500 Jews from Dărăbani and Rădăuţi-Prut. Their plight was terrible, since the Dorohoi community could no longer support them and they had arrived in Dorohoi after having been fleeced of all their possessions in the Târgu-Jiu camp. The second transport comprised 3,000 Jews, and therefore an especially long train was required to transport them.

The city of Dorohoi was thus purged of its evacuees, who, according to the local authorities, constituted a public health hazard. The order to deport the Jews of Dorohoi was issued by Gen. Corneliu Calotescu, the governor of Bukovina (5 September 1941–20 March 1943), as was revealed at the trial of Calotescu and other war criminals who held positions within the Bukovinian administration. Although Calotescu formally issued the order, however, in a centralized state such as Antonescu's such an order could not have been issued without his knowledge or consent, especially as the order was relayed by army headquarters and violated the promise Antonescu had given Filderman in the presence of Nicolae Lupu, the president of the High Court of Appeals. The document has since been traced to the Czernowitz city archive. The 1945 trial of Bukovinian war criminals unearthed several other facts, of which the most important was that "a group of important officials from Dorohoi, headed by the prefect, came especially to Czernowitz to ask Calotescu to evict the Jews of Dorohoi."[8]

The decision to deport the Jews of the Regat originated from local government officials, such as members of the military, civil servants, and lawyers, who were never associated with the Legionary movement and some of whom were (erroneously) considered friends of the Jews, such as Mayor Jean Pascu, who was on good terms with the Jews. The trial also showed that as soon as the deportation policy in southern Bukovina became public citizens bombarded the prefecture with requests to deport the Jews from Dorohoi, too, on various pretexts. The director general of the prefecture, Mihail Popescu, wrote a special report, signed by the mayor and the prefect, Col. Ioan Barcan (who after the deportation was promoted to the rank of general), asking for the transfer of Jews from Dorohoi on the grounds that they were a public nuisance and that the prefecture had received numerous requests for their removal. General Calotescu approved the request and issued a deportation order "but allowed the prefect to leave certain Jews behind, at his discretion."[9]

Until 3 December, when the deportations from Dorohoi ended, Antonescu was unavailable, and therefore any complaints of breach of promise were futile. Although Filderman submitted his "Report on the Deportation of Jews from the Dorohoi District" to Nicolae Lupu, the latter was granted an audience with the Conducător only on 3 December.[10] At that meeting Antonescu informed Lupu "that he was moved by what was happening, that he had ordered an inquiry, and that the deportees would be brought back."[11] There was no inquiry, and no Jews were brought back (until December 1943). The only Jews who were spared this terrible fate were the Jews of the last convoy, who were saved at the last minute, when they were already waiting on the platform.

Between 9 and 11 November 1941 the Sorting Committee (Comisia de triere) — an extortionist apparatus similar to its namesake in Czernowitz — was set in motion. This committee — chaired by the prefect, Colonel Barcan, and comprising the mayor; Police Commander Pamfil; the head of the Chamber of Commerce, Timoş; the craftsmen's representative, Titus Onofrei; and two army commanders from Czernowitz — met in the prefecture. An unknown number of requests for exemption from deportation were submitted by Jewish "merchants, university graduates, the disabled, the elderly, recipients of war decorations, war widows and orphans."[12] The antisemitic climate, the hostility between Romanians and Jews, and corruption within the Romanian regime led to a replay of the events of Czernowitz. A rumor spread among the Jews that it was possible to obtain sickness certificates and thereby postpone the deportation by several hours or even days. Many Jews paid huge sums to Mihail Popescu and to Dr. Felix Nădejde, the district doctor, for these permits. These two officials colluded in charging hundreds of thousands of lei for each permit, which was valid for a few days only, or demanding gold watches, gold brooches, or gold jewelry of any kind or shape in lieu of lei. Many Jews paid in the belief that Popescu, who was a close friend of the prefect, could save them from deportation altogether.

On 13 November the second convoy of Jews left Dorohoi. After the police spread the rumor that this was the last convoy to leave and that anyone subsequently found without a permit would be executed, many more Jews reported for deportation.[13] About 3,000 Jews were deported in the two convoys. A total of 1,756 Jews were left in the city, some without permits, and another 800 or so men were left in labor detachments in the Brăila district. The authorities tried to calm the distraught wives of the forced labor conscripts: "The women were told that their husbands would follow. Clad in skimpy shirts, clutching their children's hands, these women were marched out of Dorohoi. This explains why the highest mortality rate occurred among the deportees of Dorohoi."[14] These sentences were written by Filderman in a memorandum he submitted to the minister of the interior on 12 December 1943 in an attempt to persuade the minister to permit the survivors of the Dorohoi district to return to Romania. On 14 November a large convoy comprising all the Jews of Dorohoi who had no permits reached the train station. The train was waiting in the station, but at 9 a.m. the masses who were sitting on their luggage were informed that an order had been given to delay the departure because of a shortage of wagons. The order abolishing the transport had been telephoned through from Czernowitz the previous evening, but the prefect and his accomplices on the committee chose to evict the Jews from their homes in order to turn them into state property and only then to announce the delay.

After the deportation the community was almost liquidated. All community leaders who had not been arrested or held hostage and almost all rabbis, including Chief Rabbi David Schechter, were deported.

One convoy, the fate of which came to light only recently, consisted of hundreds of youth and men from the district who had returned from Târgu-Jiu and labor camps in southern Romania and were being held under guard in the school building and in a synagogue. This convoy was marched from Dorohoi to Atachi, heavily guarded by gendarmes, who traveled in wagons, shooting at any stragglers. "Anyone who lagged behind or sat down for a moment was shot on the spot. The route became littered with corpses. We constantly heard gun reports. With each report, we knew that somebody else had been shot." The gendarmes looted the few goods owned by the youths and even tortured them on the way because "they were convinced we were hiding gold and jewelry."[15] The gendarmes did not let the youth bury their friends but kept them marching for three days and three nights. Some of the youth were forced into the Dniester and mowed down with machine guns.

When the leaders of the Dorohoi community in Mogilev found out that the deportations had ceased, they telegrammed the Jewish Federation in Bucharest on 26 November begging it to take swift action to ensure the return of the deportees—some of whom were in Transnistria "even though they belonged to the Regat"—to Dorohoi. According to the telegram most of the deportees were women and children whose husbands and sons were still being kept in work detachments.[16] Should this request be denied, the community leaders continued, the federation should ensure that the deportees be allowed to stay in Mogilev, at least until their fate was decided. By then some Jews of Dorohoi were no longer alive, having been murdered or drowned in the Dniester.

Ironically, that very same day the federation received a telegram from the husbands of these women, who had been sent back to Dorohoi, asking to be allowed to join their families in Transnistria.[17] These Jews were not permitted to enter their homes or apartments, which were now state property. Although this strange request was not granted at the time, it was not forgotten and was retrieved from the files in the summer of 1942. On 21 March 1942 Clara Sofer appealed to Antonescu (in a letter that was passed on to Radu Lecca, commissioner for Jewish affairs) to allow 400 women and their children back to Dorohoi.[18] These women were the survivors of the 800 women who had been deported in November 1941 and whose husbands had been kept behind in the work detachments. Their request was rejected. Around the same time 270 men from Dorohoi appealed to the authorities and to Filderman to bring back their families from Transnistria—some 1,104 survivors, of whom 69 were war invalids, war orphans and widows, or decorated war veterans.[19] At the time, however, Filderman could no longer intervene on their behalf, since on 17 December 1941 the Jewish Federation was disbanded and replaced by the Judenrat (the Jewish Center).

In Dorohoi there were more available apartments (some of them ruined) than prospective occupants. In April 1942 the local branch of the National Romanization Center reported to Bucharest that there were 601 vacant houses that had belonged to deported Jews: 338 had been handed over to Romanians, another 19 were commissioned for government use, and 244 houses remained vacant, of which 79 were on the verge of collapse.[20]

In Dorohoi, too, the Romanization and looting of Jewish property took place in two waves, the first spontaneous and the second organized. During the first wave neighbors and ordinary Romanians broke into Jewish apartments as soon as the Jews were taken to the railway station, while municipal clerks and policemen were busy stamping documents. On 20 May 1942 Barcan, the prefect, was asked to submit a written justification to the commission of inquiry that had been set up following the disappearance of "state property" from Jewish homes: "Despite all precautions, it was impossible to completely prevent thefts because of the haste in which the deportation operation was conducted, and [because] the property to be supervised was so vast and dispersed. In the interim, in order to prevent theft, the municipality removed certain items from apartments that ran the greatest risk of theft, and stored them in warehouses."[21]

In Dorohoi, as in Kishinev and Czernowitz, much of the property that was stored in warehouses disappeared due to the defective inventorying of goods. On 22 November 1941, when it was clear that the deportation was final, Jewish "absentee" property was officially transferred to the National Romanization Center, the local branch of which was headed by attorney Marcel Adam.

The deportation of Jews from the Dorohoi district was a very important chapter in the history of the Holocaust in Romania. It proved that, in the autumn of 1941, conditions were ripe for the deportation of Jews from the Regat to Transnistria or elsewhere. The deportation plan was entirely a Romanian—not a German—initiative. The central and local Romanian authorities who gave the orders belonged to the traditional Romanian establishment and were not identified with the Romanian fascist party. Among them were officers (regulars and reserves), mayors, government officials, civil servants, railroaders, policemen, soldiers, and gendarmes. They were backed by most of the local Romanian population.

The deep impact left by the antisemitic parties of the thirties; antisemitic propaganda in the press in 1940–41; official antisemitic incitement during the Legionary government; statements by Antonescu, his deputy, Mihai Antonescu, and ministers and prefects; the aftermath of the 1940 pogroms; the heavy losses sustained by the Romanian army during the Battle of Odessa in September–October 1941; and Nazi influences on the Antonescu regime all laid the groundwork for the deportation of the Jews of the Dorohoi district with impunity. This extreme measure did not meet with any opposition from members of the public or the intelligentsia. In September 1941 Gheorghe Alexianu, the governor of Transnistria, was informed by two colonels from War Headquarters, who visited him in Tiraspol and transmitted orders verbally in the Conducător's name, that the deportation of Bessarabian and Bukovinian Jewry would be followed by the deportation of the Jews of the Regat.[22] In August 1941 Antonescu's plan to transfer sixty thousand Jews from the Regat to Bessarabia to pave roads was thwarted by Killinger, the German ambassador.[23] Killinger's intervention sprang from the Nazis' preference for implementing the Final Solution in a planned and organized manner.

A leader of the Jews of the Regat described the situation as follows: "Soldiers, officials, and even civilians—people who for generations lived peacefully with Jews, have been swept along on the current of antisemitism, and have robbed and murdered innocent people whom the authorities have failed to protect and who have been deprived of any means of self-defense."[24] Clearly, by the autumn of 1941 conditions were ripe for the deportation of all of Romania's Jews.

In November 1943 Gen. Constantin Vasiliu, undersecretary of state for police and security in the Ministry of the Interior, estimated the number of Jews deported from the Dorohoi district (including those deported in the summer of 1942) at 10,368, excluding Herța, and at 12,000 or more, including Herța.[25]

Table 7 shows the demographic changes that occurred among the Jews of Dorohoi between 1930 and 1942.

During the first deportation in November 1941, 9,367 Jews were deported (3,480 men, 3,596 women, and 2,291 children). A total of 2,556 Jews (1,404 men, 569 women, and 583 children) were left in Dorohoi.[26] In 1942 the authorities planned to deport 1,838 Jews and leave behind 718 (231 men, 226 women, and

TABLE 7. JEWS IN THE DOROHOI DISTRICT, 1930–42

Town	1930[a]	1939[b]	1941[c] April	1941[d] October	1942[e] May	1942[e,f] June
Dorohoi	5,820	—	5,389	—	3,010	2,316
Dărăbani	1,917	—	—	—	—	—
Saveni	1,774	—	6,157	—	—	—
Mihăileni	1,490	—	—	—	—	—
Herța	1,940	—	—[g]	—	—	—
Villages	1,931[h]	—	—	—	—	—
Total	14,872	15,248	11,546	11,923	3,010	2,316

[a] Centrala Evreilor, *Breviarul statistic*, 26–30; Congresul Mondial Evreesc, *Populația evreească*, 42–43, 45, 114.

[b] Congresul Mondial Evreesc, *Populația evreească*, 53, including an estimate of the number of Jews in the Dorohoi district in 1939.

[c] Congresul Mondial Evreesc, *Populația evreească*, 42. Data on the Dorohoi district were taken from the official census conducted in April 1941; see pp. 39–40, n. 2. For the number of Jews in the city of Dorohoi in April 1941, see data on the Jewish population in 1941, p. 211.

[d] Governor of Bukovina to the Presidency of the Council of Ministers, including a table, 9 April 1942, USHMM/RMFA, RG-25.006M, roll 10, "The Jewish Problem," vol. 21, p. 131.

[e] Centrala Evreilor din România, Rezultatele recensământului locuitorilor având sânge evreesc efectuat de Guvernământul Bucovinei, Situația încheiată la 20 iuliu 1942 [Results of the census of residents of Jewish blood in Bukovina, conducted by the government of Bukovina, 20 July 1942], pamphlet, p. 5; copy in Ancel, *Documents*, vol. 1, doc. 42, p. 291.

[f] See also Congresul Mondial Evreesc, *Populația evreească*, 42. There were 2,316 Jews remaining in Dorohoi after the deportations. Taking into account the 10,368 Jews who were deported according to 1943 Ministry of the Interior statistics and the 1,938 Jews from Herța, there were 14,642 Jews in the district on the eve of the deportations, about 230 less than in 1930 (approximately equivalent to the victims of the 1940 pogrom). Note that the Jewish population hardly increased during the 1930s. Note further that although the authorities deported Bessarabian- and Bukovinian-born Jews residing in the Regat and southern Transylvania, Dorohoi-born Jews residing in other parts of Romania were not deported.

[g] Herța was part of the Soviet Union after June 1940.

[h] Congresul Mondial Evreesc, *Populația evreească*, 114.

261 children) who were considered vital to the economy or who enjoyed special exemptions. On 11 June 1942 the deportations resumed. This time only 360 Jews (196 men, 82 women, and 82 children) were deported.[27] A total of 2,196 Jews—or 2,316, according to the census of citizens of Jewish blood conducted in the summer of 1942—remained in Dorohoi.[28]

23

The National Bank of Romania

On 4 December 1941 Marshal Antonescu convened a special meeting with the participation of Constantin Stoicescu, minister of justice; Gen. C. Pantazi, the deputy minister of defense; Gen. Constantin Calotescu, the governor of Bukovina; Alexandru Otulescu, the governor of the National Bank of Romania (Banca Națională a României, BNR); Stroe Ștefan, the military attorney general; and other senior officials. Antonescu informed them that events in Bessarabia, especially those for which members of the military were responsible, had blackened the regime's name: "This is the greatest disappointment I have experienced in my career—that such events can take place under my rule. . . . What makes matters worse is the fact that many members of the military are implicated." Antonescu berated General Voiculescu, reminding him that he had already warned him on two occasions not to repeat the anti-Jewish measures that had been introduced in 1918 when the Romanian army entered Bessarabia for the first time. At that time, stated Antonescu, members of the Romanian military arrested Jews, took them to the Dniester, robbed them of their possessions, murdered them, and threw their corpses into the river. Antonescu openly accused the governor of Bessarabia of dereliction of duty, especially since he was "literally two steps away from the [Kishinev] ghetto. Had I been there, things would have been different. I would immediately have put an end to such disgraceful behavior. You have tainted not only your own name, but also my name and that of the entire Romanian nation. . . . Our enemies' propaganda is based on our attitude toward the Jews. And this took place at a time when I was making an effort to enhance the standing of the Romanian nation. . . . Now I have no choice but to track down the culprits and punish them suitably."[1]

Antonescu informed his ministers and the BNR governor that he had summoned them to a special meeting in order to set up a commission of inquiry that would, on the basis of instructions it received from those present, reach swift conclusions. It was clear to all present that the disgrace he was referring to was not the murder of Jews but rather the BNR's failure to confiscate their gold—which, as Antonescu was at pains to explain, was ill gotten and therefore not their legitimate property. Antonescu clarified the point: "When I decided to take the gold and transfer it to State control, I meant taking something that did not belong to the Jews. I decided to take it for the State, and only the National Bank should have received it."[2]

Documentation available as of 1994 enables us to understand the BNR's role in the looting of Jewish property and its transfer to the Romanian Finance Ministry. The BNR operated simultaneously on five fronts. The bank was empowered by Ion Antonescu, and in one case by Mihai Antonescu, to carry out each of the five stages of this operation, as follows:

1. Romanian lei owned by the Jewish residents of Bessarabia and Bukovina prior to their deportation in October 1941 were changed into rubles at the rate of 40 lei per ruble instead of 1 leu per ruble, the going rate for the population as a whole. Rubles and any other currency owned by Jews were then changed into special German occupation marks (Reichskreditkassenscheine, RKKS) at the rate of 60 rubles per mark. The Jews of Czernowitz, for example, owned 1 million lei ($6,134, according to the official exchange rate) in July 1940, which they changed into rubles under the short-lived Soviet regime at the rate of 1 ruble per leu; they were then forced to change them back into lei upon the resumption of Romanian rule at the rate of 40 lei per ruble. In other words, what had formerly been 1 million lei was now worth only 25,000 lei. Moreover, in October 1941, on the eve of their deportation, the Jews were ordered to hand over all their money to the BNR representative in the ghetto, for which they were supposedly paid a total of 600 rubles—at a time when the ruble was no longer legal tender in Transnistria. To make matters worse, once they reached Transnistria, and even at the crossing points, the deportees were forced to change their rubles into RKKS at the rate of 60 rubles per RKKS. In the final analysis, their money was so devalued that it sufficed to buy a single loaf of bread only. The above calculation was made by clerks working for the Jewish Federation during the Holocaust itself.[3] The Jews of southern Bukovina and the Dorohoi district, having never been under Soviet occupation, were spared only the Soviet stage of this exchange operation, but their money was still confiscated by this method.

2. All foreign currency was confiscated on the spot. There was no pretense of changing it.

3. Gold and silver jewelry and items made of precious metals, as defined by the BNR clerks, including ritual objects, gold and silver coins, gold

bullion, and gold watches, were all "sold" at the rate of 211 lei per gram, when the black-market price for gold was 1,060 lei per gram.[4]

4. Pictures and other works of art were confiscated from Jewish homes after their owners were evacuated to the ghetto or deported directly to Transnistria.

5. In order to destroy all evidence of the deportees' identity, all personal documents were confiscated. These included documents relating to securities and bonds, savings books, promissory notes, or any document testifying to ownership of bank accounts, savings funds, pension schemes, or real estate in Romania or abroad.

The leu-ruble exchange rate for the population as a whole in the liberated territories was fixed immediately after the liberation by Antonescu, based on his experience during the First World War and guided by his antisemitism. Antonescu informed his ministers as well as the BNR governor how, during the First World War, Romanian officers and politicians used to smuggle money out of Austria and Russia, causing heavy losses to the Romanian state, which was forced to buy currency from the public at the fixed rate, known also to the smugglers:

> In order to foil these attempts [at smuggling], I introduced measures concerning the exchange of rubles. I determined the rate of a leu per ruble to prevent the Yids from racketeering. Now, the time has come to give the peasants [in the liberated territories] an increment of 5 lei per ruble. We shall sell our rubles to the Yids who are about to be transferred to the Ukraine, at the rate of 8 lei per ruble. . . . Thus, Mr. Finance Minister and Mr. Vulcănescu, we have adopted measures to prevent a repeat of what happened in the last war when all sorts of "vultures" engaged in racketeering. I have adopted all the requisite political precautions. The technical problems I leave up to you.[5]

Even though he explicitly blamed "officers and politicians" for racketeering in the previous war, this time Antonescu accused the Jews of endangering the stability of the national currency, even though the Jews had no freedom of movement but were being murdered or interned in camps awaiting deportation. By determining an exchange rate of 8 lei per ruble, Antonescu was clearly intending to fleece the Jews of their money. Deputy Finance Minister Mircea Vulcănescu and members of the BNR who were responsible for resolving technical problems, however, went even further and determined an exchange rate of 40 lei per ruble. The money thus confiscated from the Jews served to pay compensation to the Romanian peasants in these territories. None of the ministers dared contradict the Conducător, whose decisions were fueled not by logic but rather by his antisemitic delusions.

Antonescu, who kept an eye on the progress of the confiscation operation just as he kept an eye on developments on the front, realized—too late—that he was being duped. In early October he ordered the Finance Ministry "to put a stop to any attempt to change rubles belonging to Jews or to Germans."[6] This measure was designed to prevent German officers stationed in Romania from changing rubles they had obtained from Bessarabian, Bukovinian, and even Transnistrian Jews and gentiles into lei. At the same time that Antonescu issued secret instructions to War Headquarters to prepare for the deportations, he also issued secret instructions to the governors of Bessarabia and Bukovina, on 5 October 1941, to "organize" in concert with the national bank the "exchange" of jewelry and valuables owned by Jews for rubles or RKKS, both of which were worthless currencies, "at the official rate" and by "reliable elements" and to change their money into RKKS.[7] This order was confidentially relayed by the governor of Bessarabia to military headquarters in Kishinev and to the Kishinev branch of the national bank.[8]

After adding clarifications to Antonescu's order, the finance minister sent it on—this time not classified as confidential—to the governor of Bessarabia. The clarifications stated that jewelry or precious metals owned by Jews who were "evacuating" would be paid for in rubles at the new rate of 40 rubles per leu. Valuables would be purchased by local BNR branches. Gold would be weighed and evaluated by weight and quality at the official rate. Diamonds and precious gems would be evaluated by an expert and would be purchased at only 20 percent of their value. The Ministry of Finance, anxious to avoid any potential litigation, asked the governor of Bessarabia "together with local BNR branches, to confiscate all receipts for rubles paid out to Jews before their departure [i.e., deportation]."[9]

This order was simply a legal cover for defrauding the Jews. Within two months of the occupation the BNR set a special exchange rate for Jews of 40 rubles per leu as against 1 ruble per leu for Romanians and other Aryans. Moreover, from the date the order was issued the ruble was no longer legal tender in Transnistria (although it was still used). Jews had no option but to change their rubles into RKKS at the rate of 60 rubles per RKKS. This exchange took place in Transnistria itself and at the crossing points over the Dniester, under conditions that have already been described. In Transnistria itself it was possible to purchase the RKKS for 6 or 7 rubles.

Meanwhile, Deputy Finance Minister Vulcănescu set 25 October as the new deadline for the end of the exchange operation in the liberated territories. In a circular he sent to prefects, mayors, and other public figures, he stated that by this date all declarations concerning the amount of rubles to be changed into lei must be submitted. In the circular he also referred to lists of rubles that had been drawn up in the various camps.[10] The instructions sent by the finance minister, Gen. Nicolae Stoenescu, to the local authorities on 18 October 1941 concerning the end of this exchange operation drew a clear distinction between Jews and non-Jews: "Jews in the camps shall submit their statements to the camp commanders, specifying the date of their incarceration and the date of completion of the exchange operation in the region."[11]

The camp commanders were required to submit lists of money owned by Jews in the camps. The Finance Ministry threatened to abort the exchange operation if information was withheld. Nevertheless, no convoy of Jews was held up for this reason, and no Jew reported to the camp commander with a bundle of undeclared rubles.

The vaults of the Kishinev, Czernowitz, and Bucharest banks began filling up with crates of jewelry and gold, some of which had been discovered in the homes of search officials or their relatives, in the Regat or in apartments they rented in Bessarabia. On 14 November, in a confidential letter to the management of the BNR, Antonescu's military cabinet asked for instructions regarding the "legal" transfer of this property, and "the sale of gold owned by Jews."[12] The Conducător himself, it should be noted, was scrupulously honest in his legal handling of state property, and his name was never associated with acts of corruption. Quite simply, his concept of legitimacy did not include Jews.

Two managers of the national bank sent a confidential letter to the military cabinet, stating, "The BNR has the right to purchase all gold in the form of bullion or coins. There is no obligation to sell gold or jewelry to the BNR. The BNR is not entitled to force the owners [of these items] to sell their jewelry. Those who own jewelry do not volunteer to sell it to the BNR, since we pay only the official price, i.e., 211 lei per gram."[13]

This was a mere subterfuge, since the bank governor and some of his aides regularly participated in Antonescu's special ministerial sessions on the confiscation of gold and its transfer to the BNR, as well as in sessions at which it was decided to set up commissions of inquiry, such as the session of 4 December 1941. The traditional financial circles that controlled the bank and the Finance Ministry were closely linked to the world of Anglo-French finance and took care not to leave behind any written evidence of their direct involvement in the looting of Jewish property or in the "purchase" of gold from Jews. All receipts handed out by the bank to Jews in southern Bukovina and in the Dorohoi district, where the exchange operations were carried out in a more orderly fashion, were confiscated on the banks of the Dniester. These attempts to shrug off responsibility failed, however. The complexity of the operation and the need to give it a legal front generated documents that clearly implicate the bank and the Finance Ministry in the operation. "Anything to do with economics in [my] regime was in the hands of the liberals," stated Antonescu in 1946, in the interrogation leading up to his trial. He also named all the people whom Brătianu had agreed to "lend" him to manage economic and monetary affairs, including Alexandru Otulescu, the governor of the National Bank of Romania.[14]

On 12 January 1942, after all of Bessarabia and Bukovina, excluding Czernowitz, had been purged of Jews and no more transports were crossing the Dniester, Law no. 21 was passed, empowering the BNR "to sell rubles to the Jews who were being evacuated according to the rate determined by the Bank with the Finance Ministry's approval."[15] The phrasing of the law and the accompanying explanations testified that this was the work of the liberal financial circles (affiliated with the National Liberal Party) of the former regimes that felt a need to create a semblance of retroactive legality for the organized acts of looting.

On 12 January, with the deportation of the Jews of Odessa to the death camps set up by the Romanians near the Bug River, the BNR found a new channel for its looting operations.[16] The commander of the gendarmerie in Transnistria reported the establishment of a "commission to evaluate property, jewelry and currency exchanges" (to RKKS).[17] Since the looting of foreign citizens, even under occupation, was not condoned by international law, the BNR made sure that no document that left its hands mentioned money or valuables belonging to the Jews of Odessa or any other place in Transnistria. However, local officers and representatives of the General Staff who conducted the operation were not as sensitive to these finer points, and their reports emphasized the BNR's involvement in the theft of property of Jews sentenced to death in Odessa. For example, Major Apostolescu, who was dispatched to Odessa by the General Staff's Second Section "to supervise the evacuation of the Jews," stated in his report of 18 January 1942, at the height of the deportations, that representatives of the BNR and the Finance Ministry were present during the operation:

> The ghetto has seven commissions to match the number of police precincts. All Jews report to these commissions, which are run by an officer, and include a BNR agent, a Finance Ministry representative, two local civilians, and a midwife, who reports on cash and valuables [discovered by means of gynecological examinations]. The Jews are searched, and any gold, silver or precious stones found are evaluated by the commission, and exchanged for cash. Rubles are exchanged at the rate of one ruble per leu, up to a ceiling of 5,000 rubles. Any valuables or cash that have not been declared are confiscated. Corruption is impossible, since any member of the commission who is tempted to steal, would have first to reach a prior understanding with all other members of the commission.[18]

The Jews of Odessa who were brought to these commissions were given RKKS, if anything, not lei, for their rubles, at a rate of 60 lei per RKKS — that is, RKKS 83 at the most. The rest of their money was confiscated. Major Apostolescu's confidential report further pointed out that the BNR and the Finance Ministry representatives were stealing jewelry and valuables from the Jews. For example, a handmade gold watch worth 60,000 lei was priced by members of the bank and the commission at RKKS 20 (1,200 lei). A gold necklace was evaluated at 420 lei, and so on. Apostolescu added that he had received complaints from Jews that they were being openly robbed by the local population and Romanian soldiers. At the end of the report he pointed out that many Jews had died even before they boarded the trains, "and some of them had died en route." Major Apostolescu reported that "hardly any" valuables or cash were found among the Jews.[19] Note that the commission's searches took place after about four thousand Jews were hanged in the streets of Odessa and another twenty thousand murdered on the city outskirts (see chap. 27).

The Antonescu regime's lust for gold was rooted not only in its desire to strip the Jews of all their possessions but also in its economic outlook. The BNR managers did not accept the Nazi thesis that Europe was entering a new era in which national wealth would be measured by the German mark. They were convinced, as Mircea Vulcănescu testified, that gold bullion and the U.S. dollar — not the German mark — would remain "the standard purchasing force in every market."[20] On 10 April 1941 Vulcănescu prepared a detailed memorandum for the finance minister, who passed it on to Antonescu. The memorandum stated that gold would continue to serve as the token of economic power and independence and that Romania must continue amassing gold so as to be able to join the economic systems of free-economy states "once we are free of the constraints of war": "All members of the BNR continued to think in gold and dollar terms, even though we were allied with Germany, which wished [to introduce] the Mark as the basis for measuring wealth in Europe. Their assumption was that when peace came, the Anglo-American economy would once again determine the prices of raw materials." Antonescu and the regime, continued Vulcănescu, accepted this basic assumption, despite "ostensibly" embracing the new economic order.[21]

The scope of this operation — which entailed the confiscation of local and foreign currency, gold items and coins, silver objects, ritual objects, objets d'art, jewelry, diamonds and precious gems, bank deposits and savings, securities, bonds, insurance policies, and the like — is impossible to assess due to the circumstances under which it took place and to the fact that the BNR managers were careful not to leave any incriminating evidence behind of the bank's involvement in the looting of Jewish property. Some of these items were hidden in the belongings of Jews who were sent to Atachi and Mărculeşti and were forced, by various methods, to leave them behind. A report by a commission set up by Antonescu stated that the Jews "were not permitted to take anything but the most basic items with [them], and that the rest of their luggage was stockpiled by gendarmes and representatives of the BNR in Atachi and Mărculeşti."[22] This luggage contained large amounts of valuables, jewelry, and cash, some of which was transferred to the BNR and much of which was handed over to the Welfare Council run by Maria Antonescu, the Conducător's wife.

Some idea of the scope of Jewish property confiscated by the BNR is offered by an official government publication that came out in the autumn of 1943, glorifying the achievements of the Antonescu regime during its three years in power. The chapter titled "Currency and Credit" vaunted the stability of the leu during the war: "In recent years, the National Bank, with the State's invaluable backing, has managed to preserve the reputation of our national currency both at home and abroad." This claim was correct at the time. Despite the global slump in gold production, the publication stated, the national currency's gold coverage rose by 2.1 billion lei in 1941 and by 11.3 billion lei in 1942 (the gold Germany sent Romania in order to even out the trade balance between the two countries arrived only toward the end of 1943). In that period deposits in the large banks rose from 3 billion lei in 1940 to 5.6 billion lei in 1941 and 11.9 billion lei in 1942. Reserves in the National Savings Fund rose from 3.3 billion lei in 1940 to 5.4 billion lei in 1941 and 9 billion lei in 1942.[23] These financial developments took place in part at a time when Romania had lost over a third of its territory and a third of its population, was engaged in large-scale conscription to the army and military activity, and had suffered losses on the front. At Antonescu's trial the prosecutor summed up this chapter of Romanian history in a single sentence. "The Jews," he said, "provided the raw material" for the enrichment of the Romanian fascist state and members of the regime.[24]

The disappearance of some of this "raw material" led to the establishment of commissions of inquiry, and it was their reports that shed light on what had really happened. Self-justification by those responsible for the liquidation and deportation of the Jews has left us with the strongest proof of all of the regime's policy toward the Jews and has exposed most of the secret, verbal orders that the regime was so careful to hide. The commissions' reports, as official documents, constitute incontrovertible proof of the regime's policies. In December 1941 a commission, in an attempt to justify irregularities, determined:

> The situation of the Jews, who were subject to restrictions imposed by orders from above, in itself served as a trigger for lawlessness [on the part of the gendarmes, military, inspectors, etc.]. Moreover, the general feeling that the

Jews had been placed outside the protection of the law induced all those with some authority to enhance their strength and encourage lawlessness. [This happened] especially during the deportations, before [the convoys] left and also on the way, when the convoys of Jews literally turned into anonymous herds bereft of personality or identity, whose lives were not worth protecting. This climate of lawlessness reached epidemic proportions, and tainted the honesty of people [who participated], on or off duty, in the operations. None of them felt accountable, and this lack of accountability awakened primitive instincts. Even those who had formerly been paragons of integrity were affected. The unrest that overtook the Jews was also a factor. Their despair and their natural desire to survive caused them to mobilize all the hereditary mores that typify them.[25]

Although the looting of Jewish property by the BNR was instigated by the antisemitic Antonescu regime, it was in part implemented and supervised by traditional economic and financial circles that had always arrogantly claimed to represent Romanian democracy. On 15 January 1946 Alexandru Alexandrini, Romania's last liberal finance minister before the advent of Communist rule, exonerated all members of the BNR who had participated in the looting of Jewish property in Bessarabia and Bukovina, the Dorohoi district, and other parts of the country in 1941–42. In a special circular he sent to bank staff, Alexandrini emphasized that the operations "had been carried out by the Finance Ministry, on behalf of the Romanian government, through a power of attorney granted you at the time."[26] The looting of Jewish valuables was never raised, not even at the 1946 Paris Peace Conference, and the Romanian government's special memorandum on the situation of the Jews in Romania in 1940–44, distributed to the conference participants, never even alluded to this shameful chapter of Romanian history.[27]

24

Transnistria under Romanian Occupation

Transnistria was the name given to the part of the Ukraine that Hitler awarded Antonescu as a prize for Romania's participation in the war against the Soviet Union.[1] The territory stretched over forty thousand square kilometers and was bordered by the Dniester in the west, the Bug in the northeast, the Black Sea in the south, and the Liadova River in the west (from the Dniester north to Zhmerinca and then east to the Bug).[2] The 1939 Soviet population census reported 3 million people in the area, most of whom were Ukrainians and Russians, and a few Jews (about 331,000), Romanians (300,000), and Germans (125,000).[3]

In 1924 the Soviet Union set up an artificial political entity on this territory, known as the Autonomous Republic of Moldavia, as part of the Ukrainian Soviet Republic, with Balta as its capital, in order to remind the Romanians of its claim to Bessarabia. Transnistria (meaning "across the Dniester") was a special, ad hoc term coined during the period of Romanian-German occupation of the area. For many Romanians the name was reminiscent of northern Transylvania (meaning "beyond the forests"), which had been annexed to Hungary.

The Romanian government favored annexing Transnistria to Romania. However, the opposition, headed by Iuliu Maniu, strongly opposed the expansion of Romania beyond its ethnic borders. In particular, it feared that the annexation of this area could be interpreted as a renunciation of northern Transylvania. Consequently, Transnistria remained an occupation zone held by the Romanians.

From a geographical standpoint Transnistria was part of the fertile Podolian plateau, most (70 percent) of which was rich arable land used to grow wheat, corn, vines, fruit trees, and tobacco. Odessa, southern Transnistria's largest city, was its natural capital. In 1939 it had six hundred thousand inhabitants, most of them Russians; the rural areas were populated mainly by Ukrainians. Transnistria had many towns with populations ranging from four thousand to thirty thousand, such as Mogilev-Podolski (known also as Mogilev), Ovidiopol, Zhmerinca, Balta, and Ananyev. Some of them, such as Tiraspol, Rybnitsa, and Dubossary, had a sizeable Romanian (Moldovan) minority. These towns were, at the time of the occupation, undergoing the initial stages of Soviet industrialization and had simple factories and many workshops.

About 30 percent of Odessa's population was Jewish—200,961 people, according to the 1939 census.[4] In the early months of the war this number rose by tens of thousands due to the influx of refugees from the surrounding area and from southern Bessarabia. The remaining Transnistrian Jews lived mainly in towns, particularly in the north and the central area. Some of these towns—Krasnoye, Olgopol, Krivoye Ozero, Bershad, Shargorod, Kopygorod, and Ochacov—had a Jewish majority. When German and Romanian troops entered Transnistria, there were an estimated 331,000 Jews there, and data on the number of Jews who were murdered or who survived corroborate this figure (provisionally, at least; see chap. 38).

Most of the local Jews did not flee in the short period following the invasion when it was still possible to do so—the month to month and a half that it took for the troops to reach their areas. There were many reasons for this. Soviet propaganda had concealed that war with Germany was imminent. Even when the invasion began, the Soviets did not divulge the defeats sustained by their army. The Jews in the area were unaware of the existential danger posed by German or Romanian occupation. Right from the start, the pincer-like advance of the German army from the Lvov area to the Black Sea precluded any chance of a mass escape by the Jews (or indeed, non-Jews) in the area. The general chaos that prevailed hindered the orderly evacuation of hundreds of thousands of Jews by train, which was in any case not given priority by the Soviet authorities. For all of these reasons, the Jews as a whole were unable to escape. There were a few exceptions. An unspecified number of Jewish youth were drafted into the Soviet army, and a number of Jews were evacuated along with the factories, hospitals, and Communist Party institutions. Not all, however, reached their destinations safely.

Generally speaking, events in Transnistria were a replay of events in Bessarabia and Bukovina. The main differences were that more youth and men in general were conscripted into the Red Army and thousands of Jews managed to escape from Odessa, mainly by sea, before and during the four-month siege, including several hundred Bessarabian Jews who had escaped to Odessa in the false belief that the city was safe.

The Romanian administration was set up on 19 August 1941. All its decrees and resolutions were based on Ordinance no. 1 for the Administration of Transnistria, issued by Antonescu on 19 August, and Ordinance no. 4 for the Administration of Odessa, issued by Supreme Army Headquarters on 17 October 1941.[5] Officially, the establishment of the administration was declared only after the conquest of Odessa on 16 October 1941. In January 1942, after leaving Tiraspol, the province's interim capital, the administration requisitioned the Vorontzov princes' palace near the Black Sea, set amidst the magnificent municipality and opera buildings and other palaces belonging to aristocrats of the Czarist era. The administration was headed by Gheorghe Alexianu, together with a secretary general and nineteen ministers (see chart 3).

Transnistria was divided into thirteen districts, on the lines of the Romanian system. Each district was governed by a prefect—an army officer or gendarme of colonel rank. The gendarmerie and police were responsible for law and order. The sixty-four Soviet subdistricts (*raion*) were preserved (later, a sixty-fifth was added). Each district had two deputy prefects (pretors), usually Russian-speaking Romanians, one of whom was a native Transnistrian and the other a native Romanian. The subdistricts were governed by pretors—Romanian officers, jurists, or civil servants from the Regat.

The pretor (head of the subdistrict) played an important part in the Romanian administration of Transnistria. He enjoyed even greater powers than the prefect—in particular, control of the police and gendarmerie in the subdistrict. A special circular issued by the Gendarmerie Inspectorate to the Romanian authorities in Transnistria clarified that in areas under military jurisdiction the pretor had the authority of a police officer while on the home front, and he was the highest police authority in the absence of regular police.[6]

Pseudohistorical studies published in this period date the Romanian presence there to ancient times and claim that the region had ties with the principality of Moldova in the Middle Ages. These studies inflate the Romanian minority, which numbered about three hundred thousand, beyond all proportion, both quantitatively and qualitatively. The Antonescu regime, which planned to annex the territory and assimilate the Ukrainians, encouraged the study of the Romanian language and Romanian history in this part of the Ukraine and took every opportunity to stress the Christian ties between the two peoples. In a speech delivered on 29 November 1941 before the pretors, Alexianu emphasized Romania's long-range goals in Transnistria:

CHART 3. STRUCTURE OF THE TRANSNISTRIAN ADMINISTRATION

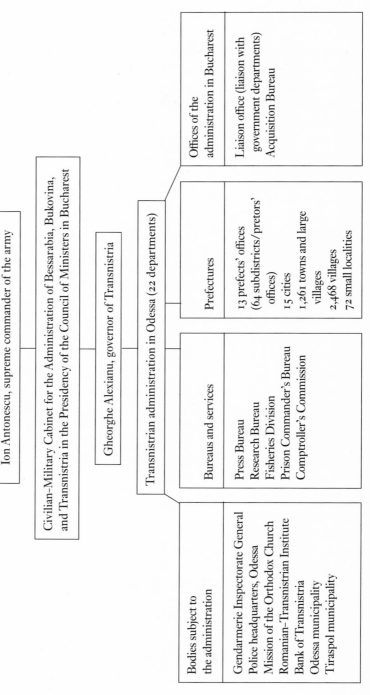

Ion Antonescu, supreme commander of the army

Civilian–Military Cabinet for the Administration of Bessarabia, Bukovina, and Transnistria in the Presidency of the Council of Ministers in Bucharest

Gheorghe Alexianu, governor of Transnistria

Transnistrian administration in Odessa (22 departments)

Bodies subject to the administration

Gendarmerie Inspectorate General
Police headquarters, Odessa
Mission of the Orthodox Church
Romanian–Transnistrian Institute
Bank of Transnistria
Odessa municipality
Tiraspol municipality

Bureaus and services

Press Bureau
Research Bureau
Fisheries Division
Prison Commander's Bureau
Comptroller's Commission

Prefectures

13 prefects' offices
(64 subdistricts/pretors' offices)
15 cities
1,261 towns and large villages
2,468 villages
72 small localities

Offices of the administration in Bucharest

Liaison office (liaison with government departments)
Acquisition Bureau

SOURCE: Ordinance no. 8 on the Administrative Division of Transnistria, 12 September 1941, Odessa Archives, 2359-1-1, pp. 7–8; Guvernământul Transnistriei, Transnistria, 26, 35.

[Whoever thinks] that our presence here is temporary or for exploitative purposes only, is wrong. Our presence here is justified by casualties and blood. . . . It is justified by the presence of a million and a half Romanians in the province, and many others across the Bug. We are here with a purpose—to rehabilitate and rebuild the province. We are here as a creative element, disseminating culture and bringing about an economic and intellectual rehabilitation. We are attempting to build a new country on the ruins of the old one left by the Bolsheviks.[7]

Although proclamations made by rulers in occupied territories are of questionable sincerity, this declaration of intent was made before the pretors, not before the representatives of the Ukrainian people. If we compare it to declarations by contemporary German leaders and German members of the administration in the Ukraine—Hitler, Himmler, Goering, Rosenberg, Koch, and others—it is clear that Romania's attitude toward Transnistria differed from Germany's attitude toward the Ukraine. From the start, dreams of annexation, where they existed, encountered strong resistance on the part of Iuliu Maniu and broad circles of the opposition. The latter did not believe in Nazi Germany's victory and in particular feared that Germany would consider the fate of northern Transylvania not open to negotiation. Mihai Antonescu rejected insinuations in Budapest to the effect that the Romanian expansion beyond the Dniester would compensate for Romania's claim in the west (Transylvania), thereby bringing an end to the dispute between Romania and Hungary. As he told the U.S. ambassador: rights in the east cannot compensate for loss of land in the west.[8] Transnistria therefore remained a quasi-occupied zone with an indeterminate future, which could not be considered part of Romania proper and whose inhabitants could not be enslaved to the Romanian state if the Romanians wished to befriend them and earn their trust.

On the other hand, the Ukrainian and Russian population did not relate seriously to Romanian dreams of annexation and felt less fear toward the Romanian occupier than toward the German occupier, as the historian Alexander Dallin so deftly put it: "It was generally felt that the Romanian occupation, unlike the German . . . was a transitory phenomenon that could not possibly be permanent—it was an aberration of history and one had to accept it as one accepted and adjusted to droughts, wars, and pestilence."[9]

During the first months of the invasion the Third and Fourth Romanian Armies operated in Transnistria. When Antonescu thought that Romania's part in the war had ended most of the armed forces were withdrawn, with the exception of the Third Army's liaison headquarters.[10] On 29 September its powers were transferred to the Fourth Army's liaison headquarters, whose units overlooked the whole of Transnistria, while Third Army units returned to Romania for a while.[11]

At the start of the occupation the Romanian army headquarters issued "directives regarding behavior toward the civilian population in the occupied territory east of the Dniester." These directives stated that the army had to protect not only the local Germans but also the local Romanians, most of whom were concentrated in the triangle formed by Yampol, Balta, Ananyev, and Tiraspol. The Romanian army warned the Ukrainians not to harm members of these two minority groups or their property, under penalty of death. The army commanders were ordered "to help the administrative bodies perform their tasks as well as possible, especially when it came to suppressing agitation by the local population."[12] These directives were relayed to the Gendarmerie Inspectorate in Transnistria, border guard units, the Ministry of the Interior, and Alexianu, the governor of Transnistria.

The directives determined "that the commanders of the Liaison Headquarter are the military aides of the Transnistrian Administration" and were to be given "complete freedom and initiative" in the context of army headquarters' directives. The commanders were expected to help the administration implement its ordinances and decrees.[13] The administration relayed its ordinances and decrees to Fourth Army headquarters, which was responsible for passing them on to the commanders in the customary manner.[14] The Fourth Army, at its own initiative, informed Alexianu that it had been ordered "to help supervise the implementation of all orders, both those issued by army headquarters, and those issued by the Transnistrian administration." Army headquarters asked for three hundred copies of each order issued by the administration.[15]

The Romanian army outdid the gendarmerie and police in its persecution of Transnistrian Jews. Divisional commanders and officers stationed in Transnistria initiated anti-Jewish measures, ensured their implementation by the civilian authorities, reported slack implementation of orders, and sought ways of punishing those who were lax in persecuting Jews. They warned against any relaxation of control, and whenever they noticed a hiatus in the enforcement of the terror policy against Jews or saw Jews outside the ghetto they urged the administration and army headquarters to tighten their measures against Jews and to discipline those responsible for the oversights.

From August to October 1941 the Romanian army cooperated with the German army and with members of the Einsatzgruppen in the murder of Ukrainian Jews and the arming of local Ukrainian militias. The Romanian divisions that were garrisoned in Transnistria, including units of Bessarabian Romanians who were recruited later (after the liberation of Bessarabia), helped the administration implement orders for the incarceration, deportation (over the Bug), and ghettoization of Jews in general and local Jews in particular. The prefects used the soldiers to preserve law and order as well as to carry out anti-Jewish measures.

The prefects and the administration in general had no need to convince the army commanders of the justice of their anti-Jewish campaign. Certainly members of the officer rank suffered no pangs of conscience. On the contrary, the army commanders made sure that the anti-Jewish policy was implemented to the letter; correspondence between the military and civil authorities in the Balta district on the subject of the Jews, most of which has been preserved, corroborates this conclusion.

The abundant documentation in the archives of the former Soviet Union and in Romania itself shows that neither the German defeat at Stalingrad nor their defeat at Kursk-orel in the summer of 1943 brought any respite in the spate of anti-Jewish directives, decrees, and ordinances issued by the army. On the contrary, the army even issued a series of new anti-Jewish decrees. For example, on 12 June 1942 the Third Army instructed all units in Transnistria to prevent the Jews from leaving the ghettos and the detention camps. "The ghetto heads had to sign [a document stating] that they would be executed if the Jews . . . failed to obey instructions," and the army was permitted to execute one Jew from each ghetto from among those who made a habit of leaving the ghetto.[16] On 12 September 1943 the Third Corps ordered the Gendarmerie Inspectorate to ensure that all Jews were issued with identity papers "to facilitate the identification of Jews who fled from one ghetto to another, or who moved around for various reasons."[17]

In February 1943 the Third Army Corps further warned of "the danger arising from the relaxation of the ghetto regime, and from Jews employed outside the ghetto."[18] It effectively advised against the hiring of Jews outside the ghetto as employees of the administration, in accordance with the governor's ordinance of December 1942, or as forced laborers. The military commanders found the employment of Jews outside the ghettos unsettling. They therefore hastened to report the change in policy, warning of the danger of employing Jews outside the ghetto, and seeking further instructions. The correspondence on this issue—insignificant from a military perspective—was colored by the basic view in Romanian military headquarters that the Jews constituted an immediate danger to the Romanian home front and therefore had to be constantly kept under the strict supervision of the ghetto and camp commanders. On 11 April 1943 the Romanian army headquarters' Second Section issued a decree concerning the handling of "dangerous" Jews.[19] As a result, Lt. Col. Dimitriu Comănescu, head of the Fourth Army liaison headquarters, addressed a query to the commander of the Berezovka gendarmerie legion regarding the status of Jewish gardeners, tailors, or other professionals who worked outside the ghetto—a phenomenon, he stressed, that contradicted orders he had received.[20]

The commander of this corps opposed the employment of Jews outside the ghettos. On 27 August 1943 the Third Army Corps issued a circular to all administrative departments to "closely" supervise all Jews who were working for various branches of the administration outside the ghetto and to incarcerate dangerous elements in camps. "Any Jew found living outside the ghetto shall be tried by a military tribunal," the circular stated.[21] This case is illustrative of how the army took the law into its own hands and even overrode the decisions of the Transnistrian administration, which authorized the employment of Jewish craftsmen outside the ghettos.

The Antonescu regime's policy of isolating the deportees from the rest of Romanian Jewry and the ban on correspondence between the deportees and the Jews of the Regat resulted in a total—albeit temporary—disruption in communications among them. In December 1942 the Jewish Center complained that it had not received any communication from the deportees for over two months and was therefore unable to send them help. Such communications, emphasized the center's head, serve "as a valuable tool in organizing aid operations for the deported Jews."[22]

Nevertheless, army headquarters continued issuing alerts that "Jews were divulging secret information in letters" that passed the censors because they were written in "ordinary language" (i.e., in a way that did not arouse suspicion). In June 1943 army headquarters, the Transnistrian administration, and the Romanian Postal Service together issued new directives concerning the mailing of letters, parcels, and aid. These directives stated that all personal letters written by Jews that had not been first submitted to the gendarmerie commands, the civilian censor, the military censor, and so on would be destroyed.[23]

Army headquarters' most important anti-Jewish initiative took place in the summer of 1942, with its proposal to expel from the Regat some 12,588 Jewish youth who had failed to report for forced labor, had absconded, or had disobeyed orders. Army headquarters even called a special meeting to discuss the confiscation of their property and which belongings they should be allowed to take with them. Army headquarters planned to send these youth and their families—around 40,000 Jews—to the death camps along the River Bug and were prevented from doing so only by the suspension of the plan to deport all Romanian Jews.[24]

These were only some of the initiatives adopted by the Romanian army in Transnistria after the mass killing operations in the winter of 1941–42. These measures were, above all, rooted in the army's antisemitic tradition, in the hostility of the command toward Jews as soldiers, and in the absolute control enjoyed by Antonescu, who, throughout the war, acted as a kind of supreme chief of the General Staff. At his trial Antonescu argued that he personally had had no part in the preparation of the extermination plan and blamed army headquarters: "I myself have never decided the liquidation of any person. In my house, we never even slaughtered a chicken. It was not I, but the Army Headquarters, that adopted these measures."[25]

THE ROMANIAN GENDARMERIE AND POLICE AND THE UKRAINIAN POLICE

The gendarmerie units, which had been organized while still on Romanian soil and which were responsible for implementing the secret order to "cleanse the ground" in Bessarabia and Bukovina, were attached to the Romanian military units that were deployed throughout Transnistria immediately after its occupation. They were entrusted not only with maintaining law and order but also with exclusive responsibility for security matters. The police were authorized to fight Communists, prevent terrorism and espionage, stop the spread of propaganda and tendentious rumors, thwart actions that ran counter to Romania's interests, and conduct "surveillance of the Jews who were being moved from densely populated areas to sparsely populated ones."[26]

The Ukrainian police played an instrumental role in the mass murder of Jews perpetrated by the Transnistrian administration in the winter of 1941–42 in the extermination camps along the Bug.[27] The composition of the Ukrainian police was not exclusively Ukrainian. Local Romanians (Moldavians) in areas populated by them and Russians (in Odessa, where they formed the majority of the population) were also enrolled in the so-called Ukrainian police. There was also a Romanian police in Odessa, Tiraspol, Balta, and other cities with police officers sent from Romania. The Ukrainian police officers were not "members of the Gendarmerie's Security Service." The security service, or Siguranța, was formed only from Romanians. They wore no special uniforms, the only distinguishing mark being an armband striped red, yellow, and blue (the colors of the Romanian flag) or other colors and bearing the word *poliția* (police). The Ukrainian police acted as guards in the ghettos, death camps, and labor camps of Transnistria and were sometimes deployed within the ghettos themselves during surprise raids and arrests by the Romanian authorities. A local constabulary (Gărzi comunale), which was subordinate to the gendarmerie, also operated in the villages. Sporting a white armband inscribed with the word *police*, the constabulary was responsible for keeping law and order and guarding property.[28]

The gendarmes had sole responsibility for security and in Transnistria served as an arm of the Siguranța—the dreaded institutions that instilled terror into the hearts of Romanians even before the war. The Transnistrian Gendarmerie Inspectorate set up its own security service (Serviciul de Siguranță) in which each gendarmerie legion had its own security bureau (*birou de siguranță*). These bureaus were responsible for gathering information on public morale and on events that took place at the district level and reporting this information to the authorities. They were also responsible for supervising the implementation and application of all decrees issued by the Transnistrian administration and military headquarters.[29]

The gendarmerie's security service recruited mainly local Romanians (*moldoveni*) but also Russians and Ukrainians, who were paid in money or kind. In early December 1941 Mihai Petală, inspector general of the Transnistrian gendarmerie, reported that the security service had been successfully organized. The Gendarmerie Inspectorate General in Transnistria, under Col. Emil Broșteanu, served as the umbrella organization for the gendarmerie and police. When the administration moved from Tiraspol to Odessa, the Inspectorate General moved with it. The gendarmerie in Transnistria was divided into six battalions, of which three were stationed in Odessa. Four of the battalions were subdivided into district legions. Each battalion had three legions, except for the Odessa battalion, which had four district legions and one mobile squad. The legions were divided into platoons (*pluton*), which operated mostly in the villages and whose members were known as agricultural gendarmes (*jandarmi agricoli*). The platoons were further subdivided into groups (*grupă*). This hierarchy resembled the hierarchy that had been introduced into Bessarabia and Bukovina, with the exception of the battalion, the umbrella organization that oversaw several legions. In addition, a battalion of about 150 professional policemen was specially imported into Odessa from Romania. Apart from these, about 800 gendarmes, based in nine city subdistricts, were deployed throughout the Odessa subdistricts.

At the outbreak of war against the Soviet Union the Antonescu regime adopted Nazi racist ideology and declared that the impending confrontation would be a confrontation between the races in general and with the Slavic race — "a race with an amorphous culture and primitive cultural concepts" — in particular. "We must fight [this race] resolutely," said Antonescu in a special memorandum he sent Hitler on 11 June 1941, prior to their meeting in which Antonescu portrayed the Romanians as a buffer against Slavic expansionism over the generations.[30] At the meeting itself Antonescu pointed out the need to eliminate "once [and] for all" the Slavic danger that had threatened Romania and Europe for centuries. "Because of its racial qualities," added Antonescu, "Romania can continue to play a role as an anti-Slavic buffer for the benefit of Germany." At the meeting Hitler, on his own initiative, promised Romania "unlimited" territorial compensation in the east.[31]

Transnistria was thus the product of Antonescu's ideological identification with Hitler's Slavophobia and antisemitism. It was the result of Antonescu's willingness to join the Reich's all-out war against the Slavic race and Hitler's personal conviction that Antonescu had set his mind on solving the Jewish problem. Mihai Antonescu expressed this clearly to Hitler when he argued that the Slavic problem was a biological, not an ideological, one. "The Romanian person," he added, "is, and always has been, anti-Slavic, just as it has always been viscerally antisemitic."[32] In order to further emphasize the ideological resemblance between the Romanians and Germans, Mihai Antonescu informed Goebbels that the Romanians, unlike the Hungarians, were "antisemites by birth and conviction" (*antisemiți din naștere și din convingere*).[33] The uncomfortable fact that the Romanians did not belong to the Nordic race was solved by Mihai Antonescu in his description to Hitler of "his vision" for recruiting the Latin nations "in the racial sense" to the German struggle against the Slavs. "Any formula for the separation, neutralization and occupation of Slavic territories is legal," he added.[34]

Mihai Antonescu's description of military goals in the east met with Hitler's approval, as the following excerpt on his views on the future of the Slavic people in the east indicates:

You are right. . . . Tomorrow's Europe shall abide two races only — the Latin [nations] and the Germans. . . . Russia cannot be dealt with through legal or political formulations, since the Russian problem is far worse than is generally thought. We must adopt principles of colonization and of the biological removal of the Slavs. . . . My objective, if it succeeds, is to destroy the Slavs. I launched my struggle against the Jews and their international [organizations], but because the Anglo-Saxon world failed to understand or help me, I was obliged to fight them, too.[35]

The Antonescu regime, whether spontaneously or for reasons of national expediency, paid a huge ideological price for Transnistria and hastened to prove itself worthy of the task of ruling over a portion of Slavic land.[36]

Nevertheless, Romania's policy and interests in the Ukraine were not identical to those of Nazi Germany. On the contrary, over time the gap between them widened, both ideologically and practically.[37] Unlike Germany, which for a while encouraged Ukrainian nationalism, Romania shared no common interests with the Ukrainian people and considered both the Ukrainians and the Russians a threat to its territorial integrity. Because Romania saw the Ukrainians as supporters of Russian nationalism, it made no attempt to incite them against the Russians. Romania was opposed to the activities of Ukrainian nationalistic organizations in its territory and in Transnistria. Although the Romanians, like the Nazis in the Ukraine, considered Transnistria to be a convenient source of food and possibly raw materials, for historical and religious reasons that we cannot go into here, they did not treat the Ukrainians like the Germans did. The Romanian authorities in Transnistria did not consider the Ukrainians or Russians *Untermenschen*, that is, they considered them an inferior race incapable of attaining the developmental level of the Romanians and unworthy of having its own state. For centuries the Slavs in the east had inspired fear — not contempt — in the Romanians' hearts. The early victories of the German and Romanian armies on the eastern front did nothing to dispel this fear.[38] Finally, Romania did not see Transnistria merely as a source of labor that could be brought over to Romania by trickery or force and exploited under conditions of slavery.

25

The Arrest and Deportation
of Jews in Transnistria

IDENTIFYING THE LOCAL JEWS

The first stage of the murder of Transnistrian Jewry was carried out by Einsatzgruppe D, which arrived with the soldiers of the German Eleventh Army and the Romanian Third and Fourth Armies. Both German and Romanian soldiers participated in the murders. This chapter in the Holocaust of Ukrainian Jewry shall not be discussed here. We do not know how many Jews were murdered by the Einsatzgruppe, although according to Otto Ohlendorf, the Einsatzgruppe commander, tens of thousands and possibly over one hundred thousand Jews were murdered.[1] The murderers of Einsatzgruppe D did not manage to kill all the Jews of Transnistria because of the huge tracts of land in which they operated and because of the need to stay close to the storm troopers. Their failure to complete their mission may also have been due to the fact that they left Transnistria after the signing of the Tighina Agreement, which transferred responsibility for the Jews to the Romanians. Ohlendorf had to leave his headquarters in Ananyev in early September 1941 without completing his campaign to exterminate the Jews of Transnistria and Podolia. Apparently the Romanians even prevented him from helping them deal with the Jews of Odessa after it was captured on 16 October 1941 (see chap. 27). The commanders of Einsatzgruppe D were critical of the way the Romanian soldiers handled the murder of the Jews, especially the acts of looting and rape in which they indulged and their failure to bury the corpses. In his report of 14 August 1941 Ohlendorf wrote that the solution to the Jewish problem between the Dniester and the Dnieper had been placed in "incompetent hands."[2] When the first deportees from Romania arrived in Transnistria the local Jews showed them the mass graves where tens of thousands of Jews had been buried. Jews from forced labor detachments who were brought over from Romania in 1942 also uncovered mass graves.

With the lull in the first wave of massacres perpetrated by the Einsatzgruppe units and after their retreat across the Bug, the remaining local Jews who had hidden among the Ukrainians or in the forests returned to their homes, which had been looted and destroyed. According to estimates based on the reports of the gendarmerie and the Romanian authorities and on personal testimonies, approximately thirty-five thousand Jews remained in the northern and central districts of Transnistria—Mogilev, Tulchin, Yampol, Balta, and Rybnitsa. At that time there were still over seventy thousand Jews living in other districts in southern Transnistria and approximately another one hundred thousand Jews in Odessa.[3]

The governor of Transnistria issued a directive requiring residents to report and register with their municipality, which would issue them identity cards. This order, however, did not apply to Jews, who had ceased to be free human beings.[4] The gendarmerie commanders, armed with Directive no. 1 of 8 September 1941, sent out their men to comb the villages of Transnistria. This directive ordered them "to ascertain the number of Yids in each locality, to set up ghettos, [and] to place Yids who are caught in the ghettos . . . under strict surveillance to ensure that they do not escape across the Dniester (westward). Suspects or those liable to carry out acts of terrorism are to be sent, following interrogation . . . to the nearest detention center."[5]

The incarceration of the local Jews in the northern and central districts of Transnistria was completed in October with the deployment of the Romanian authorities up to the banks of the Bug. The gendarmes established a network of informers in the villages and gathered whatever information they could about the whereabouts of Jews, half-Jews, and Jewish children, even those who had been baptized at birth. Most of them were arrested and sent to camps.[6] In mid-October 1941 the inspector general of the gendarmerie in Transnistria, Colonel Broșteanu, reported to the governor that the roundup of the local Jews had been completed and that "the Jews have been concentrated in ghettos and camps and are extremely upset by the measures that are being adopted against them."[7]

Not only military personnel and the gendarmerie and police in Odessa participated in the protracted effort to locate Ukrainian Jews. The pretors did, too. As stated, the pretors had the authority of police officers once they settled in their subdistricts and became familiar with the terrain. The pretor of the subdistrict of Chichelnik (Balta district), for example, noted in his activity report of November 1941 that he had moved to the subdistrict on 8 October 1941, as ordered, and stressed that he had restored peace and order and put an end to the acts of pillage and theft perpetrated primarily by the Ukrainian police: "The Jews were scattered around the city and none of them were working. I rounded them up, assigned them to a ghetto, and gave them work based on their skills. It was these Jews who were threatening our security, because once I rounded them up in the ghetto, peace was restored and I was able to concentrate on rehabilitation activities. I restored the buildings in the subdistrict with the [forced] labor of the Jews."[8]

In Odessa the police were ordered to locate Jews who had hidden before or after the onset of the deportations.[9] Until April 1942, when the Presidency of the Council of Ministers ordered a census of Jews based on certain categories, the number of Jews who had survived the liquidation campaigns of Einsatzgruppe D, and the number of Romanian Jews in general, was unknown. For example, Isopescu, prefect of the Golta district, replied to the Presidency of the Council of Ministers, in his own handwriting, that there were no more local Jews in his district.[10] On 9 September 1942 the Gendarmerie Inspectorate of Transnistria informed the Transnistrian administration that there were sixty-five thousand local Jews in the Odessa district and four thousand in the Mogilev district and that all the Jews of the Berezovka, Ananyev, Ovidopol, and Ochakov districts had "disappeared" (*dispăruți*) — that is, had been exterminated.[11]

THE CONVOYS

From late July 1941 to the spring of 1943 approximately three hundred thousand Romanian Jewish citizens and local Jews were moved from place to place in convoys that wandered throughout Transnistria. This was part of an overall plan consolidated by the Romanian General Staff and the result of verbal instructions by Ion Antonescu to Alexianu at their meeting in Tighina in late August 1941, prior to the signing of the Tighina Agreement between the Romanian and German armies. Antonescu presented this policy on 11 October 1941 to the district prefects in Romania at a session attended also by the interior minister, Gen. Dumitru Popescu, and the deputy interior minister, Gen. Ion Popescu:

Gentlemen, you are aware that one of the campaigns I have taken on is to change this people. I will turn the Romanian nation into a homogeneous body. Anything alien to it shall have to go. I have begun to implement this wish by removing the Jews. If the Jews still continue to move around freely, and go about their business, this is due to the weakness and duplicity of our Administration. . . . I have begun with Bessarabia. No trace of the Jews shall remain in Bessarabia. Bukovina shall also be purged of eighty percent of the Jews who live there. The entire suspect Jewish element, all Jewish Communists, shall be sent back to where they came from. *I shall drive them to the Bug, and they will carry on from there.*[12]

The ultimate objective was to transfer all Jews in Romania and Transnistria who were still alive after the first wave of massacres to improvised—as yet non-existent—camps in the vicinity of the River Bug, until the time was ripe for dispatching them across the Bug, in order to cleanse Transnistria, too, of Jews. To this end the General Staff established five crossing points over the Dniester and four transit points along the Bug.

The roads were practically impassable, and the gendarmes ruthlessly shot to death anyone who lagged behind, leaving trails of corpses all the way to the Bug, which they did not bother to bury, thereby angering the Germans. The gendarmes led the convoys of thousands of starving and exhausted Jews on a wild goose chase, searching for bridges that had disappeared in floods or crossing points over frozen rivers. Many of the Jews reached the breaking point and collapsed in the knowledge that they would be shot. Children were orphaned en route and adopted by other families, or they insisted on staying with their dying parents and were shot to death along with them. Gangs of Ukrainians operated throughout Transnistria, particularly in the Mogilev district, falling upon the convoys of Jews to rob and kill them and often leaving hundreds of naked Jews in their wake, who subsequently froze to death. Many Jews, especially the elderly, were too weak to lift their feet out of the deep mud and remained where they were until they were shot by the gendarmes who brought up the rear of the convoy. Each convoy was robbed first by the gendarmes—who usually were furious at the meager spoils—and then by the Ukrainian escorts and citizens. In each convoy young women were raped by ordinary gendarmes and especially by gendarmerie officers, who ordered nightly stopovers in places suitable for conducting orgies. The convoy commanders were not required to be responsible for the lives of the Jews. Their job was simply to transfer them from place to place, without names or identities. The gendarmes, who were as yet unfamiliar with the terrain, were assisted by local policemen, whom they partially entrusted with the task of guarding and accompanying the convoys. Many of these Ukrainians had already been armed by members of Einsatzgruppe D during July and August, when they had helped them murder tens of thousands of Jews.

About fifteen days after the start of the deportation, the inspector general of the gendarmerie in Transnistria, Colonel Broșteanu, informed the Transnistrian administration that the deportation plan had collapsed due to disorganization and the lack of guards, accommodation, and food for the deportees. Moreover, he stated, Romanian and German army units were also involved in the operation, as well as the gendarmes, and "constantly brought over new groups of Jews for whom there was no room." The gendarmerie companies were forced to set up provisional ghettos pending further instructions. "We received no instructions concerning the feeding and upkeep of these Jews, and the prefectures we turned to could not give us any constructive answer." The gendarmerie commander asked the governor for instructions as to how to feed and maintain "these Jews."[13] The prefectures used to cable the administration in Tiraspol regarding the progress of the convoys toward the River Bug. On 2 October 1941 the prefect of Rybnitsa, Colonel Popescu, reported to the administration that "the convoys of Jews continue as per schedule. To date, I have dispatched 3,764 [Jews]."[14]

The transfer of the convoys of Jews to the Bug continued, in total disarray, during October and November. No attempt was made to keep to the original plan of directing the convoys to specific localities along the Bug. Thousands of Jews were left in towns and villages that had never been intended to serve as ghettos or labor camps. The final destinations remained unchanged, however, and from time to time a convoy that had been abandoned in a certain locality was collected and taken to the Bug. The deportation routine was shattered in early October when the gendarmerie escorts contracted typhus from the Jews, who had contracted it already in Bessarabia. The gendarmerie reported that "dozens of case[s] of typhus" had been identified among the gendarmes, who had caught it "from the Jews in the convoys they escorted across the Dniester." Several gendarmes died from the epidemic, and immediate and strong measures were required to "protect the gendarmes' health."[15]

The convoys moved over dirt tracks or paths that had been washed away by the first rains. The first summary report of the Gendarmerie Inspectorate referred to the concentration of Jews in ghettos and camps and their panic at "the strict measures that were being adopted against them." It made no reference, however, to the murder of thousands of Jews who had been abandoned on the roadsides.[16]

Antonescu, who followed the deportation of the Jews as if it were a military campaign, pointed out at a cabinet session on 13 November 1941 that Iaşi's Jewish population had been downsized due to "congestion." He had had many problems, he added, "with those I sent to the Bug. *Only I know how many died on the way.*"[17] This statement confirms that Antonescu knew about the murder of the freezing and starving Jews in the convoys. Statistical data that he ordered provided him with an accurate picture of the scope of the extermination.

In contrast to his apathy toward the murder of the deported Jews, Antonescu showed extreme concern for the transportation of fifteen thousand cows taken as war spoils from Transnistria to Romania. He had originally ordered the transportation of twenty-five thousand cows to serve as food for the Romanian army. Following the conquest of Odessa, however, and the decline in the number of soldiers, only ten thousand cows were needed. The remaining fifteen thousand cows and an unknown number of pigs and sheep were transported via transit points that were utilized also for the deportation of Jews—but in the opposite direction: Tiraspol, Rybnitsa, Yampol, Mogilev, and Dubossary.[18] Antonescu followed this campaign personally and himself gave written instructions to the secretary general of the Presidency of the Council of Ministers, Ovidiu Vlădescu, to oversee the operation and "in particular, not to endanger the cows due to cold or negligence."[19] Cows and horses were transferred from Romania to Transnistria for the army's use on the very same rafts that were used to transfer Jews across the Dniester. Many survivors testified that they were jammed together with the livestock on the rafts, and while not a single cow was harmed during the crossing, many Jews were thrown alive into the waters of the Dniester. When a typhoid epidemic broke out among the livestock being transferred to Romania as spoils of war (including pigs and sheep), Governor Alexianu ordered a halt to their shipment until they received the appropriate treatment.[20]

ORDINANCE NO. 23

In early November, after the massacre in Odessa, the Transnistrian administration itself concluded that it was impossible to keep bringing Jews to the Bug because the Germans were refusing to accept them. Alexianu therefore ordered the gendarmerie commander to draft an ordinance on the status of the Jews, their duties, and the living conditions in the ghettos. Alexianu drew the Conducător's attention to the fact that the deportations from the motherland and the uprooting of Transnistrian Jews from their places of residence had resulted in huge concentrations of Jews in Transnistria: "Until a *final solution* is found for these colonies of Jews, we must provide them with some kind of provisional structure, work opportunities and subsistence, otherwise we will be forced to support them at the expense of the kolkhozes and sovkhozes [state farms], which will result in a huge expenditure for us."[21]

The introduction to the draft ordinance that Alexianu submitted to Antonescu emphasized that the decision to deport the Jews was a Romanian initiative, the purpose of which was to cleanse the towns and villages of Moldova, Bessarabia, and Bukovina of the presence of Jews. In this instance, too, the final objective was to bring all convoys to the vicinity of the Bug. The administration absolved itself of all responsibility for the fate of the Jews. It merely emphasized the various prohibitions that applied to Jews and their duty to serve the authorities in every respect, thereby turning them into slaves of the Romanian state. Procedures for registration, roll call, reporting for work, and reporting outbreaks of epidemics or infectious diseases were set out in detail. The gendarmes were ordered to "keep the Jewish colonies [*colonii*] under constant surveillance," while the prefects were responsible for the strict application of the directives. Any Jew leaving the ghetto "would be considered a spy" and executed. For all other offenses, Jews would be court-martialed.[22]

The draft ordinance was sent to Antonescu for approval and was returned as Ordinance no. 23, which determined the living conditions of the Jews in Transnistria until their subsequent deportation or liquidation. The ordinance remained in effect until the liberation of Transnistria by the Soviet army. It did not distinguish between local Jews and deportees. It authorized the gendarmerie "to settle" the Jews in abandoned homes and private houses in selected locations, forbade the Jews to leave these locations, ordered all Jews to be listed in a special register of Jews, and defined the ghettos as "colonies." The ordinance authorized the pretors to select a Jewish "head of colony" and other officials who would be responsible for carrying out the instructions and orders of the Romanian authorities. The fact that the Jewish "head of colony" and other "officials" had to report to the authorities turned them into informers.[23]

Unskilled Jewish laborers were required to "work for the public good" (a euphemism for forced agricultural labor) or repair bridges and roads, cut down trees in the forests, and carry stones, as well as restore Transnistria's ruined industry by renovating and running factories. Professionals and craftsmen were made to work for the municipalities or any of the Romanian authorities in exchange for a meager daily wage—a "food coupon" worth one RKKS for unskilled laborers, and two RKKS for skilled laborers. The prefect was authorized to transfer Jews from place to place within the district as requested by the authorities, while the administration was authorized to transfer Jews between districts based on the demand for labor. The administration was authorized to use Jews at will for the rehabilitation of Transnistria.[24]

Ordinance no. 23 subordinated the Jews to various authorities: the gendarmerie, the administration and its various institutions, the prefects, and the pretors, as well as various foremen, agronomists sent over from Romania to run the farms, and the commanders of army units from the garrison, who exploited the Jews for their own purposes. The resulting duplication and overlap of powers favored the adoption of totally arbitrary measures against Jews and went hand in hand with the notorious corruption that characterized Romanian officials, army personnel, and gendarmes.

26

"The Kingdom of Death"

THE ROMANIAN ADMINISTRATION AND THE
DEPORTATION OF JEWS TO THE GOLTA DISTRICT

On 17 October 1941, after the fall of Odessa, Gustav Richter, Eichmann's envoy in Romania, reported to his superiors in Berlin that Marshal Antonescu had ordered 110,000 Jews from Bessarabia and Bukovina to be concentrated in two forests in the Bug region in preparation for their extermination.[1] Richter knew of this plan from Radu Lecca, who was, at the time, a director of the Siguranța as well as a veteran Nazi agent. This document, as well as various directives issued by Antonescu and the Romanian administration in Transnistria over the following months, confirms that it was Antonescu who masterminded the plan to concentrate and exterminate so many Jews. Even though—in true Romanian fashion—this plan was bungled (most of the Jews who were exterminated in this area were local Jews), at the end of the day its objectives (the extermination of most Bessarabian and Bukovinian Jews) were achieved. The decision to deport the Jews of Bessarabia and Bukovina was made by Antonescu alone, without German pressure, as Mihai Antonescu testified in his interrogation in 1946. Similarly, it was the Conducător himself who, in late August 1941, instructed the governors of Bessarabia and Bukovina (Generals Voiculescu and Calotescu, respectively) to march the deportees toward the Bug River. Moreover, in early December 1941 Antonescu took the two governors to task for having failed to confiscate the deportees' gold, emphasizing that they had had ample time to prepare for the operation.

Antonescu insisted that the offensive against Odessa, which began on 18 August 1941, be carried out by his army, independent of German forces. He was sure that Odessa could be captured easily, but the Romanian army soon encountered difficulties because of the fortifications built by the Soviet army and the citizens of Odessa, the strength of the Russian artillery, and the determination and self-sacrifice of the soldiers and the city's defenders. Romanian headquarters continuously added new divisions until they totaled twenty-one. On 24 September Antonescu was forced to ask the Wehrmacht for help. Heavy bombing by the German air force, the concentration of German land forces in the area (which in the end did not intervene), and the threat that the Eleventh German Army posed to Crimea convinced the Soviet command to evacuate the city by sea.[2] On 16 October 1941 the Romanian and German armies entered Odessa, after having lost so many men that the Romanian army came to call the fields around Odessa the Vale of Tears.[3] The difficulty in conquering Odessa triggered unexpected reactions in Romania, as Romania's military attaché (later, ambassador) in Berlin testified: "The war exacted victims on an unprecedented scale. Daily, the people grew more impatient . . . and began grumbling: 'After the city's fall, the Romanian army should have returned home!' . . . or 'What is the Romanian army doing in Odessa?' In this war, Romania achieved its objective: to win back Bessarabia and Bukovina. What more do the Romanian forces want across the Dniester? . . . If the Germans enjoy it, let them continue fighting the Russians alone."[4]

Antonescu's fury was directed at all Jews, whether "Russian" or Romanian. In a letter he wrote to Filderman on 19 October 1941 Antonescu turned down Filderman's appeal to halt the deportation of Jews to the Bug on the grounds that this was tantamount to murdering innocent people simply because they were Jewish. He moreover accused the Jews of Bessarabia of having assaulted Romanian soldiers during the hasty withdrawal of Romanian troops in the summer of 1940, of assaulting Romanian civilians and soldiers in the summer of 1941, and of setting towns ablaze before fleeing with the Soviet army. He also blamed the "Russian" Jews for the heavy losses incurred by the Romanian army in the battle for Odessa:

> Your Jews, who have become Soviet commissars, are driving Soviet soldiers in the Odessa region into a futile bloodbath, through horrendous terror techniques as the Russian prisoners have themselves admitted, simply to cause us losses. In the Sea of Azov region, our forces, forced temporarily to retreat, left behind some wounded officers and soldiers. When they returned, they found these soldiers brutally butchered. . . . Their eyes were gouged out and their tongues, noses and ears severed. . . . Do you, Mr. Filderman, realize what is going on? Are you shocked, or upset? Do you wonder why the Russian Jews, with whom we have no quarrel, feel so much hatred [toward the Romanian army]. This hatred is shared by all [Jews], you [included].[5]

The Romanian administration in the Golta district was established in early October 1941. From its establishment until the evacuation in March 1944 it was headed by Modest Isopescu, a lieutenant colonel of the gendarmerie. The commander in charge of the Romanian administration's largest murder operation was an ordinary antisemitic officer who had been randomly appointed and who, unlike his Nazi counterparts, had not undergone any indoctrination. Isopescu chose Aristide Pădure, who at the time was only twenty-four, as his deputy. Pădure was a corrupt policeman, womanizer, and sworn and violent hater of Jews.

On 28 October the Romanians and Germans divided the city of Pervomaisk ("1 May") between them. The city was situated on either side of the Bug, with the River Bug running through it. Isopescu preferred the former name of the city from the Czarist era — Golta.

The gendarmes were deployed in the Domanevka subdistrict (the Kingdom of Death), where the death camps were set up, in late October and early November 1941. On 27 October the prefect ordered Sgt. Maj. Constantin Pelivan to Domanevka with a unit of forty gendarmes. That afternoon the unit reached Seneva, a village about fifteen kilometers south of Golta. On 2 November the unit was divided up. Sgt. Maj. Vasile Iorgulescu and eight gendarmes were sent to Akmechetka, near the bridge over the Bug. Another sergeant major and eight gendarmes were sent to the village of Marinovka; Cpl. Dumitru Antoniu and one gendarme were sent to the village of Nikolayevka; Sgt. Doru Voicu and one gendarme were sent to the village of Karlovka; Cpl. Constantin Leonte and one gendarme were sent to the village of Alexandrovka; and five gendarmes were sent to other villages. Of the full complement of forty gendarmes (of which two were regulars), twenty-nine were deployed in villages, ten in Domanevka as backups, and one, who was sick, was hospitalized. Their main objective was to examine the situation of the collective farms (kolkhozes) and take an inventory of agricultural products in the warehouses. Isopescu ordered flour production and the distribution of kolkhoz property to be suspended and ordered the potato crops to be buried underground to protect them from frost and the cabbages to be kept for transportation by cart to Golta. He also ordered the gendarmes to patrol all the villages of the subdistrict by cart.[6]

Since there were not enough Romanian gendarmes for the vast tracts of land involved, local Ukrainians volunteered their services. In his second report the commander of the Domanevka subdistrict complained that, in many places, he served as Romania's sole representative, acting simultaneously as pretor, judge, and agronomist. Moreover, he was besieged daily by Ukrainian villagers reclaiming property that had been seized from them some ten to twelve years before. Nor did he have any regular gendarmes to send out for patrols. "We need to issue permits . . . deal with [released] prisoners . . . draw up orders for patrols, send out patrols, command the unit and maintain discipline. Who will do all this, when we are so isolated and short [of staff]?"[7] It should be pointed out that in the early months the Golta prefecture had only one company of gendarmes, unlike all other districts, which had four to five.

To compensate for the shortfall in gendarmes the Twentieth Infantry Regiment of the Fourth Division was posted to the district. A large unit was sent to the Romanian village of Lubashevka, near the Vazdovka camp, and a company of this unit was sent to Golta, where it was responsible for maintaining law and order and providing security. Isopescu even asked that the soldiers of this company act as gendarmes in the villages and as border guards in the Bug region.[8]

The Romanian army units were responsible for the fate of the Jews from the arrival of the convoys until the gendarmes took over, and in many places even afterwards, due to the shortage of gendarmes and the lack of explicit instructions from the administration to the civilian authorities on the handling of the Jews. The district's military headquarters issued firearm permits to Ukrainian policemen in the villages, who had already been armed by the Germans. The Romanian soldiers, aided by these policemen, "cleansed" the district's villages of local Jews. On 16 October military headquarters in Krivoye Ozero reported to the prefect that local Jews "still remained in 15 out of the district's 380 villages."[9]

The army commanders in the district were worried about the unburied corpses that were piling up in the roads and fields and the danger of an outbreak of disease in the improvised camps that were set up for the Jews on the way to the Bug. The commander of the Twentieth Infantry Regiment asked the prefect to deal with these problems. On 2 November the prefect replied that so far "the prefecture had not received any instruction concerning the camps of the Yids, and that even guarding the Jews was not the prefecture's responsibility."[10]

In early November the village of Vazdovka had the largest camp, comprising about fifteen thousand Jews. Isopescu, in response to the request of the regiment (some soldiers of which were stationed in the village) and the mayor, decided to transfer the Jews from Vazdovka to Bogdanovka. He also asked the Fourth Division (which was responsible for maintaining law and order in the district) to supply soldiers to accompany the Jews to Bogdanovka. "As to the burial of corpses, the mayor has received my instructions."[11]

Nevertheless, the mayor of Vazdovka informed Isopescu that the army had not assigned anyone for the transfer operation. The prefect again begged the regiment commander for help, "so that we can get rid of them." He asked some of the soldiers to accompany the Jews to Bogdanovka "so that they do not remain in a Romanian area, near our unit, since they constitute a constant danger for the spread of contagious disease." The prefect had one more modest request: "That the Yids that die during the transfer should not be left unburied. If they [the soldiers] don't have time to bury them, they should instruct the mayors of the localities through which they pass to organize groups to bury [the Jews]."[12]

Even in Golta on the Bug, Isopescu's new capital, the prefect had problems with the Jews. He arranged for 1,500 Bessarabian and local Jews whom he had incarcerated in his previous capital, Krivoye Ozero, to be transferred to Golta. Only 800, however, reached the new camp. The rest perished or were killed during the transfer. Isopescu, who still hoped that the Germans would agree to deal with all the Jews of the district, had a convoy ready to leave. The gendarmes, however, set up a makeshift camp next door to the municipality, much to the chagrin of Michael Freulich, an ethnic German who had been appointed mayor by the German commissar across the Bug. Freulich complained to Isopescu that the Jews were "contagious and living in unsanitary conditions. People are dying each day. Their corpses are buried in a courtyard in the camp, and sometimes are not even covered with earth." This situation, emphasized Freulich, endangered the soldiers' health. Therefore, he requested the Jews be transferred and Jewish corpses be buried in deeper graves.[13] The prefect immediately instructed Second Lieutenant Bivolaru, the commander of the small gendarmerie unit that had been dispatched to Golta, to ensure that all corpses were buried in sufficiently deep graves. He further instructed him to ensure that "all sick Yids, the elderly and children be sent to Bogdanovka the very next day, 5 November, and that the remainder be sent to the large red building."[14]

These orders confirm that by early November the Bogdanovka camp had become an extermination camp, a camp where Jews who were no longer fit for work or who were dying were transferred. At the same time the Transnistrian administration was also notified of the problem of the corpses by the Germans, and on 6 November the administration sent telegrams to the prefects' offices in Berezovka and Golta urging them "to adopt urgent measures to bury all corpses remaining after the battles or for other reasons, for the sake of public health."[15]

It should be noted that atrocities—such as the assault, murder, and looting of deportees and the rape of women and girls—were not restricted to the Ukrainian policemen only. The gendarmes, too, felt that they had reached a place where everything was permissible: "They get drunk, quarrel with the citizen[s], shoot at night . . . confiscate goods, etc."[16] Many gendarmes and gendarmerie commanders could not resist the tremendous temptation of robbing the Jewish convoys pouring into the district. This triggered a critical power struggle between Isopescu, the commander of the gendarmerie battalion in the district (who had just been appointed interim prefect), and Lieutenant Georgescu, the commander of the gendarmerie company in Golta, who was obsessed by the possibility of stealing money and jewelry from Jews immediately upon their arrival. Georgescu was no novice when it came to looting. He had originally confiscated corn from the kolkhozes and later pocketed the toll fee collected from Ukrainians crossing over the Bug. He refused to return the company's seal to Isopescu and, aided by gendarmes and Ukrainian policemen from the Domanevka subdistrict, looted hundreds of Jews and murdered dozens on the spot. When Isopescu demanded that the loot be returned Georgescu fled to the Dniester, making off with all the money and jewelry and the company's seal.

The looting and rape were not confined to gendarmes, policemen, and ordinary Ukrainians. A group of Romanian soldiers who had defected from their unit stayed in the village of Vazdovka, where for seventy-five days they went on a rampage of looting, murder, and rape. Military headquarters at Krivoye Ozero reported that two groups of deserters, each comprising five soldiers, were operating in the place.[17] Only in mid-December did the gendarmes, with the help of soldiers in the area, manage to apprehend them and seize the "jewelry and money they had looted from Jews in the local camp," according to Isopescu's report to the military tribunal in Tiraspol.[18] When they were finally caught, three deserters had contracted typhus and had to be hospitalized. The deserters and four large bundles of jewelry and money were sent to the military tribunal in Tiraspol.[19]

In mid-November Prefect Isopescu faced a "Jewish nightmare" that he was unable to cope with: the imminent arrival of tens of thousands more Jews, even before he had managed to bury the thousands of corpses of Jews who had already been slaughtered or shot. Isopescu composed a personal, handwritten confidential report to Alexianu on 13 November 1941 in which he described the situation in his "kingdom." This report is evidence that he already understood that his domain was to become the Kingdom of Death:

> When I took over the district I found several camps of Yids here, some [of whom] had been rounded up in the towns, but most of whom [had been] sent from across the Dniester. Approximately 15,000 were gathered in the Romanian village of Vazdovka in the Lubashevka subdistrict, while there were 1,500 each in Krivoye Ozero and Bogdanovka. They were sick with typhus in Vazdovka and approximately 8,000 of them died, along with those who died of starvation. To prevent the civilians from coming into contact with them, I made a special appeal to Infantry Regiment no. 20, asking for escorts to transfer them to Bogdanovka, a village situated on the banks of the Bug, to be subsequently dispatched across the Bug. Those from Krivoye Ozero were sent to Bogdanovka, too, and were housed in the pigsties on the state farm.
>
> Before the convoy of Yids from Vazdovka arrived, however, 9,000 Yids were sent from Odessa. This means that, counting those who were already there and

those who have meanwhile arrived, there are currently 11,000 Yids housed on the state farm in pigsties that could barely accommodate 7,000 pigs. The village mayor and the manager of the state farm approached me today, desperate, because they were told that over 40,000 more Jews are on the way from Odessa.

The state farm cannot hold them all, and the new arrivals are killing those inside [the sties] in order to take their place. Since the police and gendarmes are unable to keep up with the pace of burial, and [since] the waters of the Bug are being used as drinking water, an epidemic will soon spread over the entire region.

They are not strong enough to work. . . . Most [of the Jews in the camp] are ill with tuberculosis and suffer from dysentery and typhus. To prevent the entire region from becoming infected, I implore you to stop ordering Yids to be sent to this region.[20]

The prefect's words clearly indicate that prior to the "swamping" of Bogdanovka and the Kingdom of Death with tens of thousands of Jews (i.e., before the arrival of transports containing forty thousand Jews), there were already twenty-eight thousand Jews in the Domanevka subdistrict, of whom eighteen thousand were alive and ten thousand were dead. Most of the corpses were not buried or were buried only randomly.

In November 1941 a new player came on the scene: the units of the Twentieth Division, which were responsible for traffic safety in the Bobryk subdistrict. The commander of Company no. 4 reported to the prefect on the spread of typhus among the inhabitants of Vazdovka and the area, due to their proximity to the camp and the piles of unburied corpses. He claimed he had instructed the inhabitants on how to protect themselves from the foci of contamination, but in vain. The inhabitants of the villages did not take precautions but "out of ignorance, buy lice-infested objects and clothes." The lice spread and infected others. "This valley will soon be entirely contaminated, sowing disaster among the Army as well." Indeed, the commander of the Road Guards described the backwardness of the villagers in the Kingdom of Death. They had no idea about personal and environmental hygiene, and even their sanitary workers were no better educated than the ordinary population. The villages, the officer added, had no doctors; there was not a single doctor in the entire area. For months they had had no soap. Reluctantly, the soldiers got down to work despite their natural revulsion: "The Vazdovka camp was cleansed, with the help of local villagers and soldiers of the Fourth Regiment."[21]

Third Army headquarters turned into a kind of watchdog for the implementation of the cleansing of southern Transnistria of Jews, along the Dubossary-Golta line (including the districts of Dubossary, Tiraspol, Ovidopol, Odessa, Ananyev, Ochakov, and Berezovka), due to fear of the spread of typhus. The decision was made after inspections on the ground and at the recommendation of the army's Medical Department. On 12 December the Third Army again asked the administration to transfer five to eight Jews who were working for the administration and the municipality and were still in Tiraspol "to a concentration camp on the Bug," despite their usefulness. It transpired that the authorities were holding thirty-six Jewish girls and women age fifteen to thirty-five in a special building, a fact "that triggered unflattering comments about the authorities." Third Army headquarters even asked the gendarmerie legion in Tiraspol to lend it carts to evacuate the children and the elderly. Alexianu himself sanctioned the request and issued a written instruction: "All Jews are to be taken to the Bug."[22]

The commanders of the Third Army, particularly in southern Transnistria, believed that the way to protect their soldiers, and even the Ukrainians, from typhus was by transferring the Jews eastward to the Kingdom of Death. Under prevailing conditions, when thousands of corpses were being buried on the one hand and new convoys of Jews continued to arrive on the other, it was impossible to contain the epidemic. Even in the Kingdom of Death the army asked the prefecture "to transfer the Jewish camp." There was, however, nowhere for it to go: Antonescu's Ukraine ended at the Bug.[23]

In late November the situation in the Bogdanovka camp and in other makeshift camps became intolerable. It was impossible to cram more Jews into these camps and prevent the spread of typhus, prevent contact between Ukrainians and Jews, and safeguard the soldiers' health. On 30 November Isopescu sent a telegram to the administration in Tiraspol stating that Bogdanovka was full to capacity and that he had nevertheless been informed that there were more convoys on the way. "Please see to it that they are sent to other places. Golta is also at risk," emphasized the prefect.[24] Meanwhile, he adopted the recommendation of Colonel Broșteanu, the inspector general of the gendarmerie in Transnistria, to set up new camps in the villages of Zakhariyevka and Nazarov "in order to prevent Bogdanovka being swamped."[25]

Isopescu, however, was too impatient to wait for advice from afar. In early November he gave orders for the first convoys arriving from Odessa to be put up in an improvised camp in the village of Domanevka, on the road to Odessa. The camp comprised two ruined stables and several pigsties belonging to a kolkhoz. When these could not accommodate any more people, the Jews were assigned to several ruined houses that were open to the elements. Domanevka, unlike Bogdanovka, was set up as a labor camp, a reservoir of labor for local farms. Able-bodied

Jews were sent to work in the fields, for which they received a little food. Men staved off starvation by offering their services to the peasants, thereby extending their lives. Even women worked on the farms in return for a few potatoes. The camp, however, did not have even the minimal living conditions required to survive the difficult winter, and Isopescu "prevented the inmates from making even the most basic arrangements."[26]

In a matter of weeks typhus broke out in Domanevka, too, as filth piled up knee-high before freezing in the frost. After the outbreak of typhus the deportees were not allowed to leave contaminated buildings, which were not cleaned even from animal droppings. Jews who were brought in the new convoys to the Bogdanovka and Domanevka camps had to remain outdoors day and night until they were allowed into the pigsties and stables. Fights broke out as people strove to obtain the most basic shelter requirements, as Isopescu pointed out in his report to Alexianu.

THE MASSACRE AT BOGDANOVKA

It was the Transnistrian administration, with Antonescu's backing, that made the decision to massacre tens of thousands of Jews in Bogdanovka and Domanevka, after attempts to transfer these Jews—over seventy thousand, most of whom were sick with typhus—to the Germans failed. On 19 November Isopescu still believed such a transfer possible: "There are still some Jews hiding in the villages. I have ordered a search and for all Jews thus caught to be brought to Bogdanovka pending their shipment across the Bug. We are negotiating with the Germans over this issue."[27]

Although the negotiations failed (see chap. 27), the administration did not abandon the idea even in 1942. The decision to exterminate the Jews was made in concert with the Transnistrian administration's Department of Health and the army's medical service. The Department of Health was run by Dr. Gheorghe Tătăranu, a reserve army physician (major), expert epidemiologist, and senior researcher and director of the laboratory at the Bucharest Institute of Hygiene. He was sent to Transnistria as head of a special epidemiological team attached to the army corps that launched the offensive against Odessa. After Odessa's overthrow Tătăranu accepted Governor Alexianu's invitation to run the administration's Department of Health—a position he held from early October 1941 to 1 November 1942—after which he remained in Odessa as the governor's advisor on health affairs.[28]

The decision to exterminate the Jews and burn their corpses was contingent on the consent of Dr. Mihai Negoescu, chief medical inspector of the Romanian army, who had seen reports on the Bogdanovka tragedy by military physicians serving in the Golta and Berezovka districts. But for Tătăranu's vanity, which prompted him to publish a special booklet on his "medical" achievements in Transnistria, and the physicians' field reports, there would have been no official Romanian document testifying to who was responsible for the operation of burning the corpses. Even the Germans had not yet begun to burn the corpses of Jews (it was only in mid-1943 that they did so). The Jews who were shot by the Nazis in the ravines of Babi Yar on 12 and 30 September 1941, in a manner reminiscent of the Bogdanovka operation, were subsequently buried under a thin layer of soil.

The corpses that piled up after the Bogdanovka and Domanevka operations were a health hazard to the Romanian army, the gendarmerie, local German concentrations across the Bug, and the local Ukrainian population, and therefore they had to be burnt. Even had they wished to help the Jews (who were no longer considered human beings), the army and the Romanian authorities in Transnistria did not have sufficient means to contain the typhus epidemic. In any case, the Jews were already doomed. Alexianu made it quite clear that the removal of the Jews was a prerequisite for Transnistria's rehabilitation.

On 16 December 1941 the government held a special session in Bucharest to discuss the fate of the Jews of Odessa and southern Transnistria. Although the minutes of the session did not refer to Bogdanovka, Antonescu made his position on the Jews of Odessa, and the Ukraine in general, quite clear. He gave Alexianu carte blanche to act as he saw fit, "as if Romania had been ruling these regions for two million years." Antonescu was not prepared to delay action against the Jews until negotiations with the Germans or the Final Solution got off the ground: "The question of the Yids is being discussed in Berlin. The Germans want to transfer the Yids from Europe to Russia and settle them in certain regions. However, it will take time until this plan is implemented. What shall we do with them meanwhile? Shall we wait for a decision from Berlin? Shall we wait for a decision concerning us? Shall we ensure their safety? Pack them into catacombs! Throw them into the Black Sea! [For my part] a hundred can die, a thousand can die, all of them can die."[29]

The order to shoot the Jews of the Bogdanovka camp was transmitted to Isopescu by the administration, through a special envoy who arrived in mid-November.[30] As far as is known the order was transmitted personally and verbally, but specifications concerning the incineration of corpses were given in writing by the Transnistrian administration. Isopescu, who had no qualms about exterminating the Jews in his realm, which was far from the Dniester, acted like an absolute despot and transmitted the order verbally to his deputy, Aristide Pădure, who had exclusive responsibility for Jewish affairs in his territory. Pădure, who was not aware of the enormity of the crime that was about to be committed, issued a written order to Vasile Mănescu, the pretor of the Domanevka subdistrict. Mănescu transmitted it verbally to Sgt. Maj. Nicolae Melinescu, commander of the Bogdanovka gendarmerie post. Melinescu, who had been allotted only nine gendarmes, panicked and balked, demanding to be shown the order in writing: "At that moment, Melinescu experienced a spark of humanity. Although he had looted, tortured, beaten and even shot Jews, he could not comprehend the extermination of 48,000 people, and even informed [Mănescu] that he could not carry out [this order]."[31]

Indeed, Melinescu used to beat and torture Jews into disclosing where they had hidden their property or gold. He beat and even killed Jews "for disobeying orders regarding the purchase of food." He personally flogged naked men and women. He used to work Jews hard without food and beat them up when they collapsed from exhaustion and weakness. Melinescu was far from being a Righteous Among the Nations, but when he was given the order to exterminate the Jews of the Bogdanovka camp he refused to carry it out and was therefore dismissed later from his post.[32]

The extermination campaign was a Romanian operation through and through. The indictments and the testimony of the few survivors show that the Germans neither intervened nor were present at the executions. As we shall see, the German administration on the other side of the Bug demanded the removal of the Jews, not their murder. In view of Melinescu's refusal to obey the orders Isopescu and Pădure decided to make use of the Ukrainian police. To this end, all the Ukrainian police in the district — about seventy policemen — were assembled in Golta. The Ukrainian policeman Afanasie Andrushin — a fifty-one-year-old native of Kishinev — was charged with implementing the order. Before launching this massive operation he received a written order from Pădure to shoot all Jews in the city of Golta, including craftsmen who were sick with typhus. After most of the Jews of Golta were shot to death Andrushin received a written order, signed by the deputy prefect Pădure, to shoot all the Jews in the Bogdanovka camp.[33] In Bogdanovka the operation was supervised by Pretor Mănescu, with Andrushin's help. The Ukrainian policemen did not wear uniforms, but a white armband emblazoned with the words *Romanian police* (*poliția română*) or simply *police*.

About thirty thousand Jews were shot before Christmas. There were still many more. Thousands had already been removed from the pigsties and were waiting in the forest or by the frozen river for their turn to die. The screams of Jews rang out from the valley and the pits, testifying to the fact that not all had died.

The policemen finished off the job by throwing grenades into the piles of Jewish corpses. In the three nights during which these Jews awaited their doom (24–27 December), several thousand froze to death. Several daring Jews took shelter from the freezing winds in pits that they covered with frozen corpses.

The massacre resumed on 28 December, when the policemen returned to work, and continued until 30 December. This stage of the operation was slower since the policemen were tired of working so hard and were more interested in having fun and getting drunk on *samagoon*, a local liquor made from beets, which was in plentiful supply. Several dozen women and girls were selected and kept in a special section of the kolkhoz to prepare food and serve the Ukrainian policemen. Several of them survived, including Esther Gobelman, a fifteen-year-old Jewish girl, who saw her brother and mother murdered before her eyes.[34]

During the months of December 1941 and January 1942 approximately twenty thousand Jews were concentrated in the Domanevka camp. The murders there began after the conclusion of the murder operations in Bogdanovka, on or around 10 January 1942, and lasted until 18 March 1942.[35] In Domanevka the actions were carried out in series—that is, against groups of three hundred to four hundred. The operation lasted more than two months because there was a break of several days after each action.[36] The burning of the bodies began at the end of March 1942 and continued for more than two months, until the end of May.[37] All in all eighteen thousand Jews were killed in Domanevka.[38] Old people, sick people, children, and those who were unfit for work were sent to the Akmechetka camp on the Bug, about eighteen kilometers south of Bogdanovka and a similar distance from Domanevka. Healthy Jews were also sent there as punishment for insubordination, as were several hundred orphans and abandoned children. In the early days of April 1942 about four thousand Jews were incarcerated in the camp in four large pigsties that were open to the elements and the snow and in a long warehouse without doors or windows. The main purpose of the camp was to liquidate the Jews there without the use of force, by totally isolating them from the local population. Even then Akmechetka was known as a death camp. After several weeks of isolation most of the Jews died of hunger, while the remainder succumbed to exhaustion. Of about four thousand Jews, only several hundred were still alive in May 1942. There were always several hundred Jews in the camp, since Isopescu used it as a garbage dump for all the "human dregs" that the administration sent to the Kingdom of Death.[39]

Toward the end of the murder operation Isopescu prepared a report on the mood of the population in the district. He pointed out that "the population felt a great relief following the elimination of Jews from political life, and were currently awaiting the dismantling of the kolkhozes. . . . In Golta, only forty Yids were left."[40]

In late January 1942 Isopescu informed the administration of his plans in each of the subdistrict capitals — Krivoye Ozero, Lubashevka, Domanevka, and Vradiyevka. "These cities [actually towns] were destroyed as a result of the Jewish-Bolshevik war," he claimed. Isopescu added, "The Christian population's unbridled hatred toward anything Jewish [is a hatred which,] even before the establishment of the [Romanian] Administration, caused them to raze houses belonging to Jews." Isopescu wished to rebuild the towns "and give them a character that would reflect the special Romanian [attributes] in this land." He therefore asked for Romanian architects to be sent over to build, inter alia, a Romanian cathedral and church.[41] At the height of the extermination operation the prefect instructed the pretor of the Vradiyevka subdistrict to immediately confiscate "all cows left by Jews" and fleeing residents and bring them to the sovkhozes and kolkhozes.[42]

As far as the administration was concerned, the resumption of agricultural labor, not mass murder, was by far the most important activity in the district. A telegram from the governor urged Isopescu to send the heads of the Agricultural Department and the foremen of the sovkhozes and kolkhozes to a conference in Tiraspol on 18 January 1942 to report on labor, crops, livestock, machinery, and tractors, so as to be able to resume farming in the spring.[43] This was at a time when tens of thousands of Jewish corpses were being burnt in Bogdanovka.

The few Jews who were still alive and those whom the administration had funneled into the Kingdom of Death were subjected to a selection process by Pădure and occasionally also by Isopescu, during which some were sent to Akmechetka and others to the kolkhozes and sovkhozes. Isopescu himself selected "able-bodied Yids" from among the new arrivals in the spring and summer of 1942 and sent them to the sovkhozes, which became Romanian state farms. The Jews worked in the farms under slave conditions and were housed in cowsheds guarded by gendarmes and two or three local policemen.[44]

Since Isopescu believed that the main obstacle to the normalization of life in Transnistria was the Jews, he and his aides and the army and gendarmerie commanders who were subordinate to him were convinced that they had solved the Jewish problem. The administration, however, considered the Golta district (as well as nearby Berezovka) a garbage dump for the remaining Jews that the gendarmerie, army, and police had managed to round up in southern Transnistria. Throughout 1942 there were arguments between the Transnistrian administration and Isopescu, who demanded, "Don't send me more Yids!"[45] His cries intensified as the typhus epidemic, which he had thought was eradicated, resurfaced and threatened the entire district.

The new outbreak of typhus—which no longer constituted a threat to Jews since most of them had been murdered but was a threat to Romanian soldiers, members of the administration, and the Ukrainian population in general—intensified the hatred toward the few Jews who were still alive. Lieutenant Găletaru, commander of the gendarmerie in the Domanevka subdistrict, sought to rid the Romanian soldiers and civilians in the subdistrict of the presence of several hundred Jews in the town, who no longer generated income. On 16 April 1942 he reported to the pretor that "information he had obtained" showed that the Jews of the Domanevka ghetto "are disposing of lice near the wells" from which they drew water "and sometimes even in the wells themselves." Since these wells also served the gendarmes and the Ukrainian population "and sometimes also soldiers passing through Domanevka," which was located on the Odessa-Golta road, "these elements [the Jews] constituted an immediate danger for the spread of typhus, which originated only from these Jews." In view of the above, Găletaru asked his commanders to request that Isopescu "move the Jews of this ghetto to Akmechetka or Bogdanovka," where "suitable buildings" awaited them, so that the Jews could be isolated from the civilian population.[46]

In mid-June 1942 the Kingdom of Death received new blood. A secret order signed by Alexianu informed Isopescu that the Council of Ministers had decided to expel the Gypsies from Romania to Transnistria and ordered him to absorb some of them. Accordingly, Isopescu set aside four locations in the Golta district and one in the Berezovka district to accommodate them. One of these places was Akmechetka.[47] The administration's directives concerning the Gypsies' living conditions resembled those it had issued for the Jews. Alexianu's background as a law professor allowed him to make cynical use of the Romanian language in order to evade all moral responsibility: "Measures shall be adopted to ensure that, upon the arrival of these [Gypsies] to the region, they will be able to obtain accommodation, work and food." The gendarmerie commander in Transnistria, Colonel Iliescu, also sent a secret communiqué to the prefect explaining that "the operation was launched in June in order to give them [the Gypsies] a chance to find accommodation in the summer and to hoard the means of subsistence for the following winter."[48]

The Gypsies were resettled in a similar manner as the Jews and were robbed in the same way and by the same people.[49] Although they reached the Kingdom of Death in a relatively healthy condition, less than a month later the district's military physician, Capt. Dumitru Tomescu, reported to the prefect that they were "the district's new plague." The physician visited Domanevka, Bogdanovka and Akmechetka, Novo-Cantacuzino (Novo-Kantakuzenko), and other villages and found that "the gypsies, the district's new plague, are not receiving food. Their hygiene is inadequate, and this, together with starvation, turns them into an immediate epidemiological threat."[50]

Indeed, a typhus epidemic erupted in the three districts containing Gypsies with the same virulence, under the same circumstances, and for the same reasons as with the Jews a year earlier. The Transnistrian administration and the Romanian army, which had meanwhile set up centers for the prevention and treatment of epidemics, had learnt nothing, or rather they had no desire to learn anything that might help Jews or Gypsies. In September 1943 Leonida Popp, the prefect of Berezovka, reported that all the Gypsies who had survived in the district "were naked and barefoot. They have no clothes, no shirts, and no shoes," and he demanded that they be supplied with clothes from Romania.[51]

In early 1944 a law court in Romania demanded to see death certificates for four Gypsies. The deputy prefect of the Berezovka district informed the court that 7,500 Gypsies had been crammed into one large village (Trihati) and one small village (Kovalevka), which under normal circumstances could accommodate only 800–1,000 people: "In mid-December 1942, the typhus epidemic erupted, and about 200–250 [Gypsies] were dying each day. Because of the large daily death count, it was impossible to identify the bodies. Likewise, the gypsies threw the corpses into houses and cowsheds that were set ablaze, in bushes, or [left them] in the streets. These bodies swarmed with lice the size of a finger. Because of the above, it was not possible to keep records either of the living or of the dead. After the epidemic, 1,800–2,400 gypsies remained in the village."[52]

The tragedy of the Gypsies in Transnistria has become a topic of research in recent years, particularly in Romania.[53] Their fate during the fascist regime was described and included in the final report of the Wiesel Commission, the International Commission on the Holocaust in Romania established at the initiative of president Ion Iliescu in October 2003.[54] The Transnistrian administration and the Romanian army did not wage an extermination campaign against the Gypsies as they did against the Jews. In practice, however, many of them died because of their appalling living conditions, and this matched the objectives of the Romanian regime.

From the second half of 1943 the number of Jews in the Kingdom of Death remained more or less stable, while the number of Gypsies dropped. The Jews, only a few of whom had survived the large extermination operation and most of whom had been deported in the summer and autumn of 1942 from other regions of Transnistria or the Regat, still lived in terrible conditions, but some of them worked. With the help that began trickling in from their brothers in Romania, they fought each day to survive, fearful of what the future held.[55] In late September 1943 there were 2,980 Jews in the entire Golta district, scattered among thirty-six localities—ghettos, labor camps, villages, and sovkhozes. Of these, 25 were in Akmechetka, 541 in Domanevka, 116 in Bogdanovka, 205 on the Duca Vodă farm, 543 on the Marshal Antonescu farm, 299 in the Golta ghettos, and so on.[56] At the time, when the defeat of the German and Romanian armies was no longer in doubt, Pădure and Isopescu suggested concentrating all Jews of the district in the Akmechetka camp and even sent over a delegation to examine and repair the pigsties in order to enable them to accommodate all the Jews. Three (out of four) of the main pigsties still housed about 40 Jews. A petition submitted by the Committee of Golta Jews to the Transnistrian administration stated, inter alia:

> The village has three sties that served exclusively to house pigs. There are still, at present, forty sick, elderly and infirm Jews who have been sent there from other localities in the Golta district. . . . These sties have fallen into almost total disrepair, and even if they were repaired, could not possibly hold a population of 3,000. . . . Akmechetka is far from all localities in the Golta region, making it extremely hard to obtain food, and during [snow]storms, altogether impossible. There is no local market . . . there is no drinking water even for the sixty local [Ukrainian] families. . . . The concentration of such a large number of Jews represents a serious epidemiological threat. . . . Most of the Jews in the district work on farms, and those in cities work in workhouses . . . and their services are required.[57]

The committee invoked all possible arguments in an attempt to avert the terrible decree. The only reason the administration in Odessa failed to sanction Isopescu and Pădure's final extermination plan was that Alexianu and his aides were busy hiding the evidence of their previous crimes. Before the Akmechetka camp was closed down Isopescu paid a last visit to the camp he had been so fond of visiting: "Before the closure of the camp . . . on a Sunday morning, after a banquet, all the top-ranking officials came to the death camp to see how Jews were dying. They included Prefect Isopescu and his wife, deputy prefect Pădure, Lieutenant Dumitrescu from the Gendarmerie, the pilot, Irina Burnaia, Alexianu's mistress, and the German Advisor to the prefecture, Fletscher. They had barely reached the camp's perimeter fence when the following sight met their eyes: Naked Jews, on all fours, nibbling grass."[58]

Isopescu and his aides acted, in their small kingdom, with resolve and persistence in order to implement the Antonescu regime's long-range policy. As the prefect of the Mogilev district put it in an order issued on 5 July 1942: "We shall stay here with the Ukrainians, not with the Jews."[59]

ROBBING AND EVIDENCE OF THE EXTERMINATION CAMPAIGN

In the Kingdom of Death—as in Kishinev, Czernowitz, and all regions in which the perpetrators of the secret orders for the extermination of Jews operated—property, money, and valuables belonging to Jews were confiscated in the name of and on behalf of the Romanian state and the National Bank of Romania. Many officials kept the loot for themselves, however, instead of handing it over to the state. In the course of this operation they perpetrated additional crimes out of sheer malice, which greatly intensified the victims' suffering and turned the execution itself into the less painful and frightening part of the process and sometimes even into a deliverance from suffering.

During the investigation and trials of those accused of looting and theft, all bureaucratic precautions adopted to hide the evidence of the massacre of Jews (which were already less rigorous than those adopted by the Nazis) were thrown by the wayside. The Jews were robbed by all those involved in their arrest, concentration, transfer, and internment in the death camps, from Romanian soldiers and gendarmes, Ukrainian policemen and ordinary civilians, and prefecture personnel to Romanian agronomists and clerks. These criminals were accused, officially, of robbing the Romanian state and the National Bank of Romania, not the Jews.

Official looting in the name of the Romanian state was done both at the initiative of the prefect of Golta and by order of the Transnistrian administration. In early November 1941 Isopescu gave a written order, at his initiative, to confiscate Romanian money from the deportees and hand it over to him in the prefecture.[60] The Governor of Transnistria, for his part, ordered the prefect on 21 November 1941 to assign a committee to each camp, comprising the pretor, the gendarmerie commander, and the village mayor, to collect jewelry and valuables "that the Jews were willing to sell for food" and deliver them to the representatives of the National Bank, stressing that everything belonged to the Romanian state.[61]

All attempts by the Transnistrian administration and Isopescu to hide the evidence of the extermination operation—such as the transmission of verbal orders to Isopescu and from Isopescu to Pădure by special envoy or the destruction of written orders regarding the looting and shooting of Jews—were of no avail in the end. The greed of the Romanian authorities in Transnistria gave the game away. As early as 1943 a Romanian military tribunal that was exempt from secrecy explicitly stated that "Jews were executed [shot] in the Golta district."[62]

In his letter of June 1943, sent in reply to the caution issued by the military tribunal, Isopescu admitted that it was not he but rather the administration that had dismissed Pretor Mănescu on 15 March 1942.[63] Moreover, despite his ouster Mănescu had remained in the district for a further two months, until 10 May 1942. As to the valuables stolen from Jews, Isopescu advanced a new explanation—concern for the state's interests—and attempted to limit the problem to his district only while shifting the blame onto the administration in Odessa:

> As to the measures adopted for collecting valuables from the Jews, I beg to inform you that the report I submitted to the governor on 19 November 1941 stated that, as the Yids from the district villages and towns were sent to Bogdanovka to protect them from the whims of the local population, who, in cooperation with the [Ukrainian] police, exploited and looted them, and considering that their property belongs to the Romanian State, I decided that the pretor [Mănescu], the mayor and the commander of the gendarmerie in the subdistrict keep a written record of all goods deposited by the Jews in exchange for food. The governor ratified this step, and all property listed in the inventory was handed over to the Administration via the prefecture.[64]

This time Isopescu failed to mention the huge convoys of Jew that had arrived from all over Transnistria as well as from Bessarabia and Bukovina, as he had in a previous report.[65] He referred only to the Jews of the Golta district, hoping thereby to play down the amount of property looted. Likewise, he made a point of referring to the so-called committees that he had set up and played down his role in the looting operation, claiming he had taken none of the property for himself but had simply passed it on from the prefecture to the administration. He failed, however, to specify the dates and amounts of property he had transferred in this way. To make matters worse, he portrayed the theft of jewelry, wedding rings, gold earrings, gold teeth, and the like on behalf of the Romanian state as a legitimate form of bartering. In his reply to the court he failed to even mention the "knepelech" (Yiddish for "buttons," referring here to Tsarist gold coins) that the Jews traded for bread or the thousands of gold coins that were stolen by his accomplices.

In the summer of 1943 the investigation of Mănescu, Bobei, Iliescu, and Blănaru and indirectly also of Isopescu and Pădure took an unexpected turn, much to the embarrassment of the administration in Odessa, due to the testimony of a Jewish woman named Matilda, who had escaped from the Golta ghetto but was caught by gendarmes and sent to a law court in Tiraspol. In the course of her cross-examination she described how the gendarmerie officer, Maj. Romulus

Ambrus, with the help of his Jewish accomplices, Avraham Creştinu, Alfred Follender, and others, had robbed Jewish prisoners. Following this the ssi's Section Two, headed by Col. Alexandru Ionescu-Alion, launched an investigation. Section Two, the only institution that did not become corrupt, ordered the arrest of the three heads of the Jewish Committee in Golta.[66] Ionescu-Alion traveled to Golta, where he personally arrested Ambrus and his Jewish accomplices. "These criminals managed to amass huge sums of money, millions [of lei], as well as gold, foreign currency, precious stones, etc. through extortion, terror and torture, by establishing a reign of terror among the Jews in the camps."[67]

Rumors of the investigation even reached Bucharest, where the minister of police, Piki Vasiliu, asked to see its findings. During the trial in Tiraspol, which began in January 1944 (when the front collapsed before the Soviet offensive), Haim Kogan, a survivor of the mass extermination, was asked to testify.[68] The military tribunal, perhaps under orders from their superiors, brought charges against Mănescu, the gendarmerie officers, and several minor clerks of the prefecture only. Isopescu got away scot-free. The detailed report of 16 January 1943 that Isopescu sent the military tribunal provides insight into the way of thinking and the behavior of members of the Romanian administration in Transnistria, especially their attitude toward the masses of Jews they had concentrated on the banks of the Bug in the winter of 1941–42, in preparation for their extermination:

> When, around November, I discovered what was going on in the Jewish camps, especially the way in which local citizens traded food for gold, I set up a committee comprising the pretor, the primar [village mayor] and a gendarme, and also a representative [of the Jews]. This committee took the gold and jewelry from those who wished to purchase food. I delivered the gold collected in this way to the Administration together with legal invoices. I took this step in order to ensure that the gold the Jews brought with them from Romania would return to our national coffers, and to prevent dozens of kilograms of gold finding its way to local [Ukrainians] as a result of profiteering, and illegal transfers to the left side of the Bug [i.e., to the Germans]. . . .
>
> The Administration sent no written or *verbal* order [i.e., secret order] objecting to the above measure, and did not order me to halt the operation or to return the *gold*. On the contrary, the Administration received the entire amount of gold that was confiscated. This operation continued throughout the winter, and then, more sporadically, until the autumn [1942]. . . . The last time, we handed over the gold [to the administration] was in late October 1942.[69]

The above indicates that the operation to rob the Jews of their gold overlapped the extermination campaign.

27

Odessa

On 16 October 1941 the Romanian army and a few auxiliary German units discovered that Odessa lay open to them and that the city's last defenders had sailed away in the night. Although the Romanians and Germans were aware of the evacuation of soldiers and equipment from Odessa, they were still surprised to find the city completely devoid of armed forces. The Romanians entered a city partly ravaged by the protracted siege, some of whose population—including those elements most loyal to the Soviet regime—had been evacuated by sea. Prior to the city's evacuation, various Soviet agents blew up and mined factories and installations that could not be evacuated. Toward the end of the siege, when the Soviet government was losing its grip, gangs of criminals and defectors robbed passers-by with impunity and looted warehouses, stores, clinics, and public buildings. The spread of crime in the city center attested to the Soviet government's powerlessness during the city's last days.

Contrary to the claims of Romanian propaganda, the city's two hundred thousand Jews were no darlings of the Soviet regime. Hundreds were executed during and even before the siege on various trumped-up charges.[1] The antisemitic atmosphere intensified during the siege, peaking on the eve of the city's evacuation, particularly in the working-class neighborhoods. In mid-September, after German planes dropped antisemitic leaflets over the city, a group of young hooligans, during an anti-Jewish rally in one of the neighborhoods, chanted an old antisemitic czarist slogan: "Beat the Jews and save Russia."[2]

The Romanian soldiers who entered Odessa in the fall of 1941 did not resemble their German counterparts who were, at the time, capturing city after city. The locals viewed the weak and beaten army that finally entered the silent and depleted city as a horde of "hungry and contemptible foreigners." The Romanian soldiers lost no time in looting, stealing, and breaking into houses and shops and conducted raids that inevitably ended in theft, rape, and other violent crimes.[3]

On the first night of the occupation (16–17 October) and the following day the Romanians carried out a massacre the scale of which has not been clarified to this day. Soviet sources claim that eight thousand people—most of them Jews—were executed. Some murders took place near the port and no doubt included victims who had not managed to board the last boats leaving Odessa.[4] Since chaos reigned during the first days of the occupation, this estimate is hard to corroborate. On 16 October the Tenth Division was ordered to "round up Jewish men aged 15–50 and Jews who had fled from Bessarabia (to Odessa)," an order that subsequently became a death sentence.[5] On 17 October the Romanian military authorities announced that they were conducting a general census. Romanian soldiers shot at Soviet citizens who registered for the census or who had been arbitrarily arrested and found to be in possession of membership cards for the Communist Party or military ID cards.[6] Among those executed in the early days of the occupations were sixty-one Jewish physicians.[7]

On 17 October checkpoints were set up in schools and public buildings, and all the male population of Odessa was ordered to report to these checkpoints with their Soviet documents for inspection by Romanian military headquarters. Most of those who reported were barred from leaving by military guards. About seven thousand youth were arrested on the pretext that they were conscripts or defectors and sent to Romania for forced labor. About four thousand Jews were arrested on the spot. Some were classified as dangerous Communists, Bolsheviks, or Commissars according to criteria devised by the police and SSI and were shot or hanged. Although the exact number of fatalities during the massacre is unknown, it almost certainly extended into the thousands. Dr. Israel Adesman of Odessa described one of the checkpoints in a school where he was held on the night of 17–18 October:

> Some were taken to gallows or trenches, while others were jailed. A few were allowed to return to their looted homes, but only for the time being. . . . We were over 500 people. We were kept standing the whole night jammed against one another. We were overwhelmed by fatigue, hunger, and thirst and [fear] of the unknown. All night long we heard children crying and adults groaning. The following day . . . a group of 300–400 people was taken to prison. Our group included old men, the disabled on crutches, and women with babes in arms. Many died in prison of exhaustion or of wounds they sustained from beatings. Many committed suicide.[8]

All Jewish men and youth who reported to these centers, apart from those who were interrogated, tortured, and killed, were ordered to clear away the rubble in the ruined city. Convoys of Jews and prisoners of war could be seen making their way separately to the work sites under strict supervision. On 18 October the Romanian soldiers, following the German example, began taking hostages as a way of ensuring calm in the city. Many of the hostages were Jews who had been evicted from their homes or who had reported to the checkpoints. The city's prison became a large camp for Jews awaiting interrogation, torture, abuse, and execution by the SSI, police agents, and the military.

"THE KINGDOM OF TERROR"

On 17 October 1941 Antonescu and Governor Alexianu decided that, at least to start off with, the "civil authorities—the prefect, mayor, etc.—would report to the military authorities."[9] From 18 October 1941 until the middle of March 1942 the Romanian military authorities in Odessa—helped by the gendarmerie, the police, and the civil authorities—waged a campaign of terror, execution, and deportation against the city's Jews, resulting in the murder of at least twenty-five thousand Jews and the deportation of another sixty thousand. This campaign was planned and executed by the Romanians alone—the German army and Einsatzgruppe D never even set foot in the city.[10]

On the evening of 22 October the Romanian military general headquarters exploded, killing sixty-six Romanian officers (including the city's military commander, Gen. Ion Glogojanu). Tenth Division headquarters took over the building that had formerly served as headquarters of the NKVD (the Soviet secret police). Immediately upon learning of the disaster Antonescu ordered Gen. Iosif Iacobici, chief of staff and commander of the Fourth Army, to "take drastic punitive measures."[11] Meanwhile, Gen. Nicolae Tătăranu's deputy, Col. Ion Stănculescu, deputy chief of the General Staff and chief of staff of the Fourth Army, reached Odessa in the morning with a secret order from Antonescu, which he personally handed to Gen. Nicolae Trestioreanu, deputy commander of the Tenth Division. Antonescu ordered "immediate retaliatory action, including the liquidation of 18,000 Jews in the ghettos and the hanging in the town squares of at least 100 Jews for every regimental sector."[12] The same day (23 October) Stănculescu again cabled Tătăranu, with details of the punitive measures: "Retaliatory action has been taken within the city via shooting [and] hanging. . . . The execution of the Jews in the ghettos is well on the way to reaching the aforementioned number."[13] Stănculescu also reported that although the German liaison officer had offered the help of an SS regiment to rid Odessa of "Jews and Bolsheviks," the Romanian authorities chose to act alone. Soldiers from the Tenth Division and from the Tenth Machine Gun Battalion and military gendarmes shot at Jews in the streets and hung them on tram posts, on improvised planks on street corners, on balconies overlooking the main streets, or simply on streets, after first conducting a hasty search.[14] The main executions took place in the municipal penitentiary and in Dalnic—a village near Odessa that was designated as a ghetto and to which tens of thousands of Jews were taken. According to Gherman Pântea, the Romanian mayor of Odessa, the convoy to Dalnic consisted of some fifty thousand Jews.[15] Thirty thousand or more Jews were rounded up by the gendarmes, some of whom were mounted. Shooting into the air and at people and lashing their whips, they led the massive convoy northward along the Odessa-Katarzi highway to an improvised camp in Berezovka. The deportees were then marched for about two weeks to the Bogdanovka camp, where they were liquidated.

The twenty-five thousand Jews who were the first to reach Dalnic were lined up near the antitank trenches that had been dug during the siege and shot in the head. About forty to fifty Jews were shot in one go. The operation was carried out in total chaos and disorder. Although we do not know the exact number of Jews shot, it ran into the thousands.[16] The method they used was slow and inefficient. On the afternoon of 24 October, when the liquidation operation was at its height, Personal Order no. 563 arrived, determining new punitive measures. Antonescu ordered General Tătăranu "to execute all Bessarabian Jews who had fled to Odessa" and herd all Jews "who had not yet been executed [by the previous order]" into a mined building and explode it.[17] About twenty-two thousand Jews of all ages who had been taken to Dalnic were packed like sardines into nine huge stone warehouses and slaughtered: "One by one, the warehouses were riddled with machine gun and rifle fire, doused with gasoline and ignited, except for the last warehouse, which was blown up. The chaos and the horrifying sights that followed defy description: wounded people burning alive, women with their hair on fire coming out through the roof or through openings in the burning storehouses in a desperate search for salvation. . . . Others tried to escape, climbed on to window ledges or on to the roof amidst the flames, and begged to be shot."[18] The operation continued all night and over the next day. Of about twenty-two thousand Jews, there remained only charred or blown up body parts that were collected and buried in late November by Soviet prisoners of war.[19]

In September 1944, after he was extradited to the Soviet Union along with Antonescu and his close aides, Alexianu blamed the army for the Odessa massacre. During his cross-examination he accused Gen. Nicolae Macici and General Trestioreanu of bearing sole responsibility for the massacre in Dalnic and for all actions against the Jews of Odessa in October 1941.[20] There was some basis for his claim. In Odessa, even more than in Bessarabia and Bukovina, the Romanian army was guilty of war crimes and crimes against humanity. It was responsible for implementing genocide orders, for arresting, shooting, and hanging thousands of Jews, and for burning about eighteen thousand Jews to death, as its reports testify. It coordinated the gendarmerie, the police, and the civil authorities to

CHART 4. CHAIN OF COMMAND FOR REPRISALS
AGAINST THE JEWS OF ODESSA

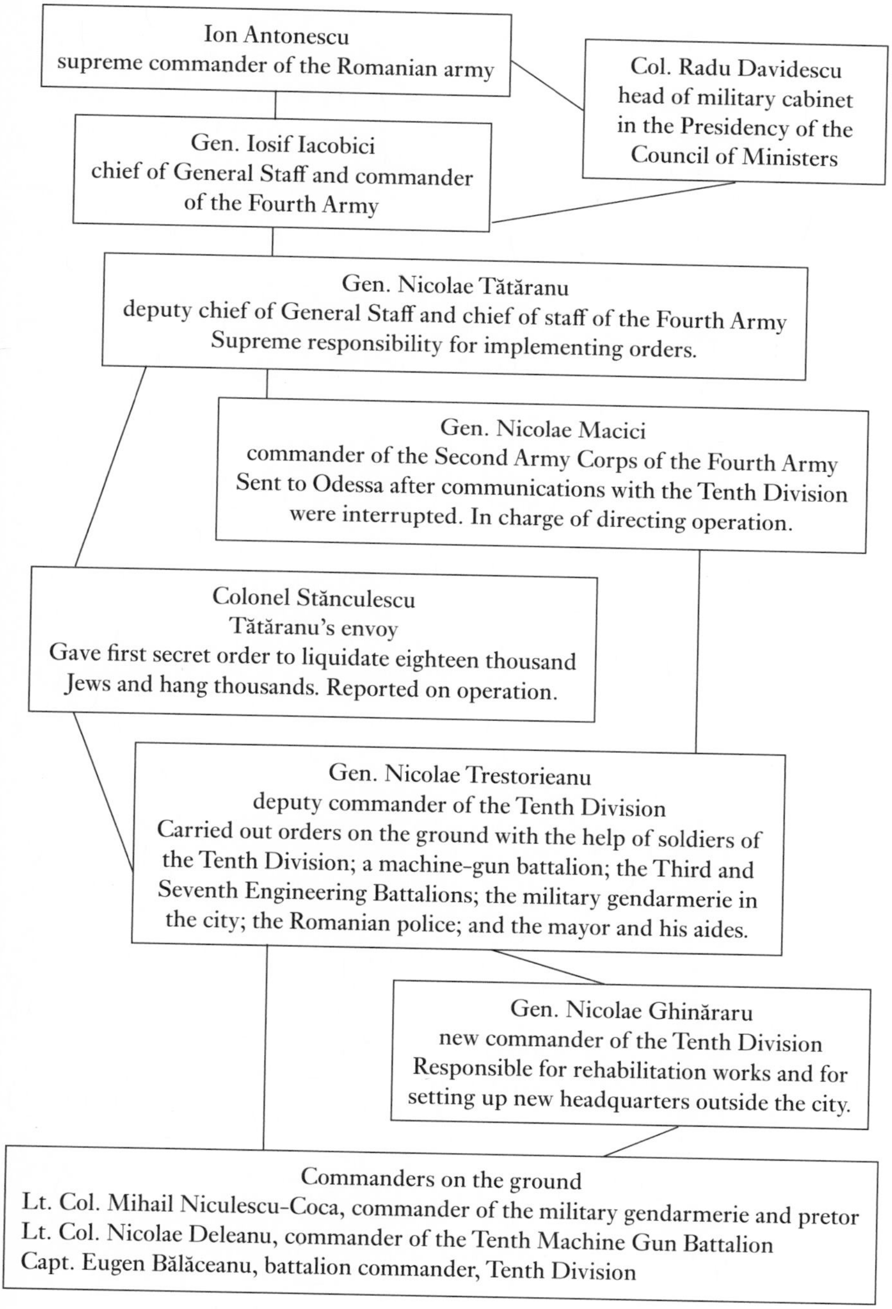

Ion Antonescu
supreme commander of the Romanian army

Col. Radu Davidescu
head of military cabinet
in the Presidency of the
Council of Ministers

Gen. Iosif Iacobici
chief of General Staff and commander
of the Fourth Army

Gen. Nicolae Tătăranu
deputy chief of General Staff and chief of staff of the Fourth Army
Supreme responsibility for implementing orders.

Gen. Nicolae Macici
commander of the Second Army Corps of the Fourth Army
Sent to Odessa after communications with the Tenth Division
were interrupted. In charge of directing operation.

Colonel Stănculescu
Tătăranu's envoy
Gave first secret order to liquidate eighteen thousand
Jews and hang thousands. Reported on operation.

Gen. Nicolae Trestorieanu
deputy commander of the Tenth Division
Carried out orders on the ground with the help of soldiers of
the Tenth Division; a machine-gun battalion; the Third and
Seventh Engineering Battalions; the military gendarmerie in
the city; the Romanian police; and the mayor and his aides.

Gen. Nicolae Ghinăraru
new commander of the Tenth Division
Responsible for rehabilitation works and for
setting up new headquarters outside the city.

Commanders on the ground
Lt. Col. Mihail Niculescu-Coca, commander of the military gendarmerie and pretor
Lt. Col. Nicolae Deleanu, commander of the Tenth Machine Gun Battalion
Capt. Eugen Bălăceanu, battalion commander, Tenth Division

carry out Antonescu's order for reprisals against "Russian" Jews. Among those involved in this crime were high-ranking Romanian army officers such as General Iacobici, chief of General Staff and commander of the Fourth Army (the highest ranking official in the army after Antonescu); General Tătăranu, deputy chief of General Staff and deputy commander of the army; General Macici, commander of the Second Army Corps; and General Trestioreanu, deputy commander of the Tenth Division; as well as gendarmerie and police commanders in Odessa, battalion and brigade commanders, officers, and regular soldiers.

What began as an antisemitic delusion harbored by Antonescu — who blamed the Jews for the heavy losses the Romanian army sustained in the battle for Odessa and in the war in general and who defined the Jews as a Satan that maneuvered the Slavic nations at will — inevitably ended in the unbridled massacre of Odessa's Jews. Despite the secrecy of the orders Bucharest soon learned of the massacre, and the French ambassador reported to the Foreign Ministry in Vichy on 10 November 1941 that the Romanian army had carried out reprisals against the Jews: "Following the explosion on 22 October in Odessa, 25,000 Jews were herded into warehouses, shot by machine guns and cannons, and set fire to by the Romanian units."[21]

During the cabinet session of 13 November Antonescu and Alexianu casually brought up the subject of the reprisals in an aside: "Were the reprisals against the Jews sufficiently severe?" Antonescu inquired. "Indeed," replied Alexianu, "many of them have been killed and hanged in the streets of Odessa." The two then went on to discuss other matters.[22] In 1943, after the defeat at Stalingrad, the subject of the massacre was again raised after War Minister General Pantazi's appeal: "The atrocities of Odessa must be concealed. The corpses of these wretched people must be removed and disposed of elsewhere." To which Antonescu, feigning ignorance, replied: "What's got into you, Pantazi? What on earth are you referring to?"[23] None of the ministers dared remind the Conducător that it was he who had ordered the reprisals against the Jews of Odessa.

ODESSA'S FIRST GHETTO

Some of the Jews who escaped the Dalnic massacre returned home, or rather, returned to what was left of their homes after they had been ransacked or occupied by their neighbors in the belief that no Jew would return. Not all of Odessa's Russians participated in the looting, however, or even hated Jews. Over the following months many of them helped Jews find hiding places or obtain false papers and saved them from deportation, although we do not know how prevalent this phenomenon was.

On 26 October 1941 the Siguranţa reported: "The return of the evacuated Jews has led to deep dissatisfaction among the Christian inhabitants who took over their abandoned houses in the belief that the explosion in the military head-quarters would result in a radical purge of Jews." The Siguranţa and the SSI were the architects of much anti-Jewish incitement. They portrayed the Jews as a risk to public order, security, and the consolidation of Romanian rule in Transnistria in general and in Odessa in particular. They were no doubt instrumental in influencing the decision makers to purge Odessa of its Jews. A Siguranţa report, for example, berated Jewish propaganda for "threatening the Christians with a ten-fold punishment when the time came." Although the Christians were still wary of the Romanian administration, the report stated, "The Russians, happy to be rid of the Jewish vermin, are well-disposed toward us."[24] From the reorga-nization of the municipality until and even after the deportation of the Jews, the municipality was bombarded with letters—anonymous and signed—informing on Jews who had held important positions in the Soviet regime and during and after the deportation from Odessa, Jews who were hiding, Jews who had adopted fictitious identities, and Jews who had false papers.[25]

The Siguranţa, and the police in general, considered not only Jews as danger-ous; on the day after the massacre they determined that "many Christians married to Jews who are concealing their identity shall be considered dangerous." The Siguranţa advised the administration in general, and concierges and housing managers in particular, to tighten their surveillance of Jews. The Siguranţa recom-mended "the tightening of registration and classification procedures, and a search of all attics, cellars, and other places of concealment used by Yids, especially Jewish partisans."[26] Many Odessan Jews did not return home but were escorted by gendarmes to Slobodka, a village in the Odessa area chosen by the Fourth Army to serve as a ghetto.[27] Once the ghetto was set up, policemen, gendarmes, and Romanian and German soldiers began deporting Jews to Slobodka. Forty thousand Jews were concentrated in the village for ten days under exceptionally harsh conditions.

During these ten days, hundreds and even thousands of Jews died, mainly from exposure and overcrowding. A sudden drop in temperature, leading to freezing weather and snowstorms, killed many Jews who were sleeping out in the open. Only a few Jews found shelter in the homes of local citizens. On 3 November, ten days after their incarceration in the Slobodka ghetto, women, children, and the elderly were allowed home, while the men were imprisoned in the city jail, at Alexianu's orders. On 7 November the authorities began cracking down on men who had managed to avoid imprisonment and were hiding in the city. Although some escaped detection with the help of Russian friends, others were betrayed by informers.

The attitude of the local population toward the Jews was not uniform. Although antisemitism had existed prior to the Romanian occupation, the Romanians fomented and disseminated it. The Russian-language newspapers issued by the Transnistrian administration accused the Jews of terrorist acts, whether real or fictitious. Not everyone, however, was deceived by this antisemitic incitement. Generally speaking, the intellectual circles were less tainted by the scourge of antisemitism. The port city of Odessa, however, unlike other Transnistrian cities, had a large criminal element that was only too happy to betray, rob, and even murder Jews, for antisemitic reasons or simply for profit. Their ranks were soon swelled by antisemitic Russian collaborators who, as diehard anticommunists, had been forced into hiding under Soviet rule but now began crawling out of the woodwork. The local Russian-Ukrainian police force, organized by the Romanian authorities, also participated in the great Jew hunt. All these elements devalued the lives of Jews even before they were deported to the death camps.

ANTONESCU AND THE JEWS OF ODESSA

Order no. 23 of 11 November 1941 turned Transnistria into a large Jewish penal colony and turned all Jews, whether local or deportees, into slaves of the Romanian state. As a result of the law all Odessan Jews became temporary guests whose incarceration in ghettos or camps was a mere logistic exercise. Alexianu, who, despite the massacre, still believed that the city was overrun with Jews, ordered the Odessan police to carry out a population census. Alexianu was not reassured by the results of the census, which found only thirty-five thousand Jews in Odessa, and ordered a repeat census: "I did not consider the statistics, which were based on personal declarations, serious and therefore ordered the Odessa municipality to conduct a new census through the concierges. . . . [The latter] were ordered to inform us of any Jews residing in their buildings. These statistics, as yet uncompleted, place the overall number of Jews in Odessa at about 100,000."[28] When the Romanian army entered Odessa the city did have more than one hundred thousand Jews, but when Alexianu wrote the above only forty thousand remained, the rest having been slaughtered or deported.

On 13 November Antonescu held a cabinet session in Bucharest to discuss, inter alia, the massacre in Odessa and the fate of the Jews.[29] The general consensus at the session was that Romania would remain in Transnistria indefinitely and that they must gear up accordingly. Alexianu boasted to Antonescu of his success in setting up the Romanian administration in Transnistria so swiftly — in a mere three months—and getting it to run so smoothly. Each of the thirteen districts had its own prefect and each subdistrict had two pretors, one of whom was brought over from Romania. "The Administration is operating under optimum conditions," Alexianu concluded. Even Dr. Innen, the German advisor who had come to teach Alexianu how to set up an administration in occupied territory based on the German model in the Baltic countries, informed him, after a two-day visit, that he was superfluous: "Everything that could be done has been done."[30]

The lack of clear demarcation lines between the various authorities operating in Odessa came to light during the massacres in the city and impelled Antonescu to define the role of the army in Transnistria as a whole: "The sole purpose of the army is [to preserve] security, while Mr. Alexianu's role is political, economic and administrative." Gen. Nicolae Dăscălescu, whom Antonescu appointed to liaise between Alexianu and the army, was authorized to give orders to the army in Transnistria. As far as Odessa was concerned, Antonescu clarified that the Tenth Division "was a body in the service of the Administration," namely, Alexianu.[31] In matters relating to the Jews, both the army and Alexianu continued to receive orders directly from Antonescu while the Tenth Division received orders also from the General Staff in Bucharest.

Antonescu's inquiry concerning the reprisal operation resembled a teacher inquiring into disciplinary measures adopted against naughty pupils more than a dictator inquiring into the progress of a massacre he had ordered, as the following indicates:

ANTONESCU: As far as the Jews of Odessa are concerned, what's done is done. From now on, let them toe the line! Were the reprisals sufficiently harsh?
ALEXIANU: Yes, Mr. Marshal.
ANTONESCU: What do you understand by "extremely harsh"? You have a tendency to be merciful to others, and not to the Romanian nation.
ALEXIANU: They were very harsh.
ANTONESCU: I told you to shoot two hundred Jews for each person killed, and a hundred for each person wounded. Was that done?
ALEXIANU: Many were shot and [many] were hanged in the streets of Odessa.
ANTONESCU: That is just as well, since I have a responsibility toward history. Let the Jews of America sue me, if they will. We must not show mercy to the Jews, because, given the chance, they would show us no mercy—neither to me, you or the nation. . . . Therefore, don't be lenient with the Jews. Be assured that, given the chance, they will take their revenge. In order to ensure that no Jew is left to take revenge, *I shall make sure to destroy them first*. I shall do this not for my sake, but for the sake of our people. Now, as far as the war spoils are concerned . . .[32]

After the enactment of Order no. 23 and after the cabinet session of 13 November it was clear that the ghetto could not serve as a long-term solution. Although Jews continued to be concentrated in Slobodka, some Jews were also taken to the village of Dalnic or even concentrated in Odessa pending their deportation. This waiting period was marked by a wave of suicides, particularly among the Jewish intelligentsia. Most of those committing suicide did so before being forcibly evicted from their apartments, but many suicides also took place in the ghetto. A Russian refugee from Odessa who fled to the United States described the situation: "The establishment of the ghettos was announced in November. Then the suicides began; doctors, lawyers, teachers killed themselves by drowning or hanging, leaving short, tragic notes. Some went berserk. Those deported to ghettos walked as if [in a] funeral procession from their homes toward their new accommodation."[33] Although there are no written records, it is clear that dozens—and as the date of the deportations drew near, hundreds—of Jews died daily. The hospital set up in the Slobodka ghetto was flooded with dying people.

THE SSI'S SPECIAL UNIT IN ODESSA

On 23 October 1941, several hours after the explosion of a bomb in Romanian army headquarters in the city, the Special Intelligence Service's Special Unit sent a cable to Antonescu's military cabinet notifying it of the disaster. The Special Unit (Eşalonul I Operativ SSI) was an autonomous intelligence unit that was subordinate neither to the army nor to the police but directly to the Presidency of the Council of Ministers. A kind of umbrella organization, it kept the Conducător informed of developments within the army and also within the opposition.

Set up in early June 1941 by SSI head Eugen Cristescu, the Special Unit was modeled on the Einsatzgruppe and comprised both military and civilian personnel. The unit's commander in chief was Cristescu, and his deputy commander was Lt. Col. Mihail Ion Lisievici. Among its commanders were Lt. Col. Vasile Palius-Ionescu, a native of Bessarabia; Curelaru, a gendarmerie captain; reserve lieutenant Gheorghe Cristescu (Eugen Cristescu's brother); and Gheorghe Patrovici-Guţă, a policeman (Cristescu's nephew). Although not actually officers, many of them wore officers' uniforms. The Special Unit helped plan the Iaşi pogroms and actively participated in the massacres in Bessarabia. Both the SSI and the Special Unit collaborated with the Abwehr (the German army's intelligence service), the SD (Nazi security service), and the German embassy in Bucharest. The Special Unit also cooperated with agents of the German security services in Bucharest, Hermann Von Rittgen and Gustav Richter, the latter

Eichmann's envoy and advisor on Jewish affairs in Romania and at one point also advisor on police affairs.

The ssi played a key role in Romania's anti-Jewish policy in Transnistria. First, it considered all Ukrainian Jews as Communist agents of the Soviet regime and the Soviet army who promoted Soviet ideology and, as such, a constant source of danger that had to be eradicated in time. It followed, therefore, that all means were justified against them. Second, it strongly influenced Antonescu's appraisals of the Jewish threat in case of a Soviet landing from the sea.

The ssi, itself influenced by Antonescu's antisemitic opinions and sentiments, in turn fed his antisemitic delusions—which were also fueled by the losses in Odessa. In the climate of the early months of the war, when it seemed that victory was right around the corner and all means against the Jews were justified, these factors were instrumental in the Conducător's decision to deport and exterminate Odessa's forty thousand Jews—all that were left after some thirty thousand Jews had been deported and at least another thirty thousand exterminated.

During his cross-examination in 1946 Cristescu testified that the ssi's role in Odessa was to identify activities and people that threatened the security of the Romanian army. The ssi in Odessa also evaluated the general mood of the population and the structure of Soviet society and gathered information on offenses committed by members of the Romanian administration in Transnistria. As Cristescu pointed out, the army, "obeying orders, naturally," launched a retaliatory operation in which twenty-five thousand to twenty-six thousand Jews lost their lives, apart from "subsequent executions during the evacuation of the Jews from Odessa and their transfer to the Germans."[34]

Reports submitted by Cristescu and by the Special Unit's commander describe the small-scale executions carried out by ssi agents, with or without the army's help. In addition to the ssi's Special Unit, the General Staff had its own special unit in Odessa. Very little is known about this unit, which was mentioned only twice during the war criminals' trials—once by Cristescu himself in an appeal he submitted after he was sentenced to death and once by Victor Ionescu, one of the deputy ministers of defense. At his trial Ionescu testified that the reprisals were carried out by an ssi unit hiding behind the name of the Military Police Section (Secția de Poliție Militară), headed by Col. Ion Perju, Cristescu's confidant. According to the witness, Perju acted according to the personal instructions of Cristescu and Lt. Col. Traian Borcescu, head of the ssi's Counterespionage Bureau, which was responsible for tracking down and killing partisans and suspects.[35] In hand-written depositions he submitted to the court, Cristescu claimed that Ionescu was ignorant of events in Odessa because he had no authority outside Bucharest and therefore all his information was based on rumor alone. Cristescu, unaware that Ionescu had omitted all mention of the ghetto, wrote, "The ssi had no ties with the ghettos. . . . The ssi did not participate in the interrogation of suspects in Transnistria [because] it had only 200 agents [and they were scattered] between the Prut and Nikolayev. Those responsible were: the gendarmes, the police, and the secret agents of the General Staff's *Field Police* [Poliția de Campanie a M. St. M.], who operated on the home front, and who are not referred to in the indictment."[36] Cristescu shifted the blame for the liquidation of Odessa's population from his men to institutions such as the General Staff's Field Police, a unit, he complained, that had not even been mentioned in the indictment and trial. Apart from these references, nothing is known about this special unit.

The ssi agents referred to their liquidation operations as "turning suspects into little angels [îngeraș]."[37] Thanks to them many partisans and suspects, particularly if they were Jewish, were "turned into little angels." As far as we know no Odessan Jew arrested by ssi agents was ever set free. Other euphemisms for extermination were "completing inquiries" or "final" interrogation, as the prosecution files indicate. These euphemisms were used mainly in connection with non-Jewish suspects and partisans. The extermination of Jews was always reported verbally, never in writing.[38]

As stated, even before the occupation of Odessa ssi reports to Antonescu on the situation in Odessa portrayed Jews as sworn enemies of the Romanian state and army who were urging the Soviet soldiers to fight to the bitter end. A report of 12 October 1941 accused the Jews of killing Romanian officers who were being taken prisoner. The report stated that a young Romanian officer who was lightly wounded "was shot to death by the [Soviet] regiment's Jewish medic who, before shooting him, cried out: 'Now you'll get a taste of your own medicine.'"[39]

Another report of 12 October, delivered to Antonescu's war cabinet, the chief of staff, War Headquarters, the Fourth Army, and the Abwehr, stated, "According to a reliable source . . . Odessa's defense will be conducted only by local Jews wearing military uniform," and added that barricades had been erected.[40] The following day the Special Unit reported that the evacuation of Soviet forces from the city had intensified and that rumor had it that "all commanders, Jews and heavy artillery had been evacuated from Odessa" and surrender was imminent.[41]

Another report emphasized that the Soviet soldiers also hated the Jews, on the pretext that most were reluctant to serve in combat units, shirked combat duty, gravitated toward hospitals "or well-paid administrative jobs," and "carried false medical documents issued by Jewish physicians testifying to illness or disability."[42] This statement, which corresponded to Antonescu's view of Jewish soldiers, found a receptive audience.

The activities and reports of the SSI's Special Unit and other intelligence organizations were instrumental in fomenting Antonescu's "natural" hatred of Jews in general and "Russian" Jews in particular. This, together with the heavy losses sustained by the Romanian army in the battle for Odessa, shaped his decision not only to drive the Jews out of Odessa but also to exterminate them.

As far as the Third Army was concerned, the plan was to deport not only the Jews of Odessa but also the Jews of southern Transnistria, as Gen. Nicolae Ghinăraru, commander of the Tenth Division and (for a short time) military commander of Odessa, stated in Order no. 2. This order, which was drawn up even prior to the cabinet session of 16 December 1941 and issued in three languages — Romanian, Russian, and German — instructed all Jews of Odessa and of the Odessa, Ovidopol, Ochakov, and Berezovka districts to send an inventory of all their valuables — jewelry, gold coins, gold artifacts, and the like — to the authorities in writing within forty-eight hours, under penalty of death.[43] Given that the Jews had already been stripped of all their possessions by soldiers and gendarmes in broad daylight, among other things, this order was totally absurd.

ORDER NO. 35

In early January the administration's Research Division handed Alexianu "a draft order concerning the deportation of Jews from Odessa and the vicinity" and directives for implementing the order. After ratifying these documents in his own handwriting Alexianu instructed that they be transmitted "to all those authorized to carry out the assignment, and that their contents be brought to the attention of General Dăscălescu, the Third Army, and the General Staff, and by a special communication, to Marshal Antonescu."[44]

Order no. 35 was the legal basis for the implementation of Antonescu's directive for the deportation of Odessan Jewry. The order reflected the original plan to deport the Jews and settle them "in the northern part of the Ochakov district and in the southern part of the Berezovka district," in localities to be determined by the local authorities.[45] Alexianu chose those specific areas because they were convenient for the expulsion of the Jews across the Bug (both Nikolayev and Voznesensk had makeshift bridges). Alexianu decided that until the Germans agreed to take over the Jews the latter should be concentrated in ethnic German regions, such as the Landau subdistrict and the southern part of the Berezovka district. He did not send them to the Kingdom of Death because it was already bursting at the seams and most of the Jews who were concentrated there had typhus.

The order instructed Jews to hand over their possessions "only in offices set up in police precincts." These possessions were to be auctioned to the local population, with the proceeds from the auction to be handed over to the Jews (a promise that was never kept). The Jews were allowed to take clothes and food with them but were warned that they would be responsible for their "living expenses" in the "relocation areas" (i.e., they would be left to starve to death). The inspector general of the gendarmerie in Transnistria, the prefects of the Odessa, Ochakov, and Berezovka districts, and the commander of the Odessa police were jointly responsible for carrying out the order. The start of the deportation was set for 10 January 1942.[46]

The "Directives for the Evacuation of the Jewish Population from Odessa and the Vicinity" briefed all those involved in the massive operation to transfer forty thousand Jews some 150–200 kilometers to their death. The directives mandated the establishment of a central bureau (*birou central de evacuare*) in the police inspectorate building in Odessa and six regional bureaus that would match the city's six police precincts and would operate concurrently. The central bureau was run by the prefect of the Odessa district together with the army's chief prosecutor, the commander of the Odessa police, an officer from military headquarters in the city, and the mayor of Odessa. The central bureau determined, together with the prefects of Ochakov and Berezovka, the destination of the Jews of Odessa. The regional bureaus (*birou de circumscripție*) were run by jurists who were army officers, the regional police commander, and an officer from military headquarters in the city.

The deportation of the Jews of Odessa differed from that of the Jews of Bessarabia and Bukovina in that a representative of the National Bank of Romania or the Finance Ministry as well as two residents of Odessa, who acted as the mayor's representatives, were formally and openly included on each committee. These public representatives helped the representative of the national bank trace and evaluate Jewish possessions. The regional bureau was responsible for identifying and registering Jews, conducting body and home searches, drawing up an inventory of property and valuables that had been confiscated, reimbursing Jews in RKKS, transmitting the inventories to the supervisors of Jewish homes and property, and sealing houses, workshops, or buildings that had served Jews.

The Jews were allowed to take up to twenty-five kilograms of clothes, food, and medicines with them as well as the RKKS they had received in return for their confiscated property. The convoys were accompanied by policemen or gendarmes working in shifts. The directives ordered the Jews to report to the Odessa railway station, where, under heavy guard, they were placed on freight trains bound for Berezovka. At Berezovka the convoys continued by foot to the relocation areas, which they were forbidden to leave under penalty of death. Col. Marcel Petală, inspector general of the gendarmerie, and Constantin Ciurea, inspector of the administration, were authorized to oversee and monitor the deportation operation on the ground.

The directives were translated into Russian and posted alongside Order no. 35 and also were published by the local Romanian- and Russian-language *Gazeta Odessei*.[47] On 10 January Alexianu was able to inform the commander of the Third Army that "steps have been taken for the immediate removal of all Yids from Odessa."[48] By 3 January 1942 copies of the order and the directives had been sent to Third Army headquarters.

THE JEWS OF THE ODESSA DISTRICT
AND SOUTHERN TRANSNISTRIA

The deportation of the Jews from the Odessa district began in late October 1941 and resumed in February 1942, after the deportations from the city began. The first convoys reached Berezovka in early November 1941 and after a day or two were marched to the Bogdanovka camp.[49] The directives for the orderly deportation of the Jews were issued in early February 1942, about a month after Order no. 35 was issued. The Central Evacuation Bureau, headed by Col. Matei Velcescu, prepared and sent special directives to all pretors of the subdistricts. The directives were mimeographed and signed by Velcescu. Only the name of the subdistrict had to be filled in. This bit of paper was tantamount to a death sentence for thirty thousand to forty thousand Jews in the Odessa district and an unknown number of Jews in southern Transnistria.[50] In mid-February a reminder was sent to the pretors to implement the order meticulously: "In order to complete the evacuation of the Jews, I order you to carry out further raids on the villages, arrest Jews who are still there, and evacuate them to Berezovka, in accordance with the directives I sent you."[51]

Although there are no exact figures for the number of Jews in the southern districts who were liquidated by the Romanians, they certainly ran into the tens of thousands. In the cabinet session of 13 November Alexianu reported that eighty-five thousand Jews were sick with typhus "in the villages which they had come to," adding that they had to be deloused to prevent contamination of the Romanian soldiers. Antonescu's response to this was: "*Let them die.*"[52] This number evidently included the thirty thousand Bessarabian Jews who were sent to the Kingdom of Death, but not the Jews of Odessa, whose deportation began on 12 January 1942. A report from the Gendarmerie Inspectorate to the Transnistrian administration on 9 September 1942 on the deported Jews states that the Jews of the Berezovka, Ananyev, Ovidopol, and Ochakov districts "had disappeared" (*dispăruți*; i.e., had been exterminated), without specifying their numbers. The sixty-five thousand Jews of the Odessa district, the report stated, had also "disappeared."[53] Thus tens of thousands of Jews from the four southern districts disappeared, just as the Jews of Odessa had disappeared. These numbers also included Jews who had survived the military operations and first massacres perpetrated by the Einsatzgruppe units and the German and Romanian soldiers.

Judging by the reports of all the Romanian institutions that monitored the deportation operation, the local Russians rejoiced at the decision to deport the Jews. The General Staff's Second Section, which at the time was Antonescu's main source of information on the progress of the operation, portrayed the deportation as a security need in its reports. It claimed that the local population, troubled by the malicious rumors spread by the Jews and Communists regarding the progress of the war, breathed a sigh of relief upon learning of the establishment of the ghetto: "The Christian population is extremely satisfied with the decision to intern the Jews in the ghetto," while the Jews, who had expressed their hatred of Christians and threatened to wreak "a terrible revenge" on them, were now being contained. In summing up the report that supposedly expressed the sentiments of the local population the General Staff added that the decision to intern them in the ghetto "had come just in time."[54] The General Staff in particular was convinced that most Jewish men avoided reporting for deportation because they harbored plans to fight the Romanian army, and they believed that this was why most Jews reporting to the ghetto were women, children, and the elderly: "The Jews became increasingly depressed and despondent as, despite the inclement weather, their evacuation proceeded in an orderly fashion. Most of those reporting were children aged under 15 or people aged over 50. The vast majority of Jews aged 18–50 were in hiding or had disappeared from the city. Efforts were made to find them. With the start of the evacuation, the intensity of the slander [campaign] abated."[55]

The vast majority of Jewish men had been conscripted to the Soviet army at the outbreak of war, hanged in the streets of Odessa, shot in the city jail or in the trenches of Dalnic, or burnt alive in the wheat silos. As we shall see below, even when the police, the gendarmerie, and soldiers raided building after building they did not find many Jews age eighteen to fifty because by then hardly any Jews remained. For example, the same source reported that by 24 January 1942 (i.e., twelve days after the start of the deportations) 15,794 Jews, "most of them elderly people or destitute children," had been deported from Odessa, despite the continuation of the surprise raids.[56]

The first convoys of Jews left Odessa in late October 1941. They left Dalnic by foot for Bogdanovka, passing through Berezovka in early November. Jews from localities in the Odessa district that were situated close to the deportation routes were made to join the convoys. Milea Morduhovici, one of the few survivors of this deportation, age sixteen at the time, testified that the convoy was so large that she could not see "where it began and where it ended."[57] The convoys were accompanied by Romanian gendarmes and Ukrainian and Russian volunteer police. The deportees were marched along the Odessa-Berezovka road for several days. After stopping over in Berezovka for a few days they continued on foot to Mostovoye and then to Domanevka via Nikolayevka. Convoys of Bessarabian Jews who had been deported from Katarzi via the Tiraspol district as well as local Jews also ended up in Berezovka. These convoys were then taken to the Bogdanovka extermination camp (the Domanevka camp was not yet serving as an extermination camp but rather as a small labor camp).

It took the convoys two weeks to cover the 150 or kilometers so to Bogdanovka, mostly in pouring rain and bitterly cold weather. The deportees were given no food or water, and anyone unable to keep up was shot by the gendarmes. At night the Jews were taken to fields and forced to sit in the mud. The gendarmes searched the Jews for valuables and took anything they could lay their hand on, even clothes, and—together with the Ukrainian policemen—raped Jewish women and girls. In the morning the convoys re-formed. Anyone unable to stand up was shot by the gendarmes and left where he or she was, unburied. Despite the trail of bodies littering the deportation route, the number of deportees remained constant or even rose as Jews from the Odessa district who had been concentrated by the gendarmes on either side of the route took their place.[58]

The arrival of about forty thousand Jews from the Odessa district swelled the population of Bogdanovka to fifty-eight thousand, according to accurate data provided by Isopescu. In mid-November the army doctor from the unit stationed in the Domanevka subdistrict, where the Bogdanovka camp was situated, reported that "very large convoys, some of them comprising 10,000–12,000 people," had been brought over and constituted a source of typhus contamination.[59] These facts give some idea of the scope of the preliminary deportations from Odessa in October and the first half of November 1941.

The second stage of the deportations—the deportation by train—began on 12 January 1942 with the departure of the first convoy of 856 Jews for Berezovka. At the start of this phase gendarmerie headquarters estimated that 40,000 Jews remained in Odessa.[60] The operation was directed by: Gendarmerie Inspector

Petală, who oversaw the operation in Odessa; Constantin Ciurea, inspector of the Transnistrian administration, who directed the next stage of the operation from the Berezovka prefecture; and Col. Matei Velcescu, who coordinated the various authorities in Odessa in order to ensure that the deportations were carried out as rapidly as possible and who effectively conducted the operation on the ground.[61]

Many Jews who survived the atrocities of Odessa broke down in Berezovka. The burning of corpses at the terminus was another method adopted by the administration's medical service to prevent the spread of typhus, since the earth was as hard as metal in the terrible cold that prevailed and it was impossible to dig a mass grave and bury them. The sight of the crackling flames pressed home to the Jews that they were doomed. The fire and the stench of burnt flesh extinguished any lingering will to survive: "The car door creaked open, and we were blinded by roaring flames. I saw people shriveling in the flames. There was a strong smell of gasoline. People were being burnt alive."[62] Although most Jews thrown on the pyre were already dead, some were simply frozen stiff. The heat of the fire revived them briefly before taking their lives.[63]

Not all transports ended at Berezovka. An unknown number of deportees were taken farther north to Veselinovo, a German-Ukrainian locality controlled exclusively by the local SS, who expelled all Ukrainians from the town in order to create a purely German locality.[64] In both Veselinovo and Berezovka angry Romanian gendarmes awaited the deportees, beat them with clubs to hurry them along, and ordered them to remove the bodies from the trains and arrange them in piles, though the deportees were half-frozen themselves. The deportees were ordered off the train into a nearby field, where they were divided up arbitrarily, with no attempt to keep families together, and marched in different directions. Although the gendarmes allowed the Jews no respite, they themselves changed shifts frequently to avoid freezing.

On 17 January, five days after the start of the operation, Col. Emil Broşteanu, the commander of the Transnistrian gendarmerie, sent a progress report to the Transnistrian administration and gendarmerie headquarters in Bucharest describing the logistics of the deportation operation. The report is quoted here in full:

I have the honor of informing you that on 12 January 1942, the evacuation of the Jews from Odessa began. In accordance with the order of the Transnistrian Administration, the Jews about to be evacuated have been assembled in the ghettos, after each [Jew] has appeared before the Committee for the Assessment of Property [jewelry; Comisia de Evaluare a Averilor-bijuterii] and surrendered his money in return for RKKS. Convoys of 1,500–2,000 individuals are formed inside the ghetto and loaded onto German trains, which take them to Mostovoye-Veselyevo [Veselinovo], in the Berezovka district. From the Berezovka station, they are escorted to the relocation area. To date, 6,000 have been evacuated, and the transports are continuing daily.

It is very hard to find shelter for them in the relocation villages, because the Ukrainian population does not accept them. Consequently, many end up in the stables of the collective farms. The freezing temperature of -20 degrees, hunger, age and infirmity cause many of them to fall frozen by the wayside. The [gendarmerie] legion in Berezovka was recruited for this operation, but due to the freezing weather, the escorts must be constantly replaced. Bodies are strewn along the routes and buried in anti-tank trenches. It is almost impossible to find locals who are willing to bury the bodies—most are unwilling to undertake such tasks. We shall continue reporting on the progress of the operation.[65]

In its first summary report on the deportation operation gendarmerie headquarters repeated this version almost verbatim, updating only the number of deportees: "As of 22 January, 12,234 Jews have been evacuated out of a total of 40,000," the report stated.[66]

The depleted convoys proceeded to various destinations. An estimated four thousand to five thousand Jews were taken to the Bogdanovka and Domanevka camps in the Kingdom of Death—where tens of thousands of Odessan Jews had already been slaughtered. In Bogdanovka the burning of corpses was at its peak, and some of the new arrivals were taken straight to the pits, where they were shot and burnt. In Domanevka the liquidations continued, and the latest convoys met the same fate as their predecessors.

Several transports were directed to the local state farms, which had passed into Romanian hands in the part of the district that was not populated by ethnic Germans. Most of the convoys, however, were taken to makeshift camps in ethnic German villages in the Berezovka district, such as Chichrin, Huliyevka, Catousea, Suha-Verba, Gradovka, Bernadovka, Lisinovka, and Rastadt. The march to these camps was drawn out as long as possible in order to thin out the ranks along the way or, as one survivor put it, so that as many as possible would die a "natural death."[67]

Convoys sent to camps eighteen kilometers from the Berezovka train station were marched in circles for three days in the frozen, snow-covered wasteland. Most of the exhausted adults and children died in the fields. Each convoy was robbed by gendarmes, who seized anything of value: "They stripped us of our last possessions. By the time we reached Domanevka, we were paupers."[68] Although the freezing weather impeded rape, it did not stop it altogether.

On 16 March 1942 the Second Army Corps issued Special Order no. 9, the exact contents of which are unknown. The order instructed the garrison in Odessa to round up Jews—especially Jewish men—who had failed to report for deportation. Velcescu, who received a copy of the order, tried to wriggle out of it by claiming that such an assignment exceeded the brief of his committee, which in any case would be dissolved after the operation.[69] The order included instructions on how to "deal with" the Jews who were thus arrested, including the incarceration of men age sixteen to forty-eight in the central jail in Odessa "for endangering public order and security" and their transfer to a special camp in Vapniarca, central Transnistria. The order further contained provisions for the sorting of the remaining Jews, who were to be taken first to Berezovka and then "to their new destination"—the Kingdom of Death.[70]

In line with the order, several hundred Jewish men were transferred from the prison to the Vapniarca camp. Twenty-seven who were too sick to be moved were left behind. The order also included a secret directive concerning the execution of Jews who were found guilty during the screening operation. Most of the men arrested after the completion of the deportations were considered spies, tried, and executed. These executions were carried out in accordance with the provisions of Order no. 23, as interpreted by General Dăscălescu in an official communication he sent to the governor of Transnistria: "Yids who have hitherto escaped imprisonment shall be considered spies, in accordance with paragraph 8 of Order 23 issued by your Administration, and shall be punished accordingly."[71] On 11 April Velcescu informed General Dăscălescu that "the execution of [suspects] found to be of Jewish extraction shall be carried out by the Pretorate in the garrison in Odessa, as determined by the Second Army Corps."[72] On 15 May the Transnistrian administration ordered the execution of twenty-two Odessan Jews "who had been convicted." The execution was carried out in the Ochakov prison.[73] Although the number of Jewish youth and men arrested and executed under the order is unknown, the army was given carte blanche to treat the fugitives as spies and execute them without trial.

THE ABANDONED CHILDREN

The children left behind in the ghetto after each transport were yet another aspect of the enormous calamity the Romanians brought upon the community of one hundred thousand Jews. It also testified to the splintering of Jewish solidarity and to public and individual helplessness in the face of such cruel circumstances. The abandoned children continued to bother the Romanian occupation authorities even after the end of the deportation operation. In the

Central Evacuation Bureau's summary report Velcescu proposed a practical solution to the problem. "The abandoned children, 479 in all, aged 6–7 at the most, shall be evacuated as circumstances permit, together with the various convoys that shall still be leaving, by handing over each child to each healthy, able-bodied woman [*femeie validă*]."[74] The term *able-bodied woman* designated a relatively young woman who was not suffering from frostbite, was not encumbered by frozen parents, and had no young children of her own. No such women were to be found, however, either because the operation was nearing its end or because there were no more women left capable of looking after a child on their final journey.

In Odessa local policemen continued to arrest abandoned Jewish and half-Jewish children who had escaped deportation. As stated above, the directives determined that any Jew arrested after the end of the deportations was to be considered a criminal and court-martialed. The correspondence between Velcescu and the administration indicates that the military tribunal in Odessa that "heard" the cases decided to intern "all Jewish children under ten" in the Jewish hospital in the former Slobodka ghetto.[75] The military prosecutor, Col. Soltan Chirilă, even sent a written clarification to the prefecture, stating, "In accordance with the Administration's directives, Jewish children under 10 shall not be evacuated, but shall, for the time being, be sent to the Children's Hospital in Slobodka."[76] Most of these children were eventually sent to Akmechetka and exterminated.

OTHER PROBLEMS

The deportation of Odessan Jewry gave rise to a number of special problems, of which the abandoned children were but one. Another problem related to Jews of mixed marriage and half-Jews (*Mischlinge*). Order no. 9 of 16 March 1942 — a secret order issued by the Second Army Corps — referred to Jews who were caught toward the end of and after the deportation operation as "suspects." The order mandated that these suspects were to be imprisoned in the central jail, and after being put through a selection process, the men were to be executed. The order called for the establishment of "a selection committee" to "check the prisoners' Jewish nationality."[77] These checks, which were conducted inside the prison, were designed in part to ascertain whether the prisoners were circumcised. Since most Jewish men in the Ukraine were, the prisoners were doomed from the outset.

The intelligence and counterespionage agencies run by the army, the Siguranța, the gendarmerie, and the Transnistrian administration continued their anti-Jewish incitement even after Odessa was Judenrein. Their accusation that Jews were responsible for disseminating "Communist propaganda among the civilian population, the workers and the army" fueled Antonescu's hatred of Romanian Jews and Jews in all places under Romanian control. Antonescu believed that that the Romanians had to be warned of this Jewish conspiracy: "The radio and press must notify the population not to be led astray by criminal elements that are backed by the Yids and other enemies of the nation that aspire to undermine the nation by all means."[78]

The various declarations and directives issued by Antonescu in cabinet sessions and on other occasions confirm that he hated the Jews of Odessa most, even after they were deported and murdered in Berezovka and in the Kingdom of Death. The policy of rendering Odessa Judenrein succeeded beyond all expectations. Only Karaite Jews—an estimated one thousand families—and a few thousand individuals who possessed false papers managed to survive.

Odessa at the time was not large enough for Jews to hide in or remain anonymous without arousing suspicions, and denunciations were commonplace throughout the Romanian occupation, although some Russians and Ukrainians risked their lives to hide and feed Jews. As the authors of the *Black Book* put it: "Under such circumstances, a mere word of comfort, a gentle look, a sip of water or crust of bread proffered to a Jewish child endangered the lives of the Russians or Ukrainians."[79] Uncircumcised Jewish boys around the age of ten who had left their former neighborhoods had the best chance of surviving. After the deportations the Romanian authorities, as stated, arrested many circumcised children and sent them to the Children's Hospital in the abandoned Slobodka ghetto.[80]

THE LOOTING OF JEWISH PROPERTY IN ODESSA

In a cabinet session of 13 November 1941 in which the question of the property of the Bessarabian Jewish deportees was debated Antonescu declared, "Jewish property belongs to the Romanian State."[81] If this were true for Bessarabian Jews, whose Romanian citizenship had not been revoked by any law, it was even more true for the Transnistrian Jews, who were citizens of an enemy state. Indeed, on 21 January 1942 the Transnistrian administration sent a telegram to all its prefects notifying them of the imminent arrival of the representatives of the national bank and explaining that all Jewish property "belongs to the State."[82] Concomitantly, measures were taken, albeit somewhat belatedly, "to prevent the transfer of looted goods" to Bessarabia and beyond. On 4 December 1941 Antonescu's military cabinet established transit checkpoints and ordered the prefects, who were authorized to deliver transit permits, to describe "items the holders of permits may take with [them]" to the homeland.[83]

Although the looting of Jewish property in Odessa was no secret both during and after Antonescu's rule, its full extent came to light only after materials in Soviet archives became available after the collapse of the Soviet Union. Due to space limitations, we shall mention only a small part of the documentation that has recently come to light. Suffice it to say that in Odessa, too, the looting took place on two levels: official looting on behalf of the Romanian state and unofficial looting by members of the Romanian administration and the army to line their own pockets. Tens of thousands of Jews who were marched from Odessa in October–November 1941 were robbed by local gendarmes and policemen. The property thus confiscated never reached the vaults of the National Bank of Romania. The authorities learned their lesson. When the second wave of deportations (by train) began in January–March 1942, seven Committees for the Registration and Confiscation of Property were set up to conduct physical and gynecological searches, among other things. In the cabinet session of 16 December 1941 Antonescu himself, driven by his fanatical hatred of Odessan Jewry, ordered Alexianu to draw up a list of valuables taken from the Jews prior to their deportation.

The official looting was implemented with the help of representatives of the National Bank of Romania and of the Finance Ministry and was supervised by the Romanian General Staff. The theft of valuables and money from the Jews of Odessa prior to their deportation by train and Antonescu's personal involvement in the operation have been described in the chapter on the National Bank of Romania (chap. 23). It is worth noting that the deportation did not begin until the representatives of the national bank arrived on the scene. On 13 January 1942 Alexianu cabled the Presidency of the Council of Ministers to notify Antonescu that the representatives of the national bank had arrived.[84] Toward the end of the operation Alexianu informed all prefects (who had not been visited by representatives of the national bank) that "all valuables taken from the Jewish population" must be stamped, sorted, registered, and described before being delivered to the administration.[85]

Apart from valuables and cash, abandoned Jewish homes were also looted. Some apartments were robbed by Russians when the Jews were ordered to move to the first ghetto. On 13 January, a day after the first convoy left Odessa, Pântea, the mayor of Odessa, issued Order no. 18, stating that the apartments of Jews "that had been abandoned during the evacuation without having been registered" would be sealed by the housing supervisors and their contents preserved "in their entirety," pending further instructions. Meanwhile, the housing supervisors and neighborhood commissioners were ordered to monitor the inventory of all objects remaining in the houses. Any infringements of the order were punishable under martial law.[86] Needless to say, these laws never deterred members of the administration, the municipality, the police, or the gendarmerie from stealing Jewish property. Jewish apartments and property were up for grabs. The first claimants were officials from the government and municipal authorities who came in the thousands from Romania. Velcescu cabled Alexianu at the height of the deportation asking if "in principle, the apartments left behind following the evacuation of the Jews could be used by civil servants arriving from the homeland." Alexianu authorized the Central Evacuation Bureau to allocate Jewish apartments, but only "after their contents had been registered and transferred [to warehouses]."[87]

Friction arose between the Romanian administration in Odessa and the Germans — military officials and the Volksdeutschen — concerning Jewish property. Velcescu, who by virtue of his position was also in charge of Jewish property that was left in the city, was asked by the Germans, too, to give them a share in the looted property. The issue of the distribution of Jewish property even reached Antonescu's military cabinet.

In the case of Odessa the General Staff reported irregularities to the German military mission in Bucharest. Alexianu himself informed Oberführer Horst Hoffmeyer (commander of Sonderkommando Russland; see chap. 28), who was stationed in the German town of Landau in the Berezovka district, that the deputy prime minister, Mihai Antonescu, and the German military mission were handling the matter. Alexianu asked Hoffmeyer to instruct his men in Odessa to address requests for apartments to the mayor rather than to act on their own initiative.[88]

In June 1942 an agreement between Alexianu and Hoffmeyer turned the Jewish theater in Odessa into the German House (Deutsche Haus), a recreation facility for German visitors to the city. On 14 June 1942 Alexianu was invited to attend the inauguration of the German House. A few days earlier he had agreed to equip hostels for German NCOs with furniture, mattresses, lamps, and the like "from the municipal warehouses."[89] The Alexianu-Hoffmeyer agreement of August 1942 allowed ethnic Germans in Odessa to take over the apartments of Jews who "had left," after paying the Romanian authorities for the furniture. In Odessa there were more vacant Jewish apartments than prospective occupants. In October 1942 a Romanian-German committee was established to examine, register, and redistribute Jewish property that had been confiscated or looted in Odessa.[90]

After February 1942 the Transnistrian administration, the various offices of which had gradually been transferred to Odessa, coordinated the looting operation throughout Transnistria. It issued instructions for the confiscation of Jewish property for the state and for the National Bank of Romania and received progress reports on the operation. The administration's files on the looting operation have been preserved intact. No less than four of its sessions were devoted to "the completion of an inventory of valuables of the Jewish population."[91] All in all, the looting of Jewish property was such an important issue that both the prefects' instructions and his reports were cabled to Alexianu to enable him to assemble the data swiftly and report back to Bucharest on the progress of the operation.

The massacre of Odessan Jewry and the deportation of sixty-five thousand Jews infused new life into the Odessan economy. The reduction in the number of inhabitants and the elimination of Jews as a productive element in economic life eased unemployment. Living conditions improved and with them, public satisfaction, especially in light of rumors of German brutality in parts of the Ukraine under German occupation. Some even went so far as to call the economic "miracle" in Odessa the new NEP.[92] Shops selling goods looted by local citizens or Romanians proliferated. Coins, jewelry, and gold objects changed hands. The government in Bucharest, in an attempt to restore this precious metal to the state treasury, even launched an operation to purchase gold on the black market.[93]

The correlation between the liquidation of the Jews and Odessa's economic revival was stressed in the Romanian press in the city, which was overtly anti-semitic and vilified the Jews even after Odessa was Judenrein. All Russian, Ukrainian, and Romanian radio stations, newspapers, and printing houses were subordinate to the administration's Cultural Department, run by the renowned Romanian sociologist Traian Herseni, a former member of the Legionary movement. An antisemitic article in the Romanian press in Odessa reported:

> Yesterday's Odessa greeted its visitors with the stench of the Yids filthy diapers and mountains of putrid garbage. . . . A constant hum filled the air, like a hornets' nest. It was easy to believe that the place was inhabited by Yids only. They scurried around in its streets, piled into its shops, gathered in herds by the doors. . . . Their increasing arrogance has rendered them abhorrent. . . . Their women walk through the street with unkempt hair, and soiled dresses worn inside out. The men . . . walk around with their shirts untucked, and their ties askew. [Under the Soviets] Yiddish became the official language. The theaters were closed down, and cultural life came to a complete standstill.[94]

The fate of Odessan Jewry was sealed by Antonescu and the Romanian military and civilian authorities in the city, who harbored a profound hatred of the Jews, whom they considered Communists and enemies of the Romanian state. The Jews of Odessa were turned into scapegoats for the ignominious defeat of the

Romanian army during the battle for Odessa and for the painful and excessive losses it sustained in this battle. This Romanian reprisal operation was made possible once the Romanians had discarded their humanitarian "constraints" — following the Nazi example, from the moment they crossed the borders of the Soviet Union. In this way the Romanians may be said to have both "killed and even inherited" the Jews of Odessa and southern Transnistria.[95]

28

The Berezovka District

Most of the thirty-four thousand Jews who were deported by train from Odessa by the Romanians between January and March 1942 were murdered and buried in the Berezovka district. They were killed by special units of the local Germans under orders from ss officers, with the full acquiescence of the Romanian authorities. The corpses of most of those murdered were burnt, not buried. A railway line ran 180 kilometers through the district linking Odessa with the Reichskommissariat Ukraine: Odessa–Berezovka–Veselinovo–Voznesensk. The farthest station, Voznesensk, was on the far side of the Bug (in the Reichskommissariat). The Berezovka district bordered the Odessa and Ochakov districts to the south, the Ananyev district to the west, the Golta district to the north, and the River Bug to the east. Across the Bug was the Generalkommissariat Nikolayev, part of the Reichskommissariat Ukraine, headed by a generalkommissar. The Nikolayev region, which under German occupation was equal in size to the whole of Transnistria and was itself divided into districts (*Kriegsgebiete*), was headed by a gebietskommissar. The Berezovka district was divided into three subdistricts—Berezovka, Mostovoye, and Landau. It comprised 53 large villages, 171 kolkhozes (collective farms), and 5 sovkhozes (state farms). Although it stretched over an area of 2,816 square kilometers it had only 58,499 inhabitants, of whom 20 percent (about 11,700) were Germans, 70 percent Ukrainians, 5 percent Romanians, and 4 percent Russians.[1]

On 10 August 1941 units of the German Eleventh Army captured the town of Berezovka and stayed there for a while. Berezovka's Jews, who in 1926 had numbered 3,223, or about 42 percent of the total population, disappeared entirely from the town. Some fled, others were murdered. Starting in October 1941 whoever was caught was deported northward to the Kingdom of Death in massive convoys that were marched through the district. After the Romanian administration established itself in the area in early September it conducted a census that showed that there were 4,750 inhabitants in the town, of whom 75 percent were Ukrainians, 10 percent Russians, and approximately 20 percent Germans. Since there were no longer any Jews there, there was no need to establish a ghetto. To the north, in the village of Krivorushiko, in the Veselinovo subdistrict, the gendarmes came across a camp containing about 500 Jews that had been set up by the Germans.[2] The second most important town for our purposes was Mostovoye, twenty-six kilometers northeast of Berezovka on the route to the Kingdom of Death. Prior to its capture several hundred Jews had lived in this town, which, at the start of the Romanian occupation, had 1,013 inhabitants, of whom 93 percent were Ukrainians. Most of its Jews were murdered by the German and Romanian occupiers, while those who remained were marched northward to Domanevka. On 27 August 1941 Alexianu appointed Col. Constantin Loghin as prefect of the district.[3] With the failure of the original plan to dump the Jewish convoys across the Bug, as stipulated in the Tighina Agreement, the Berezovka district was selected as the extermination site for the Jews of Odessa.

THE ETHNIC GERMANS

In 1941 Transnistria had the largest concentration of ethnic Germans in the Ukraine. A census conducted by the Germans in early 1943 determined that there were 130,866 ethnic Germans living in Transnistria out of a total of 169,074 in the entire territory of the Reichskommissariat Ukraine.[4] About 100,000 of them were scattered in villages and towns throughout the expanded Odessa district (which encompassed most of southern Transnistria under Soviet rule) and surrounded Odessa on all sides.[5] The ethnic Germans in the Odessa region comprised about 40 percent of the Soviet Germans in the territories under German occupation. According to the 1926 census ethnic Germans comprised 8.3 percent of the population of the Odessa district and 15.3 percent of its rural population. Based on German wartime data, there were more than thirty German villages in Transnistria, each with a population exceeding 1,000.

Convoys of Jews from Bessarabia were marched past German villages north of the Dniester estuary, northwest of Odessa, and east of Tiraspol. Convoys of Jews being marched from Odessa and from southern Transnistria passed by dozens of German villages on their way to the Kingdom of Death. One witness, whose testimony is quoted in the chapter on the Kingdom of Death, described the bloodthirstiness of the new German recruits to the SS units and how they shot directly into the Jewish masses.[6]

The units of Einsatzgruppe D operated within the ethnic German population in the Odessa district and stationed themselves in the German villages. The Einsatzgruppe comprised about five hundred men. Secondary units of Einsatzgruppe D arrived in the German areas of the Odessa district in the second half of August 1941, after conducting killing operations in Bukovina and Bessarabia.[7]

The assignments of Einsatzgruppe D in the Ukraine were, first, to purge the area of Jews, Communists, and groups of partisans; and second, to defend and look after the German localities. Einsatzgruppe units moved about, as mentioned, in concert with and attached to army units; as they entered an area they immediately set about exterminating civilians, first and foremost Jews and Jewish prisoners of war, as well as commissars and Communists in general. An Einsatzgruppe activity report stated in simple terms that "the area of operations of the commando units had become empty of Jews."[8] The Communist witch hunt also included ethnic Germans (*Volksdeutschen*), and those who were Communists or suspected of being such were also executed. Moreover, in the German localities the Einsatzgruppe and the Sonderkommando executed Jews who were married to Germans as well as their children, in keeping with the policy of preserving the purity of the German race.[9]

Another Nazi institution, which replaced Einsatzgruppe D and organized and deployed the ethnic Germans in Transnistria, turning them into part of the extermination machinery for the liquidation of the Jewish people, was the Volksdeutsche Mittelstelle, known as the VoMi, or Liaison Office for Ethnic German Affairs. Founded at the start of 1937, this organization was headed by SS Gen. Werner Lorenz. The VoMi was placed under the SS's control and had authority over all ethnic German organizations in the Reich and neighboring countries. In 1939, for example, the VoMi was involved in the transfer to Germany of Germans from the Baltic countries that were annexed by the Soviet Union. The VoMi was subordinate to Himmler in his capacity as commissar for the strengthening of German ethnicity. In Transnistria the VoMi established on 20 September 1941 Sonderkommando Russland (SkR), an extermination unit composed of ethnic Germans. Himmler entrusted the VoMi with the task of "controlling the local Germans in the occupied territory of the Soviet Union," or in other words, recruiting them for the purposes of the German motherland.[10] The members of the SkR in Transnistria were therefore members of the SS.

Even before any agreements were signed with the Romanian authorities the SkR established a "state within a state" in Transnistria, recruiting the local population in the service of the Reich. The gendarmes did not set foot in the territory under SkR control other than to carry out patrols. This area encompassed more than just the German villages and towns, because the Germans regained some of the lands that had belonged to them before the Bolshevik Revolution. The Berezovka district had forty-two German villages (with a population totaling

16,200), of which twelve were in the Landau subdistrict and the remainder in other subdistricts.[11] The Ochakov district had twenty-two German villages with 7,720 inhabitants.[12] The Ovidopol district had sixteen large German villages, ten of which were in the Franzenfeld subdistrict and five in the Bilaevka subdistrict, and five smaller villages.[13] The Dubossary district had eighteen German villages and one state farm (sovkhoz).[14] The Tiraspol district had three German villages.[15] The Golta district had only one German village. The Odessa district had thirty-one German villages scattered throughout its subdistricts.[16]

The process of *Gleichschaltung*, or the imposition of Nazi ideology over German organizations and people, was very rapid. The liquidation of Communists and *Mischlinge* (the offspring of mixed Jewish-German marriages), the SS's billeting in the villages, intensive military exercises, and the hatred of the Soviet regime that had ousted so many from their land and exiled thousands to Siberia all created the conditions for the rapid recruitment of ethnic Germans to the Nazi organizations, casting terror over the Ukrainians as well as the Jews.

AGREEMENTS WITH THE ROMANIANS

Initially the VoMi completely ignored the presence of the Romanian authorities and acted as they saw fit. They drove out the representatives of the Romanian authorities, gendarmes, army officers, and administrative staff who tried to settle in the villages as well as collectors of confiscated property and supply officers and ordered the German inhabitants to obey only their men and the village mayors, appointed by them from among the local Germans. On 30 November 1941 the pretor of the Birzula subdistrict in the Rybnitsa district, bordering Bessarabia, which was also populated by thousands of Romanians, reported to the district prefect that a representative of Hoffmeyer had informed him directly that "all Germans in the Birzula subdistrict shall obey the Birzula German authorities only. We are forbidden to take anything from their . . . kolkhozes and they will not even pay taxes to the [Romanian] State. . . . He did not present any written document, but said this was the order of Marshal Antonescu."[17]

The officer in charge of the unit for the collection of confiscated property in Transnistria left a faithful description of the "state within a state" that Himmler's envoys established within the German-populated areas of Transnistria: "The German inhabitants who are organized in each locality into Gaue [subdistricts] carry green identity cards indicating in both German and Romanian that they are under the protection of the Great Reich and that the civilian and military authorities are required to assist them whenever they ask for help. They spurn every ruling of the Romanian authorities, and if they are taken in for questioning, German soldiers immediately spring to their defense."[18]

Under the guidance of the VoMi officers the SkR implemented a German plan to concentrate ethnic Germans in specific locations, forcibly evict Ukrainians as well as Romanians from these locations, take over land, and confiscate livestock, agricultural implements, and machinery. German families were evicted from more than 200 villages in which they constituted a minority and were transferred to 228 villages and to Odessa (from which Ukrainian and other inhabitants were evicted as necessary) with the objective of turning those areas into pure German localities. The evictions and resettlement were carried out under orders of the VoMi in total disregard of anyone's wishes, even those of the Germans themselves.[19] The operation, carried out in parallel with military exercises, received post factum recognition by the Romanian authorities in executed agreements. It is also worth noting that the SkR did not recognize the borders of Transnistria and therefore moved freely back and forth across the Bug, between Transnistria and the Reichskommissariat Ukraine.

The ethnic Germans in Transnistria participated as necessary in the mass murder operations that were carried out in nearby areas. German military trucks transported them from place to place with impunity — the Romanian soldiers of the border guard did not dare stop or even search them. Thus, for example, in the summer of 1942 the commander of the gendarmerie legion in Ovidopol reported that young Germans from German villages had been recruited and taken to German military headquarters in Odessa for transfer to the garrison in Kiev.[20]

As the war continued the ethnic Germans in Transnistria became the focus of increasing attention from Dr. Georg Leibbrandt, the deputy of Alfred Rosenberg, minister for the occupied eastern territories, who was himself an ethnic German, a native of Odessa. In the summer of 1942 SS General Lorenz visited the ethnic German communities in Transnistria and sent a positive report to Himmler regarding their economic achievements and the great improvement in their condition compared with the ethnic Germans in the part of the Ukraine that was under the Reich's control. These achievements were due to the privileges granted the local Germans by the Romanian authorities through various agreements, the structure and discipline the VoMi imposed on them, and the horror their units inflicted on the surrounding area.[21]

The Tighina Agreement made no reference to the ethnic Germans. It granted Romania the right to benefit from the economic exploitation of Transnistria but forced upon it administrative advisors, economic advisors, German army liaison headquarters in Odessa, and joint accounting of war booty. The agreement ensured the removal of agricultural officers of the German Eleventh Army from Transnistria. These agricultural officers collected booty, crops, and other goods.[22]

The status of the German communities in Transnistria was determined by contacts and negotiations that took place between Bucharest and Odessa. Correspondence between the German ambassador, Manfred von Killinger, and Mihai Antonescu in November 1941 made it clear to the Romanians that the VoMi would be the sole representative of the ethnic Germans in Transnistria. Governor Alexianu and his prefects were called upon to cooperate with Hoffmeyer and with the commanders of the subregions on all issues relating to the status of the Germans.[23] Following this correspondence, Alexianu and Hoffmeyer met in Odessa on 8 December, and on 13 December 1941 they signed an understanding in Tiraspol officially recognizing the existence of "a state within a state" that the SS representatives had already established in Transnistria. The understanding determined that the administration of the Volksdeutschen was entrusted to the VoMi, which would have sole authority to decide who belonged to the German race and to issue certificates attesting to this. The Romanian authorities agreed retroactively to the resettlement of the Germans and the transfer of non-Germans but objected to the resettlement of Romanians who had not yet been evicted from those communities selected to become purely German. It was the VoMi that appointed the village mayors and oversaw the administration of the villages. Eventually the Romanian administration recognized the existence of the self-defense units that were "armed and trained by the VoMi's SS headquarters and subordinate only to it."[24] The understanding preserved the kolkhozes, to the Volksdeutschen's chagrin, prohibited the division of land, permitted fourteen German firms of the Reich to do business with Transnistria and export their products to Germany, and exempted the Germans from paying taxes. Its sole requirement was that the ethnic Germans transfer 50 percent of their agricultural output to the Romanian administration through the VoMi. The understanding formally recognized the "extension of the sovereignty of the Romanian State over all German subdistricts," a right that in theory was denied it until the agreement. Yet even after this formal recognition the SS acted as if Romanian sovereignty was nonexistent.

THE LIQUIDATION OF THE JEWS OF ODESSA

In the deposition he submitted to the People's Court prior to the delivery of its verdict, Alexianu claimed that he was not in any way responsible for the massacre of the Jews of Odessa. He admitted, however, that he "was aware" at the time that fifteen thousand to twenty thousand Jews had been massacred.

According to him, the remaining ten thousand to twelve thousand Jews were considered a danger by both the Romanian and German armies and were therefore rounded up by the gendarmerie and incarcerated in the Slobodka ghetto.[25]

Antonescu was not willing to wait for an overall German solution to the Jewish problem (as decided, in the final analysis, at the Wannsee Conference) and said as much in the government session of 16 December 1941, in which he announced that he had decided to evacuate the Jews from Odessa. He told Alexianu that, as far as he was concerned, Alexianu could throw them into the Black Sea. He was not bothered by how many would die. For his part, all of them could die.[26] Alexianu kept silent on this issue. The correspondence between the Transnistrian administration and the gebietskommissar of Nikolayev (area commissioner in the German occupied zone), as revealed after the Soviet archives became available, clarifies one of the little-known aspects of the genocide perpetrated by the Romanians. Contrary to previously held views, the first convoys of Jews who were taken to Berezovka and Veselinovo were not immediately relocated to German villages in the Berezovka district but were marched directly to the Bug for transfer to the German side, come what may. In a telegram he sent on 5 March 1942 Gebietskommissar Shlutter warned the prefect of Berezovka about the immense epidemiological catastrophe created by the Romanian authorities on the banks of the Bug: "70,000 Jews have been concentrated on the Romanian side of the Bug and abandoned to their fate. They are dying of hunger and cold. Typhus has spread among the Jews . . . and they are also endangering German territory."[27] Alexianu requested that the terms of the Tighina Agreement, which provided for the evacuation of Jews to the German occupied zone, be honored and asked to know "if the convention [the Tighina Agreement] could be applied."[28] Generalkommissar Oppermann of Nikolayev, Schlutter's superior, sent a second telegram to Alexianu on 14 February, asking "that immediate measures be adopted in order to save the army units, and the German Administration and population [the Volksdeutschen]. . . . Each day a large number of Jews die and are superficially buried."[29] On 16 February, when the translated telegram was presented to Alexianu, he jotted on the telegram, "And what was our answer?" Alexianu's deputy, Emil Cercavschi, wrote back, *"We answered Commissioner General Oppermann that we have taken measures to burn the Jewish corpses."*[30] The German legation in Bucharest was not officially advised of the decision to burn the corpses, and on 13 March the German legation's adviser, Dr. Gerhard Steltzer, asked that the Romanians stop driving Jews from the Berezovka district to the German occupied zone across the Bug. He added that, so far, two convoys of 14,500 Jews had been sent over and another 60,000 were ready to be moved.[31]

Was anyone aware that the Romanians intended to apply the Bogdanovka method for stopping the spread of the typhus epidemic to the Berezovka subdistrict, too? The exchange of telegrams between Generalkommissar Oppermann and Alexianu's deputy, Cercavschi, at the end of February is instructive. The Romanian response was communicated only verbally to the senior representative of the Wehrmacht in Transnistria, Gen. Panthen von Rottkirch, commander of liaison headquarters, who was in no apparent hurry to inform Oppermann or Rosenberg of the Transnistrian administration's decision to burn the corpses of the Jews who had died or been murdered in the Berezovka district, near the Bug. Oppermann sent another telegram to Alexianu on 25 February in response to the first telegram he had received, in which he stressed that Article 7 of the Tighina Agreement was not valid "since the military campaigns in the East had not yet ended." He requested that the concentrations of Jews on the western side of the Bug be moved fifty kilometers away.[32] Cercavschi's response, on behalf of Alexianu, is instructive. Instead of informing Oppermann of the Transnistrian administration's decision, Cercavschi referred him to "Lieutenant General von Rottkirch."[33]

The practical arrangements for the monitoring of the murders and burial or burning of corpses were concocted in periodic meetings between Alexianu and Hoffmeyer. These arrangements were summarized orally. No documents were left. Nevertheless, Alexianu and the leaders of the administration never imagined that the administration's files would one day be open to historians. They therefore took the liberty of jotting notes and instructions in the margins of documents, reports, and telegrams concerning the burning of Jewish corpses, the disposal of corpses scattered in the fields, agreements that allowed them to drive convoys of tens of thousands of Jews across the Bug, and so on.

The murder of the Jews was not the most important item on the Transnistrian administration's agenda or in its practical arrangements with the VoMi. Once the procedures for cooperation over the extermination of the Jews were established in the Berezovka district and most Odessan Jews were no longer alive, Eichmann produced a memorandum on "the deportation of *Romanian* Jews to the Reichskommissariat Ukraine." In it, Eichmann, the Nazi expert on the extermination of Jews, analyzed the differences between the extermination methods used by the Nazis and those adopted by the Romanians. After repeating the error that the seventy thousand Jews who were concentrated in the vicinity of the Bug were "Romanian" Jews, Eichmann praised the Romanians' aspirations to be rid of the Jews (*Entjudungbestrebungen*) but added that "at present" their campaign was not welcome. Although Eichmann agreed with the deportations "in principle," he censured the "lack of order and supervision" in the deportation of thousands of Jews to the Reichskommissariat Ukraine, which placed both the German forces and the local inhabitants at risk of epidemics, food contamination, and so on. "Among other things, these *unplanned and premature* evacuations of Romanian Jews to the occupied territories in the East seriously endanger the [operation] of the deportation of the German Jews, which is presently being carried out. I therefore request the intervention of the Romanian government to put an immediate end to these *illegal* transports of Jews."[34]

Eichmann recommended that if the Romanians continued to drive Jews across the Bug the SD should be given a free hand to deal with the situation. To put Eichmann's comments into perspective, it should be recalled that this senior official of Reich security had no jurisdiction over the security police in Ukraine, the Einsatzgruppe men, or the VoMi, which were accountable to Himmler alone.[35] After Ambassador von Killinger contacted Mihai Antonescu on this matter, Antonescu summoned Alexianu to Bucharest to report to him and promised him a prompt reply.[36] On 12 May 1942 the Foreign Ministry in Berlin informed Rosenberg that it had contacted the Romanian government and that the embassy in Bucharest had cabled that Governor Alexianu would shortly be arriving in Bucharest to report to Mihai Antonescu, following which "the Deputy Head of State will clarify the Romanian position." However, a Foreign Ministry official added to Franz Rademacher's letter (Rademacher was head of the Jewish desk at the Foreign Ministry) that "meanwhile, 28,000 Jews had been brought to German villages in Transnistria and liquidated."[37] He was referring to the majority of Odessa's Jews, who had been deported by train.

THE TRANSFER OF DEPORTEES FROM
ROMANIA TO SS UNITS ACROSS THE BUG

The Transnistrian administration handed over Jewish deportees from Romania as well as Ukrainian Jews to the German administration in Ukraine and to the SS units of ethnic Germans. After exterminating the majority of local Ukrainian Jews the Germans found themselves without laborers when, in 1942, they began construction of the Durchgangstrasse IV, the vital strategic highway linking Poland with the southern Ukraine. The highway began at Lvov and extended to Stalino, north of the Sea of Azov, east of Rostov—the gateway to the Caucasus and Stalingrad. The highway also passed through localities on the eastern bank of the Bug in which labor camps had been set up. These labor camps later became death camps for deportees from Romania who were handed over to the Nazis by the Transnistrian administration: Nemirov, Bratslav (to the west of the Bug), Gaysin, Ivangorod, Uman, and Kirovograd, among others. The German construction company Todt, which carried out building projects in the territory occupied by Germany, supervised this project. The German companies it hired as subcontractors brought engineers, technicians, craftsmen, and supervisors into the region.

SS units comprising ethnic Germans, which had been established on the German side of the Bug, periodically crossed over to the Romanian side and brought back thousands of Jews handed over by the gendarmes (including Jews from the Dorohoi district in the Regat) to carry out the construction work. Ukrainian policemen on the German side and Lithuanians from the volunteer units that were brought over from Lithuania helped guard and exterminate the Jews. Although we do not know exactly how many Jews were handed over by the Romanians for this purpose, there were at least fifteen thousand.

In spring–summer 1943, after the battle of Stalingrad, the Romanians suspended their mass murder operations in Transnistria. A witness captured in one sentence the difference between the two administrations: on the German side the Jews knew they were doomed at the outset, whereas on the Romanian side, after Stalingrad, they retained a flicker of hope of staying alive. The encounter between the Jews, usually whole families deported in the summer of 1942 whose mother tongue was German, and the ethnic Germans and Germans of the Reich who became their overlords, worked them to death, and set the date of their extermination is a chapter in its own right that has yet to be recorded: "In addition to the indescribable suffering, there was the constant fear of death, because every day they made it clear to us that eventually they would exterminate us—shoot us dead. . . . The Germans murdered incessantly . . . these SS assassins, devout Christians, Catholic and Protestant Bible-lovers, received quality food and high salaries. Fear of God ceased to exist. None of them even attempted to prevent acts of cruelty or murder. They were all the same, they all murdered to satisfy their blood lust, with the justification that they were merely carrying out orders from above."[38]

Although the topic of the German labor camps across the Bug is beyond the scope of this study, it deserves to be researched in its own right. Access to the archives in the Ukraine facilitated research, for the first time, into the Romanian authorities' complicity in turning Jews over to the SS units in the Reichskommissariat Ukraine. What is clear is that the Romanian administration in Transnistria knew the implications of handing over Jews to the SS units, and no transfer was done without its knowledge and approval. The governor of Transnistria considered the transfer of Jews both as a means of exterminating them and as a punitive measure designed to force the deportees to work. At the Eighth Conference of Prefects and Senior Officials of the Administration, which was convened in Odessa on 20 September 1942 in order to review the administration's achievements during the first year of occupation, Governor Alexianu addressed the prefects: "Those prefects who have *Jews and Gypsies* under their jurisdiction must put them to work, regardless of the framework, in accordance with Order [no. 23] and other directives that have been issued. Those who are unwilling to work shall be transferred across the Bug where they are accepted."[39]

SOVIET SOURCES ON ROMANIAN
EXTERMINATION OPERATIONS

On 10 April 1944 the Soviet army entered Odessa after a short but tough battle on the city outskirts. On 12 April Tiraspol was captured, and by 16 April the whole of Transnistria was in Soviet hands. Prior to the liberation, however, the inhabitants of Odessa (and all Transnistria) had a taste of life under German occupation after the city was handed over to the Germans in February 1944. Before withdrawing the German army blew up the port as well as most of the factories and some other important buildings. Likewise, before leaving, the Transnistrian administration and many Romanian officers looted treasures and large amounts of property for the Romanian state and for themselves, which they shipped to Romania in trains and trucks. The British journalist Alexander Werth, who lived in the Soviet Union during the Second World War, visited Odessa immediately upon its liberation and again in March 1945. "One could live," a young Russian inhabitant of the city told him. The Romanians did not interfere too much in the citizens' lives. There was plenty of food in the markets, and the Romanian soldiers always had something to sell. When Werth inquired what happened to the Jews, however, he received the following reply: "[The Romanians] say they bumped off an awful lot of them, but I didn't see it. Some were allowed to escape—with a little money, you could buy *anything* from the Romanians. . . . They said that if so many Jews were bumped off, it was because the Germans had demanded it. 'No dead Jews, no Odessa,' they said. Anyway, that's what the Romanians told us."[40]

Werth never met a single Jew who had hidden in Odessa during the period of Romanian rule, although there were a few. It should be noted in this context that as the liberation approached "a non-totalitarian image" of the Romanian administration, as the historian Alexander Dallin put it, emerged in Transnistria. Although this administration was corrupt through and through, it did not establish any extermination or concentration camps in its territory nor arrest inhabitants and exile them to Romania. Although it plundered the country, it left its citizens enough food and, most important, its representatives did not behave as if they were members of a superior race. Finally, it was an administration that, in its final days, was viewed "with contempt and almost pity" by the local population.[41] The Romanians, wrote Dallin in his chapter on Transnistria, "were considerably more lax than the Germans. Romanian rule lacked much of the extremism, racism, superciliousness and rigidity of German rule."[42]

This image of a nontotalitarian Romanian administration in Transnistria is reinforced by Soviet sources. On 13 June 1944 the official report of the Soviet special commission of inquiry into crimes committed by the Romanians in Transnistria, headed by A. C. Kolybanov, was published.[43] Unlike reports on other occupied territories, this document focused mainly on the corruption of the occupying Romanian authorities and German acts of destruction before they left Transnistria and Odessa in April 1944. Only at the end were "atrocities" referred to. The Soviet commission of inquiry failed to mention that most of the victims of the atrocities perpetrated by the Romanians were Jews. "On the contrary, the document took considerable pains to give non–Jewish names of a few sample victims as if to reinforce the reader's impression that the Soviet citizens were exposed to murder and abomination." Although the report stated that some two hundred thousand citizens were liquidated in Transnistria, it did not clarify whether this number included prisoners of war, Jews who were not local inhabitants, or other groups. Again, although the report confirmed that several Romanian and German generals and officers (whose names it managed to get wrong) were "war criminals," it never mentioned that they murdered or instigated the murder of Jews. The strongest accusations made in the report were in connection with the looting of institutions and facilities, works of art, and private property.[44]

Throughout the war the Soviet press remained virtually silent on events in Transnistria. During the defense of Odessa, prior to its surrender, and thereafter numerous articles were published about the battles and the defenders of the city, many of which subsequently received awards. Almost no article, however, discussed Romanian rule in the region, its nature, or its crimes. On the eve of the city's liberation Ilya Ehrenburg published a derisive article on the Romanian authorities in Odessa, the designs of the "Daco-Romanians" on Transnistria, and "the achievements" of the pioneers of "Greater Romania," the crowning glory of which was, according to him, the establishment of brothels in Odessa.[45]

Immediately after the liberation the regional committee of the Communist Party in Odessa (Obkom, for short) set up a committee of inquiry to investigate "the damage and casualties of the Fascist occupation of the region during the Great Patriotic War," as the Soviet Union called the war against Nazi Germany. The committee's report was completed in late 1944 but remained secret until 1994. Note that in this report, too, the word *Jew* is not mentioned at all, and all casualties referred to in the report were "peaceful citizens" of the Soviet state.

Although the great killing operation in the Kingdom of Death was described as "a torture campaign surpassing any act of murder in the annals of history," it was attributed to the Germans as well as the Romanians. In early November 1941 an Obkom regional committee report stated that Romanian gendarmes had accompanied convoys of "Soviet citizens" to Bogdanovka, including old people, women, and children who had been driven out of the Odessa district and the Soviet Republic of Moldova (Bessarabia) under orders of the Romanian occupying authorities. These convoys reached Bogdanovka in batches of 1,500–5,000, where they were turned over to the local gendarmes under the supervision of Sgt. Maj. Nicolae Melinescu and his aide Ghirescu. It is worth noting that almost all the names of the gendarmes and Romanian army personnel were distorted, sometimes unrecognizably so. The report referred to the liquidation method employed by the gendarmes; the murder of enfeebled Jews, the elderly, and children in the marches; and the deliberate prolonging of marches so as to increase the number of fatalities. The gendarmes turned a five-day march into a twenty-day march so as to "thin out the ranks." In Bogdanovka 55,000 "Soviet citizens" were herded into pigsties of collective farms located approximately half a kilometer from the village itself and exposed to the elements in the bitter winter of 1941–42.[46]

The report quoted the testimony of Kalimov Boris Filipovich, a survivor of the Bogdanovka camp, who also failed to mention that all its inmates were Jews: "The inmates' living [conditions] were dreadful. 2,000 people lay on moldy straw in a pigsty designed for 200 pigs, with no other covering. Among them were elderly people and children. Many lived out in the open. The prisoners received no food or water, and ate snow to quench their thirst."[47]

The report also mentioned the issue of the bread that was sold for five golden rubles, although it claimed that Isopescu himself (or Ionescu Modest, as he was erroneously called) and another Romanian officer sold the bread and seized the gold and other valuables. The bread, according to the report, was taken from the villagers of Bogdanovka. On 18 December 1941 two German officers visited Bogdanovka to inspect the site selected for liquidation: "A deep valley sloping down to the River Bug, 15 meters from the edge of the forest, to the east of the collective farm." This evidently constitutes the most accurate description of the site of the massacre of fifty-five thousand Jews. According to the Obkom's confidential report the executions were carried out by "a disciplinary unit of 60 men under the command of Hegel, a German who arrived there on 20 December, and continued its work until 15 January 1942. The carnage peaked on 21, 22, 23, 27, 28, and 29 December 1941."[48] Indeed, almost all the details were accurate. The murder squad comprised seventy people but was headed by a Ukrainian named Andrushin, and all the murderers were local Ukrainians. The participation of

Ukrainians in crimes against the Jewish nation has been well hidden, and in this case there was no mention that they were also Soviet citizens.

As stated, the massacre was perpetrated by Ukrainians and Romanians only—the Germans took no part in it at all. The report noted the existence of other camps in the Domanevka subdistrict in which 115,038 people were murdered. The Communist Party's commission of inquiry reported the imprisonment of 6,603 people in Berezovka, 4,722 in the Krasnooknian subdistrict (in the Berezovka district), 35,000 in the Mostovoye subdistrict, and more. The deportation from Odessa of some 30,000 Jews by foot and another 36,000 by train is not mentioned at all, perhaps because all of the deportees were Jews and there was no way of pretending otherwise.

The report did not mention the Odessan Jews who were deported by train in their own right but merely included them in the thirty-five thousand citizens murdered in the Mostovoye subdistrict. Likewise, the report never mentioned the Domanevka camp, in which, according to Romanian sources, eighteen thousand Jews were murdered. On the other hand, the report described at length the Germans' brutality toward and murder of Ukrainian peasants as they withdrew. The report likewise failed to mention that the "Fascist bandits" who tortured the inhabitants of two villages were "Vlasov volunteers"—Russian prisoners of war who volunteered to serve in units of Nazi collaborators. Only once, at the very end of the report, is the word *ghetto* slipped in casually, without reference to the Jews or their fate: "During the 29 months and 27 days of the occupation of Transnistria, 279,631 Soviet citizens were shot, hanged, torched or burnt alive, tortured, sent into slavery or incarcerated in the ghettos; 22,169 of them were children." Of the total, 56,101 were sent to Germany or Romania.[49] This number apparently includes those who voluntarily left Transnistria and many thousands who chose to flee with the Germans and Romanians.[50]

The Black Book (*Cartea neagră*), a collaborative effort by four Jewish authors from the Soviet Union—Ilya Ehrenburg, Vasily Grossman, Lev Ozerov, and Vladimir Lidin—that was published only in Romania in 1946, is proof of the existence of a deliberate Soviet policy to conceal the uniqueness of the Jewish fate during the Second World War. Immediately following the liberation of various parts of the Soviet Union, Ehrenburg and other Jewish authors were inundated with survivors' letters, testimonies, and diaries. The authors compiled this material, which contained the names of witnesses, into what they assumed would become a black book of crimes perpetrated against the Soviet peoples, including the Jews, in the short period in which the Soviet press permitted news of the extermination of the Jews. Publication of the book was delayed, however, due to Soviet censorship.

During Ehrenburg's visit to Romania in 1945 he or his hosts proposed the publication of a Romanian edition of the book. A much-abridged version appeared in 1946 in Romania, which eventually became the only edition, since the Soviet authorities banned publication of the book. The Romanian version remained the only proof of the efforts of the Jewish authors to publish a book on the tragedy of the Jews, written by Jews themselves, until Yad Vashem published the entire book in Russian in Jerusalem in 1980. The book has many testimonies about the murder operations and the deportation from Czernowitz as well as about the large-scale killing operations perpetrated by the Romanians and Germans in Transnistria.

Vera Inber's chapter on Odessa, based on documents and testimonies of the citizens of Odessa, documents the massacre of the Jews of Odessa stage by stage, including Dalnic and the Slobodka ghetto, Romanian reprisals in the streets of Odessa, the hanging of thousands, executions in the city jail, the murder of the Jewish doctors, the deportations by foot and by train, the pillaging of Jewish property by the Romanians (but not by their Russian neighbors), the second ghetto, and the daily transports. The Jewish authors also provide a detailed description of the Domanevka camp, although it was not mentioned in the commission's report, and of the march to Berezovka in freezing cold weather designed to "thin out" the ranks. Already at that time the authors concluded that "the number of Jews exterminated in Odessa totaled approximately one hundred thousand."[51]

True to Communist ideology, Ehrenburg and his colleagues used every opportunity to emphasize the assistance the Russians and Ukrainians offered the Jews but failed to mention the local collaborators' contribution to the massacre of the Jews. The policemen whose crimes they sometimes described remained anonymous. Around 1949 the book was banned in Romania, too, and thus few even knew of its existence, while those who had a copy of the book hurriedly disposed of it.[52]

In 1946 an official Soviet publication about Nazi atrocities in Soviet territory appeared in English translation.[53] It contained the findings of the special commission headed by Kolybanov that investigated Nazi crimes after the liberation, updated in the two years following its original publication.[54] In the chapter on Transnistria titled "The Romanian Administration and Justice," the authors castigate the Romanians principally for looting and for the Romanization policy introduced in the region. The book describes instances of torture during interrogations by the police and the Siguranţa and the prosecutions in the Odessa military tribunal, citing the testimony of those who were interrogated, none of whom were Jews (Jews who were interrogated were summarily executed).

Based on this report the commission determined that the German and Romanian war criminals exterminated two hundred thousand Soviet citizens—namely "Ukrainians, Russians, and Moldavians"—from the Odessa district. Twenty-five thousand "Soviet citizens and their children" were burnt alive in the gunpowder depots. One eyewitness described how the Romanians sprayed the warehouses with gasoline and burnt "Soviet citizens" to death. Judging by their names, all the eyewitnesses quoted were Ukrainians and Russians. Although the Bogdanovka massacre was mentioned again, the fact that the victims were Jews was concealed. The total number of victims there was set at fifty-four thousand, of whom two thousand were burned in barracks.[55]

This time the commission attributed the executions not to the Germans but to the Romanian gendarmes, glossing over the fact that the majority of the murderers were Ukrainian policemen. The "brutal extermination of peaceful Soviet citizens by Romanians on the grounds of the Bogdanovka state farm" was confirmed also by a committee of legal and medical experts, including professors of medicine. This time the commission also revealed the extermination site at Domanevka, where twenty-two thousand "citizens" were murdered. It failed, however, to mention the deportation of the Jews of Odessa by train, probably because of the difficulty in explaining why all these "citizens" were exclusively Jews. It did refer to their extermination, namely, to the thirty-five thousand "Soviet citizens" whom the "occupiers" murdered in the Mostovoye subdistrict. The commission also identified the corpses of seventeen "Soviet citizens"—none of them Jewish—who were tortured to death by "the German and Romanian monsters." It is worth noting that while the section describing the acts of rape and sabotage took up two pages of the report, the slaughter of the Jewish people in the region merited a mere one and a quarter pages.[56]

Romania outdid the Soviet Union in its attempts at deliberate obfuscation. It never even published the findings of the Soviet special commission of inquiry and never used the findings as a basis for indicting war criminals or for conducting research related to that period. No footnote of any book, study, or article every referred to the findings of this report.

The incorporation of Romania into the Soviet bloc greatly mitigated the Soviets' attitude to these crimes, particularly as the majority of them were perpetrated against the Jewish people—a people who did not exist in the reports of the various committees of the Communist Party and the Soviet state. Finally, despite the efforts of a few survivors, for many years the banks of the Bug had no memorial commemorating the crimes committed against the Jews there. It was only in 1990 that Jewish organizations in Odessa were able to erect a modest memorial in Bogdanovka.

29

The Typhus Epidemic

The comprehensive report Alexianu sent to Marshal Antonescu on 11 December 1941 on the situation in Transnistria stated, "A typhus epidemic has erupted in many Jewish camps due to the filthy conditions in which they live." The report later seems to contradict this assertion by stating, "Despite sporadic outbreaks of epidemics, especially typhus, the general level of sanitation in Transnistria is satisfactory."[1] Despite the virulence of the typhus epidemic (the same disease that had, in the First World War, killed tens of thousands of Romanian civilians and servicemen) that was claiming the lives of tens of thousands of Jews, Alexianu reported that the epidemic was under control since only several thousand cases of typhus had come to light. Unlike most members of the Romanian administration in Transnistria Alexianu was a gifted intellectual and must have been aware of the contradiction in his report.[2]

To understand this contradiction we must remember that Alexianu, the prefects, the pretors, the military doctors, and the physicians of the administration saw the Jews of Transnistria as cattle rather than human beings, to be shipped over the Bug to the Germans for extermination, according to the Tighina Agreement. Every Romanian administrator was aware that the moment the Jews were transferred to the German occupation authorities on other side of the Bug, in Reichskommissariat Ukraine, they would be killed. The governor of Transnistria mentioned the Tighina Agreement in almost every report to Antonescu. In early November 1941, after the massacre in Odessa, the Transnistrian administration itself concluded that it was impossible to keep bringing Jews to the Bug because the Germans were refusing to accept them. Alexianu therefore ordered the gendarmerie commander to draft an ordinance on the status of the Jews, their duties, and the living conditions in the ghettos. Alexianu mentioned in his report to Antonescu the need to implement a "final solution" (see chap. 25).

In early December 1941 the "radical solution" to the Jewish problem in Transnistria was, according to Alexianu, their transfer to the Germans under the terms of the Tighina Agreement. When this plan failed to materialize the Romanian authorities decided to take matters into their own hands and eradicate the source of the epidemic. In southern Transnistria, through which the Romanian units passed on their way to the front, the Romanian authorities adopted a radical approach with the backing of the Romanian military and civilian medical establishment and with Marshal Antonescu's approval. "Let them die," countered Antonescu at the cabinet session of 13 November 1941 when Alexianu notified the ministers that he had eighty-five thousand sick Jews in the villages of southern Transnistria and proposed delousing procedures to prevent them from infecting Romanian servicemen.[3]

This chapter shall focus on the ravages of the typhus epidemic in the ghettos and camps of northern and central Transnistria where the Romanian administration did not apply the extermination option. It shall also discuss how the Jews contended with the epidemic and the Romanian medical authorities' response to the crisis.

Typhus was already identified in the camps set up by the Romanians in Bessarabia before the deportation of Jews began. Jews were not infected with the disease before being evicted from their homes. Typhus, which had exacted such a heavy human toll during the First World War, had not been entirely eradicated from the region. The way the Romanian authorities treated the Jews (transferring them from place to place, depriving them of food and water, housing them in stables and pigsties, depriving them of shelter, subjecting them to physical and psychological abuse, and constantly marching them from place to place) weakened them and rendered them vulnerable to the disease. In Bessarabia the Romanian authorities did not lift a finger to stem the epidemic or treat the disease, since the Jews were in any case earmarked for deportation and extermination. They shifted responsibility for dealing with the epidemic on to the Jews themselves, without supplying them with disinfectants, medicines, or vaccines.

On 26 August 1941, after the Ministry of Health in Bucharest was informed of the outbreak and spread of the epidemic among the inmates of the Bessarabian ghettos, it issued the following directive: "In the Jewish ghettos that were established in Bessarabia [which accommodate] local Jews as well as Jews from the Ukraine, one or more doctors shall provide medical treatment, and shall adopt, under supervision of the [state's] Sanitary Institutions, all measures to prevent the spread of disease [and to maintain] hygiene and introduce a program of prophylaxis. Likewise, the competent authorities must ensure the provision of food to these ghettos."[4] This directive meant that Jewish doctors — themselves prisoners — had to treat the epidemic without any means at their disposal and, above all, had to prevent it from spreading. The Romanian Ministry of Health, aware of the correlation between weakness and susceptibility to disease, hoped that if they ceased to starve the Jews, fewer people would be infected. The recommendation to provide food, however, was never implemented. The convoys of Jews leaving for Transnistria were already starving and thus susceptible to disease. This was the sum total of efforts to tackle the disease in Bessarabia—a sovereign Romanian territory.

The typhus epidemic soon spread throughout Transnistria. Most Jews from Bukovina and the Dorohoi district who contracted the disease had been healthy at the time of their deportation, as all the survivors testified. In dealing with the problem the Romanian administration in Transnistria attempted to differentiate between the deportees and the local population. The Balta district, which served both as a transit camp for convoys heading for the Kingdom of Death and as a final destination for other convoys, can serve as a test case for examining the way in which the Romanian authorities dealt with the epidemic.

In early November the prefect Col. Vasile Nica issued a special directive, stating:

1. No Jew, local or otherwise, may leave the camp to which he is assigned.
2. Only one transit point shall be assigned for all Jews arriving [who were brought] from other localities, and the itinerary may not be altered.
3. All sanitary personnel in the subdistricts irrespective of rank shall be recruited for the war against typhus; anyone refusing to help will be severely punished.
4. All citizens are forbidden to purchase or wear clothes belonging to Jews, or to come into contact with Jews. Anyone [who violates this order] shall be punished.
5. Jews caught outside the camps shall be punished by implementation of Order 23.[5]

Similar orders issued by other prefects accused the Jews of spreading the disease, ordered them to be quarantined in camps and ghettos, forbade them to have contact with the Christian population, and introduced preventive measures in the villages. The quarantine and ban on trading clothes for food led to the starvation of tens of thousands of Jews. The order authorized the gendarmes, Ukrainian policemen, and other officials to shoot Jews found outside the camps and ghettos. Many Jews who had left the ghetto in search of food were shot dead. The implementation of Order 23 signified permission to execute Jews found outside the ghettos.

The way the typhus epidemic was handled in the Kingdom of Death put an end to the problem in southern Transnistria, despite renewed outbreaks of the disease, mainly in the Berezovka district, among the few local Jewish survivors or those who were sent there later. By late January 1942 the typhus epidemic was raging through the ghettos and camps of northern Transnistria, apart from Djurin, Murafa, and Zhmerinca, where housing conditions were slightly better.[6]

From the outbreak of the epidemic in October 1941 until approximately March 1942 the authorities assumed that the typhus epidemic, together with a policy of starvation and isolation, was the best way of getting rid of the Jews, provided the epidemic was confined to the ghettos. The fact that tens of thousands of Jews succumbed to the disease in the winter and spring of 1942 seemed to prove their point. It was only when the Romanian authorities realized that the epidemic was not confined to Jewish localities that they finally decided to take action and allowed the Jews to receive help from their coreligionists in Romania. At a convention of Jewish doctors held in January 1943 in Mogilev to discuss ways of preventing the renewed spread of the epidemic in the ghettos, a Romanian military doctor summed up the conflict between the desire to exterminate the Jews and the need to keep the area free of contagion: "We sent you here to die, but at the same time, there must be no epidemics."[7]

THE JEW AS CARRIER AND CAUSE OF INFECTION

In April 1942 Dr. Gheorghe Tătăranu, who compiled a special report on the problem of typhus in Transnistria, determined that "this epidemiological topic is of decisive importance for military operations in the next campaign." The report followed an all-out attempt by the Romanian gendarmes and Ukrainian policemen in the winter of 1941–42, at Tătăranu's behest, "to solve" the problem of typhus in the Kingdom of Death and "to prevent epidemics" in the Berezovka district, as Tătăranu described the liquidation of Odessan Jewry in his district. Clearly, all Romanian physicians considered the Jews to be the primary source of infection and dissemination of the disease, with the Gypsies a close second: "Typhus was imported from northern Bessarabia by the Jews and later spread [by them] in the districts adjoining the Bug, in the localities in which they were settled," emphasized Tătăranu in his report. In his opinion this catastrophe was not the result of the deportation per se but rather of the bungled way in which it was carried out (the failure to delouse Jews before they crossed the Dniester). This was "because the number of Jews who were brought [to the river] far exceeded the capabilities of the Disinfection Centers."[8]

Many survivors testified that no delousing operations were carried out prior to crossing the Dniester. The only "sanitization" operations that were carried out consisted of throwing the Jews off the rafts into the river or shooting into the masses waiting to cross over. Although disinfection centers were set up by the army in late October 1941, they did not cater to the Jews, who were considered as good as dead. In his report Tătăranu admitted that during the large wave of deportations "there had been no contact between the Deportation Committee and the Disinfection Centers."[9] In short, the Jews were deported to Transnistria without being subjected to any delousing procedures or physical checkups.

The Obodovka ghetto—a collection of stables and pens at the local collective farm into which several thousand Jews were crammed—was declared an infected area, surrounded with barbed wire, and guarded by the gendarmes and Ukrainian police. The fact that no one was allowed to enter or leave, even to obtain food, meant that many Jews died of hunger as well as typhus.[10] This proves that there was a third option, besides the two proposed by Sergeant Major Steflea, the commander of the gendarmerie post in Obodovka (improving their living conditions or killing them). The lack of drinking water was due to the peasants' fear of contact with infected Jews. "The wells belonged to peasants, and they often prevented us from drawing water. The lack of drinking water and the terrible living conditions exacerbated the typhus epidemic. Hundreds of deportees contracted it," wrote a survivor from Obodovka.[11] Another survivor testified that most of the Jews who arrived in Obodovka with her convoy from the Edineți camp were not infected with typhus and that the epidemic broke out a week or two after their internment. "There was no doctor there. Hunger and cold gnawed at us. . . . Many perished in the typhus epidemic in Obodovka, as well as in the neighboring camp of Tzibulevka."[12]

In the space of about three to four months, about 1,000 of the 1,200 Jews who were brought to Obodovka in the middle of winter perished: "We were herded like cattle into a large stable of an abandoned collective farm. There were approximately 1,200 of us. . . . The stable had no doors, windows or beds. We slept on the floor. The camp was guarded by [Romanian] gendarmes and Ukrainian police. It was not long before a typhus epidemic broke out in the camp. It lasted three to four months, and claimed the lives of a thousand people. The only doctor among the deportees also perished."[13] Romanian documentation and survivors' testimonies create an authentic picture of what went on in the Obodovka ghetto. Presumably, a similar situation prevailed in the other ghettos set up by the Romanians in the winter of 1941–42.

In the nearby ghetto of Tzibulevka the typhus epidemic claimed the lives of 35–40 Jews per day. Their corpses were piled on sleighs and unceremoniously dumped in mass graves. The gendarmes were interested only in keeping a tally of survivors: "The gendarmes came once every two days, took us out to a vacant lot, and counted us. We were ordered to wear the yellow star and forbidden to leave the ghetto, which was guarded by a militia of local Ukrainian peasants."[14] By 20

January 1942, of the 2,000 or so Jews who had been brought over in November 1941 only 180 (100 men, 76 women, and 4 children) were still alive, most of them suffering from severe frostbite. In the nearby village of Budey, 450 Jews out of 1,200, half of whom were deported from Storojinetz in northern Bukovina, perished. During the winter about 10–12 Jews died daily from the epidemic.[15]

The reports always portrayed the Jews as carriers of the disease, never as its victims. The Romanian authorities referred to the typhus epidemic as it related to the Jews only in orders restricting Romanians from entering the ghettos and camps and forbidding both Romanians and Ukrainians from trading or having contact with Jews. Until April 1942 local residents were forbidden to travel by train in order to protect Romanian servicemen. The prefect of the Balta district, where the epidemic was most virulent, sent the following directive to the district gendarmerie legion and to the police of Balta, both of which were directly subordinate to him: "It has been brought to my notice that throughout the city Jewish children are going from house to house begging, and spreading typhus. They walk around freely without any impediment and do not even wear the yellow star. Please take steps to ensure that no Jew leaves the ghetto without a special permit, [including] forced laborers and craftsmen [who work outside the ghetto]. As far as the organization and implementation of the above is concerned, the provisions of Order 23 must be rigorously applied."[16]

An in-depth study of the typhus epidemic in Transnistria would, to a large extent, be tantamount to writing a monograph on each ghetto and camp — an endeavor that is beyond the scope of this study. Of the 165 or so camps and ghettos that were identified in Transnistria and the dozens of collective and state farms that were turned into makeshift camps for the Jews, the three ghettos that were hardest hit by the epidemic were Shargorod, Bershad, and Mogilev. We shall focus on Mogilev and Bershad and on the Berezovka district as a whole — the scene of the extermination of Odessan Jewry.

THE TYPHUS EPIDEMIC IN MOGILEV

The typhus epidemic was identified in Mogilev in late December 1941. It was preceded by an outbreak of typhoid fever, imported by the deportees from the Edinetz camp, which did not inflict huge casualties. The first case of typhus showed up in the barracks that, after the deportations, served as a temporary shelter for Jews who had fled from the small camps in the surrounding villages, Jews without a permit, and "tramps, beggars, and down-and-outs."[17] The number of fatalities climbed steadily until they peaked at 150 a day. Many deportees who had previously made every effort to remain in Mogilev left for other ghettos despite the freezing weather and the risk of being murdered on the way. One of the survivors who fled to Tropova pointed out that "the typhus caught up with us there, too."[18] Families disintegrated due to the death of either or both parents, while many of those who remained alive were in the grips of a burning fever and too sick to realize what was happening. The Transnistrian gendarmerie and the Bessarabian administration tightened up inspection procedures at the Dniester to prevent correspondence or parcels being sent to the Jews of Mogilev from relatives in Romania, for which the latter paid the Romanian couriers a very high price.

In December "two couriers acting for the Jewish deportees" who had entry permits to Mogilev were caught with 72 letters from Bucharest and 174,000 lei earmarked "for the Jews of Mogilev." In December and January another four couriers were caught transporting 315 letters. Letters from Mogilev that were translated from German painted a grim picture of hunger, disease, and death.[19] On 15 January 1942 a Romanian sergeant major was arrested in Mogilev for delivering money to the deportees from their relatives in Romania. The money found on him was seized, while the money he had managed to allocate to the Jews was confiscated, too.[20]

Attempts by the Judenrat's Hygiene Department to combat the epidemic failed, and in March 1942 it conceded defeat. The official tally of the sick totaled 3,777 in April, rising to 4,451 in May; 1,133 Jews died in April and 254 in May (28 percent of those officially registered as sick). No house or family was untouched by the disease. Until 17 April 1942 the Romanian authorities refused to help fight the disease, either directly or indirectly.[21] On 26 January 1942, at the height of the epidemic, all Jewish men and youth who were still able bodied were sent out, "mostly naked," in the freezing cold to build a road some ten kilometers from Mogilev.[22] Since the gendarmes refused to go anywhere near the Jews, the Jewish police were entrusted with the dirty work of removing the dead from their crowded and rundown quarters.

Although the Judenrat set up a hospital it served as little more than a quarantine center, as a survivor from Dorohoi described:

People were dying like flies. Even committee workers who came to take away the corpses could not keep up with the rate. Frequently, bodies lay there for days before being removed. Gradually, we all fell ill. I saw people walking to work and suddenly falling down. . . . For the month I was stricken with the disease, I fought for my life.

A makeshift hospital was set up in a former school, where Jewish doctors, prisoners like us, began quarantining the sick. At the height of the epidemic, hundreds of people were dying daily. Those who pulled through resembled ghosts, and could barely stand on their feet. I saw many walking corpses in the streets. I, too, was one of them. Even under such appalling conditions, the brutes refused to exempt us from forced labor.[23]

On 7 April 1942 Mogilev was ravaged by typhoid fever. "At the start of the hot season, the typhus epidemic abated, but with the advent of fresh fruit and vegetables, it was replaced by an outbreak of typhoid fever."[24] In late April, after the typhus epidemic had claimed thousands of Jewish lives, the district medical establishment finally agreed to support the Jewish Committee's fight against the epidemic. The Romanian military physician Maj. Dr. Constantin Chirilă, head of the district sanitation services, was the only Romanian official who showed some empathy toward the deportees. But for the Bucharest Autonomous Assistance Commission and self-help efforts the epidemic would have continued until it burnt itself out or wiped out all Jews. On 22 March the first shipment of medicines from the Bucharest Autonomous Assistance Commission reached Mogilev, but about half of the sick (3,500 people) still died.[25] Despite the dramatic drop in the number of casualties Alexianu decided on 19 May 1942 to move 4,000 Jews from Mogilev to an improvised camp in Skazinets, since "the typhus epidemic, which was now endemic in the Mogilev district, was being spread principally by the Jewish deportees." About half of them died. The gendarmerie was given carte blanche to solve the typhus crisis in Mogilev in the way it thought fit.[26]

The typhus epidemic was particularly fierce in the ghettos and camps along the Bug in the Mogilev, Tulchin, and Balta districts and had tragic results. The terrible hardships the Jews endured left them too weak to fight the epidemic. As Carp stated, "The epidemic ran its course until it burnt itself out. All in all, the disease claimed the lives of 20,000 victims in the city and subdistrict of Mogilev."[27]

THE TYPHUS EPIDEMIC IN BERSHAD

Bershad, a town in the Balta district that had four thousand to five thousand Jews before the war, became the largest ghetto between the Dniester and Bug, accommodating some twenty thousand Jewish deportees. The first deportees to be taken there were Jews from Bessarabian camps who, after weeks of marching, were easy prey for disease. Next were deportees from Czernowitz and southern Bukovina, who were taken to Mărculeşti by train and then were marched to Bershad via the Coşăuţi forest, Soroca, Yampol, Krizhopol, Obodovka, and other places. Some deportees from the town and district of Dorohoi were also taken to Bershad. Some deportees had to pay the pretor 10,000 lei each for the privilege of staying in Bershad rather than continuing on to camps along the Bug or collective farms in the vicinity.

The ghetto was established on 29 July. When the German and Romanian forces entered Bershad they killed about ten thousand Ukrainians and Jews. The remaining Jews were concentrated in the lower part of the town of Dolina, which was declared a ghetto before the arrival of the large convoys from Bessarabia. The waves of deportees were herded into houses in the small ghetto. The large ghetto, which was set up in another part of the town, comprised twelve narrow parallel lanes with 300–350 dilapidated clay houses belonging to the local Jews, each of which accommodated about sixty people.

A Jew from Czernowitz who was deported to Bershad via the Mărculeşti camp described the journey and the ghetto itself: "In the kolkhoz, we found deportees from Bessarabia who had been on the go almost since the start of the war. They were infested with lice, neglected, almost naked and barefoot, and in a state of total despair. One collective farm in which we spent the night had the remains of previous convoys: sick people, dying people who had been left behind because they were unable to continue, as well as corpses."[28]

Although the typhus epidemic that erupted in the Balta district in December 1941 followed the same pattern as in other districts, the fact that thousands of Ukrainians instantly contracted the disease necessitated the intervention of the authorities. In April 1942 the Health Department estimated the number of infected Ukrainians at about six thousand and in November 1942 at ten thousand — "about half the total figure" in Transnistria, declared the Health Department, totally omitting the Jews in their calculations.[29] The spread of the disease among the Ukrainians was due to several factors: the fact that the Jewish convoys were being driven on toward the Bug, the establishment of thousands of improvised camps along the river, and Alexandrescu's greed (the pretor sold permits to deportees in Bershad and punished those who could not afford to pay him by expelling them).

The epidemic spread rapidly along the routes the convoys had taken in and out of Bershad, affecting mainly the northeast section of the district, where about ten ghettos had been established. Nica, the district prefect, and Maj. Dr. Gheorghe Filipaş, the army commander of health services, visited the northern subdistricts on 6 and 12 December 1941 in order "to evaluate sanitary conditions" there and ordered measures to be taken to contain the epidemic and treat the sick. The epidemic continued to rage through Bershad and neighboring ghettos until it claimed over 15,000 Jewish lives in Bershad alone. Until recently, estimates of the number of casualties in Bershad ranged from 10,000 to 20,000, based on calculations of the Jewish Committee and on survivors' testimonies. Today we have official data on which to base calculations. These data show that by early January 1942, 35,276 Jews had passed through Yampol on their way to Bershad and other ghettos on the Bug (in the Balta district).[30] Of these, many thousands were shot on the way or were left to die of typhus in transit camps. When the convoys arrived from Romania the district had about 6,000–7,000 Jews (of which 5,000 were in the town itself). To these should be added an unknown number of Jewish deportees who passed through transit points in Rybnitsa, although most of them were deported to the Kingdom of Death. All in all, by December 1941 the district had a total of about 42,000 Jews.

After the epidemic the prefecture of the Balta district ordered a census of the entire population in the district by ethnic group. The census was conducted in the spring and summer of 1942 by local Ukrainian doctors and heads of the local health services (their signatures appear on the census), since Romanian doctors were reluctant to enter the ghettos and camps. The census shows that in the Balta district 15,232 Jews survived the typhus epidemic and forced marches.[31] It follows that about 27,000 Jews perished in the Balta district in the winter and spring of 1942. According to survivors' testimonies, at least 20,000 deportees were taken to Bershad, which had about 4,000–5,000 local Jews. Thus, at the outbreak of the typhus epidemic Bershad had a total of about 24,000–25,000 Jews. Since, according to the official data, only 8,014 survived the epidemic, about 16,000 perished.[32]

THE JEWISH DOCTORS

The typhus epidemic claimed the lives of tens of thousands of Jews, most of whom died an anonymous death. Especially heartrending was the tragedy of the Jewish doctors who perished in the epidemic. They were the first to realize the true scope of the calamity. They were the first to take action, albeit in vain, and were also among the first to succumb to the disease. In most cases their wives committed suicide—a decision made easier by the fact that they had access to poisons. Although we do not know exactly how many doctors were deported, they ran into the hundreds. (The Romania of April 1941—which excluded all of Bessarabia, northern Bukovina, and northern Transylvania—had 8,403 doctors, of which 2,078 were Jewish.[33])

A survivor from Shargorod summed up the plight of the Jewish doctors: "The doctors were prepared to help, and tried hard to contain the epidemic. Most of them succumbed to the epidemic."[34] The doctors had no equipment to help them. They had no medicines, no laboratories, no antiseptics for getting rid of lice—not even the most crude antiseptics such as soap or kerosene—and no hot water for boiling clothes and destroying lice or for personal hygiene. The disinfection centers and delousing ovens used by the Romanian army and subsequently by the Romanian administration ignored the Jews and their doctors alike.

It took some time until the doctors were able to identify the epidemic, since they had no experience with the disease. Even after they identified the disease, however, there was not much they could do apart from quarantining the sick.[35] The Jewish Committees of several large ghettos, which tried to organize self-help activities, set up improvised hospitals. However, they were unable to equip the hospitals, obtain medicines, or even cover the windows of the derelict buildings that were converted into hospitals in the terrible winder of 1941–42, since the authorities still prevented any contact between the deportees and their brethren in Romania. Meanwhile, the number of sick rapidly outgrew the available hospital places. The few hospitals that were set up housed the sick, the dying, and sometimes even the dead, when the cold prevented their burial. Under these conditions the admission of infected people to the ghetto hospitals spelled certain death. Consequently, relatives sometimes concealed a family member's sickness to prevent him or her from being sent to the hospital. The aforementioned survivor from Shargorod added, "I also caught typhus. The landlord kept my condition a secret. After a while, those infected with typhus were sent to hospital where a certain death awaited them. In the hospitals the sick were not treated, no one cared for them, and people were dying primarily of starvation and filth."[36] The small ghettos, and even some larger ones that were in more remote locations, had no doctors or medicines.[37]

The Jewish doctors of Shargorod caught typhus a month after the outbreak of the epidemic.[38] In the barracks in Mogilev, three doctors who had been sent by the Jewish Committee to treat the infected fell ill one after the other, and one died. The Jewish Committee in Mogilev, with the help of the Jewish doctors, wrote special reports to the authorities describing the risks of the epidemic, but "the authorities, especially the District Sanitation Service, remained indifferent." One by one all the Jewish doctors who had set up the ghetto hospitals succumbed to the disease: "With tears in his eyes, the only doctor who was not struck down by the disease begged [the Judenrat] not to send him more patients, since they would simply die there."[39] Many Jewish doctors realized that they were unable to contain the epidemic or be useful in any way, and many lost the will to live even before they succumbed to the disease.

On 8 January 1942 Dr. Lazăr Greif died of typhus in Bershad, following which his wife, Beatrice, and their only son committed suicide. On 13 January 1942 Dr. Marbek and her brother, the former judge Dr. Robinson, committed suicide in the Shargorod ghetto beside the dead body of their sister, Therese Marbek, another typhus victim. Dr. Abraham Reicher, head of the Shargorod Jewish Committee, who did his best to contain the epidemic in the ghetto, contracted the disease and died on 3 March 1942. The doctor who treated him, Dr. Hart from Vama, in southern Bukovina, also caught the disease and died a few days later, following which his wife committed suicide.[40] In February 1942 twenty-five doctors contracted the disease in Mogilev, while twenty-three out of twenty-seven contracted the disease in Shargorod and a total of twelve died of it.[41] In the Bershad ghetto, which housed twenty thousand deportees in its few streets, dozens of unnamed doctors and doctor's wives succumbed to the disease.[42] The only fact we know for certain about the dozens of doctors who tried desperately to fight the disease in the camps and ghettos of Transnistria (mainly the northern part) is that they perished during the first winter.

SELF-HELP ACTIVITIES TO FIGHT THE DISEASE

The deportees soon realized that the typhus epidemic was the means invented or adopted by the Romanian authorities for their extermination. The need to create a disease-free zone along the transit and supply routes of the Romanian and German armies, together with Antonescu's pathological hatred of "Russian" Jews, forced the Romanians to find and implement a swift solution. In the north they decided to let events run their course by preventing ties between the deportees and the Jews in Romania, a step that meant closing all avenues of aid: "What the fascist beasts began," wrote a survivor of the first massacres, "this calamity completed."[43]

In the winter of 1941–42 the Romanian authorities were no longer concerned about the fate of Transnistrian Jewry, as long as they died without a fuss and without endangering the military, the gendarmes, or the civil servants brought over from Romania.[44] The top government echelons were waiting for the end of the fighting in the east in order to expel all Jews from Transnistria over the Bug, as specified in the agreement with the Germany army. "We shall remain here with the Ukrainians, not the Jews," wrote Col. Constantin Năsturaș, prefect of the Mogilev district, when he ordered the continued expulsion of Jews from the district.[45]

The only way the deportees could prevent their total annihilation was through self-help activities and aid from Romanian Jewry. This chapter does not discuss the activities of the Jewish leadership in Transnistria or even in Romania itself. Rather, it focuses on Jewish self-help efforts to fight the typhus epidemic and ward off the fate that the Romanian authorities had determined for them—a fate that did not involve the use of killing units but rather the adoption of the Romanian way of solving the Jewish problem.

Self-help activities began in the communities of southern Bukovina, which were transported en masse by train together with their renowned leaders and rabbis, unlike their fellow Jews who were made to wander for months through Bessarabia and Transnistria. The leaders and rabbis of these communities immediately organized help for the poorest members of the communities in the ghettos to which they were brought. With the help of community members who still had some means, they set up soup kitchens that provided a hot plate of soup each day. Such expressions of Jewish solidarity were rare in Transnistria at the time. The deportees from Bessarabia and northern Bukovina, who reached the ghettos after months of brutality, humiliation, abuse, and murder, had no leaders. Most of them had been exiled by the Soviet authorities to Siberia and other remote areas about two weeks before Operation Barbarossa began.

The considerable efforts to help to the deportees in Transnistria in the period between initial awareness of their fate toward the end of October 1941 and the establishment of the Jewish Center in early February 1942 were, on the whole, abortive. Although Filderman and a small federation committee, the Autonomous Assistance Commission, managed to send over sums of money with trustworthy Romanians, most of it, totaling tens of millions of lei, either got lost or was not funneled into organized relief efforts.

On 10 December 1941, the Presidency of the Council of Ministers approved in Antonescu's name "the official dispatch of aid in the form of money and medicines to the Jews who were deported to Transnistria."[46] The letter reached its destination on 17 December 1941, the day on which the federation was disbanded and the Jewish Center, the Judenrat of Romanian Jewry, was set up. The Jewish Center's main function, in the Nazis' eyes, was to prepare for the deportation of Romanian Jewry to the death camps.

In Bucharest the Jewish leaders focused their efforts on turning Antonescu's authorization in principle into a de facto one that would specify practical ways of helping the deportees, with Alexianu's approval. Note that when this campaign took place the relationship between the Jewish leadership and the Romanian government had changed radically due to the neutralization of Filderman, the representative par excellence of the Jews. The directors of the newly established Jewish Center clarified at the outset that their duties did not include looking after the deportees. The minister of the interior, for his part, explicitly stated that his jurisdiction extended only as far as the River Prut.[47] Alexianu himself lived in Tiraspol—an area that was exterritorial for the Jews. After Antonescu's authorization of 10 December 1941, Col. Vasile Gelep, the secretary general of the Ministry of the Interior, with whom Filderman had ties, signed a permit for a delegation of five Jews to leave for Transnistria "in order to organize aid for the Jewish deportees." The delegation, which was approved by the ministry, was to be headed by Fred Șaraga, one of Filderman's men. Colonel Gelep, relying on "the authorization granted by the Presidency of the Council of Ministers," allowed the delegation to visit ghettos in the Mogilev and Balta districts in coordination with Governor Alexianu.[48]

Alexianu refused to allow the delegation to visit Transnistria and wrote the reason for his refusal in his own handwriting: "Due to interests of State, I do not think it would be good for them to visit the camps."[49] In a meeting with a delegation of Jews including H. St. Streitman, the president of the Jewish Center, and representatives of the aid institutions and the Autonomous Assistance Commission, Alexianu summarily dismissed the possibility of Jewish delegates visiting his kingdom and declared that aid "would be limited to sending only money and medicines, in accordance with the approval that had been granted."[50]

From the summer of 1942 on the Autonomous Assistance Commission was officially allowed to send help to the deportees in Transnistria, thereby saving the lives of the deportees who remained in northern Transnistria. Approval of such aid was, however, obtained at a high price. The Jews of Romania had to pay taxes and levies that were tens or even hundreds of times more than the actual sums sent to the deportees.[51]

In early 1943 money began arriving from the American Jewish Joint Distribution Committee via the International Red Cross. Not all of it reached Transnistria. Some was stolen before it left Bucharest, some was stolen from the trains en route, some was pocketed by officials of the Transnistrian administration, and some was used by the committee heads to bribe officials into providing permits.

In late December 1942, when two Romanian armies had been defeated in Stalingrad, the Romanian administration agreed to allow the Autonomous Assistance Commission's delegation to visit several ghettos, with the proviso that it refrain from making direct contact with the deportees. This visit, in early 1943, constituted the first direct contact between Romanian Jewry and the remnants of the deportees in northern Transnistria.

The first shipments of money and medicines for the deportees arrived in February 1942, but the national bank, and later the Transnistrian administration, was in no hurry to transfer them to the Jewish Committee in Mogilev.[52] "The sums of money and medicines that were sent to the Jews," wrote the secretary of the governor's office, were received on 25 February 1942.[53] On 17 March the Secretariat of the Governors' Office in Tiraspol wrote itself a note to remind the governor to send on "the money and medicines designed for the Jews in the camps."[54] The first shipment of medicines, comprising "76 packages of medicines" and a sum of money, were sent to Tiraspol, Alexianu's capital. On 15 March the medicines were sent to the prefect of Mogilev for distribution "to the Jewish Committees."[55] The first shipment of medicines arrived only toward the end of March, a month after they were received, and the first sums of money about a fortnight earlier.[56]

On 7 April 1942 there was a new outbreak of typhoid fever in Mogilev, due to the lack of vaccinations.[57] Although a serum for vaccines against typhus already existed, it was impossible to obtain on the free market in Romania, as the Autonomous Assistance Commission pointed out in its first report in September 1942. The serum did not protect the deportees from typhus in the winter of 1941–42. It was only in March 1943, after many delays, that the supply of typhus vaccines sent by the Autonomous Assistance Commission in Bucharest reached Mogilev.[58] This shipment helped stem the second round of typhus that erupted in the city and district.

The committee managed to send substantial amounts of medicine to Mogilev to treat tuberculosis, dysentery, and other intestinal disorders as well as vaccinations against paratyphus (a milder form of typhus), disinfectants, calcium, painkillers, and sedatives and an assortment of ointments. Nevertheless, the committee found it hard to meet the enormous needs of Transnistrian Jewry: "Taking into account the tremendous shortage of medical equipment and the large number of patients, the aid that was sent was, to our regret, far from adequate. Moreover, a recent shortage of medicines has further exacerbated matters. Many items are unobtainable even for large sums of money. It is becoming daily more difficult to supply medicines."[59]

In late May 1942, after the true dimensions of the typhus epidemic in Transnistria became known, Radu Lecca, the commissioner for Jewish affairs in the Presidency of the Council of Ministers, instructed the Jewish Center to send "money and medicines" to the deportees in Transnistria.[60] This was Lecca's way of informing the Jews that they—not the government—were responsible for their own fate. In a parallel move, the Presidency of the Council of Ministers—in an attempt to hide the scope of the tragedy from Romanian Jews—revoked the permit allowing Jews to send money to relatives in Transnistria via the national bank.[61] (Since many of the recipients were no longer alive, the bank was obliged to notify the senders that the money had not been transferred.)

Although the Jewish leadership in Romania knew of the typhus epidemic in the ghettos of north and central Transnistria almost at the outset, the Romanian administration stymied its attempts to help the deportees. Sums of money and small amount of medicines began to trickle into Transnistria officially only in late March or early April 1942, when the epidemic had already claimed the lives of over sixty thousand deportees.

The leaders of the ghettos in Transnistria did not wait idly until help arrived but under indescribable conditions, with the meager means available to them and the little money trickling in from Romania or collected locally, undertook measures for combating the epidemic. These measures, which were adopted only in ghettos that had recognized leadership (usually in the Mogilev area), were partially successful. In ghettos near the Bug and in villages where tens of thousands of Jews were crammed into stables and sties the epidemic was allowed to run its course. The fittest survived, while the majority perished. Some of those who died were buried only the following spring.

Initially the Jewish leadership in Transnistria directed its efforts at setting up hospitals that effectively became hospices for dying patients in order to protect relatives of the sick or people sharing the same room from infection. The leadership also tried to introduce personal hygiene measures (clean drinking water, soap, and kerosene), set up public bathhouses, repair and operate delousing ovens, and launch public clean-ups in the streets of the ghettos. On 5 December 1941 the Jewish Committee of Mogilev set up a hospital for contagious diseases on the ruins of the local hospital, catering to thirty patients. The wards of this hospital were unheated and open to the elements. It was here that the first typhus victims were quarantined. In early January the Jewish Committee decided to set up another typhus wing. On 11 January 1942 the Jewish Committee, in a meeting with doctors, decided to introduce quarantine measures and to begin fighting the disease without any help from the Romanian authorities and without medication, food, or heating. Needless to say, their efforts failed.

A slight change in the war on typhus occurred on 13 April 1942 with the arrival in Mogilev of Dr. Constantin Chirilă, the new commander of the army's Forty-Seventh Mobile Disinfection Center and director of the city's medical services. Upon his arrival he called a meeting of Jewish doctors and accused them of negligence in the battle against typhus. When the Jewish doctors protested that they had no disinfectants or medicines, Chirilă promised to help them. Chirilă kept his word. He was the only member of the Romanian medical establishment to make an effort on behalf of the Jews. In June 1942 the Jewish Committee acknowledged that "from the day of his arrival, the major set to work, introduced measures to curb the epidemic and supervised their implementation."[62] With his help another isolation wing was set up in the Jewish hospital and equipped with 100 beds, raising the total number of beds to 164. Thanks to him, houses and clothes were disinfected and the delousing ovens had sufficient fuel to work uninterruptedly. Chirilă and his assistant, Captain Dr. Stuparu, also arranged for three hundred workers from the Jägendorf foundry, using tools they had forged themselves, to clean and disinfect houses and remove garbage and excrement from the streets.

It was only in June 1942 that the epidemic was totally eradicated, thanks in part to the committee's efforts to manufacture soap secretly, purchase kerosene, install delousing ovens, and bury the dead. On 10 January 1943 a senior army medical officer called a meeting of Jewish doctors in Mogilev to warn them to do everything within their power to prevent a new outbreak of typhus. Although the Jewish deportees had been brought to Transnistria to be exterminated, he said, it was their duty to keep the area free of disease.[63] Compared with this attitude, Chirilă's humanitarian approach was all the more remarkable.

The Jewish Committee of Shargorod did not sit by idly waiting for help, either. In December 1941 it repaired the local primitive delousing ovens and reopened a public bathhouse. The first attempt to fight the epidemic failed, however, mainly because of the shortage of medicine, and the number of casualties climbed steadily. Most doctors themselves caught the disease, and about half of them succumbed. In February the Jewish Committee set up a hospital with one hundred beds in the ghetto and ordered all the sick hospitalized. "People were forcibly taken to the public bathhouse, but despite all efforts by the few doctors who had not yet contracted the disease, the epidemic continued unabated, and even intensified." The mortality rate peaked in March; in April 36 percent of those infected died. Provisional help arrived from Romania in April, enabling the repair and operation of several delousing ovens. Clothes were disinfected and people were taken to the bathhouse. Men's heads were shaved and women's hair was treated with kerosene. In May 1942 the ghetto was divided into quarters, with a medical and sanitary team assigned to each quarter "to inspect the houses on a daily basis."[64] In the summer a general delousing campaign was launched. These measures were so successful that although several cases of typhus erupted in October 1942 the autonomous Jewish medical establishment managed to stem the epidemic, and only four Jews died.

From April 1942 the Jewish Committee in Shargorod managed to mobilize Jews for the battle against typhus. That month all the town's wells (not only those in the ghetto) were repaired. "With the ghetto's encouragement and at its expense" the power station operating the water pumps was repaired. A soap factory was set up. The committee ordered the population to boil water. A general vaccination against typhoid fever was introduced, a pharmacy was set up in the ghetto, and six public lavatories were built. "All the town's ruins that had become foci of contagion were destroyed and disinfected." Finally, the synagogue, which had become a shelter for hundreds of dying typhus patients in the winter of 1941–42, was demolished. The survivors were disinfected and assigned to alternative quarters in the ghetto. An outbreak of typhoid fever in June 1942 was controlled and caused only a few fatalities. It was only in November 1943, however, that all epidemics were totally eradicated.[65]

In Bershad and in the northern and eastern subdistricts of the Balta district the epidemic ran its course until it burnt itself out. In these areas the Jewish Committees were unable to bury all the dead in the winter. There were several recurrences of the epidemic in Tulchin and in the various labor camps, where the disease again claimed many lives in 1943.

The typhus epidemic served as a pretext for several expulsions of Jews by the prefect of Mogilev in order to "thin out" the ghetto population. These included the expulsion in 1942 of about 4,000 Jews to the Skazinets camp and of over 3,000 Jews to the Pechora death camp on the banks of the Bug. As stated, the typhus epidemic claimed more lives, proportionally, in the camps along the Bug than in camps in other districts. "The extreme squalor did not allow the deportees to improvise any protective measures. The epidemic followed its natural course until it burnt itself out." In the Ustia ghetto, five kilometers from the Bug, 1,600 out of 2,500 deportees died of typhus.[66] The following excerpt by a survivor of the Nazarinetz ghetto, who was sent there from Mogilev, describes the typhus epidemic and the general mood in the ghetto during the winter of 1941–42: "People were dropping like flies. We had no food, medicine or means of survival. We fought the epidemic with primitive means, and if I survived, it was only thanks to nature. Our calls for help fell on deaf ears. We were cut off from the rest of the world. We felt like castaways on a desert island, without help, abandoned by God and man."[67] The situation described here was common to all the small ghettos and camps along the Bug.

The desperate attempts by the Jewish Committees that existed only in some ghettos (mostly in the Mogilev district) to fight the epidemic single-handedly, even before receiving any help from Romanian Jewry, failed. In the initial stages of the epidemic the Romanian administration prevented or hindered the transfer of aid. It was only the arrival of large consignments of money, medicine, and goods, and of summer weather, that enabled the epidemic to be contained and successful self-help efforts to continue to combat typhus and other epidemics.

The problem of the burial of the tens of thousands of typhus victims in the winter and spring of 1942 epitomizes the savagery of the Holocaust in Romania. The problem of the burial of the dead was first encountered in Bessarabia in July–October 1941 during the mass executions perpetrated by the army and the Romanian gendarmerie with the help of local peasants; the problem was even larger in Transnistria in September–October 1941.

As early as October 1941 the Romanians' indifference to this issue angered the commanders of Einsatzgruppe D. They protested that "the Romanians usually left the victims' bodies where they were shot, without trying to bury them."[68] As stated, the gendarmes accompanying the convoys did not allow the Jews to bury those who died on the way. In a convoy near Yampol, for example, a Jew had to pay a large bribe to a gendarme for permission to bury one of his parents.[69] Many graves throughout Bessarabia remained exposed, and corpses strewn along the roads had to wait until the spring or summer of 1942 to be buried. It was due only to the stench and risk of epidemics that the authorities began recruiting peasants to sprinkle earth over the bodies. The problem of burial placed the entire Jewish community under an enormous moral strain, and the breaking of the taboo concerning respect for the dead caused permanent psychological damage.

Several ghetto communities found their own ways of burying their dead in winter. They thawed the ground with bonfires that were stoked day and night with straw and wood, to be able to dig mass graves. On 6 February 1942 the first attempt to dig a mass grave at the Shargorod cemetery during the winter was made: "In a temperature of minus 40, a bonfire was made and kept alight for 24 hours and thus [the undertakers] managed to dig a mass grave" and bury 165 corpses.[70]

The situation in Ivascauți, a village about ten kilometers from Shargorod where 2,000 Jews were assigned to stables and sties, was even worse. In the absence of a Jewish cemetery the local authorities allowed the deportees to bury their dead in a cemetery for horses. At first the corpses were buried in separate graves, but the graves were too shallow, and scavenger dogs soon mauled them to pieces. In late December 1942 the village still had some 600 Jewish survivors. In January 1942 sixty bodies were piled up in one of the courtyards, and a committee member, "after much pleading and weeping," obtained three carts from the Ukrainian mayor to transport the bodies to the cemetery. "We had to clear away the snow and heat the ground with a straw fire before we could dig the graves."[71] In Tarkanovka, near Obodovka, where 450 out of 550 Jews perished in the winter of

1941–42, the survivors were forced to rekindle the bonfires repeatedly on the frozen ground in order to be able to dig mass graves.[72]

In Tropova, a village about thirty kilometers from Mogilev, a youth spent three days digging two graves in the frozen ground for his mother-in-law and brother, both of them typhus victims. He had had to bribe the village head with a watch for permission to dig "a private grave." When he died, there was no one left to bury him.[73]

In the collective farms where thousands of Jewish deportees were abandoned until the spring burial was a random affair. In a collective farm near Bershad, seventy-seven out of the seventy-eight Jews who had been crammed into a single room in the early winter of 1941 contracted typhus. Since nearly all of them died we have no record of those who perished or even of the name of the farm.[74]

A Jewish woman from Czernowitz who was taken to Balki in northern Transnistria, near the German occupied zone, and was interned with six hundred deportees in a barrack described the fate of her family as follows: "While I was in a typhus coma, my three children perished. There was no one to take care of them. . . . They died of hunger. I do not know how they died, what their last moments were like, or how their little souls were snuffed out. I do not know whether they were buried or where."[75] Her husband was shot to death by the local guards when he left the ghetto in search of medicine.

In 1943 the Jewish artist Arnold Dagani from Czernowitz, who was deported to one of the ghettos, drew a picture on a scrap of paper of survivors' communing with the memory of their dear departed ones. The picture shows mounds of earth (the mass graves), by which a few Jews—the few survivors—stand, praying or weeping. This picture is a testimony to that terrible first winter the deportees experienced in Transnistria.[76]

Typhus and other epidemics lingered in Transnistria because the Romanian authorities took no action to eradicate the diseases among the Jews. Without the Jews' self-help efforts the typhus epidemic would have continued to claim lives until the end of the Romanian occupation of Transnistria. In the second winter of the occupation (1942–43) the epidemic struck mainly at the Gypsies. Without any external support or self-help, they died in the thousands. Sufficient material exists for a study of this topic, which is beyond the scope of this book. It is worth noting, however, that just as with the Jews, the Romanian government in Bucharest and the Romanian administration in Transnistria did nothing to contain the epidemic among the Gypsies, and for the same reason: it proved an excellent and convenient extermination method. The Romanian administration and army doctors, who numbered several dozen, were the watchdogs of this policy and among its initiators. Although these doctors did not conduct medical experiments, perform selections, or test the human limits of endurance as their Nazi colleagues did, they nevertheless helped implement a policy that assumed that Jews were less than human. They treated the masses of deportees in the camps and ghettos of Transnistria as if they were laboratory animals being used in a major experiment. They did not relate to them as human beings who deserved medical care, protection against disease, or even food and shelter. The Romanian doctors also participated in the grand venture of making Bessarabia and Bukovina Judenrein without any pangs of conscience. In so doing they violated the Hippocratic oath and humanitarian values. They were instrumental in helping to implement a policy of genocide.

SUMMARY OF FATALITIES

In November 1943 the deputy minister of the interior, Constantin Vasiliu, estimated that on 1 September 1943, 50,741 of a total of 110,033 Jewish deportees had survived. The remaining 59,292 had fallen victim "to the epidemic, and to the impossibility of providing medical aid and containing the epidemic in war-stricken zones."[77] The figures in this statement were inaccurate and were designed to conceal both the true number of deportees and the killing operations in the Kingdom of Death. As we shall see, the number of deportees ranged from 175,000 to 180,000. Vasiliu did not even mention the Jews who were murdered in the convoys, died of exhaustion, or were handed over to the Germans.

Today, sufficient documentation is available to evaluate the true number of Romanian Jews who perished in the large ghettos and camps of Transnistria from the winter of 1941 to the summer of 1942. This estimate is not entirely accurate because it is hard to differentiate between those who died of typhus and those who died of starvation, exposure, and other diseases. Likewise, it is hard to identify all the collective and state farms to which thousands of Jews were sent, where many of them perished without even being buried. Statistics relating to the ghettos described in this chapter serve as some indication of the extent of deaths from typhus: about 27,000 Jews died of typhus in Bershad and the entire Balta district, about 4,000 in Shargorod, and about 3,500 in Mogilev—a total of about 34,500 deaths.

The representatives of the Autonomous Assistance Commission who visited Transnistria in early 1943 found 72,214 deportees.[78] Since the total number of deportees was about 180,000, some 100,000 Jews must have been killed on the way or have died of typhus and other causes. One fact is certain: about 30,000 Romanian Jews were killed in the Kingdom of Death.[79] The remaining 70,000–75,000 died of typhus, starvation, and exposure between November 1941 and June 1942 (most of them in the winter). Thus the deputy interior minister's estimate was an attempt to conceal the massacre of Romanian Jewry in the Kingdom of Death. To add insult to injury, Alexianu's deposition to the People's Court on 29 April 1946 referred to the casualties from the typhus epidemic as follows: "During the winter of 1941–42, in Transnistrian villages where the Jews were *allegedly* located in camps, several *thousand* Jews died, due to disease, in particular typhus, exhaustion and exposure, just like ordinary civilians and Romanian soldiers."[80]

30

The Hunt for Residents
of Jewish Blood

Had there been a way of measuring exactly how much Jewish blood
the deportees from Bessarabia and Bukovina had, many humanitarian problems — of both an ideological/juridical and a practical/administrative
nature — facing the Transnistrian administration might have been avoided. The
definition of the Romanian nation and of individual citizens on the basis of blood
and Christian faith dated back to the Jewish Statute of 9 August 1940, at the end
of King Carol II's reign, even before the alliance with Nazi Germany. According
to this statute a Jew was defined by his or her religion and ethnic origins and a
Romanian by his or her blood. Then-Minister of Justice Ion Gruia boasted, "We
have devised a wholly Romanian formulation that defines Romanian blood as an
ethnic and moral factor."[1] The Jewish Statute and attendant legislation frequently
referred to "persons of Jewish blood" irrespective of whether they had converted
to Christianity, saw themselves as atheists, or considered themselves Christian
in all respects (see chap. 7).

The deportation from Bessarabia and Bukovina was supposed to affect only
persons of Jewish blood, who, according to the Romanian Orthodox Church,
popular prejudice, and antisemitic folklore were endowed with negative and
even abhorrent genetic traits. Elimination of this nuisance was tantamount to a
physical and spiritual purification — an idea that was reiterated, both wittingly
and unwittingly, in the correspondence relating to the deportations and other
actions to remove the Jews. In summarizing his achievements before resigning
Col. Dimitru Tudose, the military commander of Kishinev, boasted, "I cleansed
the city of Jews and of the remnants of the enemies, and I endowed it with a
Romanian, nay a Christian, character. I established a ghetto for the Jews under
conditions that ensure that they will no longer constitute a danger, either now
or in the future."[2]

The Bessarabian administration kept a file on all Jews, alleged Jews, Christians
of Jewish blood, and children of mixed marriages who remained in the province.

The local pretor of Bolgrad reported the existence of a seven-year-old boy who had not been baptized and was staying with his Russian mother, a seven-year-old girl who had been baptized and was also staying with her Russian mother, a four-year-old girl who was the offspring of a mixed marriage and had been baptized, and two Jewish women who had converted. A list of names attached to the report shows that there were five mixed couples in the town — two with Jewish women and three with Jewish men. The Jewish women in these mixed marriages were not deported because they had been converts for many years. Of the three Jewish husbands, one disappeared, one died, and the third was deported to Transnistria along with his grown-up son who had not converted.[3]

In late July 1942 the governor of Bessarabia published an order instructing all "residents of Jewish blood" still remaining in Bessarabia to report immediately to the police and register for a special census of residents of Jewish blood. This category included all offspring of mixed marriages who had escaped deportation to Transnistria and Jewish women who were married to non-Jews and were long-term converts. Most residents of Jewish blood were not even Jews, and there were so few of them that a special rider was attached to the order that lightened their lot: "The duty to report and register does not apply to Romanians who, [albeit] having Jewish blood, have one non-Jewish parent, were Christian, or converted to Christianity before 9 August 1940."[4]

In Bessarabia and Bukovina residents of Jewish blood were hounded until the provinces were recaptured by the Soviet army. A witch-hunt-cum-census of this kind was conducted in Bessarabia in the summer of 1943, when police chiefs in urban areas were ordered to report the presence of residents of Jewish blood. One of the gendarmes' first tasks in the towns and villages of Transnistria was to track down Jews who were still in hiding — a task they accomplished with the help of informers, of which almost every village had its fair share, at least at the start of the Romanian occupation. Information on people who were in hiding or who had assumed false identities was considered confidential, and the gendarmerie commanders, after collecting data on these cases, sent them on to the Transnistrian Gendarmerie Inspectorate, the district prefecture, the gendarmerie battalion, or the army division or even the army corps stationed in the region. Residents of Jewish blood were divided into several categories: Jewish or half-Jewish children who had been handed over to Christians for safekeeping, children who had been in hiding, children who had been baptized for their own safety but were still considered Jewish, Jewish spouses of mixed marriages (Romanian, Ukrainian, or Russian), Jews who had converted, and finally, Jews posing as Christians.

On 20 November 1941 the police of the city of Balta reported to the prefect that Jews from the ghetto, "hoping one day to return to the city," had entrusted their children to Ukrainian residents, left them money, and even "agreed to their baptism." The Balta police sent local policemen to track down these children and sent them with other convoys to the Kingdom of Death. The police commander recommended that "priests not be allowed to baptize Jewish children."[5]

Paying Ukrainians to look after Jewish children was a common practice among Ukrainian Jews who lived near the routes leading to the Kingdom of Death, in the Rybnitsa, Balta, and Berezovka districts. Although we do not know how widespread this phenomenon was, there were almost certainly hundreds of such cases. The local priests, unlike their Romanian counterparts who were sent to Transnistria, agreed to baptize Jewish children. In December gendarmerie agents reported that Jews from two villages in the Rybnitsa district "had handed over children to Christian families for adoption, and had married off [Jewish] girls to Christian boys, after first baptizing them, to save at least them from deportation."[6] According to the commander of the Transnistrian gendarmerie, who discovered these details on 20 December 1941, the wedding ceremonies were conducted by Russian priests.

A similar attempt by Jews in the Berezovka district who were being marched to camps along the Bug was foiled by gendarmes who managed to catch four children. "The children were arrested and interned in the camp," reported Colonel Broşteanu on 29 March 1942. In Ochakov the deputy chief of the local police himself adopted a Jewish child, but the matter came out into the open and this child, too, was "interned in the camp."[7]

Hundreds — perhaps thousands — of Jewish children were separated from their parents or were handed over to Ukrainians in Transnistria and to Russians in Odessa for adoption or fostering. The Romanian administration sent out agents to track them down. Initially they were interned in the camps and, after mid-1942, in the ghettos. Since their status was determined by race, not religion, it made little difference if a child was baptized or not. Bessarabian children who assumed Christian identities had greater chances of surviving than Bukovinian children, since they spoke Ukrainian or Russian.

The administration operated in two stages with respect to Jewish or half-Jewish children. First, it devised a legal definition of a Jew to determine the status of these children, which was applied in Transnistria, too. Second, it dealt with each category (abandoned children, children posing as Christians, children in hiding, children from Odessa, etc.) separately.

The administration's Research Bureau drew up a draft decree for determining who was a Jew, based on the Jewish Statute of 9 August 1940. This draft decree stated that in Transnistria the following categories would be considered Jewish: those who believed in the Jewish faith; those born to parents of the Jewish faith; baptized children born to parents of the Jewish faith, irrespective of whether the latter had converted; baptized children whose mother was Christian and father Jewish, irrespective of whether the father had converted; illegitimate children whose mother was Jewish; a woman considered Jewish according to the above criteria who was married to a Christian, if she had not converted at least two years before 22 June 1941 (the date of the invasion of the Soviet Union); atheists of Jewish blood; people of Jewish blood who had converted to any other faith; and anyone who converted to Christianity after the decree was enacted. A Christian wife could ask for a separation from a Jewish husband who had not converted. Governor Alexianu did not sign the decree on the grounds that it had come too late.[8] Indeed, most of the local Jews had already been deported and liquidated in the death camps on the Bug or were incarcerated in ghettos, and there was no longer any need for a decree to determine who was a Jew.

Prefect Isopescu asked for instructions regarding the case of half-Jewish children:

> Following the implementation of Order No. 23 issued by the Administration, we await instructions regarding the following cases:
> 1. Children born to a Jewish father and non-Jewish mother;
> 2. Children born to a Jewish mother and non-Jewish father.
> Since these children must *suffer the same fate as their parents*, please instruct us what to do with a child whose deceased father was Jewish, and whose mother is non-Jewish.[9]

According to the draft decree, which was never published and was more a directive than an official order, a child whose mother was Christian and father Jewish was considered Jewish even if he or she had been baptized and had to suffer the same fate as his parents. If, however, the father was deceased, it was impossible to ascertain whether he belonged to one of the categories that defined him as a Jew. In such a case the fate of the children might depend on whether the father had been baptized in his childhood or not, for example. These cases usually arose after local residents volunteered information or the gendarmerie commanders in the villages conducted investigations. Such investigations were commonplace during the second and third years of the Romanian occupation. During the first two years of its regime the administration had been busy tracking down Jewish children who were abandoned, adopted, or hiding.

The Transnistrian Gendarmerie Inspectorate submitted a special case to the administration for a decision-in-principle regarding the status of three children born to an unmarried Ukrainian mother and a Jewish father. After the father was interned in a camp in 1942 the mother quickly had her children baptized. When the gendarmerie inspectors tracked down the children, the mother informed them that "she could not know for sure who the father of her children was, because she had had relations with several men before she became pregnant." The Gendarmerie Inspectorate therefore asked the administration to clarify "what was to become of the three children." After the matter was brought before the Transnistrian administration's Labor Department, its director, Dr. Gheorghe Balcaş, issued the following ruling on 23 March 1943:

> Whereas the woman's statement is ambiguous, and cannot in itself serve as a basis for determining the children's paternity; and
>
> Whereas even had she been married, her husband's paternity would have been hypothetical only; and
>
> Whereas the only fact that is certain is that she is the mother; and
>
> Whereas only recognition of the children by the father through marriage [to the mother] can determine that their status is such that they must suffer the father's fate, and
>
> Whereas no such marriage has so far taken place,
>
> Therefore, in view of the above, we determine that the children of the woman Matroana Culik are illegitimate children only, and therefore have the same nationality and ethnic origins as their mother, that is, Ukrainian.[10]

As a general rule, as long as the children of mixed marriages were minors and were baptized before being discovered, the Romanian authorities tended to leave them with the mother, provided she was not Romanian and the father was imprisoned or dead. (The Germans, on the other hand, had no scruples about executing such children in ethnic German villages, particularly in the Berezovka district.)

The search for residents of Jewish blood did not cease until the eve of Transnistria's liberation. On 2 March 1944 the Transnistrian administration rejected a request by a Russian woman whose stepdaughter had been imprisoned in the Domanevka ghetto on the grounds that both parents "were of Jewish ethnic origin."[11] The mother, who claimed that the daughter was her husband's illegitimate child, requested her release on these grounds, promising to adopt and support her. On 14 February 1944 the administration began investigating the case, and on 2 March it turned down her request. There is no way of knowing whether this decision ever reached the ghetto, since on 28 March 1944 Domanevka was liberated by the Soviet army.

In Odessa the authorities found 479 abandoned Jewish children, of which 211 were ill, most of them no older than six or seven (see chap. 27).[12] They were interned in the hospital of the Slobodka ghetto together with 933 other Jews—including the physically or mentally sick and women who had just given birth—and later transferred to an orphanage the administration had provided for them in Berezovka; later still, some were transferred to Akmechetka. Most of these children perished. The Odessa police continued tracking down and arresting abandoned Jewish children until mid-1943.

Although there were apparently many children of mixed marriages, their chances of disappearing in the large city were greater. This is why they were hardly mentioned in the Romanian documents.

MIXED MARRIAGES

Among the survivors of the first terrible winter in Transnistria were many Jewish women who were married to Romanians and had been deported with their children. After having survived the typhus epidemic and the cold, they now sought permission to return to their husbands. Intermarriage was even more prevalent among Ukrainian Jews in Transnistria. Twenty years of Soviet rule, Communist ideology, and the industrialization process had brought together many youngsters of different nationalities and had led to intermarriage. The massacres in Odessa and the deportations affected all persons who were considered Jewish or who were associated with Jews. In the camps there were hundreds of non-Jewish spouses who had stood by their families. The violence and speed that characterized the incarceration and deportation of Jews left no time for devising alternative strategies that could have saved families of mixed marriages from a similar fate. In many cases it was impossible for mixed couples to disappear due to the prevalence of informers who, right to the end, informed on Jews, half-Jews, and their children and even invented Jews where there were none.

On the basis of a decision issued by the Presidency of the Council of Ministers, Radu Lecca, the commissioner for Jewish affairs, rejected requests by Jewish women who had converted to Christianity to be allowed to return to their husbands in Romania. On 25 November, for example, it rejected a request by Eugenia Marcu, who had married a Romanian in 1933 and had converted around the same time, to be reunited with her husband.[13] Such requests were rejected even when submitted by Romanian husbands.[14] Jewish women who were married to Romanians and survived the deportations to the Kingdom of Death or to the Berezovka district were imprisoned with their children pending clarification of their status. If they could prove that they had been baptized and their children had been baptized at birth, they were freed, but they were not allowed to return to Romania and were placed under police surveillance.[15]

In sum, if one of the partners of a mixed marriage was Romanian the administration took strict measures to preserve "racial purity." Jewish husbands or wives and their children were deported summarily, irrespective of their religion at the time of deportation. The fate of Jewish women who had long converted to Christianity and had escaped deportation was decided on an individual basis, depending on when they and their children had converted, police recommendations, and the husbands' wishes. Such cases were rare since only 157 women of Jewish blood (i.e., a half or a quarter Jewish) remained in Bessarabia. In the case of Ukrainian women married to Romanians from Bessarabia, on the other hand, Antonescu agreed in late March 1942 to allow them to return to their husbands, at their husbands' request.

As Romanian rule became more established the authorities invested greater effort in investigating complaints by local residents concerning the incarceration in camps and ghettos of non-Jewish women married to Jewish men. It is worth noting that non-Jewish spouses who were interned in camps in the Golta and Berezovka districts (hundreds or even thousands of whom chose to stand by their families) suffered the same fate as the Jews. In early February 1942 the "Christian Russian" residents of an entire building block in Odessa sent a telegram to the governor asking for the release of Maria Selecenko, who had mistakenly been deported with her two little children.[16] Col. Matei Velcescu, the chairman of the Central Evacuation Bureau, reported to the administration that investigations showed that the woman was of "Jewish ethnic extraction." In Romanian racist jargon, this meant that she was half-Jewish or a long-standing convert to Christianity.[17] Most Odessan Jews who had been deported by train were no longer alive when the Evacuation Bureau completed its investigation of Maria Selecenko. In a few cases female deportees were released after months of investigations proved beyond a shadow of doubt that they were not Jewish.[18] A point worth noting is that most of these cases were investigated in the second half of 1942, after tens of thousands of Jews had already been killed or perished.

The Romanian occupation authorities took each case of questionable identity very seriously and in some cases even approached the German authorities in the Ukraine when an ethnic investigation was required in the territories under their control. Particularly complex cases were brought before the military tribunal in Odessa. On 5 June 1942, for example, the military tribunal heard the case of Nadejda Iladi and her fifteen-year-old daughter, Maria. Nadejda's Russian husband was demanding they be released after he proved that his wife had converted in 1915, that they had been married by a priest in 1920, and that their daughter had been baptized at birth.[19] The military prosecution in Odessa, however, ruled as follows:

> In accordance with our doctrine and legislation, we find no cause for exempting [the mother] from the provisions of Orders 7 and 9 of the Romanian Army in Odessa [namely, incarceration and deportation from the city]. Maria Iladi [the daughter], on the other hand, was born to a Ukrainian-Russian father and to a Jewish mother and was baptized in the first year of her life. We, therefore, do determine as follows:
>
> Since in Berta's case [Nadejda's Jewish name] there is no cause for exoneration, while in Maria Iladi's case, the provisions of decree-law 1091 of 17 December 1941 are applicable, since she was baptized in the first year of her life, we do therefore recommend that:
> 1. Berta Tubianski be sent to the pretorate which will implement Order 9 in her regard;
> 2. Maria Iladi be handed over to her father.[20]

After approval by General Trestioreanu, the mother was sentenced to incarceration and the daughter released. There is no way of knowing the exact contents of Order no. 9 issued by Second Army Corps headquarters since the order was never made public. It should be noted that the military judges based their ruling on a racist decree-law issued in Romania and signed by Antonescu alone—Decree-Law 1091, which ordered a general census of all "residents of Jewish blood." This was the first time that the legal racist formula of Jewish blood appeared in legislation. This law was not adhered to implicitly, since affiliation with the Christian faith was also a factor in respect to children who had some Jewish blood but who had been baptized before age one. Paragraph 3 of the decree-law stated, "Children of Jewish blood who were not baptized in the first year of their lives shall be considered members of the Jewish faith."[21] The opposite inference was that children of Jewish blood (even if only one of the grandparents was Jewish) who had been baptized at birth and whose parents were Christian were considered Christian, not Jewish. We see from the above that the Transnistrian courts based their rulings about mixed marriages and the offspring of such marriages on Romanian racial laws.

The relative novelty of the Romanian (later Transnistrian) racial laws and the absence of clear provisions gave rise to different and even contradictory rulings concerning converts and similar categories. In Romania the issue was even more complex, since not only blood but also religion was a factor. Consequently, Antonescu was forced to intervene.

In this, as in all matters relating to the purity of the Romanian race, it was Antonescu who set the limits of Romanian and Christian tolerance. In early 1942 he ordered that all Jews "who were long-standing converts no longer be held in the ghettos."[22] This order was given after most converts from Bessarabia, Bukovina, and the Dorohoi district had already been deported. In Romania proper only two ghettos remained: the "small" Kishinev ghetto, with about two hundred Jews, and the Czernowitz ghetto, with about sixteen thousand Jews. Antonescu's order applied only to Jews who had converted to Orthodox Christianity.

In Transnistria gendarmerie agents tracked down converts with the help of informers and investigations. SSI agents considered them a potential security threat and reported them to Romanian army headquarters in Transnistria. In April 1942 a copy of an SSI report on a Jewish woman who had converted to Christianity in 1917 and a Jewish man who had converted in 1914 was sent to Third Army headquarters.[23] Col. Eugen Chirnoagă, chief of the Third Army General Staff, sent the report on to the administration, asking it "to regulate their legal status and to inform us if they should be considered Jewish, since, if so, they are about to be interned in the ghettos."[24] It took almost a month for the administration to reply that "Jews who had converted long before current events would not be sent to ghettos and would not be evacuated."[25]

The Third Army was informed of Antonescu's directive only after the mass deportations, during which converts had also been evacuated and shared the fate of "pure" Jews. Those who managed to escape deportation did so at their own initiative — through bribery, a timely escape, assimilating into the ambient society, and the like. The directives regarding converts were not sent to all Romanian authorities. Even when they were, no prefect or commander of a gendarmerie legion dared take matters into his own hands but referred each case to the administration. Within the administration it was Alexianu who laid down the law, much as Antonescu laid down the substantive law on such matters in Romania. Alexianu, for example, turned down Isopescu's request for the release of Emilia Ambos, a young girl who, "despite being baptized at birth, was nevertheless incarcerated in the ghetto," despite directives exempting converts from birth.[26]

One rule was strictly adhered to: no convert deported from Romania was allowed to return. The administration refused to free the parents of Valentina Popovici from Kishinev—Jews who had converted in 1916—and referred her to the Presidency of the Council of Ministers, "the only authority entitled to deal with such cases."[27] It subsequently transpired that they had been held in the Kishinev ghetto despite their conversion, released, and rearrested and deported with the other Jews of the ghetto.

Hundreds of files on racial and religious issues piled up in the administration, and hundreds of gendarmes and officials were employed to investigate the cases brought to the administration's attention. One such case was a request by a Ukrainian woman from Golta for the release of her niece who was being held in the Berezovka camp. The prefect passed the request on to the administration, which sent it on to the Golta gendarmerie legion, which handed it on to the commander of the Golta gendarmerie post. At the end of an investigation that lasted two months and five days, the girl, who was half-Jewish, was still alive.[28] In most cases requests by residents of Odessa whose relatives had been deported in the large waves of deportation were not granted. Some requests even went unanswered or were answered evasively because the administration knew that the people in question were no longer alive.[29]

JEWS POSING AS CHRISTIANS

In October 1941 a local Ukrainian with typhus was admitted to the hospital in Balta. Local gendarme agents reported to their superiors that, "while delirious with fever, he said that his [true] name was Zeindlblatt Suma from Kishinev, a prisoner-of-war who had been liberated by the Germans."[30] The impostor was transferred to the ghetto before he even recovered. This Jew was one of many who tried to escape the fate of thousands of Jewish prisoners of war whom the Romanian army, emulating its Nazi counterpart, was executing, after first separating the Jewish from the non-Jewish prisoners of war.[31]

The administration devoted much effort and time—sometimes several months—to solving the cases of Jews posing as Christians or suspected of doing so. One case involved Frosia Onischenko, a young girl who was imprisoned in the Suha-Balca camp in the Berezovka district in the summer of 1942. After her arrest Onischenko claimed that she was a Ukrainian from a village near Kiev and even listed the names of members of her family and relatives. The pretor referred the case to the prefecture, which referred it to the gendarmerie and the administration. The administration asked German army liaison headquarters in Transnistria (located in Odessa) to check whether the girl's parents and relatives lived in the villages of Milev and Gorodişte in the Cerkavski district near Kiev, as she claimed. The pretor meanwhile reported that a special investigation was being conducted to determine the woman's "ethnic origins." The German army liaison headquarters informed the Transnistrian administration that the German authorities had been unable to trace her parents or relatives in the aforementioned villages and that Onischenko was a common name in the region. In the absence of solid proof that the girl was of Ukrainian stock, she remained incarcerated the camp. In December 1942, when her fate still hung in the balance, she was probably still alive.[32]

The rule regarding Jews who assumed Christian identities was consistent. No one suspected of masquerading as a Christian was released unless convincing proof showed he or she was not Jewish. Alexei Karasik, for example, who was interned in the Mostovoye camp in late 1942, was not released from the camp "due to this Jew's doubtful origins," which the authorities were unable to clarify.[33]

In Odessa anyone suspected of pretending to be a Christian was deported, even if he was uncircumcised. Some suspects were even executed on suspicion that they were Soviet spies or saboteurs. The case of Alexandru Varsaski, for example, reached the Presidency of the Council of Ministers, and the General Staff sent a special envoy to Odessa to investigate the matter. Varsaski was arrested on suspicion that he was Jewish. Although he claimed he was of Romanian extraction, "he failed to present any documents" and was eventually deported to the Vapniarca detention camp "for endangering the security of the State and Army."[34] Had he been found circumcised during the initial prison inspection he would have been executed, as were all Jewish men who were arrested in Odessa after the end of the deportation operation.

The Romanian authorities were quick to arrest those suspected of masquerading as Christians, usually on the basis of rumors spread by informers. Even when an in-depth investigation showed that the rumors were false, the authorities continued to keep an eye on the suspects. In April three girls from the Ananyev district were arrested on suspicion that they were Jewish. All three were imprisoned in a labor camp, from which they later managed to escape and return to Ananyev, where they were rearrested. Even when an investigation showed that at least two of the girls were not Jewish, the Transnistrian governor told the SSI bureau in Odessa, "In order to prevent incidents, we have ordered them to remain in Ananyev under surveillance, until further notification."[35] The case was so important that even the SSI took an interest in it.

The fate of Jewish children whose parents left them behind in the villages in order to save their lives, who survived the mass executions, or who fled or were told to flee by their parents when they realized that there was no other hope of surviving is beyond the scope of this book. Suffice it to say that hundreds of such children—most of them girls—lived like hunted animals in or around the villages. Many of them were later taken into the Jewish orphanages that were set up beginning in early 1943. Many died of hunger and disease. An unknown number of such children were taken in by Ukrainian families and survived but were lost to the Jewish nation.

THE MOLDOVANS (ETHNIC ROMANIANS)

As early as September 1941 gendarmerie agents gathered information on the situation of the Moldovans and their attitude toward their Romanian brethren. The Transnistrian administration was convinced that the Moldovans supported the extermination operations and that the removal of Jews from their midst led to an immediate improvement in their situation. It is worth noting that the regions inhabited by the Moldovans, mainly near the Dniester, were by then almost entirely purged of Jews.[36]

Indeed, ethnic Romanians in Transnistria were harnessed to the Romanian extermination effort, and many of those who were appointed mayors of villages and towns showed an exceptional degree of cruelty. One such ethnic Romanian, Mihail Kazakievici, directed the executions in Domanevka and participated in the massacres in Bogdanovka. Nevertheless, the ethnic Romanians in Transnistria were less supportive of and committed to the occupation regime than were the ethnic Germans, who became an active branch of the SS in Transnistria.

The administration provided the Moldovans with special documents testifying to their Romanian origins, issued initially by Romanian army headquarters and later by the village mayors.[37] In order to encourage assimilated Moldovans to reclaim their ethnic roots, the administration published an order in February 1942 encouraging them "to revert to their original Romanian name" through a personal affidavit, a church certificate, or any other official document or through witnesses.[38] In May 1942 a "committee for examining applications to revert to Romanian names" was set up. Most of the members of this committee were Moldovans.[39] Although there is no way of ascertaining how many ethnic Romanians availed themselves of this offer, an increasing number applied to the committee in late 1943 and early 1944, many of them collaborators seeking to be evacuated to Romania in order to escape punishment for their crimes. In January 1944 the administration issued an order limiting the number of applicants.[40]

The Romanian administration in Transnistria protected and promoted the Romanian minority there and offered its youth key positions within the administration, including those relating to security and the extermination of Jews. To some extent the Romanian administration's attitude toward the ethnic Romanians was based on the German administration's policy toward ethnic Germans. The Romanian administration wished to turn ethnic Romanians in Transnistria as well as the Romanian officials it sent over into Transnistria's future lords, once the Jews had been eliminated and the Ukrainian population diluted. It relocated Romanians from occupied southern Russia and the Ukraine to localities along the Bug and Dniester — localities that also served as large extermination sites. In this way it not only "killed" but also "inherited" (1 Kings 21:19).

31

The Romanian Church and the Christianization Campaign

The Antonescu regime, which defined itself as a Christian regime, saw Transnistria as a territory that had been defiled by the godless Bolsheviks and, right from the start, launched a campaign to bring the people back to Christianity (*recreştinarea poporului transnistrian*).[1] In August 1941, before the occupation of Transnistria had been completed or its borders finally determined, Patriarch Nicodim met with Antonescu. At this meeting they decided to send a mission of the Romanian Orthodox Church to Transnistria in order to bring the people back to Christianity. For about one and a half years, 250 priests who called themselves missionaries were sent over to reinforce the 219 local Orthodox priests. Three hundred nine churches and prayer halls—twenty-two in Odessa alone—were renovated. The administration and the church mission launched a missionary campaign in the villages by distributing leaflets, prayer books, and calendars. They published primers on matters of faith that addressed the skeptical youth who had been exposed to antireligious Communist ideology. These articles were also directed against the various Christian sects. On each visit to Transnistria Antonescu made a point of visiting renovated churches, genuflecting, kissing ancient icons, crossing himself, and having himself photographed in the presence of Romanian and local priests and worshippers.

Antonescu's attitude toward the Ukrainians and Slavs in general was full of contradictions. For him the war against the Soviet Union was a huge confrontation between Christianity and Judaism, between good and evil, between Christ and Antichrist (Satan). In directives he sent Mihai Antonescu from the front on 3 September 1941 he emphasized, "Everyone must understand that this is not a war against the Slavs, but against the Jews. A life and death war: Either we win and the world is purified, or they win and we will be their slaves. . . . [T]he Jew is Satan. . . . This explains our heavy losses."[2] In this war, argued Antonescu, the Slavs were also the victims of the Jew, who was urging them to fight against the Christian Romanian army.

The campaign to bring the Ukrainians back to Christianity was no simple matter, although it was well received by a large percentage of the population. The Ukraine was religiously divided. In the east and, generally speaking, in the parts that belonged to the Soviet Union until the invasion of Poland (September 1939) Orthodox Christianity prevailed, while in Galicia the Eastern (Unitarian) Greco-Catholic Church, a strongly nationalistic Ukrainian church and a legacy of Austrian rule, prevailed. The Unitarian Church extended the influence of the Catholic Church by integrating eastern Christianity with recognition of the pope as the supreme religious authority. The Ukrainian Orthodox Church, despite its seniority and its strongly independent center in Kiev, was subject to the patriarchate in Moscow. Toward the end of the First World War the political struggle for independence gave rise to a religious movement that campaigned for the establishment of an independent Ukrainian church not subject to Moscow. The rebellion against the Russian Church led to the establishment of two independent, rival Ukrainian churches in addition to the official church.[3]

THE CHURCH, THE ADMINISTRATION, AND THE JEWS

The Jews were never a bone of contention between the administration and the Romanian Orthodox Church in Bucharest, or its mission in Odessa. The church never raised moral issues concerning the administration's policy toward the Jews, while the administration treated the church as its subordinate on this issue. Indeed, the church—not to mention the gendarmerie, the police, and the Bank of Transnistria—was directly subordinate to the administration (see chart 3). Thus, for example, when Archimandrite Iuliu Scriban (the superior of a large monastery) asked Patriarch Nicodim whether it was permissible to baptize Jews seeking to convert, the patriarch replied that this was not an ecclesiastic or spiritual issue but rather an administrative one under the governor's jurisdiction: "As far as the baptism of Jews is concerned, please note that in the Regat this is forbidden according to a decree-law on the conversion of Jews, for reasons of protecting the race. On the issue of whether this decree-law, which is valid in the Kingdom, shall or shall not be applied in Transnistria—you must approach the Governor of Transnistria, and together with his Excellency, solve the problem of the baptism of Jews in these territories."[4]

On the basis of this letter Radu Lecca, the commissioner for Jewish affairs, directly informed various departments of the administration that the Holy Synod prohibited the baptism of Jews, although the patriarch's decision actually allowed the administration considerable room for maneuver.[5] The heads of the church mission interpreted the letter in a similar manner. In principle the administration did not approve the baptism of Jews of "pure" Jewish blood, while the church mission, which the patriarch's decision subordinated to the administration even on matters of dogma, did not even approach the administration on the issue. The mission's dependency on the administration was even more obvious on the issue of the baptism of children with Jewish fathers and Ukrainian mothers who had not been baptized as infants (in the first year of their lives). These cases became an issue only after the consolidation of the Romanian Church in Transnistria and the subordination of the local priests to the Romanian Orthodox Church Mission. Prior to that the local priests had never had a problem with baptizing the children of mixed marriages. In June 1942 the mission's secretary, Archimandrite Antim Nica, asked the governor on behalf of the mission to permit the baptism of two children of a Ukrainian woman whose husband had been drafted into the Red Army in 1941. As he put it, "Was there any civilian obstacle to granting the Mysteries of Holy Baptism" to the two children?[6] As usual, the governor presented him with a written refusal, in his own handwriting.

From the administration's perspective the Jew did not exist as a religious entity. The administration's Order no. 89 of September 1942 recognized seven religions, including Islam, forbade the establishment of religious sects, and referred to the Jews only en passant. Paragraph 8 allowed those age eighteen and over to convert (but only to one of the seven recognized religions), while paragraph 10 forbade Jews to convert to any of the recognized religions "until further notice." Another paragraph ordered the Orthodox Church in Transnistria to adopt the new calendar.[7]

Christianity and the church as expressions of divine support for the Romanian experiment in Transnistria and the victory of the cross over Communism and Satan as a living proof of this support were incorporated into all ceremonial speeches delivered by the governor or the administration's representatives. This form of presenting events and wars that the Romanian people were involved in was part of the Romanian state's religious tradition and was not borrowed from the Nazis. The Nazis did not harness Jesus to their propaganda machine. This way of presenting events and actions and the willingness of the Orthodox Church and its clergy to help realize the administration's goals freed individual Romanians from the need to weigh up their actions against universal humanistic values, which had, in any case, been ridiculed by at least two generations of nationalist and fascist intellectuals, who identified them with Jews and Judaism.

In early 1942 Vasile Mănescu, the pretor of the Domanevka subdistrict, reported that "the day of the birth of our Lord" had been in the subdistricts of Domanevka and Bogdanovka and in other places.[8] In Bogdanovka the executions were called to a halt to allow the celebrations to take place, and the Ukrainian policemen in charge of the slaughter of Jews were granted a four-day leave beginning in the early hours of 24 December 1941 to celebrate Christmas. That same morning Prefect Isopescu, dressed in his holiday best, arrived to inspect the camp. Thirty thousand corpses were thrown into the valley or strewn along the roads leading to the camp. Afterward he returned to Golta to celebrate Christmas and the New Year with friends he had invited from Bucharest, to the accompaniment of a Gypsy band. Midnight Mass was conducted in the newly renovated churches by six priests who had been sent over from Bessarabia: the head of the district church, Ion Sârbu (from Hotin), who was assigned to the Golta cathedral; his deputy, Eutichie Rudnai, from the Ismail district in southern Bessarabia, also assigned to the Golta cathedral; Pavel Bondurovschi, also from the Ismail district, who served as priest in the Moldovan village of Lubashevca; Gheorghe Ilaș from the Hotin district, who served as priest in the church of Krivoye Ozero; a priest from Kishinev, who conducted the service in Shirovo; and a monk from Kishinev who conducted the service in Bobric. Two local priests held services in Akmechetka and in the St. Nicolae Church in Golta. Sârbu and Rudnai led the Christmas and New Year's services in Golta in Romanian in the presence of Prefect Isopescu, his deputy Pădure, and all the officials and gendarmerie commanders as well as the commander of the Romanian garrison in the city, in a church that was hard to heat due to the freezing weather (minus thirty-five degrees). There were four churches in the Domanevka subdistrict, two of which (those in Bogdanovka and Akmechetka) were in a state of disrepair and needed renovation.[9] The clergy and church authorities were more upset by this than they were by the extermination of eighty thousand Jews in the same subdistrict.

On 1 July 1942, a month after the burning of corpses in Bogdanovka came to an end, Mihail Melnic, a Romanian priest, reached the erstwhile Jewish town of Domanevka. In his efforts to rehabilitate religious life he visited the villages that served as graveyards for tens of thousands of Jews. Having visited Akmechetka (where dozens of Jews were dying of starvation daily), he noted "that Christian life and tradition still occupied a central place in the villagers' consciousness." The inhabitants of Akmechetka, unhappy that the service was conducted in Romanian, tried to bring in a local priest to lead the prayers in Ukrainian but were stopped by the gendarmes. The Akmechetka church lacked ritual adornments, priestly robes, and silver-plated prayer books. Less than two months after Melnic's arrival, he already knew who had spearheaded the struggle against the church under the Communists: "The religious [i.e., antireligious] propaganda was conducted mainly by the Jews. Presently, the population is angry because it is forced to work on festivals, particularly on Sundays."[10] This last sentence reveals the paradox that underlay the Christianization policy. On the one hand churches were renovated, Christian propaganda was disseminated, and church-going was encouraged, while on the other hand peasants were forced to work even on Sundays in order to cultivate the land. This being so, church services were attended mainly by old folk who looked as if they were preparing themselves for the Day of Reckoning.

In the village of Bogdanovka (where local Ukrainians had traded with Jews in the overcrowded camp prior to their execution and were unable to sleep after their execution for the smell of burnt flesh) Melnic found that "the people are God-fearing and joyously await the priest's arrival." After the local church was destroyed by the Soviet authorities in 1938, the village and five small neighboring localities had no place of worship. "This village requires the presence of a priest who can speak the local vernacular, and who aspires with all his heart [to plough] the field of our lord," Melnic reported, and he later intervened himself in order to obtain building materials to erect a church in Bogdanovka.[11]

The town of Domanevka was considered the crowning glory of the Christianization campaign. The town — 41 percent of whose inhabitants had been Jewish before the war — was partly destroyed. In 1942 about 2,853 Ukrainians were living there. The pile of corpses in the center of the town as well as the corpses that were scattered in and around the town were buried once the snows melted. The ghetto was moved to the outskirts of the town, and the corpses were burnt in the forest so that the stench of burning flesh would not reach the town. Melnic and his colleague, Mihail Moraru from the bishopric of Kishinev, who arrived in July 1942, invested time, money, and effort in rehabilitating the town's generously sized church.

Similar achievements were recorded in all the villages, the very names of which sent a shiver among the Jews who were interned there or passed through them on their way to Bogdanovka or Domanevka. Christian life in the villages of the Berezovka district flourished alongside the extermination of Jews by the Romanian gendarmes and Sonderkommando R. On 20–21 May 1943, after most Jews had been killed, their corpses burnt, and all the churches renovated, Metropolitan Iancu Vissarion, head of the Orthodox Church in Transnistria, visited the district.[12]

The ethnic Germans in the Landau subdistrict and the Berezovka and Odessa districts also led Christian lives and needed their churches renovated and Catholic and Lutheran clergy imported from Germany and Romania. The local Germans in Transnistria renovated their Catholic and Lutheran churches voluntarily and also celebrated the Christian festivals, went to confession, and received absolution. Meanwhile, their murder squads continued murdering Jews until around the autumn of 1943, when all the Germans were evacuated to the Reich.

Thus the Romanian Orthodox Church and the Romanian priests who were sent over to Transnistria consistently pursued the goal of creating a normal society in Transnistria by renovating its churches and bringing the Ukrainians back to the Christian faith. Never once did they see or mention Jews. Even before the Antonescu regime, when Miron Cristea (the most antisemitic figure after Corneliu Codreanu, the Iron Guard leader) was patriarch, the church initiated and conducted an antisemitic campaign with a Christian bias that denied the Jewish roots of Christianity. In the eyes of the clergy the Jews in Transnistria ceased being humans and became instead nonentities or, even worse, Satan's assistants or Satan himself, as Antonescu put it. The clergy's ability to differentiate between Christian values and their application to Jews is a subject worth studying in its own right. At the height of the war the patriarch and the various metropolitans published special epistles designed to encourage the soldiers. These epistles, which were printed in the ecclesiastical printing houses in an ancient script, all ended in famous verses from the Book of Psalms.[13]

Even though the Romanians considered the local Ukrainian and Russian Christians enemies of the Romanian state, their attitude toward them was quite different. Occupiers and occupied prayed in the same churches, bowed to the same God, celebrated the same festivals, and even intermarried.[14] Although the entire Transnistrian population was under Romanian occupation, the Jews suffered a different fate from that of the Christians. The war waged against the Jewish people negated their existence on Christian-antisemitic and racist-biological grounds. The Romanian concepts of blood and Christianity were the equivalents of the Nazi concepts of an inferior and defective race.

32

The Degradation of Judaism and Jews

The war against the Soviet Union was declared a holy war to rid Romanian territory of the Bolsheviks and Jews, who tried to eradicate the Christian faith from it during the year the Soviets ruled. Right from the start the war took on the character of a crusade against Judaism and the Jews, who were identified as the architects and proponents of Bolshevism. Although anti-Communist and anti-Jewish themes were not new, they now became the official position of the Romanian regime. The regime considered itself the heir of the nationalist current of Romanian political and social thought and also adopted the antisemitic legacy of the Iron Guard, despite having ousted it from government. From the first day of the war the regime's leaders, the heads of the Romanian Orthodox Church, journalists, and part of the Romanian intelligentsia issued the battle cry for a crusade against Judaism. All barriers—whether humanitarian, Christian, or legal—that might have limited this crusade had already been breached and were now totally removed.

The open campaign against Judaism was launched by Mihai Antonescu, who announced the beginning of the campaign to "purify the nation" and rejected the principles of humanism that "masked the interests of a race aspiring to rule over everyone," behind which "stood an exploitative religion," namely Judaism.[1] Mihai Antonescu used Christian themes to sanction genocide. In a radio speech at the outbreak of war he drew parallels between the suffering the Russians caused the Romanians in the occupied land and the passion of Christ. He described the Jews as "accomplices in the Bolsheviks' crime" who rejoiced at "our Christian crucifixion" and added "their Jewish insult" (*ofensă iudaică*) to the suffering of the Romanian people. Vengeance would be complete, he emphasized, only when the "evil foreigners" were expelled. Only then would it be possible to say, "Bessarabia, I have avenged you."[2]

The Romanian press translated Mihai Antonescu's directives into clear and unequivocal language. Adopting the images Antonescu, who was also the propaganda minister, bandied about, it launched a slander campaign against everything Jewish: the religion, the synagogue, rabbis, and Jewish values. All Romanian newspapers participated in this campaign, the only differences between them being ones of emphasis and vehemence. As a standard antisemitic paper wrote, the holy war was being waged against those "who had profaned the altar on the holy land," against "the Yids and Bolsheviks who had devastated the Redeemer's home, and crucified the [Christian] faith on the cross of their iniquity."[3] The antisemitic press presented the problem in simplified terms: "The war is between two worlds: the world of Christianity and the World of Judaism." In a few months, the paper continued, the Soviet Union would be defeated and Radio Moscow would issue a new call: "Christians of the world unite." The world would cast out Judaism "and Israel [the Jewish people] will cease to exist."[4] Bolshevism, explained one paper, "is simply a satanic invasion by international Judaism in its desire to rule the world. . . . They have replaced the icons of Jesus [in the church] with Lenin's picture."[5] Incitement against Judaism was rabid and delusional: "Stalin is actually a Galician Jew, a cousin of Anna Pauker [a Romanian Jewish Communist]. Stalin, the butcher from the Kremlin, is the brother of Moritz Gutman, Jabotinski's nephew."[6]

The regime's ideologues and the Romanian press found loyal allies in the war against Judaism: the heads of the Romanian Orthodox Church, the patriarch, the metropolitans, and the rank-and-file priests. Patriarch Nicodim called on the faithful to support the Conducător, to enlist as one man in the war alongside the Germans allies and fight together "in the holy crusade against Bolshevism." He exhorted the public to strike at "the criminal souls [of the Bolshevik] lackeys . . . the despicable lackeys of Satan, who are mainly foreigners, [members] of the people that has brought upon itself a divine curse ever since it crucified the son of God."[7] For the Romanian soldiers, most of whom were peasants or children of peasants, the words of the patriarch (and of the metropolitans, as we shall see) were gospel truth.

Upon the liberation of the territories another accusation was leveled against the Jews. They were accused of having set fire to the cathedrals in Czernowitz and Kishinev (and other churches), fueled by a blind hatred of Christianity. "Which satanic mind, you may wonder, that grew up in the shadow of the Talmud and in the warrens of the Free Masons, could have conceived and perpetrated such destruction."[8]

The degradation of Judaism took several forms: extreme abuse of rabbis, ritual slaughterers, and all Jews with beards and sidelocks prior to their execution; the desecration and destruction of synagogues; the desecration of Torah scrolls; the use of scraps of Torah parchment for sacrilegious purposes; the conversion of synagogues that were still standing into stables (for the army's horses), cowsheds, and warehouses; the choice of Jewish festivals as days of retribution (for violence against rabbis, liquidations, and deportations); the desecration of cemeteries, removal of bones, and obliteration of any hint of Jewish existence in the place; the paving of streets with Jewish tombstones; the use of synagogue ruins to restore and renovate churches; the sale and desecration of ritual objects; and last but not least, the rape of Jewish woman and girls on a scale and in a manner unprecedented in the Romanian state.

It is important to differentiate between what took place in Bessarabia and Bukovina and what took place in Romanian territories from which the Jews were not deported. In Bessarabia and Bukovina the deportations were preceded by a massive looting and murder operation in which the local population was encouraged to take part. The administration's policy toward the Jews varied depending on whether they were in extermination and deportation zones (Bessarabia and Bukovina), evacuation zones (the Regat and southern Transylvania), or cities or towns from which the Jews were not deported or evacuated.

THE DEGRADATION OF JEWISH WOMEN

This aspect of the Jewish catastrophe in Bessarabia and Bukovina is less well known, for obvious reasons, although immediately after the liberation it began to be aired. It fell in with the Romanian authorities' deliberate decision to release the soldiers and the Romanian people in general from all moral and legal reservations and deal with the Jews, their property, their homes, their faith, and their bodies as they wished. The degradation of Jewish girls was not considered a crime but rather a prize awarded the Romanians—the very realization of Cuza's and Codreanu's promises to expel the Jews from Romania and distribute their property among the righteous Romanians. In June 1941 it was evident that Jewish women were considered spoils of war. Although the Romanian soldiers also raped Russian and Ukrainian women, as far as Jewish women were concerned it was clear that the soldiers could do with them whatever they wished since Jewish women were no longer considered human and were going to die anyway. The freedom granted the soldiers to give free rein to their desires and the encouragement granted the peasants and the civilian population to attack Jews led in Bessarabia and Bukovina to the bestialization of an entire nation, irrespective of individuals' social class, and absolved the Romanians of all moral, legal, Christian, or cultural restraints.

One aspect of this topic relates to the attitude toward racist theories and the definition of a Jew in the Jewish Statute of 8 August 1940, passed during King

Carol II's reign. Since the Romanian nation was not defined as a pure nation from a racial point of view but rather as a nation that had coalesced on the basis of a shared history, language, blood, and faith, raping Jewish women was not considered a stigma or stain on Romanian purity of race but rather as normal behavior in time of war and as an additional opportunity for degrading Jews and Judaism.

Hadassah Goldberg

Hadassah Goldberg, from the town of Secureni in Bessarabia, was nineteen years old when she committed suicide. The Romanian and German units launched their first pogrom against the Jews on the night they occupied the town. This was followed by a looting and raping rampage. "The [Romanian] officers sent soldiers to search the houses for young women and girls, who were then brought back to the officers and cruelly raped." Hadassah was one of these girls: "She was taken away by force, amidst her mother's distraught shrieks, and brought to the Romanian officer who . . . satisfied his perversions by beating her cruelly and afterward raping her. The following day she was sent home in a terrible state. . . . She and her mother shut themselves in their home and put an end to their lives in the attic by swallowing poison."[9]

Hadassah Goldberg is one example of the many Jewish girls who committed suicide in the towns of Bessarabia after being raped and humiliated. She is a memorial to all the anonymous Jewish girls of Bessarabia and Bukovina who suffered indescribable psychological and physical torture and abuse before they committed suicide or were shot to death after being abused, as were the girls of Mărculeşti. We know the names of dozens of girls who hanged themselves or chose other ways of ending their misery.

Defending the Honor of the Girls

In Edineți, a typical Jewish town in Bessarabia, the pogrom followed no prescribed order and it was hard to know what came first: looting, killing, or rape. These crimes were perpetrated not only by local inhabitants but also by inhabitants of the surrounding villages of Ruseni, Golieni, Gordieşti, and Trabana. During the rampage, which lasted several days, girls were raped in houses, courtyards, gardens, and cellars, in the presence of members of their families. In Edineți there were several instances of men trying to prevent the rape of their daughters and sisters, but all of them ended tragically.

Hirsh Kuzminer, a teacher, organized a self-defense group for Jewish men to protect their families and forty women who were hiding with their children in a cellar. Although they managed to prevent the soldiers from breaking into the cellar to rape the women, they were all shot on the spot. Shimon Kavel, a blacksmith, fought with all his might to prevent peasants from raping his daughters, but he too was killed, together with his family. Eizic Libec and his relatives tried — in vain — to protect their wives and daughters but suffered the same fate as their predecessors. Velvele Ludmir and a group of youths were all murdered trying to protect the honor of their wives, daughters, mothers, and sisters. All the butchers of Edineți and an additional forty or so men organized an armed resistance group using the tools of their trade — knives and cleavers — to protect their wives and daughters and their property. Although they fought fearlessly, they too were overpowered.

In a particularly savage act of brutality the Romanians raped the three young daughters of David Mutzelmacher, who owned a haberdashery store in the market square, in his presence. Following this barbaric act the girls went up to the attic and hanged themselves, while their father jumped into a deep well in the churchyard. The Klufman family suffered a similar fate. The daughters all committed suicide after being brutally raped. The mother, too, tried to hang herself, but the rope tore, and she survived. She subsequently became crazy.[10]

Although there were many cases in Bessarabia of men defending the honor of their womenfolk, only a few such cases are known since none were left to tell the tale. In the provisional camps set up in Bessarabia pending the deportation to Transnistria, Romanian officers continued to humiliate Jewish girls who arrived on foot from the towns and new arrivals by train from southern Bukovina and from Czernowitz. In the Vertujeni camp that was set up in September 1941 the entire camp staff was involved in these vile acts. Altogether, the Jewish family was disintegrating on a daily basis. The older members could not keep up with the convoys and were shot to death. Young men were handpicked from the convoys to carry out various jobs and later shot. Little children died of starvation or from the hardships on the journey. In the Vertujeni camp about 130 Jews died daily.

The gendarmerie officers and the representatives of the National Bank of Romania who came to steal the Jews' last belongings organized orgies in the camp compound. Their modus operandi was simple: in the evening the gendarmes rounded up the girls and took them by force to houses in the Romanian village of Vertujeni, where the officers lived. At the 1945 trial of the camp commanders a Romanian peasant testified, "On several occasions, Captain Rădulescu and an officer of second lieutenant rank brought young Jewish girls over forcibly and slept with them. The women screamed and wailed all night long. Almost every evening women were raped. Captain Sever Buradescu also participated in these orgies, and often brought Jewish women home with him." After the Vertujeni camp was closed Buradescu and Mihăescu were transferred to the Mărculeşti camp, where they continued to rape girls.[11]

In Mărculeşti the degradation of women and girls began as soon as they stepped off the trains. At the entrance to the camp they were subjected to gynecological searches—an invasive and degrading procedure that the Romanian gendarmerie and police had perfected to a fine art—in an attempt to discover money and jewelry. During these humiliating searches Buradescu and gendarmerie officers chose young virgins and forced them into huts where they and the gendarmerie commanders and their subordinates gang-raped them.[12]

Throughout the Romanian occupation of Transnistria the soldiers, and especially the officers, had an endless supply of Jewish women. The workshops that were erected throughout the province to serve the administration's civil servants also served the army officers in all matters relating to the procurement of women. In October 1943 the Siguranţa office in Odessa reported to the administration that Cracovianu, the overseer of Jews in the Birzula workshops, "forced [Jewish] women to have sex with officers of the garrison attached to the Thirty-fifth Infantry Division." Later on he reported how a captain had asked for "all young women" to be brought to him and had selected Anna Binder, who "was placed at his disposal."[13]

Aristide Pădure, the deputy prefect of the Golta district, was in the habit of visiting the district camps and selecting beautiful Jewish girls for himself. He would then offer them a choice between the Akmechetka death camp and the chance to live a little while longer in his private home in Golta. As the indictment put it, "He sent whomever he wished to Akmechetka, and those he fancied to his harem."[14] A Jewish survivor of the Golta ghetto invested this dry legal description with some life: "Pădure would yell like a madman, hit us brutally until we bled, send people to the Akmechetka death camp at will . . . rape Jewish women, especially young ones . . . drink all night long, turn up at the camp in the morning drunk, and beat us mercilessly."[15]

The court cited a number of other methods the gendarmes used to rape Jewish girls. For example, NCO Ion Nastase, commander of the gendarmerie camp in Bershad, "was constantly drunk and hit anyone at sight. At night, he would walk through the ghetto streets breaking windows in order to force [Jewish] women out into the open, and then rape them."[16]

In the Large Ghettos of Kishinev, Czernowitz, and Odessa

The Jews of Czernowitz remembered how the Romanian (and also German) army was given three days "to loot, kill and rape Jewish women."[17] They were preceded by a mob of local residents and peasants from the area, who began raiding Jewish homes immediately after the Soviet army's withdrawal from the city and continued on the rampage even after the city's occupation.[18] Soon the streets were littered with the corpses of Jews who had been driven out of their homes and shot on the spot. "What terrified us the most was the fact that the Romanians went from house to house, picking out girls whom they then raped and murdered. We had two sisters we were extremely anxious about. We did not know what to do or where to hide them."[19]

German soldiers also participated in the murder and looting spree. "We were fair game," said a Jew from Czernowitz. "The Jewish quarter became a killing zone. The Germans and Romanians broke into Jewish homes and shot everyone on sight. They raped Jewish girls and women, and then murdered them. . . . Dead Jews lay in the streets in pools of blood."[20] However, the murder of thousands of Jews by Einsatzgruppe D, the army, and the Romanian police and the deportation of thirty thousand Jews in the autumn of 1941 made the problem of rape pale in comparison.

Second Lieutenant Enăchiță oversaw a transport of Jews from Czernowitz, deported in May 1942 to the Cariera de Piatră stone quarry, near Ladizhin: "Already on the train to Ladizhin he selected a beautiful girl, and a few months later, ordered an abortion to be performed for her on a makeshift table in the camp. His arrival in the camp was a signal for orgies. Lederman [the head of the ghetto], would each time select a girl for Enăchiță who would fire his gun during orgies. If we were lucky, he missed."[21] Eventually most of these Jews were handed over to the commanders of the German labor camps on the German side of the Bug.

In Kishinev raping began the day the Romanian army entered the city. The looting, rape, and murder rampage that took place in Kishinev proved that here, too, the soldiers had been given free hand for forty-eight hours to do with the Jews as they pleased. "It is impossible to draw up a list of all those who raped, looted and perpetrated other crimes in the city, since Kishinev was invaded by [whole] army units," testified one of the survivors.[22] Thousands of Jews were shot on the roads from Kishinev to the Dniester, and hundreds in the city itself. Only the need to bury the corpses because of the hot weather forced the soldiers to suspend the rampage.

The Kishinev ghetto, with over eleven thousand Jews and average room occupancy of twenty-five to forty people, became the playground of Romanian soldiers and policemen—particularly officers—on the way to the front.[23] "Each day, officers arrived at the ghetto, conducted searches, looted, and raped all the girls," testified a Jewish girl who was seventeen years old at the time.[24] Since the ghetto area was small and each wretched house contained hundreds of Jews, the Romanian and German soldiers were not able to carry out their designs on the spot. The ghetto became a hunting ground where young girls were abducted from their parents and taken away in military vehicles, never to return. The Jews of the Kishinev ghetto were murdered on the way to the transit points in Rezina, along the deportation route to Bogdanovka, and in the Kingdom of Death. There were hardly any survivors. Although all the Jews suffered, rape made the fate of Jewish women far worse.

The (second) Odessa ghetto was hell on earth. It was set up after the two waves of execution of the city's Jews, in the first of which several thousand Jews were shot or hanged and in the second of which twenty-two thousand were shot; most of the corpses were burnt. The ghetto was set up during the freezing Ukrainian winter, and many Jews froze to death in the streets. Some were even ordered to bring their dead with them to the train station when they were deported from the ghetto.

The rape of Jewish women was not that common in Odessa. Apparently in the early days of the Romanian occupation more Russian than Jewish women were raped by Romanian soldiers simply because most Jews had already been killed. In the period between the Romanian occupation and the establishment of the ghetto, however, the Romanian police, whose units had been brought over from Romania, ruled Odessa with a total lack of restraint. In this period, which lasted about two months, the Jews of Odessa, particularly Jewish women, were turned into the abject slaves of the Romanian administration.

The inspector of the gendarmerie in Transnistria, Col. Marcel Petală, who supervised the deportation operation, could not recall cases of murder, rape, or robbery in the streets of Odessa. Petală testified in his own handwriting that no one had reported any reckless acts and that "no one against whom such acts were supposedly perpetrated" complained. Nor was there a report, "let alone a rumor," of anyone being injured.[25] He was not lying. No Jew stayed behind in Odessa to complain. They all meekly boarded the train that carried them to their death. The administration's official photographer recalled how the commanders of the Odessa police occasionally asked him "to photograph them in the nude with [local] girls from Odessa." The commissars and police agents, including the commanders of the subdistricts, "would round up girls, even virgins . . . and bring them, through devious means, to parties that turned into orgies."[26]

Jewish families from Odessa who were deported in that period by foot to Mostovoye and Domanevka faced complex moral dilemmas. Izu Landau, a Bessarabian Jew who was arrested in Odessa and deported from Dalnic to the Kingdom of Death on 27 October 1941 in a convoy of ten thousand Jews, described one of the choices Jewish families faced: "After each [night] stop, dozens of Jews who were unable to get up were shot to death in front of the others. The remainder continued on. Mothers abandoned their children and children their parents. Girls aged 14–15 were raped in their parents' presence. Many parents allowed their daughters to be raped in exchange for a night's shelter in any room or cowshed."[27]

Who could judge a Jew faced with a "choice" between "surrendering" his teen-age daughter or letting the rest of the family freeze to death in a field? The fact that rape and death went hand in hand, and the facility with which the Romanian soldiers abused Jewish girls before their execution, was fully demonstrated in the night preceding the liquidation of the Jews of Sculeni in the Iaşi district.[28] That night the girls were gang-raped in front of their parents before being mowed down by machine guns, together with their families. There were no human feelings, no public expression of aversion, and no fear of retribution either in this or the next world. Such acts could never have taken place without the dehumanization of the Jews and the disintegration of moral—and even Christian—values.

The memorial book published by the Association of Deportees to Transnistria in 1945 had four pictures illustrating Jewish suffering in Transnistria. One of the pictures shows two children standing near their murdered parents. The three others are of girls and women: "Women who were raped and disgraced, two women in the throes of death; the innocent [female] victims of Transnistria."[29]

The suffering of the Jewish women did not end with the liberation. Romania was infected with sexually transmitted diseases and TB (tuberculosis).[30] At the time STDs, particularly syphilis, were incurable. Consequently many Jewish girls became infertile, while others never got married or else committed suicide.

33

The Iaşi Pogrom, 29 June 1941

ANTECEDENTS

The pogrom against the Jews of Iaşi was carried out on the express order of Ion Antonescu to cleanse the city of Jews and to ruthlessly liquidate any Jew who might open fire on Romanian or German soldiers.[1] The Second Section of Romanian army general headquarters and the Romanian SSI laid the groundwork for the Iaşi pogrom and supplied the pretext for punishing the city's Jewish population, while German army units stationed in the city helped the Romanian authorities carry out their antisemitic fantasy. The planning of the massacre was modeled on the pogrom in Dorohoi in the summer of 1940 and not on Nazi massacres in Eastern Europe (such as the pogrom in Lvov in early July 1941), which were only just beginning. However, without the presence of the German army in Romania the Antonescu regime would never had dared to concoct such a plan and on such a scale. A comparison between the Dorohoi and Iaşi pogroms shows that, apart from the participation of German soldiers in the Iaşi pogrom and the scale of the butchery, the recipe for carrying out pogroms against Jews had not changed. Although the scale of the Iaşi pogrom was much larger, its orders more explicit, and more Romanians participated in it, it basically followed the same pattern as the Dorohoi pogrom.

The evacuation of Jews from Iaşi was part of a "greater plan" that was supposed to rid Moldova of its Jews, together with the physical elimination ("cleansing the ground") of the Jews from Bessarabia and Bukovina. On 29 June, the day chosen for the evacuation of all Iaşi's Jews, there were at least 45,000 Jews living there.[2] In May 1942 there were 32,364 Jews, according to the census of people of Jewish blood.[3] Thus, at least 12,000 Jews were slaughtered in the pogrom.

The formal order to evacuate the Jews from the city was given by Ion Antonescu by telephone directly to Col. Constantin Lupu, commander of the Iaşi garrison, on 27 June 1941. Lupu was required, among other things, to take steps "to evacuate Iaşi's Jewish population."[4] On the night of 28–29 June, as army, police, and gendarmerie units began to arrest and execute Jews, Antonescu telephoned Lupu again and repeated the evacuation order. Thanks to Lupu, who wrote down Antonescu's verbal instructions, we have a record of what was said in that fateful telephone conversation:

1. You shall issue a signed instruction in your capacity as military commander of the city of Iaşi, based on existing government orders, with the following addendum: "Given the state of war . . . if anyone opens fire from a building, it shall be surrounded by soldiers and all its inhabitants, barring children, shall be arrested. Following a brief interrogation, the guilty parties shall be executed. Anyone hiding individuals who have committed the above offenses shall be punished in a similar manner."

2. The evacuation of the Jewish population from Iaşi is essential, and shall be carried out in full, including women and children. The evacuation shall be implemented in batches [*pachete pachete*], first to Roman and later to Târgu-Jiu. You are to coordinate the operation with the Ministry of Interior and the county prefecture. Suitable preparations must be made.[5]

Before these orders were issued an understanding was reached with the Abwehr envoy at the German legation in Bucharest and with the commander of the German army corps in Iaşi about the methods to be used against the Jews. However, since Colonel Lupu, the city's military commander, was unable to control the situation and faithfully carry out Antonescu's order, he was dismissed on 2 July 1941. The court-martial by the Fourth Army Corps in January 1942 brought to light the order he had received from the marshal and his deputy. It took until July 1996, however, for the contents of the order to be revealed (the trial itself was heard behind closed doors, and documentation on the trial and the pogrom came to light only in July 1996).

THE PLANNING OF THE POGROM

The Iaşi pogrom was planned by the same people who planned the liquidation of the Jews of Bessarabia and northern Bukovina, namely those who ordered the gendarmerie units to "cleanse the ground," those who issued special orders to the army units, and those who planned to incite the peasants of Bessarabia against the Jews even before the territory was occupied by the army. The initiator of the pogrom was Ion Antonescu himself, who issued a secret order to General Şteflea. This order formed the basis for directives to the Ministry of Interior, which controlled the gendarmerie and police, and to the Ministry of

Propaganda, headed by Mihai Antonescu. These directives were then translated into a plan of action by military command structures (the military cabinet and the Second Section) and the SSI in coordination with the two ministries.

The Romanian army supreme command was the prime mover behind the pogrom, while War Headquarters' Second Section was responsible for the planning of the pogrom, based on Antonescu's secret order to General Şteflea of 19 June 1941. Antonescu's second order to Colonel Lupu to evacuate the city's forty-five thousand Jews and his instructions to execute any Jew who attacked the army effectively gave the gendarmerie and police carte blanche to torture and murder Jews and to evacuate thousands of them by train to southern Romania.

The SSI, under instructions from Antonescu and the General Staff, established a special unit shortly after Antonescu's meeting with Hitler on 11 June 1941. Operational Echelon no. 1 (Eşalonul I Operativ)—also known as the Special Echelon—comprised some 160 operatives. Their assignment was to "protect the home front from acts of espionage, sabotage, and terror."[6] We now know that this special unit was modeled on Einsatzgruppe D, which arrived in Romania around 22 June 1941.[7] On 18 June the Special Echelon left Bucharest for Moldova accompanied by Maj. Hermann Stransky, a Romanian-speaking officer from the German army's intelligence service who served as liaison between the Abwehr and the SSI.

On 26 June antisemitic agitation in the local press suddenly intensified and effectively became an incitement to riot. At the same time the police were flooded with reports from Romanians claiming that Jews were signaling enemy aircraft, hiding paratrooper agents, holding suspicious gatherings, and the like. The emergence of this psychosis was no accident; it was contrived by the Second Section and the Special Echelon and explained in advance to Fourteenth Division headquarters and the commanders of the police and gendarmerie. It was meticulously planned so that the transition from rumor to action would be swift and lethal.[8]

On 26 June, against a backdrop of threats issued by Gen. Nicolae Stavrescu, commander of the Fourteenth Division, in the local press, Romanian soldiers (most of whom were drunk) began breaking into Jewish flats near their camps on the city outskirts.[9] Although some rioters were former Legionnaires and their sympathizers who were recruited by SSI envoys, most were civilians who armed themselves or were armed in advance of the anti-Jewish action.[10] It should be noted that Legionnaires and their followers as well as supporters of Cuza's antisemitic movement and others was merely tools that the planners of the pogrom used to launch it. It was the Antonescu administration, not the Legionary movement, that was responsible for the pogrom.

During the pogrom, army, police, and gendarmerie units attacked the Jewish population of Iași under orders from the highest military and civilian authorities, such as: War Headquarters, the commander of the Fourth Army, the grand pretor of the army, the Ministry of the Interior, the Gendarmerie Inspectorate General, and even Ion and Mihai Antonescu themselves. During the three days leading up to the pogrom (approximately from 26 June) tension escalated as Romanians, especially local intellectuals, began leaving the city and Romanian friends and acquaintances of Jews began uttering vague admonitions of an impending disaster. "Many Christians who knew of the pogrom in advance left Iași and went to stay with relatives, so as not to witness to the hideous acts of murder."[11]

Another sign of the impending violence was the appearance of crosses daubed on Christian houses. Deputy police commander Gheorghe Leahu began receiving police reports that "crosses were being daubed or whitewashed on houses inhabited by Christians, and that recently these crosses were appearing more and more frequently in many neighborhoods."[12] This practice of daubing houses with crosses was not a voluntary or spontaneous act. It began before the city was bombed. Without fully comprehending the significance of the phenomenon, many Jews realized that the Romanians who had left the city on the eve of the pogrom had marked their apartments with crosses. Once the arrests and executions began the community leaders understood, albeit belatedly, that "all Christian houses had been marked with a cross."[13]

On 27 June the authorities officially accused the Jews of responsibility for the Soviet bombardments.[14] Soviet planes first bombed Iași on 24 June, without causing serious damage. But the bombing sowed panic among the population, and rumors spread that the Jews were signaling the Soviet pilots and directing them to their targets. When the city was bombed a second time, on 26 June, various targets in the city were hit and lives were lost. About one hundred Jewish houses were damaged, and thirty-eight Jews were killed.

Worried about the rumors of the impending pogrom, Iosef Iacob, the Jewish community's president, went to see Constantin Chirilovici, the police commander, and asked him to take measures to contain the unrest.[15] In the best Romanian tradition (whereby you cannot ask a favor from an official empty-handed), Iacob offered the police commander a bribe of 2 million lei.

On 27 June, all heads of the administration in Iași convened at the prefect's palace—ostensibly to discuss law and order but actually to deploy the forces that were to participate in the pogrom.[16] Phony attacks on soldiers were organized on the evening of 28 June to incite the soldiers and create the impression of a Jewish uprising that had to be quelled. Jewish culpability was thus already a fait accompli. Before the start of the bogus attacks deputy police commander Leahu convened the local police and forbade them "to interfere with whatever the Army does in the city's streets, for better or worse," as Commissar Gratian Sprînceană, commander of regional Police Station no. 2, recalled in 1945.[17]

At 9:00 p.m. a phony air alert was sounded. Several German aircraft flew over the city, one of them firing a blue flare. This was the signal. Immediately shots were heard throughout the city, from both rifles and automatic weapons, chiefly from the main streets where army units were now marching on their way to the front.[18] The numerous shots fired wherever soldiers, mostly Romanian, were posted in full battle dress created the impression of a great battle, particularly in the city center.

Many Jews who lived in the areas where the shots were sounded now realized that this was a show deliberately staged to sow panic among them, a prearranged signal to attack them, a sign that their lives and property no longer held any worth. Indeed, soldiers accompanied by civilians—some of them supplied with arms and others who armed themselves—began looting and killing that evening among wealthy Jews in the center of town, in the streets where the phony shootings had taken place.[19] Looting, rape, and murder of Jews took place also in the city's outskirts on the night of 28–29 June, but from the outset these activities took the form of a mob bent on attacking defenseless individuals, an unleashing of depraved urges—similar to what had taken place on the second and third days of the rioting in Bucharest on 21–23 January.

At 11:00 p.m. on the night of 28–29 June the final authorization to slaughter the Jews was received. Antonescu telephoned directly to Colonel Lupu, whom he knew personally, and granted him—and through him the various other bodies—a free hand to massacre Jews. The fact that the Romanian state and its leader were the architects of the pogrom and that German army units actively supported it ensured a death toll that ran into the thousands.

As well as informing on Jews, directing soldiers to Jewish homes and refuges, and even breaking into houses themselves, many Romanian residents of Iaşi also took part in the arrest and humiliation of Jews on their way to the Chestura (police headquarters). The extent to which they helped "prune" Iaşi's Jewish population—as the pogrom was described at a cabinet meeting in Bucharest—is a topic in itself that deserves a separate study.[20] The Communist regime went out of its way to prove that the population of Iaşi—barring the riffraff or Legionnaires—had mobilized to save Jews. Survivors' testimonies, however, gathered by the Romanian courts immediately after the collapse of the Antonescu regime, point rather to a collective hatred, large-scale participation in looting, and initiatives to liquidate Jews. Many survivors described how the Jews were abused as they were led to their death in the Chestura courtyard. Leon Reicher, an attorney, wrote of one such event: "The Christian residents cursed us on the way, and demanded that we be killed on the spot, since we were to blame for the disasters and bombings, and since we had shot at Romanian and German soldiers in the night. Some were raring to lynch us."[21] Although there were hundreds of Romanian war criminals, not all of them were tracked down or identified after the war.[22] These criminals comprised Romanians from the entire social spectrum, as well as "riffraff," as the amorphous, anonymous mobs were called.

The petty murderers were the neighbors of Jews, known and lesser-known supporters of the antisemitic movements, young people (including high school students), junior-level officials with low incomes, numerous railway workers, and craftsmen frustrated by competition from the Jews but also so-called white-collar workers—government and tax clerks, engineers and laboratory technicians, business owners (some who owned in partnership with Jews), retirees, former military men, and the like. Romanian women and young girls participated in the Iași pogrom, as they had in the Bucharest pogrom. In many instances couples instigated arrests, informed on Jews, directed the authorities to their homes, and always—without fail—looted the empty homes, sometimes even before the Jewish families had been forced out.

Although not all residents participated in the pogrom, there are plenty of examples regarding the massive participation of Romanians from all social strata of Iași in the pogrom. There were enough criminals to turn 29 June 1941 into the greatest tragedy the Jews of the Regat had ever experienced. The soldiers and gendarmes, who were unfamiliar with the terrain, would never have been able to round up Jews and organize them into convoys without the help of Romanian civilians, although, for this purpose, their full mobilization and participation in the pogrom was not essential. Therefore, attempts to highlight the behavior of a few residents who helped or hid Jews or misled the soldiers cannot alter the general picture. None of Iași's residents denounced the pogrom. No one spoke out against it, either during or after it. No one called it a crime. The few who helped the Jews did so despite the atmosphere, despite the determination of the majority to back the attempt to liquidate the Jews. To a large extent the Iași pogrom was the first big test that the alumni of the Romanian antisemitic movements in Iași passed with flying colors. It is clear that in addition to the police and gendarmerie units and the Romanian and German armies thousands of local Romanians—from all walks of life—actively participated in the Iași pogrom.[23]

According to non-Jewish sources, on the first day of the pogrom about five thousand Jews were killed in the Chestura courtyard and another two thousand in the surrounding streets and along the road leading to the railway station. Antonescu's explicit order specified that forty-five thousand Jews were to be rounded up in the Chestura pending their evacuation from Iaşi. The building, which was situated in the city center fairly near the railway station and at the junction of almost all roads from the suburbs, stood in the middle of a huge courtyard.

The Jews who were taken to the Chestura on the night of 28–29 June viewed the roundup as merely the final stage in the campaign of humiliation and looting unleashed by the Romanian authorities against the city's Jews. Despite being humiliated, beaten, and shot on the way, they still never imagined they were being led to their death. As one Jew, Samuel Boghiu, noted, it was common practice for "the Jews to be taken in long convoys, beaten by their escorts, humiliated on the way, and spat at by passers-by."[24] However, panic escalated before they entered the Chestura courtyard, for the following reasons: the presence of women and children among the evacuees, the violence of the attacks (many Jews were beaten so hard that their faces turned into bloody pulp), and the sporadic shooting of Jews along the way. "Women carrying children, or nursing babes completed the sorry sight of the convoys that were being led away by the soldiers." The Jewish community's intellectuals, who began collecting and compiling testimonies from survivors immediately after August 1944, described the Chestura in the following terms:

> The Chestura was the place where the Jews of Iaşi who had been taken there were concentrated by the sentries, soldiers, policemen and the like, under a hail of blows and terrible abuse. The action began on the night of 28/29 June. Jews who could no longer squeeze into the large basement of this building were herded into the huge courtyard which, at one point, contained over 20,000 people. . . . While the Jews were being taken to the Chestura, all the riffraff of the suburbs, non-combatant soldiers, and policemen [who were recruited] for the success of this venture, looted houses that had been abandoned, or which were inhabited only by terrified women and children.[25]

The explicit orders that allowed Jewish homes and property to be seized, Jews to be searched, arrested, rounded up in the Chestura, and shot on trumped-up charges of insurrection, women and children to be sorted and released, and men to be evacuated in the death trains were issued by War Headquarters or Bucharest or directly by Ion and Mihai Antonescu. Some of these orders disappeared or were concealed and were not included in the indictments issued by the various courts that tried the war criminals after the war, as part of an attempt to pin the blame for the atrocities on the Germans and their Romanian collaborators rather than on the Romanian state or nation.

THE GREAT MASSACRE

At approximately noon on 29 June many policemen and their commanders took a lunch break. When they returned they found Germans from Todt units in the Chestura courtyard resolutely attacking and killing Jews, along with their Romanian counterparts.[26] In the Chestura building itself the Germans took over as the Romanians took a break. What they lacked in numbers they made up for in stamina.

The Germans from the Todt units who helped their Romanian colleagues smash Jewish bones were not numerous, as Colonel Lupu pointed out: they constituted "about fifty people who worked in the airport."[27] Jews who survived the pogrom corroborated that the Todt contingent, which arrived after an ad hoc commission for sorting and release of women and children broke off for lunch, comprised no more than ten to twenty men. "Wielding large wooden clubs they, and about twenty Romanian soldiers armed with rifles, were ranked on either side of the gate." What they lacked in quantity they made up for in persistence: "Soon, the dead and wounded piled up in the middle of the courtyard. Those who continued to be pushed in by the savage sentries at the entrance had no choice but to trample them."[28] "They were frenzied with fear," stated a Jewish attorney, describing the Jews who were forced to trample on bleeding bodies as the Romanians and Germans chased them to the other side of the courtyard in order to make room for more people.[29]

A survivor of this "entrance exam" described how he was shoved into the courtyard at about three o'clock and made to run the gauntlet of club-wielding Romanian gendarmes and policemen and German soldiers. "We were forced, with arms raised, to run the gauntlet in order to enter the courtyard of the Chestura. . . . We were hit on the back of our necks and on our heads, and many of us fell to the ground, dead or wounded, with split skulls. There was a huge mass of people and the horrendous sound of smashing skulls."[30]

This was no mere figure of speech. The sight of smashed skulls was the first thing that greeted the Jews as they were pushed into the courtyard. "They split open our skulls, smashed our shoulders, and broke our hands. If we tried to escape, Germans who were hiding behind the steps [of the Chestura building in the courtyard] pursued and attacked us. Many fell unconscious with fractured legs, but we were carried along by the wave of terrified people in the courtyard." The Jew who provided this handwritten account was able to identify colleagues who were less fortunate than him: "In the courtyard of the Chestura, I identified the industrialist Schneier, whose brains were spilling out of his skull, the insurance agent Freitag, with a smashed skull and fractured shoulder, the merchant Glückman, battered to death, with a gouged-out eye."[31]

At three o'clock the massacre proper began, making the acts of carnage hitherto perpetrated look like child's play by comparison. Machine guns were used and an air siren went off near the Chestura building to signal the start of the massacre. "The siren was staged. There were no planes visible in the skies."[32] Police officers standing near the gate closed the entrance and left. "Immediately afterwards, a barrage of shots was directed at the [courtyard] of the Chestura."[33] The shots came from all the buildings surrounding the Chestura and from the Chestura itself. The start of the shooting was almost simultaneous with the staged air siren. "As soon as the alert was given, soldiers began firing machine guns and rifles at the Jews packed inside the Chestura. Those who tried to escape were shot to death."[34]

Despite the killings, the gendarmes and police continued to bring convoys of Jews to the Chestura, although there was virtually no room for them. Able-bodied Jews were ordered to pile up some of the corpses to make room for the new arrivals. From prearranged positions, the Romanians and Germans directed their fire mainly at Jews who were trying to escape from the courtyard to the adjacent street. Many Jews were mowed down by machine guns in the courtyard of the church opposite the Chestura. The killing operation continued until 7:30 p.m., although the Romanian soldiers and gendarmes ceased shooting at the masses before then to direct their fire instead at Jews attempting to escape over the perimeter fence. On several occasions hundreds of Jews were murdered in one go.

The head of the sanitation services in the city, Vlad Marievici, who arrived on the morning of Monday, 30 June 1941, to organize the removal of corpses from the courtyard, testified: "When the gate opened, I saw a pile of corpses stacked high like logs that impeded the progress of the garbage truck into the courtyard proper. The floor was awash with blood that reached the gate; *the blood came up to the soles of my shoes*."[35]

PARTICIPATION BY THE GERMAN ARMY IN THE POGROM

The idea for the pogrom crystallized in the headquarters of the General Staff and its secret branch, the Second Section, and in the SSI, which was directly subordinate to Antonescu. These offices collaborated with the Wehrmacht in Romania and the headquarters of the German Thirtieth Army Corps in Iaşi. During the pogrom the Romanian authorities lost control of developments, and the city of Iaşi became a huge killing field in which soldiers of both armies, gendarmes, policemen, and civilians—both organized and unorganized—hunted down, robbed, and killed Jews. This is not what Ion Antonescu had envisioned when he gave his soldiers a free hand to slaughter Jews who opened fire on the army or when he gave the orders to evacuate Jews from the city and "to dilute" the Jewish presence in the city, as his ministers later stated in a government session.

The understandings the Second Section reached with the commander of the German army in Romania are unknown or have disappeared—like all the documents relating to the planning of the Iaşi pogrom, which disappeared from the SSI archives. Presumably some of these understandings were ad-hoc verbal agreements between the representatives of the two armies. A study of documents that have recently come to light shows that those who knew of the order to "cleanse the ground" in Bessarabia—such as Maj. Nicolae Scriban, pretor of the Fourteenth Division—also knew of the understandings with the Germans.

The German soldiers were divided into cells and sent out to arrest Jews, assigned to escort convoys, and stationed at the entrance to the Chestura. They broke into homes, either alone or together with Romanian soldiers, and robbed, beat, and murdered Jews there and during the forced march to the Chestura. They shot into crowds of Jews and committed the same acts as their partners in crime, the Romanians. In addition, they photographed the pogrom and even staged scenes for this purpose. For the German army, however, Iaşi itself was not a target. The pogrom was not part of any German plan of operation. At most it was a case of the Germans helping an antisemitic ally to rid itself of its Jews, as the ally itself had planned.

It is important to note that the units of Einsatzgruppe D—although operating in territories reclaimed by Romania after 22 June 1941—*did not operate in Romania itself* (including Iaşi). Nor did any other SS unit.[36] Antonescu's administration did not allow the SS or the Gestapo to operate in Romanian territory following the Legionnaires' revolt. The movements of Einsatzgruppe D on Romanian soil are well documented.

The local authorities (police, gendarmerie, and prefecture) were not let in on the secret understandings between the two armies regarding the pogrom. These authorities received orders and directives from the Interior Ministry and, on the day of the pogrom itself, from Mihai Antonescu, acting president of the Council of Ministers while the Conducător was busy directing the war.

Today we know that both sides—the Romanian and German armies or, more explicitly, the Fourteenth Division of the Romanian army and the Thirtieth Corps of the German army under Gen. Hans von Salmuth—acted in concert and in accordance with an oral understanding that came to light only in 1996. In February 1942 the military tribunal of the Fourth Army Corps court-martialed Colonel Lupu following complaints that he defended a number of Jewish business colleagues. During the trial it transpired that he had ordered the arrest of a number of Romanians who continued to rob and raid Jewish homes after 30 June. During the trial, which took place behind closed doors, Lupu presented the military tribunal with the secret order he received from Antonescu before the pogrom. Similarly, all the heads of the military and civilian authorities testified in the trial to their part in running the pogrom and incidents during the pogrom.[37]

THE DEATH TOLL

About fifteen thousand Jews perished in the Iaşi pogrom—eight thousand in the city itself and about seven thousand on the two death trains. Out of eight thousand Jews who boarded the two death trains, six thousand perished on the way and several hundred more perished in Iaşi itself before even boarding the train. Thousands of bodies were unloaded from the first train at Târgu Frumos, Mirceşti, Săbăoani, Roman, and Inoteşti as well as at the last station, Călăraşi. About two thousand corpses were dumped at Podu Iloaiei.

The community census that was conducted clandestinely in May 1942 listed 14,850 Jewish victims by name.[38] On 23 July 1943, at the memorial service for the victims of the Iaşi pogrom held in the city's synagogues, the ssi, on the basis of data collected from memorial plaques in synagogues, set the number of dead at 13,266, including 40 women and 180 children.[39]

In August 1942 the Iaşi Recruitment Center reported 13,868 Jewish forced laborers missing. Of these, 7,000 had not been issued death certificates.[40] This was part of a deliberate policy by the Antonescu regime to play down the scale of the pogrom. It lied about the number of victims, falsified documents, blamed others—mainly the Germans and Legionnaires—for the crimes it committed, and denied its part in devising and planning the pogrom. It conducted a protracted campaign to underplay the number of casualties—a trend continued by successive regimes for fifty years.

Why did the Antonescu regime choose Iaşi as a test case for implementing its decision to murder Jews, as the place to begin its campaign of murder, deportation, degradation, starvation, and systematic liquidation of hundreds of thousands of Jews? The answer to this question was given in 1948 by Matatias Carp, historian and secretary of the Federation of Jewish Communities:

> The roots of the pogrom in Iaşi lie deep beneath the rotting system of Romanian pseudo-democracy. This was not an outbreak of isolated passions, neither was it some sort of momentary lapse of reason. It did not come about through autogenesis in the beastly depths of some criminally disposed beings. . . . In Iaşi, people's souls and consciences had been saturated and devoured by this poison for more than three quarters of a century. In the hometown of A. C. Cuza and Corneliu Codreanu, the bastion of the National Christian Defense League, the cradle of the Iron Guard movement, it was only natural that the germs [of hate] could find the most suitable culture-medium and transform even the most moderate and unassuming people into a mob seething with hate.[41]

34

The Antonescu Regime and the Final Solution in the Regat and Southern Transylvania

"I want to cleanse the land of Jews," declared Antonescu to Gen. Ion Topor, the army's grand pretor and the commander of the military gendarmerie, in early July 1941. At a celebratory meal on 24 July in Czernowitz to mark the liberation of the city and province, in the presence of King Mihai, Antonescu asked Gen. Constantin Calotescu, the governor of Bukovina, to "cleanse Bukovina of Jews."[1]

There was a Romanian plan to rid Romania if its Jews, a plan that was formed in May 1941 under Germany's influence, but not pressure, and sometimes even against its wishes. The plan for getting rid of the Jews in Romania itself was envisaged before 22 June 1941 and was exposed by Mihai Antonescu in a cabinet session and mentioned later on various occasions. The plan was known to the Germans in Berlin and the German legation in Bucharest, but they hampered it because of their concerns about planning and organization.

"We must take advantage of this moment to achieve the cleansing of the population. Therefore Bessarabia and Bukovina will be reminiscent of the policy of Titus . . . and not only in regard to the Jews," stated Mihai Antonescu in the government session of 17 June 1941, five days before the outbreak of the war.[2] Lt. Col. Traian Borcescu, head of the of the counterintelligence section of the SSI, testified on 12 November 1945 that he and his colleagues were aware at the time of the existence of a "big plan" (*planul mare*) that referred to the Jews of Moldova: driving away the Jews of Moldova, or in other words, extending the order to "cleanse the ground" of the entire Romanian territory, was part of the "big plan."[3] The German legation in Bucharest intervened with Mihai Antonescu before 12 August 1941, asking him "to proceed with the elimination of the Jewish element only in a systematic and slow manner."[4]

Mihai Antonescu announced at the end of August 1941, during a reception at the Foreign Ministry, that General Antonescu's government intended to solve the Jewish problem in the entire country: "[The problem] is being taken care of *throughout* the country. In many towns and villages the Jews have been gathered in special quarters, or concentrated in labor camps. They are wearing the yellow Jewish star as a distinctive mark and face the disgust of the Romanian people."[5] This unwritten plan was explicitly mentioned by Ion Antonescu in the guidelines he sent to Mihai Antonescu from the front on 3 September 1941.

In early September Ion Antonescu explained his plans concerning the Jews of Romania to Mihai Antonescu. The former was furious to find out that while he had been on the front Jews of Moldova had been released from camps in southern Romania, not to their homes but into the county capitals. "All Jews shall be taken back to the camps, preferably to those in Bessarabia, *because from there we shall push them into Transnistria*, as soon as I free myself of the current concerns."[6]

Had it not been for the Nazis, who restrained Antonescu's excessive zeal for reasons of planning and organization, the big plan would have been put into practice by 1941. The preparations were renewed in the spring of 1942. On 10 July 1942 Antonescu himself ordered preparations to proceed for the deportation of all the Jews from southern Transylvania "to the Bug, to make room for the sheltering and accommodation of the Romanian refugees from the ceded Transylvania."[7] On 11 September 1942 the Presidency of the Council of Ministers prepared a detailed plan regarding the evacuation operations, "which should include the entire Jewish population," setting forth the exceptions.[8]

This plan was rigorously applied until October 1942 and abolished only in March–April 1943. The plan included not only the murder and removal of Jews (those who had not been summarily executed) from Bessarabia and Bukovina but, in the first stage, also the deportation of Moldovan Jewry, to be followed by the deportation of most Jews from all over Romania. It also, however, permitted emigration to Palestine or any other place, provided the Jews left all their property behind. The plan was to deport the Jews from Romania to Transnistria, which was to serve as a human dumping ground. The Jews would be deported only to the Golta and Berezovka districts, the Kingdoms of Death of the Transnistrian administration, where they would be liquidated in one way or another by Romanian gendarmes, Ukrainian policemen, and ethnic German killing squads in the process of repeated attempts to deport them over the Bug. This plan was in no way linked to the German plan to deport Romanian Jewry to the death camps of occupied Poland. The Romanian plan became clear only after archives in Romania and the former Soviet Union became accessible.

Ion Antonescu saw the war primarily as a struggle between the Romanian nation and the Jews—all Jews, irrespective of locality, rights, and degree of assimilation into the Romanian nation. He wished to create a "homogeneous" Romania, a sovereign nation without Jews. His first target for the application of this policy in Romania itself was Moldova. "It is my intention to conduct a policy to purge the Romanian nation [of foreigners] . . . to create an integrated and homogenous Romanian nation, both in Bessarabia *and in Moldova*, if we live. And if we do not, others shall [implement the plan], *in Transylvania, too*," stated Antonescu to his ministers. Although he understood that the expulsion of Jews from Romania could be detrimental to the national economy, in the long term it would be worth it:

> Do not think that I am not aware of the [implications]. Do not think that I do not realize that I shall precipitate a huge economic crisis by deciding to cleanse the Romanian nation of Jews. I told myself, however, that this was a war initiated by me, and in a war, the nation inevitably suffers. If I win this war, the nation will benefit. True, by expelling the Jews we shall be precipitating a crisis, but the Romanian nation must prepare itself to face this crisis, in order to rid itself of this parasite. If I fail to take advantage of this great historical moment, the results will be felt forever, and if the Jews win this war, we shall cease to exist.[9]

The plan was to deport the Jews to Transnistria, not the Nazi extermination camps in Poland (where the mass extermination machinery had not yet begun to operate). "There are tens of thousands of Jews I intend dumping in Russia," stated Antonescu.[10] In late August Killinger, the German ambassador in Bucharest, informed Berlin that Antonescu had rounded up sixty thousand Jewish men from the Regat as forced laborers and that he was intending to send them eastward — "to the areas we have just conquered."[11] This was the first allusion to the fact that Antonescu had resolved to find an immediate solution to the Jewish problem in the Regat, too. The army's grand pretor, General Topor, clarified the government's policy to his subordinates: "The country does not need Jews, and must be cleansed of Jews."[12] He used exactly the same words as Antonescu. Antonescu himself ordered the army and police to kill Jews from Galicia who were trying to flee to Romania: "We must prevent any penetration of Jews [from Galicia] to our territory. All Jews who crossed the border or shall attempt to cross the border, shall be considered spies and executed."[13] As far as the fathers of Romanian antisemitism were concerned, Galicia was merely a place from which Jews had invaded Romania in the mid-nineteenth century.

The plan for the deportation of the Jews of Romania proper, which had been formulated in the highest echelons of government, was foiled by Nazi Germany via its German military delegation in Bucharest and the German Foreign

Ministry, on the grounds that it was too wild and unplanned. Furthermore, the Germans had reached the conclusion that such a move would paralyze parts of the Romanian economy and harm Romania's ability to meet its economic commitments toward Germany.[14] Antonescu was forced to suspend his plan, but he announced in public that he had not abandoned it. Unsigned editorials that were published in the Romanian press in late October 1941 — editorials that reflected the official line — informed the Romanians that "the Jewish problem was entering the final stages of a solution, and nothing on earth, not even a miracle, could prevent it." The government announced that Romania "was one of the nations that were prepared to cooperate resolutely for a final solution to the Jewish problem — not only on the local level, but on the European level, too."[15]

Romania announced that it was also amenable to the Nazi solution to the problem. In a letter he sent to an antisemitic nationalist intellectual who praised his policy, Antonescu promised to rid Romania of all Jews: "As long as I am alive, nobody and nothing can prevent me from carrying out the task of cleansing [the country of Jews]."[16] In a summary report on the assignment of Jews to forced labor detachments, the General Staff stressed that forced labor was a temporary situation: "Forced labor is only a temporary solution — a postponement of the *complete solution* of the problem, namely, the total expulsion of all Jews without exception, even if this operation is carried out *in stages*." Although the General Staff predicted that the deportation of the Jews would cause substantial damage to the national economy, "the radical solution of the problem should not be renounced on the grounds that the state revenue shall suffer. The Jews must leave, to a man, and leave as they came. They must leave behind all the assets they amassed in this country."[17] The General Staff was merely mimicking the Conducător's thoughts. Antonescu informed his ministers of the war's domestic objectives: "Sirs, as you know, one of the struggles I undertook to wage is to reshape this nation. I shall turn this nation into a homogenous group. Anything foreign — must leave, bit by bit. . . . Any suspect Jewish element, all Jewish Communists, must go back to where they came from. I shall drive them to the Bug, and from there they will be transferred further."[18] The Antonescu regime assigned the extermination camps on the Bug and the extermination areas in the Ukraine under Nazi rule as the dumping grounds for the Jews in order to solve the Jewish problem in Romania.

Although the deportation of the Jews was the subject of public debate, censorship prevented its full coverage in the press. Many circles accepted the planned deportation and awaited the fulfillment of the promises of a regime that saw itself as Cuza's and Codreanu's heir, at least as far as the Jews were concerned.

But German pressure, their refusal to allow the Jews over the River Bug, the subsequent concentration of about seventy thousand Jews in the Golta district, the need to kill them and burn their bodies in order to present the spread of typhus, the outbreak of the typhus epidemic in the ghettos, the planned deportation of the Jews of Odessa, and the freezing winter all persuaded Antonescu to postpone the deportation operation until the spring. An order to this effect issued by Antonescu on 10 December 1941 simply stated, "Marshal Antonescu decided to leave all the Jews there until the spring."[19]

On 17 December 1941 Antonescu ordered the dissolution of the Federation of Jewish Communities and its replacements by a Jewish Center modeled on the lines of similar institutions set up by the Nazis in occupied France and in Slovakia. This step further fueled fears of an impending deportation. This decision, however, was triggered by Nazi Germany, which was equally bent on the destruction of Romanian Jewry. The evacuation of the Jews from their villages and towns, their incarceration in camps, the extermination operation in Bessarabia and Bukovina, and clear references to the impending deportation of the Jews of the Regat all served as a suitable backdrop to the extortion of Jews practiced by the regime at the time through the imposition of taxes, the obligation to hand over clothes, and the obligation to purchase war bonds.

THE NAZI FINAL SOLUTION

In mid-March 1941 a delegation "from the Reich Government and Himmler," as Mihai Antonescu defined it three years later (in March 1944), arrived in Bucharest (see chap. 16). The deputy president of the Council of Ministers also specified the names of the members of the delegation: Eitzen, Gustav Richter, Karl Hoffmann, and Karl Pflaumer. "They presented . . . an official request that responsibility for the handling of Romanian Jews be handed over to the Germans exclusively, since Germany was preparing the international solution to the problem. I refused."[20] Mihai Antonescu lied. He cooperated with the delegation and agreed to an international solution of the Jewish problem.

The Reich delegates proposed a final solution ("activity of an international character," as Mihai Antonescu called it) that would include transferring the Jews to death camps in occupied Poland in 1942 ("organizing emigration," or *Aussiedlung*). In August 1941, in the belief that Germany was on the verge of victory, Mihai Antonescu informed his ministers that he had discussed the solution to the Jewish problem with the Reich representative: "I can inform you that I have already conducted in-depth negotiations with a high-ranking German representative of German organizations concerning the Jewish problem. [They] understand that the Jewish problem requires, in the final analysis, an international solution, and they want to help us prepare this international solution."[21] The German organizations were those Himmler oversaw: the SD (Nazi security service), the SS, the Gestapo, and the RSHA. The Nazis wanted to help, and the Romanian gratefully acquiesced. As early as March 1941, after the start of talks with the RSHA delegation, Ion Antonescu instructed his minister of the interior, who in turn instructed all prefects throughout the country, to prepare ghettos for the Jews. Although the ghettos were not set up, Jews were indeed evacuated from certain neighborhoods and relocated to Jewish neighborhoods, where this was possible.

Romania's agreement in principle to contribute its part to the international solution of the Jewish problem found expression in a joint understanding with Richter even before the outbreak of war against the Soviet Union, in connection with the drafting of a new Jewish Statute by the General Staff and the justice minister.[22] On 2 September 1941 Mihai Antonescu informed the ministers that it was not merely a question of legally defining who was a Jew: "This does not interest us." The purpose of the talks was "to organize a *transitional regime* for the Jewish communities in our country, so that when the time comes, we shall extend this system as a framework for an *international solution*. We were however unable to move forward with this plan because of the replacement of the German representative with whom I worked."[23] The German representative was Gustav Richter, who was provisionally recalled to Berlin in the summer of 1941. Romania enthusiastically applied the final solution in the liberated territories, as Martin Luther, from the Foreign Ministry in Berlin, stated in a letter to Ambassador Killinger: "Under these circumstances, the activity of the Advisor on Aryanization Affairs in Bucharest" is superfluous.[24] That day Richter's main function was redefined as advisor on Aryanization affairs rather than advisor on Jewish affairs. At the time, although the extermination machinery was not yet operating in occupied Poland, both Germans and Romanians were killing Jews in the tens of thousands. Richter returned to Bucharest in October 1941 at Mihai Antonescu's request.[25] On 11 September 1941 Killinger asked the Foreign Ministry in Berlin to send Richter back to Romania, since the Romanian government "has agreed, on the basis of activity previously begun and preparations he had made with the Romanians, *to solve the Jewish problem in Romania*."[26]

When he resumed talks in October 1941 Richter acted according to instructions he received in Berlin and according to the policy he had submitted in writing on 16 May 1941 to General Zwiedinek, then undersecretary for Romanization affairs (see chap. 16). What he effectively asked was for Romania to entrust him with exclusive jurisdiction over the affairs of Romanian Jews. With his customary insolence, he demanded, among other things, that all draft proposals on Romanization issues be submitted to him for approval before being submitted to Antonescu. He demanded a law for the dissolution of Jewish organizations in Romania (apart from the communities) and for the establishment of a new organization known as the Jewish Center. He demanded the confiscation of Jewish property and the establishment of an emigration fund (*Aussiedlungsfond*) to finance the imminent emigration of Romanian Jews. Richter asked for an accurate evaluation of the true number of Jews in Romania, as defined by race, and for the centralization of all information concerning their property and assets.[27] He emphasized at the time (May 1941), before the outbreak of war against the Soviet Union, that he was acting with the final solution in mind, a term whose full significance was to come to light only later. The question arises as to whether the Aussiedlung of May 1941 was any different from those incorporated in his extermination plan of September 1942.

When he returned to Romania, and perhaps even before, Richter (and Killinger, too, acting on behalf of the German Foreign Ministry) followed "the directives for the handling the Jewish problem" that were drawn up in Berlin evidently in May 1941, shortly before the invasion of the Soviet Union.[28] The final objective of all the measures that were included in the directives was the deportation "eastwards" of all Jews from Romania, Slovakia, Croatia, Bulgaria, and Hungary. Himmler's agents were ordered to clarify whether the Romanian government, among other things, was prepared to deport their Jews eastward—a slip of the tongue, given that the deportation from Romania was supposed to be carried out northward, to the General Government.[29]

On 17 December 1941 the press published a decree-law ordering a census of "people of Jewish blood," signed by the marshal, as promised to Richter. The law defined a Jew in the spirit of the Nuremberg laws, as a German newspaper hastened to point out. A Jew was someone with one parent or even grandparent who was Jewish. Children of Jewish blood up to age one who were not baptized were considered Jewish.[30]

On 23 January 1942, two days after the Wannsee Conference, Richter asked Mihai Antonescu to stop the deportation of Jews from Romania "in view of the *imminent final solution* to the Jewish problem in Europe." Mihai Antonescu agreed to this request, thereby agreeing in principle to the final solution in Romania. He promised an immediate stop to the emigration of individuals, not only of groups. In the end the twenty-nine-year-old Richter criticized Marshal Antonescu for spending "three quarters of an hour" in a meeting with "that Jew, Clejan," who, according to him, dared to set conditions before agreeing to head the Jewish Center.[31] Both Ion and Mihai Antonescu found it hard to overlook

Richter's insolence, and he lost face with them. Negotiations between Richter and Lecca continued over the next few months, and in late April 1942 Richter emerged from his anonymity to inform Romanian Jewry, over the heads of the Romanian government, that their fate had been sealed. He published an article in the German legation's mouthpiece in Bucharest advising the Jews not to cling "to the vain hope" of preventing "the final solution" (*Endlösung*). "The Jewish problem in Romania shall be solved within a European framework," declared Richter. He took the opportunity to attack those he considered his enemies and the enemies of Nazism—in particular, Filderman. He also berated Zionism and Haim Weizman, who was giving anti-German speeches in New York at the time. At the end of the article he recalled the führer's promise of 24 February 1942 that the end of the war would also spell the end of Judaism.[32] On 12 May 1942 Rademacher of the Foreign Ministry noted that the legation in Bucharest had asked the Romanian government to halt the "uncontrolled" deportation of Jews across the Bug.[33] This was yet another move toward the preparation of the Nazi version of the final solution, as against the Romanian one.

THE BLOOD PRINCIPLE

As well as drafting a law defining Jews, the Ministry of Justice drew up a draft bill defining Romanians. This turned out to be harder than it seemed, since there was no such thing as a pure Romanian. "No country in the world has a definition based on ethnic origin," declared Minister of Justice Constantin Stoicescu, adding, "There is talk of determining ethnic origin. It is very hard to prove one is of Romanian stock. Each one of us will find it hard to prove this. We have prepared a draft [bill] that can answer the problem [from another angle]—[namely] who is a Jew."[34]

This obsessive concern with the problem of Jewish blood and with criteria for defining Jews was proof that the regime was about to cleanse itself of Jews. Those affected by the new law—primarily the children of mixed marriages or those with one Jewish grandparent, most of whom did not consider themselves in any way Jewish—objected to it. Romanians with one Jewish grandparent were told they could report to the police station rather than to the Jewish Center to fill out the necessary forms for people of Jewish blood and thereby be spared the degradation of reporting to a Jewish institution.[35] A special register (*registru de evidență*) was held for those "contaminated" with Jewish blood, namely Romanians with one Jewish grandparent.[36]

The census was supposed to facilitate the deportation by dividing Jews into those who were useful and those who were not. This division, together with the

Jewish Statute and the racist definition of a Jew, was designed to further facilitate practical preparations for the deportation of the Jews. The Siguranţa and the ssi immediately reported that the census was considered by many Jews in the provinces and even in the capital as a prelude to deportation. However, Jews were not the only ones who were disturbed by the census. Many Romanians of Jewish blood began to petition the leaders of the regime to spare them the curse of being considered Jewish under the December 1941 law.

Instructions sent to Romanian diplomats and consuls throughout the world regarding the definition of a Jew left no doubt as to the new racist principles governing the definition of Romanian nationality. These principles formed the basis for determining who was a Jew and therefore who was a candidate for deportation, in the final analysis. The guidelines concerning "the application of the law on the granting or revoking of Romanian citizenship" of 16 April 1942 declared that Romanian nationality was based on the principle of *jus sanguinis* (the principle of blood) and that the Romanian state had the sovereign right to determine who was a Romanian. However, the directives clarifying "the practical implications of the *jus sanguinis*" issued to the Romanian diplomats also stated that according to famous jurists, sociologists, and anthropologists there was no such thing as a "pure race" and that "the infusion of foreign blood was not always detrimental."[37]

Richter took a keen interest in the results of the census and visited the Central Bureau of Statistics on several occasions, meeting with bureau directors who provided him with provisional (and later conclusive) data on the number of Jews. Based on these statistics, he summed up the Jewish problem in Romania as follows: in May–June 1942 Romania had 292,149 Jews, of which 272,573 lived in the Regat and southern Transylvania, 19,475 in Bukovina (Czernowitz, Dorohoi, and Khotin), and 101 in the whole of Bessarabia. There were 4,681 converts to Christianity, 4,145 mixed marriages, and 2,942 children of mixed marriages. Richter also provided a breakdown of Jews by age and gender.[38]

In May–June 1942 rumor spread among the Jews that after completion of the census the Jews would be divided into three groups: "useful, desirable, and undesirable" (*utili, dezirabili, şi indezirabili*).[39] The rumor, albeit belated, was correct. This categorization of Jews was the last stage in the planned deportation of Romanian Jews according to both the Romanian and German plans. The statistics, together with the groundwork for the statute, convinced Antonescu in the summer of 1942 not to wait for the completion of negotiations with the Nazis but to resume the deportation of Jews that had been interrupted in December 1941.

On 27 March 1942 the Cabinet for the Administration of Bessarabia, Bukovina, and Transnistria sent a special order to the governors of these provinces to provide the latest data on the number of Jews there, according to the following categories: Jews who had been deported; Jews who had not yet been deported; and Jews who would not be deported. On 9 April the governors of Bessarabia and Bukovina sent their findings to the cabinet. Calotescu, the governor of Bukovina, reported that 91,845 Jews had been deported from the province and 23,250 were still living there, mostly in Czernowitz. Of these, 17,271 would not be deported, while 4,031 would be deported with the "first transport, because they were no longer useful or desirable." The governor added that the data on Jews awaiting deportation were not final "since we are still sorting Jews into categories. We shall then be in a position to decide who will be allowed to stay in Bukovina and who shall be expelled on account of being undesirable and unemployed."[40] As far as possible, the data included a breakdown of all categories by gender and children.

It was Antonescu who ordered the resumption of the deportations, in Order no. 462 of 30 March 1942 to the governor of Bessarabia. Order no. 508 of 27 March 1942 stated that the data on deportees should include a breakdown by gender and children.[41] The governor of Bessarabia, which was practically Judenrein, tried to determine on the basis of these data where to send the remaining Jews in Transnistria.[42] On 20 May 1942, 204 Jews were sent by train from Kishinev to Vardievka in the Golta district. On 10 July another 27 Jews were deported. All in all 231 Jews—81 men, 105 women, and 45 children, of which 14 had converted to Catholicism in 1942—were deported.[43] On 12 June the Bukovinian administration began reporting the start of the deportation operation from the province and the manner of its implementation.[44]

Had the deportations continued through the autumn of 1942 Czernowitz would have been left with less than the ten thousand Jews that remained—mainly forced laborers who were left behind in order to run the factories, their families, and a number of Jews who held individual resident permits. This had been Antonescu's original intention in October 1941, when he ordered ten thousand Jews to be left in the city out of over one hundred thousand Jews who had lived in the province (including the Dorohoi district). In the spring of 1942 Bessarabia was Judenrein by all standards, and there were no more Jews to deport. The only "Jews" left behind were long-standing converts, half-Jews, converted women married to Romanians, and their children, all of whom had been granted individual residence permits. In the summer of 1942 Antonescu decided, independently of the Nazis, to implement his original plan to deport the Jews of the Regat and southern Transylvania, too.

CZERNOWITZ, SUMMER OF 1942

In Czernowitz deportations were carried out on Sundays. On three successive Sundays (7, 14, and 28 June 1942) a total of five thousand Jews (including Polish Jews) were deported to the accompaniment of church bells and Gypsy bands in what was the penultimate stage of the campaign to purge the city of Jews. Although rumor spread on 5 June that the Jews were about to be deported, only a few Jews bothered to hide. A Jew who was deported in the first transport described how only "a few people realized how serious the situation was." Many Jews whose physical condition would have allowed them to escape were deluded by "vain hopes."[45] Even though entire families were being rounded up some still believed, even at this late stage, that they would be sent to the Regat for forced labor. Even when they were boarding the trains they failed to grasp the true nature of their fate, even though the large deportation of October 1941 was still fresh in their minds. Despite the constant stream of reports on how the Jews were being shot in Transnistria or were dying of cold, starvation, typhus, and filth, there were still Jews in Czernowitz and in the Regat who were unable to perceive the enormity of the catastrophe in Transnistria. "No-one in Czernowitz was able to conceive that such a disaster had overtaken the deportees. Jews there and in the Regat in general believed that the deportees were being sent to Transnistria for hard labor, and that at least they would be provided with [food for] sustenance. Only a few suspected that the deportees were being allowed to die of starvation."[46] For whatever reason, the Jews of Czernowitz, who were used to the relatively civilized Austro-Hungarian regime, or Jews in general, denied the reality that was staring them in the face.

The deportation squads, equipped with pre-prepared lists, stormed the homes of Jews who held "Popovici permits" (permits granted by Mayor Traian Popovici to individual Jews) and Jews who had not yet been deported due to the halt in deportations. Those who held "Calotescu permits" (permits personally signed by Governor Calotescu) were not immune either. Jews who held Calotescu permits were convinced—wrongly—that they would not be deported. Stere Marinescu, the administration's chief of staff, ordered the arrest of all those who held "valid" permits. He then proceeded to invalidate said permits: "No more documents. You must pay instead." Marinescu, who was also in Governor Calotescu's pay, spread the word that he was able to ease the Jews' lot (*să înbunătăţească eventual*)—in other words, that he was open to bribery.[47]

On the night of 6–7 June a detention squad broke into the Jewish hospital, arrested the patients, doctors, and nurses, and took them to the former sports ground of the Zionist movement (the Macabi sports ground) in which all the deportees were concentrated. The medical staff were deported in the clothes they were wearing at the time and due to the suddenness of the arrest were unable to take with them any belongings.[48] The hospital's sixty-six psychiatric patients and their caretakers were also taken to the sports ground, but not before they had entertained the citizens of Czernowitz with their antics. Clad only in shirts, they were led to the stadium to the strains of a Gypsy band. "To the population's delight, the patients were made to dance."[49] Their presence in the Macabi stadium, their irresponsible behavior, the strains of the Gypsy band, and the hilarity of the Romanian and Ukrainian residents of the city underscored the enormity of the Jews' calamity and intensified their despair. But nothing could compare to the delight afforded by the gynecological searches of women, as bands of policemen, gendarmes, and students (who participated in the deportations) formed circles to watch the spectacle (see chap. 32).

Before the third transport left Czernowitz the heads of the Jewish Committee were summoned by the administration and ordered to organize the deportation themselves—namely to select Jews for deportation and bring them to the railway station. The committee refused.[50] This transport, which left on 28 June 1942, included many Jewish intellectuals, despite the fact that their services were necessary to the city: "It included mainly university graduates—physicians, doctors from the Jewish hospital, pharmacists, teachers, and lawyers."[51]

The deportation of the Jews of Czernowitz also affected the Jews of Dorohoi. Dorohoi was part of the Regat but was annexed to Bukovina after the invasion of the Soviet Union in the summer of 1941. On 11 June, 308 Jews (176 men, 70 women, and 62 children) were deported from Dorohoi.[52] Most of the deportees were the husbands of women deported in November 1941, who had been drafted into the forced labor battalions. The deportation took the Jews by surprise, as soldiers went from house to house evicting inhabitants. Although the deportees were not allowed to take anything with them, even food, they were nevertheless all searched at the train station in case they had somehow managed to take with them money or valuables, and anything that was found was confiscated. "This operation was undertaken in a spirit of humanity," emphasized Governor Calotescu in his first report on the resumption of the deportations from Bukovina.[53]

The plan to liquidate the Jews of Czernowitz came to light on 18 August 1942 when an SS officer accompanied by German guards came to recruit Jews for work in German camps across the Bug, in Reichskommissariat Ukraine. According to an eyewitness, after the officer ordered "alles heraus" (German for "everyone out," German being the mother tongue of the Jews of Czernowitz), "we all went out in the yard. An SS officer and the gendarmerie commander were seated at the table, and standing near them was the [Jewish] camp head, Dr. Kamilo Hart. They carried out a selection."[54] The Jews who were delivered to the Germans were marched with their wives and children to the German side of the Bug. The following day the gendarmerie commander, Captain Poenaru, ordered twelve Jews "to fish out the bodies of Jews who had been shot by the Germans while crossing the Bug."[55] Those who were not shot were put to work as forced laborers and subsequently liquidated in a series of selections that began with the children and the elderly and ended with the adults. By late 1943 there were hardly any Czernowitz Jews among the Jews delivered to the Germans in the various transports.

The Tighina Agreement that was concluded with the German army on 30 August 1941 was the Romanian solution to the Jewish problem in Romania. The agreement stated that deportations to the German side of the Bug would resume after the fighting was over. In the summer of 1942 the Bucharest government tried to resume the deportations to the German side, and most of Czernowitz's Jews were deported there. The deportation of psychiatric patients and of doctors symbolized, more than anything, the Romanians' resolve in the summer of 1942 to purge Bukovina—and the Regat—entirely of Jews.

35

Toward the Implementation of the Final Solution

In early 1942 Ion Antonescu decided that, having liquidated most of the Jews of Bessarabia and Bukovina, it was now the turn of the Jews of the Regat. On 12 February he met in Berlin with Hitler, who praised him generously for the Romanian army's contribution and bravery in the war and attempted to explain away the defeat on the outskirts of Moscow. He further promised that "he was resolved to complete the destruction and final rout of the Russians from the battlefield that summer."[1] Antonescu agreed to send three-quarters of the Romanian army, most of which had already been demobilized after the 1941 campaign, to fight on the eastern front. As a token of his gratitude the führer presented Antonescu with a Mercedes-Benz. In the summer of 1942 Antonescu truly believed that victory was around the corner and that all that was needed was one final effort to defeat the Soviet Union.

It was this belief that fueled his policy toward the Jews. His desire to turn Romania into a homogeneous nation, as he had promised his ministers, affected not only the Jews but Slavs, Gypsies, and other minority groups, too. Believing that he was serving the highest interests of the Romanian nation, he was determined to forge ahead with his plans, irrespective even of the Nazis' plans. As far as the Jews were concerned, Antonescu went berserk. He constantly—sometimes even daily—issued orders to deport, detain, shoot, punish, or rob Jews in the Regat and southern Transylvania, as well as Gypsies, members of Christian sects, or any Jew who happened to irritate him at the time.

On the face of it Antonescu was bound by his promise to Filderman of 2 September 1941 to grant the Jews of the Regat preferred status. Before the start of the battle of Odessa, he agreed to abolish the yellow badge and, believing he would shortly capture Odessa, issued vague promises to the effect that he would grant a privileged status to the Jews of the Regat. "He draws a distinction between the Jews of the Regat [and other Jews], and he plans a privileged status for them."[2]

Only a month later the marshal broke his promise by ordering the deportation of the Jews of the Dorohoi district and most of the Jews of the city of Dorohoi (Dorohoi had always belonged to the Regat). In the last months of 1941 the Romanian press, under directives from Mihai Antonescu's Ministry of Propaganda, published daily announcements about the impending deportation of the Jews of the Regat. It is clear from these activities that Antonescu's promise was not made in good faith. As a despot who did not have to account for his behavior, Antonescu was free to do as he pleased. On 10 December 1941 he decided to dismiss Filderman from his post and from that point on refused to grant him an audience.

As a preliminary step to the deportations of 1942 Antonescu drew up "categories" (*categorii*) of Jews earmarked for deportation, such as so-called lawbreakers, enemies of the state, and evaders of forced labor. By the end of the summer, however, he had drawn up a plan to deport all the Jews of southern Transylvania, irrespective of category. The introduction of categories led, in the final analysis, to the attempted deportation of ninety-five thousand to one hundred thousand Jews in 1942. In late February 1942 Antonescu informed his ministers that circumstances had never been so ripe for implementing Romanization, and "we would be wrong not to exploit them." Romanization, however, was merely one aspect of the struggle he waged on the battlefront and against the Jews. "No one was so naïve as to believe, when the struggle against the Yids began, that it would be easy. Just as no one was so naïve as to believe, when we launched [the war] against Russia, that ten bullets over the Prut [would be enough] to end the war without bloodshed. Through this battle, we shall build a new path for the Romanian nation and new life for the coming generations. Romanian society will be built on this struggle and on the victims we are sacrificing today."[3]

Antonescu's message was clear: the war against the Soviet Union and the war against the Jews were one and the same thing. The new Romanian society would be built on the ashes of these two enemies. On the very day that he presented his views the Jewish problem in Bessarabia had already been solved, and in Bukovina it had almost been solved. It was he who personally instructed the resumption of the deportations of Bessarabian and Bukovinian Jewry. To whom, then, was Antonescu referring when he spoke of his war against the Jews? Both his actions and his decisions until October 1942 (and in certain cases even after that) clearly showed, as he himself admitted, that his aim was to deport as many Jews as possible in 1942. He also gave Mihai Antonescu a free hand to discuss the Nazi solution to the Jewish problem in Romania with Richter. Thus, in 1942 Romanian Jewry was doomed to destruction, whether by the Romanian or by the Nazi solution.

On 22 May 1942 Antonescu drew up principles determining exceptions to the categories of Jews who were detailed for deportation to the camps. Among the predisposing factors for the publication of these principles were: delays in preparing the Jewish Statute, Romanian preparations for deportation, problems triggered by the Romanian race laws, Antonescu's monopoly over the fate of the Jews, and the number of appeals that were submitted to him. The principles were basically a list of exceptions to the Antonescu regime's general deportation program and, with certain modifications, also to Gustav Richter's deportation program. Antonescu exempted the following categories from deportation: war invalids, their children, and their parents; war widows and orphans; parents of soldiers who had fallen in battle; wounded or decorated war veterans who had actively participated in Romania's wars on the firing lines; members of Romania's former standing army; retirees who had contributed to the state; Jewish spouses of mixed marriages, irrespective of whether they had children; Jews who had converted prior to 1920; and those age seventy or over who had family in Romania that could support them. Jews of outstanding merit who did not fit into any of these categories could still be exempted, but only at Antonescu's discretion.[4] As soon as Antonescu published the principles, they became an integral part of the as yet unpublished Jewish Statute, the Romanian deportation plan, and the Nazi deportation plan, since Richter had to take Antonescu's wishes into consideration.

From Hitler's visit in February 1942 until September of that year Antonescu issued a series of orders against the Jews, mandating their deportation to Transnistria. On 19 February he instructed the minister of the interior to imprison and deport active Communists, particularly from the capital and the oil field area (an order that was implemented in September) and all Jews who had settled in Bucharest illegally over the past two years. Although he mentioned his promise "to safeguard the life and freedom of the local Jews," this was counterbalanced by the need to take action against those endangering "public order, security and our interests. We must take steps against the culprits, and possibly against the entire [Jewish] public."[5] On 18 April he assigned a special ten-day period for the Jews to clean up the streets in cities in which there were still Jews.[6] On 24 April he ordered Lt. Col. Mihail Lisievici of the SSI to execute Communist partisans operating in Transnistria and "in other areas the Soviet Union had lost."[7] In March and April he ordered the deportation of the remainder of the Jews from the Kishinev ghetto and the continued deportation of Jews from Czernowitz. On 2 May he ordered any Jew from Hungary who crossed over into Romania illegally to be deported to Transnistria.[8]

On 3 July 1942 the General Staff published a communiqué in the press and radio ordering the Jewish Center and its branches to inform the army recruitment centers of the current addresses of all Jews age eighteen to fifty. The General Staff announced that all Jews who tried to avoid forced labor or who failed to perform their assignments properly would be deported to Transnistria.[9] After a while they extended the punishment to all family members of those slated for deportation. This communiqué was merely the tip of the iceberg of the General Staff's anti-semitic activities aimed at deporting forty thousand Jews to Transnistria.

On 10 July 1942 Antonescu introduced measures that indicated the start of the deportation from Romania proper. About thirty thousand Jews from southern Transylvania were to be deported to the Kingdom of Death in Transnistria.[10] On 16 and 17 July, in an uncontrollable but not random burst of rage, Antonescu decided to deport tens of thousands of Jews from the Regat, depending on the various categories of real or imaginary offenses they had committed. The military cabinet opened a special file titled "The Problem of the Deportation of the Jews to the Bug" ("Chestiunea deportărei evreilor pe Bug").[11] From his villa in Predeal, where he was recovering from a new bout of his mysterious disease (syphilis), Antonescu ordered Radu Davidescu, head of the military cabinet, to deport "all Jews who had infringed current price regulations, restrictions on the sale of certain products . . . and similar offenses . . . over the Bug." Antonescu added a number of explanations that shed light on the impulsive nature of his anti-Jewish decisions. For example, he ordered the deportation of "Jews from Galați who had been discovered in possession of cotton reels" that they had failed to report to the authorities. In a fit of pique, Antonescu stressed that this order merely complemented his previous orders concerning the deportation of Communist Jews, converted Jews, work-shy Jews, and the like. "These measures are designed not only for criminals, but also to rid densely populated areas of parasitic Jewish elements that violate economic laws and [disrupt] internal order." Antonescu ordered a report on the progress of the deportation of Jews in the Regat and southern Transylvania by category as well as a report on "proposals for future deportations." He added that next on the list were "the Jews of Bukovina, Jews who violate trade restrictions, and the Jews of Transylvania who are being relocated [i.e., deported] in order to make room for Romanian refugees, and the like."[12]

The following day (17 July), giving full vent to his rage, Antonescu sent yet another order from Predeal via teleprinter to the military cabinet and minister of the interior for implementation. He expanded his previous directives and broadened the eligibility criteria for deportation by ordering the deportation of all Jews and foreigners who infringed economic laws: "anyone hiding medicines, fabrics, footwear, cotton, couponed goods, and food products, as well as middlemen, saboteurs of the economy, and those who fail to respect price ceilings" Antonescu ordered the Ministry of the Economy and the Ministry of the Interior to issue a formal decision regarding the new deportations and to send it to him in his villa in Predeal for signature by 25 July. "Due process shall be reduced to a minimum. Offenders shall be deported to Transnistria without trial, together with their families. This decision shall be valid retroactively." The immediate cause of the marshal's mounting rage was apparent in an order of 17 July 1942: "We must not agree to the violation of our laws . . . while Romanian officers and soldiers risk their lives on the front. Understanding and tolerance toward these *monopolizing and disruptive elements* is unthinkable."[13] The second order turned all Jews who were still wage earners into prospective deportees, without recourse to due process. The order empowered the corrupt and antisemitic Romanian administration to immediately deport all offenders and their families. While implementation of the first order would have resulted in the deportation of ninety-five thousand to one hundred thousand Jews (about nineteen thousand from Czernowitz and Dorohoi; thirty thousand from southern Transylvania; forty thousand deemed to have evaded forced labor; and five thousand who fit in other categories), implementation of the second order signified the gradual deportation to Transnistria of all Romanian Jews.

Once the decision had been made to deport all Romanian Jews the fate of Romanian Jews residing in Nazi-occupied Europe became irrelevant. The consuls in Germany "received orders on 21 August 1942 to no longer protest the measures adopted by the Germans against Romanian Jews and their property," but to monitor the confiscation of property and to draw up an inventory of items seized by the German authorities.[14] Gheorge Davidescu, secretary general of the Foreign Ministry, sent all Romanian ambassadors a clarification concerning the government's policy toward Jews whose passports had expired. He informed the Romanian ambassador in Switzerland that, regarding the Jews who had fled to Switzerland to renew their Romanian passports: "It is our country's policy to get rid of as many members of the Jewish minority as possible." He recommended that the passports of Jews be confiscated and that they be left to deal with the Swiss authorities alone.[15]

In early September Antonescu decided to deport Jews to Transnistria after reading reports on the economy in the Romanian press that groundlessly accused Jews of economic sabotage. For example, after reading such an article in *Curentul* he ordered the confiscation of the property, internment, and deportation of the "Yids and their families" whom the newspaper had accused of sabotaging the economy. Antonescu's adoption of the final solution was reflected in his vocabulary when speaking of the Jews. It was as if a mutation had taken place; whereas until June 1941 he was merely antisemitic, after June 1941 his antisemitic outlook assumed an unmistakably Nazi-racist character.

On 31 August 1942, about two weeks before the beginning of the deportation to Poland and Transnistria, Antonescu was infuriated by reading a detailed survey he had commissioned on the size and distribution of the Jewish population in Romania, and he ordered that steps be taken to prepare the general public for the deportation of Romanian Jews:

> The [data] on the population breakdown in the cities must be published in order for the country to realize the enormity of the danger facing Romania's economic life and development, due to the crimes of the Jewish-Masonic policy, as represented through parties that call themselves "nationalist" in Transylvania and the Regat. By leaving things the way they are for my heirs, I would be turning my regime into an accomplice, too. No-one and no obstacle shall alter my resolve to completely purge the nation of this pest. When the time comes, I shall condemn all those who tried (most recently Mr. Maniu), and are trying, to prevent me from carrying out the wish of the vast majority of this nation. . . . This decision should be published in its entirety together with the statistics and the present survey . . . by 10 September.[16]

It is clear that nothing could have prevented Antonescu from carrying out his design to deport Romanian Jewry to Transnistria or occupied Poland and liquidate them.

THE DEPORTATION IN THE AUTUMN OF 1942

In the autumn of 1942 most Jews in Bukovina (Czernowitz) and southern Transylvania; offenders and evaders of forced labor; Communists and their sympathizers; new converts; Jews who tried to return to Bessarabia in the autumn and winter of 1940, after its annexation to the Soviet Union; and Gypsies were about to be deported. A total of ninety-five thousand to one hundred thousand Jews faced deportation to Transnistria. At the same time, secret negotiations with the German government and with Richter concerning the wholesale deportation of Romanian Jewry to the Bełżec Nazi camp in Poland approached their final stages. Everything was proceeding as planned. In late August Antonescu's rage reached a pinnacle. The Ministry of the Interior received a list of Communists whom the police and gendarmerie had marked variously as dangerous, undercover Communists, or Communist sympathizers, as they saw fit. The General Staff drew up a list of Jews who failed to report for forced labor or whom they labeled "work-shy" (even if they had died or been murdered), who had escaped from forced labor detachments, or who simply were absent when Gen. Constantin Cepleanu, the new inspector of forced labor, conducted his impromptu raids, even if they had been granted leave of absence. The Jewish Center, as ordered, supplied the authorities with the latest addresses of Jews, including relatives and converts. In the Târgu Jiu camp, which held Communists who had been arrested without trial, preliminary preparations were made for deportation.

The Gendarmerie Inspectorate General, under General Vasiliu, was responsible for organizing the transports to Transnistria. Vasiliu instructed the General Police Inspectorate to oversee the confiscation of the deportees' (Jews and Gypsies) belongings, the arrest of those slated for deportation, and their transfer to the gendarmerie authorities. The gendarmerie legions throughout Romania were provided with timetables of the deportation trains.[17]

On 3 September the Bucharest police arrested 395 Jews, some of whom were Communist suspects but most of whom were native Bessarabians who had attempted to return to Bessarabia in late 1940, which was then under Soviet rule. On 8 September these Jews were deported in a special train to Transnistria via Tiraspol. Soon their numbers grew to 598, as Jews from other categories were loaded on to the trains at stations en route. Four hundred and seven Communist suspects from the Târgu Jiu camp and another 554 Communist suspects from all over Romania, who were neither tried nor interned, were put on the same train.[18] Eighty-five Jews who had been imprisoned for being staunch Communists or having engaged in Communist activity were likewise added to the transport.[19] It should be noted that most Communist suspects who were being held in the Târgu Jiu camp or who were arrested throughout Romania were not actually Communists.

The train reached Tiraspol two days later, and on 12 September a selection took place. Those considered Communists were sent to Vapniarca, while the Bessarabian Jews were sent to Berezovka for liquidation. The Vapniarca camp, which was meant for Jewish political prisoners, was the closest thing to a Nazi detention camp.

On the night of 15–16 September the General Staff unleashed its deportation operation. On 22 September some 160 Bucharest Jews and their families were arrested and deported to Transnistria via Tiraspol. At stations en route the train picked up several hundred more Jews from all over Romania who had been arrested under the General Staff's deportation plan.[20] The Jewish author Mihail Sebastian noted in his diary on 22 September: "The deportation plan is being implemented slowly but surely."[21] On 2 October several hundred Jews—General

Cepleanu's victims — were imprisoned in two Jewish schools in Bucharest prior to their deportation, this time without their families.

The deportation operation was huge and required careful organization and planning as well as the cooperation of the various authorities, such as the Ministry of the Interior, the Finance Ministry, the National Romanization Center, the municipalities, and the Jewish Center, which supplied the addresses of the Jews and their families. The General Staff assigned the Jewish Center the task of guarding the families until the arrest of the family heads and of loading them onto the trains. The number of those accused of evading forced labor totaled 14,247 (about 40,000 with their families). The General Staff, with Ion Antonescu's approval, planned to deport most of them in the autumn of 1942 to the Golta and Berezovka districts, where they were to be liquidated.

In early October 1942 the Antonescu regime's resolve to deport Romanian Jewry to the camps and ghettos of Transnistria appeared inevitable and irrevocable. They were not, however, the only actors on the scene. The Nazis were also competing for the privilege of liquidating Romanian Jewry, and their methods were far more organized and efficient.

DESTINATION BEŁŻEC

The Bełżec concentration camp in the Lublin district, in which Jews were asphyxiated by carbon monoxide generated by a diesel engine, was chosen by the RSHA and the German Foreign Ministry to serve as a mass grave for Romanian Jewry. In June 1942 the camp was renovated and its extermination capacity enhanced. Six large, new gas chambers were added, capable of killing 1,000–1,200 deportees at a time (half of a daily transport of 2,000) within twenty to thirty minutes. The entire procedure, from the arrival of the deportees in the camp to the removal of the corpses via the rear doors of the gas chambers for burial, took an hour to an hour and a half. This extermination method was shrouded in secrecy and duplicity. From the moment they boarded the trains until they were forced into the gas chambers, the victims were told that they were being taken to labor camps.[22]

Access to the Bełżec camp was easy. It was the terminal station on the Czernowitz-Sniatyn-Bełżec railroad (Sniatyn was on the former Polish border). It was necessary to persuade the Jews that they were being taken to a labor camp, where they would be treated in a civilized manner, in order to facilitate matters. Mihai Antonescu was fed the same story when Richter insisted that the Romanian Jews be deported to occupied Poland, not Transnistria: "Mr. Richter informed me that the Jews from Romania and other countries were being taken to Poland where they were organized into work camps, and that while the regime in these camps could hardly be called comfortable, it was nevertheless reasonable in terms of physical preservation."[23] Although Richter was aware that he was dealing with criminals and murderers like himself, he did not realize that they had already learned about the Final Solution from Hitler himself and that the liquidation of the Jews in the "labor camps" of Poland was no secret for them (although the actual method of extermination may have been). Nor did he realize that even the Romanian diplomatic legations in the Reich and in German-occupied countries were aware of what was going on, as their reports indicated.

Secret negotiations between the Nazis and the Romanian government for the implementation of the Final Solution (formerly known as the "European solution") among Romanian Jewry resumed early in the summer of 1942. The negotiations were brief and involved no more than three to four Romanians. At the Wannsee Conference it was determined that the RSHA, with the Foreign Ministry in Berlin, would handle all problems relating to Jews living abroad.[24] As well as making Richter available to the Foreign Ministry, the RSHA predicted that the German advisors on Jewish affairs in the various countries would become superfluous "once the Jewish problem . . . was solved in the German manner." The RSHA even explicitly stated that Richter would remain in Bucharest "until the practical final solution" (bis zur praktischen Endlösung in Rumänien) was completed and return to Berlin only afterward.[25] It is worth noting that at this stage Killinger—who had previously gone out of his way to encourage the Slovakian government to adopt an anti-Jewish policy—also took part in the negotiations with the Romanians concerning the Final Solution and was not averse to using pressure and threats. He reported directly to Ribbentrop on the progress of the operation and was generally more realistic than his younger SS accomplice, of whom he was not especially fond. The negotiations on the Romanian side proceeded in total secrecy, to prevent the Jews from panicking and also to hide from opposition circles (particularly from Iuliu Maniu and his associates) any hint that negotiations were being held for the deportation of Jews to another country or to a territory under Romanian sovereignty (Transnistria).

Once the secret of the impending deportation became common knowledge, Maniu indeed intervened in order to prevent it. On 22 July 1942 Mihai Antonescu informed Killinger in writing of his agreement "to the evacuation of all Romanian Jews and the immediate transfer of the Jews from the Arad, Timişoara and Turda districts," emphasizing that "this is also the will of Marshal Antonescu."[26] Radu Lecca was due to arrive in Berlin on 19 August to conduct negotiations with the head of the RSHA and the SD on the matter. On 26 July Heinrich Müller, Gestapo head and director of Section 4, informed Martin Luther, undersecretary for foreign affairs, that the deportation of Romanian Jews in special trains "to the east" would begin on 10 September 1942.[27] Luther drew up a memorandum describing the important landmarks in the negotiations with the Romanians concerning the deportation, starting with the Romanian government's agreement in November 1941 to the deportation of its Jewish citizens living in the Reich and in the protectorate: "The deputy President of the Council of Ministers has given us his approval in writing, in accordance with Marshal Antonescu's wishes, for the German authorities to carry out the evacuation of the Jews from Romania.[28] At the same time, Rintelen from the Foreign Ministry drew up a memorandum for Luther, his superior, outlining preparations for the deportation of Romanian Jewry. The political and technical preparations for the Final Solution of the problem of Romanian Jewry were completed by Richter. In accordance with the plan, transports were to leave for the Lublin area beginning around 10 September in groups of two thousand Jews per transport. Those unfit for work were to be given "special treatment." After crossing the border the deportees were to be deprived of their Romanian nationality. The Foreign Ministry was still negotiating the settlement of certain issues in Romania. Talks with the Reich Ministry of Transport had still to be finalized but were progressing smoothly. At the RSHA's behest Richter received written confirmation from Mihai Antonescu that he consented to the deportation, and Rintelen enclosed a copy of the agreement.[29]

On 8 August, even before all the practical arrangements with the Romanian government had been finalized, Richter hastened to inform both Romanians and Jews that he had succeeded. While the Romanian press kept totally silent on the subject of the deportation of the Jews to Poland, Richter published an editorial titled "Romania Is About to Become Judenrein" ("Rumänien wird judenrein"), which embarrassed Mihai and Ion Antonescu vis-à-vis the opposition. The editorial established a correlation between the way Romania was dealing with "a problem essential to its future" (i.e., the Jewish problem) and "Romania's status in the new Europe."[30] In other words, if it did not agree to kill its Jews Romania would have no special status in Nazi Europe.

Richter presented the anti-Jewish measures as voluntary operations of the Jewish Center, a kind of mobilization on its part to implement the Romanian government's antisemitic policy. Although some members of the center, notably Nandor Gingold and A. Wilman, collaborated with Richter and provided him with up-to-date information on the Jews and on the Romanian government's policy toward them, to suggest that the dispossession and deportation of the Jews was an initiative of the Jewish Center was an outrageous fabrication of the kind the Nazis resorted to in order to prevent opposition to the implementation of their goals. In his editorial, Richter presented the Nazi perception of the Jewish

Center's role: "Right from the start, the Jewish Center's role was to clarify the various directives against the Jews, conduct a census of Jews, guide Jews toward useful activities for the Romanian State and people and ultimately prepare all the groundwork for the final cleansing of Romania of Jews."[31]

Richter was satisfied with the census finding that 272,409 Jews remained in Romania (excluding Bukovina)—an achievement that had been "quietly and unobtrusively" accomplished by the Romanian government. One hundred eighty-five thousand Bessarabian and Bukovinian Jews had been deported to Transnistria, but even before that (upon their renewed reunification) "*Bessarabia was cleansed [of Jews], and subsequently Bukovina, too.*" A mere 16,000 Jews remained. This was a tremendous achievement, continued Richter. Another achievement—one that could be credited to the entire Romanian nation—was that throughout Romania there were no more than 5,000–6,000 *Mischlinge* (children of mixed marriages), who were virtually outcasts. Richter emphasized that the census had been conducted according to the Nuremberg race laws, with one exception—converted children of mixed marriages. He also boasted of another important achievement in connection with the Romanians' attitude toward the Jewish problem: "We have managed [to create a situation whereby] in Romania, too, the Jewish problem has been recognized as one of race."[32]

Richter claimed that the Jewish Center was assigned the new task of "totally purging Romania of Jews," as if it determined policy or desired the liquidation of Romanian Jewry.[33] The article was meant to throw the Jews into confusion and despair and to divert their hatred away from Richter and the Antonescu regime toward the Jewish Center. It was the kind of duplicity in which the Nazis excelled, but it carried little weight in Romania since it had no impact on the Jewish leaders (particularly Filderman).

Richter and his superiors in Berlin were premature in announcing their success. Their greatest mistake was to link Romania's future in Nazi Europe and its status in the new Europe with the liquidation of the Jews. The Antonescu regime considered the victims it had sacrificed and was still sacrificing on the front, as well as the oil, food, and raw materials it had sent Germany, as the main price it had to pay for the recovery of northern Transylvania (Romania's most important war objective), not the liquidation of 272,000 Jews. What irked the regime most was that Hungary was not being required to deport its Jews at that point.

On 11 September 1942 Radu Lecca presented Mihai Antonescu, his immediate superior, with the Romanian plan "for the evacuation of the Jewish population from Banat and from the border areas in the west."[34] Lecca's plan confirmed the Romanian agreement in principle to the deportation of all Romanian Jews to occupied Poland. Exceptions included some of those listed in Antonescu's principles, sometimes literally, and also changes resulting from the need to adapt the principles to the plan to deport the Jews. Antonescu's directives stipulated that "[work] places in the national economy that fell vacant following the deportation of Jews, would be filled by Romanian refugees from Northern Transylvania, which had been handed over [to Hungary]." Lecca explicitly stated in his plan that the deportation destination was occupied Poland, not Transnistria.

Richter decided that all Romanian Jews would be deported to Bełżec via the Sniatyn border point in transports of two thousand Jews each. The distinctive feature of the Richter plan, which was finalized on 15 September 1942, was its aim to send an entire group of Jews to their destruction. The main ingredients of this plan were ideological antecedents (Hitler's promise of 24 February 1942 in Munich to get rid of the Jewish parasites), operational instructions, duplicitous measures to calm the Jewish population, the resolution of legal problems between Romania and Germany, the utilization of the Jewish Center, and logistical and operational planning.[35] Although Richter had to take into account, to some extent at least, Romanian requirements regarding exceptions (Antonescu's principles), he stressed that "the question of the Jews in Romania will be finally resolved only after the last Jew has left." He rejected some of the Romanian demands and expanded the number of Jews slated for deportation.[36]

Some of the clauses in Richter's plan were designed to mislead the Jews right to the very end, when the gas was released into the gas chambers. For example, he told them that they could bring with them certain items, such as "a pair of working boots . . . two woolen blankets . . . a food bowl" and the like. These items were left behind in the trains in Bełżec station when their owners were taken to the gas chambers. Richter also planned to set up a transit point in Romania between Paşcani and Czernowitz. The transit camp was designed to regulate the flow of deportees, prevent a bottleneck of Jews in Bełżec, enable the smooth transfer of Jews to the gas chambers, prevent an insurrection, and mislead the terrified Jews until the last moment regarding the true nature of the camp.

Titus Dragoş, the minister of Romanization and architect of the Jewish Statute, hastily presented Lecca with an internal report on the need "to deport several hundred thousand Jews who were found to be of no use to the country, of which about a hundred thousand were in Bucharest alone, which would solve the problem [of the shortage of accommodation] for several years." Dragoş asked Lecca about "the progress of the 'dilution' policy, namely ridding the capital of Jews through deportation and emigration." Dragoş himself was unaware that the deportees were to be taken to Poland. It is clear from Lecca's laconic answer that he assumed that Dragoş was in the know: "Our plan calls for the evacuation to Poland of all Jews who are not useful to the national economy."[37] Thus Lecca ratified that the Antonescu regime planned to deport all Romanian Jews, not only the Jews of southern Transylvania, to Poland.

Note that during this critical week (20–27 September), when representatives of the Romanian Railways Administration were invited to Berlin to discuss timetables for the deportation (and even before, from early July until late September), Bucharest was effectively leaderless. Ion Antonescu's illness had drained him, and he was hardly able to function.[38] His incapacity prevented him from attending the talks to which he was invited by Hitler in his headquarters in Vinnitsa in the Ukraine, and for the first time Mihai Antonescu stood in for him to discuss military problems with the führer and his generals and to meet with Ribbentrop.

The meetings in Vinnitsa on 22 and 23 September 1942 focused not only on military problems but also on the problem of the deportation of Romanian Jewry. Ribbentrop urged Mihai Antonescu to begin the deportation — a suggestion that he did not refuse. On the contrary, he spoke of how the "evacuation" of the Jews (i.e., the liquidation of Bessarabian and Bukovinian Jewry) had been made possible at the time by the "understanding" with the ss.[39]

Unrest among Romanian Jews reached a peak in September–October 1942. All of them, except for Filderman, still thought that they were about to be deported to Transnistria, since neither Bełżec nor Poland were mentioned in any official announcement or in talks with Jewish leaders. It took a while before the penny dropped. On 18 August the police of Timişoara reported rumors in the city of the impending deportation of Transylvanian Jews to Transnistria, under pressure from ethnic German leaders. The Jews began selling off their belongings, convinced that "they would be executed even before they reached Transnistria." They did not even believe the rumor that the rich would be allowed to immigrate to Palestine but claimed that the ships would be sunk at sea. "[They were in the grips of] an unutterable despair, and most of them declared they would commit suicide."[40]

It was, apparently, only in late October 1942 that the Jews discovered that they were to be deported to Poland, not Transnistria. The true nature of the plan came to light only after Antonescu decided to defer the deportations. The ssi reported that the Jews were notified that henceforth the deportations would be to Lublin (of notorious connotations), not Transnistria. The SSI report went on to describe how the Germans "asked for the deportation be carried out swiftly: a transport of 2,000 people every 48 hours, in trains of 50 cars." Although the information in this report was correct, the Jews found out about it only after the suspension of the deportation plan.[41]

The deportation campaign initiated by Antonescu in the summer–autumn of 1942 angered Richter greatly. These deportations were done solely at the Romanians' initiative, without any coordination with the German legation, and Richter learnt about them from Gingold, Wilman, and the German consul in Czernowitz.[42] On 7 October a very tense meeting took place between Killinger and Mihai Antonescu concerning the deportations. "We cannot continue thus," Killinger began, and added that he knew that high-ranking Romanian officials were continuing to maintain ties with Jews "and are using all means to sabotage the solution to the Jewish problem in Romania."[43]

On 11 October the German legation publicly clarified to whom it was referring. Its mouthpiece published an article titled "Judenknechte" (Jewish lackeys) that included a fierce attack on anyone sabotaging the deportation plan for Romanian Jewry, without specifying places such as Poland, Lublin, or Bełżec. The article emphasized that the deportation would be carried out in a planned manner (*planmässig*), "in the spirit of the undertaking that the Romanian government had assumed toward the New Europe" — namely, toward Nazi Germany. The news of the deportation, continued the article, led naturally to agitation among the Jews. They immediately began looking for help and regretfully found people — "Jewish lackeys" — who were willing to help. The unsigned article immediately angered the Antonescu regime by linking the future of Romania and its leaders to the deportation of the Jews. One thing must be clear, the article concluded, "The situation of the countries that wish to join the New Europe will be contingent on the way in which they solve the Jewish problem within their borders."[44] The article appeared while hundreds of Romanian soldiers were falling daily in the battles for Stalingrad and added salt to the regime's open wound. The SSI analyzed its contents and informed Antonescu that political and diplomatic circles in Bucharest considered it a rude intervention in Romania's internal affairs.[45]

It was only due to German pressure that the Antonescu regime was able to announce publicly the cessation of deportations to Transnistria without risking a German response. Richter was convinced that the way was now open for deportations to Bełżec. Mihai Antonescu had other plans. The members of the RSHA and the German Foreign Ministry, who conducted talks with the Romanians, were unable to fathom the true reasons behind the cessation of the deportations. Continued pressure by the Germans merely underscored their ignorance of the true nature of Romanian politics and Richter's arrogance and stupidity. Right to the end Richter failed to realize that his threats to expose the corruption that riddled the administration and the police (namely, their acceptance of bribes from wealthy Jews who wished to escape the transports of the summer and autumn) achieved the opposite of what he intended. It was only on 22 October, when he tried to clarify why the Jews were not being deported, that Richter realized that he had been deceived by the Romanians. He reminded Mihai Antonescu that he had agreed to the deportation in September, in Ribbentrop's presence, and that Lecca had agreed in August in Berlin. In his report Richter complained that the Romanian foreign minister "was playing games" (*Spitzfindigkeit*) with him. Mihai Antonescu admitted that he had agreed to the deportation but reminded Richter that the German legation had called for a "cessation of the deportations across the Bug, and in his opinion, this was a contradiction." Richter tried in vain to argue that "there was no contradiction," since initially there had been no question of deportation across the Bug but only to the General Government. The deportation of Romanian Jewry, Richter admonished Antonescu, must be conducted "within the framework of the solution to the Jewish problem in Europe"; the German Reich was not planning to deport Jews across the Bug but "directly" to the General Government. Mihai Antonescu, added Richter, had nothing to say "after he had put him in his place." Richter obtained a photocopy of Ion Antonescu's decision to suspend the deportations and attached it to the report he sent Berlin: "The deportation from Transylvania has simply been deliberated. Its implementation has been deferred. It shall be resumed only when the time is ripe. Until then, [the deportation] shall be prepared in all its details by the Interior Minister, according to Mr. Mihai Antonescu's instructions."[46] In Richter's opinion, Mihai Antonescu was upset at the marshal's decision to halt the deportations but, as his loyal servant, was simply obeying orders.

In fact, the opposite was true. Ion Antonescu never came to terms with the decision to suspend the deportation of Romanian Jews and never formally abolished the plan to purge Bukovina of Jews. As late as September 1943 he made a last-ditch attempt to deport Romanian Jews to Transnistria. As for Mihai Antonescu, he did his best to erase his contribution to the Holocaust of Romanian Jewry from the official records and from the memory of those who knew him. He believed that, since the Jews ruled the world, Romania's Jews should be held as bargaining chips that could later be used to save Romania and himself from the consequences of their activities in 1941–42.

On 17 October 1942, perhaps at the Nazis' instigation, the Slovakian ambassador, Ivan Milecz, boasted to members of the Romanian Foreign Ministry that "the Jewish problem in Slovakia had been almost entirely solved. [Slovakia] had deported 60,000 out of its 70,000 Jews to Poland, and the Germans had paid 500 Marks for each Jew. The ten thousand Jews who remained were considered useful until the end of the war."[47] This was exactly what the Nazis were planning to do with the Romanian Jews. In August 1942 Richter had estimated that there were seventeen thousand useful Jews in Romania.

36

The Postponement of the
Nazi Final Solution

In the government session of 13 October 1942 Mihai Antonescu announced a change of policy toward the Jews:

> For the time being, the transports of Jews across the Dniester are being halted. From now on, the transportation of Jews shall be undertaken by a joint body, to be set up by the General Staff, the Interior Ministry and the Presidency of the Council of Ministers. This body shall prevent a repeat of past errors: The General Staff issues an order; the Interior Ministry implements it; the Police Inspectorate in Bucharest begins searching for [people] on the list; the Jews hide in houses; panic and a certain atmosphere is generated around this issue. . . . [The Jews] panic, they are terrorized and threatened, and propagate a [negative] atmosphere and rumors that cause panic. *For them it is a question of life and death.* They prefer life.[1]

Mihai Antonescu stressed that one of the reasons for halting the deportations was rampant corruption among Romanian officials: "Not only do the police agents receive bribes in order to save [people earmarked] for deportation to Transnistria . . . they also threaten others who do not come under this category, earning a tidy income and tainting our Administration . . . because of their brazen and unseemly bribery operations."[2]

On the face of it Mihai Antonescu unreservedly adopted Richter's advice that "it was necessary to operate systematically [*planmässig*]." He had his own agenda, however — to divest the General Staff, the Interior Ministry, and all ministries and bodies dealing with the Jews of their authority to deport the Jews. The cessation of the deportations took the ministers, apart from Vasiliu, completely by surprise, particularly the General Staff. Although in the meeting Mihai Antonescu had stressed that "Marshal Antonescu completely agrees with me," the ministers had no idea, until the last moment, of the change that was about to take place in the policy toward the Jews. Indeed, Mihai Antonescu wrested the handling of the Jews from the General Staff, curtailed Lecca's prerogatives, and appointed an inter-ministerial committee to handle the Jewish problem. The words *deportations*, *evacuation*, and *transport* disappeared from official communiqués, to be replaced by a new word: *expatriation* (*expatrieri*).

Occasional proposals formerly submitted by the General Staff calling for stricter measures against the Jews were no longer automatically approved, as Antonescu began reining in the General Staff's authority. On 21 October the Conducător officially authorized Mihai Antonescu "to exclude the General Staff from any involvement in the Administration or in political matters." On 23 October Mihai Antonescu rejected the General Staff's proposal of 18 October that the Jews be obliged to give up their Romanian names and revert to their Jewish names. As Mihai Antonescu wrote to the minister of national defense, "Had this memorandum been brought to the Marshal's attention, he would no doubt have accused the General Staff of yet again exceeding its brief and interfering in political matters that were not its concern."[3]

The connection between the halt in the deportations to Transnistria and the halt in the deportations to Bełżec was formalized by Grigore Basarabeanu, deputy director general of Antonescu's cabinet, on 4 November 1942. Basarabeanu noted on the letter sent by the director of the Romanian Railway Authority (CFR) inquiring about the deportation of Romanian Jews to the General Government, "The ministerial council of 13 October 1942 called a halt to the deportation of Jews."[4] An official communiqué announcing a halt to the deportations appeared in the newspaper *Timpul* on 16 October: "The expatriation of certain elements from the Regat has been suspended until the establishment of a special body." The order to cease rounding up Jews for deportation reached the provincial towns too late. On 7 October thirty Jewish families were arrested in Botoşani for deportation to Transnistria, including the Jewish poet Alfred Margul Sperber and his wife.[5] On 13 October Lecca informed the heads of the Jewish Center that "the latest arrests of Jews run counter to the government's intentions" and that the detainees would be classified before being deported to Transnistria.[6] In the end, they were not deported. A month earlier, on 12 September, Lecca had informed German journalists that his task was "to transfer the Jews eastwards." On the evening of 13 October several hundred Jews who were being held in two Jewish schools in Bucharest pending their deportation were released. "It was a day of rejoicing in the Jewish streets," wrote Filderman's assistant, Carp, in his journal.[7]

The change in policy toward the Jews occurred only when Ion and Mihai Antonescu came to the gradual realization that they were unlikely to be rewarded for the many human and material sacrifices they had made (and were still making) for the realization of Hitler's dream to conquer the world. The reward they expected was the return of northern Transylvania. In 1942 Antonescu and the entire Romanian nation were prepared to pay with blood, oil, food . . . and Jews, in return for northern Transylvania. In September 1942, before the defeat at Stalingrad but closely linked to the situation on the fronts, the two leaders began to wonder if they had made the right choices, after realizing that their expectation that Hitler would return northern Transylvania to Romania was unrealistic. Later in September Mihai Antonescu realized that the Romanian soldiers on the front were serving as cannon fodder and that Germany was unable to defeat the Soviet Union. By 1942 three-quarters of the Romanian army had been sent to Russia, almost all Romania's oil had been sent to fuel the German war machine, and huge quantities of food had been transferred to the Reich, at a time when Romania itself was suffering shortages, and all this to what end and for what purpose?

The crisis that occurred on the eve of the defeat at Stalingrad can be discussed on five levels: (1) the situation at the front; (2) the problem of Transylvania; (3) Romania's relationship with Hungary; (4) the views of the opposition; and (5) attempts by the Jewish Leadership to foil the deportation plan.

THE PROBLEM OF TRANSYLVANIA

On 10 July 1942 Ion Antonescu ordered preparations to be made for the deportation of the Jews of southern Transylvania to the Bug, in order to make room for the Romanian refugees who were arriving from northern Transylvania. On 15 July the SSI reported that circles close to Maniu believed that the marshal was very ill and depressed. Antonescu, the SSI report stated, had informed Dr. Nicolae Lupu (Maniu's deputy), after the latter had examined him, that "he now realized that Romania was in German hands, and that his hopes for a positive outcome to the problem of Transylvania with Germany's help, which had been the main objective of his policy, were dashed. This realization, Maniu's supporters continued, had discouraged Antonescu so much that his health had deteriorated."[8] The recognition that Hitler was deceiving Antonescu and had no intention of using his influence to return northern Transylvania—the part of the Romanian homeland that Ribbentrop and Galeazzo Ciano (the Italian foreign minister) had handed over to Hungary in late August 1940—was a turning point in Romania's attitude toward Germany.

To relinquish Transylvania was to relinquish a national dream. Unfortunately, Antonescu linked Romania's fate with the realization of Hitler's dream to rule the world. There is no way of knowing whether Antonescu's disillusionment with Hitler caused a new flare-up of his disease or merely exacerbated it. People in government circles claimed that Antonescu was suffering from malaria. In any case, the deterioration in the marshal's health in 1942 led to his impaired judgment and inconsistency of thought and action. A council of top Romanian doctors diagnosed "a new outbreak of syphilis or malaria."[9]

Although the change of heart was gradual, it almost certainly began in mid-July 1942, when Ion Antonescu was still making many of his pro-German pronouncements. Two weeks before Ion Antonescu sank into deep depression Mihai Antonescu presented the ministers with a utopian portrait of the regime's achievements during the first year of the war and repeated the regime's maxim that the war against the Soviet Union was a war to regain northern Transylvania. To this end Romania intended to mobilize over a million soldiers in 1942. Mihai Antonescu portrayed the liberation of Romanians in northern Transylvania from the Hungarian yoke after the victory in the east in Nazi racist terms: "Every blood must die in order to protect similar blood, and all blood of one kind must be under one rule."[10] In January 1942 Ion Antonescu promised to send three-quarters of the rehabilitated Romanian army to the front: ten divisions in the first stage, to be followed by another five, in addition to forces already stationed in Transnistria and on the front—a total of twenty-six divisions. He did this without consulting anyone, even the General Staff.

Antonescu and his regime considered the Second World War no different from other wars, despite being aware that they were joining the powers that divided nations into inferior and superior and aspired to destroy states, enslave their populations, and exterminate the Jewish people on racist and ideological grounds. Like the Germans, they justified their actions by claiming they were inspired by concern for the Romanian nation and used criminal methods to obtain their national goals. Right up to the end, Antonescu never understood the difference between the First World War and a war into which he dragged the Romanian nation. His sole concern was the injustice done to the Romanian people in 1940, an injustice that in his opinion legitimized any action aimed at restoring Romania's territorial integrity, including participation in Germany's war to conquer the world. The praises that Hitler heaped upon him and his army in 1941 made a strong impression on the Romanian dictator, on whom Hitler evidently had a hypnotic effect. Only after Stalingrad did he begin to break free of it. In February 1942, although entertaining strong doubts as to the Wehrmacht's ability to obtain a definitive victory on the Soviet front, Antonescu was again hypnotized by Hitler's personality and influenced by the führer's optimistic expectation that he would achieve victory in the summer of 1942.

Nevertheless, in their talks with Hitler and Ribbentrop Ion and Mihai Antonescu raised their fears of "the Hungarian menace" and demanded that Hungary, too, send a large military force to Russia. Hitler and Ribbentrop again reassured the Conducător concerning Romania's borders, including the Hungarian border. They exploited Romanian fears to extort concessions from Hungary, too, and to force it to increase its military commitments. Indeed, in the summer of 1942 Hungary sent an entire army, comprising fifteen divisions, to the front. The conflict between Romania and Hungary, Romania's hopes for the return of northern Transylvania, and Hungary's fears of a revision in the Vienna arbitration served as a springboard for extorting economic and military concessions from Nazi Germany's two allies.

What was the führer's word of honor concerning Transylvania? What had he promised Antonescu on this issue, so close to the hearts of the Romanian nation? The answer is nothing. In their second meeting, on 23 November 1940, Hitler gave some vague indication that he understood the Romanian attitude toward Transylvania when Antonescu brought up the issue of the subjugation of 1.35 million Romanians and stated that Hitler "fully understood his feelings, his indignation, and grief," adding the cryptic comment that "history would not come to a standstill in the year 1940."[11]

Although northern Transylvania was not the only issue affecting Romania and Hungary, it influenced their attitude toward Germany and the war with Russia and, in the final analysis, the fate of the Jews. After the Antonescu administration implemented its murderous antisemitic and racial objectives in Bessarabia and Bukovina the Jews still remaining in Romania became a further symbol of Antonescu's Nazi ideology, another pawn in the regime's overt and covert competition with Hungary over northern Transylvania. The ease with which Antonescu ordered the murder of Jews enhanced his standing with Hitler. The sacrifice of thousands of Romanian soldiers, the transfer of national resources and food to Germany — out of an ideological identification with the Nazis' wishes to destroy the Jewish nation — and Romania's consent that the Nazi war machinery could deal with the remnants of Romanian Jewry, in full cognizance of what this implied, were all part of Ion and Mihai Antonescu's strategy to regain northern Transylvania. Until the late summer of 1942 Romania did all it could to appease Germany and bore the gross violations of economic agreements and harm to Romanian interests in silence. Their restraint had one goal: the return of northern Transylvania.

Competition with Hungary for Germany's goodwill also had repercussions for the Jewish issue. The glib Mihai Antonescu never lost any opportunity to rebuke the Hungarian government and people for their "favorable"
attitude toward the Jews. He never failed to stress how he, the regime, and the
Romanian people were more antisemitic than the Hungarians, hated the Jews
more, and were more amenable to radical solutions to the Jewish problem than
were the Hungarians. He outlined this position very clearly during his visit to
Berlin in November 1941, particularly during his meeting with Goebbels. After
repeatedly raising the issue of northern Transylvania's return to Romania, he
stressed "Hungary's symbolic contribution to this war" and accused the Hungarians of "megalomania." He referred to Romanian sacrifices in the war against
the Russians and presented another Romanian trump card against Hungary:
"What could be the Hungarian understanding of antisemitism, of the clarity of
a nationalism unaltered by semitic tendencies? The Hungarian press is written
by Jews. The Hungarians are the last Jewish reservation in Europe. Today, the
Jews still buy urban property in Budapest. *We are antisemitic both by birth and
conviction.* In Hungary, Jews are working behind the scenes against Germany with
the government's tacit consent."[12] Mihai Antonescu also made sure to impress
the führer with the Romanian nation's lofty plans in terms meant to ingratiate
himself with the führer: "The Romanian people is, and has always been, anti-
Slav, just as it has always been antisemitic in essence."[13] All these efforts were
made on behalf of Transylvania, but in vain.

In order to break out of this ideological impasse the official propaganda propagated the idea that Transylvania would be recaptured by force after the victory on
the eastern front. Ion Antonescu impressed this point on Hitler when he asked
for weapons for his army as a condition for his participation in the campaign in
1942: "I again stressed the conditions for our participation in the forthcoming
campaign: Hungary, and providing missing equipment [to the divisions sent
to the front], especially as the conflict between us and the Hungarians shall be
settled militarily after the war with the Russians."[14] This official position, which
was based on the illusion that Germany would allow its two satellites to fight it
out between them, was absurd, ran counter to German interests, and contradicted
the official propaganda line: namely, that the Romanian army was fighting in the
east in order to liberate northern Transylvania in the west. Moreover, equipping
the Romanian army with modern weapons—modern tanks, planes, antitank
weapons, trucks, liaison systems, and the like—was dependent on Hitler's goodwill. Hitler's agreement to Antonescu's demands would have strengthened the

Romanian army and enabled it to capture Transylvania by force. Hitler had no intention of allowing this to happen but sadistically encouraged Antonescu to nourish his vain hope, as his translator Pasul Schmidt testified: "On each visit he [Antonescu] indicated pretty plainly his firm intention of one day recovering the whole of Transylvania by force. Hitler took a secret pleasure in Antonescu's outbursts against the Hungarians, and even went as far as to hint that he might perhaps give him a free hand later in his plans of conquest."[15]

The black summer of 1942, when the fate of Romanian Jewry hung in the balance, was also the summer in which the tension between Romania and Hungary peaked. Conditions were ripe for the outbreak of an armed conflict between the two states. This was primarily due to the Hungarian authorities' attitude toward the Romanian intelligentsia in the annexed territory and to other repressive measures, such as forced transfer (expatriation) from the province. Tens of thousands of Romanian refugees fled to southern Transylvania. Despite German promises to Antonescu that the Hungarians would not attack Romania — promises designed to persuade Antonescu to send most of his forces into Russia — the General Staff saw fit to draw up a war plan against Hungary, on the assumption that if Romania continued sending military forces to the front, the Hungarians would be able to eject the Romanian army from southern Transylvania.

As stated, the two countries competed for Hitler's goodwill: Hungary sought a renewed confirmation of the Vienna Arbitration and the expansion of its border in Transylvania, while Antonescu wanted the führer to translate his vague promises regarding Transylvania into action. Romanian diplomacy naturally stressed the Romanian contribution to the war, the heavy losses in Russia, and the bitter fate of the Romanians in northern Transylvania, who were being subjected to oppression, persecution, evacuation, and deportation. Romania had given everything and received nothing in return. Hungary had given only part of its army and had not handed over its Jews. In September 1942 there was nothing left for Romania to give but the Jews. The conclusion, therefore, was that there was no need to hand over the Jews, either.

THE INTERNAL BACKGROUND TO THE
FREEZING OF THE EXTERMINATION PLAN

On 25 September 1942 the prosecution general in Arad informed Mihai Antonescu of the panic that seized the Romanians in the cities of Transylvania following the announcement that the Jews were soon to be deported "and that the deportees would be replaced by Germans from Germany":

We do not know what the government's intentions are concerning the evacuation of the Jewish population, but we are sure, being familiar with local public opinion, that no one will regret their departure. On the other hand, we feel duty-bound to inform you that Romanian public opinion in general is patently unhappy with the prospect of the arrival of Germans from Germany, even provisionally, to replace the Jews, since such a measure merely intensifies the fear that the Germans, with their expansionist ambitions, may aspire to rule this region [Transylvania] of our country. This problem especially concerns public opinion in the cities.[16]

In September news spread that broad circles of the Romanian public were concerned about the implications of the deportation of the Jews from southern Transylvania. They were not concerned about the fate of the Jews as such but rather about the consequences their deportation would have on the province and on their future. As soon as the local Romanians became aware of the deportations, news began to flow into Bucharest.

The local police and Siguranţa commanders pointed out that the deportation of Jews would, in the final analysis, harm Romanian interests in Transylvania. The Siguranţa in Timişoara described the panic that seized the city's Jews as soon as they learned of the prospective deportations and their preparations to sell off property, and it reported on the attitude of various circles toward the Jews. Although some Romanian youth, particularly former Legionnaires, rejoiced, many Romanians felt sorry for the Jews and were convinced that their deportation would harm the local economy. The Romanians had only recently become active in industry and the economy and needed the Jews until they learned to run their businesses on their own. "Under such circumstances, the rapid evacuation of the Jews could undermine the Romanian economy, which will be threatened by competition from the German element." The Germans, for their part, "were eagerly awaiting the implementation of the deportation." The evacuation of the Jews, according to the heads of the Nazi organization of Volksdeutschen, would put an end to the partnership between the Romanians and Jews and would remove all obstacles in the path of the German population's right to swift economic development. The local Hungarians did not react to the news of the deportation of Jews but merely pointed out that it could not have happened in Hungary, since Hungary was a sovereign state: "The Hungarians are saying that Hungary is, relatively speaking, in a better situation as far as its internal policy is concerned, since the Reich does not intervene, while in Romania [such intervention] is prevalent, as measures for the deportation of Jews [testify]."[17]

The same source pointed out that 24,411 Jews—most of the Jews in southern Transylvania—lived in the region of Timişoara. The situation in southern Transylvania was different from that in Bukovina, from which the Jewish population had been deported. In Bukovina the Romanians had to contend with Ukrainians who had no political representation of their own, while in southern Transylvania the Romanians had to compete with the Volksdeutschen, who had their own Nazi organization (Deutsche Volksgruppe in Rumänien), which enjoyed the political and financial protection of the Reich.

Although the Romanians formed an absolute majority in Transylvania, any change in the population's composition strengthened the enemies (both overt and covert) of the Romanian nation. Even the deportation of the Gypsies undermined ethnic stability in the region. Siguranţa headquarters in Bucharest pointed out that although the deportation of the Gypsies in the Regat was "justified," Romanian circles in Transylvania claimed that their deportation would in the long term harm Romanian national interests "in the case of a referendum" on the province's future, "since the Gypsies were always counted as part of the Romanians and were not considered a separate entity." The report revealed the deep concern among leaders of the Romanian public in Transylvania that Transnistria might be used to compensate Romania in the east for the loss of northern Transylvania: "This step will have unpleasant consequences for us, since it may be considered the start of [the operation] to transfer people eastwards in order to protect the western nations [Germans and Hungarians]. The rumor has spread among the Romanians that after the prospective evacuation of all Gypsies and Jews, the Romanians themselves may be deported to Transnistria."[18] The fear of the arrival of Germans from the Reich to replace the Jews did not disappear even after the deportations were officially suspended.[19]

FILDERMAN AND ATTEMPTS TO FOIL THE DEPORTATIONS

"The eyes of all the Jews were turned toward Filderman."[20] Thus did Piki Vasiliu, the minister for internal affairs, sum up the way Filderman was perceived by the Antonescu regime, even though at the time, when the Jews of the Regat awaited deportation, Filderman no longer held a public position. Antonescu had relieved him of his functions on 10 December 1941, when the Federation of Jewish Communities was dissolved and replaced by the Jewish Center. He was ousted from the federation building by "Hitler's Jews," as the Jews initially called the heads of the Jewish Center that was set up at Richter's behest, and was expelled from the bar on the pretext that he had intervened on behalf of the Jews of Bessarabia and Bukovina. He was under surveillance by the

Siguranța and agents of the German embassy and was personally attacked in the Romanian and German press.

In the summer of 1942, however, when news began arriving of deportations from Czernowitz and preparations for deportations in the Regat itself, Filderman decided to resume his public activity. Information on the persecution of Jews throughout the country continued to flow in from various quarters. He asked his veteran aides in the Union of Jewish Communities of the Regat and the Federation of Jewish Communities of Romania to remain in their posts and not resign in solidarity with him. The heads of the communities of the Regat and the heads of the Jewish community in southern Transylvania continued to consider him the leader of the Jews and secretly kept him posted about events. The heads of the former Romanian parties, Maniu and Brătianu, and their aides treated him with respect.

It should be emphasized that during this period—the most tragic period in their history—the Jews of Romania had no real representation. The Jewish Center, far from representing the Jewish population, was set up in order to rob Jews and prepare them for deportation, and its heads carried out the duties Richter assigned them. The leaders of the Zionist movement, including the chairman of the executive, Mișu Benvenisti, joined the Jewish Center in April 1942. Three of them were appointed heads of departments, and all of them were exempted from forced labor. As such, they could hardly be said to represent the Jewish population. Last but not least, the underground Jewish leadership known as the Jewish Council did not exist at the time, despite postwar claims to the contrary.

When news began arriving of the resumption of deportations from Czernowitz, Filderman turned to Lupu, a leader of the National Peasants' Party and Maniu's deputy, and persuaded him to ask Mihai Antonescu to revoke his decision to resume the deportation. Likewise, Lupu demanded a halt to the deportation of Jews from Mogilev to the camps near the Bug and requested an end to the brutal deportation of the enfeebled and sickly Jews who had survived the typhus epidemic. He wrote to Mihai Antonescu, "Please instill some humanity into your orders. Ask them to improve the living conditions [of the Jews] and render them humane."[21] Filderman himself composed part of the letter. On 9 June he asked the architect Nicolae Clejan, "Antonescu's Jew," to sign a petition to Mihai Antonescu requesting a halt to the deportations from Czernowitz.[22]

Had Romanian Jews waited for their brethren in democratic countries to come to their aid, they would have been almost totally liquidated. World Jewry, as well as the small Yishuv in Palestine (the Jewish settlement), which was struggling for its survival at the time, were unable to come to the aid of Romanian Jewry, or of Polish Jewry for that matter. Nevertheless, one should bear in mind that the leaders of the Jewish collectivities in the free world, as well as the leaders of the Yishuv, knew of the plight of Romanian Jewry and of the plan to liquidate them.

Filderman entered in his diary almost daily the information he received from all quarters, his fears, and details on the preparations the administration was making for the deportation of the Jews of the Regat to Transnistria. Filderman was helped by a group of people who were especially close to him, including Matatias Carp, the former secretary general of the Jewish Federation; the attorney Arnold Schwefelberg, his closest aide, who monitored antisemitic legislation and decrees and organized aid operations for the Jews in Transnistria; Ferri Froimescu, a wealthy Sephardic Jew who had ties with Romanian businessmen and industrialists and other heads of the disbanded federation and about whom little else is known.

Activities to foil the deportation were at first carried out in parallel by the leaders of the communities in southern Transylvania and by Filderman. On 20 August, when Lecca was away in Berlin, Oskar Neuman, a thirty-one-year-old Jewish industrialist who had converted to Christianity, came to Bucharest from Arad. Neuman, "one of the richest people in Romania," in Richter's opinion, "with extensive connections in political and financial circles," owned a textile plant in Arad with branches in large urban centers. Some members of the titled Neuman family, including Oskar's father, who had also converted, had emigrated to the United States.[23] At the same time, the heads of the Arad, Timişoara, and Sibiu branches of the Jewish Center also arrived in Bucharest.[24] At first they tried to "obtain the good will" of personalities who were able to influence Antonescu (i.e., to bribe them), but in vain.

When the German embassy published its article on the prospective deportation (8 August), Filderman realized that the Germans had taken the question of deportation out of the hands of the Antonescu government. Until that point he had striven to stop the deportation of Jews to Transnistria. (The Nazi plan was publicized at the height of the Romanian deportation operation from Bukovina and throughout the Regat.) On 9 August, following publication of an announcement about the prospective deportation in the *Bukarester Tageblatt*, Filderman sent a terse response to Vasiliu stressing that the deportation of Jews was an interference in Romania's internal affairs and that Romania had already surpassed itself in the field of anti-Jewish persecution. Antonescu could not accuse the Jews of Transylvania of having harmed the army or the Romanian population, as he had accused the Jews of Bessarabia and Bukovina the previous year in order to justify their deportation. This time, even according to the marshal's twisted logic, the deportation could not be justified.[25]

Jewish community leaders in Transylvania informed Filderman's aide, Carp, that the headquarters of the Fourth Territorial Command in Timişoara had been ordered to obtain freight cars for the deportation operation. Carp asked Col. Ilie Dumitrescu, head of the General Staff's Jewish section, for a clarification. The clarification showed that, while such an order indeed existed, it was not clear whether the freight cars were designated for deportation in general or specifically for the deportation of Jews and Gypsies. "[The Jews] of Transylvania are seized by a great panic," wrote Carp in his journal. When I. Tenner, the delegate from the Timiş-Torontal branch of the Jewish Center, and his associates approached the Jewish Center for help, Filderman—who had no illusions concerning the willingness of Nandor Gingold, the head of the Jewish Center, to intervene—helped them compose a memorandum "requesting permission to submit our appeal to the supreme authorities."[26] The Jewish Center did not intervene. A study of Richter's documents shows that Gingold and A. Wilman were Nazi agents who were responsible for keeping Richter apprised of developments among the Jews and government measures affecting them.[27]

At the same time, Filderman drew up a memorandum pointing out the historical roots of the Jews in Transylvania and emphasizing that they had already achieved equal rights under Austro-Hungarian rule and that their citizenship had been recognized by the Romanian administration in 1918, "during the reunification," unlike the Jews of the Regat, whose citizenship had been granted under a special law. It followed, argued Filderman, that the deportation of Jews from Transylvania could prejudice the unification between Transylvania and Romania and strengthen Hungary's claim to Transylvania, since Hungary was not deporting Jews from northern Transylvania. The representatives of the Jewish public, lacking Filderman's moral courage, were less outspoken and more circumspect than him.[28]

At this point Filderman understood that if he resorted to the same kind of activity he had adopted in the autumn of 1941, when he had tried to stop the deportation to Transnistria of the survivors of the extermination operation in Bessarabia and Bukovina, he was bound to fail. Then he had used humanitarian, Christian, and emotional arguments, but Antonescu had openly rejected them. Filderman understood that as far as Antonescu and his ministers were concerned, humanitarianism was dead. They had no compunctions about killing Jews at a time when hundreds (and later thousands) of Romanian soldiers were falling daily at the front. "We do not know what might influence these madmen," said Filderman to his secretary, Charles Gruber, in September 1941, when he fought for the abolition of the yellow patch.[29]

In a series of memoranda he submitted directly to the government and to

Antonescu via Vasiliu, the minister for internal affairs, and subsequently via Dumitru Popescu, the interior minister, and also Maniu, Filderman set forth a series of logical arguments, based on his familiarity with Romanian logic in general and Antonescu's logic in particular (which set the Romanian image and Romanian sovereignty above all considerations and hated all things Hungarian), to persuade Antonescu to defer the deportation plan. Believing that if public resistance did not exist it would have to be created, Filderman composed memoranda "in the name of" Romanian intellectuals and Romanian businessmen and industrialists, particularly those from Transylvania. These memoranda, which in the end were never sent because no Romanians were willing to sign them, bore no reference to Filderman or any other Jew. He managed to enlist Maniu's (but not Brătianu's) support and persuaded him to deliver a memorandum to Antonescu setting forth Filderman's arguments against the deportation. He persuaded Maniu to gear up for a true campaign against the deportation of Jews from Romania. Filderman resisted Richter's pressure to meet with him and was not perturbed by Richter's threats to kill him. Finally, during the anti-deportation campaign itself Filderman obtained a copy of Lecca's and Richter's deportation plans and showed them to Maniu and other Romanian public figures as proof of the involvement of the Antonescu regime. Filderman was extremely discreet and never shared information he obtained with anyone, not even those who later claimed that they were in the know and that it was they who had saved the Jews from destruction. They knew nothing, as various publications over the years prove.

On 22 August Filderman delivered a detailed memorandum to Maniu, listing the main arguments against the deportation from a Romanian nationalist standpoint, not as a favor to the Jews. This memorandum and the memorandum he prepared a month later, on 22 September, persuaded Maniu to join the cause of saving the Jews and persuaded Mihai and Ion Antonescu to order a halt to the deportations.

Omitting any reference to the deportation operations conducted by the Antonescu regime itself, Filderman portrayed the proposed deportation operation as a German diversionary tactic aimed at embroiling Romania with the Allies in order to prevent Romania from trying to negotiate a separate peace with the Allies. The main points Filderman set out in his memoranda were:

> The German press was portraying Romania as the country that had adopted the most stringent antisemitic measures and laws. Why did Romania have to serve as an example to the other fascist countries by deporting all its Jews [especially when Hungary was not doing so]?

The Jews of Transylvania had been living there for centuries [the implication being that they were unlike the Jews of Bessarabia and Bukovina, who were portrayed as foreigners in Romanian propaganda].

Marshal Antonescu had justified the deportation of Bessarabian and Bukovinian Jews as a "punishment" for the hardships suffered by the Romanian population during the year of Soviet occupation. Transylvania's Jews, on the other hand, lived far from the front, had not harmed anyone, were few in number, and represented no threat.

The Jews of Romania had volunteered to join in the war the day following the general call up, even though they had been dismissed from the army.

Germany, Italy, and Hungary had not deported their Jews, while Spain was protecting Spanish Jews living in Romania.

Although Germany was deporting Jews from the occupied countries, it was not deporting Jews from Germany itself.

Even were Germany and Italy to deport their Jews, Romania must not follow suit, since very few Jews remained there [270,000 out of 780,000].

In Hungary, the number of Jews had risen, not fallen.

The Jews had cooperated economically with the Romanians, not with other minority groups, and the Romanians had prospered thanks to them.

German industries and businesses and their branches in Romania did not employ Romanians.

Should the government nevertheless *be forced* to deport its Jews, the plan should be deferred as far as possible and be restricted only to those Jews who had entered the country illegally.

Under no circumstances should children, women, and the elderly be deported.

In order to justify the deferment of the deportation to the Germans, a law could be passed stating that those designated for deportation must emigrate within a period of several months.

One of the memoranda ended as follows: "Why should Romania accept the *Bukarester Tageblatt*'s generous offer that it deport [the Jews], since Romania is already at the forefront of those nations [that have adopted] antisemitic legislation? Why shouldn't it let Germany and Italy assume the honor, *as well as the risk*, of this initiative, while we [Romanians] wait for a general peace, which shall decide the fate of the Jews, as well as that of the European nations?"[30]

On 20 August 1942 an SSI agent presented his superiors with a faint copy of a memorandum submitted to King Mihai by Romanian intellectuals, mostly university professors and writers, protesting the deportation of Jews. The memorandum was secretly photocopied by the agent, who admitted that since the list of signatories appeared on a separate sheet, there was no way of knowing who they were. The agent further revealed that the king and queen mother attached considerable importance to the memorandum.[31]

Since Filderman's attempts to persuade Romanian intellectuals to sign a petition against the deportation were abortive, one wonders whether the Romanians who signed this petition were sincerely concerned about the plight of the Jews. The answer is both yes and no. Although some of the ideas set forth in the memorandum were clearly Filderman's, the style and contents were not his. The memorandum expressed concern for the Romanian people and contempt for the dictatorial regime in an eloquent style that was alien to Filderman and his men. The petition listed all the crimes initiated by the regime against the Jews and stated that the deportation of 185,000 Jews to Transnistria in 1941 was tantamount to their murder:

> It is clear to all that the deportations [to Transnistria] were organized under such cruel conditions, that the "relocation" of the Jews to the eastern territories, as it was called, became in fact a systematic and methodical extermination operation. Over the past two years, we have soared to the top of the list of nations that persecute Jews. . . . We have turned the Jewish problem into Romania's only problem. . . . On the home front we have nurtured a kind of anarchical fanaticism [that leads to] lawlessness and that openly sanctions the right to kill, rob and abuse. By using the authority of the State, we have created a movement of social disintegration . . . [and finally we have endangered] the very foundations of our State and society.[32]

The intellectuals condemned Romania's agreement to the deportation of Jews and asked for an end to this policy in order *to prevent a catastrophe to nation and state*:

> We were, and still are, a nation that has suffered persecution. How can we condemn the oppression of our brothers, who are living outside Romania's current borders, when *we are about to exterminate a minority population* whose right to live has been guaranteed by those same visionaries who sanctified

our national borders? Concern for the future of the homeland [calls for] an immediate halt to the persecution of Jews . . . since this can only lead to . . . . a national catastrophe. We have long since breached all the limits permitted to a state governed by law and behooving human society. We must wait for the Jewish problem to be solved as part of an overall solution to the fate of all countries in the peace conference. The peace conference will determine the status of Romanian Jewry, *and the fate of Romania itself.*[33]

The petition then reverted to Filderman's arguments: that Germany, Italy, and Hungary had not deported their Jews but were deporting Jews from the occupied countries only, and the like. The petition specified the crimes perpetrated by the regime against the Jews and their destructive effect on the social and moral fabric of the Romanian people, the lies and deceits practiced by the regime in relation to the Jews, and finally, to top it all, its impulsive agreement to deliver the Jews into the Nazis' hands.

The petition expressed the blunt truth at a time when no one dared utter it in Romania. It should be borne in mind, however, that the petition was delivered to the king, who had no real power and anyway was opposed to the dictatorial regime, not to Antonescu. Would the Romanian intellectuals, one wonders, have dared to submit, let alone sign, such a text had it been addressed to Antonescu, his deputy, or even a minister?

As stated, the petition was Filderman's brainchild, although the bulk of the text was written by Romanian intellectuals, whose identity the ssi never discovered. More importantly, after the regime's collapse no one, not even the king, referred to the petition, and no Romanian professor or writer admitted to having signed it. The contents of the petition were too radical for the regimes that materialized in Romania after August 1944—regimes that denied historical responsibility for Romania's crimes against the Jewish people. The petition ran counter to the tendency to seek to exonerate the Romanian people and state for their part in the crimes against Jews. Everyone, including the king, was patriotic. Everyone behaved as if the petition had never existed.

THE ULTIMATE MEMORANDUM

On 22 September Filderman handed Interior Minister Dumitru Popescu a special memorandum for Ion Antonescu or his deputy, setting forth the most cogent arguments against the deportation of Jews. It was this memorandum, together with Maniu's intervention, Killinger and Richter's pressure, the German embassy's article of 11 October 1942 against the "Jewish lackeys," the unrest among the Romanians in southern Transylvania, the difficulties experienced by the Romanian forces near Stalingrad before the defeat, and a rare moment of sanity on the part of Antonescu that led to the decision to provisionally halt the deportations. At first Filderman set out to prove to Antonescu that he had indeed realized his dream to get rid of the Jews—some by murder and others by deportation—and that he was in a better position than other fascist dictators. Afterward, Filderman, knowing Antonescu's penchant for tables and statistics, presented tables showing that the number of Jews had been slashed by 66 percent—that is, two thirds.

The second part of the memorandum focused on the "economic aspect" of the marshal's persecutions of the Jews. Once again Filderman tried to prove that the Conducător had accomplished his plans. He had imposed government loans and levies on the Jews, dismissed them from their jobs, and subjected them to Romanization laws and the like, heedless of the resultant harm to the Romanian economy. Filderman quoted excerpts from Antonescu's own statements and even quoted from the antisemitic newspaper *Porunca Vremii*. He stressed that wherever there were Jews, the Romanians had prospered, while in places from which Jews had been expelled (in the territories that had united in 1918), minority groups such as the Germans, Hungarians, and Ukrainians, not the Romanians, had taken their place. Hence, "*Under these circumstances, the deportation of the [remaining] Jews from Bukovina signifies the destruction of Romanian industry . . . and the deportation of Jews from Transylvania and the Regat signifies the ruination of Romanian industrialists and merchants. Are we to endanger the entire Romanization enterprise?*"[34]

An uninformed reader might deduce from the above that Filderman was an ardent supporter of the Romanization operation, which had deprived tens of thousands of Jews of their livelihood, evicted them from their apartments, and barred them from professions and jobs. Clearly, however, Filderman used such arguments simply because he knew they would achieve results. He went on to demonstrate how, in respect to the looting of Jewish property and the exploitation of Jews, Antonescu had outstripped the Nazis and fascists in Germany, Italy, Hungary, and other countries.

Finally, Filderman broached the subject of the deportation of Jews from Transylvania and the Regat. He reminded the marshal how, in the autumn of 1941, he had justified the deportation (and liquidation) of the Jews of Bessarabia and Bukovina on the grounds that they had harmed the Romanian army and population. His decision to deport the remainder of the Jews, however, invalidated his rationale in 1941 for deporting (and murdering) the Jews. The Jews of Transylvania had lived there for centuries and had never harmed Romanian interests, while the Jews of the Regat were Romanian patriots.

The memorandum ended by emphasizing that Antonescu was doing too much in the Jewish field and that it was now time for those who were pressuring him to take over. Filderman did not speak to Antonescu on behalf of the Jews and used the first person plural *we* (we deported, we shall wait) as if he were an ordinary Romanian who had no personal stake in the matter. He did so knowing that any appeal by a Jew triggered automatic rejection on Antonescu's part.

Carp described the moment when the official communiqué to defer the deportations was received on 15 October 1942: "Filderman greeted me with the words 'We've won,' the orders have gone out. There are to be no more deportations. The transports have returned. . . . The article [in the *Bukarester Tageblatt*] that contained threats against the country [Romania] stood us in good stead."[35]

Filderman and his handful of aides had good cause to feel proud of themselves. Filderman was a modest man, as his statement "we've won," rather than "I've won," indicates. Romanian Jewry was abandoned to its fate. No power in the world — not even U.S. Jewry or the small Yishuv in Palestine — could protect or save it. Therefore, world Jewry cannot be accused of indifference. If the Soviet army was unable to withstand the German-Romanian onslaught in the summer of 1941, what force could the Yishuv have mobilized against the powers that were attempting to erase Romanian Jewry from the land of the living? Filderman, armed only with words, knew how to present the danger of the destruction of Romanian Jewry not as a humanitarian problem (an angle that would carry little weight with Ion Antonescu) but rather as a Romanian problem, a problem of Romanian-Hungarian relations, a problem on which Romania's future hung. In this case, Jeremiah's prophecy prevailed: "For the Lord hath ransomed Jacob; And He redeemed him from the hand of him that is stronger than he" (Jeremiah 31:11).

After the liberation the chairman of the Zionist movement, Mişu Benvenisti, and Chief Rabbi Safran claimed that it was they who had spearheaded the struggle to save Romanian Jewry. However, they were entirely ignorant of the events and of Filderman's part in them, because he never told them. When in 1949 he tried to rebuff Rabbi Safran's attempt to take credit for the rescue of Romanian Jewry, Filderman wrote, after first ascertaining that the rabbi knew nothing of his struggle to save the Jews, "My memoranda were secret. I hope to publish them one day. Then they will see that what tipped the balance was that part of the memoranda in which I established that the Jews of Finland, Hungary, Italy and even Germany [in 1941] were not deported. Only the Jews of Holland, Belgium and France [were deported]. This placed Antonescu in a dilemma: by agreeing to the deportation of Jews, Romania turned from an ally into an occupied country."[36]

Unlike the Nazi plan to deport the Jews to occupied Poland, which was revoked in October 1942, Antonescu's plan to deport the Jews to Transnistria was never abolished. Antonescu's intention to deport most of Romanian Jewry remained intact and served as a guiding principle for Vasiliu, the minister of internal affairs (who, together with the marshal and the head of the SSI, directed Romania's internal security) and was occasionally translated into decisions. Antonescu's insistence on doing with Romanian Jewry as he saw fit, despite changes in political and military circumstances, even when it was clear that Germany would be defeated, was a reflection of his character. Common sense could not prevail against his inflated self-esteem, his total identification with Romania's national goals, and his absorption of all the negative stereotypes that had been attributed to Jews since the days of the founding fathers of Romanian antisemitism.

The Presidency of the Council of Ministers, the General Staff, and Vasiliu acted in the knowledge that the deportations to Transnistria would resume whenever the Conducător decided that the time was ripe. On 22 October 1942, for example, Ovidiu Vlădescu, secretary-general of the Presidency of the Council of Ministers, issued a general directive ordering the deportation to Transnistria of all Jews who were petitioning the courts in the hope of receiving a provisional exemption from deportation pending the courts' decisions.[37] The marshal's intention to adhere to his plan of deporting all the Jews of Bukovina who remained in Czernowitz, when the time was ripe, was revealed in a letter by Minister Vasiliu to the Presidency of the Council of Ministers regarding three Jews whom Antonescu had allowed back from Transnistria to Romania. Vasiliu explained that he had ordered the Jews to be sent to Roman in the Regat, not to Czernowitz, to prevent them being deported back to Transnistria when the deportations resumed.[38]

In March 1943 the plan to deport the Jews of Czernowitz was still valid, as Vasiliu's refusal to allow a Jewish family to move from Czernowitz to Bucharest indicates: "Marshal Antonescu forbids any relocation of Jews from Czernowitz to the country [Regat]. Moreover, the petitioner and his family belong to the group of Jews who are shortly to be deported."[39] The plan to deport the Jews of Czernowitz was still valid in August 1943, although by then the Interior Ministry realized that it might not be implemented. The Interior Ministry rejected a request by the Presidency of the Council of Ministers to grant a special travel permit to a Jew from Czernowitz who had converted to Christianity, on the grounds that they could not allow exceptions, "especially in the case of the remainder of the Jews of Czernowitz, whose are simply there on sufferance *instead of being in Transnistria.*"[40]

Antonescu continued his policy of concentrating the Jews of Moldova into the main cities in order to facilitate their subsequent deportation or forced emigration when the time came. In southern Transylvania, Jews from the towns and villages were forced to leave their homes and belongings and were concentrated in district towns and sometimes in other villages. In 1942 the Jews of Podul-Iloaiei were evacuated to Iași after Antonescu became aware of their existence on one of his visits to the region. On 17 April 1943 Antonescu ordered "the Jews to be evacuated from cities that were not district capitals to cities that served as district capitals." For many this was a second evacuation, since in June 1941 they had been relocated from their villages and towns under another order issued by Antonescu. The interior minister ordered all Romanian police inspectorates to assess the number of Jews still in these cities and the advantages and disadvantages of the proposed evacuation and to facilitate the "transfer [of their businesses] to Christian hands."[41]

This time several heads of the Iași community decided to hire the services of a Romanian lawyer who had connections with Veturia Goga, the wife of former prime minister Octavian Goga. Mrs. Goga and Antonescu's wife persuaded the marshal to abandon the plan for the time being. Mrs. Antonescu needed money for her Welfare Council, while Mrs. Goga was always in need of money.[42] The lawyer was also well remunerated. The Soviet army's proximity to Romania's border also helped curb Antonescu's antisemitic outbursts, although not always. In the spring of 1944 the General Staff sought to transfer the Jews of Moldova to ghettos so that they would not "hinder" war maneuvers.[43]

Antonescu never came to terms with the fact that he had to relinquish his dream of purging the country of Jews. However, unlike the Nazis, he no longer insisted on killing them and, from October 1942, agreed to let them emigrate anywhere they wished, provided they left all their possessions behind. On 26 March 1943 the Romanian government submitted a memorandum to the German ambassador stating, "The only solution to the Jewish problem in Romania is emigration."[44] In the same month, in an interview with his friend, the antisemitic author Ioan Brătescu-Voinești, Antonescu thanked the Germans for their support in efforts to purge the country of parasites and internal enemies. These enemies, Antonescu added, "are more dangerous in my eyes than external enemies, because while external enemies may lop off parts of the homeland, internal enemies bring about the cultural and moral poisoning of our people's soul." In the interview Antonescu promised to continue the struggle until "Jewish Bolshevism was totally eradicated."[45]

On 26 September 1943, after the collapse of Mussolini's regime, Antonescu realized that the Soviet army could not be checked and began to plan the withdrawal of troops, the administration, and local collaborators from Transnistria to Romania. It was at this juncture that the marshal informed his military secretary of the necessity of examining "in parallel" the possibility of relocating (i.e., deporting) Romanian Jews to Transnistria, "in this order: Moldova, Bucharest, and other parts of the country."[46] Thanks to the rapid advance of the Soviet forces and Mihai Antonescu's (and perhaps also the opposition's) political logic, this program remained a historical document only, one that, more than anything, revealed Antonescu's intentions toward the Jews of the Regat.

In a letter he sent Nicolae Clejan, his Jewish architect, on 4 February 1944, Antonescu expressed his regret at not having managed to deport all the Jews from Bessarabia and Bukovina (14,000 Jews were left in Czernowitz and 101 in the whole of Bessarabia) and hypocritically claimed that he had been forced to carry out the deportations in order to protect these Jews from pogroms. He threatened to settle the score with the remaining Jews and the Jews of Romania: "I again draw the Jews' attention to the fact that if they continue to subvert the State, which is too tolerant by far, they will suffer even more serious consequences than those they have suffered so far."[47]

In his letter to Clejan, Antonescu also described the policy adopted by all subsequent Romanian regimes. He summed up his relationship with and responsibility toward the Jews by stating that what had happened was a global catastrophe, not just a Jewish one. "In this war, which had been waged over the entire world, the Jews cannot evade the suffering, difficulties or catastrophes that the entire world has experienced."[48]

THE ALIBI

In late March 1943 Mihai Antonescu tried to persuade the Swiss ambassador in Romania, René de Weck, who since 13 December 1941 had also represented the interests of Britain, the United States, Belgium, Greece, and Yugoslavia, "that he had finally relinquished the persecution of the Children of Israel" and that the dissemination of the latest antisemitic leaflets was perpetrated by the German embassy and its Romanian lackeys.[49] Following this, Mihai Antonescu set about building a national alibi for the regime, the Romanian people, and himself for the crimes they had committed against the Jewish people. The alibi was based first and foremost on a guilty conscience. In terms of Jewish survival, it was a positive development. Filderman immediately noticed the change and once again proved that he was a shrewd and practical Jew who was familiar with the workings of the Romanian mind. On 24 November 1942, about a week after the Soviet offensive in Stalingrad, when Romania's leaders began fearing for the fate of the Romanian army and the Romanian state, Filderman hastened to affirm his loyalty to Romania and his willingness to intervene, if asked, on the international plane with the democratic powers. He even made sure that these views reached the opposition and the government's attention.

On 24 November 1942 the SSI reported that recent developments had reopened the debate in political circles on the problem of the Jews' attitude toward the Romanian homeland in the context of the problems Romania would have to contend with in the future. The Legionnaires were spreading the idea that the Jews were enemies of the Romanian state and were waiting for an opportunity to take revenge on it. At the same time confusion prevailed among democratic circles because a rich Jew named Fischer was among the supporters of the former King Carol II. (The king had gone into exile in Mexico and hoped, with the help of the democratic powers, to be reinstated as king of Romania.) In order to refute these specious arguments, Dr. Filderman sought to bring to his friends' notice that, as former elected leader of the Jewish communities in the country, he was prepared to publish a communiqué stating the following:

(1) The Romanian Jews, despite all the suffering they have undergone, declare their identification with the Romanian people. (2) The Romanian Jews are prepared to fight, with all means at their disposal, now and in the future, for the realization of a strong and prosperous Romania. They declare that they are prepared, with the help of their representatives, to defend the higher interests of the Romanian state before any international forum that is prepared to listen to them. (3) Romania's Jews are opposed to the reinstatement of former King Carol since, in their opinion, it was he who supported and fostered the antisemitic movement. . . . Dr. Filderman is prepared to draw up a statement, at the request of any important official or institution that can be sent abroad.[50]

Filderman understood that he had to support the Romanian state and turn a blind eye to the murder of hundreds of thousands of Jews by the army and the Romanian population in order to help distance Romania from Germany's war objectives, ensure the support of world Jewry for the return of Transylvania, continue to contribute (i.e., to be robbed), not highlight the Jews as a separate group—and hope for the best until Nazi Germany was defeated. These aims tallied with Mihai Antonescu's apologetics, which related to the liquidation of the Jews of Bessarabia, Bukovina, and Transnistria as if it had never occurred.

The alibi Mihai Antonescu concocted necessitated the adaptation of documents to the new political situation. The documents relating to the Iaşi pogrom were doctored, as were minutes of meetings with leaders of the Nazi regime and its representatives in Romania. The latter were partly rewritten in order to emphasize Antonescu's concern for his soldiers' welfare, his attempts to preserve the country's resources in the face of German demands, his prediction concerning the failure of the Nazi policy in Europe, and the like. The doctoring of documents on the extermination of the Jews in Transnistria, Iaşi and other places and the trivialization of these events would have succeeded but for the existence of secret files preserved by the Foreign Ministry and the Interior Ministry, which gave an accurate picture of the true scale of the destruction.

In constructing his alibi Mihai Antonescu saw to it that all photographs or films of extermination sites, deportation sites, crossing points over the Dniester, and the ghettos of Transnistria were destroyed. The Bucharest government was concerned about the existence of photos taken by Italian and German soldiers, civilians, and propaganda teams. The Hungarian government had a collection of such photos that it collated into a special book about the massacres perpetrated by the Romanians, printed in late 1942.[51]

Official documents that were issued after October 1942 no longer included Nazi and racist ideology. On the contrary, they expressed sensitivity to human — including Jewish — life, repugnance toward the Nazis' extermination methods, and a willingness to view Jewish emigration as a solution to the Jewish problem, pending the verdict of history (or of the Allies). One could say that between October 1942 and 23 August 1944 the Antonescu regime defended Romanian Jewry against Nazi extermination ambitions.

As far as the Jews were concerned, Mihai Antonescu's alibi also included practical decisions: an end to the extermination policy in Transnistria; an agreement to allow Jewish organizations to provide more aid to the deportees; a halt to the deportations in Bukovina; an agreement in late July 1943 to repatriate all Jews of Romanian nationality remaining in Germany and occupied countries, especially France, who had survived the deportations implemented by the Germans after Antonescu himself agreed to their deportation in November 1941; and an agreement to improve the living conditions of the Jews in the labor camps (naturally, paid for by the Jewish Center, not the state).[52] A large portion of the money extorted from Jews in exchange for certificates of exemption from forced labor was channeled into relief efforts in Romania and Transnistria. Likewise, the possibility was raised of the repatriation of the deportees being held in Transnistria, who had been left there because of Antonescu's unwillingness to admit he had been mistaken and because the continued existence of the ghettos served the regime well in its relationship with Germany. In the final analysis, only the survivors of Dorohoi and about two thousand orphans were repatriated.

Once liquidation and deportation operations were halted, the option of emigration to Palestine—an option that had been promoted all along by the Zionist movement—became a serious possibility. Emigration suited the purposes of the Antonescu regime and its policy, which, despite everything, had not changed: to get rid of the Jews. On 29 September 1942 Mihai Antonescu asked Vasiliu to examine the possibility of shipping the Jews abroad, adding, "We can make a lot of money without interfering."[53] Thus, in late 1942, the seventy-five thousand plan was born, defined by Killinger as Antonescu's attempt "to kill two birds with one stone": "On the one hand, he wishes to raise the 16 billion lei he so desperately needs, and on the other, he wants to effortlessly get rid of a large segment of the Jews."[54] The plan failed, however, because its implementation was dependent on Germany and because the Romanian authorities miscalculated how much money could be extorted from the Jews.

General antisemitic and racist propaganda stopped. The greater the defeats on the front, the greater Mihai Antonescu's belief in the omnipotence of world Jewry, which, he was convinced, ruled the world in one way of another—whether in the guise of Soviet Bolshevism or in the guise of the Anglo-American plutocracy. Mihai Antonescu developed totally unrealistic and almost insane expectations concerning the ability of Jewish leaders to influence the democratic powers in his favor and in favor of Romania.

37

The Jews of the Regat and Southern Transylvania in the Shadow of the Final Solution

Ion Antonescu saw the expulsion of Jews from the villages and towns as the fulfillment of the national and spiritual legacy of the pioneers of Romanian nationalism, the outstanding intellectuals of the nineteenth century, the church leaders, and the first statesmen of the united Romanian state that was set up in 1859: to keep the villages free of Jewish penetration, free of harmful Jewish influences that distorted the healthy spiritual structure of the village and peasant, enslaved the village economically, and caused its moral decline. Antonescu, independent of the Nazis and their plans for the Jews, promised to implement A. C. Cuza's antisemitic doctrine.

On 18 June 1941 Antonescu ordered all Jews from the villages between the Siret and the Prut to be evacuated to the large towns or the Târgu-Jiu camp in southern Romania, all men age eighteen to sixty in this region to be imprisoned in the Târgu-Jiu camp, and all remaining Jews in villages throughout Romania to be evacuated to district towns. "Families that are evacuated will not be allowed to return to their villages," the order stated. The evacuees' property was handed over to the local authorities and was thereafter considered state property. The order, dressed up, as usual, in a language designed to give it a semblance of legality, stated that "the evacuees to Târgu-Jiu should be told to take with [them] underwear, household utensils, and money." The order further stated that "the district prefects must make sure that the evacuees have food and that the measures adopted against them are civilized."[1] From that point on, all those in charge of the large deportation and extermination operations implemented by the regime (the deportations from the Kishinev ghetto, from the camps of Bessarabia, and from the Czernowitz ghetto) pointed out in their summary reports that the operation was carried out in a civilized manner (*civilizat*).

Although the order was formally issued on 21 June, its implementation began

TABLE 8. EVACUATION OF JEWS FROM THE VILLAGES AND TOWNS OF THE REGAT AND SOUTHERN BUKOVINA, JUNE–JULY 1941

| Locality/community | District | No. of Jews | Destination | | Comments |
			Men (18–60)	Women, children, the elderly	
Dărăbani	Dorohoi	2,000	Târgu–Jiu (camp)	Turnu–Severin (camp)	The women were held in the synagogue building and in the Jewish cemetery building
Săveni Mihăileni Rădăuți	Dorohoi	4,000	Târgu–Jiu	Dorohoi	Only some of the men were interned in the Târgu–Jiu camp
Siret	Rădăuți	1,500	Târgu–Jiu	Calafat (camp)	
Bucecea Ştefăneşti Suliţa	Botoşani	4,000	Botoşani	Botoşani	
Lespezi Villages in the district	Baia	1,000 2,000	Târgu–Jiu Târgu–Jiu	Fălticeni Fălticeni	
Bivolari Villages in the district	Iaşi	4,000	Iaşi, Roman, Târgu–Jiu	Iaşi, Roman	
Pungeşti Negreşti Codăeşti	Vaslui	1,000	Târgu–Jiu	Vaslui	

continued

TABLE 8. EVACUATION OF JEWS FROM THE VILLAGES AND TOWNS OF THE REGAT AND SOUTHERN BUKOVINA, JUNE–JULY 1941
continued

Locality/community	District	No. of Jews	Destination		Comments
			Men (18–60)	Women, children, the elderly	
Iveşti Podul Turcului	Tecuci	1,300	Târgu-Jiu	Tecuci	
Becesti Villages in the district	Roman	1,200	Roman	Roman	
Bereşti Bujor Drăguşeni Folteşti Villages in the district	Covurlui	700	Galaţi	Galaţi	
Puieşti Plopana Villages in the district	Tutova	500	Bârlad	Bârlad	
Huşi	Fălciu	2,100	Târgu-Jiu	Locally	Only 300 men were deported to Târgu-Jiu
Vaslui	Vaslui				700 Jews were interned locally in 5 makeshift camps
Dorohoi	Dorohoi		Târgu-Jiu Craiova (camp)		Nearly all Jewish men age 18–60, including the leaders of the community, were deported

Location	District	Number	Camp	Destination	Notes
Piatra Neamț	Neamț	1,500	—	—	One member of each family was interned locally
Constanța	Constanța	2,000	Cobadin (camp)	—	Later transferred to other camps: Mereni, Osmancea, Ciobănița
Ploiești Câmpina Sinaia Villages in the district	Parhova	2,200	Teiș (camp)	Ploiești	From 1 July 1941, all men were interned in the Ploiești camps
Buzău	Buzău	1,300	Buzău (camp)	—	Women and children were not interned
Râmnicu-Sărat	Râmnicu-Sărat	100	Râmnicu-Sărat (camp)	—	A camp was set up locally
Podul-Iloaiei	Iași	1,500	Iași	Iași	On 12 April 1942
Villages in Oltenia			Bucharest	Bucharest	
Villages in Walachia			Bucharest or local camps	Bucharest or local camps	

SOURCE: Data collated by the Jewish Federation and processed by Matatias Carp. See YVA, Romania Collection, 011/49a, pp. 53–54.

TABLE 9. EVACUATION OF JEWS FROM THE DISTRICTS OF SOUTHERN TRANSYLVANIA, JUNE–JULY 1941

Locality/community	District	No. of Jews	Destination	Comments
Aiud	Alba	1,200	Alba-Iulia	In early 1942 they were allowed to return to their towns
Abrud				
Sebeş				
Villages in the district				
Villages in the district	Bihor	700	Beiuş	
Villages in the district	Cluj–Turda	1,500	Turda	
Petroşani	Huneadoara	3,000	Deva	
Villages in the district			Hațeg	
			Beleți (village)	
			Păclişa (village)	
			Ilia (village)	
Lipova	Timiş–Torontal	1,300	Timişoara	Jews from all the villages in southern Transylvania
Villages in the district				not mentioned here were evacuated to district towns

SOURCE: Data collated by the Jewish Federation and processed by Matatias Carp. See YVA, Romania Collection, 011/494, pp. 63–64. The evacuation included the entire Jewish population of the above localities.

even before, on 19 June. The effect of this order was to liquidate Jewish communities in hundreds of localities. Initially forty thousand Jews were expelled from the villages, followed later by another twenty thousand.[2]

The evacuation was accompanied by the wholesale expropriation of property: houses, furniture, clothes, household utensils, bedding, livestock, work tools, wagons, valuables, and cash. In the best case the Jews were given a few hours (sometimes only an hour) to pack some essential belongings and leave. In many cases they were ordered to report to various places under a variety of pretexts and were then forbidden to return home to collect their belongings or money. The Jews who were earmarked for deportation were also forced to pay taxes in advance to the villages, towns, and state, including income tax (usually two years' worth in advance). They were marched in line to the nearest train station or directly to the district city or town and were put up for the night in makeshift camps. In certain places (such as Dărăbani) families had to walk for hours to reach the railway station, which was dozens of kilometers from the town. In some places (such as Suliţa) the local authorities and the gendarmerie commanders, in an uncharacteristic show of humanity, allowed the Jews to hire wagons to transport their meager possessions, but the accompanying gendarmes and wagoners robbed them of all their possessions regardless. In the overnight camps Jews were threatened and beaten into handing over their possessions. Women and girls whose husbands and brothers were deported to the Târgu-Jiu camp were subjected to further humiliations.

In many places the Romanians rejoiced at the plight of their Jewish neighbors who were being marched out of the villages in convoys. Along the way the deportees were pelted with stones and hard clods of earth; water was poured on them as they were marched through the villages, to the accompaniment of curses, ridicule, and whoops of delight. The convoys were transported to internment camps in Oltenia and southern Walachia under difficult conditions in freight cars. Men, women, and children were crammed into these cars—about one hundred to a car—for a journey that lasted six days and nights, without water or food. The trains of evacuees and trains taking soldiers to the front intersected at many stations along the way, and the soldiers were delighted to have the chance to abuse the Jews. They broke into cars that were not properly sealed and beat the Jews with their rifles, bare fists, and clubs.

By 31 July an estimated forty thousand Jews had been evacuated and an estimated 75 percent of all Jewish communities in Romania had been liquidated.[3] In May 1942 the Jewish Center drew up a list of localities from which Jews had been evacuated and localities to which they had been taken, based on a survey it conducted in February 1942. It found that 441 villages and towns throughout

Romania had been totally purged of Jews.[4] Initially the Jewish Federation had no idea which communities still existed or where the Jews had been taken. The way they determined whether a community still existed was by sending it a letter. If the letter was returned, presumably the Jewish community no longer existed. In order to help the authorities control a situation they themselves had created, Filderman proposed a plan, in the federation's name, "for the rational distribution of the Jewish evacuees from Transylvania and Banat," without understanding the full significance of the government's intention.[5] In the plan Filderman listed cities that could accommodate Jews who had been housed in makeshift buildings, warehouses, open buildings, and the like. The Antonescu regime, however, did not want the distribution to be rational and considered such advice superfluous.

THE REPERCUSSIONS OF THE EVACUATION

The repercussions of the evacuation for the Jews were disastrous. All Jews became impoverished, bankrupt, and dependent on the communities' welfare services. Productive men from the small villages and towns—merchants, tradesmen, owners of food-processing factories, members of the liberal professions, and various service providers—became unemployed and were soon recruited to forced labor detachments, leaving their families without any means of sustenance. The evacuees despaired of ever returning home. In any case, their homes were not only totally ransacked but also gutted—heaters, doorposts, windows, doors, and even tin roof sheeting were all ripped up. Even headstones were stolen from cemeteries to build stairs or tiled porches for Romanian homes.

The evacuation of the Jews also had repercussions for the Romanians. What was obvious even before, namely that the Jews were the motive force behind the economic and commercial activity of many districts in Moldova, now became a certainty. The Jews provided a number of services to the peasants: they were the main purchasers of agricultural products, which they then delivered as necessary to other districts, and they offered merchants credit to buy goods, grains, fruit, and the like, which were subsequently sold throughout Romania or exported.

In March 1942 the leaders of the Moineşti and Târgu-Ocna communities, who had been evacuated to Bacău, sent a memorandum to the interior minister stating that over the past seven months economic activity in the cities and in the entire district had plummeted. The Jewish merchants had not been replaced, and no new commercial enterprises had been established, "apart from some taverns." In the absence of goods and purchasers the local peasants were forced to trudge fifty to sixty kilometers to Bacău (where all the Jews of the district had been concentrated) in order to sell their products on Thursday (fair day). Due to

the absence of management and technical cadres, the oil refineries were produc-
ing only a quarter of their regular yield, and both direct and indirect revenue
to the state had fallen.[6] The Ministry of the Interior rejected the communities'
request for repatriation on the grounds that "the reasons for removing the Jews
have not changed."[7] Antonescu was aware of the economic harm occasioned by
the expulsion of the Jews, but his Romanian antisemitic dream overrode such
considerations, as he himself explicitly stated: "It is not the economic aspect that
is important at this point in time, but rather the life of the nation itself."[8]

HOSTAGES

The taking of hostages was evidently designed to preclude Jewish
collaboration with the Soviet enemy or to prevent insurrection. In accordance
with the Interior Ministry's order of 21 June, many Jewish men — and in certain
localities all Jewish men — age eighteen to sixty were arrested throughout Romania and detained as hostages.[9] As usual, this measure was Antonescu's brainchild.
He ordered the minister of the interior to prevent any contact between Soviet
agents, "who are sometimes disguised as women," and Judeo-Communists who
were planning sabotage operations. To this end Antonescu issued the following
directive: "All Jewish men must be rounded up in [a] Jewish neighborhood and
detained — preferably in Jewish schools and large Jewish buildings — in order
to immediately punish any attempt at disruption. Security measures must be
stepped up in the Jewish neighborhoods; the movement of Jews must be banned
between 8 pm and 7 am. Some of their leaders — rabbis, slaughterers and the
like, Communists . . . shall be held as hostages in a separate building to prevent
any acts of insurrection or sabotage."[10]

On 4 July 1941 the police commander in Bucharest summoned thirty Jewish
dignitaries, headed by Filderman, and informed them that they — together with
another fifty-four dignitaries — had been declared "moral hostages." Any attempt
at sabotage by Jews, they were told, would result in the hostages' immediate
arrest, and they would pay with their lives for the actions of Jews throughout
the country.[11] The wave of arrests following this order led to the paralysis of most
economic activity in the cities of Moldova, which in turn prompted the Ministry
of the Interior to try and contain the phenomenon. The first such attempt took
place on 16 October, when the ministry ordered the prefects to limit the number
of hostages to twenty or thirty at the most in each city and town and ordered
them to be replaced each month.[12]

On 9 February 1942 the Ministry of the Interior decided to close the makeshift
hostage camps. The closure of the camps was a "provisional" measure, and the

prefects were warned to immediately report any signs of "a mood that required stricter security measures . . . in order to reopen the camps, even in cities where they had not previously existed."[13] This order also applied to the makeshift camps in southern Walachia, where women, children, and the elderly were being held.

The arrest of hostages "to ensure law and order" and prevent contact "between the Jews and the Soviet paratroopers," soon turned into a bribery operation and a means for extorting money from wealthy Jews who were designated hostages. In early 1942 a Siguranţa agent in Iaşi reported that the community leaders who had been ordered to deliver hostages to the army had reached a kind of agreement with the military authorities "that enabled the recruitment of hostages mainly from among the poorer Jews." The wealthy Jews bought their freedom by "offering the community" (namely, the army officers) 20,000–50,000 lei, while the poor were taken away, "leaving their families without any means of subsistence, with no-one to provide for them."[14] The facts, however, were slightly different. The Siguranţa agent failed to specify the sums of money the wealthy Jews had paid the army commanders and police authorities responsible for guarding the hostages. The money they offered the community was meant to pay the poor for agreeing to serve as hostages in place of the wealthy, sometimes under the names of the wealthy. In any case, the taking of hostages soon turned into a bribery operation, as did all of Antonescu's anti-Jewish initiatives that granted the authorities the power to fine, imprison, punish, detain, and deport Jews. The arrest of hostages was just one step along the path of a larger plan for the exploitation and destruction of the Jews of Moldova.

THE YELLOW BADGE

On 2 July 1941 the commander of the Huşi garrison ordered Jewish evacuees to wear a yellow badge (the order has not been preserved). Two days later the commander of the Bacău police ordered "every Jewish woman and man" in Bacău, except for Jews who were (still) serving in the army, to affix a "Jewish star" to their garments within forty-eight hours. The yellow badge was composed of two triangles of yellow fabric, each side about six centimeters long. Anyone failing to obey the directive was to be summarily arrested.[15] On 8 July the prefecture of the Covurlui district ordered all Jews to wear the yellow badge. Toward late August the obligation to wear the badge was applied to Moldova, Bessarabia, and Bukovina; Jews in Bucharest were not made to wear the yellow badge.

On 19 August it became clear that the evacuation from towns, the detention of hostages, internment in camps in southern Romania, the obligation to wear the yellow badge, and the government's intention to oblige the Jewish population to purchase war bonds were all connected. General Stoenescu, the finance minister, urged the leaders of the Jewish public to loan money to the state by purchasing the bonds, leading them to understand that it would be possible to change some of the anti-Jewish measures if they donated more money to the war effort.

The opening of archives in the former Soviet Union has enabled us to ascertain that the General Staff was behind the order to wear the yellow badge in Romania and that General Tătăranu, deputy head of War Headquarters and the man responsible for the Iaşi pogrom, was the one who sought to implement it, with Mihai Antonescu's permission.[16] General Stoenescu, whose attempts to extort money from the Jews were hampered by the introduction of the yellow badge, sought the abolition of the obligation to wear the yellow star — or so the Jewish leadership believed. In actual fact, Stoenescu met with Mihai Antonescu and both decided "that the emblem would be imposed [on Jews] after the Jews had signed the loan" — namely, after the Jews had paid a ransom for their release from the hostage camps.[17] Dumitru Popescu, the minister of the interior, informed General Tătăranu of the decision to deceive the Jews on this matter.

Popescu, who was in favor of abolishing the order, desisted when he realized it had been introduced "at the army's request."[18] Mihai Antonescu himself believed the order had originated from Ion Antonescu. After the latter abolished the order, thanks to Filderman's intervention, he asked his ministers on 9 September, "Who issued the directive? They say I did, but I knew nothing of it." Finance Minister Stoenescu had also been kept in the dark: "I was told [it came] from War Headquarters, but I objected." After Popescu informed him that General Tătăranu had given the order, Antonescu responded:

General Tătăranu is not Marshal Antonescu. He took this step without realizing its implications. . . . This is not the first measure of this kind adopted by War Headquarters, and "War Headquarters" means "the Conducător of the State." . . . Whenever you receive an order from War Headquarters that appears inconsistent with the logic and tact of the leadership [of the state], ask me directly: "Was this — or any other — decision given by you?" and I shall answer you. Always ask me.[19]

There is reason to believe that the yellow badge was introduced as part of the understanding between the German and Romanian armies on the eve of the invasion of the Soviet Union. Since the yellow badge was not part of Antonescu's antisemitic dream nor part of Cuza's heritage, as well as for other reasons, it was easy for Antonescu to abolish it. The abolition of the yellow badge was not universal, however. Special orders were issued obliging the Jews of Bessarabia, Bukovina, and Transnistria to wear the badge.[20]

After its introduction the yellow badge served as a kind of litmus test of the attitude of the Romanian public toward the Jews. The badge immediately erected an invisible—albeit tangible—barrier between Romanians and Jews, in addition to the legal, administrative, and cultural barriers that all Romanian governments since Goga-Cuza had attempted to erect. Many Romanians in each city and town went out of their way to check whether the Jews were wearing the badge, whether it was in the right place, whether it was the right size, whether women and children were also wearing it, whether it had been removed, and whether those rumored to be Jews were indeed exempt from wearing it. Jews wearing the badge who were still allowed to go out in the streets at certain hours, to ride trams, or to go shopping were ridiculed, cursed, threatened, spat upon, hustled, and hit. Not all Romanians were guilty of such behavior; as usual, the main offenders were hooligans, youngsters, Legionnaires and former supporters of Cuza, workers, and housewives. "The yellow star is an inexhaustible source of insults and violations of the public order," Filderman told the Bucharest police commander on 4 September while warning him of the consequences this measure would have on economic activity in Bucharest, based on precedents throughout the country.[21] The Jews would stay at home, economic activity would decline, and state revenues would drop. "It was almost impossible to go outdoors. We became a target of ridicule by everyone; even Gypsy children threw stones at us when they saw us in the streets," wrote a Jew from Târgu Neamţ.[22] Despite Antonescu's decision to abolish the order, it continued to be applied in Moldovan cities "depending on the locality and the whim of the local authority," wrote Arthur Axenfeld, a leader of the Bucharest community.[23]

Richter and the German embassy considered the abolition of the badge to be a setback and continued—verbally and in writing—to ask for its reintroduction. In a special article published in the German embassy's mouthpiece, Hans Muller demanded the reintroduction of the badge and refuted the arguments Filderman had raised in a memorandum to Antonescu a year earlier, when he had attempted to persuade him that even Germany had not introduced the yellow badge.[24]

THE DETENTION CAMPS

The evacuation of tens of thousands of Jews from their homes and localities in Moldova and their partial transfer to southern Romania soon led to the creation of improvised detention centers. It consequently became necessary to make arrangements for their guarding, feeding, and work assignments and to decide who was responsible for their implementation. This operation had no purpose other than the wish to make the Jews suffer as much as possible.

As usual, Antonescu was the one who issued the order, but he failed to take its implications into account.

Everything was provisional, since behind the original decision to evacuate the Jews of Moldova, launch a pogrom against the Jews of Iaşi (the capital of Moldova), and evacuate the remainder to the Târgu-Jiu camp lay a larger, more ambitious secret plan, known as the Great Plan.

In early August Col. Nicolae Petruţoiu, secretary general of the Ministry of the Interior, drew up a table for the Central Intelligence Service (Serviciul Central de Informaţii, which liaised among the SSI, the General Staff's Second Section, and the Siguranţa and coordinated their reports to Antonescu) listing the camps and the number of detainees there (see table 10). This table omitted the camps where the Jews of Constanţa and Galaţi were being held, the Teiş camp, and the makeshift camps in which Transylvanian Jews were being held. By August 1941, when the table was compiled, thousands of Jews had already been evacuated from the Târgu-Jiu camp, since it was full to capacity.

The Jews in the detention camps, including women and older children, were put to work in the surrounding localities. They cleaned streets, dug drainage ditches, worked in the fields of large estate owners, and were employed by the municipalities. The main purpose of their work was to humiliate them, to the satisfaction of the Romanian rank and file. This humiliation extended not only to the Jewish detainees but also to Jews who had not been evacuated or transferred to Moldovan cities. Filderman, for example, complained of the humiliation that the Jews of Vaslui endured: "Each day, about 400–500 Jews from all social strata and of all ages, including Jewish physicians, lawyers, and intellectuals, even children aged 13 and over, are given humiliating or difficult jobs. They are marched through city centers, holding spades or shovels."[25] The Jews of Galaţi were held in sixteen buildings scattered throughout the city, which were guarded by 178 gendarmes. Shopkeepers were ordered to donate "goods and materials required by the army" and were accompanied by gendarmes from the makeshift camps to their shops to enable them to "fulfill their civic obligations."[26] According to the Siguranţa, some of the Jews in the Covurlui district (to which Galaţi belonged) were "detained while others were free. Detainees [were allowed] to go home accompanied by gendarmes. . . . [Free] Jews met in business firms and spoke Yiddish among themselves. The Jews from Galaţi managed to flee to other cities, thereby escaping detention."[27] Only men age eighteen to fifty remained in the Galaţi camp, "and they were sent to work in the fields, [repair] roads, and the like." The community or relatives provided for the detainees.[28] Discrimination between rich and poor Jews soon occurred in the camps, as the former constituted an easy source of income for those who supervised them. An intelligence

TABLE 10. DETENTION CAMPS IN SOUTHERN ROMANIA, AUGUST 1941

Locality of camp			Men			
	Communists	Suspects	Striking miners	Legionnaires	Jewish evacuees	Total
Craiova					300[a]	300
Calafat					243[a]	243
Călăraşi		685[b]			1,006[c]	1,691
Urziceni		1,420				1,420
Turnu-Severin						
Caracal					1,319[a]	1,319
Giurgiu					250[d]	250
Videle		89				89
Turnu-Măgurele		273				273
Târgovişte	93	28			1,121[e]	1,242
Lugoj						
Târgu-Jiu	611	516	47	175	1,501[f]	2,850
Total	704	3,011	47	175	5,740	9,677

SOURCE: Reproduced from a table Colonel Petruţoiu, secretary general of the Ministry of the Interior, sent to the Presidency of the Council of Ministers, on the situation in the camps, 6 August 1941. USHMM/RSA, RG-25.002M, reel 18, PCM Cabinet, file 86/1941, pp. 18–19.

report issued by the Gendarmerie Inspectorate General in August 1941 pointed out that that the division of labor was done "in a way that was profitable to those who were in charge."[29]

On 25 August 1941 the Ministry of the Interior authorized the repatriation of 6,774 Jews who had been evacuated from the Dorohoi and Rădăuţi districts in late June 1941. A month or so later these same Jews were expelled to Transnistria.[30] Prior to the liberation of the camps Finance Minister Stoenescu, in collaboration with Mihai Antonescu and other ministers, conducted a profitable extortion racket at the Jews' expense. In early September the Ministry of the Interior ordered all Gendarmerie Inspectorates throughout the country to report "on the existence of detention camps in the legion's area, and on the behavior of the Jews in the camps." The gendarmerie commanders' reports showed that dozens of camps had been set up, accommodating ordinary Jews, suspect Jews, Jewish men age sixteen to sixty, relocated Jews (such as 801 Jews who had sur-

		Women			Children	Grand Total
Communists	Legionnaires	Jews	Suspects	Total		
		464[a]		464	289[a]	1,053
		295[a]		295	206[a]	744
						1,691
						1,420
		518[a]		518	108[a]	626
						1,319
		345[d]		3454	218[d]	813
						89
						273
						1,242
			261	261	238	499
48	6		71	125		2,975

[a] Jews from Dorohoi.
[b] Russians from the Tulcea district.
[c] Death train from Iaşi.
[d] Jews from Bălţi-Bessarabia.

[e] Jews from Ploieşti.
[f] 112 from Lespezi, 266 from Dorohoi, 229 from Botoşani, 91 from Vaslui, 362 from Falciu, and 431 from the rest of Moldova.

vived the second death train from Iaşi and were left in Podul-Iloaiei), Jews who were made to work in the fields to replace conscripted farmers, Jews who were rounded up for work during the day but were allowed to spend the night at home, Jews who were evacuated from their cities and sent to central camps such as Teiş and Târgovişte, Jews in labor camps, Jews in humiliation camps, and Jews in hostage camps. These camps held tens of thousands of Jews who were guarded by thousands of gendarmes, soldiers, and policemen, as if they were an enemy force captured in the Romanian heartland.[31]

Communities whose Jews had not been evacuated almost collapsed under the financial strain of supporting Jews in the camps and evacuees, at the authorities' behest. Economic activity in these cities usually ground to a standstill. Factories owned by Jews or factories that employed Jewish skilled laborers declined or closed down. Meanwhile, Ion Antonescu, who was at the front at the time, was planning to deport about sixty thousand Jews from Moldova to Transnistria and then across the River Bug. He was, therefore, angered to discover that most Moldovan Jews who had been evacuated southward had been returned to their districts (but not to their towns and villages). By early September, however, he realized that he had gone too far. He once again ordered the Jews to be classified into "useful" and "not useful." This was his first retraction from his uncompromising Romanization dream:

> There are certain Jews who, as far as their work is concerned, are irreplaceable and if we dismiss them we shall be causing the State harm. Therefore, we must distinguish between Jews who are not useful, whose detention will not harm the State, and those who are useful to the country's economic life. *We have removed 50,000–60,000 Jews from the towns and villages and transferred them to cities, where they have become a burden on the leaders of the Jewish communities, who are obliged to feed them.* Some of these, however, held positions essential to the State in the towns from which they were removed.[32]

Antonescu asked the minister of the national economy and the minister of finance to determine "concrete cases" (i.e., as few cases as possible) of Jews who were "useful to the economy" and to repatriate them. This marked the end of the period of pointless humiliation. Until the subsequent attempt to get rid of the Jews of Moldova in the summer of 1942, the attitude toward them was determined by the possibility of exploiting "useful" Jews and extorting money from them. "What shall we do with the empty houses" of Jews who have been evacuated? asked General Zwiedenek, the minister of Romanization, of Mihai Antonescu. "Who will be in charge of them?" Mihai Antonescu explained that there would be no change regarding the evacuation of the Jews and that the evacuation was final, "regardless of the severity of this measure, or the economic difficulties it may cause." Two principles of the regime were irrevocable, stressed the Conducător's deputy: "Ethnic purity of the villages and the ban on the employment of Jews as civil servants."[33]

AN OFFER THAT COULD NOT BE REFUSED

On 30 July 1941 General Stoenescu, the minister of finance, convened the leaders of the Jews of Bucharest, some of whom had already been declared moral hostages, and, using veiled threats, informed them that the Jewish community of Romania had to contribute 10 billion lei toward the war loan. In order to concretize the choice facing the Jewish population, Stoenescu added that "Marshal Antonescu has vouched for the lives of the Jews."[34] Why did Antonescu have to vouch for the lives of the Jews, unless Romanian soldiers were slaughtering the Jews of Bessarabia and Bukovina? It was clear, therefore, that the choice facing Romania's Jews was: Your money or your life. The amount the Jews were required to pay was astronomical—over $100 million in 1941 terms.

The following day Filderman wrote to the minister of the interior that although the Jewish community wished to contribute to the war expenditure, as it had in 1940, it would be very hard to meet the authorities' demands, since three quarters of all the communities had been dispersed, forty thousand Jews had been evicted from their homes, many Jews were being held in camps, all Jews had had to stop working, men in the cities had been arrested, and Jews were allowed out only a few hours a day. If these restrictions were abolished, added Filderman, the Jews could return home and would be able to contribute more toward the loan.[35] The regime, however, had no intention of abolishing these restrictions; on the contrary, they used them, together with the threat of wholesale deportation, to extort even more money. The Mafia-style choice of paying up or being deported that the minister of finance offered the Jewish leaders on 30 July 1941 would today certainly qualify as an offer that could not be refused.

Filderman understood the choice, as did the leaders of the Zionist movement, Chief Rabbi Safran, and the heads of the communities of the Regat and southern Transylvania. The circular that the Jewish leadership sent to the heads of all existing communities calling on Jews to donate generously to the state included the following sentence: "Is money worth more than life?"[36] It was clear, however, right from the outset, that federation leaders did not believe it possible to obtain such a huge sum.

The loan operation enabled Filderman and the Jewish Federation to conduct a sort of nation-wide survey of existing communities. The severing of ties with the provincial towns on the authorities' orders, the evacuation of dozens of large communities and hundreds of smaller ones, the arrest of community heads and rabbis, the relocation of entire communities, the non-delivery of mail, and the like meant that for weeks and even months the federation heads had no real idea how many communities remained in Romania. In its eagerness to collect this tax the Ministry of the Interior allowed detained community leaders and rabbis to convene in Bucharest and federation heads to send out circulars and loan forms to the communities. In places where the Jewish community no longer existed the letters were returned. This, together with the convention of community leaders in Bucharest, enabled the federation to conduct a survey of the communities. The Ministry of the Interior even agreed to the federation's request to provide it with a list of the addresses of "Jewish taxpayers" with whom contact had been severed, ostensibly in order to ensure their contribution to the war loan but really in order to determine if they were still alive and whether they had been deported.[37]

The Jewish Federation used this extortion operation and the unique opportunity it offered for corresponding with the communities to draw up a list of communities in which everyone had been evacuated or deported and of communities that remained. This list did not include hundreds of small communities or small localities from which all Jews had been evacuated or deported.

IMPOSTS

On 1 September the prefectures and commanders of army units in a number of cities throughout Romania gave Jewish communities twenty-four hours to provide them with hundreds of beds, mattresses, blankets, pillows, bedding, and the like for military hospitals that had been set up in their localities. On 3 September the second military territorial command gave the Union of Jewish Communities twenty-four hours to collect and deliver 6,200 iron beds with mattresses and bedding for the military hospitals.[38] On 5 September the Jewish communities were ordered to deliver five thousand complete sets of clothing—including socks, underwear, shirts, suits, hats, and shoes—ostensibly "for hospitalized Jewish prisoners from Bessarabia who had no clothes."[39] This was a downright fabrication. Jewish soldiers in the Red Army who were subsequently taken prisoner were not admitted to Romanian hospitals but were executed. On 7 September the administrator of confiscated property in Bucharest gave the Union of Jewish Communities one day to deliver five hundred "bug-free" wooden beds to the army and threatened to penalize anyone who failed to obey the new order.[40] Naturally, the suits that were confiscated were never delivered to Jewish prisoners but were donated to Romanian reservists, particularly high-ranking ones, who were about to be demobilized. On 25 October a law was passed obliging Jews to deliver dozens of items of clothing to the state, "for free." The communities were ordered to collect the clothing, and anyone who objected faced a five- to ten-year prison sentence and a fine of between 100,000 and 500,000 lei. "Members of the communities [responsible for collecting items] who fail to meet their obligations shall face a similar penalty."[41] Richter, Eichmann's envoy in Romania, mockingly nicknamed this law the Underpants Law (Unterhosengesetz).[42] The law alarmed many Romanians who were considered Jewish as a result of the Romanian racial laws and were forced to hand over movable property.

Although the penalties were a sufficient incentive to comply, forty-four thousand extremely poor Jews were simply unable to provide the requested items, and the Jewish Center was forced to pay a ransom of 100 million lei to overturn their convictions.[43] The heavy penalties notwithstanding, it proved impossible to collect the enormous number of items specified. Accordingly, a new decree was issued in January 1942 that mandated a cash payment instead of goods in kind, based on an inflated price list.[44] This organized larceny—involving so-called legal taxation by means of decrees, written directives, collection centers, and receipts for taxes paid and items delivered—totaled tens of billions of lei. Huge amounts of goods were collected and enormous sums of money were amassed via special military taxes levied exclusively on the Jews, and even greater sums were extorted for exemptions from forced labor, instituted in 1942.

In May 1943 Antonescu imposed a special levy of 4 billion lei because the Jews were enjoying life while Romanian soldiers were dying at the front.[45] Before this tax was collected Antonescu launched an intimidation campaign similar to the one he had launched prior to making the demand for the 1941 loan. He ordered the evacuation of about sixteen thousand Jews—some of whom had already been evacuated in the June 1941 operation—from towns to district capitals. He also ordered Jews of German, Austrian, or Czechoslovakian nationality who were living in Romania to be deported to Transnistria. This time, too, the alternatives were clear: pay up or face evacuation or deportation.[46] Lecca's order instructing the Jews to donate 4 billion lei to the war loan threatened those who failed to pay, or to pay enough, with deportation to Transnistria and confiscation of their property, even though the government had abandoned its deportation policy in October 1942.

Apart from this levy, hundreds of millions of lei were collected in the form of rent paid to the National Romanization Center by Jews whose apartments had been expropriated and who were forced to pay rent. In all these cases receipts were issued, unlike cases of direct theft. Table 11 gives a partial estimate of the scale of this theft.[47]

Prior to his execution in 1946, Antonescu submitted a special memorandum to the People's Court justifying his actions and his policies. In it he boasted that he had kept the economy stable throughout most of the war years (until spring 1944), preserved the value of the lei (except for the final months of his regime), maintained a state of plenty in the marketplaces in 1942–43, and reduced the government's domestic debt. The public was twice called upon to contribute to war expenses, wrote Antonescu, and this enabled Romania to get by without asking other countries for loans. Public contributions totaled 30 billion lei, emphasized the Conducător.[48] A quarter to a third of this sum was extorted from the Jews with receipts provided, while many billions more was taken without receipts. The robbery with receipts was directly ordered by Ion Antonescu and had no connection with the Nazis.

The full extent of the theft of Jewish property by the Legionary movement and its members under National-Legionary rule has not yet been assessed. (This

TABLE 11. FORCED PAYMENTS IMPOSED BY ION ANTONESCU

	Lei
War loan	1,994,209,194
Value of movable property	1,800,135,650
Contribution to the Home for War Invalids	89,575,898
The 4-billion-lei tax (amount collected)[a]	734,156,308
Contributions at the authorities' behest	1,067,876,827
Snow tax	139,323,875
Levy for exemptions from forced labor	2,028,450,206
Contributions by the Jewish Center	504,186,987
Direct contributions to the Welfare Council[b]	510,000,000
Transfer of funds to the Welfare Council, 1943–44	1,264,813,800
Total	10,132,728,745

SOURCE: Estimates of income and expenditure from taxes collected from Jews, carried out by the office of Radu Lecca, commissioner for Jewish affairs, undated [May 1944], and estimates by the Jewish Center, in Ancel, *Documents*, vol. 7, docs. 586–87, pp. 750–51.

[a] The Jewish Center was unable to collect the 4 billion lei due to the pauperization of the Jews.
[b] The donation operations of the Welfare Council, established by Ion Antonescu's wife, Maria, were intended for the same purpose as other antisemitic policies: to improve the lot of the Romanian people during the war at the expense of the Jews, whose tragedy was caused by Maria's husband. Trucks laden with the clothing of Jews deported to Transnistria transported their loads day and night from Atachi (the main deportation transit point over the Dniester) to Czernowitz and from there throughout Romania. The kindhearted first lady distributed these clothes to Romanian widows, war orphans, and other unfortunates. The parcels were seized brutally from the Jews before they were deported. See unsigned report to the World Jewish Congress by a Jew from Czernowitz who immigrated to Palestine in 1943, titled "Extermination of the Jews of Bukovina," American Jewish Archives, Cincinnati, Ohio, World Jewish Congress Collection, manuscript collection H2 88/1943, Romania, p. 16.

theft was conducted by the use of torture, pistols, and clubs, and there was no pretense at legality; that is, no receipts were issued.) Even according to official publications, however, it totaled 2–3 billion lei in 1940 terms.[49] The legal theft perpetrated by the Antonescu regime was appraised in a ceremonial book published in 1943 to mark the third anniversary of the regime, which reviewed the regime's achievements in all areas. The book proudly described the theft of Jewish property under the rubric of Romanization. Below is a list of Jewish property that was expropriated and nationalized on behalf of the Romanian state and Romanian and ethnic citizens from October 1940 and its value on the date of expropriation:

3,178 agricultural properties, totaling 45,035 hectares of land	5,063,364,350
311 forests, totaling 47,455 hectares	2,585,980,700
99 sawmills	790,018,438
timber and wooden materials	77,690,833
141 industrial plants for processing farm products in liberated areas	[no estimate]
323 plants for processing farm products, flour mills, and oil, alcohol, and brandy distilleries	1,851,341,940
146 ships of all kinds	1,318,849,900
mortgage rights of 564 Jews lenders, individuals, and firms	180,000,000
75,385 apartments and buildings expropriated from Jews, of which 17,833 were in Bucharest and 57,552 in provincial towns; of these, 58,980 apartments were handed over to Romanian citizens and 1,656 to Romanian institutions	59,000,603,573
Total	70,867,849,734[50]

This amount does not reflect the true value of Jewish property that was expropriated. The authorities who carried out the expropriations had a vested interest in playing down the true value of the property so that they could rent it out to Romanians at lower prices or sell it cheaply to ethnic Romanians, thereby enabling as many Romanians as possible to become property owners (*proprietari*) at the Jews' expense, so as to implement the old dream of the various antisemitic movements from the late nineteenth century.

Some idea of the true worth of the Jewish property and assets that were confiscated is provided by a statement of income issued by the National Romanization Center following property rentals to Romanians. It should be borne in mind, however, that the rents Romanians paid for farm property, apartments, and buildings, as well as profits from the contracting of factories, firms, and the like, were ridiculously low relative to market prices. This was also due to the rampant corruption in all matters relating to Jewish property. The revenue the National Romanization Center obtained from expropriating Jewish property in 1942–44, excluding 1941, is itemized in table 12.

These data do not include other categories of Jewish property, such as stock

TABLE 12. INCOME FROM PROPERTY EXPROPRIATED FROM JEWS
(MILLIONS OF LEI)

	1942–43	1943–44	Total
Agricultural property	—	100	
Industrial property	185	68	
Forests and sawmills	—	28	
Rental of apartments and buildings	1,488.6	1,500	
Rental of factories and firms	—	23	
Leasing of forests	—	30	
Leasing of alcohol refineries	—	5	
Ships and barges handed over to the Navy Ministry	126	65	
Total	1,799.6	1,819	3,618.6

SOURCE: These data were published and delivered to the press by Titus Dragoș, minister of Romanization, toward the end of Antonescu's rule and were published in the Jewish newspaper *Curierul Israelit*, no. 2, 24 September 1944. The budget year began on 1 April.

shares; property stolen from Jews who were deported to Transnistria; the direct theft of money, jewelry, foreign currency, artifacts and Judaica; and life insurance policies, not to mention property that was stolen in the towns from which the Jews were deported, at the crossing points over the Dniester, and prior to or even after their execution.

FORCED LABOR

The practice of evicting Jews from their homes for the purpose of forced labor was initiated by the National-Legionary government and continued even after the Legionnaires were ousted from power. At that time forced labor was not anchored in law. The first step toward legalizing forced labor came with the publication of Decree no. 3984 of 5 December 1940, determining the military status of Jews, and its attendant regulations of 14 July 1941.[51] In addition (up to 1944) were ad-hoc laws issued by Antonescu, decree-laws, General Staff directives and provisions, and Ministry of Labor instructions concerning the organization of the labor camps and related issues.

The Jews' obligation to work for the state for free under conditions determined by the state was outlined by the General Staff in a meeting convened on 5 September 1941 to discuss the establishment, organization, and supervision of special labor camps for Jews (as distinct from detention camps) and the exploitation of the Jewish workforce in general. The rationale behind forced labor was that since the Jews were exempt from army service, they had to contribute in other ways, such as by paying special army taxes or carrying out special public works (*de folos obştesc*)—a euphemism for forced labor (*muncă obligatorie*). Compulsory labor, it was stated at the meeting, would continue as long as compulsory army service (regular and reserves) continued. Public works were carried out on behalf of the Ministry of National Defense or other government ministries and institutions in coordination with the Ministry of Defense and at its behest. In times of war or general conscription, Jewish labor would be required for the war effort only, at the General Staff's discretion. The regulations of 14 July 1941 stated that all Jews age eighteen to fifty were required to report for forced labor. Recruitment of Jews for forced labor took place in special bureaus within the regular recruitment centers and, in wartime, was not subject to time restrictions.

In an interministerial commission session on 5 September 1941, attended by the ministers of labor, finance, and the interior and a General Staff representative who led the discussions, it was decided to speed up the recruitment of Jews for forced labor and to set up special labor camps for Jews. The Jews would be required to strengthen and repair the railway network and help out in agriculture, public works, and the like and would be housed in shacks that were half underground. On 16 October a decree was issued regarding the establishment of forced labor camps and detachments for Jews, for which the Ministry of Labor, working with the General Staff, was responsible. To this end the Ministry of Labor set up a General Directorate of Forced Labor Camps and Detachments (Inspectoratul general al taberelor şi coloanelor de muncă obligatorie) and appointed a corrupt and notorious antisemite, Theodor Mociulschi, as its head.[52]

In late June 1942 the General Staff, in an attempt to streamline forced labor, issued general instructions regarding the forced labor of Jews. New arrangements were made for the assignment of Jews to external (remote) and internal (local) detachments, according to age, profession, and the like. An attempt was made to streamline the exploitation of Jewish craftsmen and intellectuals—particularly doctors, chemists, engineers, architects, and the like. Conditions under which Jews could be exempted from forced labor were clarified, and basic workers' rights, such as food, a daily allowance, and work hours, were specified (in theory, the workers were not supposed to work more than nine hours per day). The military authorities were also empowered to check whether "exempted" Jews were working in the factories to which they had been assigned and could revoke the exemption if they decided that these Jews were no longer necessary to the economy. Corporal punishment was sanctioned for any offense in connection with forced labor (unpunctuality, slackness, insubordination, and the like), and in certain cases the penalty was deportation of the offender and his family to Transnistria. Among the offenses punishable by deportation were: sloppiness at work, unauthorized leave of absence, failure to report a change of address, and "sexual relations with Romanian women." The instructions granted the various corps of the Romanian army the right to oblige Jewish women age eighteen to forty to undertake forced labor such as "sewing, washing and the like, as well as professional work." The Jewish communities were obliged to send Jewish women to work at the behest of the Labor Bureaus.[53] The General Staff's instructions concerning corporal punishment and deportation were implemented in the field. Corporal punishment, including flogging and clubbing, was inflicted for any offense in all work detachments. In Brăila, for example, the former community leader was beaten to a pulp for complaining in writing about a Romanian officer who was abusing Jews in his work detachment.[54]

On 28 October 1941, in response to his request "to draw up a general estimate of [the number] of Jews in the camps," the General Staff sent Antonescu a report on the number and distribution of Jews assigned to forced labor and the number of "useful" Jews who had received exemptions (this was before Lecca's operation had gotten under way).[55] The report gave the following estimates:

84,042	Jews age eighteen to fifty registered for forced labor according to the recruitment bureaus' records
47,345	Jews actively engaged in forced labor
9,365	Jews who received exemptions and were allowed to return to their jobs
15,399	Jews whose situation was unclear[56]
11,933	Jews, mainly intellectuals and community officials, available for work (as necessary)

From 1943 to 1944 the forced labor system became increasingly institutionalized. The demand for skilled Jewish labor increased as the war progressed. Exemptions, granted twice a year, became increasingly costly. Jewish and gentile informers kept Lecca and his men apprised of how much each Jew was worth—that is, the ransom his family could afford to pay for an exemption certificate. The various administrators and officials of the Jewish Center, as well as rabbis, slaughterers, and prominent intellectuals, did not have to pay for exemption certificates. The official estimate of income from exemptions represented only a fraction of the real amount. Hundreds of labor detachments were set up in large cities, while dozens were set up in nonurban areas. Youngsters, the poor, and many physicians were assigned to external (remote) labor detachments. Those who could afford to pay large bribes—mainly genuine or self-styled profession-als and experts—were assigned to local or even fictitious work detachments. In September 1942, 20,458 Jews were assigned to work detachments outside the cities, while another few thousand (mainly Jews from Bucharest) were assigned to labor detachments and camps near the capital.[57]

The number of exemptions grew commensurately with the number of Roma-nian officials and institutions receiving bribes from Lecca or directly from Jews. In the spring of 1943, 227.8 million lei were paid out for these exemptions, and in April 1943, 26,619 exemptions were granted.[58]

The Jews' plight was described in painstaking detail by Lecca, Antonescu's top expert on Jews:

> The situation of the Jews in Moldova was extremely difficult. They were all concentrated in the district capitals, without accommodation or furni-ture—which had been left behind in the towns and villages from which they had been evacuated. Most were unemployed, and had no other source of livelihood. Men aged 18–50 were assigned by the General Staff to external forced labor detachments, and the women and children became a burden on the Jewish communities in the cities. The women, as well as men who were unfit for [forced] labor, could not find any work, because of Iaşinschi's Legion-ary Romanization law. Jews who had had jobs in the past were dismissed and handed over to the General Staff by inspectors of the Central Romanization Office (CRO) in the Ministry of Labor, unless they paid a monthly bribe, which in many cases exceeded their salaries. All Jews who worked in commercial or industrial firms, or Jewish firm-owners, were assigned Romanian substitutes, who were paid a salary similar to that of the Jew. The CRO inspectors had the sole authority to determine whether the Romanian replacement was suf-ficiently trained to replace a Jew. If the Jew paid, the replacement was kept on for further training, and the Jew remained in his job. If he could not pay, the CRO inspector pronounced the replacement ready to take over, and informed the regional recruitment bureau [the General Staff] that the Jew was available for forced labor. If the Jew was aged 50 or over, and according to military law was no longer obliged to do military service [or forced labor], the General Staff resorted to another formula: It recruited the Jew for [forced] labor on the basis of the Impressment Law. The moment the Jew fell into the hands of the military, he was offered a new deal: If he paid, he would not be sent to the external work detachments, but would remain in a local work detachment, and see his family. If he paid an enormous sum of money—he could be sent back to [his job] in the factory from which he had been dismissed, and be kept

on a permanent basis. The collaboration between the CRO and the military was faultless. The whole of Romania was overrun by salaried or honorary CRO inspectors who lived, as the Germans used to say, "like gods in France," while the General Staff and regional recruitment centers dealt less with the soldier's needs than with the [forced] labor of Jews.[59]

Thus did Lecca, the commissioner for Jewish affairs, describe in his memoirs the suffering his rivals (the General Staff and the military in general) inflicted on the Jews. The reality he presented, however, was only fragmentary. He omitted, for example, his own extortion operation, which he introduced in the summer of 1942 after persuading Mihai Antonescu to let him take control of the granting of certificates of exemption from forced labor.

38

Statistical Data on the Holocaust in Romania

According to the director general of Romania's Central Bureau of Statistics, in 1940 Greater Romania had fewer than 800,000 Jews. This estimate was based on the results of the 1930 census and yearly updates published by the bureau.[1] According to the 1930 census, which also broke the data out by nationality, religion, and mother tongue, Greater Romania had 756,930 Jews (4.2 percent of a total population of 18 million).

During the Second World War era the number of Jews in Romania at any one time was a function of two variables: the size of the country and the scope of the killing and deportation operations. In June 1940 Romania was forced to cede Bessarabia and northern Bukovina to the Soviet Union, and in September, northern Transylvania to Hungary. After Bessarabia and northern Bukovina were recaptured in July 1941, a bloodbath was unleashed against the Jewish population there. Northern Transylvania remained in Hungarian hands until October 1944. In May–June 1944 the Jews of northern Transylvania were deported to Auschwitz.

On 6 April 1941 a general census was conducted of the population in Romania (excluding Bessarabia, northern Bukovina, and northern Transylvania), with the participation of a German observer, Professor Franz Burgdörfer, director of the Bavarian Bureau of Statistics. The census found 302,090 Jews in sovereign Romanian territory, corroborating the 1930 census. The Romanian press was surprised by the small number of Jews, and Antonescu, who like all antisemites believed that there were at least a million Jews in Romania, questioned the results of the census.[2] In August–September 1941, after the liberation of Bessarabia and northern Bukovina, a headcount of residents was conducted, including Jews in the camps and those not yet incarcerated. The census in truncated Romania in April 1941 and the headcount in Bessarabia and Bukovina in late August 1941 are the best evidence of the number of Jews in Romania in September 1941, just prior to the start of the large deportations to Transnistria.

In April–May 1942 a racist census of "residents of Jewish blood" in Romania

TABLE 13. JEWS OF ROMANIA IN THE OFFICIAL CENSUSES

	Walachia	Moldova	Bessarabia	Bukovina	Transylvania	Total	% of total population
1930	100,924 (6,357,658)	162,268 (2,433,596)	206,958 (2,864,402)	93,101 (853,009) — Southern[a] 24,094 Northern 64,051	193,679[b] (5,548,363)	756,930 (18,057,028)	4.2%
1941	120,045 (7,097,264)	135,729 (2,769,380)	72,623 (—)	71,950 — Southern 18,141 Northern 53,809	Southern 40,944 Northern (—) (3,332,898)	441,291 (13,535,757)	—
1942 "Residents of Jewish blood"	114,130	121,131	227	17,033	Southern Northern[c] 39,628	292,149 (16,843,539)	1.7%

SOURCE: Figures for 1930 are from the 1930 general census, in Centrala Evreilor din România, *Breviarul statistic*, 22–25. Figures for 1941 are from the April 1941 census in Romania proper, in Congresul Mondial Evreesc, *Populația evreească*, 37–39. See also pp. 37–38 for the headcount of Jews in the liberated territories in August–September 1941. Figures for 1942 are from the 1942 census of people of Jewish blood, in Congresul Mondial Evreesc, *Populația evreească*, 44–50; these figures are also available in Centrala Evreilor din România, *Breviarul statistic*, 22–25.

NOTE: Figures for the general population are shown in parentheses. The provinces listed are the historical provinces. Errors in calculation reflect the original document.

a The breakdown between the Jews of northern and southern Bukovina in 1930 was carried out arbitrarily by district, since in 1930 the province was not yet partitioned (in June 1940 the Czernowitz and Storojineț districts, as well as a small part of the Rădăuți district, were annexed to the Soviet Union). The slight discrepancy between the numbers is in the original.

b 148,294 Jews were transferred to Hungary in September 1940, according to the 1930 census.

c Transylvania belonged to Hungary at the time.

TABLE 14. JEWS IN THE CAMPS OF BESSARABIA, AUGUST–SEPTEMBER 1941

	Edineți (și Secureni)	Mărculești	Vertujeni	Kishinev	Still free	Total
According to the General Staff envoy	25,000	11,000	23,000	11,525	5,000–10,000	80,000
According to the general headcount	20,909	10,737	24,000	10,742	6,883	73,271

Source: The results of the headcount carried out by the General Staff envoy are included in "Investigative Report no. 2 on Irregularities in the Kishinev Ghetto," drawn up by a committee headed by Gen. Constantin Niculescu at Antonescu's order, December 1941. USHMM/SSARM, RG-54.001, reel 1, 706-1-69, pp. 48–55; copy in Carp, *Cartea neagră*, no. 19, 3:61. The general headcount is from "Jewish and Total Population, Inventory of Bessarabia and Northern Bukovina, August–September 1941" and "Jews Interned in Ghettoes and Concentration Camps in 1941," in Congresul Mondial Evreesc, *Populația evreească*, 37–38.

(excluding northern Transylvania) confirmed the disappearance of the Jews of Bessarabia and most of the Jews of Bukovina.

Data on the number of Jews in the liberated territories in August–September 1941 are not consistent, and there are slight discrepancies among the various censuses, depending on who carried them out. The importance of the statistical data cannot be overestimated, since they are proof of the extent of the massacre of Jews during and immediately after the occupation under Antonescu's orders to "cleanse the ground." Sources of the data include official results delivered in 1942 to the Jewish Center; data on the inmates of the camps collected by the General Staff envoy Lt. Col. Ion Palade, who was sent to Bessarabia to organize the deportation operation with the help of the army and gendarmerie; and statistics submitted to the Presidency of the Council of Ministers by the governors of Bessarabia and Bukovina in April 1942 as part of preparations for the Final Solution in Romania.[3] These data were collected by the regional authorities in the two provinces.

In late 1941, then, these sources show that the total number of Jews in Bessarabia amounted to roughly 80,000. There were more Jews, however, who were not included in the count. By the end of July 1941, before Transnistria was officially ceded to the Romanian administration, Romanian soldiers and gendarmes had concentrated tens of thousands of Jews in northern Bessarabia and forced them out of Bessarabia across the Dniester River, shooting hundreds of them and throwing their bodies into the river. Thus, 32,000 Jews must be added to the roughly 80,000 found in Bessarabia by the Romanian army (see chap. 18, note 13), In addition, as of 16 August 1941 the German army had captured at least 13,000 Jews in the Ukraine, who were trying to escape to Russia.[4] Therefore, in late July 1941, there were at least 125,000 Jews in Bessarabia at the time of its occupation.

The exact number of Jews killed from early July to late August 1941 remains unknown, as does the number of Jews who managed to escape to the Soviet Union. What is known from government documents is that most Jews from villages and towns in southern Bukovina and Bessarabia were murdered by the Romanian army and the local population. Likewise, we know that Einsatzgruppe D killed thousands of Jews in Czernowitz and in a few towns in Bessarabia (Kishinev, Bălți, Hotin, Tighina, etc.). The only statistics on the number of Jews murdered are those referred to in Romanian documents: 25,000 in Bessarabia and approximately 20,000 during the "hasty deportations."[5] Following Traian Popovici's evaluations and statistics, it's possible that some 15,000 Jews disappeared in Czernowitz and its surroundings.[6] This amounts to a total of 60,000 Jews.

THE SECRET REPORTS

As stated, the basis for evaluating the scope of the Holocaust in Romania is provided by the two aforementioned official censuses as well as the headcount conducted by the General Staff envoy in the liberated territories. These data, however, are not sufficient in themselves to calculate the number of Jews who survived the first wave of slaughter in Bessarabia and northern Bukovina, those deported to Transnistria, and those who perished there or the number of Ukrainian Jews who disappeared under the Romanian occupation regime. To make matters worse, after Stalingrad the Antonescu regime's policy was to conceal responsibility for the Jews' fate and doctor the statistics on victims in the official documents.

This problem was solved after 1995 with the discovery of secret reports that showed, beyond the shadow of a doubt, that Mihai Antonescu, vice president of the Council of Ministers, personally supervised the application of the extermination policy. It was his ministry (the Foreign Ministry) to which the governors of Bessarabia, Bukovina, and Transnistria and the gendarmerie commander submitted reports on the scope of the deportations and the number of Romanian

TABLE 15. NUMBER OF JEWS IN THE PROVINCE OF BUKOVINA

District	Evacuated Jews				Jews not yet evacuated				Jews not slated for evacuation			
	Men	Women	Children	Total	Men	Women	Children	Total	Men	Women	Children	Total
1. Czernowitz	*	*	*	33,891	7,715	10,075	2,656	20,466**	6,268	8,101	2,046	16,415***
2. Câmpulung	2,197	2,226	1,655	6,118	22	16	5	43	7	7	3	17
3. Storojineţ	1,260	1,334	1,325	3,919	15	15	9	39	10	10	6	26
4. Suceava	*	*	*	5,942	1	—	—	1	4	3	1	8
5. Rădăuţi	3,624	3,773	1,772	9,169	36	29	9	74	1	2	—	3
6. Hotin	5,180	6,038	12,221	23,439	35	35	21	91	33	34	17	84
7. Dorohoi	3,480	3,596	2,291	9,367	1,404	569	583	2,556	231	226	261	718
Total	—	—	—	91,845	9,228	10,739	3,283	23,250	6,554	8,383	2,334	17,271

SOURCE: Reproduced from a report and table by General Calotescu, governor of Bukovina, on Jews who were evacuated, Jews not yet evacuated, and Jews who would not be evacuated, 9 April 1942. USHMM/RMFA, RG–25.006M, reel 11, "Jewish Problem," vol. 20, pp. 130–31. The data relate to the historical province of Bukovina (Jews who were evacuated and Jews slated for evacuation), and the districts of Dorohoi (the Regat) and Hotin (Bessarabia). The Hotin district was administratively annexed to Bukovina after the territory was liberated.

NOTE: Table notes are from the original source.

* No data were found for the breakdown of evacuees from the districts of Czernowitz and Suceava by men, women, and children, since the evacuations were wholesale.

** In the first evacuation, a further 4,031 Jews will be removed since they are no longer useful and are undesirables.

*** Some of the 16,415 would still be evacuated, as undesirables.

TABLE 16. NUMBER OF JEWS EVACUATED FROM BESSARABIA

Details	Jews who were evacuated	Jews not yet evacuated			Jews not slated for evacuation		
	Number	In towns	In villages	Total	In towns	In villages	Total
Men	—	99	—	99	14	57	71
Women	—	114	—	114	73	123	196
Children	—	44	—	44	9	477	486
Total	55,867*	257	—	257	96	657	753

SOURCE: Reproduced from a report and tables by the Bessarabian administration on the number of Jews who were deported in 1941, 1 April 1942. USHMM/RMFA, RG-25.006M, reel 11, "Jewish Problem," vol. 20, pp. 132–34, 136.

NOTE: Table notes are from the original source.

*There are no data on the breakdown [men, women, children], because those responsible for this operation failed to list the evacuees by category as they were requested to do.

and Ukrainian Jews killed. The reports contained, among other information, a breakdown of the murderers by nationality (Romanian or German) and figures on the Jewish population of Transnistria at various times. Reports on the same topic by the minister of the interior were also discovered. Credit for this achievement goes to the U.S. Holocaust Memorial Museum and particularly to Dr. Radu Ioanid, thanks to whose expertise and persistence the Romanian State Archives were opened and many of its collections copied. The secret reports show that in August–September 1941 more Jews were alive than the official documents would have us believe, and therefore more Jews were deported than indicated by the figures quoted in the official statistics.

In April 1942 Antonescu's Cabinet for Bessarabian, Bukovinian, and Transnistrian Affairs asked the governors of the three provinces to provide it with up-to-date statistics on the number of Jewish deportees (men, women, and children) in their provinces. The purpose of this directive was to prepare for the Final Solution (the deportation of all Jews from Romania). "Now we are sorting them" in order to determine who will be allowed to remain, the governor of Bukovina reported, "and to remove all the undesirables and unemployed."[7] The data the governor supplied are both comprehensive and accurate. The original table (see table 15) was drawn up in Czernowitz and sent to the Presidency of the Council of Ministers. Note that the word *evacuation* in the table is a euphemism for *deportation*.

TABLE 17. NUMBER OF DEPORTEES TO TRANSNISTRIA, LATE 1941 (SECRET AND NEW DATA)

Northern Bukovina[a]	Southern Bukovina[b]	Bessarabia	Dorohoi district	Total
61,249	21,229	75,867[c]	9,367	167,712

SOURCE: Tables 15 and 16 herein.

[a] Czernowitz, Storojineț, and Hotin districts. The Jews in the Hotin district included in Calotescu's report were local Jews who were deported in an organized manner, broken down into men, women, and children. Those included in Voiculescu's report were Jews interned in the Edineți and Secureni camps, who were deported wholesale. See note in table 16.

[b] Câmpulung, Suceava, and Rădăuți districts.

[c] 55,867 plus 20,000 (from the "hasty deportations"; 12,600 of the 32,000 were returned to the Vertujeni camp and were included in the headcount).

This extremely detailed table put an end to the uncertainty concerning the number of Bukovinian Jews who were deported to Transnistria in 1941, some of whom were killed en route. It establishes that the vast majority of the Jews of northern Bukovina did not flee to the Soviet Union and that almost all the Jews in the villages and small towns were killed (by Romanian and Ukrainian citizens and the Romanian army) or deported immediately after the province was recaptured. (This topic has not been covered in this book due to lack of space.)

The governor of Bessarabia also submitted his findings (see table 16).

These findings are incomplete. They fail to take into account a number of Jews who were killed in Bessarabia prior to the deportation. The Commission of Inquiry set up by Antonescu to investigate "irregularities" in the conduct of the deportation operation determined that "the discrepancy of about 25,000 Jews between the 75,000–80,000 who were interned [in the camps] and the 55,867 who were evacuated" was due to the fact that these Jews "died a natural death, escaped or were shot."[8] To this figure must be added another 20,000 Jews who were shot in the hasty deportation of July 1941, since these Jews were not included in the General Staff headcount of August–September 1941 and were not in camps at the time. It should be borne in mind that many of the Jews who were traced and counted by the Romanian authorities were subsequently killed during the deportations.

After the deportations were resumed in the spring of 1942, on Antonescu's order, 231 Jews were deported from Bessarabia and 4,290 from Bukovina. Following this deportation the Jews of Bukovina excluding the Dorohoi district

TABLE 18. DEPORTATION OF JEWS FROM BESSARABIA AND BUKOVINA, SPRING–SUMMER 1942

	From Bessarabia				From Bukovina			
	Men	Women	Children	Total	Men	Women	Children	Total
20 May 1942	—	—	—	204	—	—	—	—
10 July 1942	—	—	—	27	—	—	—	—
8 June–11 June 1942	—	—	—	—	827	733	418	1,978
15 June 1942	—	—	—	—	447	503	201	1,151
29 June 1942	—	—	—	—	436	566	160	1,162
Total	81	105	45	231	1,710	1,802	779	4,291

SOURCE: For Bessarabia: Gen. Gheorge Voiculescu, governor of Bessarabia, to the Presidency of the Council of Ministers, 27 August 1942, and Report no. 3028, 21 August 1942, USHMM/RMFA, RG–25-006M, reel 11, "Jewish Problem," vol. 20, pp. 153–53b, 154–56. For Bukovina: Coded telegram from Gen. Corneliu Calotescu, governor of Bukovina, to the Presidency of the Council of Ministers, 22 June 1942, USHMM/RMFA, RG–25-006M, reel 11, "Jewish Problem," vol. 20, p. 215. Among the deportees were 308 Jews—176 men, 70 women, and 62 children—from Dorohoi (see anexa no. 5, p. 206).

TABLE 19. JEWS DEPORTED TO TRANSNISTRIA IN SEPTEMBER 1942
(FROM THE REGAT AND SOUTHERN TRANSYLVANIA)

	Men	Women	Total
Jews suspected of Communism but not tried	499	55	554
Jews interned in the Târgu-Jiu camp	355	52	407
Imprisoned Communist Jews	—	—	85
Jews who were deported on the order of the General Staff for infringing forced labor regulations	—	—	592
Jews who sought to return to the Soviet Union (Bessarabia) in 1940[a]	144	434	578
	—	—	2,216

SOURCE: The table was drawn up by the Ministry of the Interior in November 1943; see Carp, *Cartea neagră*, no. 248, 3:450–51.

[a] 562 Jews "disappeared" (i.e., were liquidated), 16 remained alive. See report of Lt. Col. C. Tobescu, director of the Siguranţa Service at the Gendarmerie Inspectorate, 16 September 1943, including nominal list of the deportees who "disappeared" and list of the 16 survivors, in Ancel, *Documents*, vol. 5, doc. 211–12, pp. 441–54.

totaled 17,159 (of which 16,794 were from Czernowitz); including the Dorohoi district they totaled 19,475.[9]

In August 1942 the secretary general of the Presidency of the Council of Ministers asked the governors of Bessarabia, Bukovina, and Transnistria, in Antonescu's name, for "proposals for further deportations."[10] In September 1942 at least 2,216 Jews were deported from the Regat and southern Transylvania. In October 1942 the governor of Bukovina proposed the deportation of 6,234 Jews from Czernowitz and 592 from Dorohoi—proposals that were never implemented due to the shelving of the Romanian and Nazi extermination plans.[11]

Thus far, data on the deportation of Jews to Transnistria have been unclear and even contradictory. These data are based on gendarmerie reports, Ministry of the Interior reports, and data collected by representatives of the Jewish Center, or rather, the Autonomous Assistance Commission. These discrepancies, too, have been resolved thanks to documents found in the archives of the Romanian Foreign Ministry, now at the U.S. Holocaust Memorial Museum, under the title "Problem 33" ("Problems relating to the Jews," as written on the files). A comparison between these reliable contemporary reports and the gendarmerie and Interior Ministry reports shows that the statistics on the deportees from Bessarabia and Bukovina were artificially reduced in order to conceal the true number of victims and thereby lessen the Romanian state's responsibility for their

TABLE 20. COMPARISON OF REPORTS ON THE NUMBER OF DEPORTEES

	Real-time reports[a]			Gendarmerie Inspectorate			Ministry of the Interior[b]
	1941	1942	Total	January 1942[c]	September 1942[d]	September 1943[e]	November 1943
From Bessarabia	55,867	231	56,098	—	—	55,867	55,867
From Bukovina and Dorohoi	91,845	4,290	96,135	—	—	43,798 (excluding Dorohoi)	54,166
Hasty deportations[f]	20,000 (approx.)	—	20,000	—	—	—	—
From Romania	—	2,016	2,016	—	—	—	—
Total	167,712	6,537	174,249	118,847	110,065	99,665	110,033

[a] For the sources in the "real-time reporting," see previous tables: tables 15, 16, and 17 for 1941, tables 18 and 19 for 1942.

[b] Ministry of Police within the Ministry of the Interior, report on the deportation and the problem of repatriation, including table, November 1943, in Carp, *Cartea neagră*, no. 248, 3:447–50.

[c] Summary report by the Gendarmerie Inspectorate for the period between 15 December 1941 and 15 January 1942, in Ancel, *Documents*, vol. 5, doc. 133a, pp. 216, 228.

[d] Transnistrian Gendarmerie Inspectorate to the Transnistrian administration, summary of the deportations, 9 September 1942, USHMM/RMFA, RG–25-006M, reel 11, "Jewish Problem," vol. 20, p. 161.

[e] Gendarmerie Inspectorate to the Ministry of the Interior, 16 September 1943, in Carp, *Cartea neagră*, no. 244, 3:438.

[f] Executed by the German SS; see chapter 18 herein.

TABLE 21. NUMBER OF DEPORTEES ACCORDING TO OTHER SOURCES

German embassy in Bucharest August 1942[a]	Major Dr. Tătăranu[b]	Zionist movement in Romania June 1943[c]	Dr. Filderman October 1943[d]	Ion Antonescu May 1945[e]
185,000	200,000	180,000	190,000	150,000–170,000

[a] "Rumänien wird judenrein" [Romania is about to become judenrein], *Bukarester Tageblatt*, 8 August 1942.

[b] Tătăranu, *Expunere de titluri*, 11. Tătăranu was head of the Sanitary Service in Transnistria.

[c] Report of the Zionist leadership in Romania to the representative of the World Jewish Congress in Geneva, Dr. Abraham Silberschein, June 1943, in Ancel, *Documents*, vol. 4, doc. 328, p. 620.

[d] Memorandum by Dr. Filderman to the Romanian government, 12 October 1943, in Carp, *Cartea neagră*, no. 247, 3:444.

[e] Memorandum by Ion Antonescu to the People's Court, 15 May 1946, USHMM/SRI, RG-25.004M, reel 31, file 40010, vol. 4, p. 16. Antonescu wrote, "According to my calculations, 150,000–170,000 Jews at the most were deported."

fate. None of the statistics include the convoys that were sent to Bogdanovka and the Bug area.

Table 20 shows data on the true number of deportees ("real-time reports," or reports produced during the war) compared to the doctored records.

Data from other sources confirm the "real-time" data on the number of deportees to Transnistria.

A study of tables 20 and 21 shows no major discrepancy in the data on the number of deportees, which totaled around 170,000–190,000. In the gendarmerie reports of January 1942 there was a manifest attempt to hide the number of deportees who were sent directly to the Kingdom of Death and later to systematically downplay, on paper, the number of deportees in general, although these data patently contradicted the data that the governors of Bukovina and Bessarabia and the SSI submitted in real time, in 1942.

Two recently discovered confidential reports—one by Constantin (Piki) Vasiliu and one prepared by the SSI in January 1942 on Jews concentrated west of the Zhmerinca-Odessa railway line—clarify certain former mysteries. They show that more Jews survived the first wave of destruction than was originally thought. They also show that more Jews were deported (at least 167,712 in 1941) than was originally thought and that the number of deportees for whose death the Romanian state was responsible was several tens of percentages higher than what was at first thought. Finally, they prove that the Romanian administration

TABLE 22. DEPORTEES FROM BESSARABIA, BUKOVINA, AND THE DOROHOI DISTRICT IN TRANSNISTRIA, DECEMBER 1941

Vasiliu's report			SSI report: Jews concentrated west of the Zhmerinca-Odessa railway line despite Antonescu's orders					Total	"Real-time" reports (1941)[a]
Tulchin	Balta	Golta	Mogilev	Yampol	Rybnitsa	Tiraspol	Other localities		
47,545	30,981	29,476	65,000	262	427	70	13,748	187,509	167,712

SOURCE: Vasiliu's report, USHMM/SRI, file 18844, vol. 3, p. 718 and map; reprinted in Ancel, *Transnistria, 1941–1942*, vol. 2, doc. 245, pp. 450–51. Report by Antonescu's military cabinet, including the results of the SSI census carried out under Marshal Antonescu's orders and the reasons for it, 4 January 1942, USHMM/RSA, RG–25.002M, reel 18, PCM Cabinet, file 86/1941, pp. 323–24.

[a] Table 20 herein.

secretly collected accurate data in real time on its activities. An examination of these two reports shows that they relate to two different regions in Transnistria, without any overlap (see table 22).

As stated, the Interior Ministry data (based on gendarmerie reports) on the number of deportees sent to the Bug and the SSI data on the number of deportees who remained in western Transnistria *against* Antonescu's orders (which is why he used the SSI rather than the Interior Ministry to gather the data) do not overlap but refer to different regions. (The SSI also reported on the number of local Jews who remained; see below.) The Odessa district was not included in the Interior Ministry report, since only local Jews remained there. By the spring of 1942 most of the Jews concentrated along the Bug had disappeared, even though the Germans refused to accept them. They were murdered and burned in the Golta district; succumbed to typhus, starvation, and cold in the Balta district; faced typhus and starvation in the Pechora death camp; and were delivered to the Germans in the Tulchin district. Their disappearance is evident from a comparison of the data in table 22 with the data obtained in April 1942 following a gendarmerie headcount of Jews in the ghettos of Transnistria (see table 23). From this point on, 108,002 Jewish citizens of Romania who were sent directly to the Bug disappeared from the statistics, as if they had never existed. The gendarmerie reports refer only to Jews who were sent to the western districts of Transnistria and Jews who were taken to the Bug and survived the large extermination operations and the terrible winter of 1941–42. Thus, for example, the fictitious reports state that only 118,847 Jews were deported, rather than the true figure of at least 167,712. The purpose of this was to minimize the number of Jews who perished in the three-month period before the census of 1 April 1942, which found 88,187 survivors (including local Jews). The comparison shows that in reality at least 80,000 Romanian Jews (in fact, even more, since the figure of 88,187 included local Jews) disappeared within that period (167,712 minus 88,187, or 79,525), while the doctored statistics imply that only 30,000 Romanian Jews perished (118,347 minus 88,187, or 30,160). The local Jews, who numbered some 200,000, disappeared from the statistics and were mentioned only in the secret reports. This deception was typical.

Since 108,002 Jews were expunged from the statistics on deportees, the only alternative available to us is to trace the decline in the number of deportees who were registered in the partial statistics, most of which were classified. The secret reports that have recently come to light, as well as reports by the gendarmerie and the Autonomous Assistance Commission, now provide a more accurate picture of the extermination trail of the deportees, who were counted for the first time in March 1942, and of the local Jews, who were included in the statistics after April 1942, following the large-scale extermination operations. A number of important sources are available: (1) the headcount of Jews in Transnistria of April 1942, conducted by the Transnistrian administration (a newly discovered source); (2) statistics on the number of deportees compiled by the Autonomous Assistance Commission in February 1942 (including local Jews); (3) statistics compiled by the Autonomous Assistance Commission on 22 March 1943; (4) gendarmerie figures on the number of Jewish deportees in Transnistria of 1 September 1943; (5) a table titled "The Situation of the Ghettos and the Number of Jews in Transnistria," drawn up by the General Staff of the Third Army Corps, 1 November 1943 (including local Jews); and (6) a summary of the number of Jews in Transnistria, 15 November 1943, drawn up by the Presidency of the Council of Ministers on the basis of gendarmerie reports, as well as some other sources. In considering the discrepancies in these statistics, it should be borne in mind that the true number of deportees from Romania was at least 174,249 (see table 20) and that the number of Ukrainian Jews totaled some 200,000. Only these two figures provide an accurate picture of the extent of the destruction wrought by the Romanian occupation authorities in Transnistria.

The data indicate a steady decline in the number of Jews who survived in northern and parts of central Transnistria after March 1942 — that is, toward the end of the typhus epidemic in areas whose Jews were not deported to the Kingdom of Death. Clearly, any significant change in the number of Jews in a certain district was a function of the regime's policies and decisions. For example, the decline in the number of Jews in the Mogilev district from 54,604 in April 1942 to 34,974 in March 1943 was due to the evacuation of Jews from Mogilev city to the camps along the Bug, particularly to the Pechora camp or to the Skazinets camp, as well as to the transfer of Jews to the German authorities across the Bug. Likewise, the delivery of Jews in the Golta and Berezovka districts to German construction companies and to Nazi extermination units (after the great extermination operation in the winter of 1941–42) slashed the number of Jews in these districts. In April 1942 only 1,544 Jews of about 36,000 who had been brought from Odessa to the Berezovka district remained alive (in addition to the liquidation of tens of thousands of local Jews). To this number must be added over 2,000 Romanian Jews who were brought there in September 1942, of whom only 425 survived in January 1943. The Romanian-German liquidation operations in the Berezovka district have been described at length in this book, and we shall not go into them in detail here. Suffice it to say that any sudden change in the statistics relating to a specific district or date can be explained. Note that in June–September 1942 a further 6,537 Jews were deported from Czernowitz and Romania, bringing the total to 94,724 (88,187 Jews from the March 1942

TABLE 23. DECLINE IN THE NUMBER OF JEWS IN TRANSNISTRIA

	Transnistrian administration headcount, 1 April 1942[a]				Assistance Commission, 1 January 1943[b]	Assistance Commission, 22 March 1943[c]	Gendarmerie Inspectorate headcount, 1 September 1943[d]		
	Men	Women	Children	Total			From Bessarabia	From Bukovina	Total
Ananyev	—	—	—	—	—	—	13	18	31
Balta	6,288	6,475	3,741	16,504	23,500	23,035	6,229	6,248	12,477
Berezovka	—	—	—	1,544	425	425	42	24	66
Dubossary	62	99	67	228	—	—	—	13	13
Golta	169	503	206	878	3,500	3,620	820	54	874
Jugastru	2,599	2,749	2,459	7,807	6,200	6,000	745	880	1,625
Mogilev	20,846	22,673	10,985	54,504	35,000	34,974	5,103	26,899	32,002
Ochakov	3	2	6	11	—	—	117	491	608
Odessa	233	225	218	676	—	60	—	—	—
Ovidopol	—	—	—	—	—	—	3	29	32
Rybnitsa	254	548	569	1,371	1,416	600	380	119	499
Tiraspol	6	18	3	27	250	—	33	137	170
Tulchin	1,009	1,873	1,756	4,638	3,500	3,500	495	1,849	2,344
Total	31,469	35,165	20,010	88,188	73,791	72,214	13,980	36,761	50,741

continued

TABLE 23. DECLINE IN THE NUMBER OF JEWS IN TRANSNISTRIA *continued*

General Staff of the Third Army Corps, 1 Nov. 1943[e]	Ministry of the Interior, Nov. 1943[f]	Presidency of the Council of Ministers, 15 Nov. 1943[g]				
		From Bessarabia	From Bukovina	From Dorohoi	From the Regat	Total
479	13	5	1	7	—	13
20,713	12,477	4,790	4,703	58	309	9,860
304	206	39	43	1	123	206
233	17	—	16	—	1	17
2,464	874	510	6	2	133	651
823	1,654	755	893	4	2	1,654
40,306	34,500	5,117	24,459	6,199	51	35,826
7	—	—	—	—	—	—
168	—	—	—	—	—	—
23	—	—	—	—	—	—
1,513	362	382	57	23	—	462
366	363	29	252	28	54	363
3,371	875	56	711	103	5	875
70,770	51,341	11,683	31,141	6,425	678	49,927

a Headcount includes local Jews. Confidential report of Governor Alexianu, including tables, submitted to Antonescu's Civilian–Military Cabinet in the Presidency of the Council of Ministers, 23 May 1942, USHMM/RMFA, RG–25.006M, reel 11, "Jewish Problem," file 21, pp. 142–43. The report explicitly states that "these Jews had not yet been deported [beyond the Bug]."

b Headcount includes local Jews. Romanian Gendarmerie Inspectorate, data on the number of Jews in Transnistria who were deported from Bessarabia and Bukovina, by district and locality, 1 September 1943, in Carp, *Cartea neagră*, no. 244, 3:439–42.

c Jewish Center, data on aid provided between 18 February and 12 December 1942, in Ancel, *Documents*, vol. 5, doc. 170, pp. 306–14. The list includes partial data on the number of deportees in the ghettos of Transnistria compiled by members of the Autonomous Assistance Commission in Bucharest from information provided by the ghetto heads, before contact with the deportees was permitted.

d Autonomous Assistance Commission, "Statistical Data on the Number of Jewish Deportees in Transnistria," by locality, subdistrict, and district, appendix 1 to the commission's report of 22 March 1943, in Ancel, *Documents*, vol. 5, doc. 185, pp. 345–48.

e Headcount includes local Jews. General Staff of the Third Army Corps, "Situation in the Ghettos and the Number of Jews in Transnistria under Gendarmerie Supervision" (including local Jews), 1 November 1943, Moscow Special Archives, 493-1-6, p. 187. (Jews from Romania were also brought to Transnistria for forced labor and were not under gendarmerie supervision.)

f Data from the Interior Ministry on the number of Jews in the ghettos of Transnistria, "without the locals," as handed over to Filderman shortly before the start of the repatriation of the deportees, 17 November 1943, in Ancel, *Documents*, vol. 5, doc. 236, p. 518.

g Presidency of the Council of Ministers, data on the number of Jews in Transnistria, by deportation area, on 15 November 1943, USHMM/RMFA, RG–25.006M, reel 11, "Jewish Problem," file 22, p. 589. The document states that 796 Jews who were interned in the Grosulovo camp had to be added to the total, bringing the grand total up to 50,633. The data were collected in order to organize the repatriation operation. Antonescu approved only the repatriation of Jews from Dorohoi and the Regat and orphans. Indeed, these Jews alone were repatriated before the Soviet liberation of Transnistria.

gendarmerie headcount plus 6,537, or 94,724). Thus, in the space of a year (March 1942–March 1943), 22,510 Jews perished or were liquidated. This death toll was in addition to the large killing operations in Odessa and the Kingdom of Death and to the 60,000 victims of the typhus epidemic.

Until recently we had no clear picture of how many Ukrainian Jews were included in these censuses, due to the administration's attempts to hide the number of Ukrainian Jews who were liquidated between October 1941 and March 1942. In March 1942, when the Transnistrian administration was waiting for an opportunity to get rid of all Jews as part of the preparations for the Final Solution, a secret census was conducted that included the remnants of Ukrainian Jews (by number, not name). After Stalingrad the Romanian authorities omitted Ukrainian Jews from the official censuses but registered them separately in secret reports. Officially the Romanian administration only kept track of Jews who were deported from Bessarabia, Bukovina, and the Regat. Toward October 1943 it began differentiating between deportees from Bessarabia and Bukovina and deportees from the Regat (including the Dorohoi district), since Antonescu agreed to repatriate only the latter. The Autonomous Assistance Commission and all other Jewish organizations (excluding the Jewish Center) did not differentiate between types of Jews but recorded them all and tried to save them all.

After the establishment of the Romanian administration in Transnistria the Romanian authorities began deporting local Jews (as well as Romanian Jews) to the Kingdom of Death and along the River Bug, in preparation for their transfer to the German occupation authorities under the Tighina Agreement. The Ukrainian Jews, like most Romanian Jews who were deported to the Bug, ultimately perished or were killed. Until recently statistics were not available for these Jews. It now transpires that the Transnistrian administration conducted a headcount of local Jews, including their breakdown into men, women, and children. The administration even made a point of indicating places where the Jews had been killed by Germans rather than by its own men. Table 24 reproduces a table bearing Alexianu's signature that was drawn up by the Transnistrian administration on 23 May 1942.

Note that "Jews who were evacuated from Transnistria" was a euphemism for Jews who were killed by Romanians because the Germans refused to accept them. The exception was two transports totaling 14,500 Jews whom the Germans accepted and murdered on the spot.[12] Transnistria was the end of the line. The only place it led to was the next world. The table shows that the Romanians murdered 32,433 Ukrainian Jews as well as 32,819 Odessan Jews. The largest number of local Jews evacuated to the Kingdom of Death came from the Rybnitsa district.

TABLE 24. NUMBER OF JEWS EVACUATED FROM TRANSNISTRIA (LIQUIDATION OF LOCAL JEWS)

District	Men	Women	Children	Total
Ananyev	80	137	10	227
Balta	—	—	—	—
Berezovka	—	—	—	480[a]
Dubossary[b]	—	—	—	—
Golta	—	—	—	—
Jugstaru	—	—	—	—
Mogilev	—	—	—	—
Ochakov	—	—	—	—
Odessa	4,315	19,299	9,205	32,819
Ovidopol	6	8	9	23
Rybnitsa	—	—	—	25,436[c]
Tiraspol	284	267	237	788
Tulchin	1,054	2,532	1,893	5,479
Total	5,739	22,243	11,354	65,252

SOURCE: Reproduced from Governor Alexianu to Antonescu's Civilian-Military Cabinet in the Presidency of the Council of Ministers, notification of completion of statistical investigation based on the prefects' reports, together with three tables—Jews deported from Transnistria, Jews not yet deported, and Jews not slated for deportation, 23 May 1942. USHMM/RMFA, RG-25.006M, reel 11, "Jewish Problem," vol. 20, p. 135 (Jews who were deported).

[a] Since the evacuation took place in November 1941, the exact breakdown of evacuees by category (men, women, and children) is unknown.
[b] Evacuated by SS units of the German army before the entry of the Romanian administration.
[c] Since the officials were not required to keep records (at the time), the exact number and breakdown are not known.

The data, however, are not complete. We know, for example, that the Romanian authorities evacuated Jews from Balta to the Kingdom of Death, as we have seen throughout this book. Likewise, we know that thousands of Jews from the district and city of Mogilev were evacuated to the Bug and slaughtered. Another gross omission is the massacre of Odessan Jews following the detonation in the Romanian army headquarters and the evacuation of tens of thousands of Jews from the city and district in October–December 1941 and from the southern districts in general. Alexianu was careful to point out that the evacuation from Dubossary was carried out by SS units (i.e., that the Germans were responsible for the death of these Jews). The 20,000 or so Jews who were evacuated from

TABLE 25. CONCENTRATION OF JEWS IN THE KINGDOM OF DEATH AND IN THE BEREZOVKA DISTRICT, ACCORDING TO ROMANIAN SOURCES

	From Bessarabia Sept.–Nov. 1941[a]	From Rybnitsa district Sept.–Nov. 1941[b]	From Odessa city and district Oct.–Dec. 1941[c]	From Golta district Oct.–Nov. 1941[d]	By train from Odessa Jan.–March 1942[b]	Total	Soviet sources
No. of Jews	29,476	25,436	65,000	10,000 (approx.)	32,819	162,731	150,038[e]

[a] Vasiliu's report, USHMM/SRI, file 18844, vol. 3, p. 718 and map; reprinted in Ancel, *Transnistria, 1941–1942*, vol. 2, doc. 245, pp. 450–51.

[b] Alexianu to Antonescu's Civilian-Military Cabinet in the prime minister's office, announcing that he assembled the required statistics on the basis of prefects' reports, including three tables—Jews deported from Transnistria, Jews not deported, and Jews not slated for deportation, 23 May 1942, USHMM/RMFA, "Jewish Problem," vol. 20, p. 135; reprinted in Ancel, *Transnistria, 1941–1942*, vol. 3, doc. 733, pp. 1370–73.

[c] Gendarmerie commander in Transnistria to the administration, 11 September 1942, USHMM/RMFA, "Jewish Problem," vol. 20, p. 161; reprinted in Ancel, *Transnistria, 1941–1942*, vol. 3, doc. 946, p. 1738.

[d] Isopescu report of 13 November 1941, USHMM/NOA, 2178-1-66, pp. 151–151b; reprinted in Ancel, *Transnistria, 1941–1942*, vol. 2, doc. 165, pp. 315–17.

[e] On 31 December 1944 the Communist Party's district committee pointed out that 115,038 people (Jews) were murdered in the camps in the Domanevka subdistrict and another 35,000 in the Berezovka district. Report by the District Committee of the Communist Party, [Obkom], Odessa, District Archive of the Communist Party in Odessa, Partinii Arhiv, Odescovo obkoma Kompartii Ukraini, fond 2, opis 2, delo 52, p. 25.

Dubossary were all buried in two mass graves. The secret document shows a large disparity between the number of men and the number of women and children who were evacuated from Odessa and murdered in Berezovka.

The data on the scale of destruction of local Jews mounted following a directive by the Presidency of the Council of Ministers on 22 July 1942 and a reminder on 14 August 1942 to the governors of Bessarabia, Bukovina, and Transnistria requesting "data on the deportation of Jews from Transnistria" and recommendations for further deportations.[13] On 11 September 1942 Alexianu submitted new data on the deportation of Jews from southern Transnistria — data that had not appeared in previous statistics on the evacuation of Jews from Transnistria. This secret document, which Alexianu titled "The Movement of Local Jews" (i.e., the liquidation of local Jews), stated that 65,000 Jews from the Odessa district "had disappeared," as well as an unspecified number of local Jews from the Berezovka, Ananyev, Ovidopol, and Ochakov districts. The governor also referred to 4,000 local Jews from the Mogilev district, without specifying their fate.[14] We know that these Jews were forcibly transferred to the Skazinets and Pechora camps in the spring and summer of 1942 and that most of them perished.

Classified Romanian documents that have only recently come to light indicate that in April 1942 about 163,000 Jews, most of them local, were concentrated in camps in the Kingdom of Death and in the Berezovka district.

Today we know that the Romanian administration found at least about 200,000 Ukrainian Jews in Transnistria: 25,436 in the Rybnitsa district (see table 24), 65,000 in Odessa (city and district), about 10,000 in the Golta district, 32,819 who were evacuated from Odessa by train (see table 24), 22,000 corpses discovered in mass graves in Dalnic (and another 5,000 at least who were shot or hanged in Odessa in late October 1941), 28,221 in western Transnistria, and 4,000 who were deported from Mogilev and perished.[15] To these official Romanian statistics must be added the thousands of Jews from the Tulchin district who were interned and liquidated in the Pechora death camp, about 7,000 Jews who were executed by the Germans in Bar and Balchi (on the Romanian side of the border with German occupied territory in northern Transnistria), and a few thousand in the Balta district who were transferred to Bogdanovka. This brings us to a grand total of some 200,000 local Jews.

Evidently, even this total understates the number of more local Jews, since statistics are unavailable for many towns in northern and central Transnistria.[16] Moreover, tens of thousands of Jews were shot by members of the Einsatzgruppe. The total is therefore closer to 300,000 than 200,000. We see, therefore, that most Transnistrian Jews (about 300,000) were unable to flee eastward due to the German army's impressive victories at the start of the war and its rapid advance.

Indeed, many testimonies indicate that most of the Jews who attempted to flee eastward were forced to retrace their steps because the German army had preceded them.

We are today in a position to form an accurate assessment of how many Ukrainian Jews were murdered by the Romanians in Transnistria or for whose death the Romanian administration was responsible. The answer can be found only in classified Romanian documents that have recently come to light and not in testimonies and evaluations. According to the aforementioned SSI report, in early December 1941, 28,221 local Jews were still alive west of the Zhmerinca-Odessa railway line: 14,000 in the Mogilev district, 4,000 in Mogilev city, 6,232 in the Yampol district, none in the Dubossary district, 987 in the Rybnitsa district, and 3,002 in the Tiraspol district (who, according to the report, had been transferred to Bogdanovka; another 70 had been left behind as useful craftsmen). There were still 44,417 Jews in Odessa city, bringing the total to 72,638. This number does not include tens of thousands of Ukrainian Jews who lived or had been transferred east of the Zhmerinca-Odessa line (the Bug region) or were in transit.

A second document on the number of local Jews is a report by the Gendarmerie Inspectorate in Transnistria dated December 1942, specifying 80,087 Jews in the province, of whom 29,971 were locals.[17] This implies that, from September 1941 (the start of Romanian rule in Transnistria) until December 1942, about 170,000 Ukrainian Jews were murdered or perished, according to official Romanian documents.

On 1 November 1943 Third Army headquarters pointed out that there were 70,770 Jews in Transnistria.[18] According to the gendarmerie headcount of September 1943 there were 50,741 Romanian Jews (from Bessarabia, Bukovina, and the Regat; see table 23) in Transnistria. In late November 1943, after the census of all deportees from Romania was taken, Radu Lecca, the commissioner for Jewish affairs, stated that all the Jews in Transnistria, apart from the 50,741 deportees, were locals.[19] It follows that in November 1943 the number of Ukrainian Jews totaled 20,000 (see table 23).

We may, therefore, infer that between September 1941 and November 1943 at least 180,000 Ukrainian Jews were liquidated. Most of them were murdered by the Romanians themselves, succumbed to starvation and typhus, or froze to death. The remainder, especially in the Berezovka district, were handed over to the Germans for liquidation.

Official Romanian documents that were compiled in real time show that there were fewer than 800,000 Jews in Greater Romania on the eve of the war and that there was no appreciable subsequent change in the number of Jews in the Regat and southern Transylvania. The 1941 census and the census of residents of Jewish blood corroborate the accuracy of this assertion.

The number of victims in the territory that remained under Romanian sovereignty on the eve of the war against the Soviet Union was relatively small. About 200 Jews were killed in the Dorohoi pogrom in July 1940, several hundred were pushed off moving trains, about 400 were shot to death during the Galați pogrom in July 1940, about 150 were killed before and during the Bucharest pogrom, about 15,000 were killed in the Iași pogrom or died from asphyxiation in the death trains, about 1,300 who were deported from Romania in the autumn of 1942 were executed or met their death in Transnistria, and several hundred more from the forced labor detachments perished in work-related accidents, from disease, or from the terrible living conditions — bringing the total up to about 20,000 Jews.

The extermination and deportation operations took place mainly in areas that Romania was forced to cede to the Soviet Union in June 1941 — Bessarabia and northern Bukovina — as well as in southern Bukovina and in the Dorohoi district of the Regat, in accordance with Ion Antonescu's decision to deport Jews from these areas. In 1930, 300,059 Jews lived in these territories, excluding the Dorohoi district (see table 13), and 312,991 including Dorohoi. Under Soviet rule (July 1940–July 1941) the number of Jews in these regions grew by several tens of thousands, but this estimate cannot be corroborated due to the lack of relevant data. Consequently, this population increase was not taken into account in the calculations made in this study.

The discovery of classified Romanian documents showed that fewer Jews were murdered in the first wave of killings than was originally thought. In July 1941 there were at least 112,000 Bessarabian Jews and 82,478 Jews in Bukovina (excluding the Dorohoi district) — a total of 195,000 (see tables 14 and 15). About 105,000 Romanian Jews of the 300,059 Jews who lived in Bessarabia and Bukovina in 1930 disappeared in July–August 1941, during and immediately after the battles to recapture the area. In Bessarabia, 25,000 were murdered.[20] About 15,000 Jews were killed in the towns and villages of northern Bukovina by the local population (Romanians and Ukrainians) and the Romanian army; about 32,000 Jews were deported in the "hasty deportations" of July–August 1941; and about 20,000 were killed on the spot. About 3,000 were killed in Czernowitz in the days following the occupation by Nazi extermination units and by the Romanian army

TABLE 26. JEWS KILLED BY ORDER OF THE ROMANIAN STATE, ACCORDING TO OFFICIAL ROMANIAN STATISTICS

Liquidation and deportation operations	The Regat and southern Transylvania	Dorohoi district	Bessarabia and Bukovina			Total victims (rounded)
			Bessarabia	Bukovina	Combined	
Victims of the 1940 and 1941 pogroms	about 18,000[a]	—	—	—	—	—
Victims of the order to "cleanse the ground"			45,000[b]	20,000[c]		
Deportees to Transnistria	2,016[d]	(11,667)[e]	—	—	174,249[f]	
Alive 1943–44	678[g]	(6,425)[g]	11,683	34,149	—	
Victims of the deportations	1,338	5,242	—	—	128,417	
Total victims (rounded)	20,000	5,000	—	—	194,000	220,000

[a] On the Bucharest pogrom, see chapter 11, "The Torture Centers"; on the Dorohoi pogrom and the practice of throwing Jews off moving trains, see chapter 6, "The Pogroms of Summer 1940"; on the Iași pogrom, see chapter 33, "The Death Toll."

[b] This figure includes 25,000 Jews who were counted and murdered in Bessarabia (Niculescu report, USHMM/RMFA, RG–25.006M, reel 11, "Jewish Problem," vol. 20) and 20,000 who were murdered in the hasty deportations. It is based on any official Romanian statistic. It is based on data submitted by the mayor of Czernowitz, the righteous of the nations Traian Popovici, whereby upon the return of Romanian rule to Czernowitz and its surroundings, there were 70,000 Jews there. He did not know where the remainder had disappeared. See Carp, Cartea neagră, 3:182. The official count showed 53,809 Jews (see table 13). Likewise, this minimum estimate of Jews who were murdered in the first wave of massacres is based on a study, discussed in detail in chapter 17 herein, on the liquidation of Jews in the towns and villages by the Romanian army and the local population immediately after the territory was occupied.

[c] This figure does not appear in any official Romanian statistic. See table 19 herein.

[d] Broken down as follows: 9,367 deportees in 1941 (table 15), 360 deportees in 1942 (coded telegram from Gen. Corneliu Calotescu, governor of Bukovina, to the Presidency of the Council of Ministers, 22 June 1942, USHMM/RMFA, RG–25.006M, reel 11, "Jewish Problem," vol. 20, p. 215; among the deportees were 360 Jews—196 men, 82 women, and 82 children—from Dorohoi [p. 206]), and 1,940 from the Herța subdistrict. The Herța subdistrict also belonged to the Dorohoi district and was annexed in 1940 to the Soviet Union. In 1930 there were 1,940 Jews there (Congresul Mondial Evreesc, Populația evreeească, 28). The number is in parentheses because it is included in the number of deportees from Bessarabia and Bukovina.

[f] Table 20 herein, real-time reports.

[g] Table 23 herein, 15 November 1943.

and police, and even more in Kishinev. The rest are unaccounted for. The only thing we know about them for sure is that most of them were killed.

This chapter also shows how the tens of thousands of Jews who tried to escape suffered the same fate as those who remained, because of the rapid advance of the German army and the explicit order to shoot them. About 76,000 Jews who survived the massacres perpetrated by the Romanian authorities and the local population in Bessarabia were deported to Transnistria (55,867 plus 20,000 killed by the German SS in the Ukraine during the hasty deportations). It has been proved that most of the Jewish population in northern Bukovina did not try to escape and that most of the Jews in the small towns and villages were slaughtered. A total of 86,408 Jews were deported from Bukovina in 1941 and 1942 and a further 11,667 from the Dorohoi district, bringing the total number of deportees to Transnistria to 174,249. In November 1943 there were about 50,000 survivors from all the deportation areas, including the Jews of Dorohoi. Thus, a total of 129,000 Romanian Jews were killed or perished in or en route to Transnistria. The Romanian occupation authority found at least 200,000 local Jews alive in Transnistria. The massive killing operations launched by the Romanian occupation regime in Odessa and the Kingdom of Death and during the deportation campaigns and the delivery of Jews to the German killing squads resulted in the death of about 180,000 of these Jews. Thus, altogether, the Romanian authorities were responsible for the disappearance of at least 400,000 Jews.

The secret documents that were discovered in the Foreign Ministry and Interior Ministry archives indicate the scale of the deportation and killing operations and prove that the Romanian government kept accurate statistics of the number of Jews, including Ukrainian Jews, it liquidated or deported. These documents further show that the Romanian government doctored the figures on paper so as to minimize its responsibility for their death. Without such data we would have been forced to rely on estimates and testimonies. Our statistical analysis must also include tens of thousands of Jews who were murdered mainly in Bessarabia when the province was recaptured and the massacre of the entire Jewish population in the villages and towns.

In conclusion, the Romanian state was responsible for the liquidation of at least 400,000 Jews, but the true figure was almost certainly several tens of thousands higher. Note that this conclusion is not based on a comparison with the number of Jews who lived in Romania in 1930 but rather on a comparison of the number of Jews who lived there in July–August 1941 with those who were there in 1944.

TABLE 27. NATURAL INCREASE OF THE JEWISH POPULATION, 1940–43

	Births	Deaths	Natural increase	Marriages
1940	2,672	4,978	-2,306	—
1941	3,738	9,767	-6,029	—
1942	1,520	4,813	-3,293	2,582
Jan.–Oct. 1943	1,292	3,302	-2,088	1,649

SOURCE: Data on births and deaths for the years 1941–43 are from Centrala Evreilor din România, "Buletinul demografic al populației evreești din România" [Demographic bulletin of the Jewish population in Romania], no. 10 (April 1944): 3, 7 (live births). Data for 1940 and on marriages are from Congresul Mondial Evreesc, *Populația evreească*, 57, 86. Figures for 1940 do not include the Jews of northern Bukovina.

SPECIAL PROBLEMS

This statistical study has omitted a number of events and issues that could affect the data on the number of Jews in Romania in the years 1940–44. These issues are: the legal basis for the definition of who was a Jew and how this affected the accuracy and reliability of the census of residents of Jewish blood, the birth and death rates among the Jewish population in deportation-free areas, and emigration to Palestine.

The 1942 census found that of the overall Jewish population of about 300,000, 2,942 were children of mixed marriages, 4,714 were Jews who had converted, and 4,214 were married to non-Jews. The vast majority of Jews from mixed marriages were Christians. Perhaps another several hundred or thousand quarter- or even half-Jews managed to avoid being registered as Jews. This situation did not, however, alter the general picture provided by the census, since these Romanians "of Jewish blood" were not Jews, did not consider themselves Jewish, and did not live as Jews. "The census was effectively of the Jewish population only."[21] The April 1941 census found that 302,050 Jews lived in the truncated area of Romania. In May 1942, 275,068 Jews were counted in the Regat and southern Transylvania and another 17,081 in Bukovina (mostly in Czernowitz), providing a total of 292,149 Jews.[22] The number of Jews continued to decline, and on 1 January 1943 was estimated at 289,952.[23] On 1 November 1943 the number of Jews throughout Romania was estimated at 287,804.[24]

Table 27 shows a negative natural increase of the Jewish population and an absolute drop of 13,716 Jews in a period of less than four years.

Although the overall number of Jews in Romania did not change, a Siguranța report pointed out certain fluctuations in the Jewish population in the provin-

TABLE 28. COMPARISON BETWEEN THE CENSUS OF RESIDENTS OF
JEWISH BLOOD AND THE SIGURANȚA STATISTICS

Locality	Census of residents of Jewish blood 20 May 1942	Siguranța statistics	Date
Arad	9,406	9,521	1 June 1941
Arad	9,406	11,882	January 1942
Bacău	13,038	12,870	Late 1941
Botoşani	17,441	20,753	Late 1942
Bucharest	98,048	120,000 (approximately)	May 1943
Fălticeni	5,085	5,569	1941
Focşani	1,440	1,425	November 1941
Hârlău	2,023	2,110	November 1941
Huşi	2,096	2,011	December 1941
Lugoj	1,241	1,662	Summer 1942
Moineşti	1	1,554	Summer 1941
Ploieşti	2,075	1,417	July 1941
Ploieşti	2,075	2,094	April 1942
Podul Iloaiei	0	1,171	March 1942
Roman	6,485	6,237	May 1942
Târgu Ocna	1	1,171	May 1941
Timişoara	11,788	11,809	Summer 1942
Oravița	401	473	Summer 1942

SOURCE: The number of Jews in cities and towns apart from Bucharest can be found in the
Siguranța files and the Interior Ministry files on "The Mood of the Population" ["Starea de
spirit a populației"] for the years 1941–42; copy in USHMM/SRI, RG-25.004M, reels 7, 8, and
9. The estimate of the number of Jews in Bucharest in May 1943 is based on the report of the
minister of the interior, C. Z. Vasiliu, to the Presidency of the Council of Ministers, 30 April
1943, USHMM/RMFA, RG-25.006M, reel 14, "Jewish Problem," vol. 25, p. 88b.

cial towns. The reasons for the discrepancies between the census data and the
Siguranța data stem from evacuations or other movement of some Jews. In July
1941, 1,893 Jews were taken to Arad after being evacuated from towns and villages in the district. Several hundred Jewish refugees from Poland had escaped
to Botoşani, and the Siguranța knew of their existence. Likewise, Jews from
towns in the Dorohoi district fled to Botoşani in order to escape deportation
to Transnistria. All the Jews of Târgu Ocna were evacuated to Bacău, as were
the Jews of Moineşti. In April 1942 all the Jews of Podul Iloaiei were evacuated
to Iaşi.

The German embassy also monitored data on the number of Jews in Romania, with the full cooperation of the director of the Central Bureau of Statistics, Sabin Manuilă, and his deputy, Arthur Golopenția. In July 1942 the deputy director reported directly to the "Right Honorable Mr. Richter" that there were about 290,000 Jews in the whole of Romania and even noted that, in the wake of the last deportations, the number of Jews had dropped "in the deportation districts" of southern Bukovina "by several hundred heads" (*einige Hundert Köpfe*).[25] Richter himself summarized the findings of the census of residents of Jewish blood, including a breakdown by age, profession, intermarriage, mixed-race children, and converts to Christianity.[26] A German government office in Vienna analyzed the results of the general census of 1941 and drew up a comparative chart of all the general censuses in Romania since 1899, in Bessarabia since 1897 (when it was part of Russia), and in Bukovina and Transylvania since 1880 (then part of Austro-Hungarian Empire). In their analysis of Romanian Jewry, the Nazis publicized what the Romanians had been afraid to, namely that "Bessarabian Jewry in the towns and villages . . . has been almost entirely exterminated in the war."[27]

In conclusion, although more Jews survived in Romania than in any other country belonging to Germany's *allies* (not occupied country, as Romanian historians, until recently, would have had us believe), contemporary Romanian sources show that the Antonescu regime and Romania itself slaughtered at least 400,000 Jews, including 180,000 Ukrainian Jews.[28] Of all of Nazi Germany's allies, Romania made the greatest "contribution" to exterminating the Jewish people. While it handed over fewer Jews to the Nazi killing machine than neighboring Hungary, Romania used its army, gendarmerie, and other forces to commit genocide — out of a desire to curry favor with the Nazi regime, out of national interest, and above all, out of a profound hatred for the Jewish people. Romania also set up an extensive network of ghettos and camps in Transnistria for the internment of those Jews who had survived the first exterminations and the hardships of deportation. The Romanians were determined to eliminate the Jews of Romania and the Jewish remnant in Transnistria by transferring them across the Bug to German-occupied Ukraine, delivering them to the Nazi extermination machine, or other methods. The tension that beset Romanian-German relations in the autumn of 1942 and the setbacks on the Russian and North African fronts changed the Romanian government's plans regarding the fate of Romanian Jewry and the surviving deportees in Transnistria.

Notes

Abbreviations

AMD   Archives of the Ministry of Defence
MSM   Marele Stat Major (Supreme General Command) Archives
NOA   Nikolyaev Oblast Archives
RMFA   Romanian Ministry of Foreign Affairs
SRI   Romanian Intelligence Service Archives
SSARM   Serviciul de Stat de Arhivă al Republicii Moldova (Central Archives of the Republic of Moldova)
USHMM   U.S. Holocaust Memorial Museum, Washington DC
YVA   Yad Vashem Archives, Jerusalem

In citations to manuscript materials, details such as "fond 2178, opis 1, delo 42" are abbreviated as "2178-1-42."

Introduction

1. See Ancel, "German-Romanian Relations"; Ancel, "Impact of the Course of the War."
2. W. Filderman, YVA, P-6/68, p. 99.
3. See Mendelsohn, *Jews of East Central Europe*; Livezeanu, *Cultural Politics*.
4. Cuza, *Jidanii în război*, 22; Vasiliu, *Situaţia demografică*, 35. The data on the number of Jews appear in different forms in the various drafts of Filderman's memoirs and in a booklet he published on the number of Jews in the ranks of the Romanian army who fell in the First World War, Filderman, *Adevărul asupra problemei evreeşti*.
5. I. B. Bârsan, "Cronica financiară," *Democraţia*, 10 October 1923, p. 54; *Procesul marei trădări naţionale*, 152.
6. *Buletinul Demografic*, 154–55, 344–45; copy in Ancel, *Documents*, 1:274–76. See also data on the number of Jews in 1930 published by the Jewish Center's statistics department in 1942: Centrala Evreilor, *Breviarul statistic*.
7. Schwarzfeld, "Evreii în literatura populară română." See also Ancel, "Image of the Jew"; and Oişteanu, *Imaginea evreului*, and the English translation, *Inventing the Jew*.
8. "Dogme şi canoane ecumenice împotriva evreilor" [Ecumenical dogma and law against Jews], *Porunca Vremii*, 2 November 1940.
9. In the 1878 Berlin Congress the European powers that had defeated Turkey demanded that the young Romanian state grant equal rights to Jews, having duly noted that Romanian Jews had taken part in the war against Turkey. Under pressure from the powers, the congress passed a resolution stating that religious faith could not serve as a pretext for the denial of civil and political rights. After a long series of antisemitic demonstrations and excesses, an antisemitic campaign in the press, an antisemitic speech by Prince Carol I (who spoke of the danger of the "Jewish invasion" of Moldova), and a series of promises that were made but

not kept, an amendment was made to article 7 of the 1866 Constitution on 7 October 1879, stating that Jews, too, could receive citizenship, but only on an individual basis, after each case had been brought before both houses of parliament and approved by a majority. This amendment effectively abolished the articles referring to the emancipation of Jews in the resolutions of the 1878 Berlin Congress. The government tried hard to phrase the article so that, formally at least, it met the conditions of the peace treaty and the conditions on which the powers' recognition of Romania's independence was based, but it introduced restrictions that altered the intentions and spirit of the powers' resolution and effectively foiled the emancipation of the Jews. Moreover, it was after this that the antisemitic concepts of foreign intervention and attempts to coerce Romania into granting civil rights to Jews crystallized.

10. Hașdeu, *Studie asupra judasimului*, 30.

11. Conta, *Cine sunt jidanii?*

12. *Apel către toți românii.*

13. Cuza, *Invățătura lui Isus.*

14. Filderman, *Memoirs and Diaries*, 336.

15. Fătu and Spălățelu, *Garda de Fier*, 33–106; *Impotriva fascismului*, 7–29.

16. Codreanu, *Circulări și manifeste*, 3.

17. Filderman, *Memoirs and Diaries*, 466.

18. Mușat and Ardeleanu, *România*, 237–38.

19. *Monitorul Oficial*, parliamentary session of 24 November 1936, p. 34.

20. Nedelcu, *Viața politiă*, 44.

21. Filderman, *Memoirs and Diaries*, 463.

22. Goga, *Precursori.*

23. Mușat and Ardeleanu, *România*, 253–54.

24. *Politics and Political Parties in Roumania*, 171–79.

25. World Jewish Congress, "Le nouveau gouvernement roumain et le problème des minorités et des israélites en particulier," report, 1938, YVA, Filderman Collection, P-6/Paris, pp. 1, 3.

26. Mușat and Ardeleanu, *România*, 257.

27. *Apărarea Națională*, 15 July 1935.

1. The Goga Government

1. Report by Neville Laski, one of the two presidents of the Joint Foreign Committee of the Board of Deputies of British Jews, 17 January 1938, on his visit to Romania and on the situation of the Jews there during the last two weeks of the Goga government, in Ancel, *Documents*, vol. 1, doc. 21, p. 223.

2. Interview with King Carol II, *Daily Herald*, 10 January 1938. This interview and speeches and interviews with Octavian Goga and Istrate Micescu were attached to the petition sent to the League of Nations by the World Jewish Congress in mid-January 1938: "La situation des juifs en Roumanie: Pétition du comité exécutif du Congrès Juif Mondial soumise au Conseil de la Société des Nations" (hereafter Petition, 1938), available in Ancel, *Documents*, vol. 1, doc. 19, pp. 188–215.

3. Ambri, *I falsi fascismi*, 245.

4. O. Goga, "Cuvântarea-program," *Timpul*, 2 January 1938 (hereafter Goga, platform speech); copy in Ancel, *Documents*, vol. 1, doc. 16, pp. 183–85.

5. *Porunca Vremii*, 5 January 1938.

6. World Jewish Congress, Petition, 1938, in Ancel, *Documents*, vol. 1, doc. 19, p. 39; see also Goga, platform speech, in Ancel, *Documents*, vol. 1, doc. 16, pp. 183–85.

7. World Jewish Congress, Petition, 1938, in Ancel, *Documents*, vol. 1, doc. 19, p. 39; see also Goga, platform speech, in Ancel, *Documents*, vol. 1, doc. 16, pp. 183–85.

8. World Jewish Congress, Petition, 1938, in Ancel, *Documents*, vol. 1, doc. 19, p. 39.

9. *Universul*, 31 December 1937.

10. World Jewish Congress, Petition, 1938, in Ancel, *Documents*, vol. 1, doc. 19, p. 39.

11. Interview with the king in *Daily Herald*, 6 January 1938.

12. World Jewish Congress, Petition, 1938, in Ancel, *Documents*, vol. 1, doc. 19, p. 41.

13. World Jewish Congress, Petition, 1938, in Ancel, *Documents*, vol. 1, doc. 19, p. 41. Goga and other antisemites argued that Romania had suffered four Jewish invasions: (1) in 1914–15 when the Jews of Galicia fled to Transylvania for fear of the Russians; (2) in 1919 when the Jews of Hungary, "who had set up the Hungarian Soviet Republic," fled to Transylvania for fear of Horthy's soldiers; (3) in 1921 when the Jews of the Ukraine fled to Bessarabia for fear of the Polish army, which had reached the outskirts of Kiev; and (4) when "about 30,000 German Jews" fled to Romania as Hitler came to power and began his persecutions. "They arranged matters so that they could stay on in Romania," stressed Goga. See *Daily Herald*, 6 January 1938; Ancel, *Documents*, vol. 1, doc. 16, pp. 209–10.

The Jewish organizations in Romania, and Wilhelm Filderman in particular, denied that these Jews had remained in Romania and showed, with the help of official data, that the numbers were inflated for purposes of incitement and that most of the Jewish refugees who had fled from the Ukraine in the early 1920s because of the civil war and the Petlyura pogroms had long since left Romania. Their efforts, however, were abortive. Antonescu, too, upon assuming power was convinced that there were about three million Jews in Romania (*Procesul marei trădări naționale*, 152).

14. *Paris Soir*, 10 January 1938.

15. *Paris Soir*, 10 January 1938; see also Ancel, *Documents*, vol. 1, pp. 211–12.

16. *Universul*, 31 December 1937; and *Curentul*, 2 January 1938.

17. *Porunca Vremii*, 5 January 1938.

18. *Universul*, 7 January 1938.

19. *Curentul*, 2 January 1938.

20. *Țara Noastră*, 5 January 1938.

21. *Monitorul Oficial*, 14 January 1938.

22. Alexandru Vaida Voevod, a minister in the Cristea government, refused to accede to the request that the Jewish leader Theodor Fischer addressed to him on this matter. "Exposé du Dr. Singer en date du 10 Mars 1938 à bord du steamer 'Polonia' faisant route vers la Palestine" (hereafter Singer testimony), in Ancel, *Documents*, vol. 8, doc. 143, p. 179.

23. *Curentul*, 2 January 1938.

24. *Curentul*, 2 January 1938.

25. *Curentul*, 2 January 1938.

26. "Decret-lege privitor la revizuirea cetățăniei," *Monitorul Oficial*, no. 18, 22 January 1938. See also separate publication with the Romanian text and its German translation in Ancel, *Documents*, vol. 8, doc. 141, pp. 162–77.

27. *Curentul*, 2 January 1938.

28. *Neamul Românesc*, 5 January 1938.

29. Report by Neville Laski, 17 January 1938, in Ancel, *Documents*, vol. 1, doc. 21, p. 220; see also Filderman, *Memoirs and Diaries*, 458–59.

30. *Universul*, 6 January 1938.

31. Transcript of Laski's talk with Romanian foreign minister Nicolae Petrescu-Comnen and Silviu Dragomir, general commissar for minorities, undated (hereafter report on talk with Comnen), in Ancel, *Documents*, vol. 1, doc. 23, p. 227.

32. *Timpul*, 21 January 1938.

33. *Timpul*, 1 January 1938.

34. *Jewish Telegraphic Agency Bulletin*, 11 January 1938.

35. *Timpul*, 1 January 1938.

36. *Universul*, 4 January 1938.

37. World Jewish Congress, "Le nouveau gouvernement roumain el le problème des minorities et des israélites en particulier," report, 1938, YVA, Filderman Collection, P-6/ Paris, p. 12.

38. *Frontul*, 5 January 1938.

39. *Țara Noastră*, 3 March 1938, quoted in Mușat and Ardeleanu, *România*, 785.

40. Goga, platform speech, in Ancel, *Documents*, vol. 1, doc. 16, pp. 183–85.

41. World Jewish Congress, Petition, 1938, in Ancel, *Documents*, vol. 1, doc. 19, p. 8.

42. World Jewish Congress, Petition, 1938, in Ancel, *Documents*, vol. 1, doc. 19, p. 8.

43. *Țara Noastră*, 6 January 1938.

44. *Paris Soir*, 10 January 1938; *Paris Midi*, 6 January 1938.

45. *Daily Herald*, 10 January 1938; *Epoque*, 5 January 1938.

46. *Apărarea Națională*, 1 May 1923; *Democrația*, 10 October 1923.

47. *Curentul*, 2 January 1938; *Universul*, 9 January 1938.

48. World Jewish Congress, "Le nouveau gouvernement roumain et le problème des minorités et des israélites en particulier," report, 1938, YVA, Filderman Collection, P-6/ Paris, pp. 15–18.

49. J. and J. Tharaud, "M. Goga se justifie par les chiffres mais ces chiffres sont faux," *Paris Soir*, 18 January 1938.

50. Memorandum on the revision of citizenship presented to the minister of justice by the Central Council of Romanian Jewry, 1938, YVA, 0-60/Romania, p. 5.

51. Report on talk with Comnen, in Ancel, *Documents*, vol. 1, doc. 23, p. 226.

52. Mușat and Ardeleanu, *România*, 758.

53. See *Politics and Political Parties in Romania*, 278.

54. Report by Neville Laski, 17 January 1938, in Ancel, *Documents*, vol. 1, doc. 21, pp. 220–21.

55. *Egalitatea*, 5 January 1938; *Renașterea Noastră*, 5 January 1938.

56. World Jewish Congress, Petition, 1938, in Ancel, *Documents*, vol. 1, doc. 19, p. 11.

57. Muşat and Ardeleanu, *România*, 781.

58. *Curentul*, 29 July 1937; see also his speech to a special convention of lawyers, in *Ţara Noastră*, 4 May 1937.

59. The activity is described at length in a classified report of the World Jewish Congress on the situation in Romania, 15 January 1938, YVA, P-6/Paris.

60. Workers' Circle Friendly Society in conjunction with Jewish trade unions, labour and cultural organisations, "Memorandum on the Position of the Jews in Romania," London, 1938, p. 7.

61. Nedelcu, *Viaţa politică*, 193, 196.

62. See *Dziennik Narodowy*, 3 January 1938; *Der Angriff*, 3 January 1938.

63. Goga, platform speech, in Ancel, *Documents*, vol. 1, doc. 16, pp. 183–85; Muşat and Ardeleanu, *România*, 778–79.

64. Savu, *Dictatura regală*, 112; *Timpul*, 1 December 1937.

65. *De Telegraph*, 11 January 1938.

66. Classified report by Laski dated 26 January 1938, on the one hundredth session of the council of the League of Nations, YVA, P-6/Paris, p. 1.

67. Report by Neville Laski, 17 January 1938, in Ancel, *Documents*, vol. 1, doc. 21, p. 221.

68. World Jewish Congress, report on the situation of the Jews in Romania, 25 January 1939 (hereafter January 1939 report), YVA, Filderman Archive, P-6/Paris, p. 3.

69. Muşat and Ardeleanu, *România*, 779.

70. Muşat and Ardeleanu, *România*, 781.

2. King Carol II's Dictatorship

1. Report on talk with Comnen, in Ancel, *Documents*, vol. 1, doc. 23, p. 227.

2. World Jewish Congress, report on the situation in Romania after the fall of Goga's government, 10 September 1938 (hereafter report on situation after Goga), YVA, Filderman Archive, P-6/Paris, p. 4; report on the meeting with the ambassador, in Ancel, *Documents*, vol. 1, doc. 22, p. 225.

3. Report on talk with Comnen, in Ancel, *Documents*, vol. 1, doc. 23, p. 227.

4. January 1939 report, YVA, Filderman Archive, P-6/Paris, p. 3.

5. January 1939 report, YVA, Filderman Archive, P-6/Paris, p. 2.

6. January 1939 report, YVA, Filderman Archive, P-6/Paris, p. 2.

7. For the content of the talks between Hitler and the Romanian ambassador in Berlin on 23 April 1938, see Ancel, *Documents*, vol. 9, doc. 6, pp. 13–15; report by the Romanian ambassador in Oslo on aggressive intentions of Nazi foreign policy toward Romania, 30 September 1938, in Ancel, *Documents*, vol. 9, doc. 10, pp. 22–24; transcript of the talk between Foreign Minister Gafencu and Helmut Wohltat, the economic attaché, 22 February 1939, in Ancel, *Documents*, vol. 9, doc. 22, pp. 42–43; transcript of the talk between Gheorghe Brătianu and Marshall Goering in Berlin on 6 November 1938, in Ancel, *Documents*, vol. 9, doc. 33, pp. 63–66; excerpt of the diary of the Romanian politician L. Argetoianu on his meetings with Goering in Berlin, 18 November 1938, in Ancel, *Documents*, vol. 9, doc. 34, pp. 67–72; directives by Foreign Minister Gafencu to a number of ministers concerning the relationship between Germany and Romania, 23 January 1939, in Ancel, *Documents*, vol. 9,

doc. 36, pp. 74–76; and transcript of the talk between the foreign minister and Fabricius, the German legate in Bucharest, 30 January 1939, in Ancel, *Documents*, vol. 9, doc. 378, pp. 77–78. Fabricius complained that Jews such as Max Auschnitt, Oscar Kaufman, and Aristide Blank were exerting too strong an influence on public opinion in Romania and claimed that Romanian policy was directed against poor Jews only, not rich ones.

8. January 1939 report, YVA, Filderman Archive, P-6/Paris, p. 3.

9. Călinescu, *Insemnări politice*, 426.

10. Călinescu, *Insemnări politice*, 400.

11. Testimony of Aureliu Weiss, YVA, O-33/785, pp. 3–4.

12. January 1939 report, YVA, Filderman Archive, P-6/Paris, p. 3.

13. World Jewish Congress, report on the situation of the Jews in Romania, 23 February 1939 (hereafter February 1939 report), YVA, P-6/Paris, p. 3.

14. World Jewish Congress, report on the situation in Transylvania, 23 August 1939 (hereafter report on situation in Transylvania), YVA, P-6/Paris, pp. 1, 3. Communist historiography claims that the dictatorship "reverted to the traditional policy whereby the Jewish problem was dealt with from a constitutional and humanitarian perspective, differing in this respect from National-Christian antisemitism." Dandara, *Romania's Attitude*, 9.

15. January 1939 report, YVA, Filderman Archive, P-6/Paris, p. 2.

16. On the visit to Romania of Rabbi Perlzweig, a British leader of the World Jewish Congress, and his talks with Prime Minister Călinescu, see Vago, *Shadow of the Swastika*, 48.

17. For the background to and description of the assassination of Codreanu and his associates and the attitude of Romanian and non-Romanian historians toward the assassination, see Muşat and Ardeleanu, *România*, 876–79.

18. Muşat and Ardeleanu, *România*, 873–74.

19. See Dandara, *România în vîltoarea*, 76.

20. Confidential report on the situation of the Jews in Romania, Paris, 16 June 1938 (hereafter June 1938 report), in Ancel, *Documents*, vol. 1, doc. 25, p. 230; and testimony of Zionist leader Mişu Weissman (Amir) on Călinescu's emigration policy, 1938–39, in Ancel, *Documents*, vol. 1, doc. 35, p. 255.

21. Muşat and Ardeleanu, *România*, 1014.

22. Filderman, *Memoirs and Diaries*, 496, 508.

23. Filderman, *Memoirs and Diaries*, 502.

24. June 1938 report, in Ancel, *Documents*, vol. 1, doc. 25, p. 230.

25. February 1939 report, YVA, P-6/Paris, p. 3.

26. June 1938 report, in Ancel, *Documents*, vol. 1, doc. 25, p. 230.

27. Memorandum by Filderman to the minister of justice on the procedures for the revision of citizenship and the attempt to divest the Jews of Bukovina and Transylvania of their citizenship, 16 July 1938 (hereafter memorandum on revision of citizenship), in Ancel, *Documents*, vol. 1, doc. 30, p. 244.

28. Testimony of Aureliu Weiss, YVA, 033/785, p. 3.

29. Filderman, *Memoirs and Diaries*, 496; report on situation after Goga, YVA, Filderman Archive, P-6/Paris, p. 2; Filderman to the minister of justice on the desperate situation of Jewish lawyers, 29 July 1938, in Ancel, *Documents*, vol. 1, doc. 28, p. 241.

30. Memorandum on revision of citizenship, in Ancel, *Documents*, vol. 1, doc. 30, p. 244.

31. Filderman's memorandum to Interior Minister Călinescu on antisemitic incitement in the press and attempts to "encourage" the emigration of 150,000 Jews from Romania, 21 December 1938, in Ancel, *Documents*, vol. 1, doc. 34, p. 252; see also report on situation in Transylvania, YVA, P-6/Paris, pp. 1, 3.

32. Filderman, *Memoirs and Diaries*, 502.

33. Directive on the situation of people [whose names] were deleted from the census of Romanian citizens on 15 November 1938, in Ancel, *Documents*, vol. 8, doc. 143, p. 178.

34. Filderman's memorandum to the minister of justice on the illegality of the Law for the Revision of Citizenship and its implementation, 4 July 1938, in Ancel, *Documents*, vol. 1, doc. 26, p. 234.

35. Filderman, *Memoirs and Diaries*, 503.

36. Report on situation after Goga, YVA, Filderman Archive, P-6/Paris, p. 1.

37. See Law no. 86, pt. 1, no. 17, in *Monitorul Oficial*, 20 January 1939; Filderman, *Memoirs and Diaries*, 246.

38. *Statutul Minorităților*—Law no. 1750b, *Monitorul Oficial*, 4 August 1938; for English and French translations, see YVA, 0-60/Romania. See also Règlement pour le fonctionnement du Commissariat Général pour les minorités, YVA, 0-60/Romania.

39. Dandara, *Romania's Attitude*, 9.

40. Report on talk with Comnen, in Ancel, *Documents*, vol. 1, doc. 23, p. 226. The internal controversy concerning the definition of Jews as a national minority of Romanian citizens of the Mosaic faith is beyond the scope of this study.

41. January 1939 report, YVA, Filderman Archive, P-6/Paris, p. 2.

42. Axenfeld, "Gezerot kalkaliyot."

43. February 1939 report, addendum, YVA, P-6/Paris, p. 1.

44. Filderman, *Memoirs and Diaries*, 498; report on situation after Goga, YVA, Filderman Archive, P-6/Paris, p. 2.

45. Filderman, *Memoirs and Diaries*, 499. In his testimony in March 1938, Singer stated that "all Jewish architects want to emigrate." Singer testimony, in Ancel, *Documents*, vol. 8, doc. 143, p. 180.

46. Filderman, *Memoirs and Diaries*, 498.

47. February 1939 report, addendum, YVA, P-6/Paris, p. 1.

48. See *Universul*, 9 February 1938; copy in Ancel, *Documents*, vol. 8, doc. 142, p. 178.

49. Report on situation after Goga, YVA, Filderman Archive, P-6/Paris, p. 1; memorandum on revision of citizenship, in Ancel, *Documents*, vol. 1, doc. 30, p. 244.

50. February 1939 report, addendum, YVA, P-6/Paris, p. 5.

51. Dandara, *Romania's Attitude*, 4–5; *Timpul*, 2 February 1938.

52. Dandara, *Romania's Attitude*, 16–20; see also pp. 20–22 for the memorandum and the responses of the various foreign ministries.

53. Filderman, French draft of the memoirs, YVA, P-6/1, p. 689b.

3. The Rhinocerization of the Intelligentsia

1. M. Eliade, "Judaism și antisemitism," *Vremea*, 22 July 1934.

2. M. Eliade, "Creștinătate față de Judaism," *Vremea*, 5 August 1934; "O problemă

teologică eronat rezolvată? Sau ce n-a înțeles d. Mircea Eliade" [A theological problem erroneously resolved? Or what Mircea Eliade failed to understand], *Credința*, 29 July 1934.

3. See the many articles that have appeared in *Adam*, a Jewish journal edited by Isac Ludo.

4. *Porunca Vremii*, 4 August 1940.

5. Brătescu-Voinești, *Huliganism*, 38, 83–84, 86.

6. Roșu, *Dialectica naționalismului*.

7. Roșu, *Orientări*, 154, 158.

8. Roșu, *Orientări*, 145–49.

9. Nae Ionescu, introduction to Sebastian, *De două mii de ani*, xxvii, vi–vii (emphasis in the original).

10. Roșu, *Orientări*, 151–52.

11. Brătescu-Voinești, *Huliganism*, 142.

12. Ionescu, introduction to Sebastian, *De două mii de ani*, xix.

13. Brătescu-Voinești, *Huliganism*, 82, 139, 141, 145–46.

14. Brătescu-Voinești, *Huliganism*, 16–17.

15. Brătescu-Voinești, *Huliganism*, 74–75.

16. See *Iuda*, a book of antisemitic poems and caricatures, excerpts from which appear in Ancel, *Documents*, 1:148–82.

17. Iorga, *Iudaica*, 6.

18. Ionescu, introduction to Sebastian, *De două mii de ani*, xxxii.

19. Roșu, *Orientări*, 218, 228.

20. Sebastian, *De două mii de ani*, 332.

4. The Romanian Orthodox Church

1. Florescu, "Inceputurile și evoluția," 104, 130.

2. Codreanu, *Pentru Legionari*, 295, 302.

3. Codreanu, *Pentru Legionari*, 420–21; Codreanu, *Circulări și manifeste*, 94. Here is the entire quotation:

> I have been asked whether our activity so far has followed along the same lines as those of the Christian Church. I answer: We make a great distinction between the line we follow and that of the Christian Church. The Church line is situated thousands of meters above us. It reaches perfection and the sublime. We cannot lower this plane in order to explain our acts. We, through our action, through all our acts and thoughts, *tend* toward this line, raising ourselves up toward it as much as the weight of our sins of the flesh and our fall through original sin permit. It remains to be seen how much we can elevate ourselves toward this line through our worldly efforts.

Codreanu, *For My Legionaries*, 311–12.

4. Marin, *Crez de generație*, 49.

5. Filderman, *Memoirs and Diaries*, 307.

6. Filderman, *Memoirs and Diaries*, 475.

7. Filderman, *Memoirs and Diaries*, 323. The event was described at length in various issues of the Yiddish weekly *Unzer Tzeit* (Kishinev), January–February 1930.

8. Bălan, *Studiu asupra Francmasoneriei*, 6–12.

9. Popescu, *Jidovii demascați*, 12.

10. *Curentul*, 5 September 1937.

11. *Porunca Vremii*, 24 August 1937.

12. *Porunca Vremii*, 19 August 1937.

13. *Porunca Vremii*, 19 August 1937.

14. *Apărarea Națională*, 24 August 1937.

5. *Nazi Influence on Romanian Political Life*

1. Petrescu-Comnen, Romanian minister in Berlin, on his meeting with Reich Minister of Economics Funk, 3 February 1938, in Ancel, *Documents*, vol. 9, doc. 4, pp. 9–10. (Germany and Romania had legations in Bucharest and Berlin. The formal title of their representatives was minister. We shall use the term *ambassador*.)

2. Petrescu-Comnen, Romanian minister in Berlin, on his meeting with Reich Minister of Economics Funk, 3 February 1938, in Ancel, *Documents*, vol. 9, doc. 4, pp. 9–10. On German plans to strengthen economic ties with Romania, see Ancel, *Documents*, vol. 9, doc. 5, pp. 11–12.

3. Rosenberg, *Das Politische Tagebuch*, 25 (29 May 1934).

4. Heinen, *Die Legion*, 331; Brestoiu, *O istorie*, 116.

5. Nedelcu, *Viața politică*, 195; Brestoiu, *O istorie*, 116.

6. Brestoiu, *O istorie*, 116.

7. Nedelcu, *Viața politică*, 195.

8. Nedelcu, *Viața politică*, 195.

9. Antonescu also returned this sum to Germany from state funds. Nedelcu, *Viața politică*, 195. See also Heinen, *Die Legion*, 339; Savu, *Dictatura regală*, 39.

10. Nedelcu, *Viața politică*, 195.

11. Report by Filderman on the situation of the Jews in Romania to the World Jewish Congress, December 1936, YVA, Filderman Archive, P-6/Paris, vol. 2 (English version), pp. 123–25.

12. Filderman, *Memoirs and Diaries*, 474.

13. Among the democratic personalities at that time were: G. Iunian, I. Iordan, D. Botez, M. Sadoveanu, H. Tonitza, A. Călinescu, C. I. Parhon, N. Titulescu, N. Iorga, M. Ralea, T. T. Braniște, V. Madgearu, D Dobrescu, G. Filipescu, and V. Iamandi.

14. Filderman, *Memoirs and Diaries*, 473–74.

15. Ambassador Fabricius to the Foreign Ministry in Berlin, telegram on propaganda issues, 29 August 1939, in *Akten zur deutschen auswärtigen Politik*, vol. 7, no. 426, p. 351.

16. See *Iuda*, a book of antisemitic caricatures and poems published in 1937 by *Universul*'s printing house, combining "classical" and Nazi antisemitic themes. The book was illustrated by the antisemitic artist Lazăr Petrică. Excerpts from the book appear in Ancel, *Documents*, vol. 1, doc. 15, pp. 148–82. The book ends with a pledge to exterminate the Jews.

17. In late December 1938 Filderman made an abortive attempt to persuade Interior Minister Armand Călinescu to put an end to the campaign of incitement that the press, "even the official press," was waging against the Jews. Judging by the press, said Filderman, the world consists only of Europe, and Europe consists only of Germany and Italy.

Press reports thereby "create a spirit of racism that will soon be impossible to curb." See Filderman to Interior Minister Călinescu, memorandum, 21 December 1938, in Ancel, *Documents*, vol. 1, doc. 34, p. 252.

18. Brestoiu, *O istorie*, 118.

19. Ambassador Fabricius to the Foreign Ministry in Berlin, telegram on propaganda issues, 29 August 1939, in *Akten zur deutschen auswärtigen Politik*, vol. 7, no. 426, p. 351.

20. A. Petri, "The Penetration of Nazi Ideology in Romania," in *Impotriva fascismului*, 102 (in Romanian).

21. A. Petri, "The Penetration of Nazi Ideology in Romania," in *Impotriva fascismului*, 99–100 (in Romanian).

22. Brestoiu, *O istorie*, 120.

23. Nagy-Talavera, *Green Shirts*, 291; Hillgruber, *Hitler, Carol und Antonescu*, 13.

24. Nedelcu, *Viața politică*, 197.

25. Nedelcu, *Viața politică*, 236. The Romanian Communist Party thought, exactly like the Nazis, that the measures the Goga government had adopted against the Jews were not serious but merely diversionary tactics, since they affected Jewish workers and intellectuals only, not Jewish capitalists, such as Max Auschnit, Aristide Blank, Oscar Kaufman, and Martin Bercovici, who played an important role "in setting up and sustaining the National Christian Party, and in bringing the Goga government to power." Nedelcu, *Viața politică*, 251.

26. Hillgruber, *Hitler, Carol und Antonescu*, 15.

27. Nedelcu, *Viața politică*, 203.

28. Hillgruber, *Hitler, Carol und Antonescu*, 15.

29. German Foreign Ministry to its embassies in Paris, London, Rome, Warsaw, and Moscow, telegram, March 1938, in Baumont, *Les archives secrètes*, doc. 166.

30. Secretary of State Weizsäcker (in Berlin) to the legation in Bucharest, 9 June 1938, in Baumont, *Les archives secrètes*, doc. 191.

31. Transcript of Hitler's talk with King Carol in Bertesgaden, 24 November 1938, in *Akten zur deutschen auswärtigen Politik*, vol. 5, no. 254, p. 256; see also report of the king's talk with Göhring, 26 November 1938, in Baumont, *Les archives secrètes*, doc. 226.

32. Filderman to the American Jewish Committee and world Jewish organizations, memorandum on the legal status of the Jews, late 1934, "Exposé sur le mouvement législatif roumain" (hereafter memorandum on legal status), YVA, Filderman Archive, P-6/Paris, p. 7.

33. Nuremberg Documents, PS-007.

34. *Apărarea Națională*, 3 February 1935.

35. Memorandum on legal status, YVA, Filderman Archive, P-6/Paris, p. 7.

36. Calafeteanu, "Les relations," 27.

37. Calafeteanu, "Les relations," 29.

38. Woodward and Butler, *Documents*, vol. 3, *London*, doc. 262, 17 November 1938, p. 232.

39. *Documents on German Foreign Policy*, vol. 4, doc. 273, 28 November 1938, p. 343.

40. See Karl Clodius, deputy director of the Economic Policy Department in the German Foreign Ministry, memorandum about the outcome of the German-Romanian economic negotiations, in *Documents on German Foreign Policy*, vol. 5, doc. 264, pp. 352–55. On 15 February 1939 Clodius reported to the Foreign Ministry that "on the basis of the latest

agreements of 10 December 1938, Germany now accounts for nearly 50 percent of Rumanian foreign trade." *Documents on German Foreign Policy*, vol. 5, doc. 294, p. 395. On the collapse of Romania's alliances on the eve of the Second World War, see Moisuc, "L'écroulement," 1–21.

41. Calafeteanu, "Les relations," 31–32.

42. Hillgruber, *Hitler, Carol und Antonescu*, 85–86.

6. Pogroms and Persecutions

1. Antonescu's answer to Filderman's request to stop the expulsion and murder of Bessarabian Jews, 19 October 1941, in Ancel, *Documents*, vol. 3, doc. 167, p. 260.

2. Bulei, "Romania's Situation," 1–2.

3. Summary report of the General Staff on the hostility of the Jewish population toward the Romanians during the retreat from the Soviet-annexed territories, 30 June 1940 (hereafter report on hostility of Jews), [former] Archive of the Historical Institute of the Central Committee of the Romanian Communist Party, Bucharest (hereafter Central Committee Archive), collection 24, file 3377, p. 2. Nobody knows exactly where the archive's files and microfilms are now.

4. Report on hostility of Jews, Central Committee Archive, collection 24, file 3377, p. 6.

5. *Raza Basarabiei*, 27 June 1940.

6. Summary report of the General Staff on the Jewish operation in Bessarabia and Bukovina during the retreat and on the Jewish response in other parts of Romania, 3 July 1940 (hereafter General Staff report, 3 July 1940), Central Committee Archive, collection 24, file 3376, p. 3.

7. Summary report of the General Staff on the Jewish operation in Bessarabia and Bukovina during the retreat, on acts of terror toward the Romanian population, on the integration of the Jews into the new regime, and on agitation among Romanian Jewry, 4 July 1940 (hereafter General Staff report, 4 July 1940), Central Committee Archive, collection 24, file 3377, pp. 1–3.

8. General Staff report, 4 July 1940, Central Committee Archive, collection 24, file 3377, p. 1; General Staff report, 3 July 1940, Central Committee Archive, collection 24, file 3376, p. 3.

9. Report on hostility of Jews, Central Committee Archive, collection 24, file 3377, p. 6; report by the commissioner of the Counterespionage Bureau in Reni (crossing point on the Prut River) on the progress of the Soviet army and on the hostile behavior of the Jews in southern Bessarabia, 30 June 1940, Central Committee Archive, collection 24, file 3377, pp. 1–2.

10. Report by the commissioner of the Counterespionage Bureau in Reni (crossing point on the Prut River) on the progress of the Soviet army and on the hostile behavior of the Jews in southern Bessarabia, 30 June 1940, Central Committee Archive, collection 24, file 3377, p. 1.

11. Report no. 7 of the Counterespionage Bureau in the General Staff in Bucharest on the evacuation of Bessarabia (hereafter Report no. 7), 5 July 1940, Central Committee Archive, collection 24, file 376, p. 1.

12. Documents on the behavior of the Jewish population toward the Romanian army and

the Romanian population during the retreat from Bessarabia and Bukovina were made available to me by the Historical Institute of the Central Committee of the Romanian Communist Party. The above institute chose selected documents from a large collection of documents, and I was not allowed to inspect the files myself.

13. Border Guard Staff report to the General Staff on the anti-Romanian behavior of the Jews in Czernowitz at the start of the retreat, 28 June 1940, Central Committee Archive, collection 24, file 3377; testimony of a Romanian refugee from Bukovina on the unrest caused by Communist Jews and Ukrainians, 30 June 1940, Central Committee Archive, collection 24, file 3376, p. 1.

14. Report on hostility of Jews, Central Committee Archive, collection 24, file 3377, p. 4.

15. Report of the Counterespionage Bureau on the agitation among the Jews of Iaşi during and after the retreat, on migration to the annexed territories, on the anti-Romanian atmosphere, and on activities by Communists, inter alia, 7 July 1940 (hereafter report on agitation among the Jews of Iaşi), Central Committee Archive, collection 24, file 3377, p. 2.

16. Report by the general directorate of the police on the response of the minorities in Cluj to the retreat from Bessarabia and Bukovina, 1 July 1940, Central Committee Archive, collection 24, file 3376, pp. 1–2.

17. General Staff report, 3 July 1940, Central Committee Archive, collection 24, file 3376, p. 6.

18. Report on hostility of Jews, Central Committee Archive, collection 24, file 3377, p. 4.

19. General Staff report, 4 July 1940, Central Committee Archive, collection 24, file 3377, p. 3.

20. General Staff report, 4 July 1940, Central Committee Archive, collection 24, file 3377, pp. 1, 3.

21. General Staff report, 4 July 1940, Central Committee Archive, collection 24, file 3377, pp. 3–4.

22. General Staff report, 3 July 1940, Central Committee Archive, collection 24, file 3376, p. 4.

23. General Staff report, 3 July 1940, Central Committee Archive, collection 24, file 3376, p. 4.

24. General Staff report, 4 July 1940, Central Committee Archive, collection 24, file 3377, pp. 3–4.

25. Report on agitation among the Jews of Iaşi, Central Committee Archive, collection 24, file 3377, pp. 2–3.

26. Report no. 7, Central Committee Archive, collection 24, file 376, p. 2.

27. Dov Levin, "Retreat of the Romanian Army," 300. On the attacks and humiliations inflicted on the retreating Romanian soldiers by Jews and Ukrainians, see also Nagy-Talavera, *Green Shirts*, 305; Prost, *Destin de la Roumanie*, 143–44.

28. Testimony of Israel Friedman, YVA, 0-3/1460, p. 3.

29. Testimony of Galina Ehrenpreis-Ciobanu, YVA, 0-33/803, pp. 5, 7.

30. Telegram from the Counterespionage Bureau to the General Staff on pogroms against the Jews of Dorohoi that were carried out by the Second Border Guards Regiment on 2 July 1940, Central Committee Archive, collection 24, file 3377; report on attempts to prosecute the

military personnel responsible for the Dorohoi pogroms, from the portfolio of the Bucharest Prosecution Service, in preparation for the trials of Romanian war criminals responsible for the Dorohoi pogroms, Jewish Federation copy, 1950, in Ancel, *Documents*, vol. 6, doc. 38, p. 346. The trials of Romanian war criminals referred to here never took place. On the Dorohoi pogroms, see Ancel, "Jassy Syndrome," 43–46.

31. Telegram from the Counterespionage Bureau to the General Staff on pogroms against the Jews of Dorohoi that were carried out by the Second Border Guards Regiment on 2 July 1940, Central Committee Archive, collection 24, file 3377.

32. *Pinkas Hakehilot, Rumania*, 1:106.

33. See names of the victims in the documents, testimonies, and reports compiled by the historian Matatias Carp in preparation for the trials of Romanian war criminals in Bessarabia, Bukovina, and Transylvania (hereafter Carp Collection), YVA, 0-11/109, p. 5.

34. Mircu, *Pogromurile din Bucovina şi Dorohoi*, 110–11.

35. YVA, Carp Collection, 0-11/109, p. 8.

36. YVA, Carp Collection, 0-11/109, p. 8

37. YVA, Carp Collection, 0-11/109, p. 10.

38. Protocol of the Jewish Federation's Central Committee session, 4 August 1940, in Ancel, *Documents*, vol. 1, doc. 77, p. 435.

39. Prost, *Destin de la Roumanie*, 143.

40. Protocol of the conversation between Ribbentrop and Romanian prime minister Gigurtu, 26 July 1940, in *Documents on German Foreign Policy*, vol. 10, doc. 233, p. 304.

41. Protocol of the talk between Hitler and Gigurtu, in *Documents on German Foreign Policy*, vol. 10, doc. 253, pp. 304–5.

42. Protocol of the talk between Hitler and Gigurtu, in *Documents on German Foreign Policy*, vol. 10, doc. 253, pp. 307–9.

43. Protocol of the union's Central Committee session, 27 June 1940, in Ancel, *Documents*, vol. 1, doc. 65, p. 410.

44. Protocol of the union's Central Committee session, 27 June 1940, in Ancel, *Documents*, vol. 1, doc. 65, p. 310; Ministry of Finance, letter of dismissal to the ministry's divisional director, a Jew named Paul Arian, 10 July 1940, in Ancel, *Documents*, vol. 1, doc. 70, p. 422.

45. Protocol of the union's Central Committee session, 16 July 1940, in Ancel, *Documents*, vol. 1, doc. 71, p. 423.

46. Protocol of the union's Central Committee session, 16 July 1940, in Ancel, *Documents*, vol. 1, doc. 71, p. 423; protocol of the union's Central Committee session, 25 July 1940, in Ancel, *Documents*, vol. 1, doc. 72, p. 426.

47. *România*, 6 August 1940, pp. 3, 5.

48. *România*, 2 August 1940, 22 August 1940; *Universul*, 17 August 1940.

49. *Neamul Românesc*, 9 August 1940.

50. *Luceafărul*, 28 July 1940.

51. Protocol of the union's Central Committee session, 25 July 1940, in Ancel, *Documents*, vol. 1, doc. 72.

52. *Timpul*, 30 August 1940; copy in Ancel, *Documents*, vol. 8, doc. 148, p. 189.

53. *Timpul*, 30 August 1940.

54. Protest by the Jewish Federation to the minister of the interior about antisemitic incitement in the press despite censorship, 17 August 1940, in Ancel, *Documents*, vol. 1, doc. 85, p. 458.

55. See, for example, "Stăpâni în casa noastră — Directivele noului statut evreilor" [Masters of our homes — The provisions of the new Jewish statute], *Universul*, 14 August 1940.

56. *Neamul Românesc*, 13 August 1940.

57. *Porunca Vremii*, 14 August 1940.

58. *România*, 16 August 1940.

59. S. Bucur, "Statutul juridic al evreilor," *România*, 20 August 1940.

60. Centrala Evreilor din România, *Breviarul statistic*, 54–55, 60–61; copy in Ancel, *Documents*, vol. 1, doc. 45, pp. 311–13. See summary of data from the 1942 census of people of Jewish blood, compiled by the German legation in Bucharest, including data on *Mischlinge* (crossbreeds), intermarriage, etc., in Ancel, *Documents*, vol. 1, doc. 114, p. 294.

61. *Curentul*, 20 August 1940.

62. *Neamul Românesc*, 21 August 1940.

63. A Jewish intellectual named Lascăr Sebastian approached Filderman for help, and Filderman found him a job as a wandering peddler of silk fabrics, which saved him from abject penury. See Sebastian to Filderman, thank you letter for helping him set up his business, 8 September 1940, in Ancel, *Documents*, vol. 1, doc. 89, p. 469.

64. *Porunca Vremii*, 26 July 1940. The newspaper published Filderman's address on several occasions and openly called on its readers to target him.

65. *New York Times*, 29 July 1940.

66. Protocol of the union's Central Committee session, 27 June 1940, in Ancel, *Documents*, vol. 1, doc. 65, p. 411.

67. Safran, *Resisting the Storm*, 51. News first arrived of events in Bessarabia and only later of the pogroms in Bukovina.

68. Protocol of the union's Central Committee session, 27 June 1940, in Ancel, *Documents*, vol. 1, doc. 65, p. 411.

69. Protocol of the Jewish Federation's Central Committee and Executive Committee, 4 July 1940, in Ancel, *Documents*, vol. 1, doc. 67, p. 417.

70. In a union board meeting, the president of the Tecuci community proposed that the union's letters be sent as private correspondence, "since the letters were not delivered to the local community." Protocol of 14 August, no. 454, in Ancel, *Documents*, vol. 1, doc. 81, p. 452.

71. Protocol of the union's Central Committee session, 25 July 1940, in Ancel, *Documents*, vol. 1, doc. 72, pp. 426, 430.

72. *Curentul*, 1 July 1940.

73. P. Şeicaru, "Apel către Români," *Curentul*, 2 July 1940.

74. Protocol of the Jewish Federation's Central Committee and Executive Committee, 4 July 1940, in Ancel, *Documents*, vol. 1, doc. 67, p. 416.

75. Protocol of the Jewish Federation's Central Committee and Executive Committee, 4 July 1940, in Ancel, *Documents*, vol. 1, doc. 67, p. 416.

76. Filderman, *Memoirs and Diaries*, 511.

77. Protocol of 14 August, in Ancel, *Documents*, vol. 1, doc. 81, p. 452.

78. Protocol of the union's Central Committee session, 25 July 1940, in Ancel, *Documents*, vol. 1, doc. 72, pp. 426, 430.

79. Protocol of 22 August, in Ancel, *Documents*, vol. 1, doc. 86, p. 459.

80. Protocol of 22 August, in Ancel, *Documents*, vol. 1, doc. 86, p. 460.

81. Protocol of 22 August, in Ancel, *Documents*, vol. 1, doc. 86, p. 460

82. Protocol of 2 September, in Ancel, *Documents*, vol. 1, doc. 88, p. 468 (author's emphasis). The scope of the problem diminished as a result of the Soviet annexation of Bessarabia and northern Bukovina.

83. Protocol of the union's Central Committee session, 16 July 1940, in Ancel, *Documents*, vol. 1, doc. 71, p. 424.

84. Protocol of 14 August, in Ancel, *Documents*, vol. 1, doc. 81, p. 453.

85. Protocol of 22 August, in Ancel, *Documents*, vol. 1, doc. 86, p. 459.

86. Protocol of 2 September, in Ancel, *Documents*, vol. 1, doc. 88, p. 467.

87. Protocol of 2 September, in Ancel, *Documents*, vol. 1, doc. 88, p. 466.

88. I. Peltz to Filderman, letter, 23 May 1940, in Ancel, *Documents*, vol. 1, doc. 63, p. 406.

89. Bikel, *Yahadut Romania*, 300. Sanielevici did not ask Filderman for help directly. Filderman approved the grant after the Romanian philosopher Constantin Rădulescu-Motru approached him. See Filderman's account of the help he gave to Jewish authors, YVA, P-6/94, p. 61.

90. Filderman, *Memoirs and Diaries*, 511–12.

7. The National-Legionary State

1. See the memoirs of Horia Sima, second commander of the Iron Guard: Sima, *Era libertății*. The book includes many documents, orders, directives, press clippings, and correspondence with Antonescu during the period of the Legionary regime.

2. Drăgan, *Antonescu*, vol. 2, no. 30, p. 290.

3. Sima, *Sfârșitul*, 282.

4. *Curierul Israelit*, 22 October 1944.

5. Simion, *Regimul politic*, 69, 131, 135–36.

6. Simion, *Regimul politic*, 68, 76.

7. Sima, *Era libertății*, 1:84.

8. Sima, *Era libertății*, 1:104.

9. In September 1941, after the suppression of the Legionnaires' rebellion, the Antonescu regime published a two-volume work that shed light on the murderous and terrorist nature of the Legionary movement and its crimes: *Pe marginea prăpastiei*; see 1:11, 130.

10. Sima, *Era libertății*, 1:194.

11. Simion, *Regimul politic*, 98.

12. Simion, *Regimul politic*, 98.

13. *Pe marginea prăpastiei*, 1:106.

14. Sima, *Era libertății*, 1:67–68.

15. *Timpul*, 18 October 1940.

16. *Pe marginea prăpastiei*, 1:11.

17. Sima, *Era libertății*, 1:340.

18. Sima, *Era libertății*, 1:603.

19. Sima, *Era libertății*, 1:125.

20. See the various tables of laws and administrative restrictions introduced between 1937 and 1944 in *Pinkas Hakehilot, Rumania*, 1:168–69.

21. Study on the Jewish problem in Romania drawn up by Division 1 of the Romanian General Staff, including the problem of the legal status of the Jews and legislation on Romanization issues and forced labor, from November 1942 (hereafter General Staff study), in Ancel, *Documents*, vol. 10, doc. 107, pp. 252–90.

22. General Staff study, in Ancel, *Documents*, vol. 10, doc. 107, p. 254.

23. For the Romanian text of the law and its German translation, see Ancel, *Documents*, vol. 8 doc. 141, pp. 162–77.

24. *Monitorul Oficial*, 24 November 1939; General Staff study, in Ancel, *Documents*, vol. 10, doc. 107, pp. 255–56.

25. *Monitorul Oficial*, 9 August 1940; copy in Ancel, *Documents*, vol. 1, doc. 79, pp. 437–45. For an English translation of the law, see Ancel, *Documents*, vol. 8, doc. 146, pp. 185–88.

26. General Staff study, in Ancel, *Documents*, vol. 10, doc. 107, p. 257.

27. *Czernowitzer Morgenblatt*, July 1935.

28. General Staff study, in Ancel, *Documents*, vol. 10, doc. 107, p. 257.

29. General Staff study, in Ancel, *Documents*, vol. 10, doc. 107, p. 258.

30. *Monitorul Oficial*, 9 August 1940.

31. *Monitorul Oficial*, 9 August 1940, p. 4086.

32. Ancel, "Romanian Jewry," 97.

33. *Pe marginea prăpastiei*, 1:165.

34. Simion, *Regimul politic*, 112; Carp, *Cartea neagră*, 1:56.

35. Sima, *Era libertății*, 1:296.

36. *Universul*, 7 October 1940; copy, with English translation, in Ancel, *Documents*, vol. 8, doc. 154, pp. 197–99.

37. *Monitorul Oficial*, 17 November 1940; excerpts from Carp, *Cartea neagră*, 1:93–94.

38. Carp, *Cartea neagră*, 1:96.

39. Simion, *Regimul politic*, 88.

40. Decree-Law no. 3361, *Monitorul Oficial*, 5 October 1940.

41. *Monitorul Oficial*, 5 October 1940; see also Sima, *Era libertății*, 1:200–201; Carp, *Cartea neagră*, 1:86–87.

42. *Monitorul Oficial*, 17 October 1940.

43. Decree-Law no. 3758, *Monitorul Oficial*, 10 November 1940.

44. Decree-Law no. 3789, *Monitorul Oficial*, 15 November 1940; see also Carp, *Cartea neagră*, 1:89–90.

45. Carp, *Cartea neagră*, 1:90–91; Decree-Law no. 3825, *Monitorul Oficial*, 16 November 1940; copy in Ancel, *Documents*, vol. 2, doc. 6, pp. 9–11.

46. Decree-Law no. 3850, *Monitorul Oficial*, 19 November 1940; Carp, *Cartea neagră*, 1:94–95.

47. Decision of the Ministry of Labor, no. 67794, *Monitorul Oficial*, 24 December 1940.

48. Decree-Law no. 121, *Monitorul Oficial*, 19 January 1941; Carp, *Cartea neagră*, 1:98.

49. *Curierul Israelit*, 31 December 1944.

50. Decision of the Ministry of Culture and Arts, no. 44400, *Monitorul Oficial*, 22 September 1940.

51. Decree-Law no. 3438, *Monitorul Oficial*, 14 October 1940.

52. Safran, *Resisting the Storm*, 59.

53. Decree-Law no. 3438, *Monitorul Oficial*, 14 October 1940.

54. Order no. 191730 of the Ministry of National Education, *Monitorul Oficial*, 16 October 1940; excerpts from Carp, *Cartea neagră*, 1:87.

55. Carp, *Cartea neagră*, 1:94. The order was published in *Monitorul Oficial*, 18 November 1940.

56. Carp, *Cartea neagră*, 1:114.

57. For the list of Jewish authors, including biographical details and their banned works, see Ancel, *Documents*, vol. 4, doc. 169, pp. 334–36.

58. General Staff study, in Ancel, *Documents*, vol. 10, doc. 107, p. 264.

59. Alexandru Dominic to Filderman, letter on the ties between Romanian and Jewish intellectuals, 26 July 1940, in Ancel, *Documents*, vol. 1, doc. 73, pp. 427–28. On the attitude of Romanian intellectuals toward their Jewish colleagues under Antonescu, see Volovici, "Romanian Intellectuals."

60. *Timpul*, 30 August 1940; copy in Ancel, *Documents*, vol. 8, doc. 148, pp. 189–91, including a list of lawyers expelled from the bar association in the Bucharest district.

61. Carp, *Cartea neagră*, 1:57.

62. Carp, *Cartea neagră*, 1:57, 103.

63. Carp, *Cartea neagră*, 1:58, 104; *Timpul*, 13 September 1940.

64. Carp, *Cartea neagră*, 1:58, 105.

65. Carp, *Cartea neagră*, 1:106.

66. Filderman's memorandum to Antonescu, 30 September 1940, in Ancel, *Documents*, vol. 1, doc. 121, p. 529.

67. Carp, *Cartea neagră*, 1:107–8.

68. Filderman's memorandum to Antonescu, 30 September 1940, in Ancel, *Documents*, vol. 1, doc. 121, p. 529; *Timpul*, 1 October 1940. Filderman calculated that Romanians, with a population of 12.5 million, had 4,000 Aryan doctors (or 1 doctor for about every 3,100 people), while the Jews, with a population of 330,090, had 1,900 Jewish doctors (1 doctor for about every 175 people).

69. *Timpul*, 1 October 1940.

70. Carp, *Cartea neagră*, 1:58n.

71. *Curierul Israelit*, 24 September 1944. The following is a list of other associations and organizations that expelled their Jewish members: Association of Dental Surgeons; Association of Contractors (10 October 1940); the Association of Engineers (AGIR) expelled its remaining Jewish members (Category B) on 10 October 1940; the Association of Romanian Architects chose to expel its Jewish members during its jubilee celebrations (11 October 1940); Syndicate of the Fine Arts; Romanian Association of ENT Specialists (12 October 1940); General Association of Chemists (17 October 1940); Tourist Association (26 October 1940); the Council of Merchants in the city of Câmpina decided to expel all non-Christian

merchants (30 October 1940); Union of Butchers of the Bucharest Abattoir (30 October 1940); Association of Publishers (5 November 1940); Association of Land Registrars and Assessors (9 January 1940); Association of University Lecturers; Deaf and Dumb Association (10 November 1940); the Mărășești Association of Combat Veterans expelled all Jewish servicemen irrespective of "category" (15 December 1940); the Faculty of Medicine expelled all Jewish students in their last academic year (the remainder had already been expelled); the Bucharest municipality changed the names of nine streets that were named after Jews (17 December 1940); and the Used Clothing and Shoe Exchange expelled all Jewish-owned factories and agents from the organization (21 December 1940). The Directorate of Boxing, Wrestling, and Other Sports also expelled Jewish boxers and banned them from sports centers. There were quite a number of Jewish athletes, some of whom represented Romania in international contests. See Carp, *Cartea neagră*, 1:108–11, 115–16, 118, 121, 124, 126, 135, 175, 177, 180.

72. Petition by the Jewish Federation to the minister of labor and health, 19 November 1940, in Ancel, *Documents*, vol. 2, doc. 9, p. 14.

73. *Renașterea Noastră*, 24 December 1940.

74. Report of Jewish Federation board session of 2 September 1940, in Ancel, *Documents*, vol. 1, doc. 88, p. 464.

75. Decree-Law no. 3789, *Monitorul Oficial*, 15 November 1940.

76. *Porunca Vremii*, 10 December 1940.

77. *Buna Vestire*, 10 December 1940.

8. Romanization

1. Sima, *Era libertății* 1:232–33.

2. Sima, *Era libertății*, 1:234.

3. Memorandum by Filderman to the minister of the national economy concerning acts of theft and looting perpetrated by the Legionnaires, 21 March 1941, in Ancel, *Documents*, vol. 2, doc. 99, p. 340.

4. *Pe marginea prăpastiei*, 1:130.

5. Copy of a sales deed made by the attorney Mușat, in Ancel, *Documents*, vol. 2, doc. 14, p. 22.

6. Jewish Federation to the director of the security policy concerning the Legionnaires' appropriation of stores and businesses, 3 December 1940, in Ancel, *Documents*, vol. 2, doc. 25, p. 35. The petition specified the localities in which the sales deeds were extorted and in which preparations were being made for the expropriation of Jewish property.

7. Sima, *Era libertății*, 1:215.

8. *Pe marginea prăpastiei*, 1:135.

9. Sima, *Era libertății*, 1:143.

10. Sima, *Era libertății*, 1:204–5.

11. Jewish Federation to the director of the security policy concerning the Legionnaires' general embargo and other matters, 16 October 1940, in Ancel, *Documents*, vol. 1, doc. 138, p. 557.

12. Petition by the Jewish Federation to the director of the security policy concerning the looting of merchants in Braşov, 25 November 1940, in Ancel, *Documents*, vol. 2, doc. 14, pp. 20–21.

13. Memorandum by the Jewish Federation to Antonescu, including a summary of terror operations in thirty-nine cities, 9 December 1940 (hereafter Jewish Federation's memorandum of 9 December 1940), in Ancel, *Documents*, vol. 2, doc. 36, pp. 72–73.

14. Carp, *Cartea neagră*, 1:104.

15. Carp, *Cartea neagră*, 1:203.

16. Sima, *Era libertăţii*, 1:505–6.

17. Report by the prefect of the Făgăraş district to the president of the council, 27 January 1941, in Ancel, *Documents*, vol. 2, doc. 67, p. 185.

18. Partial list of Jews whose businesses were expropriated and description of the tortures to which Jews were subjected in the headquarters of the Legionary Workers' Corps, in Carp, *Cartea neagră*, 1:212–13.

19. Petition by the Jewish Federation to the minister of the interior concerning the confiscation of radios by the police, 24 April 1941, in Ancel, *Documents*, vol. 2, doc. 123, pp. 392–93.

20. Petition by the Jewish Federation to the director of the security policy concerning the confiscation of radios, 30 October 1940, in Ancel, *Documents*, vol. 1, doc. 157, p. 583.

21. Petition by the Jewish Federation to Antonescu, 31 December 1940, in Ancel, *Documents*, vol. 1, doc. 163, p. 591.

22. Jewish Federation to the minister of the interior concerning the Legionnaires' general embargo and other matters, 21 October 1940, in Ancel, *Documents*, vol. 1, doc. 150, p. 572.

23. In Aiud forty radios were confiscated by Augustin, the local commander of the movement, who immediately sold them for 3,000 lei (instead of the going price of 15,000–20,000 lei) each and kept the proceeds for himself. Carp, *Cartea neagră*, 1:142. In Blaj the police confiscated all fourteen radios in the town, sold most of them immediately, and divided the proceeds. Memorandum by the Jewish Federation to General Antonescu on crimes committed by the Legionnaires between 1 December 1940 and 21 January 1941, submitted on 12 February 1941 (hereafter Jewish Federation's memorandum of 12 February 1941), in Ancel, *Documents*, vol. 2, doc. 76, p. 251.

24. Jewish Federation's memorandum of 9 December 1940, in Ancel, *Documents*, vol. 2, doc. 36, pp. 48–73; Carp, *Cartea neagră*, 1:154–55.

25. Jewish Federation's memorandum of 9 December 1940, in Ancel, *Documents*, vol. 2, doc. 36, p. 67. See also Jewish Federation's memorandum of 11 January 1941, with summary of the crimes perpetrated by the Legionnaires between 15 November 1940 and 1 January 1941, in Ancel, *Documents*, vol. 2, doc. 58, p. 139.

26. Jewish Federation's memorandum of 12 February 1941, in Ancel, *Documents*, vol. 2, doc. 76, p. 223.

27. Jewish Federation's memorandum of 12 February 1941, in Ancel, *Documents*, vol. 2, doc. 76, p. 249.

28. Petition by the Jewish Federation to the minister of the interior concerning the confiscation of radios by the police, 24 April 1941, in Ancel, *Documents*, vol. 2, doc. 123, p. 392.

29. Carp, *Cartea neagră*, 1:154–55.

30. Directive of the prefect of the Rădăuți district to the gendarmerie and police to confiscate radios owned by Jews, 30 June 1941, in Ancel, *Documents*, vol. 2, doc. 144, p. 425.

31. Minister for public works and communications to minister of the interior concerning the distribution of radios that had been confiscated from Jews, in Ancel, *Documents*, vol. 2, doc. 143, p. 424.

32. Carp, *Cartea neagră*, 1:204.

33. Carp, *Cartea neagră*, 1:159.

34. Carp, *Cartea neagră*, 1:196.

35. Jewish Federation's memorandum of 12 February 1941, in Ancel, *Documents*, vol. 2, doc. 76, p. 231.

36. Carp, *Cartea neagră*, 1:134, 208.

37. Carp, *Cartea neagră*, 1:171.

38. Carp, *Cartea neagră*, 1:207.

39. *Pe marginea prăpastiei*, 1:136.

40. Decree-Law no. 3361, *Monitorul Oficial*, 5 October 1940.

41. *Pe marginea prăpastiei*, 1:131–33.

42. Simion, *Regimul politic*, 82, 131, 135–36.

43. Fătu and Spălățelu, *Garda de Fier*, 294–97. See generally *Pe marginea prăpastiei*.

44. Sima, *Era libertății*, 1:275.

45. Sima, *Era libertății*, 1:275; Simion, *Regimul politic*, 73.

46. Sima to a delegation of miners who came to demand higher wages, in *Era libertății*, 1:277; see also Simion, *Regimul politic*, 73.

47. Simion, *Regimul politic*, 82.

48. Sima, *Era libertății*, 1:68.

49. *Muncitorul Legionar*, 8 November 1940; Simion, *Regimul politic*, 77; *Universul*, 17 September 1940.

50. Simion, *Regimul politic*, 80.

51. Simion, *Regimul politic*, 81.

52. *Pe marginea prăpastiei*, 1:214.

53. Congrès Juif Mondial, *Le régime légionnaire*, 3. One of the most famous and talented Romanian statesmen, C. Argetoianu, defined the Romanian parties in 1936 thus: "Groups of interested persons, who behind the party mask drain the State's liquid reserves and expel each other from government." *Impotriva fascismului*, 32."

54. M. Ionescu, "Terror Techniques and Fields of Activity during the Legionary Dictatorship and during Antonescu's Rule," in *Împotriva fascismului*, 198 (in Romanian).

55. *Pe marginea prăpastiei*, 1:3–4.

56. *Pe marginea prăpastiei*, 2:89, 90–101.

9. Legionary Terror

1. Rusenescu and Saizu, *Viața politică*, 109–10.

2. *Cuvântul*, 29 July 1926.

3. G. Ivașcu, "A Monstrous Ideology," in *Impotriva fascismului*, 108 (in Romanian).

4. *Pe marginea prăpastiei*, 2:85–87.

5. *Pe marginea prăpastiei*, 2:89.

6. Sima, *Era libertății*, 1:371.

7. Sima, *Era libertății*, 1:527–28.

8. Fătu and Spălățelu, *Garda de Fier*, 307; cf. Mihail Sturza, former deputy of Foreign Office, in USHMM/SRI, RG-25.004M, reel 52, Regatul României, Tribunalul Militar CMC, Parchetul Militar, Proces Verbal, file 4273/1941, p. 12.

9. Hoettl, *Secret Front*, 178.

10. Comandamentul Militar al Capitalei, *Asasinatele*, 166.

11. Sima, *Era libertății*, 1:564.

12. Sima, *Era libertății*, 1:574.

13. Sima, *Era libertății*, 1:574; USHMM/SRI, RG-25.004M, reel 52, file 9039, vol. 31, p. 74; *Universul*, no. 334/4, December 1940.

14. Sima, *Era libertății*, 1:610.

15. Simion, *Regimul politic*.

16. Sima, *Era libertății*, 1:251, 253; Carp, *Cartea neagră*, 1:203.

17. See Jewish Federation's memorandum of 12 February 1941, in Ancel, *Documents*, vol. 2, doc. 76, p. 252.

18. "Intre evoluție și revoluție," *Porunca Vremii*, 16 August 1940; *Chemarea Vremii*, 16 August 1940.

19. Appeal by the Jewish Federation to the minister of the interior concerning antisemitic incitement in the press, 17 August 1940, in Ancel, *Documents*, vol. 1, doc. 85, p. 458.

20. Appeal by the Union of Jewish Communities to the director general of the security police to prevent the expulsion of the ritual slaughterer, Joseph Fishman, 4 November 1940, in Ancel, *Documents*, vol. 1, doc. 169, p. 597.

21. Union of Jewish Communities to the minister of the interior on Legionary terror in Vaslui, 21 October 1940, in Ancel, *Documents*, vol. 1, doc. 150, p. 572.

22. Union of Jewish Communities to the minister of the interior on the evacuation from central Sibiu, 28 October 1940, in Ancel, *Documents*, vol. 1, doc. 155, p. 581; and USHMM/SRI, RG-25.004M, reel 58, file 9039, vol. 45, pp. 84–85 (two reports sent by local police from Sibiu [no. 53/5, November 1940] and Center of Legionary Students—Sibiu [no date]).

23. Petition by the Jewish Federation to Antonescu concerning the evacuation from Bucharest, 18 December 1940, in Ancel, *Documents*, vol. 1, doc. 143, p. 564.

24. Minister of the interior to the Jewish Federation concerning permission for Jews to continue living in the military zone in Bucharest, 21 October 1940, in Ancel, *Documents*, vol. 1, doc. 149, p. 571.

25. *Pinkas Hakehilot, Rumania*, 2:514.

26. Report on session of the Committee for the Management of Expropriated Jewish Property, in the village of Comănești, 10 December 1940, in Ancel, *Documents*, vol. 2, doc. 37, pp. 75–76.

27. Union of Jewish Communities to director general of the security police on forced evictions from apartments, 12 December 1940, in Ancel, *Documents*, vol. 2, doc. 42, p. 84.

28. Union of Jewish Communities to director general of the security police (Siguranța)

asking his permission for two hundred Jews from Panciu to remain in Focşani, 4 December 1940, in Ancel, *Documents*, vol. 2, doc. 28, p. 39.

29. Union of Jewish Communities to minister of the interior asking his approval for the return of six hundred Jews to Panciu, 21 March 1941, in Ancel, *Documents*, vol. 2, doc. 97, p. 333.

30. Jewish Federation's memorandum of 9 December 1940, in Ancel, *Documents*, vol. 2, doc. 36, p. 48.

31. Jewish Federation's memorandum of 9 December 1940, in Ancel, *Documents*, vol. 2, doc. 36, p. 72.

32. Dorohoi community to Union of Jewish Communities on the expulsion of the Jews of the district, 10 January 1941, in Ancel, *Documents*, vol. 2, doc. 54, p. 106.

33. Jewish Federation's memorandum to Antonescu of 12 January 1941, in Ancel, *Documents*, vol. 2, doc. 76, pp. 234–35.

34. Dorohoi community to Union of Jewish Communities on the expulsion of native youngsters from the city, 10 January 1941, in Ancel, *Documents*, vol. 2, doc. 55, p. 107.

35. *Pe marginea prăpastiei*, 1:164.

36. Government announcement of 5 October 1940, in Ancel, *Documents*, vol. 10, doc. 17, pp. 65–66.

37. *Pe marginea prăpastiei*, 1:169–71.

38. Carp, *Cartea neagră*, 1:117.

39. Jewish Federation to Prime Minister Antonescu on the expulsion of foreign Jews, 25 March 1941, in Ancel, *Documents*, vol. 2, doc. 102, p. 344.

40. Jewish Federation to minister of the interior concerning the destruction of synagogues by Legionnaires, 20 November 1940, in Ancel, *Documents*, vol. 2, doc. 10, pp. 15–16.

41. *Pe marginea prăpastiei*, 1:224.

42. Petition by the Union of Jewish Communities to Antonescu on the outcome of the investigation into the harassment of the Jews of Târgovişte, in Ancel, *Documents*, vol. 2, doc. 46, p. 89.

43. *Pe marginea prăpastiei*, 1:224–25.

44. *România*, 11 August 1940.

45. *Neamul Românesc*, 7 August 1940.

46. *Porunca Vremii*, 10 August 1940.

47. *Curentul*, 29 August 1940.

48. *Chemarea Vremii*, 8 August 1940.

49. *Porunca Vremii*, 13 August 1940.

50. *Porunca Vremii*, 20 August 1940.

51. *Porunca Vremii*, 4 September 1940.

52. *România*, 17 August 1940.

53. D. G. Mărculescu, "Inspiraţie Neromânescă" [Non-Romanian inspiration], *Cuvântul*, 30 October 1940.

54. Codreanu, *Pentru Legionari*, 475.

55. *Pe marginea prăpastiei*, 2:26–27.

56. Sima, *Era libertăţii*, 1:194.

57. Sima, *Era libertății*, 1:194.

58. *Pe marginea prăpastiei*, 2:55.

59. *Pe marginea prăpastiei*, 2:102.

60. *Porunca Vremii*, 10 December 1940.

61. *Buna Vestire*, 15 December 1940.

62. *Porunca Vremii*, 13 December 1940.

63. *Porunca Vremii*, 18 December 1940.

64. Petition by the president of the Jewish Federation and the chief rabbi to Prime Minister Antonescu concerning the illegality of the orders to close synagogues, in Ancel, *Documents*, vol. 1, doc. 94, p. 478.

65. *Timpul*, 15 September 1940.

66. *Timpul*, 16 September 1940.

67. Union of Jewish Communities to minister of the interior on the desecration and destruction of synagogues, 20 November 1940, in Ancel, *Documents*, vol. 2, doc. 10, p. 15; I. Șmilovici-Ploieșteanu, "Pogromul din Ploiești," *Mișmar* (Tel Aviv), 20 November 1985.

68. Report by envoy of the Union of Jewish Communities on the situation in Ploiești, 27 November 1940, in Ancel, *Documents*, vol. 2, doc. 19, pp. 28–29.

69. Memorandum of 9 December 1940, in Ancel, *Documents*, vol. 2, doc. 36, p. 55.

70. Carp, *Cartea neagră*, 1:150.

71. Report by envoy of the Union of Jewish Communities on the situation in Ploiești, 27 November 1940, in Ancel, *Documents*, vol. 2, doc. 19, pp. 28–29. The Union of Jewish Communities estimated the damages caused to the synagogues of Ploiești and Bucharest at 1 million lei (p. 16).

72. Union of Jewish Communities to Antonescu concerning the damage to community institutions, 9 December 1940, in Ancel, *Documents*, vol. 2, doc. 33, p. 45.

73. Carp, *Cartea neagră*, 1:149.

74. Carp, *Cartea neagră*, 1:152.

75. Carp, *Cartea neagră*, 1:167.

76. Petition by the Jewish Federation to minister of the interior concerning the arrest of the Vizhnitzer Rebbe, in Ancel, *Documents*, vol. 1, doc. 128, p. 540.

77. Carp, *Cartea neagră*, 1:154; Jewish Federation's memorandum of 9 December 1940, in Ancel, *Documents*, vol. 2, doc. 36, p. 60.

78. Union of Jewish Communities and Union of Sephardi Communities to the mayor of Bucharest on the expropriation of cemeteries, 16 October 1940, in Ancel, *Documents*, vol. 1, doc. 137, p. 554; Union of Jewish Communities to mayor of Bucharest on the expropriation of cemeteries, 11 December 1940, in Ancel, *Documents*, vol. 2, doc. 40, p. 82.

79. Carp, *Cartea neagră*, 1:118.

80. Jewish Federation's memorandum of 9 December 1940, in Ancel, *Documents*, vol. 2, doc. 36, p. 57.

81. Jewish Federation's memorandum of 9 December 1940, in Ancel, *Documents*, vol. 2, doc. 36, pp. 60, 66–67; Carp, *Cartea neagră*, 1:154.

82. Union of Jewish Communities and Union of Sephardi Communities to the mayor of Bucharest on the expropriation of cemeteries, 16 October 1940, in Ancel, *Documents*, vol. 1,

doc. 137, p. 554; Union of Jewish Communities to mayor of Bucharest on the expropriation of cemeteries, 11 December 1940, in Ancel, *Documents*, vol. 2, doc. 40, p. 82.

83. Ancel, *Documents*, vol. 1, doc. 136, p. 554.

84. Carp, *Cartea neagră*, 1:197.

85. Jewish Federation to undersecretary for colonization and refugees concerning the expropriation of cemeteries, 30 October 1940, in Ancel, *Documents*, vol. 1, doc. 158, p. 584.

86. Jewish Federation to undersecretary for colonization and refugees concerning the expropriation of cemeteries, 30 October 1940, in Ancel, *Documents*, vol. 1, doc. 158, p. 584.

87. Union of Jewish Communities to mayor of Bucharest on Antonescu's decision to halt the expropriation of Jewish cemeteries, 1 November 1940, in Ancel, *Documents*, vol. 1, doc. 165, p. 593.

88. Union of Jewish Communities to mayor of Bucharest on Antonescu's decision to halt the expropriation of Jewish cemeteries, 1 November 1940, in Ancel, *Documents*, vol. 1, doc. 165, p. 593.

89. Sima, *Era libertății*, 1:495, 496.

90. Sima, *Era libertății*, 1:496.

91. Carp, *Cartea neagră*, 1:69.

92. Jewish Federation's memorandum of 11 January 1941, with summary of the crimes perpetrated by the Legionnaires between 15 November 1940 and 1 January 1941, in Ancel, *Documents*, vol. 2, doc. 58, p. 129.

10. Antonescu and the Legionnaires

1. See the chapter on General Antonescu's connections with the Iron Guard in *Pe marginea prăpastiei*, 1:130

2. *Timpul*, 5 September 1940.

3. Simion, *Regimul politic*, 12.

4. Ion Antonescu, *Către români*; see memoranda by Antonescu to King Carol II, in particular the memorandum of 7 December 1934 on "corruption in the army."

5. YVA, Filderman Archive, P-6/47, p. 76. According to Filderman, Antonescu's father divorced his mother and then married a Jewish woman by the name of Frida Cuperman. After he became Conducător, Antonescu asked his stepmother (his father was no longer alive) to stop using the name Antonescu, but she refused (p. 72).

6. See Bernstein, *Les persécution des Juifs*, 28–29; Iancu, *Emanciparea Evreilor*, 126–35.

7. Watts, *Romanian Cassandra*, 180–81.

8. See Brătianu's letter to Antonescu of 20 May 1941, in Romanian State Archives, Bucharest, Presidency of the Council of Ministers Collection, file 81/1940, p. 161.

9. Carp, *Cartea neagră*, 1:74.

10. Drăgan, *Antonescu*, vol. 3, no. 140, p. 141.

11. Jewish Federation to Antonescu on the closure of synagogues, 11 September 1940, in Ancel, *Documents*, vol. 1, doc. 92, p. 475.

12. Report of Jewish Federation board session of 20 September 1940, in Ancel, *Documents*, vol. 1, doc. 106, p. 496.

13. Jewish Federation to minister of the national economy, 26 September 1940, in Ancel, *Documents*, vol. 1, doc. 115, p. 517.

14. Simion, *Regimul politic*, 144.

15. Carp, *Cartea neagră*, 1:75.

16. *Pe marginea prăpastiei*, 1:164.

17. *Pe marginea prăpastiei*, 1:170.

18. See Benjamin, *Problema evreiască*, 161–64.

19. Benjamin, *Problema evreiască*, 161–64.

20. *Pe marginea prăpastiei*, 1:179, 184.

21. *Pe marginea prăpastiei*, 1:215.

22. Antonescu's reply to the Jewish Federation's first memorandum of 16 September 1940, in Ancel, *Documents*, vol. 1, doc. 105, p. 495.

23. Antonescu to Sima, 14 January 1941, in Drăgan, *Antonescu*, vol. 3, no. 140, p. 141.

24. Antonescu to Sima, 14 January 1941, in Drăgan, *Antonescu*, vol. 3, no. 140, p. 141.

25. Antonescu to Sima, 14 January 1941, in Drăgan, *Antonescu*, vol. 3, no. 140, p. 141.

26. Law no. 80, 6 February 1941, in Consiliul Legislativ, "Colecțiune de legi si regulamente" [Collection of laws and regulations], tomul 19, 28 February 1941; copy in Ancel, *Documents*, vol. 2, doc. 83, pp. 264, 267.

27. *Documents on German Foreign Policy*, vol. 11, doc. 14, pp. 21–23.

28. *Documents on German Foreign Policy*, vol. 11, doc. 14, pp. 21–23.

29. *Chemarea Vremii*, 15 August 1940.

30. *Cuvântul*, 24 January 1941.

31. Sima, *Era libertății*, 1:79.

32. Record of the conversation between Hitler and Antonescu in Obersalzberg, 14 January 1941, in *Documents on German Foreign Policy*, vol. 11, doc. 652, p. 1094.

33. Transcript of government session of 21 September 1940, in National Romanian Archives, *Shorthand Notes*, vol. 1, doc. 3, pp. 70–71 (author's emphasis).

34. *Documents on German Foreign Policy*, vol. 11, doc. 276, p. 455.

35. *Documents on German Foreign Policy*, vol. 11, doc. 193, p. 325.

36. Testimony of former German ambassador Fabricius before the court in Frankfurt, West Germany, 1956, as recorded by Filderman, yva, Filderman Archive, P-6/47, p. 70.

37. On the purchase of such companies, see Hillgruber, *Hitler, Carol und Antonescu*, 157.

38. *Procesul marei trădări naționale*, 76.

39. Thanks to the commander of the Legionary police in Bucharest, Col. Ștefan Zăvoianu, and other accomplices, Tester managed to lay his hands on Jewish property as follows: 3,500 pounds sterling from an engineer; 2 million lei from a Jew; 4 million lei from a Jewish-owned company; a residential building in Bucharest; 1 million lei and a car from a factory owner in Iași; a sock factory belonging to Bela Goldstein worth 30 million lei; and cash in the amount of 7 million lei. After the suppression of the rebellion Tester returned the residential building and sock factory to their Jewish owners but not the cash. See Brestoiu, *O istorie*, 245–46.

40. See Ancel, "German-Romanian Relationship," 253.

41. *Timpul*, 30 September 1940; copy in Ancel, *Documents*, vol. 1, doc. 125, pp. 536–37.

42. U.S. ambassador Franklin Mott Gunther to the State Department in Washington, telegram, 10 February 1941, in Ancel, *Documents*, vol. 2, doc. 81, p. 260.

11. The Legionnaires' Rebellion

1. Sima, *Era libertății*, 2:282.
2. *Pe marginea prăpastiei*, 1:215–16 (emphasis in the original).
3. Gh. M. Ciocan, in *Porunca Vremii*, 11 January 1941.
4. N. M. Pop, "Ultima invazie," *Cuvântul*, 20 January 1941.
5. *Porunca Vremii*, 14 January 1941.
6. *Porunca Vremii*, 4 January 1941.
7. I. Rădulescu, "Israele, n-ai invins" [Israel, you have not prevailed], *Porunca Vremii*, 9 January 1941.
8. "Călăii adevărați au fost jidanii," *Porunca Vremii*, 9 January 1941.
9. All of the preceding quotations are taken from *Cuvântul*, 21 January 1941 (emphasis in the original).
10. Watts, *In serviciul mareşalului*, 1:40–42.
11. Ionescu, "Technique and Springs of Terror during the Iron Guard's and Antonescu's Dictatorship," *Impotriva fascismului*, 202 (in Romanian).
12. Carp, *Cartea neagră*, 1:146.
13. Watts, *In serviciul mareşalului*, 1:104.
14. *Pe marginea prăpastiei*, 2:322–25, 326.
15. *Pe marginea prăpastiei*, 2:241.
16. YVA, Filderman Archive, P-6/46, p. 70.
17. See a reprint of announcements and appeals by the Legionary movement as well as newspaper articles and Legionary publications that appeared during the rebellion, in *Pe marginea prăpastiei*, 2:233–34.
18. *Pe marginea prăpastiei*, 2:318.
19. *Pe marginea prăpastiei*, 2:319.
20. *Porunca Vremii*, 22 January 1941.
21. G. M. Ciocan, "Recensământul Jidanilor" [Census of the Yids], *Porunca Vremii*, 22 January 1941.
22. *Cuvântul*, 22 January 1941.
23. *Cuvântul*, 24 January 1941.
24. Ancel, *Documents*, vol. 2, doc. 64, pp. 159–65.
25. For a copy of this issue, see Ancel, *Documents*, vol. 2, doc. 64, pp. 159–63.
26. *Buna Vestire*, 21 January 1941.
27. *Pe marginea prăpastiei*, 2:328.
28. *Pe marginea prăpastiei*, 2:102–5.
29. Palaghiță, *Garda de Fier*, 147. Iaşinschi justified the decision on "the need to stand firm," and when he tried to revoke the order following a request by one of the Legionary heads "not to set fire to the city," he was told, "It is too late . . . the squads have already left."
30. *Timpul*, 3 February 1941.
31. Carp, *Cartea neagră*, 1:77.

32. Jewish Federation's memoir to Antonescu on the pogrom of 21–23 January, delivered on 5 March 1941 (hereafter Jewish Federation's memorandum of 5 March 1941), in Ancel, *Documents*, vol. 2, doc. 90, p. 290.

33. Report on the Legionary uprising delivered to Dr. Abraham Silberschein in Geneva, January 1941, YVA, Silbershein Archive, M-20/103 (hereafter report to Switzerland); copy in Ancel, *Documents*, vol. 2, doc. 72a, pp. 198–220. See also Jewish Federation's memorandum to Antonescu of 1 April 1941, p. 377.

34. *Pe marginea prăpastiei*, 2:253.

35. Jewish Federation's memorandum of 5 March 1941, in Ancel, *Documents*, vol. 2, doc. 90, pp. 290–99.

36. Fătu and Spălățelu, *Garda de Fier*, 354.

37. F. Brunea-Fox, *Orașul măcelului*, 70.

38. Jewish Federation's memorandum of 5 March 1941, in Ancel, *Documents*, vol. 2, doc. 90, p. 291.

39. Jewish Federation's memorandum of 5 March 1941, in Ancel, *Documents*, vol. 2, doc. 90, pp. 293–94.

40. Report by Carp to Filderman on the pogroms and on the torture he was subjected to in the Fifteenth Police Inspectorate, 28 January 1941, in Ancel, *Documents*, vol. 2, doc. 68, p. 187.

41. Jewish Federation's memorandum of 5 March 1941, in Ancel, *Documents*, vol. 2, doc. 90, p. 299.

42. Testimony of the military prosecutor Vlădescu, who investigated the Legionary crimes on behalf of the Antonescu regime and appeared for the prosecution in their trials in 1941. Vlădescu, "Ianuarie 1941."

43. Barbul, *Mémorial Antonesco*, 106.

44. Vlădescu, "Ianuarie 1941," 197.

45. A. Axelrad, "Glasul lui Bucur în cele trei zile" [The voice of Bucur in the three days], in Ancel, *Documents*, vol. 2, doc. 72, p. 202. Bucur was the legendary Romanian shepherd after whom Bucharest was named.

46. Petition by the Union of Jewish Communities to the military commander of the capital to return ritual and holy objects to the union, 15 April 1941, in Ancel, *Documents*, vol. 2, doc. 119, p. 386.

47. Jewish Federation's memorandum of 5 March 1941, in Ancel, *Documents*, vol. 2, doc. 90, p. 309.

48. For a partial list of buildings that were burnt down, see Carp, *Cartea neagră*, 1:243–44.

49. Jewish Federation's memorandum of 5 March 1941, in Ancel, *Documents*, vol. 2, doc. 90, p. 309.

50. Brunea-Fox, *Orașul măcelului*, 71–72.

51. Jewish Federation's memorandum to Antonescu of 1 April 1941, in Ancel, *Documents*, vol. 2, doc. 110, p. 376. See also statistical report of Jewish casualties during the uprising, drawn up by the Jewish Federation, in Ancel, *Documents*, vol. 2, doc. 98, pp. 334–39. For a list of names of the injured and their businesses and a financial assessment of damages, see Carp, *Cartea neagră*, 1:247–323.

52. Jewish Federation's memorandum to Antonescu of 1 April 1941, p. 377.

53. *Pe marginea prăpastiei*, 2:235. As stated, both the Antonescu regime and the Communist historians considered ordinary citizens, but not Jews, as casualties.

54. Report to Switzerland; copy in Ancel, *Documents*, vol. 2, doc. 72a, p. 199.

55. Hilberg, *Destruction of the European Jews*, 489.

56. Brunea-Fox, *Orașul măcelului*, 50.

57. *Universul*, 31 January 1941.

12. The Jewish Leadership

1. Carp, *Cartea neagră*, 1:71.

2. Ofir, *In the Lion's Den*, 166.

3. A. Yehuda, "Drum bun" [Farewell], *Renașterea Noastră*, 23 November 1940.

4. Letter from Chaim Shorer and Melech Neustadt to Meir Kotic and Frish, 21 July 1940, Labor Party Archives, Beit Berl 101/40, quoted in Ofir, *In the Lion's Den*, 168.

5. Letter from Chaim Shorer and Melech Neustadt to Meir Kotic and Frish, 21 July 1940, Labor Party Archives, Beit Berl 101/40, quoted in Ofir, *In the Lion's Den*, 143.

6. Letter from Chaim Shorer and Melech Neustadt to Meir Kotic and Frish, 21 July 1940, Labor Party Archives, Beit Berl 101/40, quoted in Ofir, *In the Lion's Den*, 161.

7. Letter by the Jewish writer Camil Baltazar to Filderman, 25 November 1941, in Ancel, *Documents*, vol. 3, doc. 246, p. 408. Baltazar emphasized that "he [Zissu] did so at the very moment when you were being searched and when your very life was perhaps in danger."

8. See Jewish Federation regulations, in Ancel, *Documents*, vol. 1, doc. 60, pp. 389–95; "Regulations Concerning the Activity of the Jewish Cult," ratified by the Jewish Federation on 14 May 1940, in Ancel, *Documents*, vol. 1, doc. 62, pp. 396–405.

9. For the names, addresses, phone numbers, and titles of the leaders of the Jewish Federation and the Bucharest community, see Ancel, *Documents*, vol. 3, doc. 8, p. 14. For a list of the heads of the aforementioned Jewish organizations, see Filderman, draft memoirs, YVA, Filderman Archive, P-6/47, p. 81.

10. Protocol of the Jewish Federation's Executive and Central Committee session, 2 September 1940, in Ancel, *Documents*, vol. 2, doc. 88, p. 467; Carp, *Cartea neagră*, 1:72.

11. The representative of the Bacău community stated in the session that "even if, on the face of it, the potential is there, the people are petty . . . and only with great difficulty managed to raise 10,000 lei." Ancel, *Documents*, vol. 1, doc. 88, p. 467.

12. Protocol of the Jewish Federation's executive session, 22 August 1940, in Ancel, *Documents*, vol. 1, doc. 85, p. 460.

13. Filderman's memorandum to Antonescu of 16 September 1940, in Ancel, *Documents*, vol. 1, doc. 99, p. 486.

14. Protocol of Union of Jewish Communities' executive, 22 August 1940, in Ancel, *Documents*, vol. 1, doc. 85, p. 460. See also protocol of the Union of Jewish Communities' executive, 15 November 1940, in Ancel, *Documents*, vol. 2, doc. 5, p. 6. Camil drew up the "Statistical Report of Jewish Casualties during the Pogrom," 21 March 1941, in Ancel, *Documents*, vol. 2, doc. 90, pp. 334–39.

15. The Filderman Archive at Yad Vashem contains several volumes of surveys of the

press. See J. Ancel, ed., *Dr. W. Filderman Archive*, record group P-6 (Jerusalem: Yad Vashem, 1974) (in Hebrew).

16. Watts, *In serviciul mareşalulu*, 2:177.

17. *Curierul Israelit*, 22 October 1944; USHMM/SRI, RG-25.004M, reel 52, Regatul României, Tribunalul Militar C.M.C, Parchetul Militar, Proces Verbal, file no. 4273/1941, p. 2.

18. Carp, *Cartea neagră*, 1:72.

19. Carp, *Cartea neagră*, 1:73. Antonescu himself was living proof of the success of this approach, as he wrote in one of the memoranda submitted by the Jewish Federation: "I do not defend the Jews who are, to a large extent, responsible for the calamities that have befallen this country. However, I will not tolerate actions that threaten the revitalization I wish to bring about through peace and order . . . [or] the impetuous acts of people who do not understand how much they are harming the country and the Legionary movement." Carp, *Cartea neagră*, 1:73.

20. Memorandum of the Union of Jewish Communities to the minister of national education concerning the expulsion of Jews from the state education system, 17 September 1940, in Ancel, *Documents*, vol. 1, doc. 103, pp. 477, 482.

21. Filderman, draft memoirs, YVA, Filderman Archive, P-6/47: 1940, p. 91.

22. Interview with Filderman in *Di idishe presse* (Rio de Janeiro), 4 June 1948.

23. Antonescu to Filderman, "Letter of Undertaking," by 18 September 1940, in Ancel, *Documents*, vol. 1, doc. 105, p. 495; Filderman, draft memoirs, YVA, Filderman Archive, P-6/47: 1940, pp. 75–77.

24. Filderman to Antonescu, "Letter of Undertaking," 16 September 1940, in Ancel, *Documents*, vol. 1, doc. 99, pp. 486–87. In his letter Filderman emphasized that "the previous government explicitly forbade shipping illegal immigrants [to Palestine] at the British legation's request."

25. *Pe marginea prăpastiei*, 2:346; Filderman, draft memoirs, YVA, Filderman Archive, P-6/54: 1940, p. 143.

26. M. Ussoskin to Filderman, 9 September 1948, in Filderman, draft memoirs, YVA, Filderman Archive, P-6/35, pp. 129–30.

13. Foundations of the Antonescu Regime

1. Antonescu's reply of 22 June 1941 to Iuliu Maniu's memoranda of 4 December 1940 and 4 April 1941 (hereafter Antonescu's reply of 22 June 1941), in Drăgan, *Antonescu*, vol. 2, no. 13, pp. 189–213.

2. Ancel, *Documents*, vol. 1, no. 79, p. 446.

3. N. Davidescu, "Rassa, naţie şi patrie," *Acţiunea*, 30 March 1941.

4. O. Vlădescu, "Naţiune si generaţie," *Timpul*, 6 May 1941.

5. For more on Antonescu's policy toward the Gypsies, see Ancel, "Tragedia romilor."

6. Watts, *In serviciul mareşalului*, 1:166.

7. Antonescu's reply of 22 June 1941, in Drăgan, *Antonescu*, vol. 2, no. 13, p. 205.

8. Antonescu's reply of 22 June 1941, in Drăgan, *Antonescu*, vol. 2, no. 13, pp. 205–6.

9. Maniu's memorandum to Ion and Mihai Antonescu, 18 July 1941, in Drăgan, *Antonescu*, vol. 2, no. 15, p. 218.

10. Brătianu's speech in consultation with his close aides, 14 February 1941, in Drăgan, *Antonescu*, vol. 2, no. 5, p. 159.

11. Simion, *Peliminarii politico-diplomatice*, 131.

12. Victor Dimitriuc, the minister of the national economy, resigned from the presidency of the government commission for economic negotiations with Germany on 11 June 1941; the general secretaries of the Ministry of the National Economy—Arthur Gorsky, Traian Nitescu, and Emil Marin—resigned in solidarity with their chief. Professor I. N. Fintescu resigned on 19 February 1943; the minister of agriculture and domains, Ion Sichitiu, resigned in March 1942; his successor, Aurelian Pană, resigned on 3 July 1943. The next head of the Ministry of Agriculture, Ion Marian, also resigned, in April 1944. The minister of finance, Alexandru Neagu, resigned in April 1944. The minister of public works and communications, Professor Constantin Bușilă, resigned on 5 August 1943. The minister of education, religions, and arts, Radu Rosetti, resigned in November 1941. The minister of justice, Gh. P. Docan, resigned in February 1941. His successor, Professor Constantin C. Stoicescu, resigned in August 1942. The chief of the Army High Command, Gen. Iosif Iacobic, resigned on 20 January 1942 because of his disagreement with the military commitments Antonescu had taken toward Germany.

13. *Porunca Vremii*, 20 April 1941.

14. *Porunca Vremii*, 20 April 1941.

14. The Government's Attitude toward the Jews

1. *Unirea*, 30 March 1941.

2. *Curentul*, 10 March 1941.

3. *Unirea*, 6 March 1941; *Curentul*, 6 March 1941.

4. Gh. M. Ciocan, "Recensământul și ideea de neam," in *Porunca Vremii*, 12 March 1941; *Luceafărul*, 27 March 1941.

5. *Timpul*, 1 March 1941.

6. "Ce devin evreii noștri?" [What will be with our Jews?], *Porunca Vremii*, 6 March 1941.

7. *Sfarmă Piatră*, 5 May 1941.

8. *Sfarmă Piatră*, 9 June 1941; Dr. Paul Mihăescu, "Front unic naționalist," *Sfarmă Piatră*, 20 June 1941.

9. I. P. Prundeni, "Antisemitismul românesc," *Porunca Vremii*, 6 April 1941. The author is implying that the Jews were responsible for the fact that Eminescu ended his life in a lunatic asylum.

10. For example, the speeches of Prime Minister Ionel Brătianu and Minister of Foreign Affairs Mihail Cogălniceanu at the 1878 Berlin Peace Congress preached against granting civil rights to Jews, and an antisemitic poem by Ion Creangă published in 1878 called for an economic boycott of Jews. See *Sfarmă Piatră*, 20 May 1941; *Universul*, 5 May 1941; *Porunca Vremii*, 3 May 1941.

11. C. Hentzescu, "Sa reînviem virtuțile românești" [Let's revive Romanian values], *Universul*, 26 April 1941.

12. N. Davidescu, "Loialitatea românească" [Romanian loyalty], *Acțiunea*, 27 April 1941.

13. *Viața*, 16 June 1941; *Curentul*, 16 June 1941.

14. Wilhelm Filderman, memoirs, vol. 2, 1940–44, YVA, P-6/58, p. 151.

15. Carp, *Cartea neagră*, 1:25.

16. Decree-Law no. 135, *Monitorul Oficial*, no. 47, 25 February 1941; Simion, *Peliminarii politico-diplomatice*, 50.

17. List of anti-Jewish measures adopted by the Antonescu regime, 24 January–22 June 1941 (hereafter Carp's list), YVA, Filderman Archive, P-6/42, p. 6. The list was drawn up by the Jewish Federation's secretary, Matatias Carp.

18. "The Treatment of Jews in Rumania," March 1941, in Ancel, *Documents*, vol. 2, doc. 109, pp. 373–74. This is a report on a study made in January 1941 by a veteran correspondent of the Jewish Telegraph Agency.

19. "The Treatment of Jews in Rumania," March 1941, in Ancel, *Documents*, vol. 2, doc. 109, pp. 373–74.

20. "The Treatment of Jews in Rumania," March 1941, in Ancel, *Documents*, vol. 2, doc. 109, pp. 373–74.

21. *Ordinea*, 30 March 1941.

22. Law for the Nationalization of Jewish Urban Property, 28 March, Decree-Law no. 842, *Monitorul Oficial*, no. 74, March 1941; *Curentul*, 28 February 1941; *Ordinea*, 30 March 1941. For a copy of Mihai Antonescu's rationale for the law, see Ancel, *Documents*, vol. 2, doc. 106, pp. 358–61.

23. Arh. Mucichescu-Tunari, "Problema Jidovească în statul antisemit" [The Yid problem in the antisemitic state], *Invierea*, 2 February 1941.

24. Filderman to the minister of the national economy on the suffering of the Jews, 7 April 1941, in Ancel, *Documents*, vol. 2, doc. 114, p. 381.

25. Decree-Law no. 236, *Monitorul Oficial*, no. 31, 6 February 1941.

26. Decree-Law no. 693, *Monitorul Oficial*, no. 65, 18 March 1941.

27. Decree-Law no. 410, *Monitorul Oficial*, no. 46, 24 February 1941.

28. Decree-Law no. 1195, *Monitorul Oficial*, no. 100, 30 April 1941; *Viața*, 19 April 1941.

29. *Universul*, 26 March 1941.

30. Union of Jewish Communities to the minister of the national economy, asking him to overrule the Bucharest municipality's decision to remove all Jewish meat merchants from the abattoirs so as to improve the supply of meat to the city, 7 April 1941, in Ancel, *Documents*, vol. 2, p. 382.

31. *Timpul*, 3 March 1941.

32. *Universul*, 13 March 1941.

33. Decision by the Disciplinary Committee of the Buzău Physicians' Association concerning the Jewish doctor Boris Camerman, in Ancel, *Documents*, vol. 10, doc. 193, pp. 540–42.

34. Decree-Law no. 968, *Monitorul Oficial*, no. 85, 9 April 1941.

35. Central Committee Archive, collection 24, file 3371, 10 February 1941, p. 104.

36. Lists of civil servants married to Jewish women, Central Committee Archive, collection 24, file 3371, pp. 121, 123, 135–37.

37. Decree-Law no. 1867, *Monitorul Oficial*, no. 147, 24 June 1941. The law was amended about four days later to allow marriages to Germans and Italians but not Hungarians. Decree-Law no. 1909, *Monitorul Oficial*, no. 151, 28 June 1941; see also *Acţiunea*, 10 April 1941.

38. *Luceafărul*, 18 April 1941; minister of justice to minster of the interior on the interpretation of Law no. 968 of 7 April 1941 concerning the ban on intermarriage, 12 April 1941, Central Committee Archive, collection 24, file 3371, p. 166.

39. The term the newspaper used to denote marriage to Jewish women is untranslatable, but its general sense is that the marriage was never valid in the first place.

40. "The Treatment of Jews in Rumania," March 1941, in Ancel, *Documents*, vol. 2, doc. 109, p. 375.

41. *Renaşterea Noastră*, 14 April 1941.

42. *Universul*, 15 April 1941.

43. Decree-Law no. 711, *Monitorul Oficial*, no. 68, 21 March 1941; *Porunca Vremii*, 25 March 1941.

44. Decree of the Ministry of National Defense, no. 23325, *Monitorul Oficial*, no. 37, 13 February 1941; Consiliul Legislativ, "Colecţiune de legi si regulamente," tomul 19, pp. 31–32.

45. Filderman, memoirs, vol. 2, 1940–44, YVA, P-6/58, p. 114. The law is not known and is not mentioned in *Monitorul Oficial*.

46. Federation of Jewish Communities in Romania, *Evreii din România*, doc. 35, 1:127–28.

47. Simion, *Peliminarii politico-diplomatice*, 123.

48. "O cucerire de interior, Naţionalizarea oraşelor," *Curentul*, 3 April 1941; Pr. Gh. Butnariu, "Marele fapt de restaurare," *Porunca Vremii*, 3 April 1941; "Naţionalizarea oraşelor," *Universul*, 3 April 1941; "Naţionalizarea oraşelor," *Porunca Vremii*, 3 April 1941.

49. *Unirea*, 12 April 1941; *Timpul*, 12 April 1941; *Viaţa*, 12 April 1941; *Universul*, 17 March 1942.

50. *Renaşterea Noastră*, 4 April 1941. Note that the Marghiloman Law was passed in 1918 at the instigation of Germany and demanded that Romania, which was beaten at that stage of the war, award civil rights to its Jews.

51. *Universul*, 24 March 1941.

52. *Renaşterea Noastră*, 17 and 24 May 1941.

53. *Renaşterea Noastră*, 11 April 1941.

54. *Renaşterea Noastră*, 14 April 1941.

55. *Universul*, 14 April 1941. The wife of a Jewish officer who fought on the front and later died claimed Category 2 for her children. The court granted the request but ruled that the wife was not eligible, since she was not the child of a Jewish officer. *Renaşterea Noastră*, 7 June 1941.

56. *Universul*, 26 April 1941; 4 April 1941.

57. Cristian, *Patru ani de urgie*, 45.

58. Cristian, *Patru ani de urgie*, 45–46.

59. Decree-Law no. 1216, *Monitorul Oficial*, no. 102, 3 May 1941. For a translation of the law, see Ancel, *Documents*, vol. 8, doc. 170, pp. 230–31.

60. Decree Concerning the Organization of the Sub-secretariat of the State for Romanization, Colonization, and Inventory, Decree-Law no. 1219, *Monitorul Oficial*, no. 102, 3

May 1941. For excerpts of the law in English translation, see Ancel, *Documents*, vol. 8, doc. 173, p. 231.

61. Study of the Jewish problem in Romania compiled by Division 1 of the Romanian army's High Command, undated (hereafter Romanian army study), in Ancel, *Documents*, vol. 10, doc. 107, p. 279. After Romania ceded southern Dobruja to Bulgaria, following the Craiova Agreement of 7 September 1940, population exchanges took place between Romania and Bulgaria.

62. Excerpt of the first study on antisemitic legislation carried out by Division 2 of the High Command, [late 1941?], in Ancel, *Documents*, vol. 10, doc. 66, pp. 157–58.

63. *Unirea*, 4 April 1941.

64. *Unirea*, 17 April 1941.

65. See the introduction to M. Antonescu, *In serviciul justiției românești*.

15. Romanization (II)

1. *Curentul*, 27 February 1941.

2. *Universul*, 2 March 1941.

3. *Cuvântul*, 5 May 1941.

4. Directivele D-lui General Antonescu Conducătorul Statului [Directives of General Antonescu, leader of the state], "Noua așezare a politicii interne: Problema evrească" [The new foundations of internal policy: The Jewish question], *Universul*, 20 February 1941.

5. *Timpul*, 6 March 1941; *Unirea*, 7 March 1941.

6. Decree-Law no. 554, *Monitorul Oficial*, no. 53, 4 March 1941. See also Romanian army study, in Ancel, *Documents*, vol. 10, doc. 107, pp. 269–74. A summary of the law can be found in YVA, Filderman Archive, Romanian Collection, P-6/46, p. 70, 0-11/52a, pp. 26–27.

7. Carp's list, YVA, Filderman Archive, P-6/42, p. 7.

8. Decree-Law no. 811, *Monitorul Oficial*, no. 71, 25 March 1941.

9. Decree-Law no. 2693, *Monitorul Oficial*, no. 228, 26 September 1941.

10. Decree-Law no. 1216, *Monitorul Oficial*, no. 102, 3 May 1941. For selected English translations of the law, see Ancel, *Documents*, vol. 8, doc. 170, pp. 230–31. See also Romanian army study, in Ancel, *Documents*, vol. 10, doc. 107, p. 279.

11. Romanian army study, in Ancel, *Documents*, vol. 10, doc. 107, p. 276. See also statistical summary of the Romanization of factory workers, 14 March 1942, in Ancel, *Documents*, vol. 10, doc. 75, pp. 180–81. The summary was drawn up by the Central Romanization Office and includes data on the replacement of Jewish experts by Romanians and a breakdown by profession.

12. Romanian army study, in Ancel, *Documents*, vol. 10, doc. 107, p. 283.

13. *Universul*, 13 June 1943.

14. Romanian army study, in Ancel, *Documents*, vol. 10, doc. 107, p. 276. Decree-Law no. 64504 of Ministry of Labor, *Monitorul Oficial*, no. 303, 24 December 1940.

15. Romanian army study, in Ancel, *Documents*, vol. 10, doc. 107, p. 351.

16. *Universul*, 4 May 1942; statistical summary of the Romanization of factory workers, 14 March 1942, in Ancel, *Documents*, vol. 10, doc. 75, p. 76.

17. Simion, *Peliminarii politico-diplomatice*, 120.

18. N. Crainic, "Raporturile culturale germano-române" [Cultural ties between Germany and Romania], *Unirea*, 29 April 1941. The article first appeared in *Berliner Boersenzeitung*.

19. S. Marinescu, "N-avem ce ceti? Scriitori evrei" [Nothing to read? Jewish authors], *Porunca Vremii*, 8 May 1941.

20. On this topic, see Volovici, "Romanian Intellectuals."

21. "Noul regim al împrimarilor sonore: Comunicat" [New regulations on sound recordings: Announcement], *Universul*, 14 November 1941; copy in Ancel, *Documents*, vol. 3, doc. 240, p. 401.

22. Carp's list, YVA, Filderman Archive, P-6/42, p. 91.

23. *Universul*, 31 December 1941; copy in Ancel, *Documents*, vol. 3, doc. 301, p. 482.

16. The Final Solution, 1941–42

1. Karl Ritter, ambassador for special assignments, German Foreign Office, Berlin, to the embassy in Moscow, 22 February 1941, in United Restitution Organization, *Documentation*, 1:118.

2. Note by the British ambassador of 10 February 1941, in United Restitution Organization, *Documentation*, 3:447.

3. Note of 6 June 1941, in United Restitution Organization, *Documentation*, 3:452; see also the Italian foreign minister's diary, Ciano, *Journal politique*, 1:296.

4. Brătianu's letter to Ion Antonescu, 20 May 1941, in Drăgan, *Antonescu*, vol. 2, no. 12, p. 187.

5. Killinger to Foreign Ministry in Berlin, 5 February 1941, in *Documents on German Foreign Policy*, vol. 5, doc. 13, p. 21.

6. Killinger to Foreign Ministry in Berlin, 26 February 1941, in *Documents on German Foreign Policy*, vol. 5, doc. 94, pp. 171–76.

7. Antonescu to Field Marshal Manstein, 9 December 1942, in Drăgan, *Antonescu*, vol. 3, no. 132, p. 323.

8. *Timpul*, 23 April 1941.

9. Killinger to Ribbentrop, via Consul General Adolf Windecker (temporarily assigned to the legation in Romania), 12 February 1941, Central Committee Archive, collection 10, file 9G, p. 36.

10. Simion, *Regimul politic*, 227; Barbul, *Mémorial Antonesco*, 81–82.

11. Taylor, *Goebbels Diaries*, 236, 256.

12. Killinger to Foreign Ministry in Berlin, 5 February 1941, in *Documents on German Foreign Policy*, vol. 12, doc. 14, p. 22.

13. *Sfarmă Piatră*, 2 February 1941; *Timpul*, 2 February 1941; *Timpul*, 27 February 1941.

14. *Sfarmă Piatră*, 3 May 1941.

15. *Universul*, 21 June 1941.

16. *Gazeta Ţării*, 1 and 6 June 1941.

17. Killinger to Foreign Ministry in Berlin, 5 February 1941, in *Documents on German Foreign Policy*, vol. 12, doc. 14, p. 22.

18. The German legation to the Foreign Ministry in Berlin, 27 October 1941, in *Documents on German Foreign Policy*, vol. 13, doc. 426, p. 702.

19. Taylor, *Goebbels Diaries*, 184; see also *Hitler's Secret Conversations*, 90–91.

20. From Killinger's speech to local Germans in the small town of Cristian (near Braşov), *Curentul*, 23 May 1941.

21. *Timpul*, 6 June 1941.

22. *Viaţa*, 28 May 1941.

23. See Personenverzeichnis [Biographical sketches], in United Restitution Organization, *Documentation*, 3:11–12. Regarding Richter, Klugkist explained that "the SD's liaison officers would come to Bucharest as simple tourists, and once there, would liaise with the Iron Guard and apparently also provide them with arms." See Klugkist's testimony of 1956 before the Sachen court in Germany, as recorded by Filderman, YVA, Filderman Archive, P-6/47, p. 71.

24. Cable from Mihai Antonescu to Romanian legation in Ankara, 14 March 1944, Romanian Foreign Ministry Archive, Bucharest, Ankara file, T 1, p. 108.

25. Rosenberg's statement of 28 March 1941 on the removal of the Jews from Europe, in *Der Prozess gegen die Hauptkriegsverbrecher*, doc. PS-2889, 21:255.

26. First report by Richter, advisor on Jewish affairs, to the legate Killinger, 21 May 1941, in Ancel, *Documents*, vol. 2, doc. 129, pp. 401–2.

27. Jäckel, *Hitlers Weltanschauung*, 72–73.

28. First report by Richter, advisor on Jewish affairs, to the legate Killinger, 21 May 1941, in Ancel, *Documents*, vol. 2, doc. 129, pp. 401–2.

29. First report by Richter, advisor on Jewish affairs, to the legate Killinger, 21 May 1941, in Ancel, *Documents*, vol. 2, doc. 129, pp. 403–4.

30. Antonescu's reply of 22 June 1941, in Drăgan, *Antonescu*, vol. 2, no. 13, p. 194.

31. Nuremberg Documents, PS-1024, PS-212; see also United Restitution Organization, *Documentation*, 1:127–28, 145.

32. Nuremberg Documents, PS-1028, p. 129.

33. Nuremberg Documents, NOKW-2080, pp. 124–26; Hilberg, *La destruction des Juifs*, 247–48.

34. Hilberg, *La destruction des Juifs*, 251.

35. Nuremberg Documents, NOKW-3485; United Restitution Organization, *Documentation*, 1:130; Hilberg, *La destruction des Juifs*, 248.

36. Transcript of the talk between Hitler and Antonescu, 12 June 1941, in *Documents on German Foreign Policy*, vol. 12, doc. 614, p. 1004. Antonescu's team included Gheorghe Davidescu, secretary general of the Foreign Ministry; Col. Radu Galin, a member of Antonescu's military cabinet; Maj. Octavian Niculescu, his aide-de-camp; and Dr. Scoescu, his personal physician. See United Restitution Organization, *Documentation*, 3:454.

37. Transcript of the talk between Hitler and Antonescu, 12 June 1941, in *Documents on German Foreign Policy*, vol. 12, doc. 614, p. 1006.

38. On 16 August 1941 German soldiers forced thirteen thousand Bessarabian Jews who were captured by the Wehrmacht in the Ukraine to return to Bessarabia. Niculescu report, Kishinev Archive, 706-1-69, p. 9. General Antonescu, who wanted Bessarabia "free" of Jews, complained to Killinger that the return of the Jews to Bessarabia "contradicted the guidelines which the Führer had specified to him in Munich regarding the treatment of the eastern Jews." See *Documents on German Foreign Policy*, vol. 13, doc. 207, pp. 318–19. In a letter

dated 27 August 1941 Ritter, of the German Foreign Ministry, informed the Wehrmacht's General Staff of Antonescu's complaint and added, "I have been unable to discover anything at the Foreign Ministry regarding guidelines which the Führer gave General Antonescu with respect to the treatment of the eastern Jews. The official record of the conversation between the Führer and Antonescu in the Führer's apartments in Munich does not contain anything on this subject. However, as the Führer talked to Antonescu in Munich also on other occasions, it is entirely possible that the question of the eastern Jews was also discussed there. In any case, there is no reason to doubt the accuracy of General Antonescu's assertion. I therefore recommend that General Antonescu's wish be given consideration and that the German military authorities concerned be instructed not to move the Jews back to Bessarabia." *Documents on German Foreign Policy*, vol. 13, doc. 207, p. 319; see also doc. 332, p. 528.

39. Schmidt, *Statist auf diplomatischer Buehne*. Professor Eberhard Jäckel of Stuttgart University, who has published several works on Hitler, looked into my hypothesis that Hitler discussed the Final Solution with Antonescu as early as June 1941 and informed him of his intentions and that the translator Schmidt omitted this from the transcript of the talk. In a letter he sent me on 13 June 1987 Jäckel corroborated my hypothesis, adding, "It is surprising that Schmidt omitted the discussion of the handling of the eastern Jews." Jäckel also believed that Ritter consulted Hitler before giving the go ahead. Professor Jäckel ended by saying, "None of this detracts from the accuracy of your hypothesis that Hitler and Antonescu discussed the handling of the Jews. The discovery of this exceptionally significant fact is to your credit." The letter is in my possession. On this subject, see Ancel, "German-Romanian Relationship."

40. Report of the conversation between Ribbentrop and Mihai Antonescu of 23 September 1942, which was also attended by Ambasador Ritter, Karl Clodius, Dr. Hermann Neubacher, General Gerstenberg, Gen. Gheorghe Jienescu, and Col. Radu Davidescu, in United Restitution Organization, *Documentation*, 4:578. Mihai Antonescu effectively reneged on his prior commitment to deport all the Jews of the Regat to the Bełżec extermination camp in occupied Poland.

41. Transcript of the talk of 23 September 1942 as recorded by Mihai Antonescu, in Ancel, *Documents*, vol. 9, doc. 176, pp. 446–60.

42. Transcript of the talk between Hitler and Antonescu, 12 June 1941, in *Documents on German Foreign Policy*, vol. 12, doc. 614, p. 997; Antonescu to Hitler, 30 July 1941, in *Documents on German Foreign Policy*, vol. 13, doc. 167, pp. 266–67; *Procesul marei trădări naționale*, 53.

43. Protocol of the talk between Hitler and Antonescu in Munich, 13 June 1941, in *Documents on German Foreign Policy*, vol. 12, doc. 614, p. 1006.

44. Antonescu's reply of 22 June 1941, in Drăgan, *Antonescu*, vol. 2, no. 13, p. 197 (author's emphasis).

45. Ion Antonescu to C. Brătianu, 29 October 1942, in Direcția Generală a Arhivelor Statului, *23 August 1944*, 1:437, 438, 445 (author's emphasis).

46. *Sfarmă Piatră*, 1 June 1941; 8 June 1941; 18 June 1941.

47. I. Sân-Giorgiu, "Chestia evreească abia începe," *Chemarea Vremii*, 12 June 1941.

48. Antonescu's reply of 22 June 1941, in Drăgan, *Antonescu*, vol. 2, no. 13, pp. 205–6, 213.

49. Fabricius, who completed his term as German legate in Bucharest in February 1941, said in 1956 that Antonescu never informed him "of his intention to adopt collective [penal] measures against the Jews. If he did so after I left [Bucharest] and after the confrontation with the Legionnaires, this must have been in response to the accusations that he was influenced by Jewish circles and the Free Masons." Fabricius's testimony, given in Sachen court in Germany in 1956, as recorded by Filderman, YVA, Filderman Archive, P-6/46, p. 70; P-6/47, p. 70.

17. Romanian Solution to the Jewish Problem

1. M. Antonescu, *Pentru Basarabia și Bucovina*, 60–61.

2. Ancel, *Documents*, vol. 6, doc. 15, pp. 199–201.

3. Ancel, *Documents*, vol. 5, doc. 1, p. 1. The order is quoted in the indictment against Gen. A. Stavrat, commander of the Seventh Division, who was accused of murdering Jews in the towns of Siret, Herța, Noua Suliță, Hotin, and Lipcani, and against the mayor of Herța and his aides — the commander of the local police, officers, low-ranking officers, employees of the municipality, the mayors of the aforementioned towns and their aides, gendarmes, policemen, and local citizens — a total of thirty-five people accused of torture, murder, and looting of the Jewish population. See indictment against Stavrat, in Ancel, *Documents*, vol. 6, doc. 40, pp. 424–40; see also *Procesul marei trădări naționale*, 63–64.

4. Special orders for Operation Barbarossa issued by the German army Supreme Command on 19 May 1941, together with guidelines for the behavior of soldiers in Russia, in *Trials of War Criminals*, 10:990–94.

5. This order was reconstructed in the indictment of the People's Court against nineteen commanders, officers, and low-ranking officers of the gendarmerie sections of Czernowitz, Hotin, Orhei, Cetatea-Albă, Ismail, and Kishinev who were accused of massacring the Jewish population (hereafter indictment against nineteen commanders), in Ancel, *Documents*, vol. 6, doc. 15, p. 202.

6. Indictment against Stavrat, in Ancel, *Documents*, vol. 6, doc. 40, p. 428. General Doncea asked General Stavrat, Vartic's commander, to stay the execution of eighty Jews. In his answer Stavrat explained that Vartic had been "given personal orders" and asked the general "not to interfere," since these orders were meant specifically for the pretors.

7. Indictment against nineteen commanders, in Ancel, *Documents*, vol. 6, doc. 15, p. 214. When General Stavrat, commander of the Seventh Infantry Division, was asked to authorize the execution of fifty Jews in retaliation for an unidentified Jew having opened fire on a Romanian soldier (who was not injured), he pointed out that "we must act in accordance with the special orders." One of the provisions of the special orders issued by General Antonescu stated, "For each Romanian shot by a Jew a hundred Jews shall be executed." Indictment against nineteen commanders, in Ancel, *Documents*, vol. 6, doc. 15, p. 430.

8. Indictment against M. Boulescu, commander of the Bălți gendarmerie legion, and against commanders who were accused of helping ss units kill thirty Jewish intellectuals in Bălți, organizing the murder of eighty Jews and several Jewish hostages, and setting up the Răuțel camp, 12 April 1948 (hereafter indictment against Boulescu), in Ancel, *Documents*, vol. 6, doc. 25, pp. 268–75.

9. Indictment against Boulescu, in Ancel, *Documents*, vol. 6, doc. 25, pp. 273–74. This

issue was elucidated in the Romanian court during the trial for the murder of hundreds of Jews of Bălți (July 1941) in a place called Movila Aviației. During the trial the military commander tried to shift the blame to the prefect of Bălți, but the court determined that "the order to kill the Jews could not have come from the Prefect's Office, since at the time of the killing, the army was still present, and the Prefect's Office would not have issued an order of this kind" (274). At his trial Ion Antonescu claimed that he personally had never issued liquidation orders. "In my house, not even a chicken has been slaughtered. It was not I who ordered the [liquidation] measures, but the general staff." *Procesul marii trădări naționale*, 51.

10. Indictment against Stavrat, in Ancel, *Documents*, vol. 6, doc. 40, p. 426.

11. Indictment against Stavrat, in Ancel, *Documents*, vol. 6, doc. 40, p. 434. In Hotin, for example, a junior employee at the municipality entered "a Jewish woman's home and told her that she would have no more need of her property since she was going to die anyway. He then proceeded to load carpets, linen, curtains and quilts onto carts" (436).

12. Mircu, *Pogromurile din Bucovina și Dorohoi*, 24, 32–33, 39, 44.

13. Comisia Română de Istorie Militară, *File din istoria militară*, 5–6:84–85.

14. "He was the only foreigner whom Hitler consulted on military matters when he had problems." Schmidt, *Hitler's Interpreter*, 206.

15. In the report of 29 July 1941 on the activity of Einsatzgruppe D in Bălți and the help provided by the Romanian police in the operation against the Jews of Bălți, the commander of the security police and of the SD emphasized that it was impossible to specify the number of those shot by the Romanians. Regarding the murder of forty-five Jewish community leaders in Bălți by Einsatzkommando 10a, the same report stated, "The Romanian police acted . . . according to the commando's directives." Nuremberg Documents, no. 2952.

16. Comisia Română de Istorie Militară, *File din istoria militară*, 5–6:89, 90.

17. Comisia Română de Istorie Militară, *File din istoria militară*, 5–6:90.

18. A Romanian court declared, "In the first days after the outbreak of war, large sections of northern Bukovina and of Bessarabia were lawless, and the entire region was effectively subjected to an interregnum." Arrest warrant against Vladimir Clem and Sofia Loy, village of Banila on Ceremuș, May 1948, in Ancel, *Documents*, vol. 6, doc. 29, p. 301. In July 1941 Clem and Loy informed terrorist gangs of the whereabouts of the Katz family, resulting in the murder of the family and the looting of its property.

19. Commander of the General Staff's Second Bureau Lt. Col. Alexandru Ionescu to the General Staff, 11 July 1942, USHMM/MSM, RG-25.003M, reel 11, file 781, p. 0144.

20. "The Plan to Remove the Judaic Element from Bessarabian Ground Still under Soviet Control by Organizing Teams that Will Precede the Romanian Forces," USHMM/MSM, RG-25.003M, reel 11, file 781, pp. 0145–0146 (author's emphasis); courtesy of Dr. Radu Ioanid, a director at the USHMM, who discovered the document and made it available to me.

21. Indictment against Stavrat, in Ancel, *Documents*, vol. 6, doc. 40, p. 425. See also Gold, *Geschichte der Juden*, 2:105–8.

22. Indictment against Stavrat, in Ancel, *Documents*, vol. 6, doc. 40, p. 425.

23. Among other details relating to the murders that took place in Herța cited in the indictment against Stavrat is a reference to "Mina Rotaru, a five year old girl, who was

thrown live into a ditch and left there to die." Indictment against Stavrat, in Ancel, *Documents*, vol. 6, doc. 40, p. 427.

24. Indictment against Stavrat, in Ancel, *Documents*, vol. 6, doc. 40, p. 429. Steinberg, the last president of the Jewish community, who escaped the pogrom, told the author how Romanian soldiers took him to the cemetery to help bury the dead in a mass grave. He himself counted 975 bodies. See his testimony in YVA, Romania Collection, 0-11/89. This testimony is corroborated by two other testimonies: YVA, 03-/3446, 0-3/1915.

25. Indictment against Stavrat, in Ancel, *Documents*, vol. 6, doc. 40, p. 429.

26. Soldiers of the Seventh Division "found the city destroyed by fire, looting, slaughter and corruption, and its streets and courtyards littered with corpses. Instead of restoring order and clearing away the corpses, the soldiers set about rounding up more Jews . . . about 3,000 Jews were rounded up and taken to the distillery in Noua Suliță." Indictment against Stavrat, in Ancel, *Documents*, vol. 6, doc. 40, pp. 429–30.

27. On 8 July Vartic reported to General Stavrat that "an unidentified Jew had shot at soldiers, but no one had been hurt." Nonetheless, he asked permission to retaliate, that is, to kill five Jews in the Noua Suliță camp. General Stavrat's response was "obey orders," meaning the special orders. Indictment against Stavrat, in Ancel, *Documents*, vol. 6, doc. 40, p. 430.

28. Lieutenant Costea was given a scolding by General Stavrat: "Haven't you heard of General Antonescu's order to shoot a hundred Jews for each Romanian gunned down by a Jew?" Indictment against Stavrat, in Ancel, *Documents*, vol. 6, doc. 40, pp. 430–31.

29. Indictment against Stavrat, in Ancel, *Documents*, vol. 6, doc. 40, p. 431.

30. Indictment against Stavrat, in Ancel, *Documents*, vol. 6, doc. 40, p. 431.

31. On Sunday, 6 July, two days after the pogrom, Rabbi Horovitz of Banila was forced to march to Ciudei with the remnants of his community. He testified, "A sorry sight awaited us at Ciudei. The vile objective of liquidating the Jews had been accomplished. Of the 500 Jews who had lived there, not one remained alive. This Jewish community was liquidated at the order of the criminal, Major Carp." Testimony of Rabbi Horovitz from Banila before the People's Court on the liquidation of Jews in the villages and towns of Banila, Ciudei, Storojineț, Jadova, Berhomet, Stănești, Costești, Hlinița, Droșnița, and Vijnița, in Ancel, *Documents*, vol. 6, doc. 12, pp. 145–53. See also Carp, *Cartea neagră*, 3:29.

32. Carp, *Cartea neagră*, 3:30. Carp describes how Romanian soldiers "derived pleasure" from killing Jews in Ropcea.

33. The massacre of the Jews in the villages of Stănești, Jadova, Costești, Cireș, and Rostochi is described in detail in Carp, *Cartea neagră*, 3:30–31, and in Mircu, *Pogromurile din Bucovina și Dorohoi*, 23–51. In Hlinița soldiers killed five Jews. The synagogues were desecrated, and the local citizens used the parchment of fifteen Torah scrolls to make shoes. Rabbi Horovitz was deported with the remnants of the Banila community to Transnistria, escorted by Romanian soldiers in a convoy that collected a few survivors from other Bukovinian villages on the way. The rabbi pointed out that "in the villages of Costești, Hlinița and Droșnița, 90 per cent of the Jewish population was destroyed. The only survivor of about 400 Jewish citizens of Costești was an orphan boy." Testimony of Rabbi Horovitz from Banila before the People's Court on the liquidation of Jews in the villages and towns

of Banila, Ciudei, Storojineț, Jadova, Berhomet, Stănești, Costești, Hlinița, Droșnița, and Vijnița, in Ancel, *Documents*, vol. 6, doc. 12, p. 148.

34. The fate of the Jews in the towns of Briceni, Lipcani, Fălești, Mărculești, and Florești has been described in detail by the author. See *Pinkas Hakehilot, Rumania*, vol. 2. In Gura-Căinari, not far from Mărculești, five hundred Jews were killed by members of the Sixth Vânători Regiment at the order of Colonel Matieș. This regiment was part of the Fourteenth Division under General Stavrescu's command. The massacre was carried out by officers and a sergeant major who had previously killed Jews in the frontier town of Sculeni: Captain Stihi, Lt. Eugen Mihăilescu, and Sgt. Maj. Vasile Mihailov, all from the Sixth Regiment.

In the trial of war criminals from Iași, a Romanian officer gave an eyewitness account of events in Gura-Căinari and Mărculești:

> After entering the village, Captain Stihi ordered . . . all Jews to make their way to the outskirts of the village, men and women separately. First, the victims were stripped of their jewelry, gold and silver. Stihi took these valuables and put them in a suitcase. Afterwards, it was interrogation time. The men were interrogated in groups. Captain Stihi wanted the names of the Communists in the village. When the information was not forthcoming . . . the Captain ordered all the Jews to divide into teams and excavate an anti-tank ditch that had been dug near the village. After nightfall, Lt. Eugen Mihăilescu order[ed] the Jews into groups of ten facing the ditch, and shot them with a Russian automatic rifle that had been looted. Previously, the victims had been stripped to their underwear. After all the men had been shot, it was the women's turn. They were treated in the same way. Babies were also shot. When the last woman left the victims' assembly point and was led away to the execution site, only one dead child was left, like an unwanted package. That night, about 400–500 Jews were killed.

See indictment by the prosecutor general of Bucharest against the perpetrators of the Iași pogrom and the massacre of the Jews of Sculeni, Mărculești, and Gura-Căinari, 28 May 1948, YVA, o-11/73, p. 70. See also Ancel, *Documents*, vol. 6, doc. 39, pp. 410–11. The indictment against Ion Antonescu stated, inter alia, "In the town of Climăuți in the district of Soroca, 300 children, women and men were rounded up on 12 July 1941, shot to death, and buried in a mass grave on the outskirts of the village." *Procesul marii trădări naționale*, 36.

35. We know nothing of the last moments of the Jews of the Bukovinian villages near the Dniester, in the area known as Plasa Nistrului, since there were almost no survivors from these villages. The massacres were carried out by Romanian and German soldiers, who shot 130 Jews in the village of Zoniache and 32 in Răpujineț. See Carp, *Cartea neagră*, 3:35. In most of the villages in this area, excluding Zastavna, where a ghetto was set up, all the Jews were rounded up and forced to cross the Dniester to Galicia, where they were killed by local Ukrainians or German soldiers. Only several dozen managed to escape and reach the Zastavna ghetto; they were later deported to Transnistria. See appendix to the testimony of Jacob Stenzler, YVA, o-11/89, PKR III, pp. 261–62.

36. Twelve Jews who were being held hostage were shot in the town of Lipcani. In Lincăuți-Hotin another four hostages were killed. In Cepelăuți-Hotin all of the village's two hundred Jews were shot. See Carp, *Cartea neagră*, 3:35.

The murder of the Jews in Cepelăuți-Hotin has been faithfully recorded thanks to the testimony of Shapira, a native Jewish engineer:

After the departure of the Russians, a gang of hooligans formed under the leadership of four [Ukrainians]: Gheorghe Histruga, a peasant; Vasile Țap, a man of indeterminate profession who used to work in Jewish homes; Nicolae Dobja, the secretary of the municipality; and Parfenie Panco, a wagoner. They obtained arms from the commanders of the Romanian army units and were given *carte blanche* to act against the Jews with impunity. They ordered the Jews to assemble several kilometers from the village, and stripped them of all their valuables. Before that, they looted their homes. After these acts of theft, they ordered their victims to dig their own graves. Only two girls, who were away at the time, and a boy named Eli Luterman, who was hidden by a compassionate Christian, survived to tell the tale. . . . The babies were passed from hand to hand, and then shot. . . . A girl—a relative of mine—was stripped naked and ordered to dance on her grave before being shot.

YVA, Romania Collection, 0-11/89, PKR III, pp. 116–17.

37. Einsatzgruppe D, one of the four Einsatzgruppen that operated in Soviet territory —which included Bessarabia, the area south of Czernowitz and Mogilev-Podolski to the Black Sea, and all of Transnistria—implemented the orders for the liquidation of the Jews. On 21 June all members of Einsatzgruppe D left Düben in Germany, and they reached Romania on 24 June.

38. Carp, *Cartea neagră*, 2:36.

39. Carp, *Cartea neagră*, 2:36. See also Ancel, "Kishinev," in *Pinkas Hakehilot, Rumania*, 2:411–16.

40. Ancel, *Documents*, vol. 6, doc. 41, pp. 441–45.

41. Indictment against nineteen commanders, in Ancel, *Documents*, vol. 6, doc. 15, p. 207. The written order was submitted as testimony in the trials of the Romanian war criminals in 1950 (file 547/950).

42. Arrest warrant for V. Eftimie of the Orhei gendarmerie legion and twenty-one post commanders in the surrounding area for having carried out orders to liquidate, torture, rape, and loot the Jews of the district, 1950, in Ancel, *Documents*, vol. 6, doc. 41, pp. 441–45.

43. Second arrest warrant for Capt. C. Popoiu, low-ranking officers, and commanders of the gendarmerie sections and posts in Orhei, thirty-six in toto, accused of the ghettoization of Jews from the Orhei district, formation of the executionary platoon, and liquidation of nine hundred urban Jews and hundreds of rural Jews in the district, 1950 (hereafter second arrest warrant against Popoiu), in Ancel, *Documents*, vol. 6, doc. 44, p. 497.

44. Arrest warrant against Capt. C. Popoiu, officers, and low-ranking subordinates of the Orhei gendarmerie legion, sixteen in toto, accused of the liquidation of Jews found on rural territory, deportation (via Rezina), rape of girls and women, confiscation of the possessions of Jews, and shooting of Jews who lagged behind, 1950, in Ancel, *Documents*, vol. 6, doc. 43, pp. 512–13.

45. Indictment against nineteen commanders, in Ancel, *Documents*, vol. 6, doc. 15, p. 207.

46. Arrest warrant against gendarmerie captain I. Adamovici, low-ranking officers, sergeants, and commanders of sections and posts in the Orhei gendarmerie legion, thirty-seven in toto, accused of executing orders for the liquidation of Jews in the villages and inventing new murder techniques in order to gratify their sadistic impulses, 1950 (hereafter arrest warrant against Adamovici), in Ancel, *Documents*, vol. 6, doc. 45, p. 515.

47. Arrest warrant against two captains of the Orhei gendarmerie, K. Popoiu and I. Adamovici, and against thirty-two low-ranking officers, accused of implementing orders to liquidate the Jewish population, executing the Jews of the Teleneşti ghetto and hundreds of other Jews from the surrounding villages, and torturing, looting, and raping, 1950 (hereafter arrest warrant against Popoiu and Adamovici), in Ancel, *Documents*, vol. 6, doc. 42, pp. 467, 470–71.

48. Arrest warrant against Adamovici, in Ancel, *Documents*, vol. 6, doc. 45, pp. 513–14.

49. Second arrest warrant against Popoiu, in Ancel, *Documents*, vol. 6, doc. 44, p. 497.

50. Arrest warrant against Adamovici, in Ancel, *Documents*, vol. 6, doc. 45, p. 513.

51. Arrest warrant against Popoiu and Adamovici, in Ancel, *Documents*, vol. 6, doc. 42, p. 464.

52. Arrest warrant against Popoiu and Adamovici, in Ancel, *Documents*, vol. 6, doc. 42, p. 465.

53. Indictment against Lt. Col. N. Caracaş, commander of the Lăpuşna gendarmerie legion, and seven of his subordinates; against E. Savopol, pretor of the Third Army Corps; and against Lt. Col. D. Eliescu for having perpetrated crimes in the operational areas of the gendarmerie legions in Lăpuşna and Soroca and murdering Jews, partisans, and political suspects in the period July–September 1941, 19 August 1948 (hereafter indictment against Caracaş), in Ancel, *Documents*, vol. 6, doc. 37, p. 336.

54. Indictment against nineteen commanders, in Ancel, *Documents*, vol. 6, doc. 15, p. 211. On the day they arrived in Chiperceni the gendarmes arrested the village's twenty Jews, and several hours later they shot them. The corpses were left on the village outskirts, without burial. Second arrest warrant against Popoiu, in Ancel, *Documents*, vol. 6, doc. 44, p. 498.

55. Nuremberg Documents, NO-2651. Captain Popoiu found three members of a Jewish family on his estate. He ordered the local gendarmerie commander to execute them, and the three were buried by peasants in a ditch not far from his estate. Second arrest warrant against Popoiu, in Ancel, *Documents*, vol. 6, doc. 44, p. 499.

56. Five hundred Jews were killed in Mărculeşti by Mihailescu "with an automatic rifle of Russian make that had been looted." See indictment by the prosecutor general of Bucharest against the perpetrators of the Iaşi pogrom and the massacre of the Jews of Sculeni, Mărculeşti, and Gura-Căinari, 28 May 1948, YVA, 0-11/73, p. 410.

57. Indictment against Caracaş, in Ancel, *Documents*, vol. 6, doc. 37, p. 342; indictment against nineteen commanders, in Ancel, *Documents*, vol. 6, doc. 15, p. 208.

58. The standard murder technique was to push Jews into the river and shoot at those who attempted to swim to the other side. Most women and children did not know how to swim and drowned immediately. Carp, *Cartea neagră*, testimonies 20–26, 3:65–70.

59. Report from the Inspectorate of the Kishinev Gendarmerie to the chief pretor on the killing of two hundred Jews whose corpses were thrown into the Dniester (hereafter report from Kishinev), in Ancel, *Documents*, vol. 5, doc. 35, p. 42. The Third Army opened an investigation to determine who was responsible for the murder. Two Jewish survivors submitted an accurate description of the way in which the victims were drowned. Carp, *Cartea neagră*, nos. 23–24, 3:67–69.

60. Report from Kishinev, in Ancel, *Documents*, vol. 5, doc. 35, p. 38.

61. Report from Kishinev, in Ancel, *Documents*, vol. 5, doc. 35, p. 82.

62. Indictment against Caracaş, in Ancel, *Documents*, vol. 6, doc. 37, p. 341.

63. Vasile Lungu, commander of the Chiţcani Post, caught a Jew in his village, tied him up, took him to the bridge over the Răut River, and threw him over the bridge. Calud Marin, the commander of the Molovata Post, arrested six Jews, tied them to each other, and brought them to the bank of the Dniester. There he handed them over to Nicolae Capriceru, a soldier sent to his post, and ordered him to shoot them. "Capriceru brought the Jews to the edge of the river, and at an agreed-upon signal, he and Ismană, a local peasant, pushed them into the river so that they fell straight into the water. In order to cover up his sadistic operation, he fired several shots into the air, so as to be able to report to his commander that he had shot them." Arrest warrant against Popoiu and Adamovici, in Ancel, *Documents*, vol. 6, doc. 42, p. 470; arrest warrant against Adamovici, in Ancel, *Documents*, vol. 6, doc. 45, p. 516.

64. Arrest warrant against Adamovici, in Ancel, *Documents*, vol. 6, doc. 45, p. 517.

65. Testimony of Eugen Cristescu, former head of the SSI, in Carp, *Cartea neagră*, 2:43, 51. The Einsatzgruppen were also set up to back the combat units and strengthen the army. See indictment in Munich Court against a commander of Einsatzgruppe D, Paul Johannes Zapp, in Ancel, *Documents*, vol. 6, doc. 47, p. 545.

66. Testimony of Eugen Cristescu, in Carp, *Cartea neagră*, 2:43, 51.

67. Nuremberg Documents, NO-2851.

68. Nuremberg Documents, NO-2952, NOKW-3233.

69. Nuremberg Documents, NO-2952.

70. Carp, *Cartea neagră*, no. 14, 3:55–56.

71. Nuremberg Documents, NO-2651, NO-2943, NO-2938, NO-2949, NO-2950.

72. Nuremberg Documents, NO-2934.

73. Nuremberg Documents, NO-2934, NO-2939.

74. Nuremberg Documents, NO-4540; operational report by Einsatzgruppe D, Ereignismeldung UdSSR, no. 52, Nuremberg Documents, NO-4590.

75. Nuremberg Documents, NOKW-3453.

76. *Buletinul Demografic*, 345–46; Centrala Evreilor din România, *Breviarul statistic*, 25, 145; copy in Ancel, *Documents*, vol. 1, docs. 37, 45, pp. 274–76, 305–22.

77. See YVA, testimonies, 03-1452, p. 3; 03-1456, p. 5; 03-1536, p. 2; and 03-1537, p. 45.

78. *Die Bevölkerungszählung.*

79. I. Calafeteanu and M. Covaci, "Situation of the Jews in Bessarabia, Bukovina and 'Transnistria' in the 1941–1944 Years," mimeograph, 1983, p. 8; copy in Ancel, *Documents*, vol. 10, doc. 182, p. 487.

80. I. Calafeteanu and M. Covaci, "Situation of the Jews in Bessarabia, Bukovina and 'Transnistria' in the 1941–1944 Years," mimeograph, 1983, p. 8; copy in Ancel, *Documents*, vol. 10, doc. 182, pp. 486–87.

81. See graph showing the situation of Bessarabian Jewry on 25 September 1941, in Ancel, *Documents*, vol. 10, doc. 43, p. 100.

82. Gendarmerie Inspectorate, "Bulletin of Transnistria," referring to the 118,847 deportees from Bessarabia and Bukovina, in Ancel, *Documents*, vol. 5, doc. 128, p. 220. See also

Zaharia and Copoiu, "Le problème," 9; copy in Ancel, *Documents*, vol. 10, doc. 181, p. 481. In fact, over 170,000 Jews were deported (see chap. 38).

83. The statistical data compiled by the Jewish Center's Statistical Department, based on data provided by the Romanian Central Bureau of Statistics, present an accurate picture of the Jewish demographic situation in the two provinces. See also *Die Bevölkerungszählung*; official census of the Jewish population in the provinces of Bessarabia and Bukovina and in the Dorohoi region, 1930–42, in Ancel, *Documents*, vol. 1, doc. 40, p. 324; Carp, *Cartea neagră*, no. 1, 3:41–42; Ancel, *Transnistria, 1941–1942*, vol. 1, chap. 8.

84. *Curentul*, 27 August 1941.

18. The Camps and Ghettos

1. Memorandum by Voiculescu, governor of Bessarabia, to Antonescu, undated [late 1941] (hereafter Voiculescu report), in Ancel, *Documents*, vol. 10, doc. 61, pp. 137, 142.

2. Voiculescu report, in Ancel, *Documents*, vol. 10, doc. 61, pp. 137, 143.

3. Telegram from General Topor to the minister of the interior, 18 July 1941, in Ancel, *Documents*, vol. 5, doc. 11, p. 18; order issued by General Topor to the Gendarmerie Inspectorate in Kishinev, 22 June 1941, in Ancel, *Documents*, vol. 5, doc. 14, p. 21.

4. Carp, *Cartea neagră*, 3:80; *Pinkas Hakehilot, Rumania*, 2:346, 385.

5. Order issued by the Fourth Army to the military commander of Kishinev, 31 July 1941, in Ancel, *Documents*, vol. 10, doc. 27, p. 83.

6. Telephone communiqué by the inspector general of the gendarmerie in Bessarabia, 13 August 1941, in Carp, *Cartea neagră*, no. 27, 3:70–71; Ancel, *Documents*, vol. 5, doc. 35, p. 42.

7. Angrick, "Escalation of German-Rumanian Anti-Jewish Policy," 227.

8. Carp, *Cartea neagră*, 3:81.

9. Carp, *Cartea neagră*, 3:81.

10. German ambassador in Bucharest to the Foreign Ministry in Berlin, 16 August 1941, in *Documents on German Foreign Policy*, vol. 13, doc. 207, pp. 318–19; Karl Ritter to the German army Supreme Command, 27 August 1941, in *Documents on German Foreign Policy*, vol. 13, doc. 207, p. 319.

11. Angrick, "Escalation of German-Rumanian Anti-Jewish Policy," 221.

12. Forty-two hundred on August 27, eleven thousand on August 28, and seven thousand on August 29. Angrick, "Escalation of German-Rumanian Anti-Jewish Policy," 228. Among the Jews shot here were also Jews expelled by the Hungarian authorities.

13. Romanian documents from this period discuss the 1941 deportation of approximately thirty thousand Jews across the Dniester. See, for example, the Central Information Service report on the thirty thousand Jews from the Hotin District and Bukovina, USHMM/RSA, RG-25002M, roll 17, fond: Presidency of the Council of Ministers, Military Cabinet, file 76/1941, p. 86. This report states, "From among those sent to the other side of the Dniester by the officials, some return, but the officials keep sending over more Jews." The report also requested urgent clarification from General Headquarters on the status of the Jews as of 18 August 1941. On 19 August the SSI reported that the thirty thousand Jews were interned in a camp and that "none . . . had returned west of the Dniester" (19). On 27 August General Police Headquarters reported that the German army sent back 12,600 Jews to Bessarabia

in two convoys. These Jews were subsequently interned in the Vertujeni camp (91). These were the only survivors of the "hasty deportations."

14. *Pinkas Hakehilot, Rumania*, 2:356.

15. See testimony of Sarah Katz of Milie, northern Bukovina, on the deportation from the village and the looting and murder of Jews, in Carp, *Cartea neagră*, no. 23, 3:67–68; see also report by the pretor of the Third Army to the grand pretor on 11 August 1941, on the execution of 210 Jews in a convoy of 300 Jews (Sarah Katz's convoy), in Carp, *Cartea neagră*, no. 20, 3:54.

16. Excerpt from the testimony of the first commander of the Vertujeni camp, Colonel Constantinescu, before the People's Tribunal in 1945, in Carp, *Cartea neagră*, no. 78, 3:120.

17. Carp, *Cartea neagră*, no. 45, 3:98–99; no. 71, 3:113.

18. Guvernământul Basarabiei, *Basarabia desrobiă*, 148.

19. Bukovina Gendarmerie Inspectorate to the governor of Bukovina, 11 September 1941, in Ancel, *Documents*, vol. 5, doc. 71, pp. 82–83; Carp, *Cartea neagră*, no. 77, 3:118–19.

20. Telephone report by the gendarmerie commander in Bukovina, 10 August 1941, in Carp, *Cartea neagră*, no. 49, 3:101.

21. *Curentul*, 27 August 1941. For estimates of the number of Jews who were killed in the first stage in Bukovina, see testimony of the righteous gentile Traian Popovici, mayor of Czernowitz (hereafter Popovici testimony), in Carp, *Cartea neagră*, no. 100, 3:182. By his estimate, northern Bukovina had a Jewish population of about seventy thousand when the Romanians recaptured it in 1941.

22. Excerpts from the journal-testimony of Rabbi Mordechai Horovitz, as recorded in 1945 and submitted to the Bucharest Court, in Ancel, *Documents*, vol. 6, doc. 12, pp. 145–53. The rabbi also gave testimony at Yad Vashem in 1960 (YVA, 03-1540).

23. Operational report by Einsatzgruppe D, Ereignismeldung UdSSR, no. 52, in Nuremberg Documents, NO-4590.

24. Orders relating to the deportation of Jews from the Vertujeni camp, 11 September 1941, in Ancel, *Documents*, vol. 5, doc. 80, pp. 123–24.

25. Nuremberg Documents, PS-3319.

26. Reuth, *Josef Goebbels*, 4:1059–60.

27. Gendarmerie Inspectorate in Bessarabia to the grand pretor, 11 September 1941, in Carp, *Cartea neagră*, 3:122–23; inspector general of the gendarmerie in Transnistria, Colonel Broşteanu, to the grand pretor, 3 September 1941, in Carp, *Cartea neagră*, 3:117.

28. War Headquarters to grand pretor, 4 September 1941, in Carp, *Cartea neagră*, 3:117–18.

29. Instructions for the deportation of the Jews from the Vertujeni-Soroca camp, 11 September 1941, in Carp, *Cartea neagră*, no. 80, 3:123–24.

30. Order issued by War Headquarters at Marshal Antonescu's behest to deport all Bukovinian Jewry to Transnistria, in Carp, *Cartea neagră*, no. 86, 3:143.

31. Popovici testimony, in Carp, *Cartea neagră*, no. 100, 3:171.

32. *Procesul marei trădări naţionale*, 246; excerpt from Ion Antonescu's communiqué concerning the fate of the Jews, cabinet session of 6 October 1941, in Carp, *Cartea neagră*, 3:87, 143.

33. See, for example, testimony of Shmelke Dechner from Berhomet, Storojinetz district, YVA, Romania Collection, O-11/89, PKR III, pp. 116–17; and O-3/1443, p. 5.

34. Report no. 2 of the Committee of Inquiry into Irregularities in the Kishinev Ghetto, set up by Antonescu in December 1941, in Carp, *Cartea neagră*, no. 19, 3:61; copy in Ancel, *Documents*, vol. 5, doc. 124, p. 192; original in Kishinev Archive, 706-1-69, pp. 48–55.

35. Voiculescu report, in Ancel, *Documents*, vol. 10, doc. 61, p. 139.

36. Ministry of the Interior memorandum on the problem of the repatriation of deported Jews to Romania, 12 October 1943, in Ancel, *Documents*, vol. 4, doc. 356, p. 666.

37. Memorandum from the Presidency of the Council of Ministers, submitted to Antonescu for inspection, concerning the interventions made on behalf of Bukovinian Jewry, 24 January 1944, in Ancel, *Documents*, vol. 10, doc. 131, p. 351.

38. "Răspunsul d-lui Mareşal Antonescu la scrisoarea profesorului I. Găvănescu" [Antonescu's response to Professor Găvănescu's letter], *Curentul*, 3 November 1941.

39. *Procesul marei trădări naţionale*, 144.

40. War Headquarters to the grand pretor, 17 August 1941, in Carp, *Cartea neagră*, no. 55, 3:104.

41. Carp, *Cartea neagră*, 3:83. See also report by the pretor of the Third Army to the grand pretor, 21 August 1941, in Carp, *Cartea neagră*, no. 58, 3:105–6.

42. Confidential telegram from the pretorate to the chief of the General Staff, 20 August 1941, in Carp, *Cartea neagră*, no. 59, 3:106; results of the census of Jews in the Vertujeni camp on 25 August 1941, in Carp, *Cartea neagră*, no. 61, 3:107.

43. Indictment against Colonel Agapie, Captain Buradescu, and the envoy of the National Bank of Romania, Mihăiescu, on war crimes they perpetrated in the Vertujeni and Mărculeşti camps in the Soroca district in September–December 1941 (hereafter indictment against Agapie), in Ancel, *Documents*, vol. 6, doc. 8, p. 117.

44. Indictment against Agapie, in Ancel, *Documents*, vol. 6, doc. 8, p. 116.

45. Indictment against Agapie, in Ancel, *Documents*, vol. 6, doc. 8, p. 117.

46. Instructions concerning the deportation of Jews from the Vertujeni camp, in Carp, *Cartea neagră*, no. 80, 3:123; indictment against nineteen commanders, in Ancel, *Documents*, vol. 6, doc. 15, p. 211.

47. Testimony of Israel Perikman, who spent three months in the Vertujeni camp, YVA, Romania Collection, O-11/89, PKR III, pp. 116–17; and O-3/1460, pp. 10–11.

48. See map of the deportation route issued to the escorting officers, in Ancel, *Documents*, vol. 5, doc. 73, p. 87.

49. *Procesul marei trădări naţionale*, 124.

50. Carp, *Cartea neagră*, 3:88.

51. Carp, *Cartea neagră*, no. 80, 3:124.

52. Indictment against Agapie, in Ancel, *Documents*, vol. 6, doc. 8. For details on this sum and property amassed by Agapie, see the investigation by the military tribunal of the Third Army Corps in 1942 into breaches of conduct in the camp, apparently following complaints by the commander of the Vertujeni gendarmerie legion, Ioan Oprea. Agapie sent home 12 gold watches, 30–40 diamond rings, 180–200 gold ruble coins worth 5 or 10 rubles each,

12 gold coins worth 100 rubles each, 5 gold chains 150 mm long, 3–4 Persian carpets, 5–6 wool carpets, 4 furs, a variety of coats, and more (Ancel, *Documents*, vol. 6, doc. 8, p. 121).

53. Indictment against Agapie, in Ancel, *Documents*, vol. 6, doc. 8, p. 125.

54. Indictment against Agapie, in Ancel, *Documents*, vol. 6, doc. 8, p. 124.

55. See "Mărculeşti," in *Pinkas Hakehilot, Rumania*, 2:365–68.

56. Indictment against Romanian war criminals who perpetrated the Iaşi pogrom and massacres in Mărculeşti, Gura-Căinari, and Sculeni, in Ancel, *Documents*, vol. 6, doc. 39, p. 410; report by Colonel Matieş, commander of the Sixth Regiment, to the commander of the Fourteenth Division, 20 July 1941, in Carp, *Cartea neagră*, no. 24, 2:73.

57. Carp, *Cartea neagră*, 3:89.

58. Indictment against Agapie, in Ancel, *Documents*, vol. 6, doc. 8, p. 139.

59. Testimony of Hanna Weinraub of Czernowitz, YVA, 0-3/1539, p. 3.

60. Testimony of Haya Kizelnik, YVA, 0-3/841, p. 4.

61. Testimony of Moshe Brunwasser of Storojinetz, YVA, 0-3/1445, p. 11.

62. Testimony of Hanna Weinraub, of Czernowitz, YVA, 0-3/1539, pp. 4–5; testimony of Bertha Morgenstern of Czernowitz, YVA, 0-3/1491, p. 7.

63. Testimony of Arie Weber, of Banila-upon-Siret, YVA, 0-3/1527, p. 4.

64. Head of Army Administration, General Gheorghiu, to Ministry of the Interior, 9 February 1942, in Ancel, *Documents*, vol. 5, doc. 137, p. 242.

65. Head of Army Administration, General Gheorghiu, to Ministry of the Interior, 9 February 1942, in Ancel, *Documents*, vol. 5, doc. 137, p. 242.

66. Head of Army Administration, General Gheorghiu, to Ministry of the Interior, 9 February 1942, in Ancel, *Documents*, vol. 5, doc. 137, p. 242.

67. Report of the committee appointed by the Ministry of Defense to determine to whom Jewish property left in the Mărculeşti camp belonged, 17 February 1942, in Ancel, *Documents*, vol. 5, no. 138, pp. 243–49. The Welfare Council helped war widows, war orphans, and the needy in general.

68. Report of the committee appointed by the Ministry of Defense to determine to whom Jewish property left in the Mărculeşti camp belonged, 17 February 1942, in Ancel, *Documents*, vol. 5, no. 138, p. 249.

69. Report of the pretor of the Third Army to the grand pretor, 9 August 1941, in Ancel, *Documents*, vol. 5, doc. 28, pp. 37–38.

70. Testimony of Moritz Schechter from Ciudei, northern Bukovina, YVA, 0-3/1439, p. 9.

71. Report of the Gendarmerie Inspectorate of Bukovina to the grand pretor, 1 September 1941, in Carp, *Cartea neagră*, 3:115.

72. Carp, *Cartea neagră*, 3:87; testimony of Rabbi Mordechai Horovitz, in Ancel, *Documents*, vol. 6, doc. 12, p. 157; statement by Lieutenant Bălea of the Sixtieth Police Company, 6 November 1941, in Ancel, *Documents*, vol. 5, doc. 105, p. 150.

73. Carp, *Cartea neagră*, 3:88–90.

74. Report no. 2 of the Committee of Inquiry into Irregularities in the Kishinev Ghetto, set up by Antonescu, December 1941 (hereafter Kishinev report), in Carp, *Cartea neagră*, no. 19, 3:62–64.

75. Testimony of Dr. Zeev Shärf of Suceava, YVA, 0-3/1526, p. 12.

76. Statement by Lieutenant Bălea of the Sixtieth Police Company, 6 November 1941, in Ancel, *Documents*, vol. 5, doc. 105, p. 150; testimony of Second Lieutenant Cocuz of the Sixtieth Police Company, 6 November 1941, in Ancel, *Documents*, vol. 5, doc. 106, p. 157.

77. Testimony of Shmelke Dechner from Berhomet, Storojinetz district, YVA, Romania Collection, 0-11/89, PKR III, p. 6.

78. Statement by Lieutenant Bălea of the Sixtieth Police Company, 6 November 1941, in Ancel, *Documents*, vol. 5, doc. 105, p. 154.

79. Carp, *Cartea neagră*, 3:35.

80. Carp, *Cartea neagră*, 3:83; testimony of Zipora Țoar from Seletin, YVA, 0-3/1129, p. 3.

81. Colonel Mănecuță's report on the establishment of the Secureni camp, 10 August 1941, in Carp, *Cartea neagră*, no. 49, 3:101.

82. Grand pretor to War Headquarters on the transfer of half the internees of the Edineți camp, 15 August 1941, in Ancel, *Documents*, vol. 5, doc. 41, p. 46.

83. Federation of Jewish Communities of Romania to Ministry of the Interior, and ministry's reply, 19–20 August 1941, in Ancel, *Documents*, vol. 3, doc. 22, pp. 30–31.

84. Jewish Federation to acting prime minister Mihai Antonescu, 28 August 1941, in Ancel, *Documents*, vol. 3, doc. 48, p. 89.

85. Chief of staff to the Union of Jewish Communities of Romania, authorizing the transfer of money to the Jews in Secureni via the General Staff's Prisoners of War Division, 7 September 1941, in Ancel, *Documents*, vol. 3, doc. 72, p. 128.

86. Report by the Gendarmerie Inspectorate in Bukovina on the situation of the Jews in the camps, in Carp, *Cartea neagră*, 3:88.

87. Kishinev report, in Carp, *Cartea neagră*, no. 19, 3:64.

19. The Kishinev Ghetto

1. See Ancel, "Kishinev," in *Pinkas Hakehilot, Rumania*, 2:400–16.

2. According to a description by a Jew who remained in the city under a Romanian identity. See testimony of Michael Marian, 1959, in Ancel, *Documents*, vol. 8, doc. 495, p. 595.

3. Voiculescu report, in Ancel, *Documents*, vol. 10, doc. 61, p. 137.

4. Voiculescu report, in Ancel, *Documents*, vol. 10, doc. 61, p. 141.

5. M. Mircu, *Pogromurile din Basarabia*, 15.

6. Voiculescu report, in Ancel, *Documents*, vol. 10, doc. 61, pp. 138, 143.

7. Voiculescu report, in Ancel, *Documents*, vol. 10, doc. 61, pp. 144, 145.

8. Nuremberg Documents, NOKW-3233, p. 2; Mircu, *Pogromurile din Basarabia*, 17.

9. Anklageschrift in der Strafsache gegen Paul Johannes Zapp [indictment against Zapp, commander of Einsatzkommando 11a, for crimes in Kishinev, Nikolayev, Kherson, Simferopol, and other places], Landgericht München, Munich, I, 22 Js, 204/1961, p. 545.

10. Anklageschrift in der Strafsache gegen Paul Johannes Zapp [indictment against Zapp, commander of Einsatzkommando 11a, for crimes in Kishinev, Nikolayev, Kherson, Simferopol, and other places], Landgericht München, Munich, I, 22 Js, 204/1961, pp. 535, 545; Anklageschrift in der Strafsache gegen Hunze Heinrich, L. von der Recke, G. Mohlmeyer, K. Noa, and A. Zolner [indictment against the members of Einsatzkommando 11a, Ein-

satzgruppe D, for their crimes in Bessarabia, including Kishinev and southern Ukraine], Landgericht München, Munich, I, 22 Js, 204/1961, p. 533.

11. *Pinkas Hakehilot, Rumania*, 2:415.

12. Kishinev report, in Carp, *Cartea neagră*, no. 19, 3:61; memorandum by the commander of the Tenth Gendarmerie Regiment on the Ghidighici massacre, 28 August 1941, in Carp, *Cartea neagră*, no. 28, 3:71.

13. Copy of the petition of the Community of Jews in the Kishinev Ghetto to the military commander of Kishinev, 11 September 1941, in Ancel, *Documents*, vol. 10, doc. 40, p. 96.

14. Mircu, *Pogromurile din Basarabia*, 20.

15. Copy of the petition of the Jewish Community in the Kishinev Ghetto to the military commander of Kishinev, 11 September 1941, in Ancel, *Documents*, vol. 10, doc. 40, p. 96.

16. Filderman's secretary, attorney Charles Gruber, interview by Jean Ancel, Paris, 8 November 1982.

17. Safran, *Resisting the Storm*, 79.

18. Filderman's appeal to Antonescu, 11 October 1941, in Ancel, *Documents*, vol. 3, doc. 145, p. 234.

19. Carp, *Cartea neagră*, 3:81

20. Telegrams sent 22–30 October 1941, in Carp, *Cartea neagră*, 3:85, 129.

21. Order by Antonescu to confiscate the jewelry and gold of Jews prior to their deportation, 9 October 1941, in Ancel, *Documents*, vol. 10, doc. 46, p. 103.

22. Report of the commander of the Twenty-Third Police Company, Captain Paraschivescu, 5 December 1941, in Ancel, *Documents*, vol. 10, doc. 51, pp. 121–22.

23. Report of the commander of the Twenty-Third Police Company, Captain Paraschivescu, 5 December 1941, in Ancel, *Documents*, vol. 10, doc. 51, pp. 121–22.

24. Condemnatory letter by Governor Voiculescu to the military commander of Kishinev, Colonel Dumitrescu, in Ancel, *Documents*, vol. 10, doc. 53, p. 126.

25. Voiculescu report, in Ancel, *Documents*, vol. 10, doc. 61, p. 141.

26. Thank-you letter from Filderman to Mihai Antonescu for his promise to stop the deportation of university graduates, merchants, and craftsmen, 14 October 1941, in Ancel, *Documents*, vol. 3, no. 153, p. 242. Antonescu's promise was not honored in Bessarabia.

27. Safran, *Resisting the Storm*, 78–79; Carp, *Cartea neagră*, 3:90.

28. The author found out about the fate of the ghetto leader and his family following a conversation with Sarah Kreizel from Hadera in September 1993; she was in the convoy that was deported from the ghetto on 20 October 1941.

29. Carp, *Cartea neagră*, 3:80.

30. Reports by the commanders of the convoys, 29, 30, and 31 October 1941, in Ancel, *Documents*, vol. 5, docs. 98–100, pp. 132–34.

31. Carp, *Cartea neagră*, 3:129; Mușat's telegram, 29 October 1941, in Ancel, *Documents*, vol. 3, doc. 205, p. 314.

32. "Mass Executions of Jews, Why Does Washington Remain Silent?" *The Record* (news bulletin published by the United Rumanian Jews of America, New York) 4, no. 5 (June 1942); copy in Ancel, *Documents*, vol. 4, doc. 26, pp. 54–55.

33. Military commander of Kishinev to ghetto commander, 28 October 1941, in Ancel, *Documents*, vol. 10, doc. 55, p. 128.

34. Memorandum by G. Richter, advisor on Jewish affairs, 1 September 1942, in Ancel, *Documents*, vol. 4, doc. 78, p. 145.

35. Testimony of Mihael Kvitco from Cetatea Albă in Bessarabia, April 1962, YVA, 03/2449, p. 4.

36. *Universul*, 9 March 1946; copy in Ancel, *Documents*, vol. 8, doc. 23, p. 26.

20. Czernowitz

1. Centrala Evreilor din România, Secția Statisticii, Direcțiunea Recensământului, Recensământul locuitorilor având sânge evreesc, Rezultatele din provincia Bucovina, Situație incheiată la 20 iulie 1942 [Results of the census of citizens of Jewish blood in Bukovina], stenciled booklet, 20 July 1942, pp. 4–6; copy in Ancel, *Documents*, vol. 1, doc. 43, pp. 290–92; *Die Bevolkerungszählung* (a confidential report prepared in Vienna with data on the Romanian population in 1913–43, including special data on the number of Jews and the results of the Romanian census of August–September 1941, which were not published in Romania).

2. On the eve of the calamity the Jews of Czernowitz estimated their numbers at seventy to seventy-five thousand, according to the testimony of Regina Levin, YVA, 03-1456, p. 5; testimony of Leah Louisa Neuman, YVA, 03/1452, p. 3; testimony of Simon Rosenrauch, YVA, 03-1536, p. 2; and testimony of Sarah Grosskopf, YVA, 03-1537, p. 45. Mayor Popovici also estimated the number of Jews in Czernowitz prior to the entry of the Romanian army at seventy thousand. See Popovici testimony, in Carp, *Cartea neagră*, no. 100, 3:182.

3. Manfred Reifer, the well-known Jewish leader of Czernowitz, to Filderman, Tel Aviv, 24 June 1951, YVA, P-6/35, p. 198.

4. Memorandum by Filderman to minister of the interior concerning the fate of the 15,088 Jews who were still living in the city, 7 November 1943, in Ancel, *Documents*, vol. 4, doc. 365, p. 685; *Die Bevolkerungszählung*, including demographic data on the number of citizens and their breakdown by nationality, 1880–1941.

5. Testimony of Julius Kronenfed, YVA, 03-1468, p. 1; testimony of Anna Loebel, YVA, 03-1482, p. 2.

6. Testimony of Etty Steinberger, YVA, 03-899, pp. 1–2.

7. Testimony of Julius Kronenfed, YVA, 03-1468, p. 1; testimony of Leah Luisa Neumann, YVA, 03/1452, p. 2; testimony of Anna Loebel, YVA, 03-1482, p. 2.

8. Testimony of Sarah Grosskopf, YVA, 03-1537, p. 3; testimony of Julius Kronenfeld, YVA, 03-1468, p. 2; testimony of Moshe Kerner, YVA, 03-914, pp. 1–2.

9. Testimony of Haim Steif, YVA, 03-908, pp. 3–5.

10. See testimony of Benno Schajewitcz, YVA, 03-2474. Schajewitcz was a Jewish Communist and the director of a furniture factory who was evacuated from Czernowitz to the Tatar Soviet Republic.

11. Carp, *Cartea neagră*, 3:32.

12. On the three days, see the testimonies of Sheindel Moskowitz, YVA, 03-1231, pp. 1–3; Cili Foerster, YVA, 03-1444, p. 2; Leah Luisa Neumann, YVA, 03/1452, p. 3; Maier Max

Fekler, YVA, 03-1438, p. 2; Julius Kronenfeld, YVA, 03-1468, p. 2; and Roza Sachner, YVA, 03-910, pp. 3–4. See also Roll, "Die schwarzen Tage von Czernowitz," 54–55.

13. Nuremberg Documents, NOKW-587.

14. Testimony of Perla Mark, Rabbi Mark's wife, 26 October 1954, in United Restitution Organization, *Documentation*, 1:183. Most of the reports by Einsatzgruppe D and the various Einsatzkommando units that operated in Bessarabia and Bukovina, including Einsatzkommando 10a, were collected and published by the United Restitution Organization.

15. Mircu, *Pogromurile din Basarabia*, 73.

16. Report no. 67 of 29 August 1941, extensively quoted in the Wajner Trial (Stuttgart Magistrates Court, 1957), American Jewish Archives, Cincinnati, Ohio, World Jewish Congress Collection, manuscript collection C259/10, p. 27; Nuremberg Documents, NO-4540, p. 12.

17. Mircu, *Pogromurile din Basarabia*, 75–78.

18. Testimony of Hana Fessler, YVA, 03-761, p. 3.

19. Mircu, *Pogromurile din Basarabia*, 75.

20. Siguranța report on Marinescu's character, late November 1941, USHMM/SSARM, RG-54001, roll 1, 706-1-23, pp. 145–46.

21. Telegram from Ion Antonescu (at the front) to Mihai Antonescu in Bucharest, late August 1941, USHMM/RSA, RG-25.002M, roll 19, Presidency of the Council of Ministers Cabinet Collection, file 167/1941, p. 64.

22. Popovici testimony, in Carp, *Cartea neagră*, no. 100, 3:168–69.

23. Popovici testimony, in Carp, *Cartea neagră*, no. 100, 3:166, 168–69.

24. *Procesul marei trădări naționale*, 246; report by the Presidency of the Council of Ministers on the demographic situation of Romanian Jewry in 1941, 31 August 1942, in Ancel, *Documents*, vol. 10, doc. 91, pp. 213, 215.

25. Order given by Radu Davidescu on 5 July 1941, in Ancel, *Documents*, vol. 5, doc. 77, p. 90; Carp, *Cartea neagră*, no. 86, 3:143.

26. Order by the governor of Bukovina to the military commander of the province, 9 October 1941, in Carp, *Cartea neagră*, no. 93, 3:152.

27. Filderman to Antonescu, 9 October 1941, in Carp, *Cartea neagră*, no. 94, 3:152.

28. Governor Calotescu to the military commander of Bukovina on the deportation arrangements, 10 October 1941, in Carp, *Cartea neagră*, no. 95, 3:153; copy in Ancel, *Documents*, vol. 5, doc. 80, p. 96.

29. Popovici testimony, in Carp, *Cartea neagră*, no. 100, 3:170–71 (author's emphasis).

30. In Romanian, as in French, there is a transitive verb, *a evacua*—to evacuate—but there is no reflexive form (*a se evacua*).

31. Popovici testimony, in Carp, *Cartea neagră*, no. 100, 3:169. Popovici related only to the deliberate ambiguity in the use of nouns by government leaders but not the new verb they had invented.

32. Mircu, *Pogromurile din Basarabia*, 79–80; see map of the ghetto appended to Carp, *Cartea neagră*, vol. 3.

33. Popovici testimony, in Carp, *Cartea neagră*, no. 100, 3:172.

34. Testimony of Simon Rosenrauch, YVA, 03-1536, p. 2.

35. Mircu, *Pogromurile din Basarabia*, 81.

36. Testimony of Sarah Grosskopf, YVA, 03-1537, p. 6.

37. Testimony of Sarah Grosskopf, YVA, 03-1537, pp. 6–7.

38. Testimony of Dr. Arie Zukerman, YVA, 0-3/1439, p. 9, and 03-1538, p. 2; testimony of Pnina (Pepi) Pollack, YVA, 03-1220, p. 2.

39. Mircu, *Pogromurile din Basarabia*, 89. According to the same source, General Ionescu also received a bribe through his adjutant, a major in the border guard "who negotiated on the general's behalf."

40. All the data come from Popovici testimony, in Carp, *Cartea neagră*, no. 100, 3:122.

41. Calotescu to the Presidency of the Council of Ministers, 9 April 1942, USHMM/ RMFA, RG-25.006M, roll 6, "Jewish Problem," vol. 20, p. 131.

42. Testimony of Dr. Arie Zukerman, YVA, 0-3/1439, pp. 2–3; testimony of Regina Levin, YVA, 03-1456, pp. 5–6.

43. Dori Popovici, memorandum submitted to Marshal Ion Antonescu on the situation in Bukovina, the true culprits, the possibility of remedying the situation, and the solution to the Jewish problem, 15 November 1941 (hereafter Dori Popovici's memorandum), USHMM/ SSARM, RG-54.001M, roll 1, 706-1-23, pp. 25–26.

44. Testimony of Anna Koppelman, 23 May 1943, American Jewish Archives, Cincinnati, Ohio, World Jewish Congress Collection, manuscript collection H288, p. 12. Koppelman left Romania in March 1943 with a group of seventy-five children on their way to Palestine, Cyprus.

45. Mircu, *Pogromurile din Basarabia*, 88–89.

46. Testimony of Anna Koppelman, 23 May 1943, American Jewish Archives, Cincinnati, Ohio, World Jewish Congress Collection, manuscript collection H288, p. 12.

47. Decree-Law no. 2507, *Monitorul Oficial*, no. 209, 4 September 1941.

48. Decree-Law no. 2506, *Monitorul Oficial*, no. 209, 4 September 1941.

49. Transcript of the committee session of the Civilian-Military Cabinet for the Administration of Bessarabia and Bukovina, 25 September 1941, USHMM/SSARM, RG-54.001M, roll 1, 706-1-550, pp. 240–41.

50. Transcript of the committee session of the Civilian-Military Cabinet for the Administration of Bessarabia and Bukovina, 25 September 1941, USHMM/SSARM, RG-54.001M, roll 1, 706-1-550, pp. 240–41.

51. Transcript of the committee session of the Civilian-Military Cabinet for the Administration of Bessarabia and Bukovina, 25 September 1941, USHMM/SSARM, RG-54.001M, roll 1, 706-1-550, p. 241.

52. Confidential report on the situation in Bukovina submitted by Antonescu on 22 September 1941, USHMM/SSARM, RG-54.001M, roll 1, 706-1-23, pp. 176–78.

53. The Undersecretariat for Romanization sent a director who earned 28,000 lei a month, twenty deputy directors who earned 15,000 lei a month each, and four clerks who earned 8,000 lei a month each from Bucharest to the Suceava district in order to supervise and manage the abandoned property. See "Report of the Fact-Finding Expedition to Bessarabia and Bukovina in the Field of Economy and Administration," n.d. [late November 1941], USHMM/SSARM, RG-54.001M, roll 1, 706-1-68, pp. 1–21. See also Annex no. 5, USHMM/ SSARM, RG-54.001M, roll 1, 706-1-23, pp. 120–21.

54. USHMM/SSARM, RG-54.001, roll 1, 706-1-23, pp. 189–90. Concerning the short-age of skilled labor and craftsmen, see memorandum on the work plan of the Ministry of Labor Directorate in Bessarabia and Bukovina, with statistical tables, n.d., USHMM/SSARM, RG-54.001, roll 1, 706-1-23, pp. 155–63.

55. First Siguranţa report on dissatisfaction in Bukovina, 1 October 1941, USHMM/SSARM, RG-54.001, roll 1, 706-1-23, pp. 131–32.

56. Annex no. 5, USHMM/SSARM, RG-54.001M, roll 1, 706-1-23, p. 189; inventory of lands that were leased and those that were not in the districts of Czernowitz, Khotin, and Storojineţ, prepared by the Romanization Directorate, n.d., USHMM/SSARM, RG-54.001M, roll 1, 706-1-23, p. 164.

57. First Siguranţa report on dissatisfaction in Bukovina, 1 October 1941, USHMM/SSARM, RG-54.001, roll 1, 706-1-23, pp. 132–33.

58. Report on Jewish estates that were donated by Romaşcanu to Romanian custodians, USHMM/SSARM, RG-54.001, roll 1, 706-1-23, pp. 143–45.

59. Siguranţa report on unlawful acts allegedly perpetrated by official bodies in Bukovina, 22 November 1941, USHMM/SSARM, RG-54.001, roll 1, 706-1-23, pp. 142–43.

60. Siguranţa's second report on dissatisfaction, 2 October 1941, USHMM/SSARM, RG-54.001, roll 1, 706-1-23, pp. 136–37.

61. Siguranţa's second report on dissatisfaction, 2 October 1941, USHMM/SSARM, RG-54.001, roll 1, 706-1-23, pp. 136–37.

62. Mircu, *Pogromurile din Basarabia*, 102.

63. Mircu, *Pogromurile din Basarabia*, 98.

64. Mircu, *Pogromurile din Basarabia*, 101. Mircu quotes from the list of these factories and businesses published in the journal *Finanţe si industrie* (Bucharest), no. 195–98 (September 1944).

65. Dori Popovici's letter to Marshal Antonescu, 28 October 1941, USHMM/SSARM, RG-54.001M, roll 1, 706-1-23, pp. 2, 4.

66. Dori Popovici's memorandum, USHMM/SSARM, RG-54.001M, roll 1, 706-1-23, pp. 9–84.

67. Antonescu's notes in the margin of Dori Popovici's request for an interview, USHMM/SSARM, RG-54.001M, roll 1, 706-1-23, p. 4.

68. Dori Popovici's memorandum, USHMM/SSARM, RG-54.001M, roll 1, 706-1-23, pp. 21, 68.

69. After his visit to Czernowitz, Antonescu's envoy made the following recommenda-tion: industries must be immediately reactivated. Jews who owned factories and were cur-rently unemployed or employed in unprofitable forced labor should be made to return to the factories they once owned and operate them immediately. They should receive enough money for their upkeep. Their activities should be monitored. Confidential report on the situation in Bukovina submitted by Antonescu on 22 September 1941, USHMM/SSARM, RG-54.001M, roll 1, 706-1-23, p. 178.

70. Report of the Civilian-Military Cabinet for the Administration of Bessarabia and Bukovina on the situation in the two provinces, n.d., USHMM/SSARM, RG-54.001M, roll 1, 706-1-23, p. 180.

71. Siguranța report on the mood of the population in Bessarabia, 22 November 1941, USHMM/SSARM, RG-54.001M, roll 1, 706-1-23, p. 147.

21. Southern Bukovina

1. Decree-Law no. 790, *Monitorul Oficial*, no. 209, 5 September 1941; Decree-Law no. 873, *Monitorul Oficial*, no. 236, 7 October 1941.

2. *Pinkas Hakehilot, Rumania*, 2:455, 459.

3. Carp, *Cartea neagră*, 3:135.

4. Carp, *Cartea neagră*, 3:138.

5. Testimony of Simon Rosenthal of Câmpulung, YVA, 03-1480, p. 8.

6. Telegram sent by a Jew from Câmpulung to his daughter in Bucharest, 12 October 1941, in Ancel, *Documents*, vol. 3, doc. 150, p. 239.

7. Testimony of Laura Bartfeld from Câmpulung, YVA, 03-1451, pp. 2–3.

8. Testimony of Anna Haspel from Gura Humorului, in Ancel, *Documents*, vol. 10, doc. 277, p. 665.

9. Testimony of Hannah Scharansky from Câmpulung, YVA, 03-1216, pp. 1–2.

10. Testimony of Laura Bartfeld from Câmpulung, YVA, 03-1451, pp. 2–3.

11. Testimony of Laura Bartfeld from Câmpulung, YVA, 03-1451, pp. 3–4.

12. Testimony of Shalom Fesler from Vatra Dornei, YVA, 03-896, p. 1.

13. Testimony of Iehuda Moscovici from Vatra Dornei, YVA, 03-1229, pp. 3–4; testimony of Yitzhak Ialon (Jablonower) from Vatra Dornei, YVA, 03-1238, pp. 6–7.

14. Testimony of Shalom Fesler from Vatra Dornei, YVA, 03-896, p. 2.

15. Statement by Lieutenant Roșca, commander of the Sixtieth Police Company, 6 November 1941, in Ancel, *Documents*, vol. 5, doc. 101, p. 146. Roșca was responsible for transferring the Jews and their belongings from their disembarkation from the train to their incarceration in Atachi pending deportation.

16. Ancel, *Documents*, vol. 5, doc. 103, p. 147.

17. Statement by Lieutenant Roșca, commander of the Sixtieth Police Company, 6 November 1941, in Ancel, *Documents*, vol. 5, doc. 101, p. 147.

18. Confidential report by a special gendarmerie agent to General Topor on the acts of looting and robbery perpetrated by Lieutenant Roșca and his subordinates, 31 October 1941, in Carp, *Cartea neagră*, no. 106, 3:188–89; copy in Ancel, *Documents*, vol. 5, doc. 101, pp. 134–35.

19. Testimony of Max Enzer from Siret, YVA, 03-1237, p. 8.

20. Telegram sent by a Jew from Câmpulung to his daughter in Bucharest, 12 October 1941, in Ancel, *Documents*, vol. 3, doc. 150, p. 239.

21. Carp, *Cartea neagră*, 3:136–37.

22. Testimony of Max Enzer from Siret, YVA, 03-1237, pp. 9–11.

23. Letter from Pressner, in Carp, *Cartea neagră*, no. 161, 3:314–15 (emphasis in the original); copy in Ancel, *Documents*, vol. 5, doc. 88, pp. 111–12.

24. Testimony of Ana Cahan from Rădăuți, YVA, 03-1423, pp. 2–3.

25. Mircu, *Pogromurile din Bucovina și Dorohoi*, 54–55.

26. Memorandum from Filderman to Antonescu on the deportation of Jews from Bessara-

bia and Bukovina and the deportation of Bessarabian- and Bukovinian-born Jews from the Regat, 19 October 1941, in Ancel, *Documents*, vol. 3, doc. 169, p. 266; appeal by the Jewish Federation to the minister of the interior on the deportation of Jews from Bessarabia and Bukovina and the deportation of Bessarabian- and Bukovinian-born Jews from the Regat, 20 October 1941, in Ancel, *Documents*, vol. 3, doc. 171, p. 269.

27. Union of Jewish Communities of Romania to the director general of the Siguranța on measures adopted by the Iași police to deport Bessarabian- and Bukovinian-born Jews from Iași, 27 October 1941, in Ancel, *Documents*, vol. 3, doc. 190, p. 292.

28. Jewish Federation to the director general of the Siguranța requesting a delay in the deportation of Bessarabian- and Bukovinian-born Jews, 20 October 1941, in Ancel, *Documents*, vol. 3, doc. 175, p. 273.

29. Report by Filderman on the interview with Interior Minister Popescu, 20 October 1941, in Ancel, *Documents*, vol. 3, doc. 172, p. 270.

22. The Dorohoi District

1. Testimony of Isidor Abramovici-Băluș, head of the community, on his activities during the fascist regime, from documents of the Prosecution Service in Bucharest on attempts to bring to trial members of the military responsible for the Dorohoi pogroms, Jewish Federation's copy, 1950, in Ancel, *Documents*, vol. 6, doc. 38, pp. 360–61.

2. Testimony of Isidor Abramovici-Băluș, 1950, in Ancel, *Documents*, vol. 6, doc. 38, p. 361.

3. Antonescu's order to expel the Jews from the villages between the Siret and the Prut and to incarcerate the men in the Târgu-Jiu camp, 21 June 1941, in Ancel, *Documents*, vol. 5, doc. 5, p. 9.

4. Filderman's memorandum on his meeting with Mihai and Ion Antonescu on 8 September 1941, in Ancel, *Documents*, vol. 3, doc. 74, p. 132.

5. Filderman's memorandum of 6 November 1941 on rumors that the Jews of the Dorohoi district were about to be deported and memorandum of 7 November 1941 on the start of the deportation, in Ancel, *Documents*, vol. 3, doc. 215, p. 327.

6. Report by the Romanian lawyer Constantin Mușat on the deportation of the Jewish population from Dorohoi city and district, n.d. [around 23 November 1941] (hereafter Mușat's report), in Ancel, *Documents*, vol. 3, doc. 250, pp. 412–15.

7. Mușat's report, in Ancel, *Documents*, vol. 3, doc. 250, p. 412; Carp, *Cartea neagră*, 3:140.

8. *Actul de acuzare*, 64–65; copy in Ancel, *Documents*, vol. 6, doc. 7, p. 88.

9. *Actul de acuzare*, 64–65; Mircu, *Pogromurile din Bucovina și Dorohoi*, 143.

10. Filderman's memorandum to Antonescu, in Ancel, *Documents*, vol. 3, doc. 259, pp. 426–27.

11. Filderman's memorandum on the meeting with Nicolae Lupu after the latter had met with Antonescu, 3 December 1941, in Ancel, *Documents*, vol. 3, doc. 258, p. 425.

12. Mușat's report, in Ancel, *Documents*, vol. 3, doc. 250, p. 413.

13. Fred Șaraga, "Insemnări fragmentare . . ." [Fragmentary notes], *Sliha* (Tel Aviv), 12 July 1956; copy in Ancel, *Documents*, vol. 8, doc. 438, p. 553.

14. Filderman's memorandum on the number of deportees and survivors, 2 October 1943, in Ancel, *Documents*, vol. 5, doc. 224, p. 493.

15. Testimony of Isaia Herşcovici of Dărăbani, [Tel Aviv, 27 May 1959], YVA, 03-1476, pp. 5–6.

16. Muşat's report, in Ancel, *Documents*, vol. 3, doc. 250, p. 415.

17. Filderman's memorandum on the numerous petitions submitted by Jewish men who were released from the forced labor detachments who could not find their families and whose houses were expropriated, 22 November 1941, in Ancel, *Documents*, vol. 3, doc. 242, p. 403.

18. Appeal by Clara Sofer to Antonescu, Mogilev, 14 March 1942, in Ancel, *Documents*, vol. 7, doc. 5, pp. 5–6.

19. Filderman's memorandum on the 260 appeals by men from Dorohoi to bring back their families from Transnistria, 2 February 1942, in Ancel, *Documents*, vol. 3, doc. 321, pp. 514–15.

20. National Romanization Center in Dorohoi, report on the number of Jewish homes requisitioned by the center and the use made of them, 30 April 1942, in Ancel, *Documents*, vol. 5, doc. 146, p. 265.

21. "C.N.R.-ul a patronat la Dorohoi jefuirea populaţiei evreeşti, Locuinţe sigilate şi furturi ce nu puteau fi stăvilite" [Looting and theft of the Jewish population of Dorohoi under the auspices of the National Romanization Center], *Renaşterea Noastră* (January 1945); copy in Ancel, *Documents*, vol. 8, doc. 409, p. 445.

22. *Procesul marei trădări naţionale*, 144.

23. Nuremberg Documents, NO-3106, 12 August 1941; copy in Ancel, *Documents*, vol. 5, doc. 54, p. 53.

24. Fred Şaraga, "Insemnări fragmentare . . ." [Fragmentary notes], *Sliha* (Tel Aviv), 12 July 1956; copy in Ancel, *Documents*, vol. 8, doc. 438, p. 553.

25. Jewish Center, survey of the situation of the deported Jews in Transnistria, November 1943, in Ancel, *Documents*, vol. 5, doc. 219, p. 470.

26. Governor of Bukovina to the Presidency of the Council of Ministers, including a table, 9 April 1942, USHMM/RMFA, RG-25006M, roll 10, "The Jewish Problem," vol. 21, p. 131.

27. Governor of Bukovina to the Presidency of the Council of Ministers on the progress of the deportation operation in Bukovina, 12 June 1942, USHMM/RMFA, RG-25006M, roll 10, "The Jewish Problem," vol. 21, pp. 196–97; Appendix 5 (The Deportation from Dorohoi), USHMM/RMFA, RG-25006M, roll 10, "The Jewish Problem," vol. 21, pp. 131, 206.

28. Congresul Mondial Evreesc, *Populaţia evreească*, 42.

23. The National Bank of Romania

1. Debate on the report of the commission of inquiry in Kishinev, session of 4 December 1941, transcript of the secret discussion on the failure of the operation to confiscate gold from the Jews, USHMM/SSARM, RG-54001, roll 1, 706-1-23, p. 87.

2. Debate on the report of the commission of inquiry in Kishinev, session of 4 December 1941, transcript of the secret discussion on the failure of the operation to confiscate gold from the Jews, USHMM/SSARM, RG-54001, roll 1, 706-1-23, pp. 89, 90.

3. See Carp, *Cartea neagră*, 3:137, on the lei exchange rate in May 1941 (168 lei to the dollar).

4. First report of the commission of inquiry headed by Constantin Păunescu, inspector

general of the BNR, "to investigate irregularities and anomalies in connection with the receipt of gold and valuables from the Jews of the Kishinev Ghetto," 1 December 1941, USHMM/ SSARM, RG-54001M, roll 1, 706-1-68, pp. 47–48.

5. Transcript of cabinet session of 6 September 1941, USHMM/SRI, RG-25.004M, reel 35, file 40010, vol. 77, p. 37.

6. Telegram by Governor Voiculescu to the finance minister, at Marshal Antonescu's behest, 2 October 1941, USHMM/SSARM, RG-54001M, roll 1, 706-1-22, p. 101.

7. Col. Radu Davidescu, head of the marshal's military cabinet, to governors of Bessarabia and Bukovina, 5 October 1941, in Carp, *Cartea neagră*, no. 88, 3:144.

8. Confidential letter by the Bessarabian administration to the military commander and the BNR in Kishinev, 8 October 1941, USHMM/SSARM, RG-54001M, roll 1, 706-1-22, p. 102.

9. Finance Ministry to the governor of Bessarabia, 14 October 1941, USHMM/SSARM, RG-54001M, roll 1, 706-1-22, p. 104.

10. Circular by the governor of Bessarabia concerning the new deadline for changing rubles, 17 October 1941, USHMM/SSARM, RG-54001M, roll 1, 706-1-22, p. 105.

11. Finance Ministry to the governor of Bessarabia, clarifications concerning the exchange of rubles, 18 September 1941, USHMM/SSARM, RG-54001M, roll 1, 706-1-22, p. 106. Mircea Vulcănescu, who signed the letter, called the Jews *ovrei* (an archaic term) so as to avoid using the word *jidan*.

12. Ancel, *Documents*, vol. 5, no. 118, p. 185.

13. Confidential request by BNR managers Demetrescu and Niculescu to the Presidency of the Council of Ministers, undated, in Ancel, *Documents*, vol. 5, no. 118, p. 185.

14. Transcript from Ion Antonescu's interrogation, 16 April 1946, USHMM/SRI, RG-25.004M, reel 34, file 40010, vol. 26, p. 61.

15. Law no. 21, *Monitorul Oficial*, no. 9, 12 January 1942; copy in Ancel, *Documents*, vol. 5, doc. 130, p. 223.

16. Telegram from the Transnistrian administration to the Presidency of the Council of Ministers in Bucharest on the start of the deportations from Odessa, 13 January 1942, Odessa State Archive/Gosudarstvennii Archiv Odeskoi Oblasti (hereafter Odessa Archives), fond 2242, opis 1, delo 1486, pp. 33–34.

17. Memorandum by Gendarmerie Inspectorate in Transnistria about the progress of the deportations, 17 January 1942, in Ancel, *Documents*, vol. 5, no. 129, p. 222.

18. Report by Major Apostolescu, representative of the General Staff, on the deportation of Jews from Odessa, 18 January 1942, Odessa Archives, 2242-1-1486, pp. 9–10.

19. Report by Major Apostolescu, representative of the General Staff, on the deportation of Jews from Odessa, 18 January 1942, Odessa Archives, 2242-1-1486, pp. 10–11.

20. Vulcănescu, *Ultimul cuvînt*, 16, 88. The book includes the brilliant defense speech that Vulcănescu delivered at his trial in 1946 and the appeal he submitted on his conviction in 1947. He was convicted for his part in the Antonescu government's pro-Nazi economic policy. The issue of the theft of Jewish property was never even raised at the trial. Vulcănescu died in prison in 1952. Note that Vulcănescu had not previously been known as an antisemite.

21. Vulcănescu, *Ultimul cuvînt*, 88.

22. "Report of the Fact-Finding Mission on the Situation in Bessarabia and Bukovina,"

undated [late November 1941], USHMM/SSARM, RG-54.001, roll 1, 706-1-68, explicitly states that valuable objets d'art were left in the apartments of Jews in Kishinev who were transferred to the ghetto and that not all were registered. See appendix 1A of the report, pp. 24–25. As to securities, to sort them in Atachi the BNR appointed a reserve officer to retrieve them from all the personal documents that had been confiscated from the Jews. These too were handed over without being registered. Statement by Lt. Augustin Roşca, commander of the Sixtieth Police Company, before Major Teodorescu-Sachelarie, 5 November 1941, in Ancel, *Documents*, vol. 5, doc. 104, p. 144.

23. *Trei ani de guvernare*, 238.

24. *Procesul marei trădări naţionale*, 32.

25. First report of the commission of inquiry headed by Constantin Păunescu, inspector general of the BNR, "to investigate irregularities and anomalies in connection with the receipt of gold and valuables from the Jews of the Kishinev Ghetto," 1 December 1941, USHMM/SSARM, RG-54001M, roll 1, 706-1-68, p. 6. A summary report issued by the Presidency of the Council of Ministers on 1 December 1941, following the various inquiries, stated, for example, that members of the SSI in Kishinev had stolen 1,110 gold coins worth about 4.5 million lei from three Jews; USHMM/SSARM, RG-54001, roll 1, 706-1-68, p. 64. The military commander of Kishinev, Col. Eugen Dumitrescu, evidently dispatched seven train cars laden with valuables stolen from Jews to his home in the Regat; "Report of the Fact-Finding Mission on the Situation in Bessarabia and Bukovina," undated [late November 1941], USHMM/SSARM, RG-54.001, roll 1, 706-1-68, pp. 22, 25.

26. Circular by Finance Minister Alexandrini, 15 January 1946, in Ancel, *Documents*, vol. 5, doc. 256, p. 587. Alexandrini belonged to a faction of Gheorghe Tătărescu's National Liberal Party. Tătărescu collaborated with the Communists, and it was they who appointed the minister of foreign affairs, the finance minister, and the minister of industry and trade from the National Liberal Party. Alexandrescu, *Economia României*, 99. After the Communists consolidated their rule the liberal ministers were dismissed, and Tătărescu was imprisoned for many years.

27. "Situation des Juifs en Roumanie (1940–1944)," 1946 (memorandum submitted by the Romanian government at the Paris Peace Conference); copy in Ancel, *Documents*, vol. 8, doc. 424, pp. 487–506. See especially the section referring to confiscation of property, pp. 14–16, 360–61.

24. Transnistria under Romanian Occupation

1. "Our great ally [has demonstrated] confidence in our organizational skills and has honored us with the administration of Transnistria. We are Germany's only ally to have had such an honor bestowed upon us." These words were written by Gheorghe Alexianu, governor of Transnistria, in a special ceremonial booklet published by the Transnistrian administration two years into Romanian rule in Transnistria. Guvernământul Transnistriei, *Transnistria*, 22. Alexianu further stated, "Transnistria has been handed over to the Romanian State following the Romanian army's glorious war operations and exceptional spirit of sacrifice." See Decree no. 2212, 25 May 1943, Odessa Archives, 2361-1-46. (The archive of the Transnistrian administration is part of the Odessa state archives.)

2. Litani, *Transnistria*, 9.

3. Altshuler, *Distribution of the Jewish Population*.

4. According to Altshurer, *Distribution of the Jewish Population*, table 1, Odessa had 233,155 Jews.

5. See Antonescu's ordinance on the administration of Transnistria, issued in Tighina on 19 August 1941, Central State Archive no. 1, Moscow, Collection 492, opis 1, file 5, pp. 437–39 (for details of the archive, see chap. 27); Ordinance no. 37, issued by Antonescu on 20 December 1941, on the establishment of military tribunals in Transnistria, Odessa Archives, 2361-1-29, p. 65.

6. Ordinance no. 27, issued by Governor Alexianu, concerning the deployment of the police in urban and rural areas, 24 November 1941, Odessa Archives, 2357-1c-1, pp. 21–22; clarifications concerning the "powers of the pretor in his capacity as a police officer," with the signature of Odessa police commander Col. Ion Popovici, undated, Odessa Archives, 2351-1-1, pp. 35–36.

7. Text of Governor Alexianu's speech before the pretors, 29 November 1941, Odessa Archives, 2358-1c-9, pp. 244–44b.

8. Report by Mihai Antonescu on his conversation with the U.S. ambassador, 11 September 1941, in Drăgan, *Antonescu*, vol. 3, no. 48, p. 199.

9. Dallin, *Odessa*, 251.

10. Col. Gheorghe Magherescu, former chief of Bureau 3 operations in the military cabinet of Antonescu, wrote in his memoirs, "Once Odessa fell, for the second time the general considered Romania's war as finished. As I mentioned, he returned to the capital city, resuming the role of conducător of the state, which he had exercised through an intermediary during the [military] campaign. To publicly mark this step, *he demobilized the majority of the forces*, leaving twenty infantry divisions for guarding Transnistria and three independent cavalry brigades" (author's translation and emphasis). Magherescu, *Adevărul*, 36.

11. Directive no. 4860 of Romanian army headquarters concerning the organization and operation of the liaison headquarters in Transnistria, together with lists of units and their locations in Transnistria, 15 October 1941, Odessa Archives, 2357-1c-9, pp. 6–32.

12. Directive no. 4860 of Romanian army headquarters concerning the organization and operation of the liaison headquarters in Transnistria, together with lists of units and their locations in Transnistria, 15 October 1941, Odessa Archives, 2357-1c-9, p. 134.

13. Directive no. 4860 of Romanian army headquarters concerning the organization and operation of the liaison headquarters in Transnistria, together with lists of units and their locations in Transnistria, 15 October 1941, Odessa Archives, 2357-1c-9, pp. 16–17.

14. Transnistrian administration to the Fourth Army, 13 October 1941, Odessa Archives, 2242-1-277, p. 83.

15. Fourth Army to Governor Alexianu, 9 October 1941, Odessa Archives, 2242-1-277, p. 84.

16. First Division headquarters to the prefect of Mogilev district, 12 June 1942, in Carp, *Cartea neagră*, 3:358–59.

17. Odessa Gendarmerie Inspectorate to the administration, 10 October 1943, Odessa Archives, 2214-1-1561, p. 248.

18. Transnistrian administration to the Third Army Corps concerning the Jews of the Tiraspol ghetto, 10 March 1943, Odessa Archives, 2242-1-1946, p. 77.

19. The order was not preserved but was mentioned in correspondence by army commanders in Transnistria with the administration, as cited in the following notes.

20. Correspondence by Lieutenant Colonel Comănescu to the gendarmerie commander of the Berezovka district, enclosing the order issued by the Third Army Corps, 1 August 1943, Odessa Archives, 2361-1-591, p. 143.

21. Order no. 22817 of the Third Army Corps, 27 August 1943, Odessa Archives, 2361-1-591, p. 143.

22. Jewish Center to Governor Alexianu, 9 December 1942, Odessa Archives, 2242-1-1491, p. 288.

23. Circular no. 8614 of the Transnistrian administration's postal division, 16 June 1943, Odessa Archives, 2351-IX-52, p. 59.

24. See Protocol of meeting of army headquarters' First Section, 9 June 1942, on the deportation of "criminal" Jews and norms for transporting them to Transnistria, including the confiscation of their property, USHMM/RMFA, RG-25.006M, reel 10, "Jewish Problem," vol. 21, pp. 183–83b. See also a letter by army headquarters, signed by the deputy chief of army headquarters, General Arhip, to the Presidency of the Council of Ministers to approve army headquarters' proposals on the matter, 16 August 1942, USHMM/RMFA, RG-25.006M, reel 10, "Jewish Problem," vol. 21, p. 182; Secret Order no. 900285 of army headquarters to the Gendarmerie General Inspectorate in Bucharest, to police headquarters, to the directorate of the security police (Siguranța), and to the governors of Bessarabia and Bukovina on the impending deportation and on the types of offenders and family members to be deported, 17 September 1942, USHMM/RMFA, RG-25.006M, reel 10, "Jewish Problem," vol. 20, p. 47; letter from army headquarters to the Transnistrian administration seeking to determine the deportation route of thirty thousand to forty thousand Jews, 20 September 1942, USHMM/RMFA, RG-25.006M, reel 10, "Jewish Problem," vol. 20, p. 43; secret telegram by the secretary general of the Presidency of the Council of Ministers, Vlădescu, to the governor of Transnistria, 21 September 1942, USHMM/RMFA, RG-25.006M, reel 10, "Jewish Problem," vol. 20, p. 46.

25. *Procesul marei trădări naționale*, 51.

26. List of police duties throughout Transnistria, December 1941, Odessa Archives, 2242-4-5c, p. 3.

27. I called the local police "Ukrainian" because this is how it was recorded in Romanian documents. After it became clear that the Ukrainian populace resented the occupation regime, the commander of the gendarmerie in Transnistria, Col. M. Iliescu, issued Order no. 3124 on 8 June 1942, which stated, "There is no Ukrainian police." The order called for all "Ukrainian police" to undergo a test of loyalty and set forth guidelines regarding uniforms and papers to be carried by every Ukrainian police officer. Odessa Archives, 2359-1-67, p. 160.

28. Directives of the Odessa district bureau concerning the duties of the village mayors (*primari*) and the local police, 30 December 1941, Odessa Archives, 2359-1-13, pp. 10–10b.

29. Directives concerning the implementation of policing and security measures throughout Transnistria, October 1941, Odessa Archives, 2358-1c-8, pp. 12–13.

30. Memorandum from Ion Antonescu to Hitler, 11 June 1941, in Armin, Ardeleanu, and Lache, *Antonescu-Hitler*, doc. 14, 1:90.

31. Transcript of meeting between Hitler and Antonescu, 12 June 1941, in Hillgruber, *Staatsmänner und Diplomaten*, no. 26, pp. 277–78, 280, 288.

32. Record by Mihai Antonescu on his meeting with Hitler in Berlin, 27 November 1941, in Ancel, *Documents*, vol. 9, doc. 105, p. 381.

33. Summary of a conversation between Mihai Antonescu and Propaganda Minister Goebbels, as recorded by Antonescu, Berlin, 28 November 1941, in Ancel, *Documents*, vol. 9, doc. 106, p. 294.

34. Record by Mihai Antonescu on his meeting with Hitler in Berlin, 27 November 1941, in Ancel, *Documents*, vol. 9, doc. 105, p. 282.

35. Record by Mihai Antonescu on his meeting with Hitler in Berlin, 27 November 1941, in Ancel, *Documents*, vol. 9, doc. 105, p. 381.

36. Mihai Antonescu was already two-faced at this time. In a meeting with Mott Gunther, the U.S. ambassador in Bucharest, he did not mention the word *race* but based Romania's continued participation in the war against the Soviet Union on its wish "to strengthen its sovereignty over Bessarabia and Bukovina" and to topple the Communist regime. For an account of Mihai Antonescu's conversation with the U.S. ambassador, 2 October 1941, see Drăgan, *Antonescu*, vol. 3, no. 50, p. 200.

37. The author based his comparison of the German occupation regime in the Ukraine and the Romanian occupation regime in Transnistria on Dallin's seminal study, *German Rule in Russia*. For lack of space, I shall not analyze the various approaches toward the Ukrainian problem put forward by the Nazi leadership or the disputes between the various officials but shall focus on those aspects that directly affected the Romanian occupation regime in Transnistria.

38. In mid-November 1941 the U.S. ambassador in Bucharest reported that Ion Antonescu had expressed serious doubts concerning the German army's ability to win the war, since it had not managed to conquer Russia "as planned": "The Russian soldier fought splendidly, and Russian equipment as well as military organization was excellent. Were Russia to win this war, she would soon be in a position to dominate the whole world." Note that Antonescu was influenced at the time by the heavy losses his army had sustained in the siege on Odessa. See telegram from Ambassador Mott Gunther to U.S. State Department in Washington, section 2, 15 November 1941, in Ancel, *Documents*, vol. 3, doc. 235, p. 393.

25. The Arrest and Deportation of Jews

1. At his trial Ohlendorf acknowledged that between June 1941 and June 1942 his Einsatzgruppe had killed approximately ninety thousand Jews. According to him this number also included Jews from territories up to the River Don, including the Crimean Peninsula. See Case 9 in *Trials of War Criminals*, 4:168. On the murder of the Jews of Transnistria, see Arad, Krakowski, and Spector, *Einsatzgruppe Reports*, 72–74, 86–87, 105–11, 119, 141–43, 166–70, 194–95, 221.

2. Nuremberg Documents, NO-4540.

3. These calculations are based on documents I discovered in archives in Russia, Ukraine, Moldova, and the United States. See chapter 38 herein.

4. Ordinance no. 16 by Governor Alexianu, issued in Tiraspol on 25 September 1941, Odessa Archives, 2359-1-6, p. 15.

5. Ordinance no. 1 of the gendarmerie, 8 September 1941, copied by hand by the commander of the Fifth Gendarmerie Battalion deployed in the Golta district, USHMM, NOA, RG-31.008M, microfiche 2178, fond 2178, opis 1, delo 42.

6. See report of the commander of the gendarmerie company in Ovidopol, 28 November 1941, containing a list of fifteen Jews or half-Jews, including children and villagers, who were exposed by informers who emphasized that they should be arrested and sent to camps, Odessa Archives, 2357-1c-356, p. 3. The prefect's recommendation was to implement the administration's Ordinance no. 23, namely incarceration in camps and ghettos.

7. Report of the Gendarmerie Inspectorate on the activities of the gendarmerie in Transnistria, 15–31 October 1941, Odessa Archives, 2242-4c-2, p. 187.

8. Activity report of the pretor of the subdistrict of Chichelnik for November, 28 November 1941, Odessa Archives, 2358-1c-9, pp. 128–28b.

9. For example, see Bulletin no. 29 of police headquarters in Odessa concerning the imprisonment of suspects and the deportation of Jews by train, 29 January 1942, Odessa Archives, 2242-4c-29, p. 48.

10. Confidential letter from the administration to the prefect of Golta to conduct a census of the Jews and submit the results by 12 April 1942, including handwritten comments on the letter by the prefect of Nikolayev, USHMM, NOA, RG-31.008M, 2178-1-2, p. 44.

11. Inspector of the gendarmerie in Transnistria to the Secretariat General of the Transnistrian administration, data relating to the scope of the deportations from Romania and the "movement" [i.e., extermination] of local Jews, 9 September 1942, USHMM/RMFA, RG-25.006M, reel 10, "The Jewish Problem," vol. 21, p. 152.

12. Excerpt from the transcript of a speech by Antonescu at a meeting with the prefects, 11 October 1941, USHMM/SRI, RG-25004M, reel 25b, investigation file of Dumitru Popescu, vol. 11, no. 47/1945, p. 47 (author's emphasis).

13. Gendarmerie Inspectorate to the governor, 30 September 1941, Odessa Archives, 2242-1-1067.

14. Telegram by Prefect Popescu on the progress of the convoys, 2 October 1941, Odessa Archives, 2242-1-1067, p. 33.

15. See report by the Gendarmerie Inspectorate, 15–31 October 1941, Odessa Archives, 2242-1-2, p. 184.

16. Report by the Gendarmerie Inspectorate, 15–31 October 1941, Odessa Archives, 2242-1-2, p. 187.

17. Minutes of cabinet session of 13 November 1941, in Benjamin, *Problema evreiască*, doc. 119, p. 337 (author's emphasis).

18. Transnistrian administration to Ion Antonescu concerning the order to transfer the cows to Romania, 1 November 1941, Odessa Archives, 2242-1-677, p. 144. The operation was not as simple as it seemed. Antonescu ordered healthy cows to be brought to Romania for distribution to farmers. In return, the farmers would turn over to the army authorities milk cows that were poor yielders, as a source of food for the soldiers. Consequently, tens of thousands of cows were transferred from Romania to Transnistria alongside the deportees, via the same means, that is, rafts and narrow bridges.

19. Instruction of Marshal Antonescu, signed by Vlădescu, to Governor Alexianu concerning the proper handling of the cows, 5 November 1941, Odessa Archives, 2242-1-677, p. 143.

20. Telegram in the governor's name to the prefect of the Odessa district to temporarily halt the transfer of livestock because of an outbreak of typhus, 20 November 1941, Odessa Archives, 2359-1C-1, p. 243.

21. Governor Alexianu to Marshal Antonescu, 11 November 1941, Odessa Archives, 2359-1C-1, p. 136 (author's emphasis).

22. Draft ordinance on the status of the Jews, prepared by Broșteanu, inspector general of the gendarmerie in Transnistria, undated [early November 1941], Odessa Archives, 2359-1C-1, pp. 132–35.

23. Ordinance no. 23 of 11 November 1941; copy in Carp, *Cartea neagră*, 3:395–97, and in Ancel, *Documents*, vol. 5, doc. 112, p. 176. For the original ordinance signed by Governor Alexianu, see Odessa Archives, 2242-1-1, pp. 28–30.

24. Ordinance no. 23 of 11 November 1941; copy in Carp, *Cartea neagră*, 3:395–97, and in Ancel, *Documents*, vol. 5, doc. 112, p. 176. Article 8 allowed the gendarmerie to consider escaping Jews as "spies who should be punished on the spot in accordance with the provisions of martial law." On 30 September 1941 the Gendarmerie Inspectorate in Transnistria reported to the Transnistrian administration that it had executed Communist propagandists and terrorists "in accordance with the provisions of martial law." The same laws applied to Jews.

26. "The Kingdom of Death"

1. Nuremberg Documents, excerpt from document PS-3319. For the entire document, see *Der Prozess gegen die Hauptkriegsverbrecher*, 32:183–84.

2. Hillgruber, *Hitler, Carol und Antonescu*, 128.

3. Although we do not know exactly how many casualties the Romanian army sustained in Odessa, at least 30,000 soldiers died. On 6 October 1941, ten days before the fall of Odessa, Romanian War Headquarters stated that 70,000 soldiers had fallen and another 100,000 had been wounded in the battles to capture Transnistria. Hillgruber, *Hitler, Carol und Antonescu*, 128. These data were evidently inflated to impress the Germans with the extent of Romanian losses in the war vis-à-vis German losses. Foreign Ministry circles in Berlin estimated Romanian casualties in the Battle of Odessa at 20,000 dead, 15,000 missing, and 76,000 wounded. Hillgruber, *Hitler, Carol und Antonescu*, 319n207. An official publication by the Antonescu regime in 1943 indicates that 10,486 soldiers fell in the battles to liberate Bessarabia and Bukovina, while 26,892 soldiers fell in the occupation of Transnistria and the Battle of Odessa. See *Trei ani de guvernare*, 21. Data compiled by Romanian army headquarters after the war show that from 26 June to 17 October 1941 Romanian army casualties totaled 27,061 dead, 14,624 missing, and 89,632 wounded—a total of 22.4 percent of all Romanian forces participating at that time in the war (585,930 soldiers). USHMM/MSM, RG-25003M, file IV:160, p. 4. All these figures are very high in comparison with the losses sustained by the German army up to 30 September 1941: 116,908 dead, 24,484 missing, and 409,647 wounded. Hillgruber, *Hitler, Carol und Antonescu*, 138.

4. Gheorghe, *Rumäniens Weg*, 189–90.

5. Antonescu's letter to Filderman, 19 October 1941, in Ancel, *Documents*, vol. 3, doc. 167, p. 262. The letter's contents and tenses indicate that it was written before the fall of Odessa, at the height of the battles for the city. Antonescu added a note in his own handwriting: "A wounded soldier from Piatra Neamț was buried alive, at the order and under the eyes of the Soviet Commissar Yids even though the unfortunate [soldier] begged for his life, saying he was the father of four children." The letter, which was published in the Romanian press on 27 October 1941, unleashed a virulent antisemitic campaign "that marked the psychological climax of antisemitism during the war." Carp, *Cartea neagră*, 3:138–39.

6. Report no. 18 by 1st Sgt. C. Pelivan, commander of Gendarmerie Platoon no. 3, Domanevka, to the prefecture of the Krivoye Ozero district, USHMM, NOA, RG-31.008M, 2178-1-12, pp. 48–48b.

7. Report no. 34 by 1st Sgt. C. Pelivan to the prefecture of Golta-Pervomaisk, 5 November 1941, USHMM, NOA, RG-31.008M, 2178-1-12, pp. 143–43b. Pelivan was willing to step down if the prefecture thought him unequal to the task and even pointed out that for several years he had been suffering from an ulcer.

8. Summary report by Prefect Isopescu to Governor Alexianu, 19 November 1941, USHMM, NOA, RG-31.008M, 2178-1-9, pp. 1, 55.

9. Military headquarters in Krivoye Ozero to the prefect on the arming of Ukrainian policemen, on Jews who were left in the villages, and on the shortage of priests and icons in the villages, 16 October 1941, USHMM, NOA, RG-31.008M, 2178-1-66, p. 36.

10. Prefect Isopescu to the Twentieth Infantry Regiment, 2 November 1941, USHMM, NOA, RG-31.008M, 2178-1-66, p. 138.

11. Prefect Isopescu to the Twentieth Infantry Regiment, 2 November 1941, USHMM, NOA, RG-31.008M, 2178-1-66, p. 138.

12. Prefect Isopescu to the commander of the Twentieth Infantry Regiment in the Romanian village of Lubashevka, 8 November 1941, USHMM, NOA, RG-31.008M, 2178-1-66, p. 132.

13. Golta municipality to the district prefect, 4 November 1941, USHMM, NOA, RG-31.008M, 2178-1-66, p. 89.

14. District prefect to Second Lieutenant Bivolaru, 4 November 1941, USHMM, NOA, RG-31.008M, 2178-1-66, p. 90.

15. Telegram from the administration in Tiraspol to the prefecture in Berezovka on the burial of corpses, 6 November 1941, Odessa Archives, 2361-1-600, p. 67; telegram on the burial of corpses to the prefecture of the Krivoye Ozero district, 6 November 1941, received on 11 November 1941, USHMM, NOA, RG-31.008M, 2178-1-66, p 125. Following this, Isopescu issued a directive instructing all pretors to bury corpses; USHMM, NOA, RG-31.008M, 2178-1-66, p. 126.

16. Complaint by Prefect Isopescu to the commander of the Fifth Gendarmerie Battalion in Balta [who was also in charge of the gendarmes in the Golta district], 13 November 1941, USHMM, NOA, RG-31.008M, 2178-1-9, p. 30.

17. Military commander in Krivoye Ozero to the prefect, 16 October 1941, USHMM, NOA, RG-31.008M, 2178-1-66, p. 30b.

18. Appeal to the military tribunal in Tiraspol, with the file opened against the lance cor-

poral who deserted and Vasile Marin, who robbed Jews in the Vazdovka camp, early December 1941, USHMM, NOA, RG-31.008M, 2178-1-12, p. 204.

19. Confirmation of receipt of parcels with jewelry and money and their transfer to the military tribunal in Tiraspol, 23 December 1941, USHMM, NOA, RG-31.008M, p. 203.

20. Report by Isopescu to the administration regarding the transport of Jews with a request that the administration stop sending them, 13 November 1941, USHMM, NOA, RG-31.008M, 2178-1-66, p. 151. Quoted from Ancel, "Romanian Campaigns of Mass Murder," 113.

21. Report by Lieutenant Moşoiu, commander of Company no. 4, to his superiors, November 1941, USHMM, NOA, RG-31.008M, 2178-1-12. The report was brought to Isopescu's notice, and he asked the officer to report to him.

22. Third Army headquarters to the Transnistrian administration, 12 December 1941, Odessa Archives, 2242-1-1486, p. 2. On 26 January 1942 the administration informed Third Army headquarters that the twenty-one craftsmen who had been separated from the other Jews and held in Tiraspol "will be evacuated to the concentration zones immediately after their release from quarantine." Odessa Archives, 2246-1-1486, p. 74.

23. Commander of the Twentieth Infantry Division to the prefecture, 4 December 1941, USHMM, NOA, RG-31.008M, 2178-1-12, p. 221. Isopescu's comment in the margin of Colonel Georgescu's request (written 6 December 1941) shows that the prefect did not, in fact, know how many ghettos had been set up in his district: "Please phone the subdistricts to find out how many ghettos they have, where they are situated, and how many Yids are in each [of the subdistricts]. Escapees must be shot."

24. Telegram by Isopescu to the Transnistrian administration in Tiraspol, USHMM, NOA, RG-31.008M, 2178-1-12, p. 224.

25. Report by Colonel Broşteanu, inspector of the Transnistrian gendarmerie, to Alexianu, on the need to set up three new camps for Jews because Bogdanovka was overflowing with Jews, 13 December 1941, USHMM, NOA, RG-31.008M, 2178-1-12. The governor wrote his approval of the proposal in the margin of the report, 20 December 1941.

26. *Actul de acuzare*, 26.

27. Summary report of 19 November 1941, USHMM, NOA, RG-31.008M, 2178-1-9, p. 52.

28. USHMM, NOA, 3363-1C-2: Tătăranu, *Expunere de titluri*, 11.

29. *Procesul marei trădări naționale*, 35; Ciucă and Ignat, *Stenogramele sedinţelor*, doc. 22, pp. 462–63.

30. "Top secret" communication, signed by Alexianu, concerning the envoy's arrival, with a copy of a document identifying the envoy, undated, USHMM, NOA, RG-31.008M, 2178-1-8. Although the communication took the form of a circular sent perhaps also to other prefects, the author examined the secret files of all the prefectures in southern Transnistria and found this circular only in the Golta district archive. Isopescu evidently made sure that the circular was not destroyed. The envoy's identity papers stated that he belonged to the SS of the Transnistrian administration—the Serviciul Special, or Romanian Special Service, not the Nazi SS. Nevertheless, the attempt to emulate the Nazis in this period is interesting. The Special Intelligence Service, headed by Eugen Cristescu, was directly answerable to Antonescu and called itself the SSI.

31. *Actul de acuzare*, 68; see also p. 27. During the cross-examination, Melinescu, who was spared execution in 1945 thanks to his refusal to obey the orders, described at length the looting operations, the liquidation operation, and the involvement of the prefect, his deputy, and all those who had a vested interest in the executions perpetrated by the Romanians in the district.

32. *Actul de acuzare*, 32–33. Melinescu burnt a Russian partisan alive and also stripped a Jewish girl and gave her seventy lashes because she dared ask him to behave more humanely (79–80).

33. *Actul de acuzare*, 74.

34. Esther Gobelman's testimony sheds light on the Bogdanovka atrocities. She witnessed the burning of corpses, an operation that according to her lasted almost until the summer, because the stench of rotting corpses gave away their location. After the Ukrainian police left the district Jewish girls who had been kept alive served the gendarmes and local policemen. Those who survived were subsequently put to work in the *sovkhoz*. Testimony of Esther Gobelman, Tel Aviv, 1990, YVA.

35. Isopescu's report regarding activities in Golta district, May 1943, USHMM, NOA, RG-31.008M, 2178-1-71, p. 38.

36. Carp, *Cartea neagră*, 3:225.

37. Report by Vasile Mănescu, pretor of the Domanevka subdistrict, to the prefecture in Golta, 19 March 1942, regarding the situation in the Domanevka camp after the conclusion of the murder operations; and Prefect Isopescu's decision, written in the margin of the report, to burn the bodies, 25 March 1942, USHMM, NOA, RG-31.008M, 2178-1-58, pp. 358–58b.

38. *Actul de acuzare*, 29, 70; see also Carp, *Cartea neagră*, 3:225. Ehrenburg's black book cites the murder of fifteen thousand Jews in Domanevka and fifty-four thousand in Bogdanovka. Ehrenburg et al., *Cartea neagră*, 100. The slaughter in Bogdanovka, Domanevka, and Akmechetka was also described during the trials of Antonescu and his government; see *Procesul marei trădări naționale*, 299–300. For more about the murder campaign in Domanevka, see Ancel, "Romanian Campaigns of Mass Murder," 120–25.

39. For more details on the death camp at Akmechetka, see Ancel, *Transnistria, 1941–1942*, 1:150–71.

40. "The Mood of the Population in the Krivoye Ozero District," copy of report signed by Isopescu, undated, USHMM, NOA, RG-31.008M, 2178-1-2, p. 75.

41. Report by Prefect Isopescu to the Transnistrian administration on the rehabilitation of cities in the district, 28 January 1942, USHMM, NOA, RG-31.008M, 2178-1-5, p. 264.

42. Directive by the prefect to the pretor of the Vradiyevka subdistrict [a subdistrict that had no extermination camps], 14 January 1942, USHMM, NOA, RG-31.008M, 2178-1-5, p. 47.

43. Telegram from the administration, 17 January 1942, USHMM, NOA, RG-31.008M, 2178-1-5, p. 40.

44. In the summer of 1942 thirteen Jews worked on the Bukovina state farm that was set up by Isopescu on 10 January 1942, in the middle of the winter, during the liquidation operation. Among them were thirteen-year-old Dora Rabinovici and fourteen-year-old Izia Burtman. The farm was guarded by a gendarme and two Ukrainian policemen. Bukovina farm dossier, note of 4 July 1942, USHMM, NOA, RG-31.008M, 2084-2-111, pp. 136, 182–83.

45. 13 November 1941, USHMM, NOA, 2178-1-66, pp. 151–56.

46. Secret report by the gendarmerie commander in Domanevka to the pretor of the subdistrict, 16 April 1942; and attached letter by the pretor to the prefect, 20 April 1942, USHMM, NOA, RG-31.008M, 2178-1-15, pp. 207, 208.

47. Secret communication by Governor Alexianu on the decision to deport the Gypsies and on resettlement zones in the Golta district, 16 June 1942, USHMM, NOA, RG-31.008M, 2178-1-31, p. 78. The localities were Tridubi, Crasnencoe, Vituldov-Brod, Ahmecet, and Novo-Cantacuzenco. Gypsies were also deported to the Balta, Berezovka, and Ochakov districts.

48. Secret communication by the commander of the gendarmerie to the prefect of the Golta district, 16 June 1942, USHMM, NOA, RG-31.008M, 2178-1-31, p. 77.

49. The looting perpetrated by members of the prefecture against the Gypsies was also alluded to in the indictment. Isopescu was forced to bring in the gendarmerie because the Gypsies refused to hand over their horses and carts to the prefecture. In the end the horses and carts were delivered to the kolkhozes and sovkhozes. "They died like flies." *Actul de acuzare*, 76. It was Alexianu who decided to take their horses and carts in order to prevent them from traveling around and spreading diseases. Alexianu's directive to the Balta prefect, 29 July 1942, Odessa Archives, 2358-1c-19, p. 41.

50. Report by Capt. Dumitru Tomescu, the district military physician, to the prefect of the Golta district, 10 July 1942, USHMM, NOA, RG-31.008M, 2178-1-27, p. 150.

51. Prefect of Berezovka, Leonida Popp, to the governor of Transnistria, 24 September 1943, Odessa Archives, 2361-1-591, p. 51.

52. Vasile Petrenciu, deputy prefect of the Berezovka district, to the legal department of the military administration in the territory between the Dniester and Bug [the new name of the Transnistrian administration, after January 1944], 10 February 1944, Odessa Archives, 2361-1-512, p. 151.

53. The Romanian historian Viorel Achim has published many studies and a comprehensive collection of documents on the deportation of the Gypsies to Transnistria. See Achim, ed., *Documente privind deportarea*, vols. 1–2; see also Achim and Iordachi, *Romania și Transnistria*.

54. Frieling, Ioanid, and Ionescu, *Final Report*, 223–43.

55. See report by the Labor Service in the district, 22 October 1943, on its findings during its visit to the three Golta ghettos and the labor camp: "Everywhere there is indescribable filth, and terrible overcrowding. . . . The Jews are all filthy. They do not wash . . . people are sick . . . everywhere you look you encounter a revolting sight." USHMM, NOA, RG-31.008M, 2178-1-362, p. 150.

56. Golta prefecture, list of ghettos in the Golta district and the number of Jews they contain, 6 October 1943, Odessa Archives, 2242-1-1561, pp. 198–99.

57. Appeal by the committee of Golta Jews to the governor of Transnistria to prevent the implementation of the directive of the Golta prefecture to concentrate all Jews of the district in the Akmechetka camp, 22 October 1943, USHMM, NOA, RG-31.008M, 2178-1-370. Cf. Pădure's proposal to concentrate all the Jews in the Domanevka subdistrict, in Pădure's report to Isopescu of February 1943, USHMM, NOA, RG-31.008M, 2178-1-77, proposing

the "decongestion" (*descongestionarea*) of the ghettos in the city by sending all Jews to the Domanevka camp, "so that they will available to the pretors for all sorts of skilled and unskilled labor, in accordance with Decree no. 23." In fact, he was asking for the survivors to be placed in the same situation they were in on the eve of the executions.

58. Testimony of Mihael Cvitco from Cetatea-Albă, Jerusalem, 27 April 1962, YVA, 03-2449, pp. 15–17.

59. Prefect Colonel Nesturaș's order to dismiss Jews from plants, 5 July 1942, in Carp, *Cartea neagră*, no. 193, 3:351.

60. Prefect's instructions to the pretors to collect money from the deportees, early November 1941, USHMM, NOA, RG-31.008M, 2178-1-12, p. 212.

61. Telegram from the governor of Transnistria to the prefect of Pervomaisk (Golta) concerning Jewish property, 19 November 1941, USHMM, NOA, RG-31.008M, 2178-1-12, pp. 218–18b.

62. Tiraspol military tribunal to the Golta prefecture, 6 April 1943, USHMM, NOA, RG-31.008M, 2174-1-74, p. 235.

63. Pretor Vasile Mănescu, in collaboration with the prefect, confiscated large amounts of gold coins, valuables, and money from the Jews who were executed in Bogdanovka but handed over only a fraction of the spoils to the authorities. He was arrested and interrogated by the Tiraspol Military Tribunal. Pretor Iliescu, who replaced Mănescu on 15 March 1942, was also implicated in the theft of valuables from Jews, and some two months later he was dismissed from his post. At the start of the interrogation Isopescu, wishing to exonerate himself of all suspicion of collaborating in the theft, claimed that it was he who had dismissed Mănescu from his post.

64. Prefect Isopescu to the Military Tribunal in Tiraspol, 18 June 1943, Odessa Archives, 2178-1-59, p. 339. This letter was in response to a caution sent by the Military Tribunal to the prefecture dated 16 June 1943 (p. 338). Apparently, the correct date was 16 January 1943. Clearly the month was erased in the original document and replaced with June. In this way Isopescu could claim that he had not received the letter and meanwhile cover his tracks. Other sources show that the official interrogation opened in January 1943, not June.

65. Draft of Prefect Isopescu's reply to the administration's Manpower Department at the start of the interrogation into the disappearance of gold and valuables confiscated from Jews, 12 January 1943, Odessa Archives, 2178-1-457, p. 43.

66. Testimony of Mihael Cvitco from Cetatea-Albă, Jerusalem, 27 April 1962, YVA, 03-2449, pp. 21–22. The office investigated corruption and theft by the heads of the Romanian administration in Transnistria and members of the military and the gendarmerie and was given carte blanche by Antonescu himself.

67. Testimony of Mihael Cvitco from Cetatea-Albă, Jerusalem, 27 April 1962, YVA, 03-2449, p. 21. According to Cvitco, he made this statement to Colonel Ionescu-Alion during his interrogation, during which he was not subjected to torture or humiliation. The colonel actually saved his life when gendarmes in Tiraspol tried to kill him because of his testimony (see pp. 22–23).

68. Haim Kogan's testimony, Bat Yam, May 1963, YVA, PKR/V, p. 48. (Part of a collection of testimonies that served as the basis for *Pinkas Hakehilot, Rumania*, vol. 1.)

69. Detailed report by Isopescu to the Military Tribunal in Tiraspol, 16 January 1943, USHMM, NOA, RG-31.008M, 2178-1-62, pp. 44–45 (author's emphasis).

27. Odessa

1. Tens, perhaps hundreds, of such cases were tried in special courts that sentenced Jews to death on various pretexts after the outbreak of war. These are documented in the district archive of the Communist Party in Odessa. This topic has not been discussed in this study. See Partinii Arhiv, Odescovo obkoma Kompartii Ukraini, fond II. The party archive in Odessa was transferred to the Odessa District Archive. The current name of this archive is Gosudartsveni Arhiv Odeskoi Oblasti, Ukraina.

2. Dallin, *Odessa*, 42.

3. Dallin, *Odessa*, 44, 71–72.

4. Excerpt from a letter sent by Soviet foreign minister Molotov on 6 January 1942 to all embassies in Moscow, in Carp, *Cartea neagră*, no. 117, 3:207.

5. Rotaru, Burcin, et al., *Mareşalul Ion Antonescu*, 177.

6. Dallin, *Odessa*, 76. According to one Jew, "the first night passed peacefully" in his neighborhood. Starodinskii, *Odesskoe Getto*, 7. According to another source, the night of 16–17 October was catastrophic for Jews who had not managed to vacate their homes, and it was on this night that dozens of Jewish doctors were executed. Ehrenburg et al., *Cartea neagră*, 94–95. In May 1943 the Romanian authorities in Odessa announced the discovery of a mass grave in Tatarca, a village near Odessa, claiming that the victims had been killed by the Soviets in 1939. Dallin, however, argues that this was a mass grave for Jews murdered by Romanian soldiers. In the final analysis, the Romanians did not turn the discovery into a propaganda tool (as the Germans did in the Katin affair) and themselves glossed over the matter. Dallin, *Odessa*, 39–40.

7. Ehrenburg et al., *Cartea neagră*, 95.

8. Ehrenburg et al., *Cartea neagră*, 95.

9. Secret telegram from the Presidency of the Council of Ministers to Fourth Army headquarters, 17 October 1941, 20:30, USHMM/AMD, RG-25.003M, reel 12, fond: Armata 4a, file 870, p. 684.

10. Dallin, *Odessa*, 310.

11. Telegram from the military cabinet to Fourth Army headquarters, signed by the head of the military cabinet, Colonel Davidescu, 22 October 1941, USHMM/AMD, RG-25.003M, reel 12, fond: Armata 4a, file 870, p. 634.

12. Telegram from Colonel Stănculescu to General Tătăranu, 23 October 1941, 7:45 a.m., USHMM/AMD, RG-25.003M, reel 12, fond: Armata 4a, file 870, 651–53.

13. Telegram from Colonel Stănculescu to General Tătăranu, 23 October 1941, 23:00, USHMM/AMD, RG-25.003M, reel 12, fond: Armata 4a, file 870, 640.

14. *Actul de acuzare*, 52–53; Ehrenburg et al., *Cartea neagră*, 96.

15. Certified court copy (1945) of Gherman Pântea's memorandum to Ion Antonescu on the punitive measures adopted against the Jews of Odessa, USHMM/SRI, RG-25.004M, reel 30, file 21401, vol. 2, pp. 119b–200.

16. *Actul de acuzare*, 48. Dallin mentions two thousand who were murdered in the antitank trenches. Dallin, *Odessa*, 77.

17. Order no. 563, 24 October 1941, USHMM/AMD, RG-25.003M, reel 12, fond: Armata 4a, file 870, p. 688.

18. Arrest order of 10 May 1948 by 2nd Lt. Eustaţiu Mărculescu, platoon commander of the Tenth Machine Gun Battalion, who participated in the liquidation of citizens in Odessa, in Ancel, *Documents*, vol. 6, doc. 26, pp. 281–82.

19. Obkom report, Partinii Arhiv, Odescovo obkoma Kompartii Ukraini, fond 2, opis 2, delo 52, p. 22.

20. *Actul de acuzare*, 53–54.

21. Report by the French ambassador (Vichy France) in Romania to the foreign minister, 10 November 1941, in Ancel, *Documents*, vol. 3, doc. 229, p. 376.

22. *Procesul marei trădări naţionale*, 64–65.

23. *Procesul marei trădări naţionale*, 289.

24. Report no. 213 of Siguranţa police headquarters in Odessa, Odessa Archives, 2242-4c-4, p. 78.

25. These letters and betrayals were too numerous to be specified. For further details, see files in the Odessa Archives, collection 2242, opis I, especially files between November 1941 and November 1942. Many of the "White" Russians (the anticommunists) who fled to Romania or went underground during Soviet rule revealed their identity and asked the governor or municipality to return their property — houses, land, factories — to them.

26. Report no. 213 of Siguranţa police headquarters in Odessa, Odessa Archives, 2242-4c-4, p. 79.

27. Report by Governor Alexianu to Marshal Antonescu on his visit to Odessa, 7 November 1941, Odessa Archives, 2242-1-671, p. 120.

28. Report by Governor Alexianu to Marshal Antonescu on the situation in Transnistria, Tiraspol, 11 December 1941, Odessa Archives, 2242-1-677, p. 197.

29. The session was attended by Mihai Antonescu; Interior Minister Dumitru Popescu; Finance Minister Gen. Nicolae Stoenescu; Professor Petre Tomescu, former senator of the National Liberal Party and then minister of labor, health, and social services; Professor Alexianu, governor of Transnistria; Professor Enric Oteteleşanu, minister of culture and religion; Deputy Minister of National Defense Gen. Pantazi; Dr. Ovidiu Vlădescu, secretary general of the Presidency of the Council of Ministers and former member of the National Liberal Party; Professor Constantin Buşilă, a head of National Liberal Party finances and then minister of public works and transportation; retired general Ion Sichitiu, who in the thirties had been a member of the executive of the National Peasants' Party and was now minister of agriculture; Mircea Vulcănescu, one of the most outstanding intellectuals of the thirties, a renowned financial expert, and then deputy minister of finance; Deputy Romanianization Minister Eugen Zwiedeneck; Deputy Minister of National Economy D. D. Negel; Deputy Agriculture Minister Aurelian Pană; Deputy Minister of Labor and Health Dr. Constantin Dănulescu; and governor of Bukovina Calotescu. For a transcript of the cabinet session of 13 November 1941, see Ciucă and Ignat, *Stenogramele sedinţelor*, doc. 8, pp. 121–22, 159.

30. Cabinet session with the governors of Bessarabia, Bukovina, and Transnistria, 13 November 1941, in Ciucă and Ignat, *Stenogramele sedinţelor*, doc. 7, p. 103. The question

of Romanian jurisdiction over all of Transnistria, as reported to Antonescu in this session, is important since both Alexianu and Antonescu claimed during their interrogation and in their trial in 1946 that Romanian rule did not extend over all of Transnistria until February 1942. Districts such as Golta and Berezovka, they claimed, were not under Romanian rule, and therefore everything that happened there was done by the Germans.

31. Cabinet session with the governors of Bessarabia, Bukovina, and Transnistria, 13 November 1941, in Ciucă and Ignat, *Stenogramele sedinţelor*, doc. 7, p. 120.

32. Cabinet session with the governors of Bessarabia, Bukovina, and Transnistria, 13 November 1941, in Ciucă and Ignat, *Stenogramele sedinţelor*, doc. 7, p. 120 (author's emphasis). In this session the problem of the relocation to Transnistria of Romanians scattered throughout Russia and the Ukraine was also briefly discussed.

33. Quoted from Dallin, *Odessa*, 311–12.

34. Transcript of Cristescu's interrogation, n.d. [August 1946], USHMM/SRI, RG-25004M, reel 32, file 40010, vol. 9, pp. 5–6.

35. Deposition of Victor Ionescu, USHMM/SRI, RG-25004M, reel 32, file 40010, vol. 9, pp. 117–18. According to another witness, Victor Ionescu himself, a former Siguranţa agent, was section head of Borcescu's department and "a very active man . . . a man who carried out his assignments with obsessive zeal, without taking anyone into consideration, and without allowing anything get in his way." See deposition of SSI agent attorney Florin Begnescu, 22 August 1945, USHMM/SRI, RG-25004M, reel 32, file 40010, vol. 9, p. 112.

36. Deposition of Eugen Ionescu for his defense, USHMM/SRI, RG-25004M, reel 32, file 40010, vol. 4, p. 319 (author's emphasis).

37. Deposition of SSI agent attorney Florin Begnescu, 22 August 1945, USHMM/SRI, RG-25004M, reel 32, file 40010, vol. 9, p. 112.

38. Testimony of Traian Borcescu, commander of SSI Section Two, on the activity of the operational unit in Odessa, 24 September 1945, USHMM/SRI, RG-25004M, reel 32, file 40010, vol. 9, p. 122.

39. Intelligence Report no. 1766bis by the SSI's Special Unit no. 1, 12 October 1941, Moscow Special Archives [former OSOBYI Archives], fond 490, opis 1, delo 2, p. 40.

40. Intelligence Report no. 1810, 12 October 1941, Moscow Special Archives [former OSOBYI Archives], fond 490, opis 1, delo 2, p. 39.

41. Intelligence Report no. 1819, 13 October 1941, Moscow Special Archives [former OSOBYI Archives], fond 490, opis 1, delo 2, p. 66.

42. Intelligence Report (no number or date), Moscow Special Archives [former OSOBYI Archives], 492-1-25, p. 45.

43. Order no. 2 issued by General Ghinăraru, military commander of Odessa, 15 November 1941, Odessa Archives, 2242-1-227.

44. Memorandum by Research Division to Alexianu and handwritten comments on the document, 2 January 1942, Odessa Archives, 2242-1-1486, p. 1.

45. Order no. 35, signed by Alexianu, 2 January 1942, Odessa Archives, 2242-1-1, pp. 42–43.

46. Order no. 35, signed by Alexianu, 2 January 1942, Odessa Archives, 2242-1-1, pp. 42–43.

47. Instruction to evacuate the Jewish population from Odessa and the surrounding area, signed by Alexianu, undated [2 January 1942], Odessa Archives, 2242-1-1, pp. 43–45.

48. Alexianu to the Third Army headquarters, 10 January 1942, Odessa Archives, 2242-1-1486, p. 29.

49. Report by the gendarmerie legion to the district prefecture, 31 January 1942, Odessa Archives, 2361-1-39, p. 15.

50. See letter (quarter of a page) and evacuation instructions to the pretor of the Ivanovka subdistrict, 3 February 1942, Odessa Archives, 2359-1-22, pp. 109–10.

51. Directive from the Central Evacuation Bureau signed by Colonel Velcescu, sent to the pretor of the Ivanovka subdistrict, 15 February 1942, Odessa Archives, 2352-1-22, p. 87, and to the pretor of the Antono-Codincevo subdistrict, 16 February 1942, YVA, Romania Collection, 0-11/48.

52. Cabinet session of 13 November, in Ciucă and Ignat, *Stenogramele sedinţelor*, doc. 8, p. 159 (author's emphasis).

53. USHMM/RFMA, RG-25.006M, reel 11, "Jewish Problem," vol. 21, p. 161.

54. General Staff's Second Bureau, weekly intelligence bulletin, 11 January 1942, Moscow Special Archive, 492-1-5, p. 75.

55. General Staff's Second Bureau, weekly intelligence bulletin, 12–18 January 1942, Moscow Special Archive, 492-1-5, p. 82.

56. General Staff's Second Bureau, weekly intelligence bulletin, 19–26 January 1942, Moscow Special Archive, 492-1-5, p. 134.

57. Testimony of Milea Morduhovici, 31 August 1995, in author's possession, to be submitted to Yad Vashem. The description of the deportation by foot from Dalnic to Bogdanovka, October–November 1941, is based on Morduhovici's description, the sole witness the author managed to trace. Contemporary Romanian documents corroborate her account.

58. Testimony of Milea Morduhovici, 31 August 1995, in author's possession, to be submitted to Yad Vashem. After contracting typhus in the Bogdanovka camp Morduhovici escaped to her home in Odessa, despite her terrible condition, and recovered thanks to the ministrations of a Russian doctor. She was later deported again by train with her family in February 1942.

59. Authorized copy of the report of the military physician, Lt. Dr. Petre Nedelescu, 17 November 1941, USHMM, NOA, RG-31.008M, 2178-1-12.

60. Gendarmerie Inspectorate in Transnistria, summary report of activities between 15 December 1941 and 15 January 1942, in Ancel, *Documents*, vol. 5, doc. 133a, p. 216.

61. Deposition of Matei Velcescu, 1 April 1950, USHMM/SRI, RG-25.004M, reel 30, p. 171. (In Gherman Pântea's memorandum to Ion Antonescu on the arbitrary punitive measures against the Jews of Odessa, undated [early November], from the defense file, and copies of authorized documents submitted to the court in 1952 and 1956 by Gherman Pântea.)

62. Ehrenburg et al., *Cartea neagră*, 100, quoting one witness.

63. The adjutant of a Romanian officer told him that some of the Jews burnt on the first night of their arrival were still alive. See V. Luduşanu, "Trenul-Dric," *Curierul Israelit*, 12 November 1944.

64. Commander of the Wehrmacht's liaison headquarters in Transnistria to [Romanian] Third Army headquarters in Tiraspol, 20 March 1942, Moscow Special Archive, 492-1-5, p. 262.

65. Report no. 76 by Colonel Broşteanu, inspector general of the gendarmerie in Transnistria, 17 January 1942, in Ancel, *Documents*, vol. 5, doc. 129, p. 222.

66. Gendarmerie Inspectorate in Transnistria, summary report of activities between 15 December 1941 and 15 January 1942, in Ancel, *Documents*, vol. 5, doc. 133a, p. 216.

67. Ehrenburg et al., *Cartea neagră*, 99.

68. Ehrenburg et al., *Cartea neagră*, 98.

69. Colonel Velcescu, chairman of the Central Evacuation Bureau and prefect of Odessa, to the Transnistrian administration in Tiraspol, report on the end of the deportation operation, 11 April 1942, Odessa Archives, 2242-1-1487, p. 100.

70. Directive by General Dăscălescu, commander of the Second Army Corps, to the prefecture of the Odessa district, concerning the treatment of Jews who had been arrested and were being held in Odessa's main prison, 25 March 1942, Odessa Archives, 2242-1-1488, p. 78.

71. Gen. Nicolae Dăscălescu, commander of the Second Army Corps, to the governor of Transnistria, 21 January 1942, Odessa Archives, 2242-1-1486, p. 93.

72. Colonel Velcescu, chairman of the Central Evacuation Bureau, to the Second Army Corps, 11 April 1942, Odessa Archives, 2242-1-1486, p. 101.

73. See instruction in register of the administration's secretariat, 15 May 1942, Odessa Archives, 2242-1-1487, p. 107. On 10 April 1942 the prefect of Odessa announced that there were 155 Jews left in the main prison, of which 22 had been sentenced to death. Odessa Archives, 2242-1-1488, p. 77.

74. Summary report of the Central Evacuation Bureau, 13 February 1942, Odessa Archives, 1487-1-2242, p. 132b.

75. Prefect of Odessa to the administration, 13 July 1942, and administration to the prefect of Odessa, 29 July 1942, Odessa Archives, 2242-1-1489, pp. 105, 106.

76. The military prosecutor, Chirilă, to the prefecture of Odessa, 28 June 1942, Odessa Archives, 2242-1-1489, p. 107.

77. Order no. 9 was issued by a military unit code named "M.U. Pandurul." In his letter to the unit Matei Velcescu, chairman of the Deportation Committee, summarized the main points, as implemented by him.

78. Directive by Antonescu to the Ministry of National Propaganda, signed by Colonel Davidescu, head of the military cabinet, 10 March 1942, Moscow Special Archive, 492-1-17, p. 31.

79. Ehrenburg et al., *Cartea neagră*, 105–6. The book cites cases where local Russians and Ukrainians saved Jews, either by hiding them or by helping them to join the partisans (106–7).

80. Executive of the Transnistrian administration to the prefect of Odessa, Odessa Archives, 22424-1-1489, p. 105. The author does not know how many ten-year-olds were interned in the hospital or what happened to them.

81. Transcript of cabinet session of 13 November 1941, in Ciucă and Ignat, *Stenogramele sedinţelor*, doc. 8, p. 369.

82. Deposition of Matei Velcescu, 1 April 1950, USHMM/SRI, RG-25.004M, reel 30, chapter titled "The Kingdom of Death."

83. Secret circular by Governor Alexianu to the prefects, 4 December 1941, Odessa Archives, 2358-1c-10, p. 10.

84. Telegram by Governor Alexianu to the civilian military cabinet, 13 January 1942, Odessa Archives, 2242-1-1486, p. 36.

85. Telegram by the governor's assistant to the prefects of Transnistria, 25 February 1942, Odessa Archives, 2242-1-1487, p. 96.

86. Order no. 18 by Mayor Pântea, 13 January 1942, Odessa Archives, 2242-1-1486, pp. 12–13.

87. Velcescu, cable to Alexianu, January 1942, Odessa Archives, 2242-1-1486, p. 117; Alexianu's response, 5 February 1942, Odessa Archives, 2242-1-1486, p. 116.

88. Request by the governor's assistant, Cercavski, to Hoffmeyer, the commander of Vomi (Volksdeutsche Mittelstelle, or the liaison office for ethnic German affairs) in Landau, 26 January 1943, Odessa Archives, 2242-1-1486, p. 99.

89. Invitation on behalf of the commander of the SS Sonderkommando in Odessa to Alexianu, 6 June 1942, Odessa Archives, 2242-1-1087, p. 47; governor's directive to the Odessa municipality to deliver equipment from the city warehouses, 1 June 1942, Odessa Archives, 2242-1-1087, p. 14.

90. Dallin, *Odessa*, 314.

91. List of topics on the governor's agenda concerning the valuables of Jews sentenced by the administration, recorded by the administration's secretariat, 2 March, 11 March, 8 April, and 16 April 1942, Odessa Archives, 2242-1-1486, pp. 241, 254, 300; 2342-1-1487, p. 87.

92. Dallin, *Odessa*, 141, 189. The NEP was the economic policy proclaimed by Lenin in 1922 that led to an economic revival in the Soviet Union. It was based on the provisional abandonment of the policy of state control of the means of production and of land.

93. Dallin, *Odessa*, 175.

94. "Odesa de erir de astasi," *Gazeta Odessei*, 17 January 1943; reprinted in Ancel, *Documents*, vol. 4, doc. 229, p. 429.

95. 1 Kings 21:19.

28. The Berezovka District

1. All data are taken from monograph of the Berezovka district, issued by the district prefect, Colonel Loghin, undated [late 1941], Odessa Archives, 2361-1-24, pp. 50–53; monograph of the Mostovoye subdistrict, issued by its pretor, Victor Petrenciu, 21 November 1941, Odessa Archives, 2361-1-12, pp. 23–25; monograph of the Berezovka subdistrict, September 1941, Odessa Archives, 2361-1-12, pp. 19–23; organizational chart of the Berezovka prefecture, undated, Odessa Archives, 2361-1-49, pp. 2–5; organizational chart of the Mostovoye pretorate, undated, Odessa Archives, 2361-1-49, pp. 19–29b.

2. Report by second lieutenant to the Berezovka prefecture, 21 September 1941, Odessa Archives, 2361-1c-2, p. 16.

3. Letter of appointment signed by Governor Alexianu, 27 August 1941, Odessa Archives, 2361-1c-1, p. 1. Loghin's aides were Deputy Prefect Alexandru Smochină and the pretors Victor Petrenciu, Zaheu Buliga, and Nicolae Albu (p. 48).

4. Details of the 1943 census of ethnic Germans were published in Meir Buchsweiler's doctoral thesis, *Ethnic Germans*, 338–49. This is a very important study that provides a picture of German settlement in the Ukraine under Soviet rule on the eve of the German invasion, their encounter with the German army, the organization of the *Volksdeutschen* within various Nazi frameworks, their participation in ss extermination units, their relationship with the local population, and eventually their transfer to the Reich on the eve of liberation. This research and the testimonies discovered by the author of this book after the opening up of the Russian and Ukrainian archives helped complete the picture of the liquidation of Odessan Jewry in the Berezovka district. Note that Buchsweiler's work facilitates our understanding of the operations of Sonderkommando R and the Selbstschutz units in Transnistria. His work provided links to research, books, and other articles that on occasion assisted me in filling in missing details.

5. Map of German settlement in the Odessa region in 1940, in Buchsweiler, *Ethnic Germans*, map 6. For the original data and map, see Stumpp, "Verzeichnis der deutschen Siedlungen," 181–93. There is a problem identifying the German villages: the Soviet authorities changed some of the names after the 1917 revolution as part of the Soviet Russification policy, while the Nazis, and to some extent also the Romanian occupation authorities, used the pre-Soviet German names of the localities. Therefore, new names were adopted for the Ukrainian or Russian localities whose inhabitants were forcibly driven out and replaced by ethnic Germans. Eventually, after the liberation in 1944, the Soviets once again changed the names of the villages; some were given back their original names while others were given completely new names.

6. Testimony of Malca Barbălată of Bolgrad, Nahariya, 3 April 1967, YVA, PRK/V, pp. 1263–65.

7. Buchsweiler, *Ethnic Germans*, 267.

8. Buchsweiler, *Ethnic Germans*, 3. Buchsweiler quotes from the activity reports of Einsatzgruppe D issued by security police headquarters and the SD in Berlin, known as Ereignismeldungen UdSSR, report of 26 September 1941. A total of 195 such reports are known to exist, covering most of the period of operation of the extermination units from their arrival in Romania up to their arrival in Rostov, Tagenrog, and Stalino. Copies of the reports can be found in the U.S. National Archives, Washington DC, microfilm collection T175, nos. 233, 234, 235. Reports covering important events related to the activities of Einsatzgruppe D in Bessarabia and Bukovina are in Ancel, *Documents*, vol. 5.

9. Buchsweiler discovered this information in the memoirs of Germans of Ukrainian origin that were published in the West. Buchsweiler, *Ethnic Germans*, 314–18.

10. H. Himmler, "Erfassung der deutschen Volkszugehörigen in der Gebieten der europäischen Sowietunion" [Census of German nationals in the European regions of the Soviet Union], 7 November 1941, Nuremberg Documents, no. 4274.

11. List of German villages in the Berezovka district compiled by the prefecture, early 1942, Odessa Archives, 2242-1-1087, p. 114; list of German localities in the Berezovka district with details of collective farms, inhabitants, families, and lands, undated [late 1941], Odessa Archives, 2361-1c-2, p. 240.

12. Report issued by the prefect of Ochakov and table of German villages in his district,

including the number of inhabitants and lands, 19 January 1942, Odessa Archives, 2242-1-084, pp. 75–76; first list of German villages in the Ochakov district, signed by the prefect, undated, Odessa Archives, 2242-1-1087, p. 141.

13. List of German villages in the Ovidopol district, signed by the prefect, M. Botez, undated, Odessa Archives, 2357-1c-25c.

14. List of German villages in the Dubossary district, signed by the prefect, undated, early 1942, Odessa Archives, 2242-1-1087.

15. Telegram by Col. Constantin Popescu, prefect of Rybnitsa, to the administration, 21 July 1942, Odessa Archives, 2242-1-1087, p. 136.

16. List of German villages in the Odessa district by subdistrict, signed by the prefect, Colonel Velcescu, undated, Odessa Archives, 2242-1-1087, p. 140; prefect of Golta to German liaison headquarters in Transnistria, 31 July 1942, USHMM, NOA, RG-31.008M, 2178-1-42, p. 213. The German village in the Golta district was Novo-Nikolayevka in the Vradievka subdistrict. As mentioned in note 5 above, it is not always possible to identify the villages due to name changes.

17. Vasile Ioniță, pretor of Birzula, to the prefect of the Rybnitsa district, 30 November 1941, Odessa Archives, 2242-1-1083, p. 129.

18. Copy of a report by the Tiraspol office for confiscated war property to the Romanian army's service of confiscated war property in Transnistria, 23 November 1942, Odessa Archives, 2242-1-1084, p. 226.

19. Dallin, *Odessa*, 304.

20. Confidential report by the commander of the gendarmerie legion in Ovidopol to the administration, 1 August 1942, Odessa Archives, 2357-1c-32, p. 283.

21. Dallin, *Odessa*, 300–302.

22. The Tighina Agreement of 30 August 1941 has already been quoted several times. For an additional source of the agreement, see Odessa Archives, 2361-1c-2, pp. 39–39b; German version, Odessa Archives, 2361-1c-2, pp. 45–46.

23. Correspondence between Killinger and Mihai Antonescu, 14–15 November 1941, copy, Odessa Archives, 2359-1-24, p. 3.

24. Romanian text of the understanding, Tiraspol, 13 December 1941, Odessa Archives, 2359-1-24, pp. 4–8; German text, U.S. National Archives, Washington DC, collection T 175, microfilm 194, 2733072–2733076.

25. Memorandum from Alexianu to the People's Court, 29 April 1946, USHMM/SRI, RG-25.004M, reel 33, file 40010, vol. 28, p. 1. The memorandum is full of lies: on the eve of the evacuation there were about forty thousand Jews left in Odessa. The German army did not order their evacuation. It was Alexianu who gave the order to set up the ghetto. Alexianu ordered the expulsion of Jews not only from Odessa but from the whole of Transnistria.

26. *Procesul marei trădări naționale*, 34–35.

27. Telegram by the gebietskommissar of Nikolayev, Schlutter, to the Transnistrian administration, 5 February 1942, Odessa Archives, 2242-1-1486, pp. 180–80b.

28. Telegram by the gebietskommissar of Nikolayev, Schlutter, to the Transnistrian administration, 5 February 1942, Odessa Archives, 2242-1-1486, pp. 180–80b.

29. Telegram by Generalkommissar Oppermann to Governor Alexianu in Tiraspol, 14 February 1942, Odessa Archives, 2242-1-1486, pp. 200–200b.

30. Romanian translation of Oppermann's telegram, Alexianu's note of 16 February, and Cercavschi's note of 18 February 1942, Odessa Archives, 2242-1-1486, p. 199 (author's emphasis).

31. Report on the conversation between the secretary general of the Foreign Ministry, Gheorghe Davidescu, and Dr. Gerhard Steltzer, adviser to the German legation in Bucharest, 13 March 1942, USHMM/RMFA, RG-25.006M, reel 6, "Jewish Problem," vol. 16, p. 58.

32. Telegram from Generalkommissar Oppermann to Governor Alexianu, 25 February 1942, Odessa Archives, 2242-1-1084, pp. 251–52.

33. Telegram from Secretary General Cercavschi to Generalkommissar Oppermann in Nikolayev, Odessa Archives, 2242-1-1084, p. 249.

34. Eichmann to the Foreign Ministry, 14 April 1942, Nuremberg Documents, NG-4817 (author's emphasis).

35. Police D'Israël, Adolf Eichmann (Tonbandskription und Maschine) [transcript of the pretrial interrogation of Adolf Eichmann by the Israeli police], minutes of Session no. 48, YVA, pp. 1123–25, 3074, 3038 (in German); see also transcript of Eichmann's trial by the state attorney, YVA, 23 May 1961, FI, GI, II.

36. Rademacher from the Foreign Ministry to Eichmann in Berlin, 12 May 1942, Nuremberg Documents, NG-4817.

37. Rademacher to the minister of the occupied eastern territories, 12 May 1942, Nuremberg Documents, NG-4817.

38. YVA, 03-1536, p. 8. The interactions between the German-speaking Jews and their murderers — whether Germans from the Reich or ethnic Germans — in the camps across the Bug were faithfully portrayed by the Jewish artist Dagani, who fled back to Transnistria on the eve of the last *aktion*. Dagani, *Groapa*.

39. Report no. 8 from the eighth conference of heads of the Transnistrian administration, 20 September 1942, Odessa Archives, 2242-1-22, p. 69 (emphasis in the original).

40. Werth, *Russia at War*, 736.

41. Dallin, *Odessa*, 407.

42. Dallin, *Odessa*, 393.

43. "Soubschenie Chrezvychainoi Komissii po ustanovleniiu I rassledovaniiu zlodeianii: O zlodeianliakh, sovershennykh nemetsko-rumynskimi zakhvatchikami v gorode Odesse i raionakh Odesskoi oblasti" [Report by the Commission of Inquiry on crimes committed by the German-Romanian invaders in the town of Odessa and in the subdistricts of the Odessa district], 13 June 1944 (hereafter commission report of 13 June 1944), International Military Tribunal-Nuremberg Document, USSR-47.

44. Dallin, *Odessa*, 388.

45. I. Ehrenburg, *Voina*, vol. 3, *1943–1944* (Moscow: 1944), 66–67; quoted in Dallin, *Odessa*, 387.

46. Obkom report, Partinii Arhiv, Odescovo obkoma Kompartii Ukraini, fond II, opis II, delo 52, pp. 23–24. I would like to thank Mr. Simeon Shvebish for his help in tracing the report in the Communist Party Archives in Odessa.

47. Obkom report, Partinii Arhiv, Odescovo obkoma Kompartii Ukraini, fond 2, opis 2, delo 52, p. 24.

48. Obkom report, Partinii Arhiv, Odescovo obkoma Kompartii Ukraini, fond 2, opis 2, delo 52, p. 24.

49. Obkom report, Partinii Arhiv, Odescovo obkoma Kompartii Ukraini, fond 2, opis 2, delo 52, p. 27.

50. The Romanians did not deport local inhabitants to Romania. On the contrary, they did whatever they could to reduce the number permitted to enter their country. A total of eight thousand entry permits to Romania were issued, primarily to engineers, intellectuals, and artists, not all of whom managed to flee from Transnistria. The Germans, on the other hand, forcibly removed Russians and Ukrainians to Austria and Germany. Dallin, *Odessa*, 380.

51. Ehrenburg et al., *Cartea neagră*, 93, 99.

52. On the book and its impact on Romania, see Litani, *"Black Book."*

53. *Soviet Government Statements.*

54. Commission report of 13 June 1944, International Military Tribunal–Nuremberg Document, USSR-47.

55. Commission report of 13 June 1944, International Military Tribunal–Nuremberg Document, USSR-47, pp. 173, 176.

56. Commission report of 13 June 1944, International Military Tribunal–Nuremberg Document, USSR-47, p. 177.

29. The Typhus Epidemic

1. Report by Governor Alexianu to Marshal Antonescu on the situation in Transnistria, 11 December 1941, Odessa Archives, 2242-1-677, pp. 196, 198.

2. Transcript of Alexianu's interrogation, Bucharest, 14 April 1946, USHMM/SRI, RG-25.004M, reel 34, file 40010, vol. 43, p. 222.

3. Transcript of cabinet session of 13 November 1941, in Ciucă and Ignat, *Stenogramele sedinţelor*, doc. 8.

4. Order 1040/941 of the Bessarabian administration, Orhei municipality, September 1941, USHMM/SSARM RG-54001, reel 1, 666-2-165, p. 137.

5. Order no. 18 of Col. Vasile Nica, prefect of the Balta district, undated [early November 1941], YVA, Romanian Collection, 0-11/48.

6. Carp, *Cartea neagră*, 3:268.

7. Carp, *Cartea neagră*, 3:290.

8. Tătăranu's report on his struggle against typhus, April 1942, USHMM, NOA, RG-31.00 8M, 2178-1-9, p. 55.

9. Tătăranu's report on his struggle against typhus, April 1942, USHMM, NOA, RG-31.00 8M, 2178-1-9, p. 8b. Dr. Tătăranu did not know that no deportation committee operated in Romania.

10. Carp, *Cartea neagră*, 3:266.

11. Testimony of Saly Gedanski from the village of Vicovul de Sus in southern Bukovina, Ramat Gan, November 1958, YVA, 03-1126, p. 6.

12. Testimony of Mirjam Lehrer from Petrăuţi, northern Bukovina, Tel Aviv, January

1959, YVA, 03-1228, p. 7. This witness wrote down the names of over thirty Jews from her village who died of typhus in Obodovka.

13. Testimony of Chana Weinraub from Czernowitz, Tel Aviv, November 1959, YVA, 03-1539, p. 4. The typhus epidemic evidently claimed more male than female victims (although no study has been made of this phenomenon), and therefore most of the survivors' testimonies are by women.

14. Testimony of Etl Slominski from Czernowitz, Tel Aviv, March 1959, YVA, 0-3/1439, p. 4.

15. Carp, *Cartea neagră*, 3:267. Among those who died were Rabbi Shalom (Shulim) Ginsberg and his family of ten (3:266).

16. Confidential Order no. 18, issued by Col. Vasile Nica, prefect of the Balta district, to the gendarmerie legion in the Balta district and to the police in Balta, including the prefect's handwritten comments, 8 February 1942, Odessa Archives, 2358-1c-10, p. 39. The rigorous application of Order no. 23 meant shooting Jews caught outside the ghetto, who were considered spies.

17. Report by the Hygiene Department of the Jewish Committee (Judenrat) in Mogilev on the typhus epidemic in the ghetto in the winter of 1941–42, Mogilev, 10 June 1942 (hereafter report on the typhus epidemic in Mogilev), in Carp, *Cartea neagră*, no. 165, 3:328.

18. Testimony of Käthe Cohen from Vizhnitz, Tel Aviv, August 1959, YVA, 03-1483, p. 6.

19. Confidential report by gendarmerie headquarters in Bessarabia to the military cabinet of the Bessarabian administration, 31 January 1941, in Ancel, *Documents*, vol. 10, doc. 72, p. 175; Ministry of National Defense, Military Justice Directorate, Bessarabian administration, on the arrest of a Romanian lawyer from Rădăuți who was found in possession of 135 letters by Jewish deportees from Mogilev to Jews in Czernowitz and Rădăuți, in Ancel, *Documents*, vol. 10, doc. 68, pp. 168–69; see also 7 letters out of 215 from Mogilev to Bucharest (including 1 addressed to Dr. Filderman) requesting urgent aid, found in the possession of three couriers, in Ancel, *Documents*, vol. 10, doc. 63, pp. 149–55. The letters were translated from German to Romanian.

20. Carp, *Cartea neagră*, 3:267. The messengers usually received a commission of 50 percent of the money they delivered.

21. Report on the typhus epidemic in Mogilev, in Carp, *Cartea neagră*, no. 165, 3:330, 331.

22. Carp, *Cartea neagră*, 3:268.

23. Testimony of Isaia Herșcovici from Dărăbani, Tel Aviv, 27 May 1959, YVA, 03-1476, p. 8.

24. Testimony of Käthe Cohen from Vizhnitz, Tel Aviv, August 1959, YVA, 03-1483, p. 8; Carp, *Cartea neagră*, 3:271–72.

25. Carp, *Cartea neagră*, 3:274. According to Jewish Committee records, between November 1941 and 20 April 1942, 3,410 Jews, including 267 children, died of typhus. See Jägendorf, *Jagendorf's Foundry*, 69–70.

26. Order by the governor to the prefect of the Mogilev district, 19 May 1942, in Carp, *Cartea neagră*, no. 180, 3:351.

27. Order by the governor to the prefect of the Mogilev district, 19 May 1942, in Carp, *Cartea neagră*, no. 180, 3:270.

28. Testimony of Herman Picker from Czernowitz, Tel Aviv, June 1959, YVA, 03-1467, p. 6.

29. Tătăranu's report on his struggle against typhus, April 1942, USHMM, NOA, RG-31.008M, 2178-1-9, p. 3; report by the Health Department on its activities since its inception until 1 January 1943, Odessa Archives, 2242-4c-37a, p. 2.

30. Summary report by gendarmerie headquarters in Transnistria for the period between 15 December 1941 and 15 January 1942, in Carp, *Cartea neagră*, 3:320.

31. A total of 765 Jews were alive in the subdistrict of Olgopol, all in the subdistrict capital. In the subdistrict of Obodovka, 3,019 Jews were alive, 1,438 in the subdistrict capital, 738 in Verhovka, 140 in Budey, 401 in the two parts of the Tzibulevka village (out of 1,470 who had been brought there from Bessarabia and Bukovina), and so on. In the subdistrict of Bershad, 11,017 Jews were alive in the spring of 1942, of whom 8,014 were in Bershad, 499 in Balanovka, 322 in Voytovka, 302 in Krushinovka, 191 in Kosharintsa, 132 in Osiyevka, 162 in Piatovka, 77 in Romanovka, 151 in Shumovka, 390 in Ustia, 103 in Ilanetz, 180 in Florina, and so on. In the Romanian-populated subdistrict of Pesceana, 441 Jews were alive, of whom 437 were in the village that served as the subdistrict capital. See four tables of the population in the subdistricts of the Balta district, by ethnic origin, drawn up by the prefecture's Sanitation Department in 1942 [exact date unknown], Odessa Archives, 2351-1-711, pp. 7, 9, 11, 12. Data on the number of local Jews prior to the arrival of the convoys from Bessarabia are based on survivors' testimonies (YVA, collection 03, listed by name of ghetto). Likewise, data on how many Jews reached each ghetto and how many survived the epidemic are based on survivors' testimonies. Generally speaking, the official data confirm the number of Jews who survived the epidemic.

32. Data provided by the district Judenrat to the Autonomous Assistance Commission in Bucharest on the scope of the disaster in Bershad were, generally speaking, accurate. By 1943, the committees estimated, about twenty thousand Jews had died of typhus, starvation, and exposure in the Bershad ghetto and in other ghettos of the subdistrict. It was only after the archives of the former Soviet Union were opened that the accuracy of this estimate could be assessed. See Carp, *Cartea neagră*, 3:279. For data on the number of Jews in Transnistria collected by the Autonomous Assistance Commission in Bucharest, by ghetto, subdistrict, and district, 22 March 1943, see Ancel, *Documents*, vol. 5, doc. 185, pp. 346–47.

33. *Unirea*, 9 April 1941. In May of that year the Romanian General Staff found 1,082 Jewish doctors under age fifty-two. See "The Situation of the Jews," 15 May 1941, table drawn up by the Romanian General Staff, with a breakdown of Jewish labor by profession, in Ancel, *Documents*, vol. 10, doc. 20, p. 76.

34. Testimony of Zelig Asher Hoffer, YVA, 03-1453, p. 21. Dr. Laxer from the Verhovka ghetto prepared a camphor solution himself that eased the suffering of many patients; testimony of Etl Slominski from Siret, Tel Aviv, March 1959, YVA, 03-1230, p. 5.

35. Testimony of Dr. Israel Halfan, YVA, 03-1525, p. 13.

36. Testimony of Zelig Asher Hoffer, YVA, 03-1453, p. 21.

37. Testimony of Chaja Kiselnik from Czernowitz, Tel Aviv, 1956, YVA, 03-841, p. 6.

38. Monograph on the Shargorod ghetto by the ghetto leadership, 15 January 1944, in Carp, *Cartea neagră*, 3:323.

39. Report on the typhus epidemic in Mogilev, in Carp, *Cartea neagră*, no. 165, 3:328–29.

40. Carp, *Cartea neagră*, 3:266, 268, 269.

41. Carp, *Cartea neagră*, 3:270. See list of the names of the twenty-seven doctors in the Shargorod ghetto, including a list of doctors who died in the epidemic, in Carp, *Cartea neagră*, no. 179, 3:350.

42. Testimony of Trude Malik, YVA, 03-905, p. 3.

43. Testimony of Rosa Sachner from Czernowitz, Jaffa, 27 June 1958, YVA, 03-910, p. 8.

44. During the first winter not all ghettos were surrounded by fences. The authorities turned a blind eye to Jews who lived among Ukrainians and were able to pay rent. Ghettos far from the Dniester were rarely visited by gendarmes, who came only to check how many Jews were still alive. The Jews had nowhere to flee, and only the brave and strong dared move to another ghetto without permission. Anyone caught doing so was shot to death by the gendarmes, but gendarmerie patrols were rare due to the exceptionally cold winter.

45. Instruction issued by Prefect Năsturaș to the pretors, the gendarmerie legion, and mayors of the Mogilev district, 5 July 1942, in Carp, *Cartea neagră*, no. 193, 3:361.

46. Approval by the Presidency of the Council of Ministers for the provision of aid and medicines, 10 December 1941, bearing the Jewish Center's stamp of 23 December 1941, in Ancel, *Documents*, vol. 5, doc. 121, p. 189.

47. Note by Filderman, 20 October 1941, on his talk with the interior minister, Gen. Dumitru Popescu, asking him to put an end to the deportation to Transnistria of Jews who were "Romanian citizens," in Ancel, *Documents*, vol. 3, doc. 172, p. 270. Filderman described Popescu's response as follows: "He said he was sorry, that if it were up to him he would not have approved the deportation, but that his authority ended at the 1940 borders."

48. Ministry of the Interior to the governor of Transnistria via the Presidency of the Council of Ministers, 22 January 1942, Odessa Archives, 2242-1-1486, p. 158. Filderman also received a permit. For a copy of the permit, see Ancel, *Documents*, vol. 5, doc. 132, p. 226.

49. Ministry of the Interior to the governor of Transnistria via the Presidency of the Council of Ministers, 22 January 1942, Odessa Archives, 2242-1-1486, p. 158; see notes in Alexianu's handwriting in the margins of the document.

50. Filderman's note on Governor Alexianu's interview with the Jewish delegation that he agreed to receive, 28 January 1942, YVA, Carp Archive, vol. 3, p. 253.

51. See summary of aid—money and provisions obtained through fund-raising activities, the Red Cross, and so on—in the years 1942–1944, in *Activitatea Comisiei Autonome de Ajutorare*, 7–8.

52. *Activitatea Comisiei Autonome de Ajutorare*, 3.

53. Agenda signed by the director of the Registration and Archive Bureau in the governor's office, 31 March 1942, Odessa Archives, 2242-1-1486, p. 237.

54. Agenda signed by the director of the Registration and Archive Bureau in the governor's office, 17 March 1942, Odessa Archives, 2242-1-1486.

55. Telegram by the Pharmaceuticals Directorate of the administration to Governor Alexianu, 16 March 1942, Odessa Archives, 2242-1-1487, p. 116 (Alexianu noted in his own handwriting that the prefect of Mogilev should be notified accordingly); telegram by the Transnistrian administration to the prefect of Mogilev, 21 March 1942, Odessa Archives, 2242-1-1487, p. 19.

56. Matatias Carp was convinced that the first consignment of medications had arrived in February and was first distributed in March, but he did not have access to the archive of the Transnistrian administration, only the archive of the Autonomous Assistance Commission. Carp, *Cartea neagră*, 3:271.

57. Carp, *Cartea neagră*, 3:271.

58. Jägendorf, *Jagendorf's Foundry*, 137.

59. "Die Hilfsaktion fuer die nach Transnistrien deportierten Juden," report on the activity of the Autonomous Assistance Commission from the Jewish Center's inception in mid-February 1942 until late August, 2 September 1942, in Ancel, *Documents*, vol. 5, doc. 158, p. 291. The report states that there was no conclusive data concerning the number of deportees and deportation locations.

60. Radu Lecca's instruction to the Jewish Center, 30 May 1942, in Ancel, *Documents*, vol. 7, doc. 29, p. 37.

61. N. Gingold, leader of the Jewish Center, to the governor of the national bank, asking him to introduce new procedures for transferring aid, following the instruction issued by the Presidency of the Council of Ministers, 4 June 1942, in Ancel, *Documents*, vol. 7, doc. 30, p. 38.

62. Report on the typhus epidemic in Mogilev, in Carp, *Cartea neagră*, no. 165, 3:331–32. Jägendorf also referred to Dr. Chirilă's contribution to the containment of the typhus epidemic and added that the doctor offered to deliver messages and letters to Bucharest. This led Jägendorf to suspect that Chirilă was an agent of the authorities. It transpired that both Dr. Chirilă's offer and his intentions were sincere, and he proved to be a valuable ally. It further transpired that Chirilă's son-in-law had been killed by Legionnaires. Jägendorf, *Jagendorf's Foundry*, 45.

63. Carp, *Cartea neagră*, 3:290.

64. Monograph on the Shargorod ghetto by the ghetto leadership, 15 January 1944, in Carp, *Cartea neagră*, 3:323.

65. Monograph on the Shargorod ghetto by the ghetto leadership, 15 January 1944, in Carp, *Cartea neagră*, 3:324.

66. Carp, *Cartea neagră*, 3:270.

67. Testimony of Esther Burg from Czernowitz, Jaffa, 2 April 1951, YVA, 03-1417, pp. 5–6.

68. Nuremberg Documents, NO-2651, 30 October 1941.

69. Mircu, *Pogromurile din Basarabia*, 27.

70. Carp, *Cartea neagră*, 3:268.

71. Testimony of Adolf Henner, YVA, 03-1442, p. 8; *Pinkas Hekehilot, Rumania*, 2:397.

72. Testimony of Israel Parikman from Secureni, Petah-Tiqva, 12 July 1959, YVA, 03-1450, p. 11.

73. Testimony of Chaja Kiselnik from Czernowitz, Bnei-Braq, 1958, YVA, 03-841, pp. 6–7.

74. Testimony of Moshe Brunwasser from Storojinetz, Tel Aviv, July 1959, YVA, 03-1455, p. 14.

75. Testimony of Anna Loebl, YVA, 03-1482, p. 239.

76. The picture appears in Yona Maleron's diary, between pages 33 and 34. See Maleron, *Od Tetzi Mikan*. The original can be found in the Holocaust Art Collection, Yad Vashem

Museum. See also map of mass graves in Transnistria, edited by the author, in *Pinkas Hekehilot, Rumania*, 1:545.

77. Memorandum by the deputy interior minister and commander of police and gendarmerie, Constantin Vasiliu, undated, in Carp, *Cartea neagră*, no. 248, 3:447. The memorandum was prepared for the session of the Public Order Council on 12 November 1943.

78. Report to the Autonomous Assistance Commission by Fred Şaraga, a representative of the Jewish Center who visited Transnistria, with statistical data and estimates on the number of deportees from Romania (excluding local Jews) by district and subdistrict, 22 March 1943, in Ancel, *Documents*, vol. 5, docs. 184–85, pp. 342–50. Although there are no accurate figures for the number of local Jews who died of typhus, one may assume that at least ten thousand of the thirty thousand Jews who were still alive in northern Transnistria when the ghettos were set up succumbed to the disease.

79. Report by the inspector general of the gendarmerie on completion of the operation to deport Jews from Bessarabia and Bukovina, with a map of Transnistria, USHMM/SRI, RG-25.004M, reel 64, file 18844, vol. 3, p. 2. The map shows that 29,476 Jews were evacuated to the Pervomaysk district (Golta) to Bobrik, Krivoye Ozero, and Bogdanovka. All these Jews were eventually exterminated in the Kingdom of Death.

80. Deposition by Alexianu to the People's Court, Bucharest, 29 April 1946, USHMM/SRI, RG-25.004M, reel 33, file 40010, vol. 28, p. 10 (author's emphasis).

30. The Hunt for Residents of Jewish Blood

1. Decree-Law regarding the judicial status of the Jews, in *Monitorul Oficial*, no. 183, 9 August 1940, pp. 4079–81.

2. Kishinev military headquarters to the Bessarabian administration, 13 August 1941, USHMM/MSM, RG-25.003M, roll 656, file 29.

3. Mayor of Bolgrad to the pretor of the subdistrict, with a list of names, 13 November 1941; and pretor of the Bolgrad subdistrict to the prefect of the Ismail district, 30 November 1941, Odessa Archives, 7528-1c-1, pp. 236–38.

4. Order no. 94 issued by General Voicolescu, governor of Bessarabia, 28 July 1942, USHMM/SSARM, RG-54.001, reel 21, [Police Headquarters Cahul], 697-1-41, p. 21.

5. Balta police to the prefecture of the Balta district, 20 November 1941, Odessa Archives, 2358-1c-10, p. 2.

6. Commander of the gendarmerie in Transnistria to the General Gendarmerie Inspectorate in Bucharest, 29 March 1942, in Carp, *Cartea neagră*, no. 130, 3:217.

7. Commander of the gendarmerie in Transnistria to the General Gendarmerie Inspectorate in Bucharest, 29 March 1942, in Carp, *Cartea neagră*, no. 130, 3:217.

8. Unsigned decree of February 1942, Odessa Archives, 2242-2-37, pp. 82–82b.

9. Prefect Isopescu to the Transnistrian administration, 15 April 1942, Odessa Archives, 2242-1-1487, p. 183 (author's emphasis).

10. Opinion of the director of the Labor Department, Dr. Gheorghe Balcaş, 16 March 1943, Odessa Archives, 2242-2-1496, p. 180. Alexianu wrote his approval in the margin of the report.

11. Justice Department of the Transnistrian administration to Maria Remenaia of Odessa, 2 March 1944, Odessa Archives, 2242-1-1487, p. 132b.

12. Summary report of the Central Evacuation Bureau, 13 February 1942, Odessa Archives, 2242-1-1487, p. 132b.

13. Radu Lecca to the Transnistrian administration, 25 November 1942, Odessa Archives, 2242-1-1491, pp. 227–29.

14. Request by Anastase Manu of Constanța, whose wife was evacuated when he was called up to the war, 18 February 1942, Odessa Archives, 2242-1-1486, pp. 259–59b; administration's refusal of Manu's request, 27 February 1942, Odessa Archives, 2242-1-1486, p. 252.

15. Tatiana Ivanova Micinik, an Odessan doctor born in Bessarabia and married to a Romanian from Kishinev, was discovered in March 1942 after being informed upon. She and her two little children were immediately imprisoned in the city jail, even though she proved that she had been baptized together with her children and had been separated from her husband because of the Soviet occupation of Bessarabia in June 1940 (she was reunited with him in August 1941). In late April 1942 she was released "provisionally under police surveillance," and on 19 May 1942 she was allowed to remain in Odessa. See "Tatiana File," Odessa Archives, 2242-1-1487, pp. 238–67. Approval was granted because she did not ask to return to Romania.

16. Telegram by the tenants of No. 6 Bebet Street, Odessa, 6 February 1942, Odessa Archives, 2242-1-1487, p. 74.

17. Col. Matei Velcescu, head of the Central Evacuation Bureau and prefect of the Odessa district, to the administration, 25 March 1942, Odessa Archives, 2242-1-1487.

18. Transnistrian administration to Berezovka prefecture to release Dushya Ivanciuk from the Mostovoye camp after she was found to be Russian, 17 November 1942, Odessa Archives, 2361-1-42c, p. 217; prefect's directive to the Berezovka gendarmerie legion to release her, 19 November 1942, Odessa Archives, 2361-1-42c, p. 216.

19. Complaint by Nicolae Iladi from Odessa to the governor of Transnistria, 24 June 1942, Odessa Archives, 2242-1-1489, pp. 64–64b.

20. Opinion of the military tribunal in Odessa, 16 April 1942, Odessa Archives, 2243-1-1489, pp. 65–65b. General Trestioreanu noted his approval in the margins of the document. In June the matter was again brought before the military tribunal, and the prosecution recommended "granting [the woman] an amnesty," releasing her from jail, and placing her and her family under police surveillance. See opinion of the military prosecution, 14 July 1942, Odessa Archives, 2243-1-1489, pp. 64, 66.

21. Decree-Law no. 1091, *Monitorul Oficial*, no. 29, 17 December 1941.

22. The order was cited in an application by the governor of Bessarabia, General Voiculescu, to the Transnistrian administration to release from a ghetto the husband of Paraskiva Gleizer, a Romanian woman from a village in the Soroka district, 14 February 1942, Odessa Archives, 2242-1-1488, p. 224.

23. SSI intelligence report, undated, Odessa Archives, 2242-1-1487, p. 246.

24. Third Army headquarters to Transnistrian administration, 29 April 1942, Odessa Archives, 2242-1-1487, p. 245.

25. Administration to Third Army headquarters, 18 May 1942, Odessa Archives, 2242-1-1487, p. 244.

26. Prefect Isopescu to the administration, 17 June 1942, Odessa Archives, 2242-1-1489, p. 196; administration's reply, 27 February 1942, Odessa Archives, 2242-1-1489, p. 250.

27. Request by Valentina Popovici of Kishinev, 16 February 1942, Odessa Archives, 22442-1-1486, pp. 251–51b; administration's reply, 27 February 1942, Odessa Archives, 22442-1-1486, p. 250.

28. "Korchinska Darya Karpova" file, September–November 1942, Odessa Archives, 2242-1-1491, pp. 146–51.

29. Valentin Untilov, a Russian from Odessa, requested the release of his wife, who had converted to Christianity in 1912 and was nevertheless interned in the Slobudka ghetto and deported to the Berezovka district; Emilia Melnikova was deported from Odessa in February 1942 despite having converted to Christianity in 1918. Odessa Archives, 2242-1-1487.

30. Secret Intelligence Report no. 7/1941 by a gendarmerie agent to the Balta gendarmerie legion, undated, Odessa Archives, 2358-1c-10, p. 12. The German army as well as the Romanian authorities freed prisoners of war who were natives of the region after first executing the Jews and commissars.

31. The problem of the execution of Jewish prisoners of war is not discussed here. This issue is an unknown chapter of Romanian history and appears to have taken place in the Romanian prisoner of war camps only at the start of the war. It was mentioned briefly in the interrogation of Defense Minister Pantazi before the trial of Antonescu and his government but was not mentioned at the trial itself. The prisoner of war camps were under the jurisdiction of the General Staff. *Procesul marei trădări naționale*, 97. In his interrogation Ion Antonescu testified that he had given instructions that international laws be obeyed in connection with the treatment of prisoners of war and that he himself respected these laws. Minutes of Ion Antonescu's interrogation, USHMM/SRI RG-25.004M, reel 34, file 40010, vol. 36, p. 74. Defense Minister Constantin Pantazi was asked in his interrogation if the Romanian army had conducted the war in accordance with the principles of the Hague Convention, and he answered in the affirmative. Afterward he was asked directly, "Did you know that in the initial period of the war, the prisoners-of-war were divided into two—those of Jewish origin were shot to death and the rest left in the camps?" Pantazi blamed this on the General Staff, which was subordinate to the chief of General Staff and not the Ministry of National Defense. See minutes of Pantazi's interrogation, 15 and April 1946, USHMM/SRI RG-25.004M, reel 34, file 40010, vol. 43, pp. 206, 214. The Transnistrian administration compiled twelve files comprising hundreds of pages "investigating the prisoners' ethnic origins," 14 October 1946, Odessa Archives, 2242-1-19, p. 442.

32. Onischenko file, 25 August 1942–10 December 1942, Odessa Archives, 2361-1-24, pp. 56–64, 164–65. We do not know what was decided in her case.

33. Gendarmerie Inspectorate in Transnistria to the Berezovka prefecture, 19 January 1943, Odessa Archives, 2361-1-26, p. 11.

34. Governor Alexianu to the Presidency of the Council of Ministers, 22 July 1942, Odessa Archives, 2242-1-1512, p. 205.

35. Transnistrian governor to the SSI bureau in Odessa, 7 July 1942, Odessa Archives, 2242-1-1488, p. 233. The Evacuation Bureau in Odessa freed a mother and her two young children for two days under police surveillance until their Russian origins were corroborated; 11 April 1942, Odessa Archives, 2242-1-1487, p. 268.

36. Intelligence report by the Gendarmerie Inspectorate in Transnistria, 6 January 1942, Odessa Archives, 2242-4C-29, p. 12.

37. See, for example, certificate issued by the head of the village of Calaglia in the Ovidopol district to Simion Țurcan on the basis of his personal acquaintance with the applicant, 2 April 1943, Odessa Archives, 2357-1C-51C, p. 225. Col. Leonida Pop, the prefect of the Berezovka district, issued a certificate for himself and signed by him testifying that "in accordance with records in this prefecture" he "was of Romanian ethnic origin"; 16 September 1943, Odessa Archives, 2361C-1C-40C. For the contents of such a document, see General Staff instructions regarding the army's behavior in the occupied territory, 6 September 1941, Odessa Archives, 2359-1C-1, p. 134. Such documents were issued by army headquarters at the start of the occupation only.

38. Order no. 43 of the Transnistrian administration, 7 February 1942, Odessa Archives, 2361-1-29, p. 69.

39. Decision no. 659 of the Administrative and Manpower Department of the Transnistrian administration, 7 May 1942, Odessa Archives, 2242-4-10, p. 30.

40. Order no. 283, issued by the Transnistrian administration, modifying the terms of the previous order and forbidding any other authority from issuing documents testifying to Romanian ethnic origin, 23 January 1944, Odessa Archives, 2361-1-46.

31. The Christianization Campaign

1. See Guvernământul Transnistriei, *Transnistria*, 75–78.

2. Marshal Antonescu to Mihai Antonescu, 3 September 1941, USHMM/RSA, RG-25 .002M, reel 19, fond: Presidency of the Council of Ministers, file 167/1941, pp. 64–65.

3. Namely the Independent Ukrainian Church, known in Ukrainian by the acronym UAPT, and the Autonomous Ukrainian Church (the AUT). Both were established during the civil war in the Ukraine as an expression of the wish to secede from Russia — an expression of Ukrainian national awakening. The Independent Ukrainian Church no longer recognized the patriarch in Moscow as the head of the church, declared its independence, and conducted the service and prayers in Ukrainian. This church and its leaders were persecuted under Soviet rule and continued to exist only in Ukrainian territories that were under Polish rule. After the German and Romanian invasions the Independent Ukrainian Church made a comeback in occupied eastern Ukraine and tried also to extend its influence in Transnistria. It was headed by Bishop Policarp and his close assistant Bishop Ilarion. The third Orthodox Ukrainian church, the Autonomous Ukrainian Church, also abolished a number of religious practices that had been laid down by the patriarchate in Moscow but aspired to receive recognition — albeit tenuous — from the patriarchate and maintain ties with it. This church, headed by Archbishop Alexis, fought to set up a federation of Orthodox churches in which the autonomy of the Ukrainian Church would be preserved while maintaining limited cooperation with Moscow. Alexis was arrested by the Germans, released after a short while,

and in December 1941, at a convention of bishops in Lvov, was appointed metropolitan of the Autonomous Ukrainian Church. On the Ukrainian Church, see Dallin, *German Rule in Russia*, 474–75, 481–82; see also the comprehensive study by Heyer, *Die orthodoxe Kirche*, 170–227.

4. Romanian patriarchate to Archimandrite Scriban, head of the Romanian Orthodox Church Mission in Tiraspol, report on the activity of the Romanian Orthodox Church Mission in Transnistria, 1 January–31 March 1942, 20 May 1942, Odessa Archives, 2242-1-1486, p. 2; 2264-1c-40b, p. 165.

5. Radu Lecca to the Labor Department of the Transnistrian administration, 28 May 1943, Odessa Archives, 2264-1-40a, p. 58.

6. Romanian Orthodox delegation to the governor, 22 July 1942, Odessa Archives, 2242-1-1105, p. 230. The governor's refusal was noted in the margins of the document and also sent in writing: Governor to the Romanian Orthodox Church Mission, 6 August 1942, Odessa Archives, 2242-1-1105, p. 225. The ritual of the Orthodox Church included the seven sacraments—ceremonies that sanctify important religious events in a manner that defies human understanding. These events contain within them a mystery, a truth that human logic cannot embrace (*sfintele taine*). The sacraments are baptism, confirmation, the holy Eucharist, penance, matrimony, holy orders, and extreme unction. The above highlights the self-effacement of the head of the Romanian Orthodox Church Mission in asking the governor's permission to conduct one of the sacraments.

7. Order no. 89 issued by Governor Alexianu, 28 September 1942, Odessa Archives, 2361-1-29, p. 95.

8. Pretor's report, undated [January 1942], Odessa Archives, 2387-1-4, p. 182.

9. List of mission staff, in report on the activity of the Romanian Orthodox Church Mission in Transnistria, 1 January–31 March 1942, 20 May 1942, Odessa Archives, 2242-1-1486, p. 98; report by the district head of church in Golta, the priest Ioan Dinu, on the religious activity of the priests in the district in July 1943, 30 July 1942, USHMM, NOA, RG-31.008M, 2178-1-533, pp. 163–70b; Popovici, pretor of the Domanevka subdistrict, to Prefect Isopescu, "History of the Domanevka Subdistrict," 7 November 1942, Odessa Archives, 2178-1-133, pp. 376–77b.

10. Report by the priest Melnic on his visit to the religious community of Akmechetka, 17 August 1942, Odessa Archives, 2270-1c-1, p. 25b.

11. Report by the priest Melnic on his visit to Bogdanovka, 19 August 1942, Odessa Archives, 2270-1c-1, pp. 27–27b.

12. Transnistrian administration to the Berezovka prefecture on the timing of the metropolitan's visit, 18 May 1943; and thank-you letter by Metropolitan Vissarion to the Berezovka prefecture for the warm welcome he received during his visit, 29 March 1943, Odessa Archives, 2626c-1c-7c, pp. 8, 31.

13. Psalms 20, 23, 91, 130, 121. These psalms were published in their entirety with no omissions, and they mentioned King David, Jerusalem, and the Jewish people. It was obvious, however, that there was no connection between these Jews and the Jews in Transnistria.

14. Appeal by the commander of the Thirteenth Battalion of the garrison in Transnistria to the governor, 9 April 1943, Odessa Archives 2242-1-1477, p. 7, asking, "Under what

conditions may one permit soldiers stationed east of the Dniester to marry? We have many requests by soldiers seeking to marry Ukrainian women."

32. The Degradation of Judaism and Jews

1. M. Antonescu, *Pentru Basarabia și Bucovina*, 61.

2. Mihai Antonescu's radio speech, "Basarabie, vei fi răzbunată" [Bessarabia, we shall avenge you], *Universul*, 1 July 1941.

3. *Unirea*, 29 June 1941.

4. "Declinul Judaismului" [The decline of Judaism], *Sfarmă Piatră*, 2 July 1941.

5. "Suferințele Bisericii Ortodoxe sub regimul Judeo–bolșevic" [The suffering of the Orthodox Church under the Judeo–Bolshevik regime], *Curentul*, 2 August 1941.

6. "Stalin este evreu" [Stalin is a Jew], *Gazeta Țării*, 1 July 1941.

7. Nicodim, *Cuvântul Patriarhului pentru*, 5.

8. *Curentul*, 3 August 1941.

9. Testimony of Israel Parikman from Secureni, Petah-Tikva, 12 August 1959, YVA, 03-1460, pp. 5–6.

10. Reicher and Shitz, *Yad le-Yedinits*, 733–34.

11. People's Court in Bucharest, indictment against Col. Vasile Agapie and Capt. Sever Buradescu, commanders of the Vertujeni and Mărculești camps, and against Ioan Mihăescu, a senior official of the National Bank of Romania, May 1945, in Ancel, *Documents*, vol. 6, doc. 8, pp. 124, 140.

12. Mircu, *Pogromurile din Bucovina și Dorohoi*, 46–47.

13. Confidential report by Colonel Iliescu, deputy commander of the Transnistrian gendarmerie, to the Labor Department in the Transnistrian administration, 2 October 1943, Odessa Archives, 2242-1-1503, p. 390.

14. *Actul de acuzare*, 81.

15. Testimony of Leo Rapoport from Kishinev, Special Tribunal for the Investigation of War Crimes, Bucharest, 17 March 1945, USHMM/SRI, RG-25.004M, reel 65, file 40015, vol. 3, p. 177.

16. *Actul de acuzare*, 41, 42.

17. Testimony of Richard Grinberg from Czernowitz, Givatayim, 27 February 1959, YVA, 03-1130, p. 12.

18. Testimony of Shimon Rosenrauch from Czernowitz, Tel Aviv, November 1959, YVA, 03-1536, p. 1.

19. Testimony of Ernst Zuker from Czernowitz, Petah Tikva, 2 October 1959, YVA, 03-1546, p. 4.

20. Testimony of Moshe Kerner from Czernowitz, Tel Aviv, 18 July 1958, YVA, 03-914, p. 13.

21. For details on the Cariera de Piatră camp, see YVA, Carp Archive, vol. 7, p. 44; YVA, 03-1525; YVA, Romanian Collection 0-11, p. 13.

22. Testimony of Boris Schwartzman to the Legal Department of the Romanian branch of the World Jewish Congress, 22 July 1945, USHMM/SRI, RG-25.004M, reel 65, file 40015, vol. 3, p. 295 (the testimony was handed over to the People's Court).

23. Carp, *Cartea neagră*, 3:80.

24. Testimony of Olga Averbuch of Kishinev to the Bucharest police, 2 April 1945, USHMM/SRI, RG-25.004M, reel 65, file 40015, vol. 2, p. 117.

25. Testimony of Col. Marcel Petală before the Special War Crimes Court, Bucharest, 22 June 1945, USHMM/SRI, RG-25.004M, reel 60, file 73897: "File investigation Octavian Niculescu," pp. 295b–96.

26. Testimony of the photographer Alexandru Dumitrescu, 12 April 1945, USHMM/SRI, RG-25.004M, reel 60, file 73897: "File investigation Octavian Niculescu," pp. 277–77b.

27. Testimony of Izu Landau in the People's Court in Bucharest, USHMM/SRI, RG-25.004M, reel 20, file 40011: Nicolae Macici, vol. 7, p. 107. Landau was tried and sentenced with other war criminals for having served the Romanians devotedly.

28. Ancel, *Hakdamah leretsah*, 342–44.

29. Ornstein, *Suferințele deportaților*, pictures at the front of the book.

30. In his speech of 1 January 1939 to the government, King Carol II listed the main problems the country was facing: "TB, social diseases, malaria, and infant mortality are rife," he said. By "social diseases" he was referring to sexually transmitted diseases. See Tomescu, *Anul medical 1939*.

33. The Iași Pogrom

This chapter is a summary of an in-depth study on the subject by Yad Vashem. See Ancel, *Hakdamah leretsah* (in Hebrew). The English version is in press, to be published in 2011.

1. Prior to the discovery of Antonescu's secret order in July 1996, I never claimed that he ordered the pogrom against the Jews of Iași. On my views concerning responsibility for the pogrom prior to my discovery of the order and other important documents that complete the picture, see Ancel, "Antonescu and the Jews," 184–89 (subheading on Iași pogrom); and Ancel, "Jassy Syndrome."

2. Telephone communication from prefect of Iași Col. Dumitru Captaru to Ministry of Interior in Bucharest, reporting on Mihai Antonescu's order to evacuate the Jews from the city and asking for instructions on how to carry out the order, 29 June 1941, USHMM/SRI, RG-25.004M, reel 35, file 40010, vol. 89, p. 478.

3. Centrala Evreilor din România, *Breviarul Statistic*, 28; copy in Ancel, *Documents*, vol. 1, doc. 46, p. 307.

4. Personal missive by Col. Constantin Lupu to General Antonescu, complaining that he was dismissed from his position despite having faithfully carried out his orders, 25 July 1941, USHMM/RSA, RG-25.002M, fond: Presidency of the Council of Ministers, file 247/1941, p. 10.

5. "The telephone order that Marshal Antonescu gave me personally on the night of 28/29 June, 23:00," as recorded by Colonel Lupu, investigative file on Col. (res.) Constantin Lupu, 1941, USHMM/SRI, RG-25.004M, reel 48, file 108233, vol. 28, p. 183.

6. Testimony of Eugen Cristescu before the investigative judge of the military tribunal in Bucharest, 4 July 1947, USHMM/SRI, RG-25.004M, reel 44, file 108233, vol. 54, p. 226; Carp, *Cartea neagră*, no. 3, 2:42–43.

7. On the provisional stationing of Einsatzgruppe D on Romanian territory and on its operations in Bessarabia, see Ancel, "Jassy Syndrome," pt. 1, pp. 36–38.

8. Memorandum of Col. Dumitru Captaru, submitted to the prosecutor general of the Military Appeals Tribunal, May 1946, USHMM/SRI, RG-25004M, reel 43, file 40010, vol. 36, p. 46.

9. Testimony of the survivor Herşcu Wolf to the prosecutor in the High Court of Appeals, 2 January 1948, in Carp, *Cartea neagră*, no. 19, 2:68.

10. Intelligence summary report by the police commander in Iaşi on the mood and situation in the city in the period from 22 June to 22 August 1941, in Carp, *Cartea neagră*, no. 75, 2:156.

11. "Summary of the pogrom of 29 June 1941, based on testimonies by neighborhood, and also of the days leading up to it, during which the pogrom was planned," unsigned handwritten document by intellectuals from the Iaşi Jewish community submitted in late 1944 to the Iaşi police, which began investigations (hereafter "Summary of the pogrom"), USHMM/SRI, RG-25.004M, reel 43, file 108233, vol. 42, p. 325. As far as is known, no use was made of these testimonies.

12. Testimony of Gheorghe Leahu before the People's Court in Bucharest, 29 October 1945, USHMM/SRI, RG-25.004M, reel 48, file 108233, vol. 26, p. 52.

13. Testimony of attorney Marcu Moscovici before the Bucharest court, 18 June 1948, USHMM/SRI, RG-25.004M, reel 47, file 108233, vol. 1/2, p. 671.

14. Excerpt of the testimony of the deputy head of the community, Avram Hahamu, before the public prosecutor, 2 March 1945, in Carp, *Cartea neagră*, no. 16, 2:66.

15. Testimony of Iosef Iacob before the Bucharest court, 15 June 1948, USHMM/SRI, RG-25.004M, reel 47, file 108233, vol. 1/2, p. 634.

16. Report of the deputy police commander, Gheorghe Leahu, to the Interior Ministry, 2 July 1941, in Carp, *Cartea neagră*, no. 44, 2:110.

17. Testimony of police commissar Graţian Sprînceană before the special war crimes court in Iaşi, 19 July 1945, USHMM/SRI, RG-25.004M, reel 48, vol. 26, p. 48; copy in Carp, *Cartea neagră*, no. 18, 2:67. In his testimony and in all the investigations leading up to his trial Leahu denied that he instructed the police not to interfere in the army's activities. See, for example, Gheorghe Leahu's testimony before the Bucharest People's Court, 29 October 1945, in Carp, *Cartea neagră*, 2:50–55b.

18. Report of Lt. Col. Constantin Chirilovici to Interior Ministry, June 30, 1941, in Carp, *Cartea neagră*, no. 43, 2:108.

19. Report of M. Braunstein (a leader of the Iaşi Jewish community) on Jassy [Iaşi] pogrom, submitted to the chairman of the Federation of Jewish Communities, 8 February 1945, in Ancel, *Documents*, vol. 6, no. 9, p. 35.

20. Minutes of cabinet session, with the participation of the governors of the liberated territories, 13 November 1941, USHMM/SRI, RG-25.004M, reel 35, file 40010, vol. 78, p. 13.

21. Testimony of Leon Reicher before the Bucharest military tribunal, 28 May 1947, USHMM/SRI, RG-25.004M, reel 44, vol. 51, p. 353.

22. List of 286 civilians who participated in the Iaşi pogrom, USHMM/SRI, RG-25.004M, reel 43, vol. 40, pp. 115–27. The perpetrators came from all social strata and included

students, laborers, craftsmen, civil servants, school students, actors, physicians, teachers, a priest, church singers, lawyers, retirees, merchants, and the like. Especially conspicuous were the railway workers (Romanian Railway Authority, or CFR) and officials. The list does not include army personnel, gendarmes, or ordinary police, nor does it identify all the criminals. Most of them fled the city and took up residence in areas far from Iaşi, making sure to keep away from Jews who might recognize them.

23. See indictment in Ancel, *Documents*, vol. 6, pp. 384–99.

24. "Summary of the pogrom," USHMM/SRI, RG-25.004M, reel 43, file 108233, vol. 42, p. 349.

25. "Summary of the pogrom," USHMM/SRI, RG-25.004M, reel 43, file 108233, vol. 42, p. 341.

26. Ratified copy of the testimony of policeman Vasile Morcov in the special war crimes court, 28 March 1946, USHMM/SRI, RG-25.004M, reel 43, file 108233, vol. 37, p. 012. The Todt units were the most important nonmilitary, war-supporting organization of the Third Reich, named after a member of the Nazi elite. They were involved in all sorts of construction work, including roads, railroad tracks, bridges, mines, and factories. Their members wore uniforms bearing the swastika, but they were not part of the Wehrmacht.

27. Testimony of Colonel Lupu in the special war crimes court in Bucharest, 21 June 1945, USHMM/SRI, RG-25.004M, reel 48, file 108233, vol. 29, p. 9b. Lupu downplayed the number of forces at his disposal; as far as the Germans were concerned, he clearly stated that German headquarters controlled its soldiers and that only the members of the Todt unit were an undisciplined force, but they were numerically insignificant.

28. Affidavit by Aristide Rauch in the Bucharest People's Court, 14 May 1945, USHMM/SRI, RG-25.004M, reel 48, file 108233, vol. 30, pp. 79–80. Beniamin Abramovici, a survivor of the pogrom, testified that members of Todt did not wield simple clubs but meter-long wooden rods; USHMM, RG-25.004M, reel 48, file 108233, vol. 30, p. 93b.

29. Affidavit by Mayer Juhr in the Iaşi People's Court, 14 May 1945, USHMM/SRI, RG-25.004M, reel 48, file 108233, vol. 30, pp. 88–88b.

30. Testimony of Jean Shoihet as recorded by members of the Iaşi community in September–December 1944, USHMM/SRI, RG-25.004M, reel 43, file 108233, vol. 42, pp. 386–87 (the file with the testimonies was transferred to the Iaşi People's Court).

31. Testimony of Moise Shmil as recorded by representatives of the Iaşi community, 9 September 1944, USHMM/SRI, RG-25.004M, reel 43, file 108233, vol. 42, pp. 401–401b.

32. Affidavit by Jean Sigler before the Bucharest People's Court, 18 April 1941, USHMM/SRI, RG-25.004M, reel 48, file 108233, vol. 29, p. 25.

33. Affidavit by Aristide Rauch, USHMM/SRI, RG-25.004M, reel 48, file 108233, vol. 30, p. 80.

34. Affidavit by Mayer Iur, USHMM/SRI, RG-25.004M, reel 48, file 108233, vol. 30, p. 88b.

35. Testimony of Vlad Marievici, director of sanitation services in the Iaşi municipality, before the People's Court in Iaşi, 27 July 1945, USHMM/SRI, RG-25.004M, reel 47, file 108233, vol. 24, pp. 28–29.

36. This conclusion is based on a study of the Einsatzgruppe reports, some of which were published by the author in their original form, in Ancel, *Documents*, vol. 5, and the

comprehensive study by the German scholar Helmut Krausnick on Einsatzgruppen activities, which leaves no room for speculation: Krausnick and Wilhelm, *Die Truppe des Weltanschauungskrieges*, 1:195–200. See also Ancel, "Jassy Syndrome."

37. Serviciul Pretoral "Gloria," file no. 4535/1941: file concerning court investigations on activity of Col. (retired) Lupu Constantin, 29 January 1942, USHMM/SRI, RG-25.004M, reel 47, file 108233, vol. 29, pp. 199–203.

38. Second report by M. Braunstein, a leader of the Iaşi community, to the president of the Federation of Jewish Communities about the situation of the Jews in Iaşi between 29 June 1941 and August 1944, 8 February 1945, in Ancel, *Documents*, vol. 6, doc. 4, p. 49. See also affidavit by Jean Sigler to the People's Court, in which he stated that about fourteen thousand Jews perished in the pogrom, 18 April 1945, USHMM/SRI, RG-25.004M, reel 48, file 108233, vol. 29, p. 21.

39. Report by the Special Intelligence Service residence in Iaşi on the number of Jews who died in the pogrom, 23 July 1943, USHMM/SRI, RG-25.004M, reel 115, file 3041, p. 327. See also Troncotă, *Eugen Cristescu*, 118–19.

40. Col. Ion Georgescu, head of Section One of the General Staff, to Antonescu's military cabinet in the Presidency of the Council of Ministers, report on the organization and administration of the forced labor of Jews age eighteen to fifty, 8 November 1941, USHMM/RSA, RG-25.002M, fond: Presidency of the Council of Ministers Cabinet Collection, file 86/1941, p. 251.

41. Carp, *Cartea neagră*, 2:10–11.

34. The Final Solution in the Regat

1. Memorandum by Gen. Ion Topor, 7 April 1945, submitted to the prosecutor general of the People's Court in Bucharest, USHMM/SRI, RG-25.004M, reel 25, file 20725, vol. 10, pp. 337–38.

2. Transcript of the government session of 17 June 1941, in Benjamin, *Problema evreiască*, doc. 93, p. 234.

3. USHMM/SRI, RG-25004M, reel 47, file 108233, vol. 24, p. 122.

4. Nuremberg Documents, NG 3106; Hilberg, *Destruction of the European Jews*, 493. The "Jewish element" meant Romanian Jews from the Regat.

5. *National Zeitung Essen*, 2 September 1941 (author's emphasis).

6. Ion Antonescu to Mihai Antonescu, 13 September 1941, in Ancel, *Transnistria, 1941–1942*, vol. 2, doc. 31, p. 57 (author's emphasis). Ancel quotes Antonescu's original letter at full length.

7. Ancel, *Contributii*, 2:166, quotes the original order at full length.

8. See the plan in the original and quoted at full length in Ancel, *Documents*, vol. 4, doc. 85, pp. 165–67.

9. Minutes of government session of 5 September 1941, in Benjamin, *Problema evreiască*, doc. 107, p. 299 (author's emphasis).

10. Minutes of the government session of 6 September 1941, in Benjamin, *Problema evreiască*, doc. 108, p. 303.

11. Nuremberg Documents, NG-3989, 1 September 1941; copy in Ancel, *Documents*, vol. 3, doc. 51, p. 102.

12. Order issued by Gen. Ion Topor to the army and gendarmerie units in Bessarabia, 17 July 1941, USHMM/RSA, RG-25.002M, reel 16, file 133/1941, p. 5.

13. Copy of the order issued by Marshal Antonescu concerning the Jews of Galicia who were trying to flee to Romania, 6 August 1941, USHMM/SSARM, RG-54.001, reel 1, 666-2-165, p. 79.

14. Foreign Ministry advisor Helmuth Wohlthat to Reichsbankoberinspektor Hoppe, 12 August 1941, Nuremberg Documents, NG-3106; copy in Ancel, *Documents*, vol. 5, doc. 54, p. 53.

15. "Rezolvarea problemei evreieşti" [The solution to the Jewish problem], *Unirea*, 30 October 1941; copy in Ancel, *Documents*, vol. 3, doc. 208, p. 318.

16. "Răspunsul d-lui Mareşal Antonescu la scrisoarea profesorului I. Găvănescu" [Marshal Antonescu's response to Professor Găvănescu's letter], *Curentul*, 3 November 1941; copy in Ancel, *Documents*, vol. 3, doc. 219, p. 332.

17. Summary report by Colonel Georgescu, head of the General Staff's Section One, on the exploitation of Jews in the year following the introduction of forced labor, 25 November 1941, in Ancel, *Documents*, vol. 10, doc. 60, p. 135 (author's emphasis).

18. Minutes of the government session of 11 October 1941, USHMM/SRI, RG-25.004M, reel 32, file 40010, vol. 11, p. 47.

19. Presidency of the Council of Ministers to the governors of Bessarabia and Bukovina, Order no. 260, 10 December 1941, USHMM/RMFA, RG-25.006M, reel 10, "Jewish Problem," vol. 21, pp. 277–78.

20. Cable by Mihai Antonescu to the Romanian legation in Ankara, 14 March 1944, Romanian Ministry of Foreign Affairs Archives, Bucharest, file Ankara, vol. 1, pp. 108–9. On the members of the Nazi Party who came to Romania in March, see chap. 16, note 23. Unfortunately, despite considerable effort, I was unable to trace German documents on the delegation's visit, objectives, and achievements. I found no German documents on this important visit, which took place before Hitler informed Antonescu in their meetings of May and June 1941 about what he intended to do with the Soviet Jews.

21. Minutes of the government session of 5 August 1941 (excerpts), USHMM/SRI, RG-25.004M, reel 32, vol. 9, p. 40.

22. "Study and Proposals Concerning the Jewish Problem in Romania," by Gen. Nicolae Mazarini, under chief [subşef] of General Staff, (confidential document), USHMM/SRI, reel 10, file 2711, pp. 1–35; confidential letter from Mihai Antonescu to Constantin C. Stoicescu, minister of justice, undated, USHMM/RSA, RG-25.002M, reel 19, fond: Presidency of the Council of Ministers, file 476/1941, p. 37.

23. Minutes of the government session of 2 September 1941, USHMM/RSA, RG-25.002M, reel 19, fond: Presidency of the Council of Ministers, file 476/1941, p. 348 (author's emphasis).

24. Martin Luther to Killinger, 27 August 1941, Nuremberg Documents, NG-4962 (author's emphasis).

25. Killinger to the German Foreign Ministry, memorandum rejecting Heydrich's claim

that Romania was friendly to the Jews, 1 September 1941, Nuremberg Documents, NG-3989; copy in Ancel, *Documents*, vol. 3, doc. 51, p. 102.

26. Cable by Killinger to the Foreign Ministry in Berlin, Bucharest, 11 September 1941, in United Restitution Organization, *Documentation*, 3:481 (author's emphasis).

27. Richter's report to ambassador Killinger, 21 May 1941, in Ancel, *Documents*, vol. 2, doc. 129, pp. 401–4.

28. "Richtlinien für die Behandlung der Judenfrage," in *Der Prozess gegen die Hauptkriegsverbrecher*, doc. 212-PS, 25:302.

29. Agenda of the morning session with Heydrich, Berlin, 8 December 1941, Nuremberg Documents, NG-2586; copy in Ancel, *Documents*, vol. 3, doc. 270, p. 447.

30. Decree-Law no. 1091, *Monitorul Oficial*, no. 299, 17 December 1941; copy in Ancel, *Documents*, vol. 3, doc. 287, p. 467.

31. Richter's note on his meeting with Mihai Antonescu, 23 January 1942, in Ancel, *Documents*, vol. 3, doc. 311, pp. 494–95 (author's emphasis). Note that even in the war period Jews continued to emigrate from Romania to Palestine—albeit on a much smaller scale.

32. G. Richter, "Jüdische 'Fata Morgana,'" *Bukarester Tageblatt*, 26 April 1942; copy in Ancel, *Documents*, vol. 3, doc. 360, p. 588.

33. Note by Rademacher of 12 May 1942 to the Reich Office for the Occupied Territories, Nuremberg Documents, NG-4817; copy in Ancel, *Documents*, vol. 8, doc. 367, p. 597.

34. Minutes of the government session attended by the governors of Bessarabia, Bukovina, and Transnistria, 16 December 1941, USHMM/SRI, RG-25.004M, reel 33, file 40010, vol. 28, p. 401.

35. Circular of the Bessarabian administration to the Bessarabian police concerning the census of Jews in the country, 31 March 1942, Kishinev Archive, 666-2-262, p. 1.

36. Bessarabian administration to the Orhei police, 11 February 1942, USHMM/SSARM, RG-54001, reel 1, 666-2-165, p. 351.

37. Instruction booklet II.2 put out by the Romanian Foreign Ministry concerning the application of the 1939 law on the granting or revoking of Romanian citizenship, 14 April 1942, USHMM/RMFA, RG-25.006M, reel 7, "Jewish Problem," vol. 16, p. 460.

38. Judenzählung 1942, summary of data from the census of people of Jewish blood in the German legation, in Ancel, *Documents*, vol. 1, doc. 44, pp. 294–96.

39. Secret reports of the General Directorate of Police for 1942, undated, USHMM/SRI, RG-25.004M, reel 7, file 10585, vol. 31, p. 115.

40. Governor of Bukovina's reply to Secret Order no. 502/1942 put out by the cabinet, 27 March 1942, and table of data, 9 April 1942, USHMM/RMFA, RG-25.006M, reel 10, vol. 21, pp. 130–31.

41. Order no. 462 issued by Antonescu to deport the 425 Jews remaining in Bessarabia, 30 March 1942; and report by the governor of Bessarabia to the Cabinet for the Administration of the Territories citing Marshal Antonescu's two orders, 21 August 1942, USHMM/RMFA, RG-25.006M, reel 10, vol. 21, pp. 154, 176.

42. Governor of Bessarabia, Gh. Voiculescu, to the cabinet of the Presidency of the Council of Ministers (copy), 22 April 1942, USHMM/SRI, RG-25.004M, reel 35, file 40010, vol. 114, p. 46.

43. Report by the Bessarabian administration to the Presidency of the Council of Ministers on the resumption of the deportations, 21 August 1942, USHMM/RMFA, RG-25.006M, reel 10, "Jewish Problem," vol. 21, p. 155.

44. Report by the Bukovinian administration on the start of the deportation, 12 June 1942, together with five appendices, USHMM/RMFA, RG-25.006M, reel 10, "Jewish Problem," vol. 21, pp. 196–206.

45. Testimony of Arie Zukerman of Czernowitz, Tel Aviv, November 1959, YVA, 03-1533, p. 5.

46. Testimony of Chana Weinraub of Czernowitz, Tel Aviv, November 1959, YVA, 03-1539, pp. 6–7.

47. *Actul de acuzare*, 59, 60.

48. Testimony of Nechama Jirisditski, a nurse at the Jewish hospital of Czernowitz, December 1959, YVA, 03-1541, p. 2.

49. Testimony of Richard Grünberg of Czernowitz, Givatayim, 27 February 1959, YVA, 03-1130, p. 19.

50. Carp, *Cartea neagră*, 3:233

51. Testimony of Julius Kronenfeld of Czernowitz, Tel Aviv, June 1959, YVA, 03-1525, p. 13; 03-1468, p. 5.

52. Table of the number of Jews deported from Dorohoi on 11 June 1942 compiled by the military cabinet in the offices of the Bukovina administration, USHMM/RMFA, RG-25.006M, reel 11, "Jewish Problem," vol. 21, pp. 205, 206.

53. Table of the number of Jews deported from Dorohoi on 11 June 1942 compiled by the military cabinet in the offices of the Bukovina administration, USHMM/RMFA, RG-25.006M, reel 11, "Jewish Problem," vol. 21, p. 197.

54. Testimony of Arie Zukerman of Czernowitz, Tel Aviv, November 1959, YVA, 03-1533.

55. Testimony of Josef Frolich of Czernowitz, Tel Aviv, 1 December 1958, YVA, 03-1525, p. 13; 03-1127, p. 7.

35. Implementation of the Final Solution

1. Protocol of the meeting between Ion Antonescu and Hitler in Berlin, 11 February 1942 (Romanian version), in Armin, Ardeleanu, and Lache, *Antonescu-Hitler*, doc. 40, 1:179.

2. Note by Filderman and Clejan on their meeting with Ion Antonescu on 8 September 1941, in Ancel, *Documents*, vol. 3, doc. 74, p. 132.

3. Minutes of the government session of 26 February 1942, in National Romanian Archives, *Shorthand Notes*, vol. 6, doc. 6, p. 185.

4. Ion Antonescu's principles, Secret Document no. 5748, delivered to the governors of Bessarabia, Bukovina, and Transnistria, USHMM/RMFA, RG-25.006M, reel 11, "Jewish Problem," vol. 21, p. 608; note of the Presidency of the Council of Ministers, version relating to the Jews of the Regat, 17 August 1942, USHMM/RMFA, RG-25.006M, reel 11, "Jewish Problem," vol. 20, pp. 193–94.

5. Military cabinet in the Presidency of the Council of Ministers to the Interior Ministry, 19 February 1942 (copy), USHMM/SRI, RG-25.004M, reel 32, file 40010, vol. 11, p. 46.

6. Foreign Ministry circular with Antonescu's order that the Jews clean the streets, 2 April 1942, USHMM/RSA, RG-25.002M, reel 14, file 20/1942, p. 12.

7. Presidency of the Council of Ministers to the SSI, 24 April 1942, USHMM/SRI, RG-25.004M, reel 35, file 40010, vol. 123, p. 1.

8. Police of the Kishinev district to the Orhei police, 2 May 1942, USHMM/SSARM, RG-54.001, reel 2, 666-2-262, p. 7.

9. Communiqué no. 499, *Monitorul Oficial*, no. 152, 3 July 1942.

10. Col. Radu Davidescu, head of Antonescu's military cabinet, to the minister of the interior, 10 July 1942, USHMM/RSA, RG-25.002M, reel 18, file 104/1941, p. 61.

11. Heading of file no. 55, Antonescu's military cabinet, office no. 2 [last document in file, dated 6 October 1942], USHMM/RSA, RG-25.002M, reel 18, file 104/1941, p. 12. The order to deport "to the Bug" was a deliberate slip of the pen, implying deportation right to the edge of the Bug.

12. Order no. 35 issued by Antonescu on 16 July 1942 to the minister of the interior, signed [but not dated] by Davidescu, head of the military cabinet, USHMM/RSA, RG-25.002M, reel 18, file 104/1941, p. 20. See also the order as dictated by Antonescu and written down by Davidescu, including corrections he made while taking down the dictation (pp. 22–24).

13. Addendum to Antonescu's Order no. 35, 17 July 1942, USHMM/RSA, RG-25.002M, reel 18, file 104/1941, pp. 25–26 (author's emphasis).

14. Top secret report by Constantin Caragea, head of the Consular Section of the Foreign Ministry, "concerning the property that had been confiscated from Romanian Jews in Germany," 4 January 1943, USHMM/RMFA, RG-25.006M, reel 7, "Jewish Problem," vol. 16, pp. 472–72b.

15. Foreign Ministry directives on Jews holding expired Romanian passports, 12 October 1942, in Federation of Jewish Communities in Romania, *Evreii din România*, doc. 621, 3:372.

16. Internal memo of the Presidency of the Council of Ministers on the Jewish population in Romania, submitted to Antonescu, containing handwritten notes and decisions, 31 August 1942, in Ancel, *Documents*, vol. 10, doc. 91, pp. 210–15.

17. Interior Minister C. Z. Vasiliu to the General Police Inspectorate, 1 September 1942 (authorized copy), USHMM/SRI, RG-25.004M, reel 32, file 40010, vol. 11, p. 93.

18. List of the names of 414 Jews incarcerated in the Târgu-Jiu camp, their addresses, professions, and reasons for incarceration, drawn up by Col. Gheorghe Zlătescu, 1 September 1942, USHMM/RSA, RG-25.002M, reel 10, file 14/1942, pp. 131–61; 407 of the prisoners were deported. For a list of the names of the 598 Jews, see Ancel, *Documents*, vol. 5, doc. 211, pp. 442–53.

19. Ancel, *Documents*, vol. 5, doc. 232, p. 513.

20. Carp, *Cartea neagră*, 3:241; list of the names of 275 Jews who infringed the laws on forced labor throughout Romania, drawn up by the General Staff, in Ancel, *Documents*, vol. 5, doc. 205, pp. 383–89. They were deported with their families, but the names of their relatives were not included in the list.

21. Sebastian, *Jurnal*, 471.

22. *Encyclopedia of the Holocaust*, 1:190–93.

23. Note of Mihai Antonescu's talk with Gustav Richter in Bucharest, 11 November 1942, in Ancel, *Documents*, vol. 10, doc. 99, p. 242.

24. Memo by Martin Luther from the Foreign Ministry to Rintelen, on the principles

and landmarks in Nazi policy toward the Jews, Berlin, 21 August 1942, Nuremberg Documents, NG-2586J, paragraph 4.

25. Memo by Martin Luther from the Foreign Ministry to Rintelen, on the principles and landmarks in Nazi policy toward the Jews, Berlin, 21 August 1942, Nuremberg Documents, NG-2586J, paragraph 11.

26. Killinger to the Foreign Ministry in Berlin, cable on the Romanian agreement to the deportation of Romanian Jewry to the death camps in Poland, 22 July 1942, YVA, microfilm collection, JM/3124.

27. Luther to Müller, 11 August 1942, in Ancel, *Documents*, vol. 4, doc. 56, pp. 104–5.

28. Memorandum by Luther concerning negotiations for the deportation of Romanian Jewry, 17 August 1942, in Ancel, *Documents*, vol. 4, doc. 60, p. 111.

29. Note by Rintelen to Luther, 19 August 1942, in Ancel, *Documents*, vol. 4, doc. 65, p. 120.

30. "Rumänien wird judenrein," *Bukarester Tageblatt*, 8 August 1942; copy in Ancel, *Documents*, vol. 4, doc. 49, pp. 93–94.

31. "Rumänien wird judenrein," *Bukarester Tageblatt*, 8 August 1942; copy in Ancel, *Documents*, vol. 4, doc. 49, pp. 93–94.

32. "Rumänien wird judenrein," *Bukarester Tageblatt*, 8 August 1942; copy in Ancel, *Documents*, vol. 4, doc. 49, pp. 93–94.

33. "Rumänien wird judenrein," *Bukarester Tageblatt*, 8 August 1942; copy in Ancel, *Documents*, vol. 4, doc. 49, pp. 93–94.

34. Lecca's plan to deport the Jews from southern Transylvania, 11 September 1942, in Ancel, *Documents*, vol. 4, doc. 85, pp. 165–67.

35. Richter's plan to deport all Romanian Jews ("Aussiedlung der Juden aus Rumänien"), 15 September 1942, in Ancel, *Documents*, vol. 5, doc. 96, pp. 190–96.

36. For an analysis of the plans and a broad comparison between them, including a translation of the plans and other documents relating to practical measures for the deportation, see Ancel, "Plans."

37. Address by the Ministry of Romanization to Radu Lecca, enclosing the opinion of the ministry's Research Department, 29 September 1942, and Lecca's response in the margins of the document, in Ancel, *Documents*, vol. 4, doc. 138, pp. 276–78 (author's emphasis).

38. Apart from the frenzy that possessed him when it came to Jews, as reflected in directives and orders to punish and deport them, I found no document or instruction signed by Antonescu from early August until 21 October 1942.

39. Protocol from the meeting between Ribbentrop and Mihai Antonescu, 23 September 1942, in Vinnitsa (excerpts), in United Restitution Organization, *Documentation*, 4:578.

40. Report of Timişoara Police Precinct no. 1, 18 August 1942, USHMM/SRI, RG-25.004M, reel 2, file 10523, vol. 9, pp. 11–12.

41. SSI report of 13 November 1942, USHMM/SRI, RG-25.004M, reel 14, file 2909, vol. 248, p. 303.

42. The relevant documents were published in Ancel, *Documents*, vol. 4, "June–October 1942."

43. Richter's report on Killinger's meeting with Mihai Antonescu, 7 October 1942, U.S. National Archives, Washington DC, Records of the Strategic Services, RG 226, XL, 13178.

44. "Judenknechte," *Bukarester Tageblatt*, 11 October 1942; copy in Ancel, *Documents*, vol. 4, doc. 152, pp. 297–98.

45. SSI report on the article and the response it triggered in Bucharest, 12 October 1942, USHMM/SRI, RG-25.004M, reel 14, file 8180, vol. 6, pp. 84–87.

46. Richter's report, "The Situation of the Deportation of the Jews from Romania," 26 November 1942, in Ancel, *Documents*, vol. 4, doc. 186, pp. 364–65.

47. SSI note of 17 October 1942, "The Slovakian Ambassador and the Jewish Problem," USHMM/RSA, RG-25.002M, reel 16, file 368/1942 (I), p. 4.

36. Postponement of the Nazi Final Solution

1. Protocol of government session of 13 October 1942, USHMM/RSA, RG-25.002M, reel 16, Presidency of the Council of Ministers, file 473/1942 (II), pp. 859–60 (author's emphasis). In the protocol Mihai Antonescu used the neutral term *transfer of Jews* (*trimiteri*) instead of *deportation* (*deportare*). One may assume that in practice everyone used the term *deportation*.

2. Protocol of government session of 13 October 1942, USHMM/RSA, RG-25.002M, reel 16, Presidency of the Council of Ministers, file 473/1942 (II), pp. 860–61.

3. Confidential letter by Mihai Antonescu to General Pantazi, minister of national defense, 23 October 1942 (copy), USHMM/SRI, RG-25.004M, reel 32, file 40010, vol. 9, p. 89.

4. Note in the margins of the request by the director of the CFR [Romanian Railway Authority] to the Presidency of the Council of Ministers, 27 October 1942, in Ancel, *Documents*, vol. 10, doc. 96, p. 236.

5. Note by the SSI on the deportation of Jews in provincial towns, 9 October 1942, USHMM/SRI, RG-25.004M, reel 14, file 2869, vol. 208, pp. 334, 337. The note states that Romanian intellectuals had (successfully) intervened on behalf of the Jewish poet, including the literary critic Eugen Lovinescu, the poet Ion Pillat, the poet Vasile Voiculescu, and Oscar Walter Cisek from the Ministry of Propaganda.

6. Note by the SSI on the deportation of Jews in provincial towns, 9 October 1942, USHMM/SRI, RG-25.004M, reel 14, file 2869, vol. 208, p. 339.

7. Excerpt from Matatias Carp's journal, 14 October, in Ancel, *Documents*, vol. 4, doc. 152, p. 302.

8. SSI report on the marshal's illness, 15 July 1942, USHMM/SRI, RG-25.004M, reel 33, file 40010, vol. 31, p. 288.

9. A study on Antonescu published in Romania in 1993 stated that he was not ill with malaria and that in the summer of 1942 he underwent "a late and terminal stage of syphilis" after having "caught the disease in his youth." Mezincescu, *Mareşalul Antonescu*, 148–49. A late stage of syphilis cannot be discovered in serological examinations. The disease could be diagnosed only if Antonescu himself confessed to having caught it and "after a protracted follow-up of the patient and a rigorous psychiatric examination." Who, however, would have dared to conduct a psychiatric examination of the Conducător? And who could have differentiated between his megalomania and a psychiatric illness?

10. Protocol of government session of 25 June 1942, USHMM/SRI, RG-25.004M, reel

32, file 40010, vol. 9, p. 33. To King Mihai's question as to why he had sent the Romanian army to fight in Russia, Antonescu replied, "The road to Transylvania is through Russia." Gould, *Crown against Sickle*, 34.

11. Note on the talk between Chancellor Hitler and president of the Council of Ministers Antonescu, 22 November 1940, in *Documents on German Foreign Policy*, vol. 11, doc. 381, p. 670.

12. Note by Mihai Antonescu on his talks with Joseph Goebbels in Berlin, 28 November 1940, in Ancel, *Documents*, vol. 9, doc. 106, p. 294 (author's emphasis).

13. Note by Mihai Antonescu on his talk with Hitler in Berlin, 27 November 1941, in Ancel, *Documents*, vol. 9, doc. 105, p. 281.

14. Protocol of the meeting between Ion Antonescu and Hitler in Berlin, 12 February 1942 (Romanian version), in Armin, Ardeleanu, and Lache, *Antonescu-Hitler*, doc. 40, 1:183. Antonescu demanded that the Germans ask Hungary to send large forces to the front and provide the Romanian army with military equipment to enable it to participate in the battle.

15. Schmidt, *Hitler's Interpreter*, 244.

16. Report by the prosecution general in Arad to Mihai Antonescu, 25 September 1942, in Federation of Jewish Communities in Romania, *Evreii din România*, doc. 545, 3:261. Even before (and after) Antonescu's time the prosecution system of the Romanian courts compiled periodic reports on the public mood and submitted them to the Presidency of the Council of Ministers, the Ministry of Justice, or the Siguranța.

17. Report by the Siguranța in the Timișoara district on the Jewish problem, undated [September 1942], USHMM/SRI, RG-25.004M, file 2710, vol. 23, pp. 239–40.

18. Report by the Siguranța bureau in the Bucharest General Police Inspectorate, 28 September 1942 (copy), USHMM/SRI, RG-25.004M, reel 65, file 40015, vol. 2, p. 117; and reel 34, file 40010, vol. 59, p. 67.

19. Report by Siguranța headquarters in Bucharest, 16 October 1942, USHMM/SRI, RG-25.004M, reel 2, file 10523, vol. 9, p. 73.

20. Transcript of the interrogation of Piki Vasiliu, minister of police, in the People's Court, 19 April 1946, USHMM/SRI, RG-25.004M, reel 34, file 40010, vol. 39, p. 190.

21. Nicolae Lupu's letter to Mihai Antonescu, 7 June 1942 (copy), in Ancel, *Documents*, vol. 4, doc. 4, p. 10. The appeal failed. About three thousand Jews were deported by train to the notorious Pechora camp and about four thousand to a similar camp — Skazinets. Most of them perished.

22. Architect Nicolae Clejan to Mihai Antonescu, 9 June 1942 (copy), in Ancel, *Documents*, vol. 4, doc. 5, p. 11.

23. Note by Richter on Baron Neuman and his activities regarding the Jewish problem, 8 September 1942, in Ancel, *Documents*, vol. 4, doc. 82, pp. 159–61.

24. Collection of Siguranța follow-up reports on developments among the Jews [September 1942], USHMM/SRI, RG-25.004M, reel 7, file 10585, vol. 31, p. 116.

25. Note on the deportations by Filderman, submitted to the government, 5 August 1942, in Ancel, *Documents*, vol. 4, doc. 54, p. 99.

26. Memorandum by I. Tenner, delegate of the Timiș-Torontal branch of the Jewish Center (copy), undated [August 1942], in Ancel, *Documents*, vol. 4, doc. 102, pp. 221–23.

27. See, for example, notes by Richter dated 4, 8, 16, and 17 September, which explicitly mentioned "Gingold reports," in Ancel, *Documents*, vol. 4, docs. 81, 82, 105, and 111, pp. 151, 158, 226, and 238. At the time, Wilman made three requests to Filderman to meet with Richter to discuss the deportations, but Filderman refused.

28. "Memorandum to Clarify the Legal Status of the Jews of Transnistria and Banat," in Ancel, *Documents*, vol. 4, doc. 132, pp. 266–69.

29. Interview with Charles Gruber, Paris, June 1997, in author's possession.

30. Memorandum by Filderman, 22 September 1942, in Ancel, *Documents*, vol. 4, no. 69, pp. 118–25 (author's emphasis). Filderman knew that Germany had begun to deport its Jews, but since the Romanian press had failed to mention it, he claimed that the deportation was not from Germany itself, acting on the principle that "we do not know what might influence these madmen."

31. Two notes by an SSI agent in the royal palace, dated 20 August and 18 September 1942, USHMM/SRI, RG-25.004M, reel 14, file 2869, vol. 208, pp. 271–72. Pages 263–70 contain the full text of the petition.

32. Photocopy of the memorandum that a group of Romanian intellectuals delivered to the king, 20 August 1942, USHMM/SRI, RG-25.004M, reel 14, file 2869, vol. 208, pp. 264–65.

33. Photocopy of the memorandum that a group of Romanian intellectuals delivered to the king, 20 August 1942, USHMM/SRI, RG-25.004M, reel 14, file 2869, vol. 208, pp. 266–67 (author's emphasis).

34. USHMM/SRI, RG-25.004M, reel 14, file 2912, vol. 251, p. 247 (emphasis in the original).

35. Excerpt from Matatias Carp's journal, in Ancel, *Documents*, vol. 4, doc. 152, p. 302 (author's emphasis).

36. Filderman's letter to Shertok in the Center for Jewish Documentation, Paris, 18 November 1949, in Ancel, *Documents*, vol. 8, doc. 431, p. 525. Filderman added, "Following the article that Rabbi Safran published concerning his activities and mine, in which the rabbi takes sole credit for the cessation of all the deportations, I consider myself obliged to contest his claim concerning the cessation of the deportations in October 1941, and all other deportations. . . . How come the press attacked me, and I was dismissed from the Bar Association, while the press never mentioned his name, and the rabbi never suffered at all? As to other interventions, as for example the cessation of the general deportation of Romanian Jewry, on this matter too he is lying. . . . I have not yet decided when, but the day shall come in which I shall have no choice but to refute the rabbis' claims, which are totally unfounded."

37. Directive by the Presidency of the Council of Ministers, 22 October 1942, copy in the Kishinev Police Inspectorate, 28 October 1942, USHMM/SSARM, RG-54001, reel 5, 696-1-32, p. 216.

38. Note by the Presidency of the Council of Ministers, 24 October 1942, attached to Minister Vasiliu's letter on the matter, USHMM/RMFA, RG-25.006M, reel 12, "Jewish Problem," vol. 23, pp. 627–28.

39. Interior Ministry to the Presidency of the Council of Ministers, 18 March 1943, USHMM/RMFA, RG-25.006M, reel 13, "Jewish Problem," vol. 24, p. 297.

40. Interior Ministry to the Presidency of the Council of Ministers, 27 August 1943, USHMM/RMFA, RG-25.006M, reel 14, "Jewish Problem," vol. 25, p. 487.

41. Order issued by Marshal Antonescu on 17 April 1943 on the evacuation of Jews from cities that were not district capitals, copy in the Kishinev Police Inspectorate, 22 April 1943, USHMM/SSARM, RG-54001, reel 6, 696-1-84, p. 21.

42. Cristian, *Patru ani de urgie*, 91–92.

43. Memorandum by Filderman to the minister of the interior concerning the government's plan to set up ghettos in Moldova, 25 April 1944, in Ancel, *Documents*, vol. 8, doc. 33, p. 33.

44. Memorandum by the Romanian government concerning measures it adopted to solve the Jewish problem, 26 March 1943, in Ancel, *Documents*, vol. 4, doc. 285, pp. 524–25.

45. Ion Brătescu-Voineşti, "Am văzut pe Mareşal" [I saw the marshal], *Porunca Vremii*, 5 March 1943, copy in Ancel, *Documents*, vol. 4, doc. 266, pp. 491–92.

46. Directive by Ion Antonescu to the General Staff to draw up plans in the event of an evacuation from Transnistria, Bessarabia, and Bukovina, 23 September 1943, YVA, Romanian Collection, 0-11/48.

47. Antonescu's letter to architect Nicolae Clejan, 4 February 1944, in Ancel, *Documents*, vol. 8, doc. 13, p. 19.

48. Antonescu's letter to architect Nicolae Clejan, 4 February 1944, in Ancel, *Documents*, vol. 8, doc. 13, p. 19.

49. De Weck, "Journal," entry for late March 1943.

50. SSI report of 24 November 1942, USHMM/SRI, RG-25.004M, reel 14, file 2909, vol. 248, p. 373.

51. Cable by Nicolae Dumitrescu, the Romanian ambassador in Madrid, to the Foreign Ministry in Bucharest, on the terrible impression created by an anti-Romanian book published by the Hungarian government, with shocking details and pictures of crimes against Romanian Jews, 10 January 1943, in Hîncu, *Un licăr în beznă*, 56.

52. Secret directive by the interior minister in Antonescu's name to the foreign minister to allow Jews of Romanian nationality residing in Germany and in occupied countries to return to Romania, 19 July 1943, in Hîncu, *Un licăr în beznă*, 63.

53. Collection of protocols of government sessions in 1942, USHMM/SRI, RG-25.004M, reel 14, file 8180, vol. 6, p. 110.

54. Cable by Killinger to the Foreign Ministry in Berlin, 12 December 1942, in Ancel, *Documents*, vol. 4, doc. 203, p. 399.

37. Jews in the Shadow of the Final Solution

1. Urgent order by General Antonescu for the evacuation of all Jews from the villages of Moldova, the incarceration of men in the Târgu-Jiu camp, and the evacuation of Jews from the other villages of Romania and their transfer to district cities, 21 June 1941, in Ancel, *Documents*, vol. 2, doc. 126, pp. 414–15.

2. In 1942, in a survey of the Jewish population in Romania, Filderman determined that 38,920 Jews had been evacuated from their localities in June–July 1941. This number did not include subsequent evacuations. See "Data on the Jewish Population, 1942," YVA, Filderman Archive, P-6/49, pp. 6–7. See tables 8 and 9 herein for data on the communities that were

liquidated following the evacuation of the Jews from the camps in southern Romania or to cities and towns in the districts in which they resided.

3. Appeal by the Federation of Jewish Communities of Romania to the minister of the interior concerning the purchase of war bonds by Jews, 31 July 1941, in Ancel, *Documents*, vol. 2, doc. 197, p. 492.

4. Jewish Center, table of the localities from which Jews were evacuated and the places to which they were transferred, 13 May 1942, in Ancel, *Documents*, vol. 3, doc. 368, pp. 598–611.

5. Memorandum by the Jewish Federation to the minister of the interior together with proposals for the relocation to cities of the Jewish population who had been evacuated from the villages of Transylvania and Banat, 27 July 1941, in Ancel, *Documents*, vol. 3, doc. 187, pp. 479–81.

6. Joint memorandum of the Moineşti and Târgu-Ocna communities, which were evacuated to Bacău, Filderman's copy, 1 March 1942, in Ancel, *Documents*, vol. 3, doc. 342, pp. 550–52.

7. Ministry of the Interior to the Târgu-Ocna community in Bacău, 22 May 1942, in Ancel, *Documents*, vol. 3, doc. 373, p. 624.

8. Ion Antonescu to Mihai Antonescu, 3 September 1941, USHMM/RSA, RG-25.002M, reel 18, Presidency of the Council of Ministers, file 167/1941, p. 46.

9. Memorandum of the Union of Jewish Communities of the Regat to the minister of the interior on the detention of Jewish hostages in Romania, 8 July 1941, in Ancel, *Documents*, vol. 2, doc. 166, pp. 451–52.

10. Order no. 4598 of the minister of the interior, 30 June 1941, USHMM/SRI, RG-25.004M, reel 25, file 20725, vol. 9, p. 301.

11. SSI list of eighty-four Jewish dignitaries in the capital who were declared hostages, USHMM/SRI, RG-25.004M, reel 14, file 2960, vol. 300, pp. 52–57.

12. Order no. 19935 of the Ministry of the Interior, 16 October 1941, YVA, Romanian Collection, o-11/49a, p. 77.

13. Order no. 37215 of the Ministry of the Interior, 9 April 1942 (SSI copy), USHMM/SRI, RG-25.004M, reel 10, file 2699, vol. 22, pp. 486–87.

14. List by Siguranţa agent Gheorghe Năstase of Iaşi, 9 January 1942, USHMM/SRI, RG-25.004M, reel 8, file 7635, vol. 2, p. 754.

15. Order by the police commander of Bacău on the obligation to wear a yellow badge, 4 July 1941, in Ancel, *Documents*, vol. 2, doc. 157, p. 441.

16. Minutes of government session, 5 August 1941 (excerpt), USHMM/SRI, RG-25.004M, reel 32, file 40010, vol. 11, p. 45.

17. Secretary general of the Ministry of the Interior to the Presidency of the Council of Ministers on the understanding concerning the introduction of the yellow badge, 15 August 1941, USHMM/RSA, RG-25.002M, reel 17, Presidency of the Council of Ministers, file 86/1941, p. 69.

18. Report from the cross-examination of the accused, Dumitru Popescu, in the People's Court, 16 July 1945, USHMM/SRI, RG-25.004M, reel 32, file 40010, vol. 11, p. 10.

19. Minutes of the government session of 9 September 1941, USHMM/SRI, RG-25.004M, reel 35, file 40010, vol. 77, pp. 51b–52b.

20. Decree no. 3303/1941 issued by War Headquarters, obliging the Jews of Moldova, Bessarabia, Bukovina, and "east of the Dniester" [Transnistria] to wear the yellow badge, which was 7x7 centimeters, on a black background, 8 August 1941, USHMM/MSM, RG-25.003M, reel 11, fond: Fourth Army, file 799, p. 138.

21. Filderman's diary entry on the session with Gen. Radu Gheorghe, police commander of the capital, 4 September 1941, in Ancel, *Documents*, vol. 3, doc. 62, p. 115.

22. Testimony of Lieba Iţic Aizic of Târgu Neamţ, Jaffa, 28 December 1959, YVA, 03-1547, p. 2.

23. Testimony of Arthur Axenfeld, "Memoirs of a Jewish Communal Worker," Tel Aviv, 15 February 1960, YVA, 03-1550, p. 13.

24. *Bukarester Tageblatt*, 20 December 1942.

25. Appeal by the Union of Jewish Communities to the minister of the interior, 4 August 1941, in Ancel, *Documents*, vol. 2, doc. 204, p. 500.

26. Confidential report by the Ministry of the Interior on the situation in the Galaţi camp, 17 September 1941, USHMM/RSA, RG-25.002M, reel 18, Presidency of the Council of Ministers Cabinet, file 86/1941, p. 144.

27. Intelligence report issued by the Central Intelligence Service in the Presidency of the Council of Ministers on the situation of the Jews in the Covurlui district, 25 August 1941, USHMM/RSA, RG-25.002M, reel 18, Presidency of the Council of Ministers, file 86/1941, p. 141.

28. Report no. 2037, issued by the Gendarmerie Inspectorate in the Galaţi district, 8 September 1941, USHMM/SRI, RG-25.004M, reel 66, file 18844, vol. 4, p. 341.

29. Intelligence report by Col. Vasile Sachelarie, commander of the railway gendarmerie legion, 16 August 1941, USHMM/RSA, RG-25.002M, reel 18, Presidency of the Council of Ministers, file 86/1941, p. 467.

30. Order no. 7639 issued by the Ministry of the Interior to send back 6,774 evacuees to district cities, 21 August 1941, and list of camps and of Jews to be sent back, USHMM/SRI, RG-25.004M, reel 25, file 20725, vol. 9, pp. 304, 304b. About 1,000 survivors of the death train were sent back to Iaşi from Calaraşi with these Jews.

31. Collection of reports by the commanders of gendarmerie legions throughout Romania on the detention camps in the cities and the district, forced labor, supervision of the camps, the public mood, and the like, September 1941, USHMM/SRI, RG-25.004M, reel 25, file 20725, vol. 9, pp. 550–74. Since the Ministry of the Interior's order did not distinguish between the camps of Romania proper and the camps of Bessarabia, important reports were received on the fate of the Jews in detention camps in Bessarabia.

32. Minutes of the government session of 9 September 1941 (excerpts), USHMM/SRI, RG-25.004M, reel 35, file 40010, vol. 77, p. 52 (author's emphasis).

33. Minutes of the government session of 12 September 1941, in Benjamin, *Problema evreiască*, doc. 110, p. 317.

34. Memorandum by the Jewish Federation to the Ministry of the Interior, mentioning the Conducător's promise, 5 September 1941, in Ancel, *Documents*, vol. 3, doc. 63, p. 117; report on the meeting between eleven Jewish public figures and Finance Minister Stoenescu that took place at his behest, concerning the obligation to purchase war bonds in the amount

of 10 billion lei, 29 October 1941, YVA, Carp Archive, vol. 3, p. 374. In the meeting the minister repeated the Conducător's promise that "he vouched for the lives of the Jews."

35. Appeal by the Jewish Federation to the minister of the interior, 31 July 1941, in Ancel, *Documents*, vol. 2, doc. 197, p. 492.

36. Circular by the Jewish Federation to the heads of communities, 16 September 1941, USHMM/RSA, RG-25.002M, reel 17, Presidency of the Council of Ministers, file 86/1941, p. 216.

37. Order by the Ministry of the Interior to the General Police Inspectorate to provide the Jewish Federation with the addresses of Jewish taxpayers whose addresses did not appear on the list of tenants, so that they could contribute to the loan (copy), USHMM/SRI, RG-25.004M, reel 6, file 7635, vol. 2, p. 138.

38. Urgent instruction by the second military territorial command to the Union of Jewish Communities to provide the military hospitals with equipment, including a specification of the equipment (copy), 3 September 1941, in Ancel, *Documents*, vol. 3, doc. 53, p. 104.

39. Instruction by the head of the Military Center for the Collection of Confiscated Goods to the Union of Jewish Communities, 5 September 1941 (copy), in Ancel, *Documents*, vol. 3, doc. 64, p. 118.

40. Instruction by the head of the Military Center for the Collection of Confiscated Goods to the Union of Jewish Communities for the delivery of five hundred wooden beds, 7 September 1941 (copy), in Ancel, *Documents*, vol. 3, doc. 71, p. 127; list of belongings handed over by the Union of Jewish Communities up to 19 October 1941, in Ancel, *Documents*, vol. 3, doc. 168, p. 263.

41. Decree-Law no. 2909, *Monitorul Oficial*, no. 250, 21 October 1941. See also *Renaşterea Noastră*, no. 773, 25 October 1941; copy in Ancel, *Documents*, vol. 3, doc. 186, p. 285.

42. Memorandum by Matias Wilman (Grinberg) [Richter's Jewish assistant] to the People's Court, undated [1945], USHMM/SRI, RG-25.004M, reel 28, file 40017, vol. 5, p. 1.

43. Circular of 17 June 1943 from the Kishinev police, containing Justice Ministry statistics on forty-four thousand Jews who failed to hand over items and on the ransom paid in exchange, USHMM/SSARM, RG-54.001, reel 6, 696-1-157, p. 75.

44. Decree no. 152, *Monitorul Oficial*, no. 15, 19 January 1942.

45. Instruction by Radu Lecca to the Jewish Center in Antonescu's name to pay a tax of 4 billion lei, 11 May 1943, in Ancel, *Documents*, vol. 4, doc. 307, p. 566.

46. Memorandum by Filderman to the minister of the interior concerning the order to evacuate sixteen thousand Jews from the towns, 6 May 1943, including statistical data on the towns and the number of Jews to be evacuated, in Ancel, *Documents*, vol. 4, doc. 303, pp. 558–61; memorandum by Filderman to Minister Vasiliu on the order to deport foreign Jews to Transnistria, 30 April 1943, in Ancel, *Documents*, vol. 4, doc. 299, p. 550.

47. In addition to the sources cited in table 11, see Radu Lecca's directive to the Jewish Center of 1 July 1943 to provide the Welfare Council with 410 million lei from the money collected from Jews for exemptions from forced labor, 10 February 1944, in Ancel, *Documents*, vol. 7, doc. 517, p. 679; section on Radu Lecca in the indictment against the Antonescu regime quoting the sum of 1,264,813,800 lei that was transferred to the League for Social Action [Liga Operelor Sociale; formerly the Welfare Council] in 1943–44, 29 April 1946, USHMM/

SRI, RG-25.004M, reel 31, file 40010, vol. 1, p. 172. Ancel, *Documents*, vol. 7, contains most of the orders for payment, statements of income and expenditure, and instructions to donate money to institutions, organizations, municipalities, churches, and the like. It is not easy to estimate how much the taxes were in real terms. Between May 1941 and May 1944 the dollar rose fivefold or more. In September 1940 the official dollar rate was less than 100 lei, and on 20 June 1941 the official dollar rate was 200 lei. YVA, Carp Archive, vol. 3, p. 342. By March 1943 it had doubled to 400 lei. Carp, *Cartea neagră*, 3:293. The Jews also handed over numerous articles of clothing: 204,717 shirts, 203,790 pairs of underpants, 205,775 pairs of socks, 359,505 handkerchiefs, 203,373 towels, 104,841 sweaters, 80,103 suits, 67,894 pairs of shoes, 23,431 winter and summer hats, 21,441 blankets, 23,095 sheets, 65,805 duvet covers and pillow cases, and 20,139 winter coats, as well as hospital equipment (including medical instruments belonging to Jewish physicians and dentists, most of which were confiscated), Jewish hospitals with all their equipment, and the like. Thousands of homes and their contents also were turned into apartments for Romanian and German officers. No estimate has yet been carried out on the extent of the robbery, extortion, and expropriation of Jewish property by the Romanian state and its citizens.

48. Memorandum by Ion Antonescu submitted to the People's Court on 15 May 1946, USHMM/SRI, RG-25.004M, reel 31, file 40010, vol. 4, pp. 29, 32–33.

49. Partial data published by the Antonescu regime on the provincial towns merely state that Jewish property worth over 1 billion lei was sold for 216 million lei. Of this, the Jews were paid only 52 million lei—mostly from money that had been stolen from the Jews in the first place. The official data represent only the tip of the iceberg of the theft of Jewish property under the Legionary regime. See *Pe marginea prăpastiei*, 1:135.

50. *Trei ani de guvernare*, 144–45.

51. "Regulament asupra decretului—lege relativ la statutul militar al Evreilor," *Monitorul Oficial*, pt. 1, no. 164, 14 July 1941, pp. 5–8.

52. Decree-Law no. 3205, *Monitorul Oficial*, 16 November 1941.

53. General instructions by the General Staff, no. 55500, concerning forced labor for Jews, 27 June 1942, in Ancel, *Documents*, vol. 4, doc. 21, pp. 32–44.

54. Collection of laws and orders on Jewish affairs, YVA, 011-49a, p. 119.

55. Directive by Antonescu's military cabinet to the Ministry of the Interior to prepare an assessment of the number of Jews and how they were used in forced labor, 28 October 1941, USHMM/RSA, RG-25.002M, reel 18, Presidency of the Council of Ministers, file 86/1941, p. 248.

56. These Jews were not traced, despite searches, threats, and investigations that were carried out up to August 1944. This category included 13,868 Jewish men whom the Iaşi recruitment center was unable to trace in the summer of 1942 or even after (see chap. 33). Most of them were murdered in the Iaşi pogrom. The recruitment center's lists also included Jews who had died, emigrated, moved, and the like or whose addresses had not been updated due to lack of coordination, although they were recruited at their new addresses.

57. List of external forced labor detachments, testimony of Dadu Rosenkrantz, director of the Jewish Center's Department of Professional Rehabilitation, responsible for issues relating to forced labor, YVA, 011/39, pp. 32–33.

58. For a table of the number of exemption certificates granted in April 1943 and their breakdown by category, see Ancel, *Documents*, vol. 7, doc. 425, p. 583.

59. R. Lecca, *Eu i-am salvat*, 181–82. Lecca was sentenced to life imprisonment in 1946 and was released in 1964. Lecca's memoirs were written at the Securitate's request, while he served his prison sentence. Lecca's assignment was to leave an authentic document, as it were, on the Holocaust in Romania. However, the memoirs clearly contain the crude imprint of members of the Securitate, who concocted proof of the humanitarianism of the Romanian people and of the Nazis' exclusive guilt for the Holocaust of Romanian Jewry, including the Iaşi pogrom. The memoirs contain gross distortions of events, dates, and personalities, while accounts of Lecca's extortion racket and how it made him rich are interspersed with lies ordered from above and lies that he himself managed to insinuate—such as hiding the fact that in August 1942 he had visited Berlin to discuss the implementation of the general plan to exterminate the Jews (he reported this meeting as having taken place in the winter of 1943–44) and lies concerning the Iaşi pogrom, the executions in Bogdanovka, and the like. However, the memoirs also contain reliable and important details on extortion techniques, the interactions among the various authorities dealing with the Jews, the rivalries among them, and the involvement of the regime's leaders in the creation of a system of persecution of Jews. It is evident that Lecca's intelligence and cunning far surpassed those of his interrogators and jailers. The memoirs were published by a nationalist publishing house that resurfaced after the collapse of the Communist regime in Romania.

38. Data on the Holocaust in Romania

1. In 1939 Dr. Sabin Manuilă of the Romanian Academy reviewed the results of the 1930 general census of the Jewish population, data on the number of Jewish schoolchildren and the number of Jewish army recruits, and data from the 1938 revision of citizenship and reached the conclusion that "the number of Jews in 1930 was fewer than 800,000." See *Curierul Israelit*, 17 December 1944. For the survey itself, see S. Manuilă, "Consideraţiuni asupra prezentării grafice a etnografiei României," Academia Română, Bucharest, Memoriile Secţiunii istorice, seria 3, 1939, tomul 21, memoriul 14, anexa 3.

2. "Rezultatele recensământului" [Results of the census], *Universul*, 15 June 1941; copy in Ancel, *Documents*, vol. 1, doc. 133, p. 411. Romania also ceded a small territory to Bulgaria, southern Dobruja, which according to the 1930 census had 846 Jews.

3. "The census of the Jews in the camps of Bessarabia shall be supervised by the camp commander in the presence of a representative of the local recruitment bureau." Special order by the Third Territorial Command for Administering the Headcount, 15 September 1941, USHMM/SSARM, RG-54.001, reel 2, 693-2-299, p. 99.

4. Killinger to Foreign Ministry in Berlin, 16 August 1941, *Documents on German Foreign Policy*, vol. 13, doc. 207, pp. 318–19.

5. Niculescu report, USHMM/RMFA, RG-25.006M, reel 11, "Jewish Problem," vol. 20.

6. Carp, *Cartea neagră*, 3:182.

7. Letter by the governor of Bukovina to the Presidency of the Council of Ministers with data on the scale of the deportation in 1941 in Bukovina, 9 April 1942, USHMM/RMFA, RG-25.006M, reel 11, "Jewish Problem," vol. 20, p. 130.

8. Niculescu report, USHMM/RMFA, RG-25.006M, reel 11, "Jewish Problem," vol. 20.

9. Centrala Evreilor din România, Rezultatele recensământului locuitorilor având sângee evreesc efectuat de Guvernământul Bucovinei [Results of the census of residents of Jewish blood in Bukovina], booklet, 20 July 1942; copy in Ancel, *Documents*, vol. 1, doc. 43, p. 287.

10. Order to the governors, issued by Ovidiu Vlădescu, 14 August 1942, USHMM/RMFA, RG-25.006M, reel 11, "Jewish Problem," vol. 20, p. 164.

11. Report by the governor of Bukovina on the deportations at the end of the summer 1942 and proposals for further deportations, 21 August 1942, USHMM/RMFA, RG-25.006M, reel 11, "Jewish Problem," vol. 20, p. 162.

12. Protocol of the conversation between the Romanian Foreign Ministry's secretary general, Gheorghe Davidescu, and Dr. Gerhard Stelzer, advisor to the German legation in Bucharest, 13 March 1942, USHMM/RMFA, RG-25.006M, reel 7, "Jewish Problem," vol. 16, p. 58.

13. Secretary general of the Presidency of the Council of Ministers, Ovidiu Vlădescu, to the governors of Bessarabia, Bukovina, and Transnistria, 22 July 1942, and reissue of this directive, 14 August 1942, USHMM/RMFA, RG-25.006M, reel 10, "Jewish Problem," vol. 21, pp. 166, 263.

14. Gendarmerie commander in Transnistria to the Transnistrian administration, data on the stages of the deportation of Jews from Transnistria, 9 September 1942, USHMM/RMFA, RG-25.006M, reel 10, "Jewish Problem," vol. 21, p. 161. Note that he forgot to use the code word *evacuation*, and wrote *deportation* instead.

15. On figures for the Golta district, see a report by Isopescu to the administration regarding the transport of Jews with a request that the administration stop sending them, 13 November 1941, USHMM, NOA, RG-31.008M, 2178-1-66, p. 151. On the Dalnic figures, see Obkom report, Partinii Arhiv, Odescovo obkoma Kompartii Ukraini, fond II, opis II, delo 52, p. 22. On the figures for western Transnistria, see SSI report to the Presidency of the Council of Ministers on the transfer of the Jews east of the Zhmerinca-Odessa railway line, 24 December 1941, USHMM/RSA, RG-25.002M, reel 18, Presidency of the Council of Ministers, Military Cabinet, file 86/1941, pp. 325–27.

16. The findings of the population census that the Soviet authorities conducted on 17 January 1939 remained classified for over fifty years. The territory that was later called Transnistria included the district of Odessa and part of the Vinnitsa district. There were 233,155 Jews in the Odessa district at the time and 141,825 Jews in the entire Vinnitsa district. However, at least 43,444 Jews lived in a region that was incorporated into the German side of the district two years later. It is also possible to ascertain that on the eve of the outbreak of war there were 331,636 Jews in Transnistria. In Odessa alone there were 200,961 Jews. See Altshuler, *Distribution of the Jewish Population*, 11, 21, 23.

17. Report by the Gendarmerie Inspectorate General in Bucharest on the number of Jews in Transnistria, their distribution, and the places from which they were deported, as follows: Bessarabia, Bukovina, the Regat, and locals, December 1942 (copy), USHMM/SRI, RG-25.004M, reel 25, file 20725, vol. 9, p. 291.

18. Data from Interior Ministry on the number of Jews in the ghettos of Transnistria,

"without the locals," as handed over to Filderman shortly before the start of the repatriation of the deportees, 17 November 1943, in Ancel, *Documents*, vol. 5, doc. 236, p. 518.

19. Radu Lecca to Marshal Antonescu on ways of implementing the governor's decision to repatriate the deportees, 20 November 1943, in Ancel, *Documents*, vol. 7, doc. 393, p. 547.

20. Niculescu report, USHMM / RMFA, RG-25.006M, reel 11, "Jewish Problem," vol. 20.

21. Congresul Mondial Evreesc, *Populația evreească*, 39n1.

22. Congresul Mondial Evreesc, *Populația evreească*, 39.

23. Centrala Evreilor din România, "Buletinul demografic al populației evreești din România" [Demographic bulletin of the Jewish population in Romania], no. 1 (June 1943): 6.

24. Centrala Evreilor din România, "Buletinul demografic al populației evreești din România" [Demographic bulletin of the Jewish population in Romania], no. 10 (April 1944): 2.

25. Arthur Golopenția to Gustav Richter on the number of Jews in Romania and their distribution in various regions, 18 June 1942, in Ancel, *Documents*, vol. 1, doc. 39, p. 279.

26. Summary of the data on the census of people of Jewish blood conducted by Richter, undated [1942], in Ancel, *Documents*, vol. 1, doc. 44, pp. 294–95.

27. *Die Bevölkerungszählung*, 24; copy in Ancel, *Documents*, vol. 1, doc. 47, p. 332.

28. Concerning the differences between the number of the victims of the Holocaust in Romania in Ancel's evaluation and the number provided by the International Commission on the Holocaust in Romania (Frieling, Ioanid, and Ionescu, *Final Report*, 381–82), Jean Ancel explained in a letter to the editorial board of the University of Nebraska Press in March 2003: "I have not changed my conclusions about the statistics of Jewish victims of the Holocaust in Romania and Transnistria: at least 410,000 Jews of whom 220,000–230,000 were Romanian Jews and 180,000 Ukrainian. But the numbers in the Wiesel Report are the result of a compromise between my numbers and those of others. I had to choose between signing the Report or resigning. I decided to sign, because for me it was more important that for the first time the Romanian state recognized its responsibility for the crimes committed against the Jewish people."

Bibliography

This bibliography was compiled by Dr. Miriam Caloianu. Immediately below is a selection of important recent works on topics connected with the Romanian chapter of the Holocaust that have not been cited in the notes. Following that is a list of sources cited in the notes.

Deletant, Dennis. *Hitler's Forgotten Ally*. London: Palgrave Macmillan, 2006.

Dumitru, Diana. "The Attitude of the Non-Jewish Population of Bessarabia and Transnistria to the Jews during the Holocaust: A Survivors' Perspective." *Yad Vashem Studies* 37, no. 1 (2009): 53–83.

Friling, Tuvia, Radu Ioanid, and Mihail E. Ionescu, eds. *Final Report: International Commission on the Holocaust in Romania*. Iaşi, Romania: Polirom, 2005.

Hausleitner, Mariana, Brigitte Mihok, and Juliane Wetzel, eds. *Rumänien und der Holocaust: Zu den Massenverbrechen in Transnistrien 1941–1944*. Berlin: Metropol, 2001.

Heinen, Armin. *Rumänien, der Holocaust und die Logik der Gewalt*. Munich: R. Oldenbourg Verlag, 2007.

Ioanid, Radu. *The Holocaust in Romania: The Destruction of Jews and Gypsies under the Antonescu Regime, 1940–1944*. Translated by Marc J. Masurovsky. Chicago: Ivan R. Dee, 2000.

Laigniel-Lavastine, Alexandra. Introduction to *Cartea neagra: Le livre noir de la destruction des Juifs de Roumanie, 1940–1944*, by Matatias Carp. Paris: Denoël, 2009.

Solonari, Vladimir. "'Model Province': Explaining the Holocaust of Bessarabian and Bukovinian Jewry." *Nationalities Papers* 34, no. 4 (September 2006): 471–500.

———. "Patterns of Violence: The Local Population and the Mass Murder of Jews in Bessarabia and Northern Bukovina, July–August 1941." *Kritika* 8, no. 4 (Fall 2007): 749–87.

§

Achim, Viorel, ed. *Documente privind deportarea ţiganilor în Transniatria* [Documents on the deportation of Gypsies to Transnistria]. Bucharest: Editura Enciclopedică, 2004.

Achim, Viorel, and Constantin Iordachi, eds. *Romania şi Transnistria: Problema Holocaustului*. Bucharest: Curtea Veche, 2004.

Activitatea Comisiei Autonome de Ajutorare [Activities of the Autonomous Assistance Committee]. Bucharest: 1944.

Actul de acuzare, rechizitoriile şi replica acuzării în procesul primului lot de criminali de răsboi [Indictment, remarks by the prosecution, and response by the defense in the trial of the first group of war criminals]. Bucharest: Editura Apărării Patriotice, 1945.

Akten zur deutschen auswärtigen Politik, 1933–1945. Baden-Baden, Germany: Frankfurt und Göttingen, 1950–82.

Alexandrescu, Ion. *Economia României în primii ani postbelici* [Romania's economy in the early postwar years]. Bucharest: Editura Politică, 1986.

Altshuler, Mordechai, ed. *Distribution of the Jewish population of the USSR 1939*. Jerusalem: Hebrew University, 1993.

Ambri, Mariano. *I falsi fascismi: Ungheria, Jugoslavia, Romania, 1919–1945*. Rome: Jouvence, 1980.

Ancel, Jean. "Antonescu and the Jews." *Yad Vashem Studies* 23 (1993): 213–80.

———. *Contributii la istoria României*. Bucharest: Haseter, 2003.

———, ed. *Documents Concerning the Fate of Romanian Jewry*. 12 vols. Jerusalem: Beate Klarsfeld Foundation, 1986.

———. "German-Romanian Relations during the Second World War." In *The Tragedy of Romanian Jewry*, ed. Randolph L. Braham, 57–76. New York: Columbia University Press, 1994.

———. "The German-Romanian Relationship and the Final Solution." *Holocaust and Genocide Studies* 19, no. 2 (Fall 2005): 252–75.

———. *Hakdamah leretsah: Peraot Yasi, 29 beyuni 1941* [Prelude to murder: The pogrom in Jassy, 29 June 1941]. Jerusalem: Yad Vashem, 2003. (In Hebrew.)

———. "The Image of the Jew in the View of the Romanian Anti-Semite: Continuity and Change." In *Shvut 16*, 39–57. Tel Aviv: Diaspora Research Institute, Tel Aviv University, 1993.

———. "The Impact of the Course of the War on Romanian Jewish Policies." In *The Shoah and the War*, ed. Asher Cohen, Yehoyakim Cohavi, and Yoav Gelber, 177–210. New York: Peter Lang, 1992.

———. "The Jassy Syndrome." Pts. 1 and 2. *Romanian Jewish Studies* (Jerusalem) 1, no. 1 (Spring 1987): 33–50; 1, no. 2 (Winter 1987): 35–53.

———. "Plans for the Deportation of Romanian Jews, and their Discontinuation in the Light of Documentary Evidence, July–October 1942." *Yad Vashem Studies* 16 (1984): 381–420.

———. "The Romanian Campaigns of Mass Murder in Transnistria, 1941–1942." In *The Destruction of Romanian and Ukrainian Jews during the Antonescu Era*, ed. Randolph L. Braham, 87–133. New York: Columbia University Press, 1997.

———. "Romanian Jewry between 23.8.1944 and 30.12.1947." Doctoral thesis, Hebrew University of Jerusalem, 1979. (In Hebrew.)

———. "Tragedia romilor și tragedia evreilor din România: Asemănări și deosebiri." Introduction to *Romane asva: Lacrimi Rome*, by Luminița Mihai Cioabă. Sibiu, Romania: Ro Media, 2006.

———. *Transnistria, 1941–1942: The Romanian Mass Murder Campaigns*. 3 vols. Tel Aviv: Goldstein-Goren Diaspora Research Center, Tel Aviv University, 2003.

Angrick, Andrej. "The Escalation of German-Rumanian Anti-Jewish Policy after the Attack on the Soviet Union." *Yad Vashem Studies* 26 (1998): 203–38.

Antonescu, Ion. *Către români . . . chemări, cuvântări, documente*. 2nd ed. Bucharest: 1941.

Antonescu, Mihai A. *In serviciul justiției românești* [In the service of Romanian justice]. Bucharest: 1941.

———. *Pentru Basarabia și Bucovina: Îndrumări date administrației desrobitoare* [For

Bessarabia and Bukovina: Guidelines for the liberation administration]. Bucharest: 1941.

Apel către toţi românii. Bucharest: 1922.

Arad, Yitzhak, Shmuel Krakovski, and Shmuel Spector, eds. *The Einsatzgruppen Reports: Selections from the Dispatches of the Nazi Death Squads' Campaign against the Jews: July 1941–January 1943.* New York: Holocaust Library, 1989.

Armin, V., I. Ardeleanu, and S. Lache, eds. *Antonescu-Hitler: Corespondenţă şi întîlniri inedite (1940–1944)* [Antonescu and Hitler: Unpublished correspondence and meetings, 1940–1944]. Vol. 1. Bucharest: Cozia, 1991.

Axenfeld, Arthur. "Gezerot kalkaliyot neged yehudei romania bein shtei milhamot ha-olam" [Economic decrees against Romanian Jewry in the interwar period]. *Toladot* 11 (Kislev 5736/1975): 5–8.

Bălan, N. N. *Studiu asupra Francmasoneriei.* Bucharest: 1937.

Barbul, G. *Mémorial Antonesco: Le troisième homme de l'axe.* Vol. 1. Paris: Editions de la Couronne, 1950.

Baumont, Maurice, ed. *Les archives secrètes de la Wilhelmstrasse.* Vol. 5. Paris: Plon, 1950.

Benjamin, Lya, ed. *Problema evreiască în stenogramele Consiliului de Miniştri* [The Jewish problem in the Council of Ministers' transcripts]. Bucharest: Hasefer, 1996.

Bernstein, S. *Les persécution des Juifs en Roumanie.* Copenhagen: Edition du Bureau de l'Organisation Sioniste, 1918.

Bikel, Shlomo. *Yahadut Romania* [Romanian Jewry]. Tel Aviv: 1978. (In Hebrew.)

Brătescu-Voineşti, Ioan Alexandru. *Huliganism.* Bucharest: Editura Tip. Ziarului Universul, 1938.

Brestoiu, Horia. *O istorie mai puţin obişnuită: În culisele frontului secret din România* [An atypical history]. Bucharest: Editura Politică, 1987.

Brunea-Fox, F. *Oraşul măcelului: Jurnalul rebeliunei şi crimelor legionare* [City of carnage: Diary of the rebellion and Legionary crimes]. Bucharest: Luceafărul S.A.R., 1944.

Buchsweiler, Meir. *Ethnic Germans in the Ukraine toward the Second World War.* Tel Aviv: Society for Jewish Historical Research, Diaspora Research Institute, 1980. (In Hebrew.)

Bulei, Ion. "Romania's Situation in Summer 1940 and Its Repercussions on the Jewish Population." Unpublished stencil, copy in Yad Vashem Library. Paper presented at the Second Symposium of Israeli and Romanian Historians, Yad Vashem, January 1986.

Buletinul demografic al României (Bucharest) 5, no. 3 (March 1936).

Calafeteanu, Ion. "Les relations économiques germano-roumaines de 1933 à 1944." *Revue d'histoire de la 2e guerre mondiale* (Bucharest) 140 (1985).

Călinescu, Armand. *Însemnări politice.* Bucharest: Humanitas, 1990.

Carp, Matatias. *Cartea neagră. Suferinţele evreilor din România, 1940–1944* [The black book]. 3 vols. Bucharest: Atelierele Grafice Socec, 1946–47.

Centrala Evreilor din România [Jewish Center]. *Breviarul statistic al populaţiei evreeşti din România* [Results of the census of residents of Jewish blood]. Bucharest: 1943.

Ciano, Galeazzo. *Journal politique, 1939–1943.* 2 vols. Neuchâtel, Switzerland: Edition de la Baconnière, [1948].

Ciucă, Marcel Dumitru, and Maria Ignat, eds. *Stenogramele sedinţelor Consiliului de Miniştri: Guvernarea Ion Antonescu* [Shorthand notes of the Council of Ministers sessions: Antonescu's government]. Vol. 5. Bucharest: Romanian National Archive, 2001.

Codreanu, Corneliu Zelea. *Circulări şi manifeste*. Madrid: Colecţia "Omul Nou," 1951.

———. *Pentru Legionari* [For my Legionaries]. Sibiu, Romania: 1936. Translated as *For My Legionaries: The Iron Guard*. Madrid: Editura Libertatea, 1976.

Colesco, L. *La population de réligion mosaïque en Roumanie: Etude statistique*. Bucharest: 1915.

Comandamentul Militar al Capitalei, ed. *Asasinatele dela Jilava . . . Snagov şi Strejnicul, 26–27 noemvrie 1940* [The assassinations in Jilava, Snagov, and Strejnicul, 26–27 November 1940]. Bucharest: Monitorul Oficial şi Imprimeriile Statului, 1941.

Comisia Română de Istorie Militară, ed. *File din istoria militară a poporului român* [Pages from the military history of the Romanian people]. 15 vols. Bucharest: Editura Militară, 1974–84.

Congrès Juif Mondial. *Le régime légionnaire et sa solution du problème juif.* Bucharest: 1945.

Congresul Mondial Evreesc [World Jewish Congress, Division: Romania]. *Populaţia evreească în cifre: Memento statistic* [Jewish population in figures: Statistical review]. Bucharest: 1945.

Conta, Vasile. *Cine sunt jidanii? Primejdia jidovească . . .* [Who are the Yids? The danger of the Yids]. Bucharest: 1922.

Cristian, S. C. *Patru ani de urgie* [Four years of disaster]. Bucharest: Editura Timpul S.A. Sărindar, 1945.

Cuza, A. C. *Invăţătura lui Isus, Judaismul şi teologia creştină* [The doctrine of Jesus, Judaism and Christian theology]. Iassy, Romania: Editura LANC, 1925.

———. *Jidanii în război*. Bucharest: 1923.

Dagani, Arnold. *Groapa e în livada de vişini*. Bucharest: 1946. German translation: *Lasst mich leben* [Let me live]. Translated and introduced by Siegfried Rosenzweig. Tel Aviv: 1960.

Dallin, Alexander. *German Rule in Russia, 1941–1945: A Study of Occupation Politics.* London: Macmillan, 1981.

———. *Odessa, 1941–1944: A Case Study of Soviet Territory under Foreign Rule.* Santa Monica CA: Rand, 1957.

Dandara, Livia. *România in vîltoarea anului 1939* [Romania in the whirlpool of 1939]. Bucharest: Editura Ştiinţifică şi Enciclopedică, 1985.

———. *Romania's Attitude within International Talks Concerning the Situation of the Jews in Europe (1938–1939)*. Bucharest: 1986. Stencil, copy in Yad Vashem Library.

Der Prozess gegen die Hauptkriegsverbrecher vor dem Internationalen Militärgerichtshof Nürnberg. Nuremberg, Germany: 1949.

de Weck, René. "Journal, 1939–1945." Cote LD4. Bibliothèque Cantonale et Universitaire, Fribourg, Switzerland.

Die Bevölkerungszählung in Rumänien 1941. Vienna: Bearbeitet und herausgegeben von der Publicationstelle Vien, 1943.

Direcția Generală a Arhivelor Statului, Centrul de Studii și Cercetări de Istorie si Teorie Militară, eds. *23 August 1944: Documente, 1939–1943.* Vol. 1. Bucharest: 1984.

Documents on German Foreign Policy 1918–1945. Series D (1937–1945). 14 vols. London: His Majesty's Stationery Office, 1949–76.

"Dogme și canoane ecumenice împotriva evreilor" [Ecumenical dogma and law against Jews]. *Porunca Vremii* (Bucharest), November 2, 1940.

Drăgan, Iosif Constantin, ed. *Antonescu: Mareșalul României și răsboaiele de reîntregire* [Antonescu: Marshal of Romania and the reunification wars]. 4 vols. Cannaregio, Venetia, Italy: Editura Nagard, 1986–88.

Ehrenburg, Ilya. *Voina.* Vol. 3, *1943–1944.* Moscow: 1944.

Ehrenburg, Ilya, et al. *Cartea neagră* [The black book]. Bucharest: 1946.

Encyclopedia of the Holocaust. Jerusalem: Yad Vashem and Sifriyat Ha-Poalim, 1990. (In Hebrew.)

Fătu, Mihai, and Ion Spălățelu. *Garda de Fier: Organizație teroristă de tip fascist* [The Iron Guard: A terrorist-cum-fascist organization]. Bucharest: Editura Politică, 1971.

Federation of Jewish Communities in Romania, ed. *Evreii din România între anii 1940–1944.* 3 vols. Bucharest: Hasefer, 1997.

Filderman, Wilhelm. *Adevărul asupra problemei evreești în România în lumina textelor religioase și a statisticei* [The truth on the Jewish problem in Romania in light of religious and statistical data]. Bucharest: 1925.

———. *Memoirs and Diaries.* Vol. 1, *1900–1940.* Edited by Jean Ancel. Jerusalem: Tel Aviv University and Yad Vashem, 2004.

Florescu, E. "Inceputurile și evoluția mișcării fasciste in România pîna în anul 1933" [The inception and evolution of the fascist movement in Romania up to 1933]. Doctoral thesis, Universitatea București, 1979.

Gheorghe, Ion. *Rumäniens Weg zum Satellitenstaat.* Heidelberg: 1952.

Goga, Octavian. *Precursori* [The vanguard]. Ediție de exil. Madrid: Carpați, 1957.

Gold, Hugo. *Geschichte der Juden in der Bukowina. Ein Sammelwerk.* 2 vols. Tel Aviv: 1958–62.

Gould, L. A. *Crown against Sickle.* London: Hutchinson, 1953.

Guvernământul Basarabiei. *Basarabia desrobită, drepturi istorice, nelegiuri bolșevice, infăptuiri Românești* [Bessarabia liberated, historic rights, Bolshevik crimes, and Romanian achievements]. Kishinev, Bessarabia: 1942.

Guvernământul Transnistriei. *Transnistria.* Odessa: 1943.

Hașdeu, Bogdan Petriceicu. *Studie asupra judasimului, industria națională, industria străină și industria ovreiască față cu principiul concurenței* [Study on Judaism, the national industry, foreign industry and Jewish industry and the principle of competition]. Bucharest: 1866.

Heinen, Armin. *Die Legion "Erzengel Michael" in Rumänien: Soziale Bewegung und Politische Organization.* Munich: R. Oldenbourg Verlag, 1986.

Heyer, Rudolf Friederich. *Die orthodoxe Kirche in der Ukraine von 1917 bis 1945.* Cologne: Muller Verlag, 1953.

Hilberg, Raul. *The Destruction of the European Jews*. Chicago: Quadrangle, 1961.

———. *La destruction des Juifs d'Europe*. Paris: Fayard, 1988.

Hillgruber, Andreas. *Hitler, König Carol und Marschall Antonescu*. Wiesbaden, Germany: Frantz Steiner Verlag, 1965.

———, ed. *Staatsmänner und Diplomaten bei Hitler*. Pt. 1. Frankfurt am Main: Bernard und Graefe, 1970.

Hîncu, Dumitru. *Un licăr în beznă* [A spark in the darkness]. Bucharest: Hasefer, 1997.

Hitler's Secret Conversations, 1941–1944. New York: New American Library, 1961.

Hoettl, Wilhelm. *The Secret Front: The Story of Nazi Political Espionage*. London: Weidenfeld and Nicolson, 1953.

Iancu, Carol. *Emanciparea Evreilor din Romania (1913–1919)*. Bucharest: Hasefer, 1998.

Împotriva fascismului. Bucharest: Editura Politică, 1971. (Papers presented at a symposium on the critical analysis of fascism in Romania.)

Iorga, Nicolae. *Iudaica*. Bucharest: 1937.

Iuda. Bucharest: Tipografia ziarului Universul S.A., 1937.

Jäckel, Eberhard. *Hitlers Weltanschauung: Entwurf einer Herrschaft*. Stuttgart: Deutsche Verlags-Anstalt, 1986.

Jägendorf, Siegfried. *Jagendorf's Foundry: A Memoir of the Romanian Holocaust, 1941–1944*. Edited by Aron Mirth-Mannheimer. New York: Harper Collins, 1991.

Krausnick, Helmut, and Hans-Heinrich Wilhelm. *Die Truppe des Weltanschauungskrieges: Die Einsatzgruppen der Sichercheitspolizei und des SD, 1938–1942*. Stuttgart: Deutsche Verlags Anstalt, 1981.

Lecca, Radu. *Eu i-am salvat pe evreii din România* [I saved Romania's Jews]. Bucharest: Editura Roza Vânturilor, 1994.

Levin, Dov. "The Retreat of the Romanian Army from Bessarabia (1940)." In *Pinkas Hakehilot, Rumania*, vol. 2. Jerusalem: Yad Vashem, 1980. (In Hebrew.)

Litani, Dora. "*Black Book* on the Annihilation of the Jews in the Soviet Union." *Yediot Yad Vashem* 23/24 (1960).

———. *Transnistria*. Tel Aviv: Typo studio Ijak, 1981.

Livezeanu, Irina. *Cultural Politics in Greater Romania: Regionalism, Nation Building and Ethnic Struggle, 1918–1930*. Ithaca NY: Cornell University Press, 1995.

Magherescu, Gheorghe. *Adevărul despre Mareşalul Antonescu*. Vol. 2. Bucharest: Editura Păunescu, 1991.

Maleron, Yona. *Od tetzi mikan* [You'll get out of here yet]. Jerusalem: Yad Vashem, 1980.

Manuilă, Sabin. "Consideraţiuni asupra prezentării grafice a etnografiei României." *Memoriile secţiunii istorice*, Seria III, 1939, tomul XXI, memoriul 14, anexa III, Academia Română, Bucharest.

Marin, Vasile. *Crez de generaţie*. 2nd ed. Bucharest: 1937.

Mémorial Antonescu: Le IIIe homme de l'axe. Vol. 1. Paris: Editions de la Couronne, 1950.

Mendelsohn, Ezra. *The Jews of East Central Europe between the World Wars*. Bloomington: Indiana University Press, 1987.

Mezincescu, Eduard. *Mareşalul Antonescu şi catastrofa României* [Marshal Antonescu and Romania's catastrophe]. Bucharest: Editura Artemis, 1993.

Ministrul Domeniilor. *Buletinul statistic al României pentru anul 1914.* Bucharest: 1915.

Mircu, Marius. *Pogromurile din Basarabia şi alte câteva intâmplări.* Bucharest: Glob, 1947.

———. *Pogromurile din Bucovina şi Dorohoi* [The pogroms in Bukovina and Dorohoi]. Bucharest: Glob, 1945.

Moisuc, Viorica. "L'écroulement des alliances de la Roumanie à la veille de la deuxième guerre mondiale." *Revue d'histoire de la 2e guerre mondiale* (Bucharest) 140 (1985).

Muşat, Mircea, and Ion Ardeleanu. *România după Marea Unire* [Romania after the great unification]. Vol. 2, pt. a IIa, *Noiembrie 1933–septembrie 1940.* Bucharest: Editura Ştiinţifică şi Enciclopedică, 1988.

Nagy-Talavera, Nicholas M. *The Green Shirts and the Others: A History of Fascism in Hungary and Romania.* Stanford CA: Hoover Institution Press, Stanford University, 1970.

National Romanian Archives. *Shorthand Notes of the Council of Ministers Sessions Antonescu's Government.* Vol. 1, *September–December 1940.* Vol. 6, *February–April 1942.* Bucharest: Editura Mica Valahie, 1997, 2002.

Nedelcu, Florea. *Viaţa politică din România în preajma instaurării dictaturii regale* [Political life in Romania on the eve of the establishment of the royal dictatorship]. Cluj, Romania: Editura Dacia, 1973.

Nicodim, Patriarhul Romaniei. *Cuvântul Patriarhului pentru post, pentru oştire pentru ogor* [The patriarch's letter on the occasion of the fast, for the army and for the land]. Bucharest: 1942.

Ofir, Efraim. *In the Lion's Den: The Zionist Movement in Romania during World War II.* Tel Aviv: Goldstein-Goren Center for the History of the Jews in Romania, Diaspora Research Institute, Tel Aviv University, 1992. (In Hebrew.)

Oişteanu, Andrei. *Imaginea evreului în cultura română* [The image of the Jew in Romanian culture]. Bucharest: Humanitas, 2001.

———. *Inventing the Jew. Antisemitic Stereotypes in Romanian and Other Central-East European Cultures.* Lincoln: University of Nebraska Press, 2009.

Ornstein, Fabius. *Suferinţele deportaţilor în Transnistria: Gândiţi-vă la tot ce s'a petrecut în Transnistria 1941–1944* [Suffering of the deportees in Transnistria]. Bucharest: 1945.

Palaghiţă, Ştefan. *Garda de Fier: Spre reînvierea României* [The Iron Guard: Toward Romania's revival]. Buenos Aires: 1951.

Pătrăşcanu, Lucreţiu. *Sub trei dictaturi.* Bucharest: 1946.

Pe marginea prăpastiei, 21–23 ianuarie 1941 [On the brink of the abyss]. 2 vols. Bucharest: 1941.

Pinkas Hakehilot, Rumania [Encyclopedia of Jewish communities]. 2 vols. Jerusalem: Yad Vashem, 1969.

Politics and Political Parties in Roumania. London: International Reference Library, 1936.

Popescu, Marin. *Jidovii demascaţi: Lucrare de sinteză pe bază de documente.* Bucharest: 1936.

Procesul marei trădări naţionale [The great national treason trial]. Bucharest: 1946.

Prost, Henri. *Destin de la Roumanie (1918–1954).* Paris: Editions Berger-Levrault, 1954.

Reicher, Mordekhai, and Shitz Joseph-Magen, eds. *Yad le-Yedinits: Sefer Zikaron li-Yehudei Yedinits-Bessarabia* [Memorial book of the Jews of Edineți, Bessarabia]. Tel Aviv: Association of the Jews of Edineti in Israel, 1973. (In Hebrew.)

Reuth, Ralf Georg, ed. *Josef Goebbels: Tagebücher 1924–1945*. 5 vols. Munich: Piper, 1992.

Roll, Mathias. "Die schwarzen Tage von Czernowitz." *Die Stimme* (Tel Aviv) (1950): 54–55.

Rosenberg, Alfred. *Das Politische Tagebuch Alfred Rosenbergs aus den Jahren 1934/35 und 1939/40*. Edited by Hans-Günther Seraphim. Göttingen; Berlin; Frankfurt: Musterschmidt, 1956.

Roșu, Nicolae. *Dialectica naționalismului*. Bucharest: Ed. Cultura Națională, 1936.

———. *Orientări în veac* [Landmarks in the century]. Bucharest: Editura Cugetarea, 1937.

Rotaru, Jipa, Octavian Burcin, et al. *Mareșalul Ion Antonescu: Am făcut războiul sfânt împotriva bolșevismului* [Marshal Ion Antonescu: I waged a holy war against Bolshevism]. Oradea, Romania: Editura Cogito, 1994.

Rusenescu, M., and I. Saizu. *Viața politică în România, 1922–1928*. Bucharest: Editura Politică, 1979.

Safran, Alexandru. *Resisting the Storm: Romania, 1940–1947: Memoirs*. Edited by Jean Ancel. Jerusalem: Yad Vashem, 1987.

Savu, Gheorghe Al. *Dictatura regală*. Bucharest: Editura Politică, 1970.

Schmidt, Paul. *Hitler's Interpreter*. London: Heinemann, 1951.

———. *Statist auf diplomatischer Buehne, 1923–45*. Bonn: Athenaeum-Verlag, 1949.

Schwartzfeld, Moses. "Evreii în literatura populară română." *Anuar pentru israeliți* 14 (1891): 97–172.

Sebastian, Mihail. *De două mii de ani*. Bucharest: Hasefer, 1995.

———. *Jurnal, 1935–1944*. Bucharest: Humanitas, 1996.

Sima, Horia. *Era libertății, statul Național-Legionar* [The era of liberty, the National-Legionary state]. 2 vols. Madrid: Editura Mișcării Legionare, 1982, 1986.

———. *Sfârșitul unei domnii sângeroase* [The end of a bloody reign]. Madrid: Editura Mișcării Legionare, 1977.

Simion, Aurică. *Peliminarii politico-diplomatice ale insurecției romane din august 1944* [The political-diplomatic background to the Romanian Uprising in August 1944]. Cluj-Napoca, Romania: Editura Dacia, 1979.

———. *Regimul politic din România în perioada septembrie 1940–ianuarie 1941*. Cluj-Napoca, Romania: Editura Dacia, 1976.

Soviet Government Statements on Nazi Atrocities. London: Hutchinson, 1946.

Starodinskii, David. *Odesskoe Getto, Vospominaniia*. Odessa, USSR: Tpp. Haieth, 1991.

Stumpp, Karl. "Verzeichnis der deutschen Siedlungen im Gebiet Odessa [mit Karte]." In *Heimatbuch der Deutschen aus Russland, 1956*. Stuttgart, Germany: Landsmannschaft der Deutschen aus Russland, 1956.

Tătăranu, Gheorghe. *Expunere de titluri și lucrări științifice* [Description of titles and scientific works]. Odessa: 1943.

Taylor, Fred, ed. *The Goebbels Diaries, 1939–1941*. London: Hamish Hamilton, 1983.

Tomescu, Petre. *Anul medical 1939* [Medical year 1939]. Bucharest: 1940.

Trei ani de guvernare, 6 septembrie 1940–6 septembrie 1943 [Three years of government, 6 September 1940–6 September 1943]. Bucharest: 1943.

Trials of War Criminals before the Nuremberg Military Tribunals under Control Council Law no. 10. 15 vols. Washington DC: GPO, 1949–53.

Troncotă, Cristian. *Eugen Cristescu, asul serviciilor secrete românesti: Memorii, 1916–1944* [Eugen Cristescu: The wizard of the Romanian Secret Service]. Bucharest: Editura Roza Vânturilor, 1997.

United Restitution Organization. *Documentation Judenverfolgung in Rumänien.* 4 vols. Frankfurt: 1959–60.

Vago, Bela. *The Shadow of the Swastika — The Rise of Fascism and Antisemitism in the Danube Basin, 1936–1939.* London: Farnborough, 1975.

Vasiliu, E. *Situaţia demografică a României.* Cluj, Romania: Cartea Românească, 1923.

Vlădescu, I. N. "Ianuarie 1941." *Jurnalul de dimineaţă* 8, no. 57 (21 January 1945).

Volovici, Leon. "Romanian Intellectuals — Jewish Intellectuals during the Dictatorship of Antonescu." *Romanian Jewish Studies* (Jerusalem) 1 (Spring 1987): 77–89.

Vulcănescu, Mircea. *Ultimul cuvînt* [The last word]. Bucharest: Humanitas, 1992.

Watts, Larry. *În serviciul mareşalului* [In the marshal's service]. 2 vols. Munich: Jon Dumitru Verlag, 1985.

———. *Romanian Cassandra: Ion Antonescu and the Struggle for Reform, 1916–1941.* Boulder CO: East European Monographs, 1993. Distributed by Columbia University Press.

Werth, A. *Russia at War, 1941–1945.* London: Pan, 1965.

Woodward, E. L., and Rohan Butler, eds. *Documents on British Foreign Policy, 1919–1939.* Third Series. 9 vols. London: His Majesty's Stationery Office, 1949–61.

Zaharia, Gheorghe, and Nicolae Copoiu. "Le problème de la situation des juifs de Roumanie pendant les années 1938–1944." *L'historiographie roumaine* (1983).

Index

decree laws, 197, 424
De două mii de ani (Sebastian), 54–55
deicide, 58
democracy: abandonment of, 16–18, 59,
    65, 67, 105, 128, 174–75; denounce-
    ment of, by Ion Antonescu, 215–16;
    and intellectuals, 63, 64, 571n13
deportations, 3, 276, 465–66; from
    Bessarabia and Bukovina, 232–34,
    606n13; cessation of, 483–87, 502,
    508–9; deaths during, 541–45; exemp-
    tions from, 234, 244, 280, 291, 294,
    300–301, 305, 472, 481; and Final
    Solution, 463, 472–77; and genocide,
    236; messages left during, 293–94;
    to Soviet Union, 271; statistics on,
    535–38, 541–48, 552–60
detention camps (*lagăre*), 141, 232–40,
    520–22, 665n31
Deutsche Allgemeine Zeitung, 208
de Weck, René, 506–7
Diaconu, Petre, 227
Diaspora mentality, 171
Dimineaţa, 30
Dimitriuc, Victor, 91
Dniester River, 228, 234–35, 236, 237, 243
Dobrogeanu-Gherea, Constantin, 134
Doctor's Union, 98–99
"Doina" (Eminescu), 21
Dolina ghetto, 403
dollars, 312
Domanevka death camps, 336–37,
    341–50, 371, 392–94, 432–33, 628n38,
    629n55
Dominic, Alexandru, 103
Dorohoi district, 75–77, 125, 244, 289,
    298–305, 468, 471, 574n30
Dos Yiddische Vort, 30
Dragomir, Silviu, 30, 33, 39, 47
Dragoş, Titus, 481–82
Dresdner Bank, 64
Duca, I. Gh., 42
Dumitrescu, Eugen, 260–61, 264, 266–67,
    268, 620n25

Dumitrescu, Ilie, 497
Durchgangstrasse IV, 387–88

Eastern (Unitarian) Greco-Catholic
    Church, 431
Economic Council, 114
economy, Anglo-American, 312
economy, Romanian, 68–70, 182–83,
    196–201; and Antonescu regime, 177;
    and deportations, 459, 493, 516–17,
    523–24; and Final Solution, 460;
    German control of, 572n40; and
    Jewish persecution, 502; and National-
    Legionary government, 116; Roman-
    ization of, 82
Edineţi camp, 253–55
Education Ministry, 57, 100–101
Ehrenburg, Ilya, 390, 392–93
Eichmann, Adolf, 212, 386–87
Einsatzgruppe D, 2, 213, 223–24, 234,
    273, 327, 380–81, 454, 603n37, 623n1
Einsatzgruppen (mobile death squads),
    213–14, 229, 240, 559, 605n65
Einsatzkommando, 259–60, 264, 272
Eliade, Mircea, 51, 52
Elias Hospital, 184
emigration, 41, 45–46, 49–50, 166, 170,
    458, 463, 505, 591n24, 656n31
Eminescu, Mihai, 10, 180, 592n9;
    "Doina," 21
Engineer's Union, 47
Eretz Israel (Land of Israel), 166
escapes, 236, 425, 426–28
ethnic cleansing, 218, 244, 261, 290
euphemisms, 277–78, 364, 461, 482, 487,
    500, 540, 552, 613n31, 660n1
Evening Standard, 29
evidence, suppression of, 451, 454–55,
    508
evreu (Jew), term of, 140–41, 182
extortion, 109–10, 524–28, 666n47

Fabricius, Wilhelm, 65, 206–7
families, 255, 257, 295, 370, 440

Farbenindustrie, 64

fascism, 12–13, 16–19, 23, 64; and Antonescu regime, 173–74, 178; and Christianity, 22; and National-Legionary state, 89–90; and Romanian Orthodox Church, 174–75; theory of, 432

Federation of Jewish Communities of Romania, 5, 84, 165–71; and Antonescu regime, 591n19; and appropriation of property, 112; and Bucharest pogrom, 163; and camp prisoners, 256–57; and deportations, 126, 266–68, 297, 301–3; disbanding of, 303, 461; and increased oppression, 86–87; and Kishinev ghetto, 264

Filderman, Wilhelm, 3–4, 20, 30–32, 45–47, 167–71; attempts of, to help Jews, 132; and Bucharest pogrom, 162; campaign against, 83, 576n64; and cemetery desecrations, 134; on church support of antisemitism, 57; criticism of press by, 81; and denial of employment, 95; and deportations, 126, 267, 277, 296–97, 301–2, 335, 494–503, 643n47, 662n36; and European Jews, 165; and extortion operation, 525; and failure of reasoned approach, 82–83; and Federation, 407, 471; and genocide, 71; and ghetto committee, 264; and Gustav Richter, 464, 480; as hostage, 517; and increased oppression, 84–88; and intellectuals, 64; and Ion Antonescu, 131, 138, 140–42, 591n19; and Iuliu Maniu, 498; and Jewish organizations, 34; on Jewish Statute, 80; and Mihai Antonescu's alibi, 506–7; and Romanian Bar Association, 103; and Shapiro, 265; and typhus victims, 407–8; and writers, 577n89

Filipaş, Gheorghe, 403

Filipovich, Kalimov Boris, 391

Final Solution, 145, 148, 204–12, 343, 457–64, 475–79; and deportation, 463;

and genetic identity, 417–18; and Ion Antonescu, 213–14, 597n38, 598n39; in Odessa, 355, 364–65; in Transnistria, 395. *See also* "international solution"

Finance Ministry, 310–12, 314, 366, 375, 477

Foamete, Ion, 228

Follender, Alfred, 352

food shortages, 240

forced labor, 79, 85–86, 127, 186, 195, 200, 530–34, 667n56; and Army High Command, 198; and army service, 188; in Bukovina, 291; in Czernowitz, 273–74; and death of laborers, 455; and deportations, 302–3, 658n20; and detention camps, 237, 240; and Jewish Bureau, 274; on Jewish holidays, 264; and Jewish Statute, 170; and Odessa Jews, 354; on state farms, 346, 628n44; in Transnistria, 329, 333; and typhus victims, 402; in Vatra Dornei, 293

France, 13, 23, 35–38, 59, 62–63, 65–66, 69

Freemasons, 52, 58, 120, 143–44, 150–52, 154–56, 206–7, 437

Freulich, Michael, 338

Friedman, David, 132

Frigan, Major, 218–19

Froimescu, Ferri, 496

Führer's Decree (Führerbefhel), 213

Funk, Walther, 61, 571n1

Gafencu, Grigore, 40–41, 42, 64

Galaţi camp, 521

Galeş, Dimitri, 281

Găletaru, Lieutenant, 347

Galicia region, 271, 459

Gârneaţă, Ilie, 110, 114

gas chambers, 477, 481

Gavrilă, Dumitru, 226

Gazeta Odessei, 367

Gelep, Vasile, 408

gendarmerie, 370–75, 453–54; administration of, in Golta, 336–38; in camps and ghettos, 237, 240, 254; and deportations, 246–47; and genocide, 224–27, 235, 344, 603n46; and looting, 236–37, 252, 284–85, 295; and pogrom, 450; and rape, 440–41; and shooting of Jews, 246; in Transnistria, 322–24, 328, 333, 625n24

Gendarmerie Inspectorate, 320–21, 324, 329, 367, 421, 476

General Government, 276

General Staff, 363–64, 375, 454, 460

genocide, 2–3, 227–31, 234, 605n65; in Czernowitz, 272; and deportations, 246, 372; and disposal of bodies, 604nn54–55; and drowning, 228, 237, 293, 302, 604nn58–59; and Ion Antonescu, 71; in Kishinev ghetto, 262–63; in Odessa, 384–85; Romanian policy of, 217; statistics on, 537–38, 540–41, 547–48, 552–53, 555–57, 559–60; in Ukraine, 236

Georgescu, Grigore, 112, 134

Georgescu, Lieutenant, 338–39

German Foreign Ministry, 2, 3, 206, 243, 459–60

German House (Deutsche Haus), 376

German News Agency (Deutsche Nachrichten Büro), 62, 64

German occupation marks. *See* RKKS

Germans, 196–97, 201, 376, 492–93, 556

Germans, ethnic, 61, 66, 380–84, 388, 421, 428, 435, 637n4, 639n38

German secret service, 205

German Third Reich: alliance of, with Romania, 176–77; appeasement of, 40–41, 97, 183, 490, 567n7; and deportations, 483–85; disillusionment with, 488; financial support from, 63–64; and foreign policy, 67; and Goga government, 36; hegemony of, over Romania, 197; influence of, in Romania, 17–18, 61, 145–48, 217, 224,

627n30; and Ion Antonescu, 205; as military threat, 204; and Romanian Final Solution, 458–60; and Soviet Union, 214–15

German villages, 380–83, 637n5

Germany, 208, 499, 662n30. *See also* German Third Reich

Gestapo, 454, 462

Ghandism. *See* passive resistance

Ghelmegeanu, Mihail, 79, 84

Gheorghe, Ion, 153–54

ghetto committee, 263–64, 267

ghettos, 212, 232–34; in Bessarabia, 240; in Bukovina, 291; and deportation, 237; and Final Solution, 462; in Transnistria, 328–33, 624n6; typhus epidemic in, 410–11; in Vatra Dornei, 293

Ghidighici massacre, 263

Ghinăraru, Arthur, 562

Ghinăraru, Nicolae, 365

Gigulie, Dimitru, 228

Gigurtu, Ion, 78–79

Gingold, Nandor, 479, 497

Giurgiuveanu, Alexandru, 260–61

"Glasul lui Bucur în cele trei zile" (Axelrad), 161, 589n45

Gleichschaltung, 382

Glogojanu, Ion, 355

Gobelman, Esther, 345, 628n34

Goebbels, Joseph, 206, 208

Goga, Octavian, 20–22, 25–28, 36, 62

Goga, Veturia, 505

Goga government (1937–38), 25–38, 66–67, 94, 180, 565n22, 572n25

gold, 310–12, 351–52

Goldberg, Hadassah, 439

Golta district, 335–38, 344–45, 458, 477

grain trade, 186–87

Great Britain, 23, 35–36, 65–66, 69

Greater Romania, 5, 139

Great Plan, 521

Great Romanian Bank, 64

Great Synagogue, 272

International Commission on the Holo-
caust in Romania, 348
international Jewry, myth of, 37–38, 207
"international solution," 209–10, 462–63,
464. *See also* Final Solution
internment camps, 234. *See also specific
camps*
Ionesco, Eugène: *The Rhinoceros*, 16
Ionescu, Alexandru, 221
Ionescu, Nae, 53–54, 62, 571n9
Ionescu, Vasile, 277–78, 280, 614n39
Ionescu, Victor, 363–64, 633n35
Ionescu-Alion, Alexandru, 352
Ion Gigurtu government (1940), 78–80
Iordan, Iorgu, 142
Iorga, Nicolae, 10, 20, 29–31, 42, 52, 74,
96, 122, 131; *Judaica*, 83
Iron Guard (Garda de Fier). *See* Legion
Isacescu, Mihai, 20
Isopescu, Modest, 336–43, 346–52
Israel, 59
Italy, 17–18, 36, 499

Jeckeln, Friedrich, 236
Jewish Bureau (Biroul evrei), 274
Jewish Center (Judenrat), 211, 303, 322,
401–2, 461, 476–77, 479–80, 494–95
Jewish Committees, 402, 405, 410–11
Jewish Council, 495
Jewish Cultural Center, 272
Jewish Doctor's Union, 104
Jewish Party, 34, 46–47, 165
"Jewish problem," 10, 18–19, 212
Jewish Statute, 34, 44, 80–81, 94–96, 101,
175, 417, 420, 438–39, 472
Jews, 5–9, 23, 27–32, 71–76, 80–81,
94–105, 181–86, 464–66; accusations
against, 129–30, 134–35, 151–52,
363, 437, 448; appropriation of
property of, 107–15, 121–22, 143,
183, 186–90, 211, 260, 277, 352, 376,
527–29, 580n6, 667n49; as artists, 87;
and assassination of Corneliu Zelea
Codreanu, 92; as authors, 87, 101, 202,

577n89; baptism of, 431–32, 649n6;
barring of, from professions, 47–48,
200, 579n71; British, 35; businesses of,
45, 47, 171, 193; categorization of, 194,
524; children of, 372–73, 419–20, 428,
443–44; citizenship of, 23, 41, 44–46,
48, 94, 190–92, 563n9; civil rights of,
5, 32–33, 79–80, 95, 196, 497, 563n9;
in Communist revisionist history,
390–94; as craftsmen, 200, 556; deaths
of, 415–16, 455, 515, 562, 645nn78–
79, 663n2, 670n28; definition of, 175,
193, 212, 419–20; demographics on,
211–12; demonization of, 24, 51–55,
58, 430, 435; as doctors, 98–99, 118,
184, 187, 191, 195, 404–6, 642nn33–
34; emancipation of, 20; employment
of, 86–87, 113, 162–63, 177–78, 196,
577n82; eradication of culture of, 202;
ethnic identity of, 423–24, 646n20; in
Europe, 165; expulsion of, 59, 123–26,
141, 170, 179–81, 184, 211; "foreign,"
125–26; and Freemasons, 154–56;
from Galicia, 459; homeland of, 59,
166; identification of, 212, 271, 274,
281, 291, 321, 328, 399–400, 648n5;
as journalists, 44; Karaite, 374; as
lawyers, 29–30, 44–45, 81, 98, 103,
117–18, 184; leadership of, 82–84, 85,
165, 168; and Legionnaires' rebellion, 156; as minority, 46; Moldovan,
457–58, 518; as nonentities, 191, 314,
343, 415, 435; and Obkom report,
390–92; organizations of, 5–6, 34, 158;
as patriots, 507; persecution of, 164;
population of, 101, 123, 150–51, 155,
231–32, 315–16, 535–38, 547, 560–62,
563n4, 565n13, 668n1; in Regat,
470–71; Romanian, xii, 388, 559; as
scapegoats, 84, 377–78; as source of
income, 264; Soviet, 271; stereotypes
of, 8–9, 10, 27–28, 64, 571n16; and
suppression of Legion, 208; theaters
of, 100; Transylvanian, 499; and

Richter, Gustav, 147, 209–12, 269, 334, 362–63, 461–65, 472–81; and census of Jews, 562; and deportations, 483–85; and Wilhelm Filderman, 498, 662n27

Richtlinien, 224–25

right-wing movements, 174

Rintelen (German Foreign Ministry officer), 478–79

Rioşanu, Alexandru, 156, 171, 274, 275

Rittgen, Hermann Von, 362–63

ritual slaughter, 86–88, 123, 437, 517

RKKS, 266, 276–77, 307, 309, 311–12, 333, 366, 370

Romania: alliance of, with fascist powers, 176; antisemitism in, 2; culture of, 202; deportations from, 458, 497; genocide policy of, 224; Holocaust research in, xi; as homogeneous state, 459; Jewish policy of, 217; and loss of territory, 176; myth of, as tolerant nation, 131, 181; as occupied state, 204; pro-Western policy of, 61–62, 69; and suppression of documentation, 394; unification of, 61; values in, 107, 128

Romanian Bar Association, 29, 103

Romanian blood, 95–96, 193–94

Romanian Catholic Church, 59

Romanian Credit Institute (Institutul de Credit Românesc), 186

Romanian Front (Frontul Românesc), 19–20, 207

Romanian Institute of Statistics, 7

Romanian National Party, 19

Romanian Orthodox Church: and anti-semitism, 3, 54, 128, 216, 417; and campaign against Judaism, 182, 437; and Christianization of Transnistria, 430–31; and Jewish stereotypes, 8–9; and nationalism, 56–60; and National-Legionary government, 130; sacra-ments of, 649n6

Romanian Railway Authority, 291

Romanians, 193–94, 196–97, 212, 227–28, 230, 262–63, 428, 464–65, 648n37. *See also* Moldovans

Romanian Special Intelligence Service. *See* ssi (Romanian Special Intelligence Service)

Romanization, 82, 106–18, 146–47, 181–85, 192–202, 281–88, 614n53; and Bukovinian economy, 615n69; cam-paign for, 114; commissioners of, 112; of culture, 23, 201–3; of Jewish homes, 303; of land, 284; laws for, 97–98, 282; of theaters, 195, 202–3. *See also* nationalization

Romanization Administration, 260–61, 267, 282–85, 287

Romanization and Colonization, Under-secretariat for, 192

Romaşcanu, Stefan, 284

Roşca, Augustin, 254, 257

Rosenberg, Alfred, 62, 66, 210, 212–13, 383

Rosenkrantz, Dadu, 167

Roşu, Nicolae, 52, 53

Rottkirch, Panthen von, 386

RSHA (Reich Central Security Office), 2, 209–10, 214, 217, 243, 462, 478

Rüchrig, Andreas, 208

Rudnai, Eutichie, 433

Russians, 358–60, 374, 392, 632n25, 635n79, 640n50

sadism, 226–28, 388, 439, 603n46, 605n63

Safran, Alexandru, 3, 79, 83–84, 100, 264–65, 503, 525

Salmuth, Hans von, 455

Sanielevici, Henric, 87, 577n89

Şaraga, Fred, 265, 408

Sărăţeanu, Arthur Zelţer, 104

Sărbiceni forest, 255

Sârbu, Ion, 433

Scharansky, Hannah, 292

Schechter, David, 302

Schechter, Moritz, 254

Schickert, Klaus, 64, 65

Schmidt, Pasul, 214, 492, 598n39

Schobert, General Von, 213, 230

Schönfeld, Abraham, 132

schools, 100–101, 169, 195, 200–201, 284

Schor (Jew in Kishinev ghetto), 269

Schwarzer Adler Hotel, 272–73

Schwefelberg, Arnold, 496

Scriban, Iuliu, 431

Scriban, Nicolae, 454

SD (Nazi security service), 205, 262, 277, 362, 387, 462

Sebastian, Mihail, 476; *De două mii de ani*, 54–55

Secret Police, German (Schutzpolizei), 262

Secureni, 74, 255–57, 439

Securitate (Romanian Information Service), 3, 668n59

Șeicaru, Pamfil, 52, 84, 181

Selecenko, Maria, 423

sexually transmitted diseases, 444

Sfarmă Piatră, 215

Shapiro (leader of ghetto committee), 263–64, 265, 268

Shärf, Zeev, 255

Shargorod, 411

Siberia, 271

Siguranța (Romanian Security Police), 3, 157, 323–24, 359, 373–74, 465, 493

Sima, Horia, 42–44, 90–93, 106–8, 114, 148

Simion, Aurică, 90

Siret, 76, 222, 240

Skazinets detention camp, 235

skilled labor, 291, 294, 322, 333, 341, 627n22

SkR (Sonderkommando Russland), 382–84

Slavs, 325–26, 470

Slobodka Children's Hospital, 373–74, 635n80

Slobodka ghetto, 359, 362, 374, 385, 393

Slovakia region, 484–85

Sofer, Clara, 303

Soroca district, 245, 252

Sorting Committee (Comisia de triere), 301, 370

Soviets, 391–92

Soviet Union: and Czernowitz, 270–71; German failure to defeat, 623n38; and Goga government, 36–37; invasion of, 213; territorial demands of, 43, 71–75, 89; and war with Romania, 173–77, 214, 325–26, 430, 436–37, 471, 489, 660n10; weapons of, and genocide, 228, 604n56. *See also* Red Army

sovkhozes. *See* state farms (sovkhozes)

Spain, 499

Special Echelon, 229, 233, 447

Special Service, 627n30

Sperber, Alfred Margul, 487, 660n5

Sprînceană, Gratian, 449, 652n17

ss (Schutzstaffel), 209, 214, 379–80, 384, 454, 462, 468–69, 559. *See also* Waffen-ss

ssi (Romanian Special Intelligence Service), 229, 261–62; and anti-Jewish incitement, 359; and deportations, 482; and Iași, 445, 447; and looting, 352, 630n66; and Odessa, 354–55, 362–65; and religious converts, 425

Stalin, Joseph, 437

Stănculescu, Ion, 355

Stănescu (antisemitic priest), 57

Stănescu, Dan, 275, 276

Stănescu, Marin, 113, 127

Stângă, Ilie, 113

state farms (sovkhozes), 379

Stavrat, Olimpiu, 223

Stavrescu, Nicolae, 447

Ștefan, Stroe, 306

Șteflea, General, 446–47

Șteflea, Ilie, 218

Stelescu, Mihail, 42

Steltzer, Gerhard, 385

Stoenescu, Nicolae, 310, 519, 522, 524

Stoicescu, Constantin, 186, 306, 464

Storojinetz ghetto, 244, 271

Comprehensive History of the Holocaust series

The Origins of the Final Solution
The Evolution of Nazi Jewish Policy, September 1939–March 1942
by Christopher R. Browning

The Jews of Bohemia and Moravia
Facing the Holocaust
by Livia Rothkirchen

The Holocaust in the Soviet Union
by Yitzhak Arad

The History of the Holocaust in Romania
by Jean Ancel

To order or obtain more information on these or other University of Nebraska Press titles, visit www.nebraskapress.unl.edu.